Die Welthandelsorganisation und die Regulierung
internationaler Wirtschaftsdynamik

Die Deutsche Bibliothek verzeichnet diese Publikation in der Deutschen Nationalbibliografie: detaillierte bibliografische Daten sind im Internet über http://dnb.ddb.de abrufbar.

Ausgabe in 4 Bänden: Bd. 1 (Abschnitte 'A', 'B', 'C', 'D'', E'); Bd. 2 (Abschnitte 'F', 'G', 'H', 'I'); Bd. 3 (Abschnitte 'J', 'K'); Bd. 4 (Abschnitte 'L', 'M', 'N').
<u>Dies ist Bd. 4 (Abschnitte 'L', 'M', 'N').</u>

Druck: DIP-Digital-Print, 58453 Witten.
© 2008 Trade Focus Verlag, Zedernweg 45, 53757 St. Augustin
http://www.tradefocus.de
ISBN 978-3-9810240-4-3

Inhaltsverzeichnis   Bd. 4 (Abschnitte 'L', 'M', 'N')

Teil IV

L	<u>Informationen</u>	1387
1.	GATT Fallübersicht	1388
2.	WTO Fallübersicht	1397
3.	Definitionen	1411
4.	Abkürzungsverzeichnis	1412
M	<u>Literatur</u>	1415
N	<u>Tabellen</u>	1541

L   Informationen

Inhalt

1.	GATT Fallübersicht	1388
2.	WTO Fallübersicht	1397
3.	Definitionen	1411
4.	Abkürzungsverzeichnis	1412

L   Informationen

1. GATT Fallübersicht. GATT-Übersichtstabelle über 13 Gruppen und Länderpaare und thematische Schwerpunkte der Klagen, 1955-1989. Gestützt, einschließlich der Fallnumerierung, auf Hudec 1991.

Kategorie	Anzahl	Landwirtschaft	VERs	Liberalisierung	wg. US-Druck	Industriesubventionen	Erfolge der Klägerpartei (4)
USA vs. Entwicklungsländer	7	3	-	2	...	-	3
Entwicklungsländer vs. USA	11	2	-	-	3	-	2
EU vs. Entwicklungsländer	2	1	-	-	...	-	-
Entwicklungsländer vs. EU	10	6	3	-	...	-	2
Entwicklungsländer vs. kleineres Industrieland	5	2 (1)	1	-	...	-	2
USA vs. kleineres Industrieland	17	5	-	3	...	-	8
kleineres Industrieland vs. USA	6	3	2	-	-	-	1
EU vs. Japan	3	-	1	-	...	-	2
Japan vs. EU	2	-	1	-	...	-	-
USA vs. Japan	10	4	-	-	-	-	4 (5)
Japan vs. USA	2	-	1 (2)	-	-	-	-
USA vs. EU	20	14	-	-	-	2 (3)	2
EU vs. USA	15	5	1	-	-	1 (3)	3
Insgesamt	110	45	10	5	4 (2)	3	29
in Prozent:	100	41.0	9.1	4.5	3.6	2.7	26.3

(1) Hier geht es eher um tropische Früchte: Bananen, Kaffee.
(2) Auch wegen US-Druck, deshalb wäre Doppelnennung notwendig. Dies ist im insgesamten Ergebnis reflektiert.
(3) Sämtlich mit bezug zur Luftfahrt, bzw. Airbus.
(4) Aufgrund vieler Informationslücken recht subjektive Bewertung. E steht für klare erkennbare Erfolge.
(5) Die Erfolge der USA gegenüber Japan haben einen auffällig niedrigen Streitwert.
Insgesamt 67 Fälle fallen in die speziellen thematischen Kategorien, dies sind 61 Prozent.

Übersicht über Gruppen und Länderpaaren in der GATT-Streitbeilegung plus eine thematische Zusammenstellung von Klagen und Streitbeilegungsverfahren: Die Zusammenstellung erfolgt ab 1955 um frühe, offenbar nicht relevante Fälle (die sind 34 Fälle) auszuklammern. Insgesamt werden 173 Klagen und Streitbeilegungsfälle von 207 einbezogen. Davon werden 63 Fälle abgezogen, weil sie in Gruppen fallen, die nicht zur gewählten Fragestellung passen. Übrig bleiben die oben in der Tabelle zusammengefaßten 110 GATT-Klagefälle. Ausgeklammert sind die Streitigkeiten zwischen USA mit Kanada (Kanada vs. USA 93, 102, 121, 140, 147, 152, 153, 167, 194, 203 ; USA vs. Kanada, 58, 75, 108, 155, 157, 195, 205) dies sind 17 Fälle, sowie die zwischen Kanada vs. EU (73, 95, 129, 134, 145, 201) und EU vs. Kanada (128, 139, 149, 151), dies sind 10 Fälle, sowie die Auseinandersetzungen zwischen Australien vs. EU (62, 77, 86, 101, 110, 135), dies sind 6 Fälle. Ebenso nicht beachtet werden Klagen zwischen den kleinen Industrieländern, die besonders in den fünfziger und sechziger Jahren zwischen Staaten Europas erfolgten (Europa-intern: 37, 38, 39, 41, 42, 46, 47, 48, 52, 53, 56, 90), sonstige solcher Fälle, etwa zwischen Australien und England, Kanada und Japan (50, 51, 66, 74, 90, 133, 169, 177, 183, 197), dies sind insgesamt 22 Fälle. Weiterhin nicht beschrieben werden die Streitigkeiten zwischen kleineren Industrieländer und der EU, dies sind 3 Fälle (86, 135, 182) und der EU gegen kleine Industrieländer (116, 117, 130), ebenfalls 3 Fälle. Ignoriert werden die Klagen kleinerer Industrieländer gegen Entwicklungsländer (174, 181), also 2 Fälle. Korea wird als Entwicklungsland geführt.

Die Fallnummern sind identisch mit Hudec (1991). Die Beschreibungen orientieren sich an Hudec, liegen aber in der Verantwortung des Verfassers. Das folgende Schema wird verwendet: Fallnummer, Jahr, Titel der Klage, teilweise erfolgt Einordnung der Klage zu einem speziellen Abkommen. Dann wird darauf hingewiesen, ob es ein

Panelbericht (Streitbeilegungsbericht) gegeben hat. Falls dies nicht erwähnt wird, hat es diesen Bericht nicht gegeben.

Kommentar in der folgenden Liste: **E** Erfolg durch Klägerpartei, **TE** Teilerfolg, auch bei sehr geringem Streitwert, **K** Kompromiß, **N** Neutral, **B** Blockade durch Gegenpartei.

USA vs. Entwicklungsländer

44 USA vs. Chile, 1956, Auto Taxes, höhere Steuern auf US Automobile, Chile lenkt ein. E
64 USA vs. Jamaica, 1970, Panelbericht. Klärungsklage bzgl. Commonwealth Präferenzen, keine Auswirkungen auf Jamaica. N
126 USA vs. Brazil, 1983, Subsidies on Export and Production of Poultry. (Subsidies Code). Landwirtschaft. Hängt mit 106, USA vs. EU zusammen. Die drei Parteien einigen sich schließlich auf geringere Subventionen. K
163 USA vs. India, 1987, Import Restrictions on Almonds. Landwirtschaft. Nach sechs Jahren Konsultationen, die eine erste Verbesserung des Marktzugangs mit sich brachten, greifen US-Mandelexporteure zu einer Sec 301 Untersuchung, die in zwei Klagen, darunter siehe unten 164, resultierte. Ein Panel wird etabliert, ein Bericht aber nicht geschrieben. Erstmals Auseinandersetzung um die BOP-Rechtfertigung für Indiens umfassendes Quotenschutzsystem (vgl. dazu 173, 174, 181). Indien erklärt sich bereit die Quote auf 20 Millionen US$ zu erhöhen (bis 1988 hatte der Importwert bei 4 Millionen US$ gelegen). TE
164 USA vs. India, 1987, Import Restrictions on Almonds. Landwirtschaft. Siehe Klage 163 oben. TE
173 USA vs. Korea, 1988, Restrictions on Imports of Beef. Liberalisierung. Panelbericht, adopted. Durch Sec. 301 Beschwerde initiiert. Es geht um Fleischquoten, die Koreas Industrie schützen. Thematisch weitreichender Fall, der die Rechtfertigung dieser Maßnahmen durch Zahlungsbilanzprobleme (BOP) angreift und die Aktivitäten von Staatshandelsunternehmen angeht. Das Panel entscheidet, daß es die Rechtfertigung von BOP-Maßnahmen untersuchen kann, wenn sich beide Parteien darüber einig sind. Die Aktivitäten koreanischer Staatshandelsunternehmen stellen sich als nicht GATT-widrig heraus. Durch die Annahme des Berichts durch Korea kann die USA auf diesbezügliche und andere Liberalisierungen drängen. Der Landwirtschaftsaspekt tritt aufgrund der anderen Thematik zurück. E
206 USA vs. Brazil, 1989, Restrictions on Imports of Certain Agricultural and Manufactured Products. Liberalisierung. Angriff auf das gesamte brasilianische Importkontrollregime. Gegen mengenmäßige Beschränkungen, Lizenzpraktiken etc. Vermittels einer US Super 301 Untersuchung. Brasilien rechtfertigt sich mit Verweis auf BOP-Probleme. USA gibt Klage auf, weil Brasilien eine umfangreiche Liberalisierung vorbereitet (Collier Liberalisierung). Hier tritt der Landwirtschaftsaspekt ebenfalls zurück. E

Entwicklungsländer vs. USA

54 Uruguay vs. 15 Developed Countries, 1961, Panelbericht, Landwirtschaft. Gegen die Landwirtschaftspolitik der Industrieländer. Teilerfolge, die meisten Industrieländer gehen aber nicht darauf ein. TE
98 India vs. USA, 1980, Countervailing Duty without Injury Criterion. Die USA weigern sich das in der Tokyo-Runde ausgehandelte Abkommen zum Rekurs auf das "material injury"-Kriteriums bei Ausgleichszolluntersuchungen auf Länder anzuwenden, die überhaupt keine Disziplin hinsichtlich Exportsubventionen akzeptieren. Dies ist Teil einer US-Strategie Abkommen der Tokyo-Runde gegenüber Entwicklungsländer, die sich bestimmten Disziplinen verweigern, nur plurilateral umzusetzen. Die USA ziehen sich hier von ihrer Position zurück und akzeptieren offenkundig wertlose indische Zusicherungen. E
111 India vs. USA, 1982, Countervailing Duty Procedures. Schwierigkeiten bei der Berechnung eines Ausgleichszolles, den die USA gegenüber Indien erhebt, für 'industrial fasteners'. Die USA Untersuchung hat Steuerrückzahlungen für indische Produzenten im Moment des Exports als Subventionen gewertet, obwohl diese Rückerstattungen im Zusammenhang mit einem komplizierten Kaskadensteuersystem (Inputs sind unterschiedlichen Besteuerungen ausgesetzt) sind. Die USA erklären sich bereit, diese Sachlage anzuerkennen, stellen einen Ausgleichszoll ein und arbeiten mit Indien an der Lösung weiterer Fragen. E
112 Argentina vs. EU, Kanada, Australia, 1982, Trade Restrictions Falkland War. Die mächtigen GATT-Staaten machen deutlich, daß politischen Konflikte nicht vom GATT gelöst werden können.
142 Nicaragua vs. USA, 1985, Trade Measures Affecting Nicaragua. Panelbericht, blocked. Hintergrund: US-Handelsembargo aus politischen Gründen. Nicht gelöst. B
146 Brazil vs. USA, 1986, Measures on Imports of Non-Beverage Ethyl Alcohol. Brasilien produziert Ethyl-Alkohol um Automobile zu betreiben und Ölimporte zu sparen. Als Brasilien diese in die USA exportieren will, erhöhen die US in Zusammenhang mit dem U.S. Deficit Reduction Act of 1984 die Zölle und eröffnen Antidumping-Untersuchungen. Nach Konsultationen verfolgt Brasilien die Sache nicht weiter, weil es keine Ethyl-Überschüsse zum Export mehr übrig hat. Nicht gerade nötiger US-Druck. B

170 Brazil vs. USA, 1987, Tariff Increase and Import Prohibition on Brazilian Products, 'Informatics Dispute'. Weil Brazilien den Verkauf eines Softwareprogramms verbietet, drohen die USA am 13. November 1987 Vergeltungszölle auf Waren aus Brasilien zu erheben, die einen Verlust von 105 Millionen US$ nach sich ziehen würden. Seit 1985 lief eine Sec 301 Untersuchung gegen Brasilien. Im Dezember 1987 wird eine Einigung erzielt, die der Generaldirektor des GATT vermittelt. Im Januar 1988 erlaubt Brasilien den Verkauf der Software. Nicht gerade nötiger US-Druck angesicht dem Versuch Brasiliens eine Computerindustrie aufzubauen. B

178 Chile vs. USA, 1988, Quality Standards for Grapes. Landwirtschaft. Thema ist eine saisonbezogene Verordnung, die Untersuchungen vorsieht, um Trauben in einem bestimmten Zeitraum nur in höchster Qualität auf den US-Markt zu lassen. Dieser Zeitraum wird vorgezogen, sodaß weitaus mehr chilenische Trauben als sonst unter die Qualitätskontrolle fallen. Mexiko wird es eingeräumt, Qualitätsuntersuchungen in der Nähe der US-Grenze auf eigenem Territorium, stattfinden zu lassen. Die Exporte aus Chile werden nicht in Chile untersucht, sondern erst in den USA. Würde die Untersuchung in Chile vorgenommen, könnte Chile Transportkosten sparen, wenn Früchte ausgesondert werden. Ergebnis: Die USA ziehen den Termin nicht vor, keine weiteren Folgen. N

185 Brazil vs. USA, 1988, Collection of Countervailing Duty on Non-Rubber Footwear. (Subsidies Code), Panelbericht, blocked (by Brazil). Komplexer Fall um Ausgleichszölle. Brasilien bekommt hier unrecht, später aber, in DS18/R, recht. USA zieht seine GATT-widrigen Maßnahmen nicht zurück. B

198 Brazil vs. USA, 1988, Import Restrictions on Certain Products from Brazil, 'Pharmaceuticals Retaliation'. Die USA wenden 100 Prozent Zölle auf brasilianische Produkte an, weil, vermittels einer Sec 301 Beschwerde der mangelnde Patentschutz für US-Pharma- und Chemieprodukte in Brasilien beklagt wird. Die Vergeltung der USA für den mangelnden Patentschutz (der gar nicht unter das GATT fällt, es handelt sich um eine GATT widrige Vorgehensweise) wird ab 20 Oktober 1988 effektiv. Ein Panel wird zwar etabliert, ist aber verunsichert über seine Terms-of-Reference und wird schließlich abgebrochen, denn die Parteien schlichten ihren Streit. Am 27 Juni 1990 erklärt sich Brasilien bereit im nächsten Jahr eine Patentgesetzgebung zu veranschieden, daneben findet die umfassende Liberalisierung der Collier-Regierung statt. Bis Mitte 1992 ist die Patentgesetzgebung noch nicht verabschiedet. Nicht nötiger US-Druck, im Zusammenhang mit den Verhandlungen der Uruguay-Runde über das TRIPs-Abkommen. B

190 Brazil vs. USA, 1988, Export Enhancement Program (EEP) Subsidy. (Subsidies Code and Art. XXIII). Landwirtschaft. Anlaß sind Subventionen für Sojabohnenexporte. Kein Lösung des Konflikts. B

EU vs. Entwicklungsländer

131 EU vs. Chile, 1984, Import measures on diary products. Landwirtschaft. Durch einem Minimum-Importpreis, von dem aus Chile einen Wertzoll kalkuliert, erhöht sich der Zoll auf EU-Milchprodukte aus 60 Prozent. Chile hat aber verbindlich in seinen Zolllisten 30 Prozent festgelegt. Die EU wird von Chile davon in Kenntnis gesetzt, daß sie auch ein Antisubventionszoll (bzw. ein Ausgleichsverfahren anstrengen könnte) gegen die EU-Milchsubventionen veranschlagen könnte. Daraufhin zieht die EU die Klage zurück. B

207 EU vs. Chile, 1989, Internal Taxes on Spirits. Unterschiedliche Steuerraten auf ausländische und lokale Spirituosen. Streit wird nicht weiter verfolgt. N

Entwicklungsländer vs. EU

54 Uruguay vs. 15 Developed Countries, 1961, Recourse to Article XXIII, Panelbericht, Landwirtschaft. Gegen die Landwirtschaftspolitik der Industrieländer. Teilerfolge, die meisten Industrieländer gehen aber nicht darauf ein. TE

82 Chile vs. EU, 1978, Export Refunds on Malted Barley. Landwirtschaft. Gegen EU-Roggensubventionen, die chilenische Exporte verdrängen. Chile verfolgt die Klage nicht weiter. Zweimal 1980 und 1981 erfolgen unter dem Subventionskodex der Tokyo-Runde weiter Konsultationen, auch hier wird dieses Thema nicht weiterverfolgt. B

83 Korea vs. EU, 1978, Article XIX Action on Imports into the U.K. of Television Sets from Korea. VER. Während Verhandlungen der Tokyo-Runde zum Thema Schutzklausel und der länderspezifischen Anwendung dieser. Die asiatischen NICs waren damals dagegen. Eine Studie des GATT-Sekretariats wird statt des Streits in Auftrag gegeben. 1979 verkündet Korea, daß ein VER bezüglich TV-Sets ausgehandelt wurde und zieht die Klage zurück. Die länderspezifische Anwendung der Schutzklausel ist bis heute in der WTO erlaubt. B

87 Brazil vs. EU, 1978, Refunds on Exports of Sugar, Landwirtschaft. Panelbericht, adopted. Hintergrund. EU Zuckerexporte steigen von 8.5 Prozent des Weltmarktes auf 14.3 Prozent 1978. EU weigert sich dem Internationalen Zuckerabkommen beizutreten, daß Zuckerexporte einschränken soll. Obwohl "serious prejudice" festgestellt wird, weigert sich die EU dies anzuerkennen, ändert später ihre Maßnahmen in Produzentendirektzahlungen, womit dem Panelbericht die Argumentationsbasis entzogen wird. Keine Einigung. Weitere Fälle zu diesem Thema 86 (Australien vs. EU, 1978, mit demselben Ergebnis), 109, 110. B

89 Chile vs. EU, 1979, Restictions on Import of Apples, Landwirtschaft. Panelbericht, adopted. Moderater Panelbericht mit Verständnis für die EU, der in weiteren Auslegungen der GATT-Regeln zu diesem Thema

rückgängig gemacht wird und nur das geringe Quotenvolumen anprangert, nicht aber die EU-Subventionspolitik. EU schafft die Apfelquote ab, deshalb keine weiteren Auswirkungen des Panels, später gibt es aber neue Apfelquoten, die in Klage 180 zum Thema werden. B

104 Hongkong vs. EU, 1981, Quantitative Restrictions on Imports of Certain Products from Hongkong. VER. Panelbericht, adopted. Hongkong wehrt sich gegen restriktiver werdende französische Quoten für Quartz-Uhren aus Hongkong. Die EU argumentiert, daß die Quoten, die in diesem Falle aus früheren BOP-Einschränkungen resultieren, sozusagen gewohnheitsrechtlich ('law creating facts') gerechtfertigt sind. Das Panel folgt diesem Argument nicht und verweist darauf, daß der Text des GATT-Abkommen gültig bleibt, der in Art. XI:1 mengenmäßige Beschränkungen verbietet. Am 16 Juni 1987 meldet Hongkong, daß den Forderungen des Panelberichts entsprochen wurde. E

110 Argentina et al. vs. EU, 1982, Sugar Regime. Landwirtschaft. Et al. bedeutet: Australia, Brazil, Columbia, Cuba, Dominican Republic, India, Nicaragua, Peru, Philippines. Siehe USA vs. EU 109. Es geht darum, die EU zum Beitritt zu einem internationalen Zuckerabkommen zu bewegen, um die Subventionspraktiken der EU und deren Weltmarktanteile angreifen zu können. Die Verhandlungen scheitern. B

166 Argentina vs. EU, 1987, Enlargement of EEC – Accession of Spain and Portugal. Landwirtschaft. Der Beitritt von Spanien und Portugal erhöhte deren Schutzbarrieren bezüglich landwirtschaftlicher Produkte, senkte aber die Zölle für Industriewaren auf das niedrige EU-Niveau ab. Während der Art. XXIV:6 Konsultationen beharrt die EU darauf, die Vorteile und Nachteile 'global' zu betrachten, kurz: davon auszugehen, daß die niedrigen Industriezölle ausreichend für die Erhöhung im Landwirtschaftbereich kompensieren. Mit den USA hatte die EU schon eine Abkommen abgeschlossen, daß Mais und Sorgumexporte in die beiden Länder zu erhöhten Mengen vorsah. Argentinien gelingt es, gestützt durch diese Klage, ein ähnliches Abkommen auszuhandeln, das überdies auch eine Erhöhung der Fleischqouten vorsieht. E

180 Chile vs. EU, 1988, Restrictions on Imports of Dessert Apples. Landwirtschaft. Panelbericht, adopted (EU veröffentlicht längeres Statement, daß es nicht mit den Argumenten übereinstimmt). Panelbericht stellt unter anderem Verstoß gegen Art. XI Ausnahmen, 2 (c) (i) und (ii) fest. Die EU läßt Maßnahmen auslaufen und weigert sich Kompensationen zu zahlen. Ob die Maßnahme später wieder genutzt wurden ist nicht bekannt, jedoch wahrscheinlich. B

199 Hongkong vs. EU, 1989, Antidumping Duty on Video Cassettes. (Antidumping Code). VER. Steht in Verbindung mit den Verhandlungen um das Antidumping-Übereinkommen der Uruguay-Runde. Konkretes Ergebnis unklar. TE

Entwicklungsländer vs. kleineres Industrieland

55 Brazil vs. UK, 1961, Margin of Preferences Bananas, Landwirtschaft. Panelbericht, UK zieht zusätzliche Präferenzen für Jamaica zurück. Erfolg für Brasilien. E

84 Hongkong vs. Norway, 1978, Textile Import Restrictions. VER. Panelbericht, Hongkong wehrt sich gegen eine 40 Prozent Verringerung seiner norwegischen Textilquoten, sechs andere Entwicklungsländer waren nur dazu verpflichtet worden, ihre Importe einzufrieren. GATT-Panel fordert Nichtdiskriminierung von Hongkong, die VERs selbst wenden nicht angegriffen. Bericht wird angenommen, Norwegen verweigert Umsetzung, später, 1984, wird ein neues VER mit Hongkong ausgehandelt. TE

94 Brazil vs. Spain, 1980, Unroasted Coffee, Landwirtschaft. Panelbericht, adopted. Spanien lenkt ein und verzollt brasilianischen Kaffee so wie anderen 'gleichartigen' Kaffee mit 6 Prozent. E

96 India vs. Japan, 1980, Leather, In einem Schlichtung durch den Generaldirektor des GATT, eine spezielle Einrichtung der Streitbeilegung für Entwicklungsländer seit 1966, räumt Japan Indien größere Quoten ein. E

132 South Africa vs. Canada, 1984, Discriminatory Application of Retail Sales Tax on Gold Coins. Panelbericht, blocked. Die kanadische Provinz Ontario erhebt keine Steuern auf Goldmünzen aus der dortigen Produktion. Bekannter Fall in dem klargestellt wird, daß der Staat für die Handlungen der Provinzregierung verantwortlich ist. Kanada weigert durch die Blockade des Berichts Kompensationen zu zahlen, was der Bericht gefordert hatte. B

USA vs. kleineres Industrieland

35 USA vs. France, 1955, Stamp Tax, begründete US-Klage, wg. erhöhter Stempelsteuer bei Zollabfertigung: Steuer wird 1961 abgeschafft. E

40 USA vs. France, 1956, Auto Taxes, diskriminierende Steuern für US Automobile, kein Erfolg für USA, abgeschafft 1986 durch EuGH. B

56 USA vs. France, 1962, Import Restrictions (I), Panelbericht, BOP, partielle Liberalisierung erreicht. Liberalisierung. E

57 USA vs. Italy, 1962, Import Restrictions, BOP, Liberalisierung erreicht. E

60 USA vs. Italy, 1969, Gebühr bei Zollabfertigung. Später akzeptiert USA möglicherweise modifizierte Umsetzung des Gesetzes. TE

61 USA vs. Greece, 1970, Präferenzen Griechenlands für UDSSR. Ergebnis nicht bekannt. -
67 USA vs. France, 1972, Import Restrictions (II), BOP, die restlichen Quoten werden liberalisiert. E
68 USA vs. UK, 1972, Dollar Area Quotas, Landwirtschaft. Tropische Früchte, Rum, Quoten für karibischen Commonwealth Länder, ab 1975 werden die Quoten abgeschafft und US Produzenten nicht mehr benachteiligt. US-Erfolg. Proteste der karibischen Entwicklungsländer. E
70 USA vs. France, 1973, Income Tax Practices, Panelbericht, steht im Kontext des DISC-Falles (siehe EU vs. USA 69). K
71 USA vs. Belgium, 1973, Income Tax Practices, Panelbericht, steht im Kontext des DISC-Falles (siehe EU vs. USA 69). K
72 USA vs. Netherlands, 1973, Income Tax Practices, Panelbericht, steht im Kontext des DISC-Falles (siehe EU vs. USA 69). K
91 USA vs. Spain, 1979, Soybean Oil, Panelbericht, Landwirtschaft. Aufgrund von allgemeiner Ablehnung des Panelberichts durch viele GATT-Mitglieder keine weiteren Folgen. Danach allerdings weitere Konsultationen mit Spanien, ohne daß darüber weiteres bekannt wäre. -
118 USA vs. Poland 1982, Suspension of MFN. Die USA setzen MFN für Polen aufgrund der Unterdrückung der Solidaritäts-Gewerkschaft aus. Diskussion über die Auslegung eines speziellen bilateralen Abkommens dazu. Keine Auswirkung des GATT-Streits. 1987 wird MFN wieder eingeführt. E
171 USA vs. Norway, 1988, Restrictions on Imports of Apples and Pears. Landwirtschaft. Panelbericht, adopted. Es geht um temporäre Importbeschränkungen für Äpfel und Birnen, die bis zum Weihnachtsgeschäft gelten. Die USA bekommt vom Panel recht. Norwegen geht teilweise auf US-Forderungen ein, Streit erstreckt sich bis 1991, wird dann von den USA nicht weiterverfolgt. TE
172 USA vs. Sweden, 1988, Restrictions on Imports of Apples and Pears. Landwirtschaft. Gleicher Fall wie oben 171. Kein Panelbericht. Einigung mit Schweden gelingt durch Abschaffung bestimmter Quoten und einer Neuverhandlung von Zöllen. E
202 USA vs. Finland, 1989, Restrictions on Imports of Apples and Pears. Landwirtschaft. Fall wie oben 171 und 172. Finland ändert 1990 seine Quoten in Zölle um. E
204 USA vs. Norway, 1989, Oslo Toll Ring Project. (Procurement Code). Klage gegen politischen Einfluß bei der Vergabe eines Auftrags. Norwegen zahlt Präsentationskosten an amerikanisches Firmenkonsortium zurück. TE

kleineres Industrieland vs. USA

36 Australia vs. USA, 1955, Hawai Regulations. Landwirtschaft. In Hawai steht in Geschäften, die Eier verkauften zwangsweise das Schild 'we sell foreign eggs'. Erfolg für Australien. E
43 Denmark vs. USA, 1956, Export subsidy on Poultry, Landwirtschaft, unbekannter Ausgang. -
144 Portugal vs. USA, 1985, Restrictions on Imports of Cotton Pillowcases and Bedsheets. VER. Portugals Importe werden in den USA gesondert vom MFA verwaltet und eingeschränkt. In diesem Fall wird von Portugal nur eine Forderung nach GATT-Konsultationen ausgesprochen. Danach erfolgt die Aushandlung eines VERs über das keine weiteren Informationen vorliegen. B
187 Australia vs. USA, 1988, Import Restrictions on Sugar. Landwirtschaft. Panelbericht, adopted. Die mengenmäßigen Beschränkungen der USA wiederprechen GATT Art. XI: 1. Die USA wandelt ihre mengenmäßigen Beschränkungen in wirkungsgleiche 'tariff rate quotas' um und entfernen ein bestehende verbindliche Festlegung der Höhe, sodaß die Maßnahmen womöglich noch restriktiver wurden als zuvor. B
191 Schweden vs. USA, 1988, Antidumping Duties on Stainless Seamless Pipes and Tubes from Sweden. VER bezug. Panelbericht, adoptions left open. Protest Schwedens gegen eines der vielen Untersuchungen der USA im Eisen- und Stahlbereich. Schweden ist erfolgreich, weil die US-Untersuchung nicht mit dem Antidumpingkodex übereinstimmt. Die USA verweigert aber Kompensation. B
192 Finland vs. USA, 1988, Procurement of Antarctivc Research Vessel. (Procurement Code). Es geht um 'buy America'-Provisionen. Finland verfolgt die Sache nicht weiter nachdem gewisse Fortschritte in den Konsultationen erreicht wurden. Später gibt es einen ähnlichen Fall der EU gegen die USA. Die USA nimmt den Bericht nicht zu Kenntnis. B

EU vs. Japan

124 EU vs. Japan, 1983, Nullification and Impairment of Benefits. Bekannte Klage der EU, daß aus der engen Zusammenarbeit zwischen Regierung und privater Seite unter anderem handelsbeschränkende Wirkungen resultieren und das dadurch Vorteile, die eigentlich aus dem GATT resultieren sollten, nicht eintreten. Weder ein Panel noch eine Arbeitsgruppe kommen zustande. 1985 kündigt Japan diverse Liberalisierungsmaßnahmen an, ohne eine Zusamenhang mit dieser Klage darzulegen. Diese Klage wird 1989 Vorbild für die US-amerikanische 'Structural Impediments Initiative gegenüber Japan. B

154 EU vs. Japan, 1986, Restrictions on Alcoholic Beverages. Panelbericht, adopted. Erfolgreiche Klage gegen weitaus höhere Besteuerung von EU und US-Alkoholika gegenüber japanischem Reisschnaps ('sochu'). Meilenstein in der Art. III.2 Interpretation. Im Jahre 1989 wird in Japan das dementsprechende Gesetz verabschiedet, daß die Besteuerung fast angleicht. E

156 EU vs. Japan, 1987, Restrictions on Semiconductors. VER. Panelbericht, adopted. Grundlegender Panelbericht, der sich gegen den Einsatz von VERs ausspricht. Hier geht es um die EU Reaktion auf das US-Japan Halbleiter VER. Wohl unter dem Eindruck des Panelberichts wird nicht direkt ein VER mit Japan ausgehandelt, sondern erst eine Antidumpinguntersuchung eingeleitet und in Zusammenhang damit dann ein VER ausgehandelt. Ein solches sog. 'undertaking' ist vom GATT Antidumping Code zugelassen. E

Japan vs. EU

119 Japan vs. EU, 1982, Import Restrictive Measures on Video Tape Recorders. VER. Frankreich bremst den Import von japanischen Videorecordern durch Zollabfertigungtricks. Im April 1983 hat die EU einen Mindestpreis für japanische Videorekorder ausgehandelt und die französischen Maßnahmen werden zurückgenommen. TE

188 Japan vs. EU, 1988, Antidumping Regulation on Imports on Parts and Components. 'Screwdriver Assembly'. Panelbericht, adopted. Hier wird, vor der WTO Gründung, erstmals gegen Mindestinland bzw. 'local content'-Vorschriften angegangen (später im TRIMs). Die Maßnahmen gegenüber Japan, die seitens der EU angestrengt werden, damit japanischen Hersteller in der EU Antidumpinguntersuchungsvorschriften nicht durch Importe von Einzelteilen (und der Montage in der EU) umgehen können, verstoßen gegen eine Reihe von GATT-Regeln, darunter Art. III.2 und 4. Die EU verweigert sich einer Änderung ihrer Umsetzung mit Verweise auf Antidumpingverhandlungen der Uruguay-Runde. B

USA vs. Japan

81 USA vs. Japan, 1977, Import of Thrown Silk Yarn, Landwirtschaft. Panelbericht. US-Klage gegen japanische Subventionierung der Seidenproduktion. Aufgrund einer Sec 301 Beschwerde eines US Seidenherstellers. Panelbericht wird nicht öffentlich, Kompromiß ausgehandelt. Ergebnis: Japan stellt für den US Seidenhersteller eine USA spezifische Quote bereit. E

85 USA vs. Japan, 1978, Leather (I), Japan gesteht USA höhere Lederproduktquoten zu. Die Exporte nach Japan steien von 1978-1982 von 2 bis 9 Millionen US-Dollar. TE (geringer Streitwert)

92 USA vs. Japan, 1979, Tobacco. Landwirtschaft. Japan setzt sukzessive seine Zölle und anderen Beschränkungen für Tabakimporte aus. Handel mit USA steigt nur langsam an. TE (geringer Streitwert)

115 USA vs. Japan, 1982, Metal Softball Bats. (Standards Code). Hier geht es darum, daß japanischen Testvorschriften für amerikanische Metallschläger diskriminierend waren. Mit diesen Vorschriften wurden die Amerikaner 1973 vom Markt ausgeschlossen. Die Japaner lenken diesmal ein. 1984 schließlich akzeptiert die japanischen Softball-Liga amerikanische Metallschläger. TE (geringer Streitwert)

120 USA vs. Japan, 1983, Leather (II), Panelbericht, adopted. Festgehalte wird, daß die japanischen mengenmäßigen Beschränkungen gegen GATT-Regeln verstoßen. In einer komplexen Einigung liberaliert Japan und stellt teils seine Quoten auf Tariff Rate Quotas um. Den USA wird eingeräumt auf bestimmte Waren Zölle zu erhöhen. Detail: Japan rechtfertigt Maßnahmen weil dadurch eine Bevölkerungsminderheit (Dowas) geschützt werden, die Lederwaren anfertigen. TE (geringer Streitwert)

136 USA vs. Japan, 1984, Single Tendering Procedures, (Government Procurement). Japan nutzt weiterhin öffentliche Auftragsvergabe ohne eine offene Aussschreibung. Nach weiteren Konsultation mit den USA erklärt Japan 1986, daß immer weniger Aufträge ohne Ausschreibung stattfinden. E

141 USA vs. Japan, 1985, Quantitative Restictions on Imports of Leather Footwear. Wird ohne Bericht in einer Einigung geregelt, die auch Streit 120 zum selben Thema umfaßt. TE (geringer Streitwert)

148 USA vs. Japan 1986, Restrictions on Certain Agricultural Products. Landwirtschaft. Panelbericht, adopted (with reservations). Bericht, der problematisch hinsichtlich Staatshandelsunternehmen entscheidet und auch sonst viele US-Punkte übernimmt, deshalb Vorbehalte von Japan und anderen Ländern gegenüber diesem Bericht. Die Produkte um die es geht sind allerdings weniger wichtig und Japan liberalisiert einen großen Teil. E (aber wohl nicht so großer Streitwert)

150 USA vs. Japan, 1986, Restictions on Imports of Herring, Pollock and Surimi. Ergebnis, welches allerdings nicht im GATT berichtet wird, weil es GATT-Regeln widerspricht: Japan eröffnet US-Fischzulieferern Lizenzen. Anderen Ländern nicht. E

176 USA vs. Japan, 1988, Restrictions on Imports of Beef and Citrus Products. Landwirtschaft. Japan geht auf viele der US-Forderungen ein. E

Japan vs. USA

80 Japan vs. USA, 1977, Zenith, Panelbericht, Auf Wunsch der USA eingebrachte Klage zur Klärung eines USA-internen gerichtlichen Streits bezüglich Ausgleichszahlungen.
161 Japan vs. USA, 1987, Unilateral Measures on Imports of Certain Japanese Products, 'Semiconductor' Retaliation. VER. Japan wendet sich gegen höhere US-Zölle auf Halbleiter, begründet mit der angeblichen Nichteinhaltung des Halbleiter-VERs durch Japan. Zollsenkungen erfolgen danach offenbar dann, wenn Japan auf Forderungen der USA eingeht. Die letzten Zölle werden abgeschafft als es am 1 August 1991 zu einer Verlängerung des VER kommt. Siehe dazu auch die EU-Klage gegen Japan 156. K

USA vs. EU

65 USA vs. EU, 1972, Compensatory Import Taxes, Landwirtschaft. EU schafft die zusätzlichen Steuern ab, die innerhalb des landwirtschaftlichen Stützungssystem Wechselkursänderungen abfangen sollen. E
76 USA vs EU, 1976, MIPS, Landwirtschaft. Panelbericht. Die Minimum Import Price Requirements der EU werden aus internen Gründen abgeschafft. Wahrscheinlich werden ähnlich wirksame, anders benannte Maßnahmen eingeführt. TE
78 USA vs. EU 1976, Animal Feed Proteins, Landwirtschaft. Panelbericht. EU schafft die Maßnahmen, die aufgrund der Überprodution von Milchpulver eingeführt wurde und Sojatierfutterhersteller (und Importeure von Soja aus den USA) dazu anhalten, Milchpulver unterzumischen, aus internen Gründen ab. Sie war sowieso temporär angelegt. US-Klage beruht auf einer Sec 301 Beschwerde von US-Sojabohnenproduzenten. TE
97 USA vs. EU 1980, 'Spin-Chill' Requirements on Imports of Poultry, 1980, begründete U.S.-Klage. Es geht um englische Vorschriften wie Hünchenfleisch gegahrt werden muß, die erst 2 Jahre später für die eigenen Unternehmen gelten. Unklarheit ob die PPMs unter das TBT fallen. Kein Panelbericht. Wird fallengelassen, weil U.S.-Unternehmen schnell mit der Regulierung zurechtkommen. N
99 USA vs. EU, 1981, Export Subsidies by Greece, (Subsidies Code). Griechenland erstattet Exporteuren bestimmte Steuern zurück. Dies widerspricht nach Ansicht der USA dem Verbot von Exportsubventionen für Industrieprodukte der Industrieländer. Die USA wollen den neuen Subventions-Kodex ausprobieren. Dieser Fall steht im Kontext mit der Aufnahmevorbereitungen für Griechenland in die EU, bei der diese Praktiken offengelegt wurden. Aufgrund mangelnden Interesses der US-Industrie wird die Klage zurückgezogen. N
103 USA vs. EU, 1981, Wheat Flour, (Subsidies Code), Landwirtschaft. Panelbericht, blocked by EU and others. Test für Subventions-Kodex. Hintergrund. Den EU-Subventionen wird zugesprochen daß Weizenmehlexporte der EU 1959 bis 1962 für 29 Prozent des Weltmarkts aufkommen und 1978 bis 1981 für 75 Prozent, während der US-Anteil in dieser Zeit von 25 auf 9 Prozent sinkt. Die EU senkt ihre Export eigenständig ab, die USA übt davor schon Vergeltung indem sie für den Markt in Ägypten Exportsubventionen vergibt (dort hat die EU 25 Prozent ihres Weizenmehls verkauft). Mit dem Food Security Act von 1985 erhöhen die USA die Subventionen noch einmal. Dieser Subventionswettlauf erstreckt sich bis mindestens 1992. Klage 123 der EU hängt damit zusammen. B
105 USA vs. EU, 1982, Subsidies on Exports of Pasta Products, (Subsidies Code), Landwirtschaft. Panelbericht, blocked, Beruht auf einer Sec 301 Beschwerde eines US-Pasta-Produzenten. Hintergrund: EU-Pasta-Produzenten werden für die hohen internen EU Preise für Eier und Weizen kompensiert. Eine Ausgleichszahlunguntersuchung der USA kommt nicht zustande, weil "material injury" offenbar nicht erfüllt ist. Schon die Mitglieder des Panels können sich nicht einigen, weil einerseits die Meinung besteht, daß GATT Art. XVI: 4 immer schon so verstanden wurde, daß er die EU-Praktik toleriert, andererseits wird dies geleugnet. Es folgen Zollerhöhungen seitens der USA auf EU-Pasta. Die EU erhöht ihrerseits Zölle auf US-Zitronen (siehe unten 113) und Walnussexporte. Im August wird eine vorläufige Einigung erzielt und die Zollerhöhungen zurückgenommen. Die EU erklärt sich bereit darauf zu achten, daß die Kompensationen nicht größer sind als nötig, um die Unterschiede zum Weltmarktpreis wettzumachen. TE (weil die Politik nicht gänzlich geändert wurde)
106 USA vs. EU, 1982, Subsidies on the Export and Production of Poulty, (Subsidies Code). Landwirtschaft. In informellen Konsultationen einigen sich die EU, USA und Brasilien (siehe Klage 126) auf einen gemeinsamen Abbau von Exportsubventionen. K
107 USA vs. EU, 1982, Production Aids on Canned Peaches, Canned Pears, Canned Fruit Cocktail and Dried Grapes. Landwirtschaft. Panelbericht, blocked. Beruht auf einer Sec 301 Beschwerde von US-Birnenherstellern. Der Panelbericht bezieht eine moderate Stellung zu der EU-Politik. USA und EU einigen sich trotz Blockade des Berichts. Die EU baut Subventionen um 25 Prozent ab. E
109 USA vs. EU, 1982, Export Subsidies on Sugar, (Subsidies Code). Landwirtschaft. Vorläufige Einigung eine multilaterale Lösung zu suchen. Danach Fehlschlag ein solches, multilaterales, neues internationales Zuckerabkommen zu gründen. Danach wird auch die USA Ziel von mehreren GATT-Klagen, weil sie ihrerseits Importbeschränkungen für Zucker intensivieren (Klagen 140, 186, 187). B

113 USA vs. EU, 1982, Tariff Treatment of Citrus Products from Certain Mediterranean Countries. Landwirtschaft. Panelbericht, blocked. Die USA greift regionale Präferenzen für Mittelmeerländer an, die die EU diesen einräumt. Der Bericht ist dezidiert pro-USA, denn solche Präferenzabkommen müssen im dazugehörigen Ausschuß des GATT bewertet werden, es wird aber festgestellt, daß eine Zunichtemachung und Schmälerung von Vorteilen die der USA zustehen vorliegt. Der nachfolgende Streit wird in einem Paket mit dem Pasta-Streit (oben 105) verfolgt. In bezug auf Zitrusprodukte senkt die EU in der 1986 erzielten Einigung ihre Zölle für US-Produkte ab, umgekehrt senkt die USA Zölle oder andere Marktzugangsbeschränkungen für EU-Produkte ab. K

114 USA vs. EU, 1982, Value-Added Tax (VAT) and Threshold. (Government Procurement Code) Panelbericht, adopted (without recommendation). Weil in der EU ein hohes Mehrwertsteuerniveau herrscht glaubt die EU, daß die Geldwerte ihrer öffentlichen Aufräge, dadurch daß sie die Mehrwertsteuer enthalten, ein höheres Niveau erhalten und öfter unter die Disziplin der Abkommens über öffentlichen Aufträge fallen, als dies in der USA der Fall ist. Sie rechnet deshalb die Mehrwertsteuer ab. (Dazu kommt ein internes Harmonisierungsproblem, weil die Länder unterschiedliche Raten haben) Die USA wehrt sich dagegen. Der Panelbericht stützt die US-Position. Die EU einigt sich darauf, generell 13 Prozent abzurechnen und geht somit nicht auf die US-Forderung ein. B

158 USA vs. EU, 1987, Government Financing of Airbus Industries (I), (Aircraft Code). Industriesubventionen. Während der Konsultationen wird sich darauf geeinigt eine Klarstellung der Passagen des Luftfahrt-Kodex über Subventionen anzustreben. Siehe die Klage 196 später.

159 USA vs. EU, 1987, Animal Hormones Directive, (Standards Code). In komplexen Konsultationen keine Einigung ob der Code für Technische Standards Anwendung findet. Als die EU ihr Embargo für US-Hormonrindfleisch umsetzen, antwortet die USA mit 100 Prozent Zöllen auf 100 Million US$ von den EU gehandelten Waren. Die Zölle werden Stück für Stück zurückgefahren, aber nicht ganz ausgesetzt. B

168 USA vs. EU, 1987, Directive von Third-Country Meat Imports, Landwirtschaft. Hin und her bezüglich EU-Gesundheitsstandards für Schlachthäuser. Aufgrund einer Sec 301 Beschwerde. USA ist der Meinung, daß seine Standards substantiell equivalent sind. Die EU gesteht dies erst zu, zieht dies dann zurück. 1992 gelingt eine endgültige Einigung. K

175 USA vs. EU, 1988, Greek Import Restrictions on Almonds, Landwirtschaft. Es geht um einen temporäres Importembargo für Mandeln, daß die erstmals entstandene Chance zu exportieren zunichtemacht, denn es hatte eine schlechte Ernte gegeben. Das Embargo wird etwas später aufgehoben. TE (geringer Streitwert)

179 USA vs. EU, 1988, Payments and Subsidies on Oilseeds and Animal-Feed Proteins. Landwirtschaft. Panelbericht, adopted (die EU veröffentlich aber ein Papier in dem sie darlegt, daß sie mit diversen Punkten nicht einverstanden ist). Durch Sec 301 Rekurs der US-Sojaproduzenten initiiert. Die EU hatte 1962 verbindlich zugestanden, daß auf Ölsaaten kein Zoll erhoben wird. Später verliert die USA durch die Subventionierung der EU-Ölsaaten Marktanteile. Das Panel übernimmt in weiten Teilen die US-Argumentation und stellt Zunichtemachung und Schmälerung von Vorteilen fest, die der USA aus dem GATT resultieren würden und fordert von der EU eine Neuverhandlungen ihrer Zollkonzession. Die EU ändert ihre Marktordnung, dasselbe Panel stellt aber weiterhin GATT-Widrigkeit der Regulierungen fest. Die EU ersucht daraufhin Neuverhandlungen, diese sind aber schnell blockiert, weil die USA nicht zufrieden sind, mit den Kompensationen die die EU anbietet. Etwas später fordert die USA die Autorisierung Vergeltungsmaßnahmen anzuwenden, die EU lehnt dies aber ab. Danach kündigt die USA, am 5. November 1992, an Vergeltungsmaßnahmen zu ergreifen und einen 200 Prozent Zoll auf 300 Millionen US$ EU Importe anzuwenden. Am 20. November wird die Einigung verkündigt, die nicht nur Limits für die EU Sojabohnenproduktion umfaßt, sondern auch ein Rahmen für das Landwirtschaftsabkommen, das in den Verhandlungen der Uruguay-Runde seit längerem erfolglos diskutiert wird, bereithält. Deutlich wird, daß die GATT-Auseinandersetzungen im Kontext der Verhandlungen der Uruguay-Runde zu deuten sind. K

184 USA vs. EU, 1988, Restrictions on Imports of Apples. Landwirtschaft. Panelbericht, adopted. Bericht ähnlich wie Chile vs. EU, 180. Maßnahmen der EU laufen aus, keine weiteren Informationen. B

196 USA vs. EU, 1989, Government Financing of Airbus Industries (II). (Subsidies Code). Industriesubventionen. Panelbericht, blocked. Thema ist eine Wechselkursgarantie der BRD-Regierung für die Daimler-Benz GmbH, die den Regierungsanteil an Airbus übernehmen will. Diese GATT-widrige Garantie wird zurückgenommen, obwohl der Bericht blockiert wurde. Siehe auch 158. In dieser Zeit wird das Übereinkommen über Luftfahrt ausgehandelt. TE (geringer Streitwert)

198 USA vs. EU, 1989, Restraints on Exports of Copper Scrap. Die EU hatten Exportverbote für Kupferschrott aufrecherhalten. Die USA argumentiert, daß dies in der EU Weltmarktpreise artifiziell niedrig hält. Die EU schafft dieses Exportverbot ab und stellt in einem Report fest, daß diese Maßnahme nicht mehr nötig ist. TE (geringer Streitwert)

EU vs. USA

59 EU vs. USA, 1963, Chicken War, Landwirtschaft. Panelbericht, Landwirtschaft. EU hatte Zollzugeständnisse ausgesetzt, durch hohe Zölle und variable Abgaben auf Hühner, USA deshalb Zugeständnisse zurückgezogen,

Streit um Höhe dieser Zugeständnisse. U.a. resultiert ein 25 Prozent ad valorem Zoll auf leichte LkW daraus, der bis 1992 galt. B

69 EU vs. USA, 1973, DISC, Panelbericht, US-Steuervorteile für Exporteure. Zieht sich bis 1984 und endet mit einem Kompromiß. USA verändert seine Position nicht, obwohl die Maßnahmen nicht GATT-konform sind. B

88 EU vs. USA, 1978, Application of Countervailing Duties, hier geht es um die USA, die bislang keine Überprüfung auf "material injury", also der Verletzung ihrer eigenen Industrie in einem Ausgleichszahlungsverfahren einbezogen hatten. Allein die Subventionierung einer ausländischen Firma reichte aus. Mit dem Abkommen zu diesem Thema der Tokyo-Runde ändert die USA ihr Verhalten und seit dem 26 Juli 1979 ist dies US-Gesetz. E

100 EU vs. USA, 1981, Import Duty on Vitamin B12, Panelbericht, adopted. Eine bestimmte Zollhöhe der USA steht im Einklang mit dem GATT, weil die USA einen diesbezüglichen Vorbehalt niedergelegt hatten. Die EU akzeptiert dies nicht, der Bericht wird aber trotzdem angenommen. Nach der Tokyo-Runde sinkt der Zoll bis 1984 sowieso auf 16 Prozent ab. Die EU hatten 21 Prozent gefordert. Die EU droht mit einer Zollerhöhung, setzt dies aber nicht um. N

122 EU vs. USA, 1983, Manufacturing Clause in US Copyright Legislation. Panelbericht, adopted. Das US-Gesetz, das teilweise den Import von Büchern verbietet, die von US-Autoren geschrieben wurde, sollte sowieso auslaufen. Der GATT-Bericht dagegen erhöht den Druck auf den Kongress, nicht einer Verländerung zuzustimmen. E

123 EU vs. USA, 1983, Export Subsidies on Sales of Wheat Flour to Egypt. (Subsidies Code). Landwirtschaft. Siehe 103 USA vs. EU. Panel wird zwar etabliert, aber kein Panelbericht, keine sonstigen dokumentierten Ergebnisse. Die US-Subventionen werden ein Jahr später nicht mehr gewährt. TE (geringer Streitwert)

127 EU vs. USA, 1984, Tariff Classification of Machine-Threshed Tobacco. Landwirtschaft. Streit um Reklassifikation von zerkleinerten Tabak, der von EU Produzenten so behandelt wurde, um in eine niedrigere Zollkategorie zu geraten. So zumindest die US-Version. Die EU sieht eine GATT-widrige Reklassifikation. Ergebnis: USA gewährt einem Zuliefer Kompensation. TE (geringer Streitwert)

138 EU vs. USA, 1984, Ban on Imports of Steel Pipe and Tube from the European Community. VER. EU beschwert sich über US Embargo für Stahlröhren, welches nicht im VER mit den USA ausgemacht war. Ergebnis: 1985 ist ein VER für Stahlröhren aus der EU ausgehandelt.

152 EU (mit Mexiko, Kanada) vs. USA, 1986, Superfund Taxes. Panelbericht, adopted. USA wollen mit höheren Steuern auf importierte Petroleumprodukte Umweltschutzmaßnahmen bezahlen. Panelbericht stellt Diskriminierung gleichartiger Produkte fest. EU, Kanada fordern Autorisierung um Vergeltung üben zu können. USA blockiert dieses Ansinnen im General Council. EU einigt sich mit USA. Im Dezember 1989 wird die Superfund-Gesetzgebung von den USA GATT-kompatibel gemacht. E

153 EU (mit Kanada) vs. USA, 1986, Customs User Fee. Panelbericht, adopted. Die USA suchen nach Haushaltseinnahmen und erheben aus diesen Gründen ein Zollabfertigungsnutzungsentgelt von 0.17 Prozent. Auch deshalb weil diese Gebühren zu abfertigungsfremden Zwecken eingesetzt werden, entscheidet das Panel dagegen. 1990 ändert die USA diese Gesetzgebung, diesmal wird eine Minimum und Maximumsumme festgelegt, die Zweckentfremdung ausgeschlossen. Die EU protestiert zwar, verfolgt diese Sache aber nicht weiter. TE

160 EU vs. USA, 1987: Tax Reform Legislation for Passenger Aircraft. Industriesubventionen. Einstellung des Verfahren weil die Steuervorteile für U.S.-Flugzeuge bereits ausgelaufen waren. TE (in Relation zum den gesamten Subventionen geringer Streitwert)

162 EU vs. USA, 1987, Section 337 of the Tariff Act of 1930, 'Aramid Fibres' Case. Panelbericht, adopted. Es geht um Patentverletzungsverfahren nach Sec. 337 in den USA, zu denen ausländische Firmen schwerer Zugang haben als US-Firmen. Dies ist GATT-inkompatibel. Es geht hier um Maßnahmen gegenüber Maßnahmen gegen Importe. USA verschleppt die Änderung des Gesetzes. TE

165 EU vs. USA, 1987, Procurement of Machine Tools by the Department of Defense. Frühzeitige Klage gegen ein Gesetzgebungsvorhaben in den USA, das in bezug auf Käufe des Verteidigungsministeriums eine 'buy national'-Provision vorsah. Es gelingt der EU nicht, die USA davon abzubringen und aufgrund des Beharrens der USA darauf, daß es sich um eine Sache der nationalen Sicherheit handelt und für die EU keine Erfolgsaussichten bestehen, wird die Klage nicht weiter verfolgt. B

186 EU vs. USA, 1988, Restrictions unter 1955 U.S. Waiver and unter Headnote to U.S. Schedule XX. Landwirtschaft. Panelbericht, adopted (EU veröffentlich Gegenposition). Gegenstand ist die U.S.-Sondergenehmigung für ihre Landwirtschaftspolitik. EU bekommt zugestanden, daß sie auch eine Sondergenehmigung angreifen kann, solange sie detaillierte Begründungen vorlegt und dies als sog. 'nonviolation nullification or impairment'-Klage erfolgt. Dies war diesmal nicht der Fall, deshalb kein Ergebnis und keine weiteren Streitigkeiten die hieraus resultieren. TE

193 EU vs. USA, 1988, Increase in Rates of Duty on Certain Products form the EU, 'Hormones Retaliation'. Die EU protestiert gegen die Vergeltung der USA, die aus Klage 159 resultiert. Die USA blockiert Panelbildung, Blockade der GATT-Prozeduren bis Ende 1992. B

1989 EU vs. USA, 1989, Determination under Sections 304 and 305 of the Trade Act of 1974 Relating to EC Oilseed Subsidies. <u>Landwirtschaft</u>. Es geht um US-Vergeltungsentscheidungen unter Sec 301, die im Ölsaaten Fall, 179, vor dem eigentlichen Panelbericht, bereits im administrativen Prozedere angelaufen sind. Eine konkrete Vergeltung fand allerdings nicht statt. N

2. WTO Fallübersicht. Quelle für die Informationen: WTO Webseite.

Streitparteien/Kürzel	Ergebnis
DS373 China — Measures Affecting Financial Information Services and Foreign Financial Information Suppliers (Complainant: European Communities)	consultations requested
DS372 China — Measures Affecting Financial Information Services and Foreign Financial Information Suppliers (Complainant: European Communities)	consultations requested
DS371 Thailand — Customs and Fiscal Measures on Cigarettes from the Philippines (Complainant: Philippines)	consultations requested
DS370 Thailand — Customs Valuation of Certain Products from the European Communities (Complainant: European Communities) 25 January 2008	consultations requested
DS369 European Communities — Certain Measures Prohibiting the Importation and Marketing of Seal Products (Complainant: Canada) 25 September 2007	consultations requested
DS368 United States — Preliminary Anti-Dumping and Countervailing Duty Determinations on Coated Free Sheet Paper from China (Complainant: China) 14 September 2007	consultations requested
DS367 Australia — Measures Affecting the Importation of Apples from New Zealand (Complainant: New Zealand) 31 August 2007	Panel established
DS366 Colombia — Indicative Prices and Restrictions on Ports of Entry (Complainant: Panama) 12 July 2007	Panel established
DS365 United States — Domestic Support and Export Credit Guarantees for Agricultural Products (Complainant: Brazil) 11 July 2007	Panel established, single panel with DS357
DS364 European Communities — Regime for the Importation of Bananas (Complainant: Panama) 11 July 2007	Panel established, see DS27
DS363 China — Measures Affecting Trading Rights and Distribution Services for Certain Publications and Audiovisual Entertainment Products (Complainant: United States) 10 April 2007	Panel established
DS362 China — Measures Affecting the Protection and Enforcement of Intellectual Property Rights (Complainant: United States) 10 April 2007	Panel established
DS361 European Communities — Regime for the Importation of Bananas (Complainant: Colombia) 21 March 2007	Panel established, see DS27
DS360 India — Additional and Extra-Additional Duties on Imports from the United States (Complainant: United States) 6 March 2007	Panel report expected in March 2008
DS359 China — Certain Measures Granting Refunds, Reductions or Exemptions from Taxes and Other Payments (Complainant: Mexico) 26 February 2007	single Panel with DS358 etablished, see DS358
DS358 China — Certain Measures Granting Refunds, Reductions or Exemptions from Taxes and Other Payments (Complainant: United States) 2 February 2007	see DS359, memorandum of understanding between China and the U.S.
DS357 United States — Subsidies and Other Domestic Support for Corn and Other Agricultural Products (Complainant: Canada) 8 January 2007	Panel established, single panel with DS365
DS356 Chile — Definitive Safeguard Measures on Certain Milk Products (Complainant: Argentina) 28 December 2006	Panel work suspended until further notice
DS355 Brazil — Anti-dumping Measures on Imports of Certain Resins from Argentina (Complainant: Argentina) 26 December 2006	Panel report expected in August 2008
DS354 Canada — Tax Exemptions and Reductions for Wine and Beer (Complainant: European Communities) 29 November 2006	consultations requested
DS353 United States — Measures Affecting Trade in Large Civil Aircraft — Second Complaint (Complainant: European Communities) 27 June 2005	Panel report expected in July 2008
DS352 India — Measures Affecting the Importation and Sale of Wines and Spirits from the European Communities (Complainant: European Communities) 20 November 2006	Panel work suspended until further notice
DS351 Chile — Provisional Safeguard Measure on Certain Milk Products (Complainant: Argentina) 25 October 2006	Panel work suspended until further notice
DS350 United States — Continued Existence and Application of Zeroing Methodology (Complainant: European Communties) 2 October 2006	Panel report expected in September 2008
DS349 European Communities — Measures Affecting the Tariff Quota for Fresh or Chilled Garlic (Complainant: Argentina) 6 September 2006	consultations requested
DS348 Colombia — Customs Measures on Importation of Certain Goods from Panama (Complainant: Panama) 20 July 2006	mutually agreed solution
DS347 European Communities — Measures Affecting Trade in Large Civil Aircraft (Second Complaint) (Complainant: United States) 31 January 2006	other settled or inactive cases
DS346 United States — Anti-Dumping Administrative Review on Oil Country Tubular Goods from Argentina (Complainant: Argentina) 20 June 2006	consultations requested
DS345 United States — Customs Bond Directive for Merchandise Subject to	Panel report, same issue, same

Anti-Dumping/Countervailing Duties (Complainant: India) 6 June 2006	panelists as in DS343
DS344 United States — Final Anti-dumping Measures on Stainless Steel from Mexico (Complainant: Mexico) 26 May 2006	Panel report
DS343 United States — Measures relating on Shrimp from Thailand (Complainant: Thailand) 24 April 2006	Panel report, same issues, same panelists as in DS345
DS342 China — Measures Affecting Imports of Automobile Parts (Complainant: Canada) 13 April 2006	single Panel established, DS339, D340, DS342
DS341 Mexico — Definitive Countervailing Measures on Olive Oil from the European Communities (Complainant: European Communities) 31 March 2006	Panel report expected April 2008
DS340 China — Measures Affecting Imports of Automobile Parts (Complainant: United States) 30 March 2006	single Panel established, DS339, D340, DS342
DS339 China — Measures Affecting Imports of Automobile Parts (Complainant: European Communities) 30 March 2006	single Panel established, DS339, D340, DS342, Panel report expected April 2008
DS338 Canada — Provisional Anti-Dumping and Countervailing Duties on Grain Corn from the United States (Complainant: United States) 17 March 2006	no panel established nor settlement notified
DS337 European Communities — Anti-Dumping Measure on Farmed Salmon from Norway (Complainant: Norway) 17 March 2006	Panel report
DS336 Japan — Countervailing Duties on Dynamic Random Access Memories from Korea (Complainant: Korea) 14 March 2006	Panel report, AB report
DS335 United States — Anti-Dumping Measure on Shrimp from Ecuador (Complainant: Ecuador) 17 November 2005	Panel report
DS334 Turkey — Measures Affecting the Importation of Rice (Complainant: United States) 2 November 2005	Panel report
DS333 Dominican Republic — Foreign Exchange Fee Affecting Imports from Costa Rica (Complainant: Costa Rica) 12 September 2005	no panel established nor settlement notified
DS332 Brazil — Measures Affecting Imports of Retreaded Tyres (Complainant: European Communities) 20 June 2005	Panel report, AB report
DS331 Mexico — Anti-Dumping Duties on Steel Pipes and Tubes from Guatemala (Complainant: Guatemala) 17 June 2005	Panel report
DS330 Argentina — Countervailing Duties on Olive Oil, Wheat Gluten and Peaches (Complainant: European Communities) 29 April 2005	no panel established nor settlement notified
DS329 Panama — Tariff Classification of Certain Milk Products (Complainant: Mexico) 16 March 2005	mutually agreed solution, full success of Mexico
DS328 European Communities — Definitive Safeguard Measure on Salmon (Complainant: Norway) 1 March 2005	no panel established nor settlement notified
DS327 Egypt — Anti-Dumping Duties on Matches from Pakistan (Complainant: Pakistan) 21 February 2005	Panel established, mutually agreed soluation ('price undertaking')
DS326 European Communities — Definitive Safeguard Measure on Salmon (Complainant: Chile) 8 February 2005	On 12 May 2005, Chile formally withdrew its request for consultations, as the safeguard measure at issue was terminated as of 27 April 2005.
DS325 United States — Anti-Dumping Determinations regarding Stainless Steel from Mexico (Complainant: Mexico) 5 January 2005	no panel established nor settlement notified
DS324 United States — Provisional Anti-Dumping Measures on Shrimp from Thailand (Complainant: Thailand) 9 December 2004	no panel established nor settlement notified
DS323 Japan — Import Quotas on Dried Laver and Seasoned Laver (Complainant: Korea) 1 December 2004	Panel started work, but then mutually agreed solution, Korea recieves better market access: 27 January 2006 WT/DS323/5
DS322 United States — Measures Relating to Zeroing and Sunset Reviews (Complainant: Japan) 24 November 2004	Panel report, AB report
DS321 Canada — Continued Suspension of Obligations in the EC — Hormones Dispute (Complainant: European Communities) 8 November 2004	Panels established by DSB/report delayed several times, see DS320
DS320 United States — Continued Suspension of Obligations in the EC — Hormones Dispute (Complainant: European Communities) 8 November 2004	Panels established by DSB/report delayed several times, see DS321
DS319 United States — Section 776 of the Tariff Act of 1930 (Complainant: European Communities) 5 November 2004	no panel established nor settlement notified
DS318 India — Anti-Dumping Measures on Certain Products from the Separate Customs Territory of Taiwan, Penghu, Kinmen and Matsu (Complainant: Chinese Taipei) 28 October 2004	no panel established nor settlement notified
DS317 United States — Measures Affecting Trade in Large Civil Aircraft (Complainant: European Communities) 6 October 2004	Panels established by DSB/reports not yet circulated
DS316 European Communities — Measures Affecting Trade in Large Civil Aircraft (Complainant: United States) 6 October 2004	Panels established by DSB/reports not yet circulated
DS315 European Communities — Selected Customs Matters (Complainant: United States) 21 September 2004	Panel report, AB report
DS314 Mexico — Provisional Countervailing Measures on Olive Oil from the European Communities (Complainant: European Communities) 18 August 2004	no panel established nor settlement notified
DS313 European Communities — Anti-Dumping Duties on Certain Flat Rolled	mutually agreed solution,

Iron or Non-Alloy Steel Products from India (Complainant: India) 5 July 2004	EC withdrew measure
DS312 Korea — Anti-Dumping Duties on Imports of Certain Paper from Indonesia (Complainant: Indonesia) 4 June 2004	Panel report, Art. 21.5 Panel report
DS311 United States — Reviews of Countervailing Duty on Softwood Lumber from Canada (Complainant: Canada) 14 April 2004	mutually agreed solution on 23 February 2007, covering the following disputes DS236, DS247, DS257, DS264
DS310 United States — Determination of the International Trade Commission in Hard Red Spring Wheat from Canada (Complainant: Canada) 8 April 2004	no panel established nor settlement notified
DS309 China — Value-Added Tax on Integrated Circuits (Complainant: United States) 18 March 2004	mutually agreed solution, on 14 July 2004, China agreed to amend or revoke the measures at issue to eliminate the availability of VAT refunds on ICs produced and sold in China and on ICs designed in China but manufactured abroad
DS308 Mexico — Tax Measures on Soft Drinks and Other Beverages (Complainant: United States) 16 March 2004	Panel report, AB report, Mexico lost case, no justification under Art. XX (d)
DS307 European Communities — Aid for Commercial Vessels (Complainant: Korea) 13 February 2004	no panel established nor settlement notified, pursued further as DS301
DS306 India — Anti-Dumping Measure on Batteries from Bangladesh (Complainant: Bangladesh) 28 January 2004	mutually agreed solution, success Bangladesh, the contested measure has been terminated by India
DS305 Egypt — Measures Affecting Imports of Textile and Apparel Products (Complainant: United States) 23 December 2003	mutually agreed solution, no information given WT/DS305/4G/L/667/Add.125, May 2005
DS304 India — Anti-Dumping Measures on Imports of Certain Products from the European Communities (Complainant: European Communities) 8 December 2003 '27 products case'	no panel established nor settlement notified, after negotiations with the EU India abolishes or modifies several measure, see Abschnitt 'J', Antidumping
DS303 Ecuador — Definitive Safeguard Measure on Imports of Medium Density Fibreboard (Complainant: Chile) 24 November 2003	no panel established nor settlement notified
DS302 Dominican Republic — Measures Affecting the Importation and Internal Sale of Cigarettes (Complainant: Honduras) 8 October 2003	Panel report, AB report, Article 21.3 (c) arbitration, Dominican Republic brings measure into conformity
DS301 European Communities — Measures Affecting Trade in Commercial Vessels (Complainant: Korea) 3 September 2003 EU's Sec. 301 case	Panel report, at the DSB meeting of 20 July 2005, the European Communities informed the DSB that the Temporary Defense Mechanism (TDM) was not renewed when it expired on 31 March 2005.
DS300 Dominican Republic — Measures Affecting the Importation of Cigarettes (Complainant: Honduras) 28 August 2003	pursued further as DS302
DS299 European Communities — Countervailing Measures on Dynamic Random Access Memory Chips from Korea (Complainant: Korea) 25 July 2003	Panel report
DS298 Mexico — Certain Pricing Measures for Customs Valuation and Other Purposes (Complainant: Guatemala) 22 July 2003	mutually agreed solution
DS297 Croatia — Measures Affecting Imports of Live Animals and Meat Products (Complainant: Hungary) 9 July 2003	no panel established nor settlement notified
DS296 United States — Countervailing Duty Investigation on Dynamic Random Access Memory Semiconductors (DRAMS) from Korea (Complainant: Korea) 30 June 2003	Panel report, AB report
DS295 Mexico — Definitive Anti-Dumping Measures on Beef and Rice (Complainant: United States) 16 June 2003	Panel report, AB report
DS294 United States — Laws, Regulations and Methodology for Calculating Dumping Margins (Zeroing) (Complainant: European Communities) 12 June 2003.	Panel report, AB report
DS293 European Communities — Measures Affecting the Approval and Marketing of Biotech Products (Complainant: Argentina) 14 May 2003	reports DS293, DS291, DS290 of the panel, contained in one: Panel report
DS292 European Communities — Measures Affecting the Approval and Marketing of Biotech Products (Complainant: Canada) 13 May 2003	reports DS293, DS291, DS290 of the panel, contained in one: Panel report
DS291 European Communities — Measures Affecting the Approval and Marketing of Biotech Products (Complainant: United States) 13 May 2003	reports DS293, DS291, DS290 of the panel, contained in one: Panel report, implementation unclear as of early 2008
DS290 European Communities — Protection of Trademarks and Geographical Indications for Agricultural Products and Foodstuffs (Complainant: Australia) 17 April 2003	Panel report, single Panel with United States' DS174 complaint
DS289 Czech Republic — Additional Duty on Imports of Pig-Meat from Poland (Complainant: Poland) 16 April 2003	no panel established nor settlement notified

DS288 South Africa — Definitive Anti-Dumping Measures on Blanketing from Turkey (Complainant: Turkey) 9 April 2003	no panel established nor settlement notified
DS287 Australia — Quarantine Regime for Imports (Complainant: European Communities) 3 April 2003	mutually agreed solution, notified 9 March 2007
DS286 European Communities — Customs Classification of Frozen Boneless Chicken Cuts (Complainant: Thailand) 25 March 2003	Panel report, AB report, Article 21.3 (c) arbitration
DS285 United States — Measures Affecting the Cross-Border Supply of Gambling and Betting Services (Complainant: Antigua and Barbuda) 13 March 2003	Panel report, AB report, Article 21.3 (c)
DS284 Mexico — Certain Measures Preventing the Importation of Black Beans from Nicaragua (Complainant: Nicaragua) 17 March 2003	no Panel, Mexiko removed contested measure
DS283 European Communities — Export Subsidies on Sugar (Complainant: Thailand) 14 March 2003	separate but identical Panel reports: DS 265, DS 266, DS 283, joint AB report, see DS265
DS282 United States — Anti-Dumping Measures on Oil Country Tubular Goods (OCTG) from Mexico (Complainant: Mexico) 18 February 2003	Panel report, AB report
DS281 United States — Anti-Dumping Measures on Cement from Mexico (Complainant: Mexico) 31 January 2003	Panel work supsended, due to mutually agreed solution
DS280 United States — Countervailing Duties on Steel Plate from Mexico (Complainant: Mexico) 21 January 2003	Panel established by DSB/report not yet circulated
DS279 India — Import Restrictions Maintained Under the Export and Import Policy 2002-2007 (Complainant: European Communities) 23 December 2002	no panel established nor settlement notified
DS278 Chile — Definitive Safeguard Measure on Imports of Fructose (Complainant: Argentina) 20 December 2002	no panel established nor settlement notified
DS277 United States — Investigation of the International Trade Commission in Softwood Lumber from Canada (Complainant: Canada) 20 December 2002	Panel report, Article 21.5 Panel report, Article 21.5 AB report
DS276 Canada — Measures Relating to Exports of Wheat and Treatment of Imported Grain (Complainant: United States) 17 December 2002	Panel report, AB report
DS275 Venezuela — Import Licensing Measures on Certain Agricultural Products (Complainant: United States) 7 November 2002	no panel established nor settlement notified
DS274 United States — Definitive Safeguard Measures on Imports of Certain Steel Products (Complainant: Chinese Taipei) 1 November 2002	no panel established nor settlement notified
DS273 Korea — Measures Affecting Trade in Commercial Vessels (Complainant: European Communities) 21 October 2002	Panel report
DS272 Peru — Provisional Anti-Dumping Duties on Vegetable Oils from Argentina (Complainant: Argentina) 21 October 2002	no panel established nor settlement notified
DS271 Australia — Certain Measures Affecting the Importation of Fresh Pineapple (Complainant: Philippines) 18 October 2002	no panel established nor settlement notified
DS270 Australia — Certain Measures Affecting the Importation of Fresh Fruit and Vegetables (Complainant: Philippines) 18 October 2002	Panel established by DSB/report not yet circulated
DS269 European Communities — Customs Classification of Frozen Boneless Chicken Cuts (Complainant: Brazil) 11 October 2002	Panel report, AB report, Article 21.3 (c) arbitration
DS268 United States — Sunset Reviews of Anti-Dumping Measures on Oil Country Tubular Goods from Argentina (Complainant: Argentina) 7 October 2002	Panel report, AB report, Art. 21.3 (c) arbitration
DS267 United States — Subsidies on Upland Cotton (Complainant: Brazil) 27 September 2002	Panel report, AB report
DS266 European Communities — Export Subsidies on Sugar (Complainant: Brazil) 27 September 2002	separate but identical Panel reports: DS265, DS266, DS283, joint AB report, see DS265
DS265 European Communities — Export Subsidies on Sugar (Complainant: Australia) 27 September 2002	separate but identical Panel reports: DS 265, DS 266, DS 283, joint AB report: Panel report, AB report, Article 21.3 (c) arbitration
DS264 United States — Final Dumping Determination on Softwood Lumber from Canada (Complainant: Canada) 13 September 2002	Panel report, AB report, Article 21.3 (c) arbitration, Article 21.5 Panel report
DS263 European Communities — Measures Affecting Imports of Wine (Complainant: Argentina) 4 September 2002	no panel established nor settlement notified
DS262 United States — Sunset Reviews of Anti-Dumping and Countervailing Duties on Certain Steel Products from France and Germany (Complainant: European Communities) 25 July 2002	no panel established nor settlement notified
DS261 Uruguay — Tax Treatment on Certain Products (Complainant: Chile) 18 June 2002	Panel established, but parties requested it to stop its work, mutually agreed solution
DS260 European Communities — Provisional Safeguard Measures on Imports of Certain Steel Products (Complainant: United States) 30 May 2002	Panels established by DSB/reports not yet circulated
DS259 United States — Definitive Safeguard Measures on Imports of Certain Steel Products (Complainant: Brazil) 21 May 2002: 'Final Reports of the Panel'	single panel process, but eight separated reports, with particularized findings: Panel report, AB report
DS258 United States — Definitive Safeguard Measures on Imports of Certain Steel Products (Complainant: New Zealand) 14 May 2002	single panel process, but eight separated reports, with particularized findings: Panel report, AB report

DS257 United States — Final Countervailing Duty Determination with respect to certain Softwood Lumber from Canada (Complainant: Canada) 3 May 2002	Panel report, AB report, Article 21.5 Panel report, Article 21.5 AB report
DS256 Turkey — Import Ban on Pet Food from Hungary (Complainant: Hungary) 3 May 2002	no panel established nor settlement notified
DS255 Peru — Tax Treatment on Certain Imported Products (Complainant: Chile) 22 April 2002	other settled or inactive cases, Peru abolished contested measure
DS254 United States — Definitive Safeguard Measures on Imports of Certain Steel Products (Complainant: Norway) 4 April 2002	single panel process, but eight separated reports, with particularized findings: Panel report, AB report
DS253 United States — Definitive Safeguard Measures on Imports of Certain Steel Products (Complainant: Switzerland) 3 April 2002	single panel process, but eight separated reports, with particularized findings: Panel report, AB report
DS252 United States — Definitive Safeguard Measures on Imports of Certain Steel Products (Complainant: China) 26 March 2002	single panel process, but eight separated reports, with particularized findings: Panel report, AB report
DS251 United States — Definitive Safeguard Measures on Imports of Certain Steel Products (Complainant: Korea) 20 March 2002	single panel process, but eight separated reports, with particularized findings: Panel report, AB report
DS250 United States — Equalizing Excise Tax Imposed by Florida on Processed Orange and Grapefruit Products (Complainant: Brazil) 20 March 2002	no Panel, mutually agreed solution Florida changed tax law
DS249 United States — Definitive Safeguard Measures on Imports of Certain Steel Products (Complainant: Japan) 20 March 2002	single panel process, but eight separated reports, with particularized findings: Panel report, AB report
DS248 United States — Definitive Safeguard Measures on Imports of Certain Steel Products (Complainant: European Communities) 7 March 2002	single panel process, but eight separated reports, with particularized findings: Panel report, AB report
DS247 United States — Provisional Anti-Dumping Measure on Imports of Certain Softwood Lumber from Canada (Complainant: Canada) 6 March 2002	no panel established nor settlement notified
DS246 European Communities — Conditions for the Granting of Tariff Preferences to Developing Countries (Complainant: India) 5 March 2002	Panel report, AB report, Article 21.3 (c) arbitration
DS245 Japan — Measures Affecting the Importation of Apples (Complainant: United States) 1 March 2002	Panel report, AB report, Article 21.5 arbitration
DS244 United States — Sunset Review of Anti-Dumping Duties on Corrosion-Resistant Carbon Steel Flat Products from Japan (Complainant: Japan) 30 January 2002	Panel report, AB report
DS243 United States — Rules of Origin for Textiles and Apparel Products (Complainant: India) 11 January 2002	Panel report, India lost same topic as in DS151 and DS85
DS242 European Communities — Generalized System of Preferences (Complainant: Thailand) 7 December 2001	no panel established nor settlement notified
DS241 Argentina — Definitive Anti-Dumping Duties on Poultry from Brazil (Complainant: Brazil) 7 November 2001	Panel report, implementation not known
DS240 Romania — Import Prohibition on Wheat and Wheat Flour (Complainant: Hungary) 18 October 2001: 'Hungary uses DSU Art. 4.8 urgency procedures again'	not panel established, Romania withdrew measure
DS239 United States — Anti-Dumping Duties on Silicon Metal from Brazil (Complainant: Brazil) 18 September 2001	no panel established nor settlement notified
DS238 Argentina — Definitive Safeguard Measure on Imports of Preserved Peaches (Complainant: Chile) 14 September 2001	Panel report, Argentina withdrew measure
DS237 Turkey — Certain Import Procedures for Fresh Fruit (Complainant: Ecuador) 31 August 2001	Panel established, but suspended due to mutually agreed solution, Turkey withdrew contested measure
DS236 United States — Preliminary Determinations with Respect to Certain Softwood Lumber from Canada (Complainant: Canada) 21 August 2001	Panel Report, case won by Canada
DS235 Slovakia — Safeguard Measure on Imports of Sugar (Complainant: Poland) 11 July 2001 'sugar against butter and margerine'	mutually agreed solution, Slovakia agreed to a progressive increase of the level of its quota for imports of sugar from Poland between 2002 and 2004, and Poland agreed to remove its quantitative restriction on imports of butter and margarine.
DS234 United States — Continued Dumping and Subsidy Offset Act of 2000 (Complainants: Canada, Mexico) 21 May 2001	joint complaint DS234 and DS217, see DS217
DS233 Argentina — Measures Affecting the Import of Pharmaceutical Products (Complainant: India) 25 May 2001	no panel established nor settlement notified
DS232 Mexico — Measures Affecting the Import of Matches (Complainant: Chile) 17 May 2001	other settled or inactive cases
DS231 European Communities — Trade Description of Sardines (Complainant: Peru) 20 March 2001	Panel report, AB report, on 25 July 2003, the EC and Peru informed the DSB that they had reached a mutually

	agreed solution, case won by Peru
DS230 Chile — Safeguard Measures and Modification of Schedules Regarding Sugar (Complainant: Colombia) 17 April 2001	no panel established nor settlement notified
DS229 Brazil — Anti-Dumping Duties on Jute Bags from India (Complainant: India) 9 April 2001	no panel established nor settlement notified
DS228 Chile — Safeguard Measures on Sugar (Complainant: Colombia) 15 March 2001	consultation request replaced by that in dispute DS230
DS227 Peru — Taxes on Cigarettes (Complainant: Chile) 1 March 2001	Panel established but not pursued further, Peru withdrew measure
DS226 Chile — Provisional Safeguard Measure on Mixtures of Edible Oils (Complainant: Argentina) 19 February 2001	no panel established nor settlement notified
DS225 United States — Anti-Dumping Duties on Seamless Pipe from Italy (Complainant: European Communities) 5 February 2001	no panel established nor settlement notified
DS224 United States — US Patents Code (Complainant: Brazil) 31 January 2001	no panel established nor settlement notified
DS223 European Communities — Tariff-Rate Quota on Corn Gluten Feed from the United States (Complainant: United States) 25 January 2001	no panel established nor settlement notified
DS222 Canada — Export Credits and Loan Guarantees for Regional Aircraft (Complainant: Brazil) 22 January 2001	Panel report, Article 22.6 arbitration
DS221 United States — Section 129(c)(1) of the Uruguay Round Agreements Act (Complainant: Canada) 17 January 2001	Panel report, case won by U.S.
DS220 Chile — Price Band System and Safeguard Measures Relating to Certain Agricultural Products (Complainant: Guatemala) 5 January 2001	no panel established nor settlement notified
DS219 European Communities — Anti-Dumping Duties on Malleable Cast Iron Tube or Pipe Fittings from Brazil (Complainant: Brazil) 21 December 2000	Panel report, AB report
DS218 United States — Countervailing Duties on Certain Carbon Steel Products from Brazil (Complainant: Brazil) 21 December 2000	no panel established nor settlement notified
DS217 United States — Continued Dumping and Subsidy Offset Act of 2000 (Complainants: Australia, Brazil, Chile, European Communities, India, Indonesia, Japan, Korea, Thailand) 21 December 2000	joint complaint DS217 and DS234, Panel report, AB report, Article 21.3 (c) arbitration, Article 22.6 arbitration
DS216 Mexico — Provisional Anti-Dumping Measure on Electric Transformers (Complainant: Brazil) 20 December 2000	no panel established nor settlement notified
DS215 Philippines — Anti-Dumping Measures Regarding Polypropylene Resins from Korea (Complainant: Korea) 15 December 2000	no panel established nor settlement notified
DS214 United States — Definitive Safeguard Measures on Imports of Steel Wire Rod and Circular Welded Quality (Complainant: European Communities) 1 December 2000	Panel established by DSB/report not yet circulated
DS213 United States — Countervailing Duties on Certain Corrosion-Resistant Carbon Steel Flat Products from Germany (Complainant: European Communities) 10 November 2000	Panel report, AB report
DS212 United States — Countervailing Measures Concerning Certain Products from the European Communities (Complainant: European Communities) 10 November 2000	Panel report, AB report, Art. 21.5 Panel report
DS211 Egypt — Definitive Anti-Dumping Measures on Steel Rebar from Turkey (Complainant: Turkey) 6 November 2000	Panel report
DS210 Belgium — Administration of Measures Establishing Customs Duties for Rice (Complainant: United States) 12 October 2000	Panel established, but mutually agreed solution
DS209 European Communities — Measures Affecting Soluble Coffee (Complainant: Brazil) 12 October 2000	no panel established nor settlement notified
DS208 Turkey — Anti-Dumping Duty on Steel and Iron Pipe Fittings (Complainant: Brazil) 9 October 2000	no panel established nor settlement notified
DS207 Chile — Price Band System and Safeguard Measures Relating to Certain Agricultural Products (Complainant: Argentina) 5 October 2000	Panel report, AB report, Article 21.3 (c) Arbitration Report, Art. 21.5 Report in the making, not yet finished
DS206 United States — Anti-Dumping and Countervailing Measures on Steel Plate from India (Complainant: India) 4 October 2000	Panel report
DS205 Egypt — Import Prohibition on Canned Tuna with SoyBean Oil (Complainant: Thailand) 22 September 2000	no panel established nor settlement notified
DS204 Mexico — Measures Affecting Telecommunications Services (Complainant: United States) 17 August 2000	Panel report, Mexico fully complied with recommendations
DS203 Mexico — Measures Affecting Trade in Live Swine (Complainant: United States) 10 July 2000	no panel established nor settlement notified
DS202 United States — Definitive Safeguard Measures on Imports of Circular Welded Carbon Quality Line Pipe from Korea (Complainant: Korea) 13 June 2000	Panel report, AB report, Article 21.3 (c) arbitration
DS201 Nicaragua — Measures Affecting Imports from Honduras and Colombia (Complainant: Honduras) 6 June 2000	no panel established nor settlement notified
DS200 United States — Section 306 of the Trade Act 1974 and Amendments thereto (Complainant: European Communities) 5 June 2000	no panel established nor settlement notified

DS199 Brazil — Measures Affecting Patent Protection (Complainant: United States) 30 May 2000	mutually agreed solution, 'Pharma local working requirements'
DS198 Romania — Measures on Minimum Import Prices (Complainant: United States) 30 May 2000	mutually satisfactory solution
DS197 Brazil — Measures on Minimum Import Prices (Complainant: United States) 30 May 2000	no panel established nor settlement notified
DS196 Argentina — Certain Measures on the Protection of Patents and Test Data (Complainant: United States) 30 May 2000	mutually agreed solution, see DS171
DS195 Philippines — Measures Affecting Trade and Investment in the Motor Vehicle Sector (Complainant: United States) 23 May 2000	Panel established by DSB/report not yet circulated
DS194 United States — Measures Treating Export Restraints as Subsidies (Complainant: Canada) 19 May 2000	Panel report
DS193 Chile — Measures affecting the Transit and Importing of Swordfish (Complainant: European Communities) 19 April 2000	Panel established, but activity suspended, other settled or inactive cases
DS192 United States — Transitional Safeguard Measure on Combed Cotton Yarn from Pakistan (Complainant: Pakistan) 3 April 2000	Panel report, AB report, the US declared it had directed the US Customs Services to eliminate the limit on imports of combed cotton yarn from Pakistan. Success Pakistan.
DS191 Ecuador — Definitive Anti-Dumping Measure on Cement from Mexico (Complainant: Mexico) 15 March 2000	no panel established nor settlement notified
DS190 Argentina — Transitional Safeguard Measures on Certain Imports of Woven Fabric Products of Cotton and Cotton Mixtures Originating in Brazil (Complainant: Brazil) 11 February 2000	mutually agreed solution
DS189 Argentina — Definitive Anti-Dumping Measures on Carton-Board Imports from Germany and Definitive Anti-Dumping Measures on Imports of Ceramic Tiles from Italy (Complainant: European Communities) 26 January 2000	Panel report, Argentina revokes measure, success EC
DS188 Nicaragua — Measures Affecting Imports from Honduras and Colombia (Complainant: Colombia) 17 January 2000	Panel established by DSB, but Panel not yet been composed
DS187 Trinidad and Tobago — Provisional Anti-Dumping Measure on Macaroni and Spaghetti from Costa Rica (Complainant: Costa Rica) 17 January 2000	no panel established nor settlement notified
DS186 United States — Section 337 of the Tariff Act of 1930 and Amendments thereto (Complainant: European Communities) 12 January 2000	no panel established nor settlement notified
DS185 Trinidad and Tobago — Anti-Dumping Measures on Pasta from Costa Rica (Complainant: Costa Rica) 18 November 1999	no panel established nor settlement notified
DS184 United States — Anti-Dumping Measures on Certain Hot-Rolled Steel Products from Japan (Complainant: Japan) 18 November 1999	Panel report, AB report, Article 23.1 (c) arbitration
DS183 Brazil — Measures on Import Licensing and Minimum Import Prices (Complainant: European Communities) 14 October 1999	no panel established nor settlement notified
DS182 Ecuador — Provisional Anti-Dumping Measure on Cement from Mexico (Complainant: Mexico) 5 October 1999	no panel established nor settlement notified
DS181 Colombia — Safeguard Measure of Imports of Plain Polyester Filaments from Thailand (Complainant: Thailand) 7 September 1999	no panel, Columbia removed contested measure
DS180 United States — Reclassification of Certain Sugar Syrups (Complainant: Canada) 6 September 1999	no panel established nor settlement notified
DS179 United States — Anti-Dumping measures on Stainless Steel Plate in Coils and Stainless Steel Sheet and Strip from Korea (Complainant: Korea) 30 July 1999	Panel report
DS178 United States — Safeguard Measure on Imports of Fresh, Chilled or Frozen Lamb from Australia (Complainant: Australia) 23 July 1999	single Panel DS177 and DS178, see DS177
DS177 United States — Safeguard Measure on Imports of Fresh, Chilled or Frozen Lamb from New Zealand (Complainant: New Zealand) 16 July 1999	single panel DS177 and DS178, Panel report, AB report, US not amused, claims new obligations are imposed: Bridges Vol. 5 No. 19 May 22, 2001
DS176 United States — Section 211 Omnibus Appropriations Act of 1998 (Complainant: European Communities) 8 July 1999	Panel report, AB report, US refuses to implement, see: WT/DS176/11/Add.42, 5 May 2006, WT/DS176/11/Add.64 4 March 2008
DS175 India — Measures Affecting Trade and Investment in the Motor Vehicle Sector (Complainant: United States) 2 June 1999	single Panel DS146 and DS 175: Panel report, short AB report, not pursued further. On 6 November 2002, India informed the DSB that it had fully complied with the recommendations of the DSB in this dispute
DS174 European Communities — Protection of Trademarks and Geographical Indications for Agricultural Products and Foodstuffs (Complainant: United States) 1 June 1999	Panel report, single Panel with Australia's DS290 complaint
DS173 France — Measures Relating to the Development of a Flight	see DS172

Management System (Complainant: United States) 21 May 1999	
DS172 European Communities — Measures Relating to the Development of a Flight Management System (Complainant: United States) 21 May 1999	no panel established nor settlement notified
DS171 Argentina — Patent Protection for Pharmaceuticals and Test Data Protection for Agricultural Chemicals (Complainant: United States) 6 May 1999	mutually agreed solution
DS170 Canada — Term of Patent Protection (Complainant: United States) 6 May 1999	Panel report, AB report, Article 21.3 (c) arbitration. U.S. won the case.
DS169 Korea — Measures Affecting Imports of Fresh, Chilled and Frozen Beef (Complainant: Australia) 13 April 1999	see DS161
DS168 South Africa — Anti-Dumping Duties on Certain Pharmaceutical Products from India (Complainant: India) 1 April 1999	no panel established nor settlement notified
DS167 United States — Countervailing Duty Investigation with respect to Live Cattle from Canada (Complainant: Canada) 19 March 1999	no panel established nor settlement notified
DS166 United States — Definitive Safeguard Measures on Imports of Wheat Gluten from the European Communities (Complainant: European Communities) 17 March 1999	Panel report, AB report
DS165 United States — Import Measures on Certain Products from the European Communities (Complainant: European Communities) 4 March 1999	Panel report, AB report
DS164 Argentina — Measures Affecting Imports of Footwear (Complainant: United States) 1 March 1999	Panels established by DSB/reports not yet circulated, see DS123, DS121
DS163 Korea — Measures Affecting Government Procurement (Complainant: United States) 16 February 1999	Panel report, USA not successfull
DS162 United States — Anti-Dumping Act of 1916 (Complainant: Japan) 10 February 1999	Panel report, AB report, Article 21.3 (c) arbitration, see DS136
DS161 Korea — Measures Affecting Imports of Fresh, Chilled and Frozen Beef (Complainant: United States) 1 February 1999	Panel report, AB report, Korea implements
DS160 United States — Section 110(5) of US Copyright Act (Complainant: European Communities) 26 January 1999	Panel report, Article 21.3 (c) arbitration, Article 22.6 arbitration. USA does not implement. On 23th of June 2003, the US and the EC informed the DSB of a mutually satisfactory temporary arrangement.
DS159 Hungary — Safeguard Measure on Imports of Steel Products from the Czech Republic (Complainant: Czech Republic) 21 January 1999	no panel established nor settlement notified
DS158 European Communities — Regime for the Importation, Sale and Distribution of Bananas (Complainants: Guatemala, Honduras, Mexico, Panama, United States) 20 January 1999	no panel established nor settlement notified
DS157 Argentina — Definitive Anti-Dumping Measures on Imports of Drill Bits from Italy (Complainant: European Communities) 14 January 1999	no panel established nor settlement notified
DS156 Guatemala — Definitive Anti-Dumping Measure on Grey Portland Cement from Mexico (Complainant: Mexico) 5 January 1999	Panel report, Guatemala informed the DSB that in October 2000 it had removed its anti-dumping measure and had thus complied with the DSB's recommendations.
DS155 Argentina — Measures Affecting the Export of Bovine Hides and the Import of Finished Leather (Complainant: European Communities) 23 December 1998	Panel report, Art. 23.1 (c) arbitration. Implementation delayed due to economic problems in Argentina, EC retains right to invoke Art. 21.5
DS154 European Communities — Measures Affecting Differential and Favourable Treatment of Coffee (Complainant: Brazil) 7 December 1998	no panel established nor settlement notified
DS153 European Communities — Patent Protection for Pharmaceutical and Agricultural Chemical Products (Complainant: Canada) 2 December 1998	no panel established nor settlement notified
DS152 United States — Sections 301–310 of the Trade Act 1974 (Complainant: European Communities) 25 November 1998	Panel report
DS151 United States — Measures Affecting Textiles and Apparel Products (II) (Complainant: European Communities) 19 November 1998	mutually agreed solution
DS150 India — Measures Affecting Customs Duties (Complainant: European Communities) 31 October 1998	no panel established nor settlement notified
DS149 India — Import Restrictions (Complainant: European Communities) 28 October 1998	no panel established nor settlement notified
DS148 Czech Republic — Measure Affecting Import Duty on Wheat from Hungary (Complainant: Hungary) 12 October 1998	no panel established nor settlement notified
DS147 Japan — Tariff Quotas and Subsidies Affecting Leather (Complainant: European Communities) 8 October 1998	no panel established nor settlement notified
DS146 India — Measures Affecting the Automotive Sector (Complainant: European Communities) 6 October 1998	single Panel DS146 and DS175, EU joins DS 175 complaint of the U.S.
DS145 Argentina — Countervailing Duties on Imports of Wheat Gluten from the European Communities (Complainant: European Communities) 23 September 1998	no panel established nor settlement notified

DS144 United States — Certain Measures Affecting the Import of Cattle, Swine and Grain from Canada (Complainant: Canada) 25 September 1998	no panel established nor settlement notified
DS143 Slovak Republic — Measure Affecting Import Duty on Wheat from Hungary (Complainant: Hungary) 19 September 1998	no panel established nor settlement notified
DS142 Canada — Certain Measures Affecting the Automotive Industry (Complainant: European Communities) 17 August 1998	single panel DS139 and DS142
DS141 European Communities — Anti-Dumping Duties on Imports of Cotton-type Bed Linen from India (Complainant: India) 3 August 1998	Panel report, AB report, Article 21.5 Panel report, Article 21.5 AB report
DS140 European Communities — Anti-Dumping Investigations Regarding Unbleached Cotton Fabrics from India (Complainant: India) 3 August 1998	no panel established nor settlement notified
DS139 Canada — Certain Measures Affecting the Automotive Industry (Complainant: Japan) 3 July 1998	single Panel with DS 142: Panel report, AB report, Article 21.3 (c) arbitration, Canada stated that, as of 18 February 2001, it had complied with the DSB's recommendations.
DS138 United States — Imposition of Countervailing Duties on Certain Hot-Rolled Lead and Bismuth Carbon Steel Products Originating in the United Kingdom (Complainant: European Communities) 12 June 1998	Panel report, AB report, as a follow-up to this case, the EC has filed a new complaint against the US see WT/DS212.
DS137 European Communities — Measures Affecting Imports of Wood of Conifers from Canada (Complainant: Canada) 17 June 1998	no panel established nor settlement notified
DS136 United States — Anti-Dumping Act of 1916 (Complainant: European Communities) 4 June 1998	Panel report, AB report, Article 21.3 (c) arbitration, see DS 162
DS135 European Communities — Measures Affecting Asbestos and Products Containing Asbestos (Complainant: Canada) 28 May 1998	Panel report, AB report EC/France won
DS134 European Communities — Restrictions on Certain Import Duties on Rice (Complainant: India) 27 May 1998	no panel established nor settlement notified
DS133 Slovak Republic — Measures Concerning the Importation of Dairy Products and the Transit of Cattle (Complainant: Switzerland) 7 May 1998	no panel established nor settlement notified
DS132 Mexico — Anti-Dumping Investigation of High-Fructose Corn Syrup (HFCS) from the United States (Complainant: United States) 8 May 1998	Panel report, Article 21.5 Panel report, Article 21.5 AB report, Mexico lost, implementation not clear
DS131 France — Certain Income Tax Measures Constituting Subsidies (Complainant: United States) 5 May 1998	no panel established nor settlement notified
DS130 Ireland — Certain Income Tax Measures Constituting Subsidies (Complainant: United States) 5 May 1998	no panel established nor settlement notified
DS129 Greece — Certain Income Tax Measures Constituting Subsidies (Complainant: United States) 5 May 1998	no panel established nor settlement notified
DS128 Netherlands — Certain Income Tax Measures Constituting Subsidies (Complainant: United States) 5 May 1998	no panel established nor settlement notified
DS127 Belgium — Certain Income Tax Measures Constituting Subsidies (Complainant: United States) 5 May 1998	no panel established nor settlement notified
DS126 Australia — Subsidies Provided to Producers and Exporters of Automotive Leather (Complainant: United States) 4 May 1998	Panel report, Article 21.5 Panel report On 24 July 2000, the parties notified the DSB that they had reached a mutually satisfactory solution
DS125 Greece — Enforcement of Intellectual Property Rights for Motion Pictures and Television Programs (Complainant: United States) 4 May 1998	mutually agreed solution, see DS124
DS124 European Communities — Enforcement of Intellectual Property Rights for Motion Pictures and Television Programs (Complainant: United States) 30 April 1998	mutually agreed solution
DS123 Argentina — Safeguard Measures on Imports of Footwear (Complainant: Indonesia) 22 April 1998	no panel established nor settlement notified
DS122 Thailand — Anti-Dumping Duties on Angles, Shapes and Sections of Iron or Non-Alloy Steel and H Beams from Poland (Complainant: Poland) 6 April 1998	Panel report, AB report. Thailand maintains measure based on a new injury investition, see WT/DS122/9, 6 December 2001
DS121 Argentina — Safeguard Measures on Imports of Footwear (Complainant: European Communities) 6 April 1998	Panel report, AB report, pursuant to Article 21.3 of the DSU, Argentina informed the DSB on 11 February 2000 that the safeguard measure would remain in force until 25 February 2000 and, by that date, the measures aimed at complying with the DSB's recommendations and ruling would be adopted.
DS120 India — Measures Affecting Export of Certain Commodities (Complainant: European Communities) 11 March 1998	no panel established nor settlement notified
DS119 Australia — Anti-Dumping Measures on Imports of Coated Woodfree Paper Sheets (Complainant: Switzerland) 20 February 1998	mutually agreed solution
DS118 United States — Harbour Maintenance Tax (Complainant: European	no panel established nor settlement

Communities) 6 February 1998	notified
DS117 Canada — Measures Affecting Film Distribution Services (Complainant: European Communities) 20 January 1998	no panel established nor settlement notified
DS116 Brazil — Measures Affecting Payment Terms for Imports (Complainant: European Communities) 8 January 1998	no panel established nor settlement notified
DS115 European Communities — Measures Affecting the Grant of Copyright and Neighbouring Rights (Complainant: United States) 6 January 1998	mutually agreed solution notified Copyright law has been changed
DS114 Canada — Patent Protection of Pharmaceutical Products (Complainant: European Communities) 19 December 1997	Panel report, Article 21.3 (c) arbitration, at the DSB meeting of 23 October 2000, Canada informed Members that, effective from 7 October 2000, it had implemented the DSB's recommendations.
DS113 Canada — Measures Affecting Dairy Exports (Complainant: New Zealand) 29 December 1997	single Panel established for DS103 and DS113, see DS103
DS112 Peru — Countervailing Duty Investigation against Imports of Buses from Brazil (Complainant: Brazil) 23 December 1997	no panel established nor settlement notified
DS111 United States — Tariff Rate Quota for Imports of Groundnuts (Complainant: Argentina) 19 December 1997	no panel established nor settlement notified
DS110 Chile — Taxes on Alcoholic Beverages (Complainant: European Communities) 15 December 1997	Panel report, AB report, Article 21.3 (c) arbitration, joint DS87 and DS110 reports, Chile lost and complies
DS109 Chile — Taxes on Alcoholic Beverages (Complainant: United States) 11 December 1997	no panel established nor settlement notified
DS108 United States — Tax Treatment for "Foreign Sales Corporations" (Complainant: European Communities) 18 November 1997	Panel report, AB report, Article 21.5 Panel report, Article 21.5 AB report, Article 22.6 arbitration, Second Recourse to Article 21.5 Panel, Second Recourse to Art. 21.5 AB
DS107 Pakistan — Export Measures Affecting Hides and Skins (Complainant: European Communities) 7 November 1997	no panel established nor settlement notified
DS106 Australia — Subsidies Provided to Producers and Exporters of Automotive Leather (Complainant: United States) 10 November 1997	other settled or inactive cases, see DS126
DS105 European Communities — Regime for the Importation, Sale and Distribution of Bananas (Complainant: Panama) 24 October 1997	no panel established nor settlement notified, see DS27
DS104 European Communities — Measures Affecting the Exportation of Processed Cheese (Complainant: United States) 8 October 1997	no panel established nor settlement notified
DS103 Canada — Measures Affecting the Importation of Milk and the Exportation of Dairy Products (Complainant: United States) 8 October 1997	see above, single panel established for DS 103 and DS 113: Panel report, AB report, Article 21.5 Panel report, Article 21.5 AB report, Second recourse to Article 21.5 Panel, Second recourse to Article 21.5 AB, on 9 May 2003, Canada and the United States, and Canada and New Zealand informed the DSB that they had reached mutually agreed solutions
DS102 Philippines — Measures Affecting Pork and Poultry (Complainant: United States) 7 October 1997	no panel, on 12 March 1998, the parties communicated a mutually agreed solution to their disputel
DS101 Mexico — Anti-Dumping Investigation of High-Fructose Corn Syrup (HFCS) from the United States (Complainant: United States) 4 September 1997	other settled or inactive cases, see DS132
DS100 United States — Measures Affecting Imports of Poultry Products (Complainant: European Communities) 18 August 1997	no panel established nor settlement notified
DS99 United States — Anti-Dumping Duty on Dynamic Random Access Memory Semiconductors (DRAMS) of One Megabit or Above from Korea (Complainant: Korea) 14 August 1997 Alice in Wonderland case: 'likely' 'not likely' discussion	Panel report, Article 21.5 Panel report (4 pages long) not pursued further, on 20 October 2000, the parties notified the DSB of a mutually satisfactory solution to the matter, involving the revocation of the antidumping order at issue as the result of a five-year 'sunset' review by the U.S. DOC.
DS98 Korea — Definitive Safeguard Measure on Imports of Certain Dairy Products (Complainant: European Communities) 12 August 1997	Panel report, AB report, at the DSB meeting of 26 September 2000, Korea informed the DSB that it had lifted its safeguard measure on 20 May 2000 and stated that it had completed the implementation of the DSB's recommendations in this case.
DS97 United States — Countervailing Duty Investigation of Imports of Salmon from Chile (Complainant: Chile) 5 August 1997	no panel established nor settlement notified

DS96 India — Quantitative Restrictions on Imports of Agricultural, Textile and Industrial Products (Complainant: European Communities) 18 July 1997	on 7 April 1998, the two parties notified a mutually agreed solution, no panel
DS95 United States — Measure Affecting Government Procurement (Complainant: Japan) 18 July 1997	single Panel established with DS88, not pursued further
DS94 India — Quantitative Restrictions on Imports of Agricultural, Textile and Industrial Products (Complainant: Switzerland) 17 July 1997	on 23 February 1998, the two parties notified a mutually agreed solution, no panel
DS93 India — Quantitative Restrictions on Imports of Agricultural, Textile and Industrial Products (Complainant: New Zealand) 16 July 1997	no panel, in a letter dated 14 September 1998, but communicated to the Secretariat on 1 December 1998, the two parties notified a mutually agreed solution to this dispute, no panel
DS92 India — Quantitative Restrictions on Imports of Agricultural, Textile and Industrial Products (Complainant: Canada) 16 July 1997	on 25 March 1998, the two parties notified a mutually agreed solution, no panel
DS91 India — Quantitative Restrictions on Imports of Agricultural, Textile and Industrial Products (Complainant: Australia) 16 July 1997	on 23 March 1998, the two parties notified a mutually agreed solution, no panel
DS90 India — Quantitative Restrictions on Imports of Agricultural, Textile and Industrial Products (Complainant: United States) 15 July 1997	Panel report, AB report, at the DSB meeting of 5 April 2001, India announced that, with effect from 1 April 2001, it had removed the quantitative restrictions on imports in respect of the remaining 715 items and had thus implemented the DSB's recommendations in this case.
DS89 United States — Anti-Dumping Duties on Imports of Colour Television Receivers from Korea (Complainant: Korea) 10 July 1997	at the DSB meeting on 22 September 1998, Korea announced that it was definitively withdrawing the request for a panel because the imposition of anti-dumping duties had now been revoked.
DS88 United States — Measure Affecting Government Procurement (Complainant: European Communities) 20 June 1997	Panel proceedings suspended by EU, see DS95
DS87 Chile — Taxes on Alcoholic Beverages (Complainant: European Communities) 4 June 1997	Panel report, AB report, Art. 21.3 (c) arbitration. At the DSB meeting of 1 February 2001, Chile announced that implementing legislation was adopted, success EU
DS86 Sweden — Measures Affecting the Enforcement of Intellectual Property Rights (Complainant: United States) 28 May 1997	in panel established, in a communication dated 2 December 1998, the two parties notified a mutually agreed solution to this dispute
DS85 United States — Measures Affecting Textiles and Apparel Products (Complainant: European Communities) 22 May 1997	no panel established, mutually agreed solution
DS84 Korea — Taxes on Alcoholic Beverages (Complainant: United States) 23 May 1997	single panel DS75 and DS84, see DS75
DS83 Denmark — Measures Affecting the Enforcement of Intellectual Property Rights (Complainant: United States) 14 May 1997	on 7 June 2001, the parties to the dispute notified to the DSB a mutually satisfactory solution on the matter, no panel established
DS82 Ireland — Measures Affecting the Grant of Copyright and Neighbouring Rights (Complainant: United States) 14 May 1997	mutually agreed solution, no Panel established
DS81 Brazil — Measures Affecting Trade and Investment in the Automotive Sector (Complainant: European Communities) 7 May 1997	no panel established nor settlement notified
DS80 Belgium — Measures Affecting Commercial Telephone Directory Services (Complainant: United States) 2 May 1997	no panel established nor settlement notified
DS79 India — Patent Protection for Pharmaceutical and Agricultural Chemical Products (Complainant: European Communities) 28 April 1997	Panel Report, India enacts legislation to implement the recommendations and rulings of the DSB.
DS78 United States — Safeguard Measure Against Imports of Broom Corn Brooms (Complainant: Colombia) 28 April 1997	no panel established nor settlement notified
DS77 Argentina — Measures Affecting Textiles, Clothing and Footwear (Complainant: European Communities) 21 April 1997	panel not pursued further, settled or inactive case, success USA, EU
DS76 Japan — Measures Affecting Agricultural Products (Complainant: United States) 7 April 1997	Panel report, AB report, mutually satisfactory solution
DS75 Korea — Taxes on Alcoholic Beverages (Complainant: European Communities) 2 April 1997	single panel with DS84: Panel report, AB report, Article 21.3 (c) arbitration
DS74 Philippines — Measures Affecting Pork and Poultry (Complainant: United States) 1 April 1997	not panel, mutually agreed solution
DS73 Japan — Procurement of a Navigation Satellite (Complainant: European	no panel, mutually agreed solution

Communities) 26 March 1997	
European Communities — Measures Affecting Butter Products (Complainant: New Zealand) 24 March 1997	panel proceedings suspended due to mutually agreed solution
DS71 Canada — Measures Affecting the Export of Civilian Aircraft (Complainant: Brazil) 10 March 1997	no panel established nor settlement notified
DS70 Canada — Measures Affecting the Export of Civilian Aircraft (Complainant: Brazil) 10 March 1997	Panel report, AB report, Article 21.5 Panel report, Article 21.5 AB report
DS69 European Communities — Measures Affecting Importation of Certain Poultry Products (Complainant: Brazil) 24 February 1997	Panel report, AB report implementation not known
DS68 Ireland — Customs Classification of Certain Computer Equipment (Complainant: United States) 14 February 1997	joint panel, joint AB with DS62
DS67 United Kingdom — Customs Classification of Certain Computer Equipment (Complainant: United States) 14 February 1997	joint panel, joint AB with DS62
DS66 Japan — Measures Affecting Imports of Pork (Complainant: European Communities) 25 January 1997	no panel established nor settlement notified
DS65 Brazil — Certain Measures Affecting Trade and Investment in the Automotive Sector (Complainant: United States) 10 January 1997	no panel established nor settlement notified
DS64 Indonesia — Certain Measures Affecting the Automobile Industry (Complainant: Japan) 29 November 1996	joint panel, joint arbitration with DS54
DS63 United States — Anti-Dumping Measures on Imports of Solid Urea from the Former German Democratic Republic (Complainant: European Communities) 28 November 1996	no panel established nor settlement notified
DS62 European Communities — Customs Classification of Certain Computer Equipment (Complainant: United States) 8 November 1996	Panel report, AB report success EU
DS61 United States — Import Prohibition of Certain Shrimp and Shrimp Products (Complainant: Philippines) 25 October 1996	no panel established nor settlement notified, but see DS58
DS60 Guatemala — Anti-Dumping Investigation Regarding Portland Cement from Mexico (Complainant: Mexico) 17 October 1996	Panel report, AB report
DS59 Indonesia — Certain Measures Affecting the Automobile Industry (Complainant: United States) 8 October 1996	joint panel, joint arbitration with DS54
DS58 United States — Import Prohibition of Certain Shrimp and Shrimp Products (Complainants: India, Malaysia, Pakistan, Thailand) 8 October 1996	Panel report, AB report, Article 21.5 Panel report, Article 21.5 AB report
DS57 Australia — Textile, Clothing and Footwear Import Credit Scheme (Complainant: United States) 7 October 1996	no panel, case settled
DS56 Argentina — Measures Affecting Imports of Footwear, Textiles, Apparel and other Items (Complainant: United States) 4 October 1996	Panel report, AB report
DS55 Indonesia — Certain Measures Affecting the Automobile Industry (Complainant: Japan) 4 October 1996	joint panel, joint arbitration with DS54
DS54 Indonesia — Certain Measures Affecting the Automobile Industry (Complainant: European Communities) 3 October 1996	Panel report, Art 21.3 (c) arbitration. On 15 July 1999 Indonesia informed the DSB that it had issued a new automotive policy which implemented the recommendations of the DSB. Success for EU, Japan (two requests), USA
DS53 Mexico — Customs Valuation of Imports (Complainant: European Comminities) 27 August 1996	no panel established nor settlement notified
DS52 Brazil — Certain Measures Affecting Trade and Investment in the Automotive Sector (Complainant: United States) 9 August 1996	no panel established nor settlement notified
DS51 Brazil — Certain Automotive Investment Measures (Complainant: Japan) 30 July 1996	no panel established nor settlement notified
DS50 India — Patent Protection for Pharmaceutical and Agricultural Chemical Products (Complainant: United States) 2 July 1996	Panel report, AB report. At the DSB meeting on 28 April 1999, disclosed the enactment of the relevant legislation to implement the recommendations of the DSB, success USA
DS49 United States — Anti-Dumping Investigation Regarding Imports of Fresh or Chilled Tomatoes from Mexico (Complainant: Mexico) 1 July 1996	no panel, case settled by USA success probably Mexico
DS48 European Communities — Measures Concerning Meat and Meat Products (Hormones) (Complainant: Canada) 28 July 1996	separate Panel report but same AB report as DS26
DS47 Turkey — Restrictions on Imports of Textile and Clothing Products (Complainant: Thailand) 20 June 1996	consultations requested
DS46 Brazil — Export Financing Programme for Aircraft (Complainant: Canada) 19 June 1996	Panel report, AB report, Article 21.5 Panel report, Article 21.5 AB report, Art. 22.6 Arbitration, Second Recourse to Article 21.5 Panel report
DS45 Japan — Measures Affecting Distribution Services (Complainant: United States) 13 June 1996	no panel established nor settlement notified
DS44 Japan — Measures Affecting Consumer Photographic Film and Paper (Complainant: United States) 13 June 1996	Panel Report, not supporting U.S. claims.
DS43 Turkey — Taxation of Foreign Film Revenues (Complainant: United	Panel established, on 14 July 1997,

States) 12 June 1996	both parties notified a mutually agreed solution
DS42 Japan — Measures concerning Sound Recordings (Complainant: European Communities) 28 May 1996	no panel, mutually agreed solution
DS41 Korea — Measures concerning Inspection of Agricultural Products (Complainant: United States) 24 May 1996	no panel established or settlement notified
DS40 Korea — Laws, Regulations and Practices in the Telecommunications Procurement Sector (Complainant: European Communities) 5 May 1996	no panel, on 22 October 1997, the parties mutually agreed solution
DS39 United States — Tariff Increases on Products from the European Communities (Complainant: European Communities) 18 April 1996	no panel, the United States withdrew the measure on 15 July 1996 and the EC decided not to pursue its panel request, first dispute involving Sec. 301
DS38 United States — The Cuban Liberty and Democratic Solidarity Act (Short title: US - Helms Burton) (Complainant: European Communities) 3 May 1996	Panel suspended work at the request of the EC, dated 21 April 1997
DS37 Portugal — Patent Protection under the Industrial Property Act (Complainant: United States) 30 April 1996	no panel, mutally agreed solution
DS36 Pakistan — Patent Protection for Pharmaceutical and Agricultural Chemical Products (Complainant: United States) 30 April 1996	no panel, mutually agreed solution
DS35 Hungary — Export Subsidies in respect of Agricultural Products (Complainants: Argentina, Australia, Canada, New Zealand, Thailand, United States) 27 March 1996	no panel, agreement among parties that Hungary should seek a waiver
DS34 Turkey — Restrictions on Imports of Textile and Clothing Products (Complainant: India) 21 March 1996	Panel report, AB report, mutually acceptable solution: Turkey liberalizes in certains product categories
DS33 United States — Measures Affecting Imports of Woven Wool Shirts and Blouses from India (Complainant: India) 14 March 1996	Panel report, AB report, the US withdrew measure as of 22 November 1996, before the Panel had concluded its work: success India
DS32 United States — Measures Affecting Imports of Women's and Girls' Wool Coats (Complainant: India) 14 March 1996	Panel established but activities terminated on 25 April 1996 on request of India
DS31 Canada — Certain Measures Concerning Periodicals (Complainant: United States) 11 March 1996	Panel report, AB report, Canada withdrew the contested measure.
DS30 Brazil — Countervailing Duties on Imports of Desiccated Coconut and Coconut Milk Powder from Sri Lanka (Complainant: Sri Lanka) 23 February 1996	not panel established nor settlement notified, see DS22
DS29 Turkey — Restrictions on Imports of Textile and Clothing Products (Complainant: Hong Kong, China) 12 February 1996	not panel established nor settlement notified
DS28 Japan — Measures Concerning Sound Recordings (Complainant: United States) 9 February 1996	first TRIPS dispute, mutually agreed solution
DS27 European Communities — Regime for the Importation, Sale and Distribution of Bananas (Complainants: Ecuador, Guatemala, Honduras, Mexico, United States) 5 February 1996	Panel report, AB report, Article 21(3)(c) arbitration, Art. 21.5 Panel report, Art. 22.6 arbitration, mutually agreed solution 2 July 2001, new Art 21.5 Panel report 2007.
DS26 European Communities — Measures Concerning Meat and Meat Products (Hormones) (Complainant: United States) 26 January 1996	Panel report, AB report, Article 21(3)(c) arbitration, Art. 22.6 arbitration
DS25 European Communities — Implementation of the Uruguay Round Commitments Concerning Rice (Complainant: Uruguay) 14 December 1995	claim seemed similar to DS17, other settled or inactive cases
DS24 United States — Restrictions on Imports of Cotton and Man-Made Fibre Underwear (Complainant: Costa Rica) 22 December 1995	Panel report, AB report, on 10 April 1997, the US measure subject of this dispute had expired on 27 March 1997 meaning that the US had immediately complied with the recommendations of the DSB.
DS23 Venezuela — Anti-Dumping Investigation in Respect of Imports of Certain Oil Country Tubular Goods (OCTG) (Complainant: Mexico) 5 December 1995	no panel, Venezuela terminated contested measure
DS22 Brazil — Measures Affecting Desiccated Coconut (Complainant: Philippines) 30 November 1995	Panel report, AB report, but the invoked provisions were inapplicable, no success for Philippines
DS21 Australia — Measures Affecting the Importation of Salmonids (Complainant: United States) 20 November 1995	Panel work suspended, but see DS18
DS20 Korea — Measures concerning Bottled Water (Complainant: Canada) 8 November 1995	not panel established, mutually agreed solution
DS19 Poland — Import Regime for Automobiles (Complainant: India) 28 September 1995	not panel estabished, mutually agreed solution
DS18 Australia — Measures Affecting Importation of Salmon (Complainant: Canada) 5 October 1995	Panel report, AB report, Article 21(3)(c) arbitration, Art. 21.5 Panel report, implementation not known
DS17 European Communities — Duties on Imports of Rice (Complainant: Thailand) 5 October 1995	see DS25, other settled or inactive cases

DS16 European Communities — Regime for the Importation, Sale and Distribution of Bananas (Complainants: Guatemala, Honduras, Mexico, United States) 28 September 1995	no panel established nor settlement notified
DS15 Japan — Measures Affecting the Purchase of Telecommunications Equipment (Complainant: European Communities) 18 August 1995	although there has been no official notification, the case appears to have been settled bilaterally
DS14 European Communities — Trade Description of Scallops (Complainant: Chile) 24 July 1995	Panel suspended proceedings due to mutually agreed solution
DS13 European Communities — Duties on Imports of Grains (Complainant: United States) 19 July 1995	on 30 April 1997, the US informed the Secretariat that it was withdrawing its request for a panel because EC had adopted regulations implementing an agreement reached on this matter
DS12 European Communities — Trade Description of Scallops (Complainant: Peru) 18 July 1995	panel suspended proceedings due to mutually agreed solution
DS11 Japan — Taxes on Alcoholic Beverages (Complainant: United States) 7 July 1995	joint panel with DS8
DS10 Japan — Taxes on Alcoholic Beverages (Complainant: Canada) 7 July 1995	joint panel with DS8
DS9 European Communities — Duties on Imports of Cereals (Complainant: Canada) 30 June 1995	other settled or inactive cases, see DS13, USA reached agreement with EU on a similar complaint
DS8 Japan — Taxes on Alcoholic Beverages (Complainant: European Communities) 21 June 1995	Panel report, AB report, Article 21(3) (c) arbitration
DS7 European Communities — Trade Description of Scallops (Complainant: Canada) 19 May 1995	panel suspended proceedings due to mutually agreed solution
DS6 United States — Imposition of Import Duties on Automobiles from Japan under Sections 301 and 304 of the Trade act of 1974 (Complainant: Japan) 17 May 1995	not panel established, mutually agreed solution
DS5 Korea — Measures Concerning the Shelf-Life of Products (Complainant: United States) 3 May 1995	no panel established, mutually agreed solution
DS4 United States — Standards for Reformulated and Conventional Gasoline (Complainant: Brazil) 10 April 1995	joint panel with DS2
DS3 Korea — Measures Concerning the Testing and Inspection of Agricultural Products (Complainant: United States) 4 April 1995	no information available, other settled or inactive cases
DS2 United States — Standards for Reformulated and Conventional Gasoline (Complainant: Venezuela) 24 January 1995	joint panel with DS4, Panel report, AB report
DS1 Malaysia — Prohibition of Imports of Polyethylene and Polypropylene (Complainant: Singapore) 10 January 1995	no panel established, Singapore withdraws complaint

3. Definitionen

OECD Mitglieder sind: Originalmitglieder seit dem 14. Dezember 1960 sind: Österreich, Belgien, Kanada, Dänemark, Frankreich, Deutschland, Griechenland, Island, Irland, Italien, Luxemburg, Niederlande, Norwegen, Portugal, Spanien, Schweden, Schweiz, Türkei, Großbritannien, USA. Die folgenden Ländern kommen später dazu, mit Beitrittsdatum: Japan, 28. April 1964; Finnland, 28. Januar 1969; Australien, 7. Juni 1971; Neuseeland, 29. Mai 1973; Mexiko, 18. Mai 1994; Tschechische Republik, 21. Dezember 1995; Ungarn, 7. Mai 1996; Polen 22. November 1996; Republik Korea 12. Dezember 1996.

EU: Die Verträge von Paris (EGKS bzw. ECSC, 1951) und Rom (EWG bzw. EEC, 1957) werden unterzeichnet von Belgien, Niederlande, Luxemburg, Frankreich, Italien und die Bundesrepublik Deutschland und treten jeweils am 1. Januar folgenden Jahres in Kraft. Dänemark, Irland und Großbritannien kommen ab dem 1. Januar 1973 dazu. Griechenland tritt am 1. Januar 1981 bei, Spanien und Portugal am 1. Januar 1986. Und Österreich, Finnland und Schweden am 1. Januar 1995.

LDCs sind Länder mit niedrigem Einkommen (unter 900 US$ pro Kopf), mit geringer wirtschaftlicher Diversifikationsrate und schwachen menschlichen Ressourcen ('weak human resources'). Derzeit werden folgende Länder von den VN dazugezählt: Afghanistan, Angola, Bangladesh, Benin, Bhutan, Burkina Faso, Burundi, Cambodia, Cape Verde, Central African Republic, Chad, Comoros, Democratic Republic of Congo, Djibouti, Equatorial Guinea, Eritrea, Ethiopia, Gambia, Guinea, Guinea-Bissau, Haiti, Kiribati, Lao People's Democratic Republic, Leshoto, Liberia, Madagascar, Malawi, Maldives, Mali, Mauritania, Mozambique, Myanmar, Nepal, Niger, Rwanda, Samoa, Sao Tome and Principe, Senegal, Sierra Leone, Solomon Islands, Somalia, Sudan, Togo, Tuvalu, Uganda, United Republic of Tanzania, Vanuatu, Yemen, Zambia. Aus: UNCTAD 2001: 1.

Die Entwicklungsländer in der WTO werden nach einer Liste bestimmt, die keinen offiziellen Charakter hat und die Änderungen unterworfen sein kann, so ist z.B. Thailand und Malaysia weder in der Liste der Entwicklungsländer noch der Industrieländer zu finden. Der Status der Länder ist somit umstritten und wird u.a. in Verhandlungen erst festgelegt: Albania, Angola, Antigua & Barbuda, Argentina, Armenia, Bahrain, Bangladesh, Barbados, Belize, Benin, Bolivia, Botswana, Brazil, Brunei, Burkina Faso, Burundi, Cambodia, Cameroon, Central African Republic, Chad, Chile, China, Georgia, Ghana, Grenada, Guatemala, Guinea, Guinea Bissau, Guyana, Haiti, Honduras, Hong Kong, India, Indonesia, Israel, Jamaica, Jordan, Kenya, Kuwait, Kyrgyzstan, Lesotho, Macao, Macedonia (FYR), Madagascar, Niger, Nigeria, Oman, Pakistan, Panama, Papua New Guinea, Paraguay, Peru, Philippines, Qatar, Romania, Rwanda, Senegal, Sierra Leone, Singapore, Solomon Islands, South Korea, Sri Lanka, St. Kitts & Nevis, St. Lucia, St. Vincent & Grenadines, Suriname. Aus: Kasteng et al. 2004: 53.

Die Industrieländern in der WTO werden, siehe oben, als informelle Liste geführt, die keine rechtliche Relevanz hat, darunter befinden sich einige neu beigetretene Transformationsländer: Australia, Austria, Belgium, Bulgaria, Canada, Croatia, Czech Republic, Denmark, Estonia, Finland, France, Germany, Greece, Hungary, Iceland, Ireland, Italy, Japan, Latvia, Liechtenstein, Lithuania, Luxembourg, Netherlands, New Zealand, Norway, Poland, Portugal, Slovak Republic, Slovenia, South Africa, Spain, Sweden, Switzerland, United Kingdom, USA. Aus: Kasteng et al. 2004: 53.

An der ersten Verhandlungsrunde des GATT nahmen folgende 23 Staaten teil: Syrien, Libanon, Burma, Ceylon, Südrhodesien, Pakistan, Indien, China, Brasilien, Chile, USA, Frankreich, Niederlande, Norwegen, Finland, Schweden, England, Kanada, Tschechosowakei, Australien. Argentinien, Polen nehmen an den Verhandlungen teil, ratifzieren aber nicht, die Türkei verzögert die Ratifizierung. Vgl. Wilcox 1949: 46.

Das GATT trat am 1. Januar 1948 für 23 Staaten in Kraft: Australien, Belgien, Brasilien, Burma, Ceylon, Chile, China, Frankreich, Großbritannien, Indien, Kanada, Kuba, Libanon, Luxemburg, Neuseeland, Niederlande, Norwegen, Pakistan, Südrhodesien, Südafrika, Syrien, Tschechoslowakei, USA. Senti 1986a: 40. Vom Vertrag zurückgetreten sind China (1950), Libanon (1951), Syrien (1951) und Liberia (1950). Senti 1986a: 40. Die Kündigung Chinas erfolgte damals durch Taiwan. China ist seit 1984 wieder als Beobachter zugelassen. Senti 1986a: 40.

Die Havanna-Charta der ITO unterzeichneten folgende Staaten: Afghanistan, Australien, Ägypten, Bolivien, Brasilien, Burmesische Union, Canada, Ceylon, Chile, China, Columbien, Costa-Rica, Cuba, Tschechoslowakei, Dänemark, Dominikanische Republik, Ecuador, Österreich, Belgien, Mexico, Niederlande, Neuseeland, Nikaragua, Norwegen, Pakistan, Panama, Peru, Philippinen, Portugal, Südrhodesien, Schweden, San Salvador, Frankreich, Griechenland, Guatemala, Haiti, Indonesien, Iran, Irak, Irland, Italien, Libanon, Liberia, Luxemburg, Syrien, Transjordanien, Südafrikanische Union, England, USA, Uruguay, Venezuela. Hummer/Weiß 1997: 9-10.

An der Uruguay Runde des GATT, die zur Gründung der WTO führte, nahmen folgende Länder teil: Algeria, Antigua & Barbuda, Argentina, Australia, Austria, Bangladesh, Barbados, Belize, Benin, Botswana, Brazil, Burkina Faso, Burma, Burundi, Cameroon, Canada, Central African Republic, Chad, Chile, China (als Beobachter), Columbia, Congo, Costa Rica, Cote d' Ivoire, Cuba, Cyprus, Czechoslovakia, Dominican Republic, El Salvador, Egypt, European Economic Community, Belgium, Denmark, Malta, France, Germany Fed. Rep. of, Greece, Ireland, Italy, Luxembourg, Netherlands, Portugal, Spain, United Kingdom, Finland, Fiji, Gabon, Gambia, Ghana, Guyana, Guatemala, Haiti, Honduras, Hongkong, Hungary, Iceland, India, Indonesia, Israel, Jamaica, Japan, Kenya, Korea Rep. of, Kuwait, Lesotho, Madagaskar, Malawi, Malaysia, Maldives, Zimbabwe, Mauritania, Mauritius, Mexico, Morocco, New Zealand, Nicaragua, Niger, Nigeria, Norway, Pakistan, Paraguay, Peru, Philippines, Poland, Romania, Rwanda, Senegal, Sierra Leone, Singapore, South Africa, Sri Lanka, Suriname, Sweden, Switzerland, Tanzania, Thailand, Togo, Trinidad & Tobago, Tunisia, Turkey, Uganda, United States, Uruguay, Yugoslavia, Zaire, Zambia. Aus: Finger/Olechowski 1987: 241.

Von den 125 Teilnehmerstaaten der Uruguay-Runde haben 14 Staaten die Schlußakte nicht unterzeichnet: Burkina Faso, Dominikanische Republik, Gambia, Grenada, Haiti, Lesotho, Malediven, Ruanda, St. Kitts und Nevis, St. Vincent/Grenadinen, Sierra Leone, Tschad, Togo und Swaziland. Vgl. Langer 1995: 2.

Nettonahrungsmittelimporteure (net food-importing developing countries, 'NFIDCs'): dazu gehören sämtliche der am wenigsten entwickelten Länder (die LDCs) sowie Barbodos, Cote d'Ivoire, Dominikanische Republik, Ägypten, Honduras, Jamaica, Kenya, Mauritius, Marokko, Peru, Senegal, Sri Lanka, Trinidad und Tobago, Tunesien und Venezuela. WTO 1995: 448-449. Vgl. WTO Doc. G/AG/5.Gemäß FAO werden diese Länder genannt: low-income food-deficit countries, 'LIFDCs', siehe FAO 2004c: 14.

AKP-Mitgliedsstaaten sind: Africa: Angola, Benin, Botswana, Burkina Faso, Burundi, Cameroun, Cape Verde, Central African Republic, Chad, Comoros, Congo (Brazzaville), Congo (Kinshasa), Djibouti, Equatorial Guinea, Eritrea, Ethiopia, Gabon, Gambia, Ghana, Guinea, Guinea Bissau, Ivory Coast, Kenya, Lesotho, Liberia, Madagascar, Malawi, Mali, Mauritania, Mauritius, Mozambique, Namibia, Niger, Nigeria, Rwanda, Sao Tome & Principe, Senegal, Seychelles, Sierra Leone, Somalia, South Africa, Sudan, Swaziland, Tanzania, Togo, Uganda, Zambia, Zimbabwe. Carribean: Antigua and Barbuda, Bahamas, Barbados, Belize, Cuba, Dominica, Domican Republic, Grenada, Guyana, Haiti, Jamaica, St.-Kitts & Nevis, St.-Lucia, St.-Vincent, Suriname, Trinidad & Tobago. Pacific: Cook Islands, Federated States of Micronesia, Fiji, Kiribati, Marshall Islands, Nauru, Niue, Palau, Papua New Guinea, Samoa, Solomon Islands, Timor-Leste, Tonga, Tuvalu, Vanuatu. In: http://ec.europa.eu/comm/development/body/country/country_en.cfm.

4. Abkürzungsverzeichnis

AB	Appellate Body, die Berufungsinstanz der Welthandelsorganisation
DOC	U.S. Department of Commerce
DSU	Understanding on Rules and Procedures Governing the Settlement of Disputes bzw. Vereinbarung über Regeln und Verfahren zur Beilegung von Streitigkeiten (Teil des WTO-Abkommes). Zitatebeispiel: DSU Art. 22 Abs. 4.
EGV	Vertrag zur Gründung der Europäischen Gemeinschaft in der Version von Maastricht. Die Änderungen durch den Amsterdamer Vertrag sind gekennzeichnet und mit 'neu: Art. ..'
EPIL	Encyclopedia of Public International Law, Schriftenreihe
EuGH	Europäischer Gerichtshof
I.L.M.	International Legal Materials, Schriftenreihe
ITA	International Trade Administration, im U.S. Department of Commerce
ITC	U.S. International Trade Commission

IWF	Internationaler Währungsfond bzw. IMF International Monetary Fund
JWT	Journal of World Trade
JWTL	Journal of World Trade Law (neuerdings Journal of World Trade)
QRs	Quantitative Restrictions, mengenmäßige Beschränkungen
SDT	Special and Differential Treatment, Sonder- und Vorzugsbehandlung von Entwicklungsländern
U.S.T	United States Treaties and Other International Agreements, Schriftenreihe
VER	Voluntary Export Restraints, freiwillige Selbstbeschränkungsabkommen
VN	Vereinte Nationen
WTO	Welthandelsorganisation bzw. World Trade Organization
WuW	Wirtschaft und Wettbewerb

M Literatur

- Literaturverzeichnis 1416

M   Literatur

Literaturverzeichnis

A

ABA Private Anticompetitive Practices 2000: American Bar Association, Report on Private Anticompetitive Practices as Market Access Barriers. In: http://www.abanet.org/antitrust/marketaccess.html.
ABA Proposed Agribusiness Legislation 2000: American Bar Association, Section on Antitrust. Comments Relating to Proposed Agribusiness Legislation Pending Before the 106th Congress, 2000. In: http://www.abanet.org/antitrust.
Abbott 1997: Abbott, Frederick M. WTO Dispute Settlement and the Agreement on Trade-Related Aspects of Intellectual Property Rights. In: Petersmann, Ernst-Ulrich (ed.). International Trade Law and the GATT/WTO Dispute Settlement System. London, The Hague, Boston: Kluwer Law, 1997.
Abbott 1998: Abbott, Philip. Competition Policy and Agricultural Trade. COM/AGR/CA/TD/TC/WS(98)196. Paris: OECD, 1998. In: http://www.oecd.org.
Abbott et al. 2000: Abbott, Kenneth W., Keohane, Robert O., Moravcsik, Andrew, Slaughter, Anne-Marie, Snidal, Duncan. The Concept of Legalization. In: International Organization, Vol. 54, No. 3, Summer 2000. S. 401-419.
Abbott 2004: Abbott, F. M. WTO Dispute Settlement Practive Relating to the Agreement on Trade-Related Intellectual Property Rights. In: Ortino, Federico, Petersmann, Ernst-Ulrich (eds.). The WTO Dispute Settlement System 1995 - 2003. The Hague et al.: Kluwer Law International, 2004.
Abbott 2005: Abbott, F.M. Are the Competitions Rules in the WTO Agreement on Trade-Related Aspects of Intellectual Property Adequate? In: Petersmann, Ernst-Ulrich (ed.). Reforming the World Trading System. Legitimacy, Efficiency, and Democratic Governance. Oxford: Oxford University Press, 2005.
Abdullah/Rahman 1993: Abdullah, A. A., Rahman, Atiq. Bangladesh. In: Patel, Surendra J. Technological Transformation in the Third World. Aldershot: Avebury/UNU/WIDER, 1993.
Abed 1998: Abed, George T. Trade Liberalization and Tax Reform in Southern Mediterranean Countries. IMF Working Paper WP/98/49. Washington: International Monetary Fund, 1998. In: http://www.imf.org.
Abeyratne 1997: Abeyratne, R.I.R. The Settlement of Commercial Aviation Disputes under the General Agreement on Trade in Services and the ICAO Council - A Comparative Analysis. In: Petersmann, Ernst-Ulrich (ed.). International Trade Law and the GATT/WTO Dispute Settlement System. London, The Hague, Boston: Kluwer Law, 1997.
Ablin/Katz 1987: Ablin, Eduardo, Katz, Jorge M. From Infant Industry to Technology Exports: the Argentine Experience in the International Sale of Industrial Plants and Engineering Work. In: Katz, Jorge M. Technology, Generation in Latin American Manufacturing Industries. London: Macmillan Press, 1987.
Abramowitz 1956: Abramowitz, Moses. Resource and Output Trends in the United States since 1987. In: American Economic Review, Papers and Proceedings, Vol. XLVI, No. 2, May 1956. S. 5-23.
Acelor Information 2006: Acerlor. Report Annuel. Trade Barriers. 2004. In: http://www.acelor.com.
Achterbosch et al. 2004: Achterbosch, T.J., Hammouda, Ben H., Osakwe, P. N., van Tongeren, F. W. Trade Liberalization under the Doha Development Agenda. Options and consequences for Africa. Report 6.04.09, June 2, 2004. Agricultural Economics Research Institute (LEI), The Hague. In: http://www.lei.wageningen-ur.nl/.
Adamantopoulos 1987: Adamantopoulos, Konstantinos. Das Subventionsrecht des GATT in der EWG. Köln, Berlin: Carl Heymanns Verlag, 1987.
Adams 1990: Adams, James D. Fundamental Stocks of Knowledge and Productivity Growth. In: Journal of Political Economy, Vol. 98, No. 4, 1990. S. 673-702.
Adams 1998: Adams, Richard H. The Political Economy of the Food Subsidy System in Bangladesh. In: Journal of Development Studies, Vol. 35, No. 1, October 1998. S. 66-88.
Adams 2002: Adams, Ashley C. Note: Section 211 of the Omnibus Appropriations Act: The Threat to International Protection of U.S. Trademarks. In: North Carolina Journal of International Law and Commercial Regulation, Bd. 28, No. 1, 2002. S. 221-246.
Adams/Brock 1990: Adams, Walter, Brock, James W. The Automobile Industry. In: Adams, Walter (Hrg.). The Structure of American Industry. New York: Macmillan, 1990.
Adams/Mueller 1990: Adams, Walter, Mueller, Hans. The Steel Industry. In: Adams, Walter (Hrg.). The Structure of American Industry. New York: Macmillan, 1990.
Adenikinju et al. 2001: Adenikinju, Adeola, Söderling, Ludvig, Soludo, Charles, Varoudakis, Aristomene. Structural Factors Affecting Manufacturing Competitiveness: Comparative Results from Cameroon, Cote d'Ivoire, Nigeria and Senegal. In: OECD. Policies to Promote Competitiveness in Manufacturing in Sub-Saharan Africa. Development Centre Seminars within the IMF and the AERC. Kwasi Fosu, Augustin, Nsouli, Saleh M., Varoudakis, Aristomene (eds.). Paris: OECD, 2001a.
Adler 1970: Adler, Michael. Specialization in the European Coal and Steel Community. In: Journal of Common Market Studies, Vol. Viii, No. 3, March 1970. S. 177-191.

Adlung 2006: Adlung, Rudolf. Public Services and the GATS. In: Journal of International Economic Law, Vol. 9, No. 2, 2006. S. 455-485.
Afrique Express 2003: Afrique Express. Cacao. Abidjan tente de sauver 'la petite campagne', No. 271, 03/06/2003. In: http://www.afrique-express.com/archive/QUEST/cotedivoire/cotedivoireeco/271cacao.htm.
Agarwal 1976: Agarwal, Jamuna P. Bedeutung und Determinanten ausländischer Direktinvestitionen in Entwicklungsländern. In: Die Weltwirtschaft, Heft 1, 1976. S. 174-201.
Agarwal 1985: Agarwal, Suraj Mal. Electronics in India: Past Strategies and Future Possibilities. In: World Development, Vol. 13, No. 3, 1985. S. 273-292.
Agarwal 1994: Agarwal, Jamuna Prasad. The effects of the Single Market programme on foreign direct investment into developing countries. In: Transnational Corporations, Vol. 3, No. 2, August 1994.
Agarwal 1996: Agarwal, Jamuna Prasad. Does Foreign Direct Investment Contribute to Unemployment in Home Countries? – An Empirical Survey - . Kiel Working Paper No. 765, September 1996.
Agarwal et al. 1995: Agarwal, Jamuna P., Hiemenz, Ulrich, Nunnenkamp, Peter. European Integration: A Threat to Foreign Investment in Developing Countries? Kieler Diskussionsbeiträge No. 246, März 1995.
Agarwal et al. 1995: Agarwal, Jamuna P., Langhammer, Rolf J., Lücke, Matthias, Nunnenkamp, Peter. Export Expansion and Diversification in Central and Eastern Europe: What can be learnt from East and Southeast Asia. Kieler Diskussionsbeiträge, No. 261, November 1995.
Aggarwal 1985: Aggarwal, Vinod K. Liberal Protectionism. The International Politics of Organized Textile Trade. Berkeley; Los Angeles; London: The University of California Press, 1985.
Aggarwal 2001: Aggarwal, Aradhna. Liberalization, Multilateral Enterprises and Export Performance: Evidence from Indian Manufacturing. Indian Council for Research on International Economic Relations, Working Paper 69, June 2001. In: http://www.icrier.res.in/.
Aggarwal 2004: Aggarwal, Aradhna. Impact of Tariff Reduction on Exports: A Quantitative Assessment of Indian Exports to the US. Indian Council for Research on International Economic Relations, Working Paper 120, January 2004. In: http://www.icrier.res.in/.
Aggarwal/Goldar 2004: Aggarwal, Aradhna, Goldar, Bishwanath. Trade Liberalization and Price-Cost Margins in Indian Industries. Indian Council for Research on International Economic Relations, Working Paper 130, April 2004. In: http://www.icrier.res.in/.
Aghevli/Montiel 1996: Aghevli, Bijan B., Montiel, Peter J. Exchange Rate Policies in Developing Countries. In: Frenkel, Jacob A., Goldstein, Morris (eds.). Functioning of the International Monetary System. Vol. 2. Washington: IMF, 1996.
Aghion et al. 2003: Aghion, Philippe, Burgess, Robin, Redding, Stephen, Zilibotti, Fabrizio. The Unequal Effects of Liberalization: Theory and Evidence from India. London School of Economics, Harvard University. October 3, 2003. In: http://econ.lse.ac.uk/staff/rburgess/wp/abrz031002.pdf.
AGOA News 2003: AGOA News. SACU-US Negotiations: Issues around Rules of Origin. 11.8.2003. In: http://www.agoa.info.
Agosin/Ffrench-Davis 1993: Agosin, Manuel R., Ffrench-Davis, Ricardo. Trade Liberalization in Latin America. In: CEPAL Review 50, August 1993. S. 41-62.
Agreement on Multi-Chip Integrated Circuits 2005: Agreement on Multi-Chip Integrated Circuits. Brussels, 3 November 2005. In: http://europa.eu.int/comm/trade.
Ahiakpor 1985: Ahiakpor, James C. W. The success and failure of dependency theory: the experience of Ghana. In: IO, Vol. 39 No. 3, Summer 1985. S. 535-552.
Ahluwalia 1986: Ahluwalia, Isher Judge. Industrial Growth in India. Performance and Prospects. In: Journal of Development Economics 23, 1986, S. 1-18.
Ahluwalia 1994: Ahluwalia, Isher Judge. The Role of Trade Policy in Indian Industrialization. In: Helleiner, Gerald K. (ed.). Trade Policy and Industrialization in Turbulent Times. London; New York: Routledge, 1994.
Ahmad 1978: Ahmad, Jaleel. Tokyo Rounds of Trade Negotiations and the Generalized System of Preferences. In: The Economic Journal, 88, June 1978. S. 285-295.
Ahn 2000: Ahn, Dukgeun. Linkages between International Financial and Trade Institutions. IMF, World Bank and WTO. In: JWT, Vol. 34, No. 4, 2000. S. 1-35.
Ahn 2002: Ahn, Sanghoon. Competition, Innovation and Productivity Growth: A Review of Theory and Practice. OECD Economics Department Working Paper, ECO/WKP(2002)3. Paris: OECD, 2002. In: http://www.oecd.org.
Ahuja 2001: Ahuja, Rajeev. Export Incentives in India within WTO Framework. Indian Council for Research on International Economic Relations, Working Paper 72, July 2001. In: http://www.icrier.res.in/.
Aiginger 1998: Aiginger, Karl. The privatization experiment in Austria. In: Parker, David (ed.). Privatization in the European Union. Theory and Policy Perspectives. London; New York: Routledge, 1998.
Ajuja 2002: Ahuja, Rajeev. Export Incentives in Brazil and Korea within the WTO Framework. Indian Council for Research on International Economic Relations, Working Paper 79, April 2002. In: http://www.icrier.res.in/.
Akiyama et al. 2001: Akiyama, Takamasa, Baffes, John, Larson, Donald F., Varangis, Panos (eds.). Commodity Market Reforms. Lessons of Two Decades. Washington: World Bank, 2001.
Akiyama et al. 2003: Akiyama, Takamasa, Baffes, John, Larson, Donald F., Varangis, Panos. Commodity Market Reform in Africa: Some Recent Experience. World Bank Policy Research Paper No. 2995, March 2003. In: http://www.worldbank.org.
Akrasanee/Wiboonchutikula 1994: Akrasanee, Narongchai, Wiboonchutikula, Paitoon. Trade and Industrial Policies and Productivity Growth in Thailand. In: Helleiner, Gerald K. (ed.). Trade Policy and Industrialization in Turbulent Times. London; New York: Routledge, 1994.

Aksoy/Beghin 2005: Aksoy, M. Ataman, Beghin, John C. Global Agricultural Trade and Developing Countries. Washington: World Bank, 2005.
Akyüz 2005: Akyüz, Yilmaz. The WTO Negotiations on Industrial Tariffs: What is at stake for developing countries? Geneva: May, 2005. In: http://www.twnside.org.sg/akyuz.htm.
Akyüz et al. 1998: Akyüz, Yilmaz, Chang, Ha-Joon, Kozul-Wright, Richard. New Perpectives on Asian Development. In: Journal of Development Studies, Special Issue on East Asian Development. Vol. 34, No. 6, August 1998. S. 4-36.
Akyüz/Cornford 2000: Akyuz, Yilmaz, Cornford, Andrew. Capital Flows to Developing Countries of the International Financial System. UNU/WIDER Working Paper, July 2000. In: http://www.wider.unu.edu/.
Alam 2007: Alam, Shawkat. Trade Restrictions Pursuant to Multilateral Environmental Agreements: Developmental Implications for Developing Countries. In: JWT, Vol. 41, No. 5, 2007. S. 983-1014.
Albert et al. 1999: Albert, Mathias, Brock, Lothar, Hessler, Stephan, Menzel, Ulrich, Neyer, Jürgen. Die Neue Weltwirtschaft. Entstofflichung und Entgrenzung der Ökonomie. Frankfurt am Main: Surkamp, 1999.
Albrecht 1964: Albrecht, Karl. Planifikateure am Werk. Wirtschaft zwischen Zwang und Freiheit. Düsseldorf; Wien: Econ Verlag, 1964.
Albrecht 1999: Albrecht, Ulrich. Internationale Politik. München, Wien: Oldenbourg, 1999.
Alburo 1999: Alburo, Florian A. Liberalizing Manufacturing Trade. Options for the 2000 WTO Negotiations. Working Paper, World Bank. In: http://www.worldbank.org/research/trade.
Alcorta 1994: Alcorta, Ludovico. The Impact of New Technologies on Scale in Manufacturing Industries: Issues and Evidence. In: World Development, Vol. 22, No. 5, 1994. S. 755-769.
Aldrich 1994: Aldrich, George H. What Constitutes a Compensable Taking of Property? The Decisions of the Iran-United States Claims Tribunal. In: American Journal of International Law, Vol. 88, 1994. S. 585-610.
Alegria et al. 1997: Alegria, Tito, Carrillo, Jorge, Estrada, Jorge Alonso. Restructuring of production and territorial change: a second industrialization hub in Northern Mexico. In: CEPAL Review 61, April 1997. S. 187-205.
Alesina/Rodrik 1994: Alesina, Alberto, Rodrik, Dani. Distributive Politics and Economic Growth. In: The Quarterly Journal of Economics, May 1994.
Allekotte 2004: Allekotte, Bernd. New Rules on Technology Licensing. Grünecker, Kindeldey, Stockmair & Schwanhäusser, April 23, 2004. In: http://www.gruenecker.de.
Allen 1953: Allen, William R. The International Trade Philosophy of Cordell Hull, 1907-1933. American Economic Review, Vol. 43, 1953. S. 101-116.
Allen et al. 1998: Allen, Chris, Gasiorek, Michael, Smith, Alasdair. The Competition Effects of the Single Market in Europe. In: Economic Policy, Heft 1, 1998. S. 441-486.
Altemöller 2000: Altemöller, Frank. Welthandelsordnung und einzelstaatliche Umweltschutzpolitik - Ein Widerspruch? In: RabelsZ Bd. 64, 2000. S. 213-255.
Amann/de Paula 2004: Amann, Edmund, de Paula, Germano Mendes. Ownership Structure in the Post-Privatized Brazilian Steel Industry: Complexity, Instability and the Lingering Role of the State. University of Manchester. Centre for Regulation and Competition, Working Paper No. 75, June 2004. In: http://idpm.man.ac.uk/crc/.
AMD Information 2006: AMD. FAB 26 Information. 2006. In: http://66.129.71.27/en-us/about.aspx.
Amelung 1987: Amelung, Thorsten. Zum Einfluß von Interessengurppen auf die Wirtschaftspolitik in Entwicklungsländern. In: Die Weltwirtschaft, Heft 1, 1987. S. 158-171.
Amelung 1989: Amelung, Thorsten. The Determinants of Protection in Developing Countries: An Extended Interest-Group Approach. In: Kyklos, Vol. 42, Fasc. 4, 1989. S. 515-532.
American University Information 2006: American University, Kogod School of Business. China Information Technology Study. 2006. In: http://www.american.edu/ksb/mogit/country.html.
Ames et al. 1996: Ames, Glenn C. W., Gunter, Lewell, Davis, Claudia. Analysis of the U.S. European Community Oilseeds Agreement. Department of Agricultural and Applied Economics, University of Georgia, Faculty Series FS 96-11, June 1996. In: http://www.agecon.uga.edu.
Amin 1997: Amin, Samir. Die Zukunft des Weltsystems. Herausforderungen der Globalisierung. Hamburg. VSA-Verlag, 1997.
Amiti 1999: Amiti, Mary. Specialization Patterns in Europa. In: Weltwirtschaftliches Archiv, Vol. 135, 4, 1999. S. 571-593.
Amsden 1984: Amsden, Alice H. Taiwan. In: World Development, Vol. 12, No. 5/6, 1984. S. 491-503.
Amsden 1985: Amsden, Alice H. The State and Taiwan's Economic Development. In: Evans, Peter B. et al. (eds.). Bringing the State Back In. Cambridge: Cambridge University Press, 1985.
Amsden 1989: Amsden, Alice H. Asia's Next Giant. South Korea and Late Industrialization. Oxford: Oxford University Press, 1989.
Amsden 1994: Amsden, Alice H. Why Isn't the Whole World Experimenting with the East Asian Model to Develop?: Review of The East Asian Miracle. In: World Development, Vol. 22, No. 4, 1994. S. 627-633.
Amsden 1997: Amsden, Alice H. Editorial: Bringing Production Back in – Understandings Government's Economic Role in Late Industrialization. In: World Development, Vol. 25, No. 4, 1997. S. 469-480.
Amsden 1999: Amsden, Alice H. Industrialization under New WTO Law. UNCTAD X, Bangkok February 12, 2000. TD(x)/RT.1/7, 1. December 1999. In: http://www.unctad.org.
Amsden 2005: Amsden, Alice H. Promoting Industry under WTO Law. In: Gallagher, Kevin P. Putting Development First. London, New York: Zed Books, 2005.

Anastassopoulos et al. 1986: Anastassopoulos, Jean-Pierre, Blanc, George, Dussauge, Pierre. Staatliche Multinationale Unternehmen. Frankfurt; New York: Campus Verlag, 1986.

Anderson 1990: Anderson, Kym. China and the Multi-Fibre Arrangement. In: Hamilton, Carl B. Textiles Trade and the Developing Countries. Eliminating the Multi-Fibre Arrangement in the 1990s. Washington: World Bank, 1990.

Anderson 1995: Anderson, Kym. Lobbying Incentives and the Pattern of Protection in Rich and Poor Countries. In: Economic Development and Cultural Change, 43, 1995/96. S. 401-423.

Anderson 1995a: Anderson, Jeffrey J. Structural Funds and the Social Dimension of EU Policy: Springboard or Stumbling Block? In: Leibfried, Stephan, Pierson, Paul (eds.). European Social Policy. Between Fragmentation and Integration. Washington: Brookings Institution, 1995.

Anderson 1996: Anderson, Kym (ed.) Strengthening the Global Trading System: From GATT to WTO. Adelaide: Centre for International Economic Studies, 1996.

Anderson 1998: Anderson, James E. Trade Restrictiveness Benchmarks. In: Economic Journal, Vol. 198, July 1998. S. 1111-1125.

Anderson 2002: Anderson, Kym. Pecularities of Retaliation in WTO Dispute Settlement. Adelaide University. CIES Discussion Paper No. 207, March 2002. In: http://www.adelaide.edu.au/cies/.

Anderson 2004: Anderson, Kym. Agriculture, Trade Reform and Poverty Reduction: Implications for Sub-Saharan Africa. Policy Issues in International Trade and Commodities Study Series No. 22, United Nations Conference on Trade and Development. UN: New York and Geneva, 2004. In: http://www.unctad.org.

Anderson 2004a: Anderson, Kym. Agricultural Trade Reform and Poverty Reduction in Developing Countries. World Bank Policy Research Working Paper 3396, September 2004. In: http://www.worldbank.org.

Anderson 2004b: Anderson, Greg. The Canada - United States Softwood Lumber Dispute: Where Politics and Theory Meet. In: JWT, vol. 38, No. 4, 2004. S. 661-699.

Anderson et al. 1999: Anderson, Kym, Feridhanusetyawan, Tubagus Erwidodo, Strutt, Anna. Agriculture and the Next Round of WTO Negotiations. Working Paper, East Asia Workshop World Bank 1999. In: http://www.worldbank.org/research/trade.

Anderson et al. 2005: Anderson, Kym, Martin, Will, van der Mensbrugghe, Dominique. Market and Welfare Implications of Doha Reform Scenarios. In: Anderson, Kym, Martin, Will (eds.). Agricultural Trade Reform and the Doha Development Agenda. Washington: World Bank, 2005. In: http://www.worldbank.org.

Anderson/Park 1989: Anderson, Kym, Young-il, Park. China and the International Relocation of World Textile and Clothing Activity. In: Weltwirtschaftliches Archiv, Bd. 125, 1989. S. 129-147.

Anderson/Rugman 1989: Anderson, Andrew, Rugman, Alan. Subsidies in the U.S. Steel Industry: A New Conceptual Framework and Literatur Review. In: JWT, Vol. 23 No. 6, 1989. S. 58-83.

Anderson/Wager 2006: Anderson, Robert D., Wager, Hannu. Human Rights, Development, and the WTO. The Cases of Intellectual Property and Competition Policy. In: Journal of International Economic Law, Vol. 9, No. 3, 2006. S. 707-747.

Andrews 1982: Andrews, Bruce. The political economy of world capitalism: theory and practice. In: IO, Vol. 36 No. 1, Winter 1982. S. 135-163.

Andriamananjara/Nash 1997: Andriamananjara, Shuby, Nash, John. Have Trade Policy Reforms Led to Greater Openness in Developing Countries? World Bank, Policy Research Working Paper, No. 1730, February 1997. In: http://www.worldbank.org.

Anfavea Yearbook 2006: Associação Nacional dos Fabricantes de Veículos Automotores (Anfavea). Brazilian Automotive Industry Yearbook. 2006. In: http://www.anfavea.com.br/Index.html.

Antoniadis 2007: Antoniadis, Antonis. Unilateral Measures and WTO Dispute Settlement: An EC Perspective. In: JWT, Vol. 41, No. 3, 2007. S. 605-627.

Apibunyopas 1993: Apibunyopas, Preeyanuch. TNCs and Impacts on Industrialization in Thailand. In: Regional Development Dialogue, Vol. 14, No. 4, Winter 1993. S. 94-120.

Appelbaum et al. 1994: Appelbaum, Richard P., Smith, David, Christerson, Brad. Commodity Chains and Industrial Restructuring in the Pacific Rim: Garment Trade and Manufacturing. In: Gereffi, Gary, Korzeniewicz, Miguel (eds.). Commodity Chains and Global Capitalism. Westport, Connecticut; London: Praeger 1994.

Appliance Magazine 2003: Appliance Magazine. Whirlpool Special Section: India & Asia Operations: Success in India. April 2003. In: http://www.appliancemagazine.com/editorial.php?article=168.

Aquino 1978: Aquino, Antonio. Intra-Industry Trade and Inter-Industry Specialization as Concurrent Sources of International Trade in Manufactures. In: Weltwirtschaftliches Archiv, Bd. 114, 1978, S. 275-296.

Archibald 1961: Archibald, G. C. Chamberlin versus Chicago. In: Review of Economic Studies, Vol. 29 No. 78, October 1961. S. 2-21.

Arestis/Sawyer 1998: Arestis, Philip, Sawyer, Malcolm. Keynesian Economic Policies for the New Millennium. In: Economic Journal, Vol. 108, January 1998. S. 181-195.

Aricanli/Rodrik 1990: Aricanli, Tosun, Rodrik, Dani. On Overview of Turkey's Experience with Economic Liberalization and Structural Adjustment. In: World Development, Vol. 18, No. 10, 1990. S. 1243-1350.

Ariff 1994: Ariff, Mohamed. The Competitiveness of Malaysian Exports: Policy Perspectives. In: Asia-Pacific Development Journal, Vol. 1 No. 1, June 1994. S. 91-102.

Ariyoshi et al. 2000: Ariyoshi, Akira, Habermeier, Karl, Laurens, Bernard, Otker-Robe, Inci, Canales Kriljenko, Jorge Ivan, Kirilenko, Andrei. Capital Countrols: Country Experiences with their Use and Liberalization. Occasional Paper No. 90, Washington: IMF, 2000. In: http://www.imf.org.

Ark et al. 1996: Ark, Bart van, de Haan, Jacob, de Jong, Herman J. Characteristics of economic growth in the Netherlands during the postwar period. In: Crafts, Nicolas, Toniolo, Gianni (eds.). Economic Growth in Europe since 1945. Cambridge: Cambridge University Press, 1996.
Arndt 1952: Arndt, Helmut. Wettbewerb der Nachahmer und schöpferischer Wettbewerb (Original 1952). In: Herdzina, Klaus (Hrg.). Wettbewerbstheorie. Köln: Kiepenheuer&Witsch, 1975.
Arndt 1979: Arndt, Helmut. Irrwege der politischen Ökonomie. München: C.H. Beck, 1979.
Arndt 1981: Arndt, Helmut. Macht und Wettbewerb. In: Cox, Helmut, Jens, Uwe, Markert, Kurt (Hrg.). Handbuch des Wettbewerbs. München: Franz Vahlen, 1981.
Arndt 1985: Arndt, H. W. The Origins of Structuralism. In: World Development, Vol. 13, No. 2, 1985. S. 151-159.
Arnold/Bronckers 1988: Arnold, M. I. B., Bronckers, C. E. J. The EEC New Trade Policy Instrument: Some Comments on Its Application (Reg. 2641/84). In: JWTL, Vol. 22, No. 6, 1988. S. 19-38.
Aron 1969: Aron, Raymond. Frieden und Krieg. Frankfurt am Main: S. Fischer Verlag, 1969.
Arrow 1951a: Arrow, Kenneth J. An Extension of the Basic Theorems of Classical Welfare Economics. In: Arrow, Kenneth J., Debreu, Gérard (eds.). Landmark Papers in General Equilibrium Theory, Social Choice and Welfare. Cheltenham: Edgar Elgar, 2001.
Arrow 1951b: Arrow, Kenneth J. Social Choice and Individual Values. New Haven; London: Yale University Press, 1978 (1951).
Arrow 1962: Arrow, Kenneth J. The Economic Implications of Learning by Doing. In: Review of Economic Studies, Vol. 29 No. 80, June 1962. S. 155-173.
Arrow/Debreu 1954: Arrow, Kenneth J., Debreu, Gérard. Existence of an Equilibrium for a Competitive Economcy. In: Arrow, Kenneth J., Debreu, Gérard (eds.). Landmark Papers in General Equilibrium Theory, Social Choice and Welfare. Cheltenham: Edgar Elgar, 2001.
Ashley 1984: Ashley, Richard K. The Poverty of Neorealism. In: International Organization, 38, 2, Spring 1984. S. 225-285.
Aswicahyono et al. 2000: Aswicahyono, Haryo, Basri, M. Chatib, Hill, Hal. How not to industrialize? Indonesia"s Automotive Industry. In: Bulletin of Indonesian Economic Studies, Vol. 36, No. 1, April 2000. S. 209-241.
Athukorala/Hazari 1988: Athukorala, Premachandra, Hazari, Bharat R. Market Penetration of Manufactured Imports from Developing Countries: The Australian Experience. In: JWT, Vol. 22 No. 5, 1988. S. 49-65.
ATPDEA Report 2005: United States Trade Representative. Second Report to Congress on the Operation of the Andean Trade Preference Act as Amended. April 30, 2005. In: http://www.ustr.gov/Trade_Development/Preference_Programs/ATPA/Reports/Section_Index.html.
Aturupane et al. 1997: Aturupane, Chonira, Djankov, Simeon, Hoekman, Bernhard. Determinants of Intra-Industry Trade between East and West Europe. World Bank Policy Research Working Paper, No. 1850, November 1997. In: http://www.worldbank.org.
Audretsch/Yamawaki 1989: Audretsch, David B., Yamawaki, Hideki. The Allocation of R&D Expenditure and U.S.-Japanese Trade. In: Audretsch, David B., Gordon, Michael P. (eds.) The Internationalization of U.S. Markets. New York; London: New York University Press, 1989.
Auer 2005: Auer, Josef. Fertigungstechnik im Hochlohnland Deutschland. Deutsche Bank Reserach, September 2005. In: http://www.dbresearch.com.
Australia Importing Technology 1988: Bureau of Industry Economics. Importing Technology. Research report 25. Canberra: Australian Government Publishing Service, 1988.
Auto International in Zahlen, div. Jahrgänge: Das Auto International in Zahlen. Verband der Automobilindustrie (VDA) e.V., Frankfurt.
Automotive Agreement U.S. Japan 1995: Japan-United States: Automotive Agreement and Supporting Documents, August 23, 1995. In: 34 I.L.M. 1482, 1995.
AVIC 1 Information: China Aviation Industry Corporation I. Information 2006. In: http://www.avic1.com.
AVIC 2 Information: China Aviation Industry Corporation II. Information 2006. In: http://www.avic2.com.
Aw/Hwang 1995: Aw, B.-Y., Hwang, A. R. Productivity and the export market: A firm-level analysis. In: Journal of Development Economics, Vol. 47, 1995. S. 313-332.
Awuku 2004: Awuku, E Opuku. WTO Dispute Settlement Practice and Trade-Related Environmental Measures. In: Ortino, Federico, Petersmann, Ernst-Ulrich (eds.). The WTO Dispute Settlement System 1995 - 2003. The Hague et al.: Kluwer Law International, 2004.
Azzam 1997: Azzam, Azzeddine M. Measuring Market Power and Cost-Efficiency Effects of Industrial Concentration. In: Journal of Industrial Economics, Vol. XLV, No. 4, December 1997. S. 377-401.

B

Bacchetta/Bora 2003: Bacchetta, Marc, Bora, Bijit. Industrial Tariff Liberalization and the Doha Development Agenda. WTO Discussion Paper, 2003. In: http//www.wto.org.
Bacchus 2005: Bacchus, James. A Few Thoughts on Legitimacy, Democracy, and the WTO. In: Petersmann, Ernst-Ulrich (ed.). Reforming the World Trading System. Legitimacy, Efficiency, and Democratic Governance. Oxford: Oxford University Press, 2005.
Backes 1995: Backes, Peter. Die neuen Streitbeilegungsregeln der Welthandelsorganisation (WTO). In: Recht der Internationalen Wirtschaft, Heft 11. 916-919.

Badiane et al. 2002: Badiane, Ousmane, Dhaneshwar, Ghura, Goreux, Louis, Masson, Paul. Cotton Sector Strategies in West and Central Africa. World Bank Policy Research Working Paper No. 2867, Washington: World Bank, July 2002. In: http://www.worldbank.org.

Badiane/Shively 1998: Badiane, Ousmane, Shively, Gerald E. Spatial integration, transport costs, and the response of local prices to policy changes in Ghana. In: Journal of Development Economics, Vol. 56, 1998. S. 411-431.

Badura 1966: Badura, Peter. Bewahrung und Veränderung demokratischer und rechtsstaatlicher Verfassungsstruktur in den internationalen Gemeinschaften. In: Veröffentlichungen der Vereinigung der Deutschen Staatsrechtslehrer, Heft 23, 1966. Berlin: Walter de Gruyter. S. 34-104.

Baer 1989: Baer, Werner. The Brazilian Economy. Growth and Development. New York: Praeger, 1989.

Bagwell/Sykes 2004: Bagwell, Kyle, Sykes, Alan O. Chile - price band system and safeguard measures relating to certain agricultural products. In: World Trade Review Vol. 3, No. 3, 2004. S. 507-528.

Bahmani-Oskooee et al. 1991: Bahmani-Oskooee, Mohsen, Mohtadi, Hamid, Shabsigh, Ghiath. Exports, growth and causality in LDCs. In: Journal of Development Economics 36, 1991. S. 405-415.

Bailey et al. 1992: Bailey, David, Harte, George, Sugden, Roger. US Policy Debate Towards Inward Investment. In: JWT, Vo. 26, No. 4, 1992.

Bailey/Gersbach 1995: Bailey, Martin Niel, Gersbach, Hans. Efficiency in Manufacturing and the Need for Global Competition. In: Brookings Papers: Microeconomics 1995. S. 307-358.

Bain 1950: Bain, Joe S. Workable Competition in Oligopoly: Theoretical Considerations and Some Empirical Evidence. In: American Economic Review, Vol. XL No. 2, May 1950. S. 35-66.

Bain 1951: Bain, Joe S. Relation of Profit Rate to Industry Concentration, 1936-1940. In: Quarterly Journal of Economics, Vol. 65, No. 3, August 1951. S. 293-324.

Bain 1954: Bain, Joe S. Economies of Scale, Concentration, and the Condition of Entry in Twenty Manufacturing Industries. In: American Economic Review, Bd. 44, 1954. S. 15-39.

Bain 1965: Bain, Joe S. Barriers to New Competition. Cambridge: Harvard University Press, 1965.

Bakuli 1994: Bakuli, Luvisia D. Pitfalls in Technology Transfer: Kenya's Construction Industry. In: World Development, Vol. 22 No. 10, 1994. S. 1609-1612.

Balassa 1963: Balassa, Bela. An Empirical Demonstration of Classical Comparativ Cost Theory. In: The Review of Economics and Statistics, Vol. 45, 1963. S. 231-238.

Balassa 1966: Balassa, Bela. Tariff Reductions and Trade in Manufactures among the Industrial Countries. In: American Economic Review, Vol. 56, June 1966. S. 466-473.

Balassa 1967: Balassa, Bela. Trade Liberalization among Industrial Countries. New York, Toronto, London, Sydney: McGraw-Hill, 1967.

Balassa 1971: Balassa, Bela. Trade Policies in Developing Countries. In: American Economic Review, Vol. 61, 1971. S. 178-194.

Balassa 1978: Balassa, Bela. The 'New Protectionism' and the International Economy. In: Journal of World Trade Law, Vol. 12, 1978, S. 409-436.

Balassa 1979: Balassa, Bela. The Changing Pattern of Comparative Advantage in Manufactured Goods. In: Review of Economics and Statistics. Vol. 61, 1979. S. 259-266

Balassa 1979a: Balassa, Bela. Export Composition and Export Performance in the Industrial Countries, 1953-71. In: Review of Economics and Statistics. Vol. 61, 1979. S. 604-607.

Balassa 1980: Balassa, Bela. The Tokyo Round and the Developing Countries. In: Journal of World Trade Law. Vol. 14 No. 2, March April 1980. S. 93-118.

Balassa 1981: Balassa, Bela. The Newly-Industrializing Developing Countries after the Oil Crisis. In: Weltwirtschaftliches Archiv, Bd. 117, 1981. S. 142-194.

Balassa 1981a: Balassa, Bela. Trade in Manufactured Goods: Patterns of Change. In: World Development, Vol. 9, No. 1, 1981. S. 263-275.

Balassa 1981b: Balassa, Bela. Policy Responses to External Shocks in Selected Latin-American Countries. In: Baer, Werner, Gillis, Malcolm (Hrg.). Export Diversification and the New Protectionism. The Experiences of Latin America. NBER and the Bureau of Economic and Business Research University of Illinois: University of Illinois, 1981.

Balassa 1981c: Balassa, Bela. The Newly Industrializing Countries in the World Economy. New York: Pergamon Press, 1981.

Balassa 1985: Balassa, Bela. Exports, Policy Choices, and Economic Growth in Developing Countries after the 1973 Oil Shock. In: Journal of Development Economics, Vol. 18, 1985. S. 23-35.

Balassa 1986: Balassa, Bela. The Determinants of Intra-Industry Specialization in United States Trade. In: Oxford Economic Papers, Vol. 38, 1986. S. 220-233.

Balassa 1986a: Balassa, Bela. Intra-Industry Specialization. A Cross-Country Analysis. In: European Economic Review, 30, 1986. S. 27-42.

Balassa 1989: Balassa, Bela. Outward Orientation. In: Chenery, H., Srinivasan, T.N. Handbook of Development Economics, Vol. II, Chap. 31, Amsterdam; New York: Elsevier Science B.V., 1989.

Balassa et al. 1971: Balassa, Bela and Associates. The Structure of Protection in Developing Countries. Baltimore; London: John Hopkins Press, 1971.

Balassa et al. 1982: Balassa, Bela and Associates. Development Strategies in Semi-Industrial Economies. Baltimore, London: John Hopkins University Press, 1982.

Balassa et al. 1986: Balassa, Bela, Bueno, Gerardo M., Kuczynski, Pedro-Pablo, Simonsen, Mario Henrique. Toward Renewed Economic Growth in Latin America. Washington D.C.: Institute for International Economics, 1986.
Balassa/Bauwens 1987: Balassa, Bela, Bauwens, Luc. Intra-Industry Specialization in a Multi-Country and Multi-Commodity Framework. In: Economic Journal, Vol. 97, December 1987. S. 923-939.
Balassa/Bauwens 1988: Balassa, Bela, Bauwens, Luc. Changing Trade Patterns in Manufactured Goods: An Econometric Investigation. Amsterdam: Elsevier Publishers, 1988.
Balassa/Kreinin 1967: Balassa, Bela, Kreinin, Mordechai E. Trade Liberalization under the Kennedy Round: The Static Effects. In: The Review of Economics and Statistics, Vol. XLIX, No. 2, May 1967. S. 125-137.
Balassa/Michalopoulos 1986: Balassa, Bela, Michalopolous, Constantine. Liberalizing Trade between Developed and Developing Countries. In: JWTL, Vol. 20 No. 1, Jan. Feb. 1986. S. 3-28.
Balasubramanyam 1991: Balasubramanyam, V.N. Putting TRIMS to Good Use. In: World Development, Vol. 19, No. 9, 1991. S. 1215-1224.
Balasubramanyam et al. 1996: Balasubramanyam, V. N. Foreign Direct Investment and Growth in EP and IS Countries. In: Economic Journal, 106, January 1996, S. 95-105.
Baldone et al. 2001: Baldone, Salvatore, Fabio, Sdogati, Tajoli, Lucia. Patterns and Determinants of International Fragmentation of Production: Evidence from Outward Processing Trade between the EU and Central Eastern European Countries. In: Weltwirtschaftliches Archiv, Bd. 137, Heft 1, 2001. S. 80-104.
Baldwin 1969: Baldwin, Robert E. The Case against Infant-Industry Tariff Protection. In: Journal of Political Economy, Bd. 77, 1969. S. 295-597.
Baldwin 1970: Baldwin, Robert E. Nontariff Distortions of International Trade. Washington: The Brookings Institution, 1970.
Baldwin 1984: Baldwin, Robert E. The Changing Nature of U.S. Trade Policy since World War II. In: Baldwin, Robert E. Krueger, Anne O. The Structure and Evolution of Recent U.S. Trade Policy. Chicago; London: The University of Chicago Press, 1984.
Baldwin 1986: Baldwin, Robert E. Toward More Efficient Procedures for Multilateral Trade Negotiations. In: Aussenwirtschaft, 41. Jg, Heft 2/3, 1986. S. 379-394.
Baldwin 1992: Baldwin, Richard. High-Technology Exports and Strategic Trade Policy in Developing Countries: The Case of Brazilian Aircraft. In: Helleiner, Gerald K. (ed.) Trade Policy, Industrialization and Development. Study prepared for WIDER. Oxford: Clarendon Press, 1992.
Baldwin 1992a: Baldwin, Robert E. Are Economists' Traditional Trade Policy Views Still Valid? In: Journal of Economic Literature, Vol. 30, June 1992. S. 804-829.
Baldwin 1996: Baldwin, Robert E. The Political Economy of Trade Policy: Integrating the Perspectives of Economics and Political Scientists. In: Feenstra, Robert C. et al (eds.). The Political Economy of Trade Policy. Papers in Honor of Jagdish Bhagwati. Cambridge, Mass.: The MIT Press, 1996.
Baldwin et al. 1979: Baldwin, Robert E., Stern, Robert M., Kierzkowski, Henryk. Evaluating the Effects of Trade Liberalization. London: Trade Policy Research Centre, 1979.
Baldwin et al. 1995: Baldwin, Richard E., Forslid, Rikard, Haaland, Jan. Investment Creation and Investment Diversion: Simulation Analysis of the Single Market Programme. NBER Working Paper 5364, November 1995.
Baldwin/Flam 1989: Baldwin, Richard, Flam, Harry. Strategic Trade Policies in the Market for 30-40 Seat Commuter Aircraft. In: Weltwirtschaftliches Archiv, Vol. 125, 1989. S. 484-499.
Baldwin/Hilton 1984: Baldwin, Robert E., Hilton, R. Spence. A Technique for Indicating Comparative Costs and Predicting Changes in Trade Relations. In: Review of Economics and Statistics, Vol. 66, 1984. S. 105-110.
Baldwin/Murray 1977: Baldwin, Robert E., Murray, T. MFN Tariff Reductions and Developing Country Trade Benefits under the GSP. In: The Economic Journal, 87, March 1997, 30-46.
Baldwin/Ottaviano 1998: Baldwin, Richard E., Ottaviano, Gianmarco I. P. Multiproduct Multinationals and Reciprocal FDI Dumping. CEPR (Centre of Economic Policy Research) Discussion Paper No. 1851, March 1998.
Ball 1996: Ball, Carlos A. Making of a Transnationalist Capitalist Society: The Court of Justice, Social Policy, and Individual Rights Under the European Community's Legal Order. In: Harvard International Law Journal, Vol. 37, No. 2, Spring 1996. S. 307-388.
Ballon 1987: Ballon, Ian Charles. The Implications of Making the Denial of Internationallly Recognized Worker Rights Actionable Under Section 301 of the Trade Act of 1974. In: Virginia Journal of International Law, Vol. 28, 1987. S. 73-127.
Banerjee et al. 1995: Banerjee, Biswajit, Koen, Vincent, Krueger, Thomas, Lutz, Mark S., Marrese, Michael, Saavalainen, Tapio O. Road Maps of Transition. The Baltics, the Czech Republic, Hungary and Russia. IMF Occasional Paper. Washington: IMF, 1995.
Banerjee et al. 2006: Banerjee, Abhijit, Deaton, Angus, Lustig, Nora, Rogoff, Ken. An Evaluation of World Bank Research, 1998-2005. September 24, 2006. In: http://www.worldbank.org.
Bardan 1973: Bardan, Benyamin. The Cotton Textile Agreement 1962-1972. In: JWTL, Vol. 7 No. 1, Jan. Feb. 1973. S. 8-35.
Bardhan 1984: Bardhan, Pranab. The Political Economy of Development in India. Oxford: Basil Blackwell, 1984.
Bardhan 1989: Bardhan, Pranab. The New Institutionalist Economics and Development Theory: A Brief Critical Assessment. In: World Development, Vol. 17, No. 9, 1989. S. 1389-1395.
Bardhan 1995: Bardhan, Pranab. The Contribution of Endogenous Growth Theory to the Analysis of Development Problems: An Assessment. In: Behrman, J. Srinivasan, T.N. (eds.) Handbook of Development Economics, Vol. III, Amsterdam; New York: Elsevier Science B.V., 1995.

Bardhan 1997: Bardhan, Pranab. Method in the Madness? A Political-Economy Analysis of the Ethnic Conflicts in Less Developed Countries. In: World Development, Vol. 25, No. 9, 1997. S. 1381-1398.

Barnard 2000: Barnard, Catherine. Social dumping and the race to the bottom: some lessons for the European Union from Delaware? In: European Law Review, Vol. 25, 2000. S. 57-78.

Barrett 1989: Barrett, Sean. The importance of state enterprises in the Irish economy and the future for privatization. In: Parker, David (ed.). Privatization in the European Union. Theory and Policy Perspectives. London; New York: Routledge, 1998.

Barrett 1998: Barrett, Christopher B. Immiserized Growth in Liberalized Agriculture. In: World Development, Vol. 26 No. 5, 1998. S. 743-753.

Barringer/Pierce 2000: Barringer, William H., Pierce, Kenneth J. Paying the Price for Big Steel. American Institute for International Steel. In: http://www.aiis.org.

Barro 1991: Barro, Robert J. Economic Growth in a Cross Section of Countries. In: Quarterly Journal of Economics, May 1991. S. 407-443.

Barro 1996: Barro, Robert J. Determinants of Economic Growth. A Cross-Country Empirical Study. NBER Working Paper 5698, August 1996.

Barro/Sala-i-Martin 1991: Barro, Robert J., Sala-i-Martin, Xavier. Convergence across States and Regions. In: Brookings Papers on Economic Activity, 1: 1991, S. 107-182.

Barro/Sala-i-Martin 1992. Barro, Robert J., Sala-i-Martin, Xavier. Convergence. In: Journal of Political Economy, Vol. 100, No. 2, 1992. S. 223-251.

Barro/Sala-I-Martin 1995: Barro, Robert J., Sala-i-Martin, Xavier. Technological Diffusion, Convergence, and Growth. NBER Working Paper No. 5151, June 1995.

Bartá/Richter 1995: Bartá, Vit, Richter, Sándor. Die Osterweiterung der Europäischen Union aus westlicher und östlicher Sicht. In: Europa 1996 Auswirkungen einer EU-Osterweiterung. Schriftenreihe des Bundeskanzleramts. Wien: Österreichische Staatsdruckerei, 1995.

Bartels 2001: Bartels, Lorand. Applicable Law in WTO Dispute Settlement Proceedings. In: JWT Vol. 35, No. 3, 2001. S. 499-519.

Bartels 2004: Bartels, L. WTO Dispute Settlement Practice on Article XXIV of the GATT. In: Ortino, Federico, Petersmann, Ernst-Ulrich (eds.). The WTO Dispute Settlement System 1995 - 2003. The Hague et al.: Kluwer Law International, 2004.

Barth/Kürsten 1996: Barth, Henner, Kürsten, Martin. Die mineralischen Rohstoffe Afrikas – Chancen für die deutsche Wirtschaft. Hannover: Bundesanstalt für Geowissenschaften und Rohstoffe, 1996.

Bartmann 1996: Bartmann, Hermann. Umweltökonomie - ökologische Ökonomie. Stuttgart; Berlin; Köln: Kohlhammer, 1996.

Barton 2004: Barton, John H. Patents and the Transfer of Technology to Developing Countries. In: OECD. Patents, Innovation and Economic Performance. Conference Proceedings. Paris: OECD, 2004.

Barzel 1968: Barzel, Yoram. Optimal Timing of Innovations. In: Review of Economics and Statistics. Vol. 50, 1968. S. 348-355.

Bassett 2001: Bassett, Thomas J. The Peasant Cotton Revolution in West Africa. Cote d' Ivoire, 1880-1995. Cambridge: Cambridge University Press, 2001.

Bastos 1999: Bastos, Renato. Computer Hardware and Peripherals, Brazil. Industry Sector Analysis. Foreign Commercial Service and U.S. Department of State, 1999. In: http://www.corporateinformation.com/data/statususa/brazil/comphardware.html.

Basu/Pattanaik 1997: Basu, Kaushik, Pattanaik, Prasanta K. India's economy and the reforms of the 1990s: genesis and prospect. In: Journal of International Trade & Economic Development Vol. 6, 2, 1997. S. 123-133.

Bates 1981: Bates, Robert H. Markets and States in Tropical Africa. The Political Basis of Agricultural Policies. Berkely; Los Angeles; London: University of California Press, 1981.

Bates/Lien 1985: Bates, Robert H., Lien, Da-Hsiang Donald. On the operations of the International Coffee Agreement. In: IO, Vol. 39 No. 3, Summer 1985. S. 553-559.

Bathrick 1998: Bathrick, David D. Fostering Global Well-Being. A New Paradigm to Revitalize Agricultural and Rural Development. Washington: International Food Policy Research Institute, 1998.

Bauer 1954: Bauer, P.T. West African Trade. A Study of Competition, Oligopoly and Monopoly in a Changing Economy. London: Routledge & Kegan Paul Ltd., (1954) 1963.

Bauer 1971: Bauer, P. T. Dissent on Development. Studies and Debates in Developmental Economics. London: Weidenfels and Nicolson, 1971.

Bauer 2003: Bauer, Nina. Industrielle Cluster in Japan - Entstehung, Funktionalität und Wandel. Japan Analysen Prognosen Nor. 189, Oktober 2003. In: http://www.japan.uni-muenchen.de.

Bauer/Yamey 1957: Bauer, P.T., Yamey, B.S. The Economics of Under-developed Countries. Digswell; Cambridge: James Nisbet; Cambridge at the University Press, 1957.

Baumann 1998: Baumann, Helmut. Die Dienstleistungsfreiheit auf dem Gebiet der audiovisuellen Medien. Berlin: Duncker & Humblot, 1998.

Baumol 1982: Baumol, William J. Contestable Markets: An Uprising in the Theory of Industry Structure. In: American Economic Review, Vol. 72 No. 1, March 1982. S. 1-15.

Baumol 1986: Baumol, William J. Productivity Growth, Convergence, and Welfare. What the Long-Run Data Show. In: American Economic Review, Vol. 76, No. 5, December 1986. S. 1072-1085.

Baur 1980: Baur, Jürgen F. The Control of Mergers Between Large, Financially Strong Firms in West Germany. In: Zeitschrift für die gesamte Staatswissenschaft. Bd. 136, 1980. S. 444-464.

Bautista 1998: Bautista, Romeo M. Effects of Domestic Policies and External Factors on Agricultural Prices: Cassava and Soybeans in Indonesia. In: The Developing Economies, XXXVI-2, June 1998. S. 155-177.
Baxter/Crucini 1993: Baxter, Marianne, Crucini, Mario J. Explaining Saving-Investment Correlations. In: American Economic Review, Vol. 83 No. 3, June 1993. S. 416-436.
Bayoumi et al. 1996: Bayoumi, Tamin, Coe, David T., Helpman, Elhanan. R&D Spillovers and Global Growth. IMF Working Paper WP/96/47. Washington, IMF, 1996.
Baysan/Blitzer 1991: Baysan, Tercan, Blitzer, Charles. Turkey. In: The Experience of New Zealand, Spain and Turkey. Liberalizing Foreign Trade, Vol. 6. Oxford: World Bank/Blackwell, 1991.
BCC Research 2004: BCC Research. World Pharmaceutical Market to Cross US$ 900 Billion by 2008. Summary/Not full report, March 12, 2004. In: http://www.bccresearch.com.
Bean/Crafts 1996: Bean, Charles, Crafts, Nicolas. British Economic Growth sind 1945: relative economic decline ... and renaissance? In: Crafts, Nicolas, Toniolo, Gianni (eds.). Economic Growth in Europe since 1945. Cambridge: Cambridge University Press, 1996.
Beck 1996: Beck, Ulrich. Die Subpolitik der Globalisierung. In: Gewerkschaftliche Monatshefte, 11-12, 1996. S. 673-680.
Becker/Hanrahan 2002: Becker, Geoffrey, Hanrahan, Charles E. Trade Remedies and Agriculture. CRS Report for Congress, February 22, 2002. In: http://www.nationalaglawcenter.org/assets/crs/RL31296.pdf.
Becker/Womach 2002: Becker, Geoffrey, Womach, Jasper. The 2002 Farm Bill: Overview and Status. CRS Report for Congress, Updated, June 3, 2002. In: http://fpc.state.gov/fpc/c18787.htm.
Becroft 2006: Becroft, Ross. The Standard of Review Strikes Back: The US-Korea DRAMS Appeal. In: Journal of International Economic Law Vol. 9, No. 1, 2006. S. 207-217.
Been/Beauvais 2003: Been, Vicki, Beauvais, Joel C. The Global Fifth Amendment: NAFTA's Investment Protections and the Misguided Quest for an International 'Regulatory Takings' Doctrine. New York Center for Law and Business, Working Paper CLB-02-06. In: http://pepers.ssrn.com/abstract=337480
Beez 2000: Beez, Peter. Wirtschaftliche Entwicklung in Südkorea: Wachstum als Folge eines Reformprozesses. Hamburg: Institut für Asienkunde, 2000.
Begg 1997: Begg, Iain. Interregional Transfers in a Widened Europe. In: Siebert, Horst (ed.). Quo Vadis Europe? Tübingen: Mohr, 1997.
Behboodi 2001: Behboodi, Rambod. The Aircraft Cases: Canada and Brazil. In: Canadian Yearbook of International Law 2001. S. 387-431.
Behrens 1994: Behrens, Peter. Die Wirtschaftsverfassung der Europäischen Gemeinschaft. In: Brüggemeier, Gert. Verfassungen für ein ziviles Europa. Baden-Baden: Nomos, 1994.
Beise 1994: Beise, Marc. Vom alten zum neuen GATT - Zu den neuen Dimensionen der Welthandelsordnung. In: Vitzthum, Wolfgang Graf (Hrg.). Europäische und Internationale Wirtschaftsordnung aus der Sicht der Bundesrepublik Deutschland. Baden-Baden: Nomos, 1994.
Beitz 1985: Beitz, Charles R. Justice and International Relation. In: Beitz, Charles R. et al. (eds.). International Ethics. Princeton: Princeton University Press, 1985.
Beitz 1999: Beitz, Charles R. Social and cosmopolitan liberalism. In: International Affairs, 75, 3, 1999, 515-529.
Belderbos 1997: Belderbos, Rene A. Antidumping and Tariff Jumping: Japanese Firms' DFI in the European Union and the United States. In: Weltwirtschaftliches Archiv, Vol. 133, Heft 3, 1997. S. 419-457.
Bell et al. 1984: Bell, Martin, Ross-Larson, Bruce, Westphal, Larry E. Assessing the Performance of Infant Industries. In: Journal of Development Economics, Vol. 16, 1984. S. 101-128.
Bellamy/Child 2001: Bellamy, Sir Christoper, Child, Graham. European Community Law of Competition. Fifth Edition. London: Sweet&Maxwell, 2001.
Bello 2003: Bello, Walden. Multilateral Punishment. The Philippines in the WTO, 1995-2003. Focus on the Global South. In: http://www.focusweb.org.
Benda/Klein 1991: Benda, Ernst, Klein, Eckart. Lehrbuch des Verfassungsprozeßrechts. Heidelberg: C.F. Müller, 1991.
Ben-David 1993: Ben-David, David. Equalizing Exchange: Trade Liberalization and Income Convergence. In: Quarterly Journal of Economics, August 1993. S. 653-679.
Bender 1999: Bender, Dieter. Außenhandel. In: Bender, Dieter et al. (Hrg.) Vahlens Kompendium der Wirtschaftstheorie und Wirtschaftspolitik. München: Vahlen, 1999.
Bender/Sparwasser 1995: Bender, Bernd, Sparwasser, Reinhard, Engel, Rüdiger. Umweltrecht. Heidelberg: C.F. Müller, 1995.
Benedeck 1990: Benedek, Wolfgang. Die Rechtsordnung des GATT aus völkerrechtlicher Sicht. Berlin; Heidelberg etc.: Springer, 1990.
Benedeck 1998: Benedek, Wolfgang. Einführung zur Textausgabe. In: Benedek, Wolfgang. Die Welthandelsorganisation (WTO). München: C.H. Beck, 1998.
Bennell 1984: Bennell, Paul. The Utilization of Professional Engineering Skills in Kenya. In: Fransman, Martin, King, Kenneth (eds.). Technology Capability in the Thirld World. London: Macmillan, 1984.
Bennett et al. 1999: Bennet, Davis, Liu, Xiaming, Parker, David, Steward, Fred, Vaidya, Kirit. China and European Economic Security: Study on medium to long term impact fo technology transfer to China. European Commission, DG I, July 1999. In: http://europe.eu.int/comm/trade.
Berg 1993: Berg, Hartmut: Motorcars: between growth and protectionism. In: de Jong, H.W. (ed.) The Structure of European Industry. Dordrecht; Boston; London: Kluwer, 1993.
Berge 1946: Berge, Wendell. Cartels. Challenge to a Free World. Washington: Public Affairs Press, 1946.

Berger 1996: Berger, Johannes. Vollbeschäftigung als Staatsaufgabe? In: Grimm, Dieter (Hrg.). Staatsaufgaben. Frankfurt am Main: Surkamp, 1996.
Bergsten 1992: Bergsten, Fred C. The Primacy of Economics. In: Foreign Policy, No. 87, Summer 1992. S. 3-24.
Bergsten/Keohane 1975: Bergsten, Fred C. Keohane, Robert O., Nye, Joseph S. International Economics and International Politics: a framework for analysis. In: International Organization, Vol. 29, No. 1, Winter 1975, S. 3-36.
Bernard et al. 2003: Bernard, Andrew B., Eaton, Jonathan, Bradford Jensen, Bradford J., Kortum, Samuel S. Plants and Productivity in International Trade. Working Paper. In: http://www.econ.umn.edu/.
Bernard/Jones 1996: Bernard, Andrew B, Jones, Charles I. Comparing Apples to Oranges: Productivity Convergence and Measurement Across Industries and Countries. In: American Economic Review, Vol. 86, No. 5. December 1996. S. 1216-1237.
Bernard/Jones 2000: Bernard, Andrew B, Jones, Charles I. Technology and Convergence. In: Dixon, Huw David. Controversies in Macroeconomics Growth, Trade and Policy. Oxford: Blackwell, 2000.
Bernstein/Mohnen 1998: Bernstein, Jeffrey I., Mohnen, Pierre. International R&D Spillovers between U.S. and Japanese R&D Intensive Sectors. In: Journal of International Economics, 44, 1998. S. 315-338.
Bernstein/Nadiri 1988: Berstein, Jeffrey I., Nadiri, M. Ishaq. Interindustry R&D Spillovers, Rates of Return, and Production in High-Tech Industries. In: American Economic Review, Papers and Proceedings, Vol. 78, No. 2, May 1988. S. 429-434.
Bernstein/Nadiri 1989: Berstein, Jeffrey I., Nadiri, M. Ishaq. Research and Development and Intra-industry Spillovers: An Empirical Application of Dynamic Duality. In: Review of Economic Studies, Vol. 56, 1989. S. 249-269.
Berry et al. 1995: Berry, Steven, Levinsohn, James, Pakes, Ariel. Voluntary Export Restraints on Automobiles: Evaluating a Strategic Trade Policy. In: NBER Working Paper No. 5235, August 1995.
Berry et al. 1999: Berry, Steven, Levinson, James, Pakes, Ariel. Voluntary Export Restraints on Automobiles: Evaluating a Trade Policy. In: American Economic Review, Vol. 89, No. 3, June 1999. S. 400-430.
Berthelemy/Söderling 1999: Berthelemy, Jean-Claude, Söderling, Ludvig. The Role of Capital Accumulation, Adjustment and Structural Change for Economic Take-off: Empirical Evidence from African Growth Episodes. OECD Development Centre, Working Paper No. 150, CD/DOC(99)7, July 1999. In: http://www.oecd.org.
Berthelot 2001: Berthelot, Jacques. Some theoretical and factual clarifications in order to get a fair Agreement on Agriculture at the WTO. Unveröffentlichtes Papier. Symposium on issues confronting the world trading system, Geneva, July 6, 2001.
Berthelot 2002: Berthelot, Jacques. The Reform of the Common Agricultural Policy - Consequences for Developing Countries from the Mid-Term Review of the Agenda 2000. Bonn, 24 Sep. 2002. Unveröffentlichte Präsentation: Forum Umwelt und Entwicklung, German Ministry for Cooperation and Development.
Berthelot 2004: Berthelot, Jacques. How to prosecute the dumping of US and EU agri-food products at the WTO after the 'Peace clause'. Unveröffentlichtes Papier. April 7, 2004.
Berthelot 2004a: Berthelot, Jacques. Ending Food Dumping: taking the US and EU through the WTO disputes procedure after the expiry of the 'peace clause'. Unveröffentlichtes Paper, 20 May 2004.
Berthold/Fehn 1997: Berthold, Norbert, Fehn, Rainer. Aktive Arbeitsmarktpolitik – wirksames Instrument der Beschäftigungspolitik oder politische Beruhigungspille? In: ORDO, Bd. 48, 1997.
Berthold/Fehn 1998: Berthold, Norbert, Fehn, Rainer. Tarifpolitik und Arbeitslosigkeit: Löst die Europäische Währungsunion das Beschäftigungsproblem? In: Cassel, Dieter (Hrg.). 50 Jahre Soziale Marktwirtschaft. Schriften zu Ordnungfragen der Wirtschaft, Band 57, Stuttgart: Lucius&Lucius, 1998.
Bertram 1993: Bertram, Heike. Werkzeugmaschinenbau in Deutschland und die globale Konkurrenz. In: Geographische Rundschau, Bd. 45, Heft 9, 1993. S. 486-492.
Bertsch 1981: Bertsch, Gary K. U. S. Export Controls: The 1970's and Beyond. In: JWTL, Vol. 15 No. 1, Jan. Feb 1981. S. 67-82.
Bessen/Hunt 2004: Bessen, James, Hunt, Robert M. The Software Patent Experiment. In: OECD. Patents, Innovation and Economic Performance. Conference Proceedings. Paris: OECD, 2004.
Betz 1998: Betz, Joachim. Globalisierung und nationale Sozialpolitik. In: Nord-Süd-Aktuell, Jahrgang XII, Nr. 3, 1988, S. 449-457.
Beyerlin 1996: Beyerlin, Ulrich. State Community Interests and Institution Building in International Environmental Law. In: ZaöRV, Vol. 39, 56/3, 1996. S. 602-627.
BFAI 2004: Bundesstelle für Außenhandelsinformation. Mexiko öffnet den Automobilsektor. 19.02.2004. In: http://www.bfai.de.
Bhagwati 1977: Bhagwati, Jagdish. Consideration of Policy Issues at the International Level. The reverse transfer of technology (brain drain): International resource flow accounting, compensation, taxation and related policy proposals. UNCTAD, Geneva, TD/B/C-6/AC.4/2, 13. December 1977.
Bhagwati 1978: Bhagwati, Jagdish. Anatomy and Consequences of Exchange Control Regimes. National Bureau of Economic Research. Cambrigde, Mass.: Ballinger Publishing Company, 1978.
Bhagwati 1982: Bhagwati, Jagdish. Directly Unproductive, Profit Seeking (DUP) Activities. In: Journal of Political Economy, Vol. 90, No. 51, 1982. S. 988-1002.
Bhagwati 1988: Bhagwati, Jagdish. Export-Promoting Trade Strategy: Issues and Evidence. In: The World Bank Research Observer, Vol. 3 No. 1, January 1988. S. 27-57.
Bhagwati 1989: Bhagwati, Jagdish. Is Free Trade Passé after All? In: Weltwirtschaftliches Archiv, Vol. 125, No. 1, 1989, S. 17-44.

Bhagwati 1989a: Bhagwati, Jagdish. U.S. Trade Policy at Crossroads. In: Irwin, Douglas A. (ed.) Political Economy and International Economics. Jagdish Bhagwati. Cambridge: The MIT Press, 1984.
Bhagwati 1990: Bhagwati, Jagdish. Departures from Multilateralism: Regionalism und Aggressive Unilateralism. In: Economic Journal, 100, December 1990. S. 1304-1317.
Bhagwati 1990a: Bhagwati, Jagdish. Geschützte Märkte. Protektionismus und Weltwirtschaft. Frankfurt am Main: Kneip Verlag, 1990.
Bhagwati 1991: Bhagwati, Jagdish. The World Trading System at Risk. New York et al.: Harvester Wheatsheaf, 1991.
Bhagwati 2000: Bhagwati, Jagdish. The Wind of Hundred Days. Cambridge, Mass.: MIT Press, 2000.
Bhagwati 2004: Bhagwati, Jagdish. In Defense of Globalization. Oxford: Oxfort University Press, 2004.
Bhagwati et al. 1969: Bhagwati, Jagdish, Ramaswami, V. K., Srinivasan, T. N. Domestic Distortions, Tariffs, and the Theory of Optimum Subsidy: Some Further Results. In: Journal of Political Economy, Bd. 77, 1969. S. 1005-1013.
Bhagwati et al. 1984: Bhagwati, Jagdish, Brecher, Richard A., Srinivasan, T. N. DUP Activities and Economic Theory. In: Irwin, Douglas A. (ed.) Political Economy and International Economics. Jagdish Bhagwati. Cambridge: The MIT Press, 1984.
Bhagwati/Irwin 1987: Bhagwati, Jagdish, Irwin, Douglas A. The Return of the Reciprocitarians: U.S. Trade Policy Today. In: Irwin, Douglas A. (ed.) Political Economy and International Economics. Jagdish Bhagwati. Cambridge: The MIT Press, 1984.
Bhagwati/Mavroidis 2004: Bhagwati, Jagdish N., Mavroidis, Petros C. Killing the Byrd Amendment with the right stone. In: World Trade Review Vol. 3 No. 1, 2004. S. 199-127.
Bhagwati/Srinivasan 1975: Bhagwati, Jagdish, Srinivasan, T. N. Foreign Trade Regimes and Economic Development: India. National Bureau of Economic Research. New York, London: Columbia University Press, 1975.
Bhagwati/Srinivasan 1980: Bhagwati, Jagdish N., Srinivasan, T.N. Revenue Seeking: A Generalization of the Theory of Tariffs. In: Journal of Political Economy, Vol. 88, No. 6, 1980. S. 1069-1087.
Bhagwati/Srinivasan 2002: Bhagwati, Jagdish N., Srinivasan, T.N. Trade and Poverty in the Poor Countries. In: American Economic Review, Papers and Proceedings, Vol. 92 No. 2, 2002. S. 180-208.
Bhalla/Fluitman 1985: Bhalla, A. S., Fluitman, A. G. Science and Technology Indicators and Socio-economic Development. In: World Development, Vol. 13, No. 2, 1985. S. 177-190.
Bhaskar 1986: Bhaskar, K. N. Japanes Automotive Strategies: A European and US Perspective. Norwich: The Motor Industry Research Unit, 1986.
Bhattacharjea 2004: Battacharjea, Aditya. Trade and Competition Policy. Indian Council for Research on International Economic Relations, Working Paper 146, November 2004. In: http://www.icrier.res.in/.
BHEL 2006: Bharat Heavy Electricals Ltd. (BHEL). Informationen. 2006. In: http://www.bhel.com/bhel/about.htm
Bianchi/Forlai 1993: Bianchi, Patrizio, Forlai, Luigi. The domestic appliance industry 1945-1991. In: de Jong, H.W. (ed.) The Structure of European Industry. Dordrecht; Boston; London: Kluwer, 1993.
Bickenbach/Soltwedel 1998: Bickenbach, Frank, Soltwedel, Rüdiger. Produktionssystem, Arbeitsorganisation und Anreizstrukturen: Der Paradigmenwechsel in der Unternehmensorganisation und seine Konsequenzen für die Arbeitsmarktverfassung. In: Cassel, Dieter (Hrg.). 50 Jahre Soziale Marktwirtschaft. Schriften zu Ordnungfragen der Wirtschaft, Band 57, Stuttgart: Lucius&Lucius, 1998.
Bieback 1985: Bieback, Karl-Jürgen. Sozialstaatsprinzip und Grundrechte. In: EuGRZ, 12 Jg., Heft 22, 1985. S. 657-669.
Bierbaum 1992: Bierbaum, Frank. Strategisches Verhalten in stagnierenden Branchen – Eine Darstellung am Beispiel der deutschen Textilindustrie. Dissertation St. Gallen. Gronau: Druckerei Möllers, 1992.
Bierling 1999: Bierling, Stephan. Südafrikas Wirtschaft unter Mandela: Möglichkeiten und Grenzen der ökonomischen Transformation. In: Aus Politik und Zeitgeschichte, B 27/99, 2. Juli 1999.
Biermann 2001: Biermann, Frank. The Rising Tide of Green Unilateralism in World Trade Law. Options for Reconciling the Emerging North-South Conflict. In: JWT Vol. 35, No. 3, 2001. S. 412-448.
Bierstecker 1987: Bierstecker, Thomas J. Multinationals, the State, and Control of the Nigerian Economy. Princeton: Princeton University Press, 1987.
Bierstecker 1993: Bierstecker, Thomas J. International Financial Negotiations and Adjustment Bargaining: An Overview. In: Bierstecker, Thomas J. (ed.). Dealing with Debt. International Financial Negotiations and Adjustment Bargaining. Boulder: Westview Press, 1993.
Bierwagen/Hailbronner 1988: Bierwagen, Rainer M., Hailbronner, Kay. Input, Downstream, Upstream, Secondary, Divisionary and Components or Subassembly Dumping. In: JWT, Vol. 22 No. 1, 1988. S. 27-59.
Biggs et al. 1995: Biggs, Tyler, Shah, Manju, Srivastava, Pradeep. Technological Capabilities and Learning in African Enterprises. World Bank Technical Paper Number 288. Washington: World Bank, 1995.
Biggs/Shah 1997: Biggs, Tyler, Shah, Manju. Trade Reforms, Incentives on the Ground and Firm Performance in Ghana. RPED Paper No. 105, July 1997. In: http://www.worldbank.org/rped/documents/rped105.pdf.
Bigsten et al. 2001: Bigsten, Arne, Collier, Paul, Dercon, Stefan, Fafchamps, Marcel, Gauthier, Bernard, Gunning, Jan Willem, Oduro, Abena, Oostendorp, Remco, Patillo, Cathy, Sönderbom, Mans, Teal, Francis, Zeufack, Albert. Exporting and Efficiency in African Manufacturing. In: OECD. Policies to Promote Competitiveness in Manufacturing in Sub-Saharan Africa. Development Centre Seminars within the IMF and the AERC. Kwasi Fosu, Augustin, Nsouli, Saleh M., Varoudakis, Aristomene (eds.). Paris: OECD, 2001a.

Bigsten et al. 2002: Bigsten, Arne, Collier, Paul, Dercon, Stefan, Fafchamps, Marcel, Gauthier, Bernard, Gunning, Jan Willem, Oduro, Abena, Oostendorp, Remco, Patillo, Cathy, Sönderbom, Mans, Teal, Francis, Zeufack, Albert. Credit Constraints in Manufacturing Enterprises in Africa. University of Oxford: Centre for the Study of African Economies, November 2002. In: http://www.csae.ox.ac.uk.

Binswanger et al. 1995: Binsanger, Hans P., Deininger, Klaus, Feder, Gerschon. Power, Distortions, Revolt and Reform in Agricultural Land Relations. In: Behrman, J., Srinivasan, T. N. (eds.). Handbook of Development Economics. Vol. III. Den Haag: Elsevier Science, 1995.

Binswanger/Deininger 1997: Binswanger, Hans P., Deininger, Klaus. Explaining Agricultural and Agrarian Policies in Developing Countries. World Bank Policy Research Working Paper No. 1765, March 11, 1997. In: http://www.worldbank.org.

Bird 1995: Bird. Graham. IMF Lending to Developing Countries. London; New York: Routledge, 1995.

Bjurek/Durevall 2000: Bjurek, Hans, Durevall, Dick. Does Market Liberalization Increase Total Factor Productivity? Evidence from the Manufacturing Sector in Zimbabwe. Journal of Southern African Studies, Vol. 26 No. 3, September 2000. S. 463-479.

Blackhurst 1986: Blackhurst, Richard. GATT Surveillance of Industrial Policies. In: Aussenwirtschaft, 41. Jg, Heft 2/3, 1986. S. 361-378.

Blackhurst et al. 1999: Blackhurst, Richard, Lyakurwa, Bill, Oyejide, Ademola. Improving African Participation in the WTO. Working Paper, World Bank, September 1999. In: http://www.worldbank.org/research/trade.

Blackhurst/Enders 1995: Blackhurst, Richard, Enders, Alice, Francois, Joseph F. The Uruguay Round and Market Access: Opportunities and Challenges for Developing Countries. In: Martin, Will, Winters, L. Alan (eds.). The Uruguay Round and the Developing Countries. World Bank Discussion Papters 307, Washington: World Bank, 1995.

Blackhurst/Hartridge 2005: Blackhurst, Richard, Hartridge, David. Improving the Capacity of WTO Institutions to Fulfil their Mandate. In: Petersmann, Ernst-Ulrich (ed.). Reforming the World Trading System. Legitimacy, Efficiency, and Democratic Governance. Oxford: Oxford University Press, 2005.

Blaich 1970: Blaich, Fritz. Der 'Standard-Oil-Fall' vor dem Reichstag. Ein Beitrag zur deutschen Monopolpolitik vor 1914. In: Zeitschrift für die gesamte Staatswissenschaft, Vol. 126, 1970. S. 663-682.

Blaich 1974: Blaich, Fritz. Robert Liefmann und das Problem der staatlichen Kartellpolitik. In: Jahrbuch für Sozialwissenschaft, Bd. 25, Heft 1, 1974. S. 138-157.

Blankart 1994: Blankart, Charles B. Öffentliche Finanzen in der Demokratie. München: Vahlen, 1994.

Blecker 1997: Blecker, Robert A. The 'Unnatural and Retrograde Order': Adam Smith's Theories of Trade and Development Reconsidered. In: Economica, Vol. 64, 1997. S. 527-537.

Blecker/Feinberg 1995: Blecker, Robert A, Feinberg, Robert M. A Multidimensional Analysis of the International Performance of U.S. Manufacturing Industries. In: Weltwirtschaftliches Archiv, Bd. 131, Heft 2, 1995. S. 339-358.

Bletschacher 1992: Bletschacher, Georg. Strategische Handels- und Industriepolitik in der Automobilindustrie? In: Die Weltwirtschaft, Heft 1, 1992. S. 68-84.

Bletschacher/Klodt 1992: Bletschacher, Georg, Klodt, Henning. Strategische Handels- und Industriepolitik. Tübingen: Mohr, 1992.

Blind et al. 2004: Bling, Knut, Edler, Jacob, Frietsch, Rainer, Schmoch, Ulrich. Scope and Nature of the Patent Surge: A View from Germany. In: OECD. Patents, Innovation and Economic Performance. Conference Proceedings. Paris: OECD, 2004.

Bloch/Sapsford 1996: Bloch, Harry, Sapsford, David. Trend in the International Terms of Trade Between Primary Producers and Manufacturers. In: Journal of International Development, Vol. 8, No. 1, 1996. S. 53-67.

Blomqvist/Mohammad 1986: Blomqvist, Ake, Mohammad, Sharif. Controls, Corruption, and Competitive Rent-Seeking in LDCs. In: Journal of Development Economics, Vol. 21, 1986. S. 161-180.

Blomström et al. 1996: Blomström, Magnus, Lipsey, Robert E., Zejan, Mario. Is Fixed Investment the Key to Economic Growth. In: Quarterly Journal of Economics, Vol. CXI, Issue 2, May 1996. S. 269-276.

Blonigen 2000: Blonigen, Bruce A. Tariff-Jumping Antidumping Duties. NBER Working Paper No. 7776, July 2000.

Blonigen 2003: Blonigen, Bruce A. Tariff-Jumping Antidumping Duties. NBER Working Paper No. 9625, April 2003.

Blonigen 2004: Blonigen, Bruce A. Working in the System: Firm Learning and the Antidumping Process. NBER Working Paper No. 10783, September 2004.

Blonigen et al. 2002: Blonigen, Bruce A., Tomlin, KaSaundra, Wilson, Wesley W. Tariff-Jumping FDI and Domestic Firm's Profits. NBER Working Paper No. 9027, July 2002.

Blonigen/Bown 2001: Blonigen, Bruce A., Bown, Chad P. Antidumping and Retaliation Threats. NBER Working Paper No. 8576, November 2001.

Blonigen/Haynes 1999: Blonigen, Bruce A., Haynes, Stephen E. Antidumping Investigations and the Pass-Through of Exchange Rates and Antidumping Duties. NBER Working Paper No. 7378, October 1999.

Blonigen/Prusa 2001: Blonigen, Bruce A., Prusa, Thomas J. Antidumping. NBER Working Paper No. 8398, July 2001.

Blonigen/Prusa 2002: Blonigen, Bruce A., Prusa, Thomas J. The Cost of Antidumping: The Devil is in the Details. Working Paper, February 2002. In: http://darkwing.uoregon.edu/~bruceb/adpage.html.

BLS 2000: Bureau of Labor Statistics. Industry at a Glance. Overview on Employment Data. In: http://stats.bls.gov.

BMBF 1997: Bundesministerium für Bildung, Wissenschaft, Forschung und Technologie. Zur Technologischen Leistungsfähigkeit Deutschlands. 1997. In: http://www.bmbf.de.
BMWi 1999: BMWi. Wirtschaftslage und Reformprozesse in Mittel- und Osteuropa. Sammelband 1999. Berlin 1999.
Bobzin 2006: Bobzin, Hagen. Edgeworth Box im Güterraum. Februar 2004. In: http://www.uni-siegen.de/~vwlii/mikro/edgeworth-gueter.html.
Boccara/Nsengiyumva 1995: Boccara, Bruno, Nsengiyumva, Fabien. Short-Term Supply Response to a Devaluation. World Bank Policy Research Working Paper, No. 1428, February 1995. In: http://www.worldbank.org.
Böckenförde 1987: Böckenförde, Ernst-Wolfgang. Demokratie als Verfassungsprinzip. In: Isensee, Josef, Kirchhof, Paul (Hrg.). Handbuch des Staatsrechts. Bd. I. Heidelberg: C.F. Müller, 1987.
Böckenförde 1991: Böckenförde, Ernst-Wolfgang. Staat, Verfassung, Demokratie. Studien zur Verfassungstheorie und zum Verfassungsrecht. Frankfurt am Main: Surkamp, 1991.
Böckenförde 1999: Böckenförde, Ernst-Wolfgang. Staat, Nation, Europa. Frankfurt am Main: Surkamp, 1999.
Böcker/Herrmann 2002: Böcker, A., Herrmann, R. Internationale Kartelle in der Ernährungswirtschaft und die Möglichkeit der neuen Industrieökonomie zur Feststellung von Kollusionen. In: Brockmeier, M., Isermeyer, F., von Cramon-Taubadel, S. (Hrg.). Liberalisierung des Weltagrarhandels - Strategien und Konsequenzen. Münster-Hiltrup: Landwirtschaftsverlag, 2002.
Bodammer et al. 2005: Bodammer, Imme, Forbes Pirie, Mia, Addy-Nayo, Chris. Telecoms Regulation in Developing Countries: Attracting Investment into the Sector: Ghana - A Case Study. In: JWT, Vol. 39, No. 3, 2005. S. 527-558.
Bofinger et al. 1996: Bofinger, Peter, Reischle, Julian, Schächter, Andrea. Geldpolitik. München: Vahlen, 1996.
Bogdandy 1992: Bogdandy, Armin von. The Non-Violation Procedure of Article XXIII:2, GATT. In: JWT, Vol. 26, No. 4, 1992. S. 95-111.
Bogdandy 1993: Bogdandy, Armin von. Supranationale Union als neuer Herrschaftstypus. Entstaatlichung und Vergemeinschaftung in staatstheoretischer Perspektive. In: Integration, 16. Jg. 4/93, Beilage zur Europäischen Zeitung 10/1993.
Bogdandy 2001: Bogdandy, Armin von. Verfassungsrechtliche Dimensionen der Welthandelsorganisation: Entkopplung von Recht und Politik oder neue Wege globaler Demkratie? In: Kritische Justiz, Bd. 34, 2001. In: http://www.mpil.de/personal/bogdandy/index.html.
Bogdandy/Nettesheim 1996: Bogdandy, Armin von, Nettesheim, Martin. Die Europäische Union: Ein einheitlicher Verband mit eigener Rechtsordnung, EuR, Heft 1, 1996.
Böhm 1928: Böhm, Franz. Das Problem der privaten Macht. In: Die Justiz, Band III, 1927/1928. S. 324-352.
Böhm 1933: Böhm, Franz. Wettbewerb und Monopolkampf. Berlin: Carl Heymanns Verlag, 1933.
Böhm 1966: Böhm, Franz. Privatrechtsgesellschaft und Marktwirtschaft. In: ORDO, Bd. 17, 1966. S. 75-151.
Böhme 1970: Böhme, Hans. Der Weltseeverkehr. In: Die Weltwirtschaft, Heft 1, 1970. S. 175-197.
Böhme 1976: Böhme, Hans. Weltseeverkehr 1976: Nach kurzem Aufschwung eine neue Flaute? In: Die Weltwirtschaft, Heft 2, 1976. S. 148-181.
Böhme 1985: Böhme, Hans. Weltseeverkehr: Auf dem Weg in eine neue Flaute? In: Die Weltwirtschaft, Heft 2, 1985. S. 115-170.
Böhme 1987: Böhme, Hans. Weltseeverkehr: Unerwartete Belebung auf den Frachtenmärkten. In: Die Weltwirtschaft, Heft 2, 1987. S. 171-193, Tabellen S. 26-34.
Böhme 1988: Böhme, Hans. Staatliche Reglementierung der Linienschiffahrt oder Freiheit der Meere? Zur Revisionskonferenz über den UN-Linienkodex. In: Die Weltwirtschaft, Heft 1, 1988. S. 165-177.
Böhme 1996: Böhme, Hans. Weltseeverkehr: Märkte zwischen Boom und Baisse. Kieler Diskussionsbeiträge No. 275, Juni 1996.
Boltho 1996: Boltho, Andrea. Was Japanese Growth Export-Led?. In: Oxford Economic Papers, 48, 1996. S. 415-432.
Boltho/Holtham 1992: Boltho, Andrea, Holtham, Gerald. The Assessment: New Approaches to Economic Growth. In: Oxford Review of Economic Policy, Vol. 8, No. 4, 1992. S. 1-14.
Bonelli 1992: Bonelli, Regis. Growth and productivity in Brazilian industries. Impacts of trade orientation. In: Journal of Development Economics, Vol. 39, 1992. S. 85-109.
Bonelli 2000: Bonelli, Regis. Brazil: The Challenge of Improving Export Performance. In: Marario, Carla, Bonelli, Regis, ten Kate, Adriaan, Niels, Gunnar. Export Growth in Latin America. Policies and Performance. Boulder; London: Lynne Rienner, 2000.
Bonus 1979: Bonus, Holger. Öffentliche Güter: Verführungen und Gefangenendilemma. In: Stützel, Wolfgang et al. (Hrg.). Grundtexte zur Sozialen Marktwirtschaft. Stuttgart: Gustav Fischer Verlag, 1981.
Bora et al. 1999: Bora, Bijit, Lloyd, P. J., Pangestu, Mari. Industrial Policy and the WTO. WTO/World Bank Conference on Developing Countries in a Millenium Round, 20-21 September 1999. In: http://www.worldbank.org.
Bora/Graham 2005: Bora, Bijit, Graham, Edward M. Investment and the Doha Development Agenda. In: Petersmann, Ernst-Ulrich (ed.). Reforming the World Trading System. Legitimacy, Efficiency, and Democratic Governance. Oxford: Oxford University Press, 2005.
Boratav/Türel 1993: Boratav, Korkut, Türel, Oktar. Turkey. In: Taylor, Lance (ed.). The Rocky Road to Reform. Adjustment, Income Distribution, and Growth in the Developing World. Cambridge: MIT Press, 1993.
Borchart 1996: Borchart, Klaus- Dieter. Die rechtlichen Grundlagen der europäischen Union. Heidelberg: C.F. Müller, 1996.

Borchert 1994: Borchert, Manfred. Strategische Handelspolitik – alter Wein in neuen Schläuchen? In: RWI-Mitteilungen, Jg. 45, 1994. S. 205-220.

Borchert et al. 1987: Borchert, Jutta, Hayunga, Hayo, Scheewe, Winfried, Seitz, Klaus, Stahlmann, Axel, Windfuhr, Michael. Wer Hunger pflanzt und Überschuß erntet. Beiträge zu einer entwicklungspolitischen Kritik der EU Agrarpolitik. Hamburg: BUKO Agrarkoordination/Verein zur Förderung entwicklungspolitischer Zusammenarbeit, 1987.

Borchert/Grossekettler 1985: Borchert, M., Grossekettler, H. Preis- und Wettbewerbstheorie. Stuttgart et al.: Kohlhammer Verlag, 1985.

Borenstein et al. 1995: Borenstein, Severin, MacKie-Mason, Jeffrey K., Netz, Janet S. Antitrust Policies in Aftermarkets. In: Antitrust Law Journal, Vol. 63, 1995. S. 455-482.

Borensztein et al. 1994: Borensztein, E., Khan, Moshin S., Reinhart, Carmen M., Wickham, Peter. The Behavior of Non-Oil Commodity Prices. Occasional Paper 112. Washington: International Monetary Fund, 1994.

Borensztein et al. 1998: Borensztein, E., Gregorio, J. De, Lee, J-W. How does foreign direct investment affect economic growth? In: Journal of International Economics, Vol. 45, 1998. S. 115-135.

Bork 1978: Bork, Robert H. The Antitrust Paradox. New York: Basic Books, 1978.

Borkin/Welsh 1943: Borkin, Joseph, Welsh, Charles. Germany's Master Plan. The Story of Industrial Offensive. London; New York; Melbourne: John Long, 1943.

Bornschier/Chase-Dunn 1985: Bornschier, Volker, Chase-Dunn, Christopher. Transnational Corporations and Underdevelopment. New York: Praeger, 1985.

Börnsen et al. 1985: Börnsen, Ole, Glismann, Hans H., Horn, Ernst-Jürgen. Der Technologietransfer zwischen den USA und der Bundesrepublik. Kieler Studien Nr. 192. Tübingen: Mohr, 1985.

Borrmann et al. 1995: Borrmann, Axel, Fischer, Bernhard, Jungnickel, Rolf, Koopmann, Georg, Scharrer, Hans-Eckart. Regionalismustendenzen im Welthandel. Baden-Baden: Nomos, 1995.

Bortolotti et al. 2003: Bortolotti, Bernardo, Fantini, Marcella, Siniscalco, Domenico. Privatization around the world: evidence from panel data. In: Journal of Public Economics, Vol. 88, 2003. S. 305-332.

Bosworth 1995: Bosworth, Barry. Prospects for Saving and Investment in Industrial Countries. In: Brookings Institution, Discussion Papers in International Economics, No. 113, 1995, http://www.brookings.org

Bosworth/Collins 1999: Boswoth, Barry P., Collins, Susan M. Capital Flows to Developing Economies: Implications for Saving and Investment. In: Brookings Papers on Economic Activity 1, 1999. S. 143-180.

Bottasso/Sembenelli 2001: Bottasso, Anna, Sembenelli, Alessandro. Market power, productivity and the EU Single Market Program: Evidence from a panel of Italian firms. In: European Economic Review, Vol. 45, 2001. S. 167-186.

Bouet et al. 2004: Bouet, Antoine, Bureau, Jean-Christophe, Decreux, Yvan, Jean, Sebastian. Multilateral agricultural trade liberalization. The contrasting fortunes of developing countries in the Doha Round. CEPII Working Paper, No. 18 November 2004. In: http://www.cepii.fr.

Bourgeois 1997: Bourgeois, Jaques H.J. GATT/WTO Dispute Settlement Practice in the Field of Anti-dumping law. In: Petersmann, Ernst-Ulrich (ed.). International Trade Law and the GATT/WTO Dispute Settlement System. London, The Hague, Boston: Kluwer Law, 1997.

Boussemart/de Bandt 1993: Boussemart, Benoît, de Bandt, Jaques. The textile industry: widely varying structures. In: de Jong, H.W. (ed.) The Structure of European Industry. Dordrecht; Boston; London: Kluwer, 1993.

Bovard 1991: Bovard, James. The Fair Trade Fraud. How Congress Pillages the Consumer and Decimates American Competitiveness. New York: St. Martin's Press, 1991.

Bowen et al. 1987: Bowen, Harry P., Leamer, Edward E., Sveikauskas, Leo. Multicountry, Multifactor Tests of the Factor Abundance Theory. In: American Economic Review , Vol. 77 No. 5, December 1987. S. 791-809.

Bown 2004: Bown, Chad P. Trade Remedies and WTO Dispute Settlement: Why are so few challenged? Working Paper, December 2004. In: http://darkwing.uoregon.edu/~bruceb/adpage.html.

Bown 2004a: Bown, Chad P.. How Different are Safeguards from Antidumping? Evidence from US Trade Policies Toward Steel. Deparment of Economics and International Business School, Brandeis University, July 2004. In: http://darkwing.uoregon.edu/~bruceb/adpage.html.

Bown 2006: Bown, Chad P. Global Antidumping Database Version 2.0. In: http://www.brandeis.edu/~cbown/global_ad/.

Bown et al. 2003: Bown, Chad P., Hoekman, Bernard, Ozden, Caglar. The pattern of US antidumping: the path from initial filing to WTO dispute settlement. In: World Trade Review Vol. 2, No. 3, 2003. S. 349-371.

Bown/Hoekman 2005: Bown, Chad P., Hoekman, Bernard M. WTO Dispute Settlement and the Missing Developing County Cases: Engaging the Private Sector. In: Journal of International Economic Law, Vol. 8, No. 4, 2005. S. 861-890.

Boyce/Ndikumana 2000: Boyce, James K., Ndikumana, Leonce. Is Africa a Net Creditor? New Estimates of Capital Flight from Severely Indebted Sub-Saharan African Countries, 1970-1996. In: http://www.umass.edu/economics/publications/econ2000_01.pdf.

Boyd 1987: Boyd, Richard. Goverment-Industry Relations in Japan: Access, Communications, and Competitive Collaboration. In: Wilks, Stephen, Wright, Maurice (eds.). Comparative Government-Industry Relations. Western Europe, the United States, and Japan. Oxford: Clarendon Press, 1987.

Boyle/Hogarty 1975: Boyle, Stanley E., Hogarty, Thomas F. Pricing Behavior in the American Automobile Industry, 1957-71. In: Journal of Industrial Economics, Vol. 24, No. 2, December 1975. S. 81-95.

Bradford 1990: Bradford, Colin I. Jr. Policy Interventions and Markets: Development Strategy Typologies and Policy Options. In: Gereffi, Gary, Wyman, Donald L. Manufacturing Miracles. Paths of Industrialization in Latin America and East Asia. Princeton: Princeton University Press, 1990.

Bradford/Lawrence 2004: Bradford, Scott, Lawrence, Robert Z. Has Globalization Gone Far Enough? The Costs of Fragmented Markets. Washington: Institute for International Economics, 2004.

Bradford/Mead Over 1982: Bradford, Ralph M., Mead Over, A. Organizational Costs, 'Sticky Equilibria', and Critical Levels of Concentration. In: Review of Economics and Statistics, Vol. 64, 1982. S. 50-58.

Brand 2003: Brand, Ulrich. Nach der Krise des Fordismus. Global Governance als möglicher hegemonialer Diskurs des internationalen Politischen. In: Zeitschrift für Internationale Beziehungen, Vol. 10 No. 1, 2003. S. 143-166.

Brandao/Carvalho 1991: Brandao, Antonio Salazar P., Carvalho, Jose L. Brazil. In: Krueger, Anne O., Schiff, Maurice, Valdes, Alberto. The Political Economie of Agricultural Pricing Policy. Vol. 1 Latin America. Baltimore, London: John Hopkins University Press, 1991.

Brander 1981: Brander, James A. Intra-Industry Trade in Identical Commodities. In: Journal of International Economics, Vol. 11, 1981. S. 1-14.

Brander 1986: Brander, James A. Rationales for Strategic Trade and Industrial Policy. In: Krugman, Paul R. Strategic Trade Policy and the New International Economics. Cambridge, Mass.: Cambridge University Press, 1986.

Brander/Spencer 1984: Brander, James, Spencer, Barbara. Tariff Protection and Imperfect Competition. In: Kierzkowski, Henryk (ed.). Monopolistic Competition and International Trade. Oxford: Clarendon Press, 1984.

Brandt 2004: Brandt, Hartmut. Probleme und Tendenzen der Agrarpolitiken in Subsahara-Afrika. Berichte und Gutachten 8/2004. Bonn: Deutsches Institut für Entwicklungspolitik, 2004.

Brannon et al. 1994: Brannon, Jeffery T., James, Dilmus D., Lucker, G. William. Generating and Sustaining Backward Linkages between Maquiladoras and Local Suppliers in Northern Mexico. In: World Development, vol. 22, No. 12, 1994. S. 1933-1945.

Branson/Monoyios 1977: Branson, William H., Monoyios, Nicolaos. Factor Inputs in U.S. Trade. In: Journal of International Economics, Vol. 7, 1977. S. 111-131.

Branstetter et al. 2003: Branstetter, Lee, Fisman, Raymond, Foley, C. Fritz. Do Stronger Intellectual Property Rights Increase International Technology Transfer? Empirical Evidence from U.S. Firm-Level Panel Data. APEC Study Center, Columbia Business School, Discussion Paper No. 20. July 2003 In: http://www.columbia.edu/cu/business/apec/publications/Branstetter.pdf.

Brauer 1982: Brauer, Dieter. Das Lied von der Freiheit. Nach Ronald Reagan soll die Dritte Welt dem kapitalistischen Entwicklungsmodell nacheifern. Aber kann sie das? In: Deutsches Allgemeines Sonntagsblatt, Rubrik DZ-Aktuell, Nr. 1, 3. Januar 1982. S. 7.

Brautigam 1995: Brautigam, Deborah. The State as Agent: Industrial Development in Taiwan, 1952-1972. In: Stein, Howard (Hrg.). Asian Industrialization and Africa. Studies in Policy Alternatives to Structural Adjustment. London: St. Martin's Press, 1995.

Bredimas/Tzoannos 1981: Bredimas, Anna E., Tzoannos, John G. In Search of a Common Shipping Policy for the E.C. Journal of Common Market Studies, Vol. XX, No. 2, December 1981. S. 95-114.

Breitenacher et al. 1995: Breitenacher, Michael, Vieweg, Hans-Günther, Vogler-Ludwig, Kurt. Textil- und Bekleidungsindustrie in der EU: Neue Technologien erfordern neue Qualifikationen. In: ifo-Schnelldienst, 35-36/1995. S. 35-41.

Brennan/Buchanan 1993: Brennan, Geoffrey, Buchanan, James M. Die Begründung von Regeln. Konstitutionelle Politische Ökonomie. Tübingen: Mohr, 1993.

Brenton 2003: Brenton, Paul. Integrating the Least Developed Countries into the World Trading System. Policy Research Working Paper 3018. Washington: World Bank, April 2003. In: http://www.worldbank.org.

Brenton/Manchin 2002: Brenton, Paul, Manchin, Miriam. Making EU Trade Agreements Work. The Role of Rules of Origin. CEPS Working Document No. 183, March 2002. In: http://www.ceps.be.

Bresnahan 1985: Bresnahan, Timothy F. Post-Entry Competition in the Plain Paper Copier Market. In: American Economic Review, Vol. 75, No. 2, May 1985. S. 15-19.

Brewer/Young 1999: Brewer, Thomas L., Young, Stephen. WTO Disputes and Developing Countries. In: JWT, Vol. 33, No. 5, 1999. S. 169-182.

Bridges div. Jg., div. No., div. Monate, div. Jahre: Bridges. International Centre for Trade and Sustainable Development. In: www.ictsd.org.

Bridges Weekly 2006: Bridges Weekly. US, EU, Canada join forces to challenge China on Auto parts. Vol. 10, Number 20, 20 September 2006. In: http:/www.ictsd.org.

Briguglio 1998: Briguglio, Lino Pascal. Small Country Size and Returns to Scale in Manufacturing. In: World Development, Vol. 26 No. 3, 1998. S. 507-515.

Brink 2005: Brink, Gustav. The 10 Major Problems With the Anti-Dumping Instrument in South Africa. In: JWT, Vol. 39, No. 1, 2005. S. 147-157.

Brock 1990: Brock, Gerald W. The Computer Industry. In: Adams, Walter (Hrg.). The Structure of American Industry. New York: Macmillan, 1990.

Brock 1997: Brock, Ditmar. Wirtschaft und Staat im Zeitalter der Globalisierung. In: Aus Politik und Zeitgeschichte, B 33-34/97, 8. August 1997.

Brock 1998: Brock, Lothar. Die Grenzen der Demokratie: Selbstbestimmung im Kontext des globalen Strukturwandels und des sich wandelnden Verhältnisses von Staat und Markt. In: PVS, Sonderheft 29/1998. S. 271-292.
Bronckers/Goyette 2003: Bronckers, Marco, Goyette, Martin. The EU's Special Safeguard Clause in Respect of China: How will it work? In: Legal Issues of Economic Integration, Vol. 30, Bd. 2, 2003. S. 123-131.
Bronckers/McNelis 1999: Bronckers, Marco, McNelis, Nathalie. Rethinking the "Like Product" definition in WTO Antidumping Law. In: JWT Vol. 33, No. 3, 1999. S. 73-91.
Bronfenbrenner/Luce 2004: Bronfenbrenner, Kate, Luce, Stephanie. The changing nature of corporate global restructuring: The impact of production shifts on jobs in the US, China, and around the globe. Washington, DC: US-China Economic and Security Review Commission. In: http://digitalcommons.ilr.cornell.edu/cbpubs/15.
Bronfenbrenner/Luce 2004a: Bronfenbrenner, Kate, Luce, Stephanie. Offshoring: The evolving profile of corporate global restructuring. Multinational Monitor, 25(12), 26-29. In: http://digitalcommons.ilr.cornell.edu/cbpubs/18/.
Bronz 1949: Bronz, George. The International Trade Organization Charter. In: Harvard Law Review, Vol. 62 No. 7, May 1949. S. 1089-1125.
Broude 2003: Broude, Tomer. An Anti-Dumping 'To be or not to be' in Five Acts: A New Agenda for Research and Reform. In: JWT, Vol. 37, No. 2, 2003. S. 305-328.
Brown 1950: Brown, William Adams. The United States and the Restoration of World Trade. Washington D.C., Brookings Institution, 1950.
Brown 1978: Brown, Gilbert T. Agricultural Pricing Policies in Developing Countries. In: Schultz, Theodore William. Distortions of Agricultural Incentives. Bloomington; London: Indiana University Press, 1978.
Brown/Whalley 1980: Brown, Fred, Whalley, John. General Equilibrium Evaluations of Tariff-Cutting Proposals in the Tokyo Round and Comparisons with more Extensive Liberalization of World Trade. In: Economic Journal, 90, December 1980. S. 838-866.
Brownbridge/Harrigan 1996: Brownbridge, Martin, Harrigan, Jane. Positive Terms-of-Trade Shocks and Struktural Adjustment in Sub-Saharan Africa. In: Development Policy Review, Vol. 14, 1996. S. 409-427.
Brülhart 1998: Brülhart, Marius. Trading Places: Industrial Specialization in the European Union. In: Journal of Common Market Studies, Vol. 36, No. 3, September 1998. S. 319-346.
Brülhart 2001: Brülhart, Marius. Evolving Geographical Concentration of European Manufacturing Industries. In: Weltwirtschaftliches Archiv, Bd. 137, Haft 2, 2001. S. 215-243.
Brülhart/Torstensson 1996: Brülhart, Marius, Torstensson, Johan. Regional Integration, Scale Economies and Industry Location in the European Union. CEPR (Centre of Economic Policy Research) Discussion Paper No. 1435, July 1996.
Brunner 1991: Brunner, Hans-Peter. Building Technological Capacity: A Case Study of the Computer Industry in India: 1975-87. In: World Development, Vol. 19, No. 12, 1991. S. 1737-1751.
Bruno 1972: Bruno, Michael. Domestic Resource Costs and Effective Protection: Clarification and Synthesis. In: Journal of Political Economy, Vol. 80 No. 1, 1972. S. 16-69.
Bruton 1989: Bruton, Henry. Import Substitution. In: Chenery, H., Srinivasan, T.N. Handbook of Development Economics, Vol. II, Amsterdam; New York: Elsevier Science B.V., 1989.
Bruton 1998: Bruton, Henry J. A Reconsideration of Import Substitution. In: Journal of Economic Literature, Vol. XXXVI, June 1998. S. 903-936.
Buccola/McCandlish 1999: Buccola, Steven T., McCandlish, James E. Rent Seeking and Rent Dissipation in State Enterprises. In: Review of Agricultural Economics, Vol. 21 No. 2, 1999. S. 358-373.
Buch et al. 2000: Buch, Claudia M., Heinrich, Ralph P., Lusinyan, Lusine, Schrooten, Mechthild. Russia's Dept Crisis and the Unofficial Economy. Kiel Working Paper No. 978, April 2000.
Buchanan 1980: Buchanan, James M. Rent Seeking and Profit Seeking. In: Buchanan, James M., Tollison, Robert D., Tullock, Gorbon (eds.). Toward a Theory of the Rent-Seeking Society. College Station: Texas A& M University Press, 1980.
Buchanan et al. 1980: Buchanan, James M., Tollison, Robert D., Tullock, Gorbon (eds.). Toward a Theory of the Rent-Seeking Society. College Station: Texas A& M University Press, 1980.
Buchanan/Keohane 2006: Buchanan, Allen, Keohane, Robert. The Legitimacy of Global Governance Institutions. In: Ethics and International Affairs, Vol. 20 No. 4, 2006. S. 405-438.
Buchs 1996: Buchs, Thierry D. Selected WTO Rules and Some Implications for Fund Policy Advice. IMF Working Paper, WP/96/23. Washington: IMF, 1996.
Bufacchi/Garmise 1995: Bufacchi, Vittorio, Garmise, Shari. Social Justice in Europe: An Evaluation of European Regional Policy. In: Government and Opposition, Vol. 30, No. 1, Winter 1995. S. 179-197.
Buffie 2001: Buffie, Edward F. Trade Policy in Developing Countries. Cambridge: Cambridge University Press, 2001.
Buigues/Goybet 1985: Buigues, Pierre, Goybet, Philippe. The Community's Industrial Competitiveness and International Trade in Manufactured Products. Reprinted in: Jaquemin, Alexis, Sapir, André (eds.) The European International Market. Selected Readings. Oxford: Oxford University Press, 1989.
Bulajic 1993: Bulajic, Milan. Principles of International Development Law. Dordrecht, Boston, London: Martinus Nijhoff, 1993.
Bülow et al. 1999: Bülow, Wolfram von, Hein, Eckhard, Köster, Klaus, Krüger, Winfried, Litz, Hans Peter, Ossorio-Capella, Carles, Schüler, Klaus W. Globalisierung und Wirtschaftspolitik. Marburg: Metropolis, 1999.

Bundeskartellamt 2001: Bundeskartellamt. Das Untersagungskriterium in der Fusionskontrolle – Marktbeherrschende Stellung versus Substantial Lessening of Competition. Diskussionspapier für die Sitzung des Arbeitskreises Kartellrecht am 8. und 9. Oktober 2001. In: http://www.bundeskartellamt.de.
Bundesministerium für Wirtschaft 1998: Bundesministerium für Wirtschaft. Autonome Zollaussetzungen für Waren des industriellen Bereichs ab 1 Juli 1998. In: http://www.bmwi.de.
Bundesregierung 2006: Positionspapier der Bundesregierung 2006. Globalisierung gestalten: Externe Wettbewerbsfähigkeit der EU steigern - Wachstum und Arbeitsplätze in Europa sichern. September 2006.
Bundesverfassungsgericht 1997a: Grimm, Dieter, Kirchhof, Paul. Entscheidungen des Bundesverfassungsgerichts. Bd. 1. Tübingen: Mohr, 1997.
Bundesverfassungsgericht 1997b: Grimm, Dieter, Kirchhof, Paul. Entscheidungen des Bundesverfassungsgerichts. Bd. 2. Tübingen: Mohr, 1997.
Bundjamin 2005: Bundjamin, Erry. The 10 Major Problems With the Anti-Dumping Instrument in Indonesia. In: JWT, Vol. 39, No. 1, 2005. S. 125-135.
Buntzel 1998: Buntzel, Rudolf. Agrarliberalisierung, WTO und Welternährung. Die Marrakesh-Entscheidung als letztes Schlupfloch. In: Agrarbündnis (Hrg.). Der Kritische Agrarbericht. Kassel; Rheda-Wiedenbrück: ABL Bauernblatt Verlag, 1998.
Burfischer 2001: Burfischer, Mary E. Agricultural Policy Reform in the WTO - The Road Ahead. U.S. Deparment of Agriculture, Economic Research Service, Agricultural Economic Report No. 802, May 2001. In: http://www.ers.usda.gov/Publications/aer802/.
Burger 1998: Burger, Bettina. Ausländische Direktinvestitionen, technologische Spillover-Effekte und industrielle Entwicklung, dargestellt am Beispiel Mexiko. Baden-Baden: Nomos, 1998.
Burkhardt 1995: Burkhardt, Jürgen. Kartellrecht. München: Beck, 1995.
Burnett/Scherer 1990: Burnett, William B., Schwerer, Frederic M. The Weapons Industry. In: Adams, Walter (Hrg.). The Structure of American Industry. New York: Macmillan, 1990.
Burnside/Dollar 1997: Burnside, Craig, Dollar, David. Aid, Policies and Growth. World Bank, Policy Research Working Paper, No. 1777, June 1997. In: http://www.worldbank.org.
Burstein et al. 2005: Burstein, Ariel, Kurz, Christopher Johann, Tesar, Linda. Trade, production sharing and the international transmission of business cycles. American Economic Association Annual Meeting Paper 2006. In: http://www.aeaweb.org/annual_mtg_papers/2006/0106_0800_0603.pdf.
Burton/Inoue 1984: Burton, F. N., Inoue, Hisashi. Expropriations of Foreign-Owned Firms in Developing Countries. In: JWTL, Vol. 18 No. 5, Sept. Oct. 1984. S. 396-414.
Busch/Reinhardt 2000: Busch, Marc L., Reinhardt, Eric. Bargaining in the Shadow of Law: Early Settlement in GATT/WTO Disputes. Fordham International Law Journal, Vol. 24, 2000-2001. S. 158-172.
Busch/Reinhardt 2003: Busch, Marc L., Reinhardt, Eric. Developing Countries and General Agreement on Tariffs and Trade/World Trade Organization Dispute Settlement. In: JWT, Vol. 37, No. 4, 2003. S. 719-735.
Büschgen 1975: Büschgen, Hans E. Zur Diskussion um das Bankensystem in der Bundesrepublik Deutschland. In: WSI-Mitteilungen, 28 Jg. Juli 1975, 362-374.
Business Week Online 2006: Business Week Online. Intel's Eager Passage to India. December 6, 2005. In: http://www.businessweek.com/technology/content/dec2005/tc20051206_475674.htm.
Bussolo/Morrison 2002: Bussolo, Maurizio, Morrisson, Christian. Globalization and Poverty. In: Braga de Macedo, Jorge et al. (eds.). Development is back. Paris: OECD, 2002.
Byiringiro 1995: Byiringiro, Fidele Usabuwera. Determinants of Farm Productivity and the Size-Productivity Relationship under Land Constraints: The Case of Rwanda. Thesis. Michigan State University, Department of Agricultural Economics. In: http://www.aec.msu.edu/agecon/pubs.htm
Byrne 1998: Byrne, Noel. Licensing Technology. Bristol: Jordans, 1998.

C

Cable 1987: Cable, Vincent. The Impact of EEC Trade Policies on Developing Countries. In: Giersch, Herbert (ed.). Free Trade in the World Economy. Towards the Opening of Markets. Tübingen: Mohr, 1987.
Cadot et al. 2006: Cadot, Olivier, Carrere, Celine, De Melo, Jaime, Tumurchudur, Bolormaa. Product-specific rules of origin in EU and US preferential agreements. In: World Trade Review Vol. 5 No. 2, 2006. S. 199-224.
Caetano 2005: Caetano, Ana. The 10 Major Problems With the Anti-Dumping Instrument in Brazil. In: JWT, Vol. 39, No. 1, 2005. S. 87-96.
Cameron 1995: Cameron, David R. Transnational relations and the development of the European economic an monetary union. In: Risse-Kappen, Thomas (ed.). Bringing transnational relations back in. Cambridge: Cambridge University Press, 1995.
Canavese 1982: Canavese, Alfredo J. The Structuralist Explanation in the Theory of Inflation. In: World Development, Vol. 10, No. 7, 1982. S. 523-529.
Cao et al. 1997: Cao, Yuan Zheng, Fan, Gang, Woo, Wing Thye. Chinese Economic Reforms: Past Successes and Future Challenges. In: Woo, Wing Thye, Parker, Stephen, Sachs, Jeffrey D. Economies in Transition: Comparing Asia and Eastern Europe. Cambridge: The MIT Press, 1997.
Caprio/Klingebiel 1996: Caprio, Gerard Jr., Klingebiel, Daniela. Bank Insolvencies: Cross-country Experience. World Bank, Policy Research Working Paper, No. 1620, July 1996.
Carlin 1996: Carlin, Wendy. West German growth and institutions, 1945-90. In: Crafts, Nicolas, Toniolo, Gianni (eds.). Economic Growth in Europe since 1945. Cambridge: Cambridge University Press, 1996.

Carneiro/Werneck 1993: Carneiro, Dionisio D., Werneck, Rogerio L. F. Brazil. In: Taylor, Lance (ed.). The Rocky Road to Reform. Adjustment, Income Distribution, and Growth in the Developing World. Cambridge: MIT Press, 1993.
Carrol 1992: Carrol, Lewis. Alice's Adventures in Wonderland. Hertfordshire: Wordsworth, 1992.
Casella 1997: Casella, Paulo Borba. The Results of the Uruguay Round in Brazil: legal and constitutional aspects of implementation. In: Jackson, John H., Sykes, Alan O. (eds.). Implementing the Uruguay Round. Oxford: Clarendon Press, 1997.
Casella 1997a: Casella, Paulo Borba. From Dispute Settlement to Jurisdiction? Perspectives for the Mercosur. In: Petersmann, Ernst-Ulrich (ed.). International Trade Law and the GATT/WTO Dispute Settlement System. London, The Hague, Boston: Kluwer Law, 1997.
Cashin 2003: Cashin, Paul. Commodity Prices and the Terms of Trade. In: IMF Research Bulletin, Vol. 4, No. 4. Washington: IMF, December 2003. In: http://www.imf.org.
Cashin et al. 2000: Cashin, Paul, Liang, Hong, McDermott, C. John. How Persistant are Shocks to World Commodity Prices? In: IMF Staff Papers, Vol. 47 No. 2. Washington: IMF, 2000. In: http://www.imf.org.
Cashin/McDermott 2002: Cashin, Paul, McDermott, C. John. The Long-Run Behavior of Commodity Prices: Small Trends and Big Variability. In: IMF Staff Papers, vol. 49, No. 2. Washington: IMF, 2002. In: http://www.imf.org.
Cass 2001: Cass, Deborah Z. The 'Constitutionalization' of International Trade Law: Judical Norm-Generation as the Engine of Constitutional Development in International Trade. In: European Journal of International Law, 12, 2001. S. 3-38.
Cassel/Rauhut 1998: Cassel, Dieter, Rauhut, Siegfried. Soziale Marktwirtschaft: Eine wirtschaftspolitische Konzeption auf dem Prüfstand. In: Cassel, Dieter (Hrg.). 50 Jahre Soziale Marktwirtschaft. Schriften zu Ordnungfragen der Wirtschaft, Band 57, Stuttgart, Lucius&Lucius: 1998.
Castley 1996: Castley, R. J. The Role of Japanese Foreign Investment in South Korea's Manufacturing Sector. In: Development Policy Review, Vol. 14, 1996. S. 69-88.
Cavallo/Cottani 1991: Cavallo, Domingo, Cottani, Joaquin. Argentina. In: The Experience of Argentina, Chile and Uruguay. Liberalizing Foreign Trade, Vol. 1. Oxford: World Bank/Blackwell, 1991.
Cavelaars 2003: Cavelaars, Paul. Does Competition Enhancement Have Permanent Inflation Effects? In: Kyklos, Vol. 56 No. 1, 2003. S. 69-94.
Caves 1996: Caves, Richard E. Multinational enterprise and economic analysis. Cambridge: Cambridge University Press, 1996.
Cawson et al. 1987: Cawson, Alan, Holmes, Peter, Stevens, Anne. The Interaction between Firms and the State in France: The Telecommunications and Consumer Electronics Sectors. In: Wilks, Stephen, Wright, Maurice (eds.). Comparative Government-Industry Relations. Western Europe, the United States, and Japan. Oxford: Clarendon Press, 1987.
CBO AD Study 2001: Congress of the United States. Congressional Budged Office. Antidumping Action in the United States and Around the World. Juni 2001. In: http://www.cbo.gov.
CBO AD/CV Study 1994: Congress of the United States. Congressional Budged Office. How the GATT Affects U.S. Antidumping and Countervailing Duty Policy. September 1994. In: http://www.cbo.gov.
CCFA 2006: Comité des Constructeurs Francais d' Automobiles. Analyse & Faits. 2006. In: http://www.ccfa.fr.
Cecchini 1988: Cecchini, Paolo. Europa '92. Der Vorteil des Binnenmarkts. Baden-Baden: Nomos, 1988.
CEFIC 1998: European Chemical Industry Council. Facts and Figures 1998. In: http://www.cefic.be.
Celasun 1994: Celasun, Merih. Trade and Industrialization in Turkey. In: Helleiner, Gerald K. (ed.). Trade Policy and Industrialization in Turbulent Times. London; New York: Routledge, 1994.
Cerra/Saxena 2002: Cerra, Valerie, Saxena, Sweta Chaman. An Empirical Analysis of China's Export Behavior. IMF Working Paper WP/02/200. Washington: IMF, 2002. In: http://www.imf.org.
César das Neves 1996: César das Neves, João. Portuguese postwar growth: a global approach. In: Crafts, Nicolas, Toniolo, Gianni (eds.). Economic Growth in Europe since 1945. Cambridge: Cambridge University Press, 1996.
Chadha 2000: Chadha, Rajesh. GATS and Developing Countries: A Case Study of India. Working Paper, South Asia Workshop. In: http://www.worldbank.org/research/trade.
Chadha et al. 2000: Chadha, Rajesh, Brown, Drusilla K., Deardorff, Alan V., Stern, Robert M., Computational Analysis of the Impact on India of the Uruguay Round and the Forthcoming WTO Trade Negotiations. World Bank, WTO Background Paper, March 2000. In: http://www.worldbank.org/research/trade.
Chakravarthy 1999: Chakravarthy, S. Role of Competition Policy in Economic Development and the Indian Experience. In: Asian Economic Review, Vol. 41, No. 3. pp. 386-401.
Chakravarthy 2001: Chakravarty, S. Indian Competition Law on the Anvril. In: World Competition, 24 (4), 2001. S. 571-606.
Chakravatarty 1987: Chakravarty, Sukhamoy. Development Planning. The Indian Experience. Oxford: Clarendon Press, 1987.
Chamberlin 1950: Chamberlin, E.H. Product Heterogeneity and Public Policy. In: American Economic Review, Vol. XL No. 2, May 1950. S. 83-92.
Champ/Attaran 2002: Champ, Paul, Attaran, Amir. Patent Rights and Local Working under the WTO TRIPS Agreement: An Analysis of the U.S.-Brazil Patent Dispute. Yale Journal of International Law, vol. 27, 2002. S. 365-393.

Chandler 1990: Chandler, Alfred D. Scale and Scope. The Dynamics of Industrial Capitalism. Cambridge, Mass.: Belknap Press of Harvard University Press, 2001.
Chandler/Hikino 1997: Chandler, Alfred D., Hikino, Takashi. The large enterprise and the dynamics of modern economic growth. In: Chandler, Alfred D., Amatori, Franco, Hikino, Takashi. Big business and the wealth of nations. Cambridge: Cambridge University Press, 1997.
Chang 1994: Chang, Ha-Joon. The Political Economy of Industrial Policy. New York: St. Martin's Press, 1994.
Chang 2002: Chang, Ha-Joon. Kicking away the ladder. Development Strategy in Historical Perspective. London: Anthem Press, 2002.
Chang/Green 2003: Chang, Ha-Joon, Green, Duncan. The Northern WTO Agenda on Investment: Do as we say, not as we did. Geneva: South Centre, June 2003. In: http:/www.southcentre.org.
Chang/Singh 1993: Chang, Ha-Joon, Singh, Ajit. Public Enterprises in Developing Countries and Economic Efficiency. In: UNCTAD Review, No. 4, 1993. S. 45-116.
Chard/Macmillen 1979: Chard, J.S., Macmillen, M. J. Sectoral Aids and Community Competition Policy: The Case of Textiles. In: JWTL, Vol. 13 No. 2, March April 1979. S. 132-157.
Charnovitz 2002: Charnovitz, Steve. The WTO's Problematic 'Last Resort' Against Noncompliance. In: Aussenwirtschaft, Jg. 57, Heft 4, 2002. S. 409-439.
Charnovitz 2003: Charnovitz, Steve. Comment on the 'WTO Response'. In: Cottier, Thomas, Mavroidis, Petros C (eds.). The Role of the Judge in International Trade Regulation. Ann Arbor: University of Michigan Press, 2003.
Charnovitz 2005: Charnovitz, Steve. The WTO and Cosmopolitics. In: Petersmann, Ernst-Ulrich (ed.). Reforming the World Trading System. Legitimacy, Efficiency, and Democratic Governance. Oxford: Oxford University Press, 2005.
Charnovitz 2005a: Charnovitz, Steve. Belgian Family Allowances and the challenge of origin-based discrimination. In: World Trade Review Vol. 4 No. 1, 2005. S. 7-26.
Charnovitz et al. 2004: Charnovitz, Steve, Bartels, Lorand, Howse, Robert, Bradley, Janes, Pauwelyn, Joost, Regan, Douglas. The Appellate Body's GSP Decision. Internet Roundtable. In: World Trade Review Vol. 3, No. 2, 2004. S. 239-265.
Chaytor 1997: Chaytor, Beatrice. Developing Countries and GATT/WTO Dispute Settlement: A Profile of Enforcement in Agriculture and Textiles. In: Petersmann, Ernst-Ulrich (ed.). International Trade Law and the GATT/WTO Dispute Settlement System. London, The Hague, Boston: Kluwer Law, 1997.
Cheh 1974: Cheh, John H. United States Concessions in the Kennedy Round and Short-Run Labor Adjustment Costs. In: Journal of International Economics, Vol. 4, 1974. S. 323-340.
Chen 1984: Chen, Edward K. Y. Hongkong. In: World Development, Vol. 12, No. 5/6, 1984. S. 481-490.
Chen/Hou 1993: Chen, Tain-Jy, Hou, Chi-ming. The Political Economy of Trade Protection in the Republic of China Taiwan. In: Ito, Takatoshi, Krueger, Anne O. Trade and Protectionism. Chicago; London: The University of Chicago Press/NBER, 1993.
Chenery 1960: Chenery, Hollis. Patterns of Industrial Growth. In: American Economic Review, Bd. 50, 1960, S. 624-654.
Chenery 1975: Chenery, Hollis B. The Structuralist Approach to Development Policy. In: American Economic Review, Papers and Proceedings, Vol. 65, No. 2, 1975. S. 310-316.
Chenery 1979: Chenery, Hollis B. Structural Change and Development Policy. Oxford: Oxford University Press (Published for World Bank), 1979.
Chenery 1980: Chenery, Hollis B. Interactions Between Industrialization and Exports. In: American Economic Review. American Economic Association. Vol. 70, No. 2, May 1980. S. 281-287.
Chenery et al. 1974: Chenery, Hollis, Ahluwalia, Montek S., Bell, C. L. G., Duloy, John H., Jolly, Richard. Redistribution with Growth. Oxford: Oxford University Press (Published for the World Bank), 1974.
Chenery et al. 1986: Chenery, Hollis, Robinson, Sherman, Syrquin, Moshe. Industrialization and Growth. A Comparative Study. Washington: Oxford University Press (Published for World Bank), 1986.
Chenery/Syrquin 1989: Chenery, Hollis, Syrquin, Moshe. Three Decades of Industrialization. In: The World Bank Economic Review, Vol. 3, No. 2, 1989, S. 145-181.
Chenery/Syrquin 1989a: Chenery, Hollis, Syrquin, Moshe. Patterns of Development 1950 to 1983. World Bank Discussion Paper No. 41, Washington: World Bank, 1989.
Chennamaneni 1997: Chennamaneni, Ramesh. Indian Agriculture at Cross Roads: Emerging Issues of Growth, Environment, and Food Security. Working Paper, Nr. 36/1997. Humboldt-Universität zu Berlin, Wirtschafts- und Sozialwissenschaften an der Landwirtschaftlich-Gärtnerischen Fakultät. Berlin: 1997.
Chesnais 1992: Chesnais, Francois. National Systems of Innovation, Foreign Direct Investment and the Operations of Multinational Enterprises. In: Lundvall, Bengt-Ake. National Systems of Innovation. Towards a Theorey of Innovation and Interactive Learning. London; New York: Pinter, 1992.
Chiarlone 2000: Chiarlone, Stefano. Evidence of Product Differenciation and Relative Quality in Italian Trade. CESPRI Working Paper No. 114, July 2000. In: http://www.cespri.uni-bocconi.it/.
Chipman/Moore 1972: Chipman, John S., Moore, James C. Social Utility and the Gains from Trade. In: Journal of International Economics, Vol. 2, 1972. S. 157-172.
Cho 1998: Cho, Sung-joon. GATT Non-Violation Issues in the WTO Frameworki: Are They the Archilles' Heel of the Dispute Settlement Process? In: Harvard International Law Journal, Vol. 39, No. 2, Spring 1998. S. 311-355.
Cho 2005: Cho, Sungjoon. A quest for WTO's legitimacy. In: World Trade Review Vol. 4, No. 3, 2005. S. 391-399.
Cho/Hong 1999: Cho, Dongchul, Hong, Kiseok. Currency Crisis of Korea: Internal Weakness or External Interdependence. NBER East Asian Seminar, Hawai June 1999. In: http://www.nber.org.

Choi 2007: Choi, Won Mog. To Comply or Not to Comply? Non-implementation Problems in the WTO Dispute Settlement System. In: JWT, Vol. 41, No. 5, 2007. S. 1043-1071.

Choinski 2002: Choinski, Alexander Steward. Anatomy of a Controversy: The Balance of Political Forces Behind Implemenation of the WTO's Gasoline Decision. In: Law and Policy in International Business, Vol. 33, No. 4, 2002. S. 569-776.

Chomsky 2000: Chomsky, Noam. Profit over People. Neoliberalismus und globale Weltordnung. Hamburg; Berlin: Europa Verlag, 2000.

Chong Nam et al. 1999: Chong Nam, Il, Kim, Joon-Kyung, Kim, Kang, Yeongjae, Wook Joh, Sung, Kim, Jun-Il. Corporate Governance in Asia: A Comparative Perspective. Conference: OECD, Korean Development Institute. In: http://www.oecd.org/daf/corporate-affairs.

Choudhri/Hakura 2000: Choudhri, Ehsan U., Hakura, Dalia S. International Trade and Productivity Growth: Exploring the Sectoral Effects for Developing Countries. IMF Working Paper, WP/00/17. In: http://www.imf.org.

Choudhri/Hakura 2001: Choudhri, Ehsan U., Hakura, Dalia S. International Trade in Manufactured Products: A Ricardo-Heckscher-Ohlin Explanation with Monopolistic Competition. IMF Working Paper, WP/01/41. In: http://www.imf.org.

Chow 1987: Chow, Peter C. Y. Causality between export growth and industrial development. Empirical evidence form the NICSs. In: Journal of Development Economics, Vol. 26, 1987. S. 55-63.

Christakos 2002: Christakos, Helen A. WTO Panel Report on Section 110 (5) of the U.S. Copyright Act. In: Berkeley Technology Law Journal Vol. 17, 2002. S. 595-611.

Christiansen 2006: Christiansen, Arndt. Der 'more economic approach' in der EU-Fusionskontrolle - eine kritische Würdigung. Deutsche Bank Research, Working Paper Series, Research Notes 21, Januar 2006. In: http://www.dbresearch.com.

Chua 1998: Chua, Adrian T. L. Reasonable Expectations and Non-Violation Complaints in GATT/WTO Jurisprudence. In: JWT, Vol. 32, No. 2, April 1998. S. 27-50.

Cieslik 1984: Cieslik, Jerzy. Restrictive Clauses in Licensing Agreement. In: JWTL, Vol. 18 No. 5, Sept. Oct. 1984. S. 415-428.

Cisco Informationen 2006: Cisco Informationen. Yahoo, 2006. In: http://finance.yahoo.com/q/ks?s=CSCO.

Civil Aircraft Agreement 1992: Agreement between the Governments of the United States of America and the European Economic Community concerning the application of the GATT Agreement on Trade in Civil Aircraft on Trade in Large Civil Aircraft. In: http://www.ita.doc.gov/td/aerospace. Vgl. auch July 1, 1992, BNA, 9 ITR 1273-78 (1992). Siehe dazu **Hudec 1991:** 578.

Clague 1991: Clague, Christoper K. Factor proportions, relative efficiency and developing countries trade. In: Journal of Development Economics, 35, 1991. S. 357-380.

Clairmonte/Cavanagh 1990: Clairmonte, Frederic F., Cavanagh, John H. TNCs and the global beverage Industry. In: The CTC-Reporter, No. 30, Autumm 1990.

Clarete/Whalley 1994: Clarete, Ramon L., Whalley, John. Immiserizing growth and endogenous protection. In: Journal of Development Economics, Vol. 45, 1994. S. 121-133.

Clark 1940: Clark, J.M. Zum Begriff eines funktionsfähigen Wettbewerbs (englisches Original 1940). In: Herdzina, Klaus (Hrg.). Wettbewerbstheorie. Köln: Kiepenheuer&Witsch, 1975.

Clark 1950: Clark, J.M. The Orientation of Antitrust Policy. In: American Economic Review, Vol. XL No. 2, May 1950. S. 93-104.

Clark 1961: Clark, J.M. Competition as a Dynamik Process. Washington: Brooking Institution, 1961.

Clark 1993: Clark, Don P. Recent Evidence on Determinants of Intra-Industry Trade. In: Weltwirtschaftliches Archiv, Bd. 129, 1993. S. 332-343.

Clark/McDonald 1998: Clark, Peter B., McDonald, Ronald. Exchange Rates and Economic Fundamentals: A Methodological Comparison of BEERs and FEERs. IMF Working Paper, WP/98/67. Washington: IMF, 1998. In: http://www.imf.org.

Clarke 1995: Clarke, Roger R. G. More evidence on income distribution and growth. In: Journal of development economics. Vol. 47, 195. S. 403-427.

Clarke et al. 1984: Clarke, Roger, Davies, Stephen, Waterson, Michael. The Profitability-Concentration Relation: Market Power or Efficiency? In: The Journal of Industrial Economics, Vol. XXXII, No. 4, June 1984. S. 435-450.

Clarke et al. 2004: Clarke, P.A., Bourgois, J., Horlick, G.N. WTO Dispute Settlement Practice Relating to Subsidies and Countervailing Measures. In: Ortino, Federico, Petersmann, Ernst-Ulrich (eds.). The WTO Dispute Settlement System 1995 - 2003. The Hague et al.: Kluwer Law International, 2004.

Clerides et al. 1998: Clerides, Sofronis, Lach, Paul, Tybout, James R. Is Learning by Exporting Important? Micro-Dynamic Evicence from Colombia, Mexico, and Morocco. In: Quarterly Journal of Economics, Vol. CXIII, Issue 3, August 1998. S. 903-947.

Cline 1982: Cline, William R. Can the East Asian Model of Development Be Generalized. In: World Development, Vol. 10, No. 2, 1982. S. 81-90.

Cline 1984: Cline, William R. Exports of Manufactures from Developing Countries. Washington: Brookings Institution 1984.

Cline 1986: Cline, William R. U.S. Trade and Industrial Policy: The Experience of Textiles, Steel, and Automobiles. In: Krugman, Paul R. Strategic Trade Policy and the New International Economics. Cambridge, Mass.: Cambridge University Press, 1986.

Cline 1987: Cline, William R. The Future of World Trade in Textiles and Apparel. Washington: Institute for International Economics, 1987.

Cline 2004: Cline, William R. Cline. Trade Policy and Global Poverty. Washington, D.C.: Institute of International Economics, 2004.
Cline et al. 1978: Cline, William R., Kawanabe, Noboru, Kronsjö, T. O. M., Williams, Thomas. Trade Negotiations in the Tokyo Round. A Quantitative Assessment. Washington D.C.: The Brookings Institution, 1978.
Cloud/Silver 1999: Cloud, Kathleen, Silver, Dale I. Gender and Agribusiness Project (GAP): Case Study, Cargill Zimbabwe, November 1999. In: http://www.ips.uiuc.edu/gap.
Coates 1998: Coates, Barry. The Developmental Implications of the MAI: WDM Critique of the Fitzgerald Report to DFID. World Development Movement, July 1998. In: http://www.wdm.org.uk.
Coe et al. 1995: Coe, David T., Helpman, Elhanan, Hoffmaister, Alexander W. North-South R & D Spillovers. NBER Working Paper No. 5048. March 1995.
Coe et al. 1997: Coe, David T., Helpman, Elhanan, Hoffmaister, Alexander W. North-South R & D Spillovers. In: Economic Journal, Vol. 107, January 1997. S. 134-149.
Coen/Hickman 1980: Coen, Robert M., Hickman, Bert G. Investment and Growth in an Econometric Model of the United States. In: American Economic Review, Vol. 70, No. 2, May 1980. S. 214-234.
Coes 1991: Coes, Donald V. Brazil. In: The Experience of Brazil, Columbia and Peru. Liberalizing Foreign Trade, Vol. 4. Oxford: World Bank/Blackwell, 1991.
Cohen 1990: Cohen, Benjamin. The Political Economy of International Trade. In: IO, Vol. 44, 2, Spring 1990. S. 261-281.
Cohen 1993: Cohen, Daniel. Low Investment and Large LCD Debt in the 1980s. In: American Economic Review, Vol. 83, No. 3, June 1993. S. 437-449.
Cohen et al. 1987: Cohen, Wesley M, Levin, Richard C., Mowrey, David C. Firm Size and R&D Intensity: A Reexamination. In: Journal of Industrial Economics, Vol. XXXV, No. 4, June 1987. S. 543-565.
Cohen/Levinthal 1989: Cohen, Wesley, Levinthal, Daniel A. Innovation and Learning: The Two Faces of R&D. In: Economic Journal, Vol. 99, September 1989. S. 569-596.
Cohen/Zysman 1987: Cohen, Stephen S., Zysman, John. Manufacturing Matters. New York: Basic Books, 1987.
Colclough 1991: Colclough, Christopher. Structuralism versus Neo-liberalism: An Introduction. In: Christopher Colclough, James Manor (eds.). States or Markets? Neo-liberalism and the Development Policy Debate. Oxford. Clarendon Press, 1991.
Collier/Gunning 1998: Collier, Paul, Gunning, Jan Willem. Explaining African Economic Performance. WPS/97-2.2, Revised 19 June 1998. Oxford Centre for the Study of African Economies. In: http://www.csae.ox.ac.uk/workingpapers/main-wps.html.
Collins 1993: Collins, David J. Bearings: The Visible Hand of Global Firms. In: Yoffie, David B. Beyond Free Trade. Firms, Governments, and Global Competition. Boston, Mass.: Harvard Business School Press, 1993.
Collins 1998: Collins, Susan M. Economic Intergration and the American Worker: An Overview. In: Collins, Susan M. (ed.). Imports, Exports, and the American Worker. Washington D.C.: Brookings Institution, 1998.
Collins/Bosworth 1996: Collins, Susan M., Bosworth, Barry P. Economic Growth in East Asia: Accumulation versus Assimilation. In: Brookings Papers on Economic Activity, 2, 1996. S. 135-205.
Collins-Williams/Salembier 1996: Collins-Williams, Terry, Salembier, Gerry. International Disciplines on Subsidies. In: JWT Vol. 30 Bd. 1, Febuary 1996. S. 5-17.
Collyns/Dunaway 1987: Collyns, Charles, Dunaway, Steven. The Cost of Trade Restraints. The Case of Japanese Automobile Exports to the United States. In: International Monetary Fund, Staff Papers, Vol. 34, 1987. S. 150-175.
Committee Report Japan 2004: Comittee Report. Report on the WTO Consistency of Trade Policies by Major Trading Partners. 2004. In: http./www.meti.go.jp/english/report.
Conklin/Lecraw 1997: Conklin, David, Lecraw, Donald. Restrictions on Foreign Ownership during 1984-1994: Developments and Alternative Policies. In: Transnational Corporations, Vol. 6 No. 1, April 1997. S. 1-30.
Connor 2002: Connor, John M. The food and agricultural global cartels of the 1990s. Staff Paper 4, July 2002. In: http://www.agecon.purdue.edu/staff/connor/papers/index.asp.
Connor 2004: Connor, John M. Global Antitrust Prosecution of Modern International Cartels. In: Journal of Industry, Competition and Trade, Vol. 4 No. 3, 2004. S. 239-267. In: http://www.agecon.purdue.edu/staff/connor/papers/index.asp.
Connor 2005: Connor, John M. Price-fixing overcharges: Legal and economic evidence. Staff paper No. 04-17 (revised), Purdue University. In: http://ssrn.com/abstract=787924.
Conybeare 1983: Conybeare, John A. C. Tariff protection in developed and developing countries: a cross-sectional and longitudinal analysis. In: IO, Vol. 37 No. 3, Summer 1983. S. 441-463.
Cook 1998: Cook, Paul. Privatization in the UK. In: Parker, David (ed.). Privatization in the European Union. Theory and Policy Perspectives. London; New York: Routledge, 1998.
Cooney 2003: Cooney, Stephen. The American Steel Industry: A Changing Profile. CRS Report to Congress, RL31748, Updated November 10, 2003. In: http://www.fpc.state.gov/c4763.htm.
Cooper 1995: Cooper, Charles. Technology, manufactured exports and competitiveness. Background Paper ID/WG.542/5(SPEC.). Wien: UNIDO, 1995. In: http://www.unido.org.
Cooper 1999: Cooper, Richard N. Should Capital Controls be Banished. In: Brookings Papers on Economic Activity, 1, 1999. S. 89-141.
Cooper 2003: Cooper, Willliam H. Trade Remedy Law Reform in the 108th Congress, CRS Report for the Congress, Order Code RL30461, Updated July 22, 2003. In: http://www.fpc.state.gov/c4763.htm.

Corbo/Fischer 1995: Corbo, Vittorio, Fischer, Stanley. Structural Adjustment, Stabilization and Policy Reform: Domestic and International Finance. In: Behrman, J. Srinivasan, T.N. (eds.) Handbook of Development Economics, Vol. III, Amsterdam; New York: Elsevier Science B.V., 1995.

Corbo/Melo 1985: Corbo, Vittorio, Melo, Jaime de. Liberalization with Stabilization in the Southern Cone of Latin America. Special Issue of World Development. Vol. 13. No. 8. Oxford: Pergamon Press, 1985.

Corden 1966: Corden, M. W. The Strukture of a Tariff System and the Effective Protection Rate. In: Journal of Political Economy, Vol. 74, No. 3, June 1966. S. 221- 237.

Corden 1971: Corden, M. W. The Theory of Protection. Oxford: Oxford University Press, 1971.

Corden 1974: Corden, M. W. Trade Policy and Economic Welfare. Oxford: Clarendon Press, 1974.

Cornia 1999: Cornia, Giovanni Andrea. Liberalization, Globalization and Income Distribution. UNU/WIDER Working Paper, March 1999. In: http://www.wider.unu.edu/.

Cornwell/Wächter 1999: Cornwell, Christopher M., Wächter, Jens-Uwe. Productivity Convergence and Economic Growth: A Frontier Production Function Approach. ZEI-Working Paper, B 6, Bonn, April 1999.

Correa 1998: Correa, Carlos M. Patent Rights. In: Correa, Carlos M., Yusuf, Abdulquwi A. Intellectual Property Rights and International Trade: The TRIPS Agreement. London; The Hague: Kluwer, 1998.

Correa 2000: Correa, Carlos M. Intellectual Property Rights, the WTO and Developing Countries. London: Zed Books, 2000.

Correa 2000a: Correa, Carlos M. Options for the Implementation of Farmers' Rights at the National Level. South Centre Working Paper 8. December 2000. In: http://www.southcentre.org.

Correa/Yusuf 1998: Correa, Carlos M., Yusuf, Abdulquwi A. Intellectual Property Rights and International Trade: The TRIPS Agreement. London; The Hague: Kluwer, 1998.

Costello 1993: Costello, Declan. The redistributive effects of interregional transfers: A comparison of the European Community and Germany. In: European Economy, Reports and Studies, Vol. 5, Generaldirektion Wirtschaft und Finanzen. Luxemburg 1993.

Cottani et al. 1990: Cottani, Joaquin A., Cavallo, Domingo F., Khan, M. Shahbaz. Real Exchange Rate Behavior and Economic Performance in LDCs. In: Economic Development and Cultural Change, 1990. S. 61-76.

Cotterill 1991: Cotterill, Ronald W. Food Retailing: Mergers, Leverages Buyouts, and Performance. Food Marketing Policy Centre, Research Report No. 14, September 1991. In: http://www.fmpc.uconn.edu.

Cotterill 1999: Cotterill, Ronald W. Continuing Concentration in Food Industries Globally: Strategic Challenges to an Unstable Status Quo. Food Marketing Policy Centre, Research Report No. 49, October 1999. In: http://www.fmpc.uconn.edu.

Cottier 1998: Cottier, Thomas. Dispute Settlement in the World Trade Organization: Characteristics and Structural Implications for the European Union. In: Common Market Law Review 35, 1998. S. 325-378.

Cottier 2004: Cottier, Thomas. Proposals for Moving from Ad hoc Panelists to Permanent WTO Panelists. In: Ortino, Federico, Petersmann, Ernst-Ulrich (eds.). The WTO Dispute Settlement System 1995 - 2003. The Hague et al.: Kluwer Law International, 2004.

Cottier/Mavroidis 2003: Cottier, Thomas, Mavroidis, Petros C. The Role of the Judge in International Trade Regulation. Ann Arbor: University of Michigan Press, 2003.

Cottier/Mavroidis 2003a: Cottier, Thomas, Mavroidis, Petros C. Concluding Remarks. In: Cottier, Thomas, Mavroidis, Petros C (eds.). The Role of the Judge in International Trade Regulation. Ann Arbor: University of Michigan Press, 2003.

Cottier/Oesch 2003: Cottier, Thomas, Oesch, Matthias. The Paradox of Judicial Review in International Trade Regulation: Towards a Comprehensive Framework. In: Cottier, Thomas, Mavroidis, Petros C (eds.). The Role of the Judge in International Trade Regulation. Ann Arbor: University of Michigan Press, 2003.

Cottier/Schefer 1997: Cottier, Thomas, Schefer, Krista Nadakavukaren. Non-Violation Complaints in WTO/GATT Dispute Settlement: Past, Present and Future. In: Petersmann, Ernst-Ulrich (ed.). International Trade Law and the GATT/WTO Dispute Settlement System. London, The Hague, Boston: Kluwer Law, 1997.

Cotton Board News 2001: Cotton Board. Cotton News from Sub-Saharan Africa. December 2001. In: http://www.cottonboard.org.

Coughlin 1990: Coughlin, Peter. Moving to the next phase. In: Riddell, Roger C. (ed.). Manufacturing Africa. Performance & Prospects of Seven Countries in Sub-Saharan Africa. Overseas Development Institute. London: James Currey, 1990.

Council of Economic Advisors 1999: Council of Economic Advisors. America's Interest in the World Trade Organization: An Economic Assessment. November 16, 1999. In: http://www.whitehouse.gov/WH/EOP/CEA/html/about.html.

Covell 1998: Covell, Charles. Kant, die liberale Theorie der Gerechtigkeit und die Weltordnung. In: Der Staat, Bd. 37, Heft 1/4, 1998. S. 361-384.

Cowling/Mueller 1980: Cowling, Keith, Mueller, Dennis C. The Social Costs of Monopoly Power. In: Buchanan, James M., Tollison, Robert D., Tullock, Gorbon (eds.). Toward a Theory of the Rent-Seeking Society. College Station: Texas A&M University Press, 1980.

Cox 1987: Cox, Robert W. Production, Power, and World Order. Social Forces in the Making of History. New York: Columbia University Press, 1987.

Coxhead 2000: Coxhead, Ian. Consequences of a food security strategy for economic welfare, income distribution and land degradation: the Philippine case. Working Paper. Annual World Bank Conference on Development Economics. Washington: World Bank, 2000. In: http://wb.forumone.com/research/abcde/

CPT Letter 2006: Consumer Project on Technology. Letter on Thai Efavirenz License. 21 December 2006. In: http://www.cptech.org.
Crafts 1973: Crafts, N. F. R. Trade as an handmaiden of growth: an alternative view. In: Economic Journal, Vol. 83, Sep. 1973. S. 875-889.
Crafts/Toniolo 1996: Crafts, Nicolas, Toniolo, Gianni. Postwar growth: an overview. In: Crafts, Nicolas, Toniolo, Gianni (eds.). Economic Growth in Europe since 1945. Cambridge: Cambridge University Press, 1996.
Crafts/Toniolo 1996a: Crafts, Nicolas, Toniolo, Gianni. Reflections on the country studies. In: Crafts, Nicolas, Toniolo, Gianni (eds.). Economic Growth in Europe since 1945. Cambridge: Cambridge University Press, 1996.
Cranfield et al. 1998: Cranfield, John A. L., Hertel, Thomas W., Eales, James S., Preckel, Paul V. Changes in the Structure of Global Food Demand. Purdue University, Department of Agricultural Economics, Staff Paper 98-5, May 1998. In: http://www.agriculture.purdue.edu/.
Cravinho 1998: Cravinho, Joao. Frelimo and the Politics of Agricultural Marketing in Mozambique. In: Journal of Southern African Studies, Vol. 24 No. 1, March 1998. S. 93-113.
Crisil Industry Analysis div. Sektoren 2006: Crisil. Crisil India Budget 2005-2006. Industry Analysis, div. Sektoren. 2006. In: http://www.crisil.com.
Croley/Jackson 1996: Croley, Steven, Jackson, John H. WTO Dispute Procedures, Standard of Review, and Deference to National Governments. In: The American Journal of International Law, Vol. 90, 1996. S. 193-213.
Croley/Jackson 1997: Croley, Steven, Jackson, John H. WTO Dispute Panel Deference to National Government Decisions. The Misplaced Analogy to the U.S. Chevron Standard-of-Review Doctrine. In: Petersmann, Ernst-Ulrich (ed.). International Trade Law and the GATT/WTO Dispute Settlement System. London, The Hague, Boston: Kluwer Law, 1997.
Croome 1995: Croome, John. Reshaping the World Trading System. A History of the Uruguay Round. Geneva: WTO, 1995.
Croome 1998: Croome, John. The Present Outlook for Trade Negotiations in the World Trade Organisation. World Bank, Policy Research Working Paper, No. 1992, October 1998.
Cross 2006: Cross, Karen Halverson. King Cotton, Developing Countries, and the 'Peace Clause': The WTO's US Cotton Subsidies Decision. In: Journal of International Economic Law, Vol. 9 No. 1, 2006. S. 149-195.
Cuddington 1992: Cuddington, John T. Long-run trends in 26 primary commodity prices. A disaggregated look at the Prebisch-Singer hypothesis. In: Journal of Development Economics, 39, 1992. S. 207-227.
Culem/Lundberg 1986: Culem, Claudy, Lundberg, Lars, The Product Pattern of Intra-Industry Trade: Stability among Countries and over Time. In: Weltwirtschaftliches Archiv, Bd. 112, 1986, S. 113-130.
Cull 1997: Cull, Robert J. Financial Sector Adjustment Lending: A Mid-Course Analysis. World Bank, Policy Research Working Papers, No. 1804, August 1997. In: http://www.worldbank.org.
Cumby/Moran 1997: Cumby, Robert E., Moran, Theodore H. Testing Models of the Trade Policy Process: Antidumping and the 'New Issues'. In: Feenstra, Robert C. (ed.). The Effects of U.S. Trade Protection and Promotion Policies. Chicago, London: University of Chicago Press, 1997.
Curry/George 1983: Curry, B., George, K. D. Industrial Concentration: A Survey. In: The Journal of Industrial Economics. Vol. XXXI, No. 3, March 1983. S. 203-255.
Curtis/Vastine 1971: Curtis, Thomas B., Vastine, John Robert. The Kennedy Round and the Future of American Trade. New York; Washington; London: Praeger Publishers, 1971.
Curzon/Curzon Price 1979: Curzon, Gerard, Curzon Price, Victoria. The Undermining of the World Trade Order. In: ORDO, Bd. 30, 1979. S. 383-407.
Czempiel 1994: Czempiel, Ernst-Otto. Vergesellschaftete Außenpolitik. In: Merkur, Heft 1, Januar 1994. S. 1-14.

D

Dacia Logan Informationen 2006: Dacia Logan Anzeige. In: ADAC Motorwelt, Heft 3, 2006. S. 45.
Dahlman 1984: Dahlman, Carl J. Foreign Technology and Indigenous Technological Capability in Brasil. In: Fransman, Martin, King, Kenneth (eds.). Technology Capability in the Third World. London: Macmillan, 1984.
Dahlman et al. 1987: Dahlman, Carl J., Ross-Larson, Bruce, Westphal, Larry E. Managing Technological Development: Lessons from the Newly Industrializing Countries. In: World Development, Vol. 15, No. 6, 1987. S. 759-775.
Dahlman/Cortes 1984: Dahlman, Carl J., Cortes, Mariluz. Mexico. In: World Development, Vol. 12, No. 5/6, 1984. S. 601-624.
Dahlmann/Fonseca 1987: Dahlmann, Carl J., Fonseca, Fernando Valadares. From Technological Dependence to Technological Development: The Case of the USIMINAS Steel Plant in Brazil. In: Katz, Jorge M., Technology Generation in Latin American Manufacturing Industries. London: Macmillan Press, 1987.
Dalum 1992: Dalum, Bent. Export Specialization, Structural Competitiveness and National Systems of Innovation. In: Lundvall, Bengt-Ake. National Systems of Innovation. Towards a Theorey of Innovation and Interactive Learning. London; New York: Pinter, 1992.
Dam 2005: Dam, Kenneth W. Cordell Hull, the Reciprocal Trade Agreements Act, and the WTO. In: Petersmann, Ernst-Ulrich (ed.). Reforming the World Trading System. Legitimacy, Efficiency, and Democratic Governance. Oxford: Oxford University Press, 2005.
Das 1985: Das, Dilip K. Dismantling the Multifibre Arrangement? In: JWTL, Vol. 19 No. 1, Jan. Feb 1985. S. 67-80.

Das 1998: Das, Dilip K. Trade in Financial Services and the Role of the GATS. In: Journal of World Trade, Vol. 32, No. 6, 1998. S. 79-114.
Das 1999: Das, Satya P. An Indian Perspective on WTO Rules on Direct Foreign Investment. Working Paper, South Asia Workshop, December 1999. In: http://www.worldbank/research/trade.
Das 2003: Das, Deb Kusum. Quantifying Trade Barriers: Has Protection Declined Substantially in Indian Manufacturing? Indian Council for Research on International Economic Relations, Working Paper 105, July 2003. In: http://www.icrier.res.in/.
Dasgupta/Stiglitz 1980: Dasgupta, Pharta, Stiglitz; Joseph. Industrial Structure and the Nature of Innovative Activity. In: Economic Journal, Vol. 90, June 1980. S. 266-293.
Daumann/Hösch 1998: Daumann, Frank, Hösch, Ulrich. Freiheitssichernde Regeln und ihre Justiziabilität - dargestellt am Beispiel des § 1 UWG. In: ORDO, Bd. 49, 1998.
Davey 2003: Davey, William J. Has the WTO Dispute Settlement System Exceeded Its Authority? A Consideration of Deference Shown by the System to Member Government Decisions ind Its Use of Issue-Avoidance Techniques. In: Cottier, Thomas, Mavroidis, Petros C (eds.). The Role of the Judge in International Trade Regulation. Ann Arbor: University of Michigan Press, 2003.
Davey 2004: Davey, William J. Proposals for Improving the Working Procedures of WTO Dispute Settlement Panels. In: Ortino, Federico, Petersmann, Ernst-Ulrich (eds.). The WTO Dispute Settlement System 1995 - 2003. The Hague et al.: Kluwer Law International, 2004.
Davey 2004a: Davey, William J. WTO Dispute Settlement Practice Relating to GATT 1994. In: Ortino, Federico, Petersmann, Ernst-Ulrich (eds.). The WTO Dispute Settlement System 1995 - 2003. The Hague et al.: Kluwer Law International, 2004.
David 1975: David, Paul A. Technical choice, innovation and economic growth. Cambridge: Cambridge University Press, 1975.
David/Huang 1996: David, Cristina C., Huang, Jikun. Political Economy of Rice Price Protection in Asia. In: Economic Development and Cultural Change, 1996. S. 463-483.
Davidow 1994: Davidow, Joel. The worldwide influence of U.S. antitrust. In: Kovaleff, Theodore P. The Antitrust Impulse. Vol. 2. New York, London: M.E. Sharpe, 1994.
Davidow/Shapiro 2003: Davidow, Joel, Shapiro, Hal. The Feasibility and Worth of a World Trade Organization Competition Agreement. In: JWT, Vol. 37, No. 1, 2003. S. 49-68.
Davies 1979: Davies, Stephen. The Diffusion of Process Innovations. Cambridge: Cambridge University Press, 1979.
Davies/Lyons 1996: Davies, Stephen, Lyons, Bruce. Industrial Organization in the European Union. Structure, Strategy, and the Competitive Mechanism. Oxford: Clarendon Press, 1996.
Davis 1995: Davis, Donald R. Intra-Industry Trade: A Heckscher-Ohlin-Ricardo approach. In: Journal of International Economics, Vol. 39, 1995. S. 201-226.
Davis et al. 1996: Davis, Donald R., Weinstein, David E., Bradford, Scott C., Shimpo, Kazushige. The Heckscher-Ohlin-Vanek Model of Trade: Why does it fail? When does it work? NBER Working Paper No. 5625, June 1996.
Davis et al. 1997: Davis, Donald R., Weinstein, David E., Bradford, Scott C., Shimpo, Kazushige. Using International and Japanese Regional Data to Determine When the Factor Abundance Theory of Trade Works. In: American Economic Review, Vol. 87 No. 3, June 1997. S. 421-446.
Davis/Neascu 2001: Davis, Michael H., Neascu, Dana. Legitimacy, Globally: The Incoherence of Free Trade Practice, Global Economics and their Governing Principles of Political Economy. In: University of Missouri-Kansas City Law Review, Vol. 69, 2001. S. 733ff. In: In: http://papers.ssrn.com/.
Davis/Weinstein 1996: Davis, Donald R., Weinstein, David E. Does Economic Specialization Matter for International Specialization? NBER Working Paper No. 5706, August 1996.
Davis/Weinstein 1998: Davis, Donald R., Weinstein, David E. An Account of Global Factor Trade. NBER Working Paper No. 6785, November 1998.
D'Costa 1995: D'Costa, Anthony P. The Restructuring of the Indian Automobile Industry: Indian State and Japanese Capital. In: World Development, Vol. 23, No. 3, 1995. S. 485-502.
De Band 1998: de Band, Jaques. Privatization in an industrial policy perspective: The case of France. In: Parker, David (ed.). Privatization in the European Union. Theory and Policy Perspectives. London; New York: Routledge, 1998.
De Carmoy 1978: De Carmoy, Guy. Subsidy Policies in Britain, France and West Germany: An Overview. In: Warnecke, Steven J. (ed.). International Trade and Industrial Policies. Government Intervention and an Open World Economy. London: Macmillan Press, 1978.
De Castro 1989: De Castro, Juan A. Determinants of protection and evolving forms of North-South Trade. In: UNCTAD Review, Jg. 1, Number 2, 1989. S. 1-22.
De Cordoba et al. 2004: de Córdoba, Santiago Fernandez, Laird, Sam, Vanzetti. Trick or Treat? Development opportunities and challenges in the WTO negotiations on industrial tariffs. David. Draft 10 May 2004. UNCTAD Trade Analysis Branch: http://192.91.247.38/tab/Default.asp.
De Ghellinck et al. 1988: De Ghellinck, Elisabeth, Geroski, Paul A., Jaquemin, Alexis. Inter-Industry Variations in the Effect of Trade on Industry Performance. In: Journal of Industrial Economics, Vol. XXXVII, No. 1, September 1988. S. 1-19.
De Grauwe 1996: De Grauwe, Paul. Exchange Rate Variability and Slow Growth of Trade. In: Frenkel, Jacob A., Goldstein, Morris (eds.). Functioning of the International Monetary System. Vol. 2. Washington: IMF, 1996.

De Gregorio 1992: De Gregorio, José. Economic Growth in Latin America. In: Journal of Development Economics, Vol. 39, 1992. S. 59-84.
De Haen 1996: De Haen, Hartwig. World Food Security: Challenge to the FAO. In: Deutsche Stiftung für Internationale Entwicklung/Arbeitsgemeinschaft für Tropische und Subtropische Agrarforschung (Hrg.). Perspectives for World Food Security. Bonn, 1996.
De Janvry et al. 1995: De Janvry, Alain, Sadoulet, Elisabeth, De Anda, Gustavo Gordillo. NAFTA and Mexico's Maize Producers. In: World Development Vol. 23 No. 8, 1995. S. 1349-1362.
De Janvry et al. 1997: De Janvry, Alain, Sadoulet, Elisabeth, Davis, Benjamin. NAFTA and Agriculture: An early assessment. Department of Agricultural and Resource Economics, University of California at Berkeley, Working Paper No. 807, April 1997. In: http://are.berkeley.edu.
De Jong 1993: de Jong, Henk Wouter. Market Structures in the European Community. In: de Jong, H.W. (ed.) The Structure of European Industry. Dordrecht; Boston; London: Kluwer, 1993.
De Jong 1993a: de Jong, Mark W. Services Industries: Innovation and Internationalization. In: de Jong, H.W. (ed.) The Structure of European Industry. Dordrecht; Boston; London: Kluwer, 1993.
De la Torre 1981: De la Torre, Jose. Public Intervention Strategies in the European Clothing Industries. In: JWTL, Vol. 15 No. 2, March April 1981. S. 124-148.
De la Torre et al. 1978: De la Torre, Jose, Jedel, Michael Jay, Arpan, Jeffrey S., Ogram, E. William, Toyne, Brian. Corporate Responses to Import Competition in the U.S. Apparel Industry. Atlanta, Georgia: College of Business Administration, Georgia State University, 1978.
De la Torre/Gonzalez 2005: De la Torre, Luz Elena Reyes, Gonzales, Jorge G. Antidumping and Safeguard Measures in the Political Economy of Liberalization: The Mexican Case. World Bank Policy Research Working Paper 3684, August 2005. In: http://www.worldbank.org.
De Lettenhove 1984: De Lettenhove, Albert Kervyn. Steel: a Case Study in Industrial Policy. In: Jacquemin, Alexis (ed.). European Industry: Public Policy and Corporate Strategy. Oxford: Clarendon Press, 1984.
De Long/Summers 1991: De Long, J. Bradford, Summers, Lawrence H. Equipment Investment and Economic Growth. In: Quarterly Journal of Economics, May 1991. S. 445-502.
De Melo et al. 1996: De Melo, Martha, Denizer, Cevdet, Gelb, Alan. From Plan to Market: Patterns of Transition. World Bank, Policy Research Working Paper, No. 1564, January 1996. In: http://www.worldbank.org.
De Menil 1997: De Menil, Georges. Trade Policies in Transition Economies: A Comparison of European and Asian Experiences. In: Woo, Wing Thye, Parker, Stephen, Sachs, Jeffrey D. Economies in Transition: Comparing Asia and Eastern Europe. Cambridge: The MIT Press, 1997.
De Nardis et al. 1996: De Nardis, Sergio, Goglio, Alessandro, Malgarini, Marco. Regional Specialization and Shocks in Europe: Some Evidence from Regional Data. In: Weltwirtschaftliches Archiv, Vo. 132, No.1, 1994. S. 195-214.
De Paiva Abreu 1995: de Paiva Abreu, Marcelo. Trade in Manufactures: The Outcome of the Uruguay Round and Developing Country Interests: In: Martin, Will, Winters, L. Alan. The Uruguay Round and the Developing Countries. World Bank Discussion Patpers 307, Washington: World Bank, 1995.
De Vault 1993: De Vault, James M. The Impact of U.S. Unfair Trade Laws: A Preliminary Assessment. In: Weltwirtschaftliches Archiv, Bd. 129, 1993. S. 735-751.
De Walle 1994: De Walle, Nicolas. Political Liberation and Economic Policy Reform in Africa. In: World Development, Vol. 22, No. 4, 1994. S. 483-500.
De Wolf 1993: de Wolf, Peter. The pharmaceutical industry: towards on single market? In: de Jong, H.W. (ed.) The Structure of European Industry. Dordrecht; Boston; London: Kluwer, 1993.
Dean 1990: Dean, Judith M. The Effects of the U.S. MFA on small exporters. In: Review of Economics and Statistics, Vol. 72, No. 1, Feb. 1990. S. 63-69.
Dean et al. 1994: Dean, Judith M., Desai, Seema, Riedel, James. Trade Policy Reform in Developing Countries since 1985. A Review of the Evidence. Washington: World Bank, 1994.
Deardorff 1990: Deardorff, Alan V. Should Patent Protection Be Extended to All Developing Countries. In: World Economy, Vol. 13, No. 4, December 1990. S. 497-507.
Deardorff 1992: Deardorff, Alan V. Welfare Effects of Global Patent Protection. In: Economica, Vol. 59, February 1992. S. 35-51.
Deardorff 1994: Deardorff, Alan V. Exploring the Limits of Comparative Advantage. In: Weltwirtschaftliches Archiv, Vol. 130, No. 1, 1994. S. 1-19.
Deardorff 1999: Deardorff, Alan V. Patterns of Trade and Growth across Cones. Research Seminar in International Economics, Discussion Paper No. 443, July 1999. In: http://www.fordschool.umich.edu/rsie/workingpapers/wp.html.
Deardorff/Stern 1984: Deardorff, Alan V., Stern, Robert M. The Effects of the Tokyo Round on the Structure of Protection. In: Baldwin, Robert E. Krueger, Anne O. The Structure and Evolution of Recent U.S. Trade Policy. Chicago; London: The University of Chicago Press, 1984.
Debaere 2005: Debaere, Peter. Small Fish - Big Issues. The Effect of Trade Policy on the Global Shrimp Market. CEPR Discussion Paper No. 5254, September 2005.
Deccan Herald 2006: Deccan Herald. Dell mulls PC unit in India. Newspaper article, Tuesday, January 31, 2006. In: http://www.deccanherald.com/deccanherald/jan312006/business1632252006130.asp.
Defense Contracts 1999: Information on companies recieving U.S.-Department of Defense contracts. In: http://web1.whs.osd.mil/PEIDHOME/PROCSTAT/p01/fy1999/top100.htm.

Dehio 1995: Dehio, Jochen. Analyse wirtschaftlicher Aufholprozesse in Ostasien. RWI-Mitteilungen, Jg. 46, 1995, S. 317-335.

Dehousse et al. 1999: Dehousse, Franklin, Ghemar, Katelyne, Vincent, Philippe. Market Access Study to Identify Trade Barriers Affecting the EU Textiles Industry in Certain Third Country Markets. European Commission, DG Trade, Brussels, March 1999. In: http://europe.eu.int/comm/trade.

Deininger/Binswanger 1995: Deininger, Klaus, Binswanger, Hans P. Rent Seeking and the Development of Large-Scale Agriculture in Kenya, South Africa, and Zimbabwe. In: Economic Development and Cultural Change, 1995. S. 493-522.

Deininger/Olinto 2000: Deininger, Klaus, Olinto, Pedro. Why Liberalization Alone has not Improved Agricultural Productivity in Zambia. World Bank Working Paper No. 2302, March 2000. In: http://www.worldbank.org.

Deitelhoff 2006: Deitelhoff, Nicole. Überzeugung in der Politik. Grundzüge einer Diskurstheorie internationalen Regierens. Frankfurt am Main: Surkamp, 2006.

Delgado 1992: Delgado, Christopher L. Why Domestic Food Prices Matter to Growth Strategy in Semi-Open West African Agriculture. In: Journal of African Economies, Vol. 1 No. 3, 1992. S. 446-471.

Demsetz 1974: Demsetz, Harold. Two Systems of Belief About Monopoly. In: Goldschmid, Harvey J., Mann, Michael H., West, Fred J. Industrial Concentration: The New Learning. Boston, Toronto: Little, Brown and Company, 1974.

Demsetz 1982: Demsetz, Harold. Barriers to Entry. In: American Economic Review, Vol. 72 No. 1, March 1982. S. 47-57.

Denison 1967: Denison, Edward F. Why Growth Rates Differ. Postwar Experience in Nine Western Countries. Washington, D.C.: The Brookings Institution, 1967.

Denison 1985: Denison, Edward F. Trends in American Economic Growth, 1929-1982. Washington: Brookings Institution, 1985.

Denison 1993: Denison, Edward F. The Gowth Accounting Tradition and Proximate Sources of Growth. In: Szirmai, Adam, van Ark, Bart, Pilat, Dirk (eds.). Explaining Economic Growth. Essays in Honour of Angus Maddison. Amsterdam: North Holland, 1993.

Denters 1996: Denters, Erik. Law and Policy of IMF Conditionality. The Hague: Kluwer, 1996.

Denters 2004: Denters, Erik. The BOP Restrictions Case of US v. India: How the IMF may affect decision making in the WTO. In: Reflections on Emerging International Law. Essays in Memory of Late Subrata Roy Chowdhury. National Law School of India University, Bangalore, 2004.

Deparment of Commerce 2003: Department of Commerce. Memorandum Dynamic Random Access Memory Semiconductors from the Republic of Korea, 68 FR 37122, June 23, 2003. In: http://www.commerce.gov.

Department of Disinvestment India 2005: Department of Disinvestment, Ministry of Finance. Indien. In: http://www.divest.nic.in/index.htm.

Department of Information Technology 2006: Department of Information Technology. Draft Paper on National Electronics/IT Hardware Manufacturing Policy. India, 2006. In: http://www.mit.gov.in/nwpolicy.asp.

Department of Telecommunication Sanchar Bhavan 2004: Department of Telecommunication Sanchar Bhavan (Investment Policy Cell). Status Paper on Manufacture of Telecom Equipment in India. Dated 31st March 2004. In: http://www.dot.gov.in.

Deraniyagala 1999: Deraniyagala, Sonali. Comparative and Pooled Analysis of the Three Countries. In: Lall, Sanjaya (Hrg.). The Technological Response to Import Liberalization in SubSaharan Africa. United Nations University, INTECH. London: MacMillan Press, 1999.

Deraniyagala/Semboja 1999: Deraniyagala, Sonali, Semboja, Haji H. H. Trade Liberalization, Firm Performance and Technology Upgrading in Tanzania. In: Lall, Sanjaya (Hrg.). The Technological Response to Import Liberalization in SubSaharan Africa. United Nations University, INTECH. London: MacMillan Press, 1999.

DeRosa et al. 1979: DeRosa, Dean A., Finger, J. Michael, Golub, Stephen S., Nye, William W. What the 'Zenith Case' Might Have Meant. In: JWTL, Vol. 13 No. 1, Jan Feb 1979. S. 47-54.

Desta 2001: Desta, Melaku Geboye. Food Security and International Trade Law. An Appraisal of the World Trade Organization Approach. In: JWT Vol. 35, No. 3, 2001. S. 449-468.

Destler 2003: Destler, I.M. US Trade Politics and Rules of Origin: Notes Towards A Paper. May 24, 2003. In: http://www.puaf.umd.edu/faculty/paper/Destler/RoO%20(1).pdf.

Destler 2005: Destler, I.M. American Trade Politics, 4th Edition. Washington, Institute for International Economics, June 2005.

Destler/Odell 1987: Destler, I.M., Odell, John S. Anti-Protection: Changing Forces in United States Trade Politics. Washington: Institute for International Economics, 1987.

Dethier 1991: Detier, Jean-Jacques. Egypt. In: Krueger, Anne O., Schiff, Maurice, Valdes, Alberto. The Political Economy of Agricultural Pricing Policy. Vol. 3 Africa and the Mediterranean. Baltimore, London: John Hopkins University Press, 1991.

Deutsch 1968: Deutsch, Karl W. Analyse internationaler Beziehungen. Frankfurt am Main: Europäische Verlagsanstalt, 1968.

Deutsche Bank Research 2001: Deutsche Bank Research. Euroland Industries in 2001 and 2002, April 2, 2001. In: http://www.dbresearch.com.

Deutscher Bundestag 2007: Deutscher Bundestag. EU und Globalisierung. Wissenschaftliche Dienste, Nr. 1/07, 2007. In: http://www.bundestag.de.

Deutscher Zolltarif 1961: Deutscher Zolltarif 1961. Anlagenband zum Bundesgesetzblatt Teil II, Jahrgang 1960.

Deutsches Handels-Archiv, div. Ausgaben: Bundesministerium für Wirtschaft (Hrg.). Deutsches Handels-Archiv (DHA). Sammlung von Handelsabkommen, Zolltarifen und sonstigen Vorschriften über den zwischenstaatlcihen Handelsverkehr. Dieselbe Reihe ab 1983 (hier nicht zitiert): Bundesstelle für Außenhandelsinformatione (Bfai) (Hrg.). Zoll- und Handelsinformationen. Köln.
DeVault 1993: DeVault, James M. The Impact of the U.S. Unfair Trade Law: A Preliminary Assessment. In: Weltwirtschaftliches Archiv, Bd. 129, 1993. S. 733-751.
Devereaux et al. 2006a: Devereaux, Charan, Lawrence, Robert Z., Watkins, Michael D. Making the Rules. Case Studies in US Trade Negotiation, Vol. I. Washington: Institute for International Economics, 2006.
Devereaux et al. 2006b: Devereaux, Charan, Lawrence, Robert Z., Watkins, Michael D. Resolving Disputes. Case Studies in US Trade Negotiation. Vol. II. Washington: Institute for International Economics, 2006.
Devereux/Naeraa 1996: Devereux, Stephen, Naeraa, Trine. Drought and Survival in Rural Namibia. In: Journal of Southern African Studies, Vol. 22 No. 3, September 1996. S. 421-440.
Dhanani 2000: Dhanani, Shafiq. Indonesia: Strategy for Manufacturing Competitiveness. Vol. II, Main Report. Jakarta: UNDP/UNIDO, November 2000. In: http://www.unido.org.
Diakosavvas/Scandizoo 1991: Diakosavvas, Dimitris, Scandizzo, Pasquale L. Trends in the Terms of Trade of
Diao et al. 2003: Diao, Xinshen, Diaz-Bonilla, Eugenio, Robinson, Sherman. How much does it hurt? The Impact of Agricultural Trade Policies on Developing Countries. Washington: IFPRI, 1993. In: http://www.ifpri.org.
Dichmann 1997: Dichmann, Werner. Gewerkschaften und Tarifautonomie in ordnungspolitischer und evolutorischer Sicht. In: ORDO, Bd. 48, 1997.
Dicke et al. 1976: Dicke, Hugo, Glismann, Hans H., Horn, Ernst-Jürgen, Neu, Axel D. Beschäftigungswirkungen einer verstärkten Arbeitsteilung zwischen der Bundesrepublik und den Entwicklungsländern. Kieler Studien 137. Tübingern: Mohr, 1976.
Dicken 1998: Dicken, Peter. Global Shift. Transforming the World Economy. London: Paul Chapman Publishing, 1998.
Dickerson 1995: Dickerson, Kitty G. Textiles and Clothing in the Global Economy. Englewood Cliffs, New Jersey: Merrill/Prentice Hall, 1995.
Dickson 1996: Dickson, Ian. China's Steel Imports: An Outline of Recent Trade Barriers. Working Paper No. 96/6. Chinese Economy Research Unit, Adelaide, July 1996. In: http://www.adelaide.edu.au/CERU.
Didier 2001: Didier, Pierre. The WTO Anti-Dumping Code and EC Practice. In: JWT, Vol. 35, No. 1. S. 33-54.
Diebold 1952: Diebold, William. The End of the ITO. Essays in International Finance, No. 16, Department of Economics and Social Institutions, Princeton University, October 1952.
Diehl 1999: Diehl, Markus. The Impact of International Outsourcing on the Skill Structure of Employment: Empirical Evidence from German Manufacturing Industries. Kieler Arbeitspapiere Nr. 946, September 1999.
Dieter 1998: Dieter, Heribert. Die Rolle der Finanzmärkte und des IWF. Zur Genese der asiatischen Finanzkrise. In: Entwicklung und Zusammenarbeit, 39. Jg., No. 7, 1998.
Dieter 2004: Dieter, Heribert. Präferentielle Ursprungsregeln in Freihandelszonen: Hemmnisse für den Internationalen Handel. In: Aussenwirtschaft, 59. Jg. Heft III, 2004. S. 273-301.
Dieter 2005: Dieter, Heribert. Bilateral Trade Agreements in the Asia-Pacific: Wise or Foolish Policies? University of Warwick, CSGR Working Paper Series No. 183/05, December 2005. In: http://www2.warwick.ac.uk.
Dietz/Havlik 1995: Dietz, Raimund, Havlik, Peter. Auswirkungen der EU-Ost-Integration auf den österreichischen und den EU-Osthandel. In: Europa 1996 Auswirkungen einer EU-Osterweiterung. Schriftenreihe des Bundeskanzleramts. Wien: Österreichische Staatsdruckerei, 1995.
Dijkstra 2000: Dijkstra, A. Geske. Trade Liberalization and Industrial Development in Latin America. In: World Development, Vol. 28, No. 9, 2000, S. 1567-1582.
Dinopoulos/Kreinin 1988: Dinopoulos, Elias, Mordechai E., Kreinin. Effects of the U.S.-Japan Auto VER on European Prices and on U.S. Welfare. In: Review of Economics and Statistics, Vol. 70, 1988. 484-491.
Disyatat 2004: Disyatat, Piti. Rationalizing Asian's Foreign Reserves Built Up. Research Institute of Economy, Trade and Industry (RIETI). June 2004. In: http://www.rieti.go.jp.
DIW 1997: DIW, Berlin, ITC, Genf. China als Handelspartner und Produktionsstandort für deutsche mittelständische Unternehmen. Dezember 1997. In: http://www.diw.de.
DIW-Afrika 12/1997: DIW-Wochenbericht. Afrikas Stellung auf dem Weltmarkt und in der Europäischen Union. Jg. 64, 20. März 1997.
DIW-Niederlande 16/1997: DIW-Wochenbericht. Die Niederlande: Beschäftigungspolitisches Vorbild? DIW 16/1997, Jg. 64, 17. April 1997.
DIW-Osterweiterung 14/1997: DIW-Wochenbericht. Europäische Union: Osterweiterung beschleunigt Konvergenz. DIW 14/1997, Jg. 64, 3. April 1997.
DIW-Rußland 15/2000: DIW-Wochenbericht. Russlands Wirtschaftspolitik setzt auf Investitionen. DIW 15/2000. Jg. 67, 13. April 2000.
DIW-Schuhproduktion 14/1997: DIW-Wochenbericht. Schrumpfungsprozess der deutschen Schuhproduktion hält an. DIW 14/1997, Jg. 64, 3. April 1997.
DIW-Subventionsabbau 1999: Kriterien und Vorschläge für einen Subventionsabbau. DIW Diskussionspapiere (zusammen mit dem IfW Kiel), Nr. 181. Berlin, März 1999.
Dixit/Norman 1986: Dixit, Avinash, Norman, Victor. Gains from Trade without Lump-Sum Compensation. In: Journal of International Economics, Vol. 21, 1986. S. 111-112.
Dixit/Stiglitz 1977: Dixit, Avinash K., Stiglitz, Joseph E. Monopolistic Competition and Optimum Product Diversity. In: American Economic Review, Vol. 67 No. 3, June 1977. S. 297-308.

Dodaro 1991: Dodaro, Santo. Comparative Advantage, Trade and Growth: Export-Led Growth Revisited. In: World Development, Vol. 19, No. 9, 1991, pp. 1153-1165.
Dohlman/Hoffman 2000: Dohlman, Eric, Hoffman, Linwood. The New Agricultural Trade Negotiations: Background and Issues for the U.S. Wheat Sector. USDA Economic Research Service, 2000. In: http://www.usda.gov.
Döhrn 1994: Döhrn, Roland. Deutsche Direktinvestitionen in der Europäischen Union: Produktions- oder Finanzintegration. In: RWI-Mitteilungen, Jg. 45, 1994. S. 261-281.
Dolata 1997: Dolata, Ulrich. Das Phantom der Globalisierung. In: Blätter für deutsche und internationale Politik, 1, 1997. S. 100-104.
Dollar 1992: Dollar, David. Outward-oriented Developing Economies Really Do Grow More Rapidly: Evidence form 95 LDCs, 1976-1985. In: Economic Development and Cultural Change, 1992, S. 523-544.
Dollar 1993: Dollar, David. Technological Differences as Source of Comparative Advantage. In: American Economic Review, Papers and Proceedings, Vol. 83, No. 2, May 1993. S. 431-439.
Dollar/Kraay 2001: Dollar, David. Trade, Growth, and Poverty. World Bank Policy Research Working Paper No. 2615, June 2001. In: http://www.worldbank.org.
Domar 1946: Domar, Evsey D. Capital Expansion, Rate of Growth, and Employment. In: Econometrica, Vol. 14, No. 2, April 1946. S. 137-147.
Domowitz et al. 1987: Domowitz, Ian, Hubbard, Glen R., Petersen, Bruce C. Oligopoly Supergames: Some Empirical Evidence on Prices and Margins. In: Journal of Industrial Economics, Vol. XXXV, No. 4, June 1987. S. 379-398.
Domowitz et al. 1988: Domowitz, Ian, Hubbard, Glen R., Petersen, Bruce C. Market Structure and Cyclical Fluctuations in U.S.-Manufacturing. In: Review of Economics and Statistics, Vol. 70, 1988. S. 55-66.
Donges 1976: Donges, Jürgen B. A Comparative Survey of Industrialization in Fifteen Semi-Industrial Countries. In: Weltwirtschaftliches Archiv, Bd. 112, 1976, S. 626-659.
Donges 1981: Donges, Jürgen B. Außenwirtschafts- und Entwicklungspolitik. Die Entwicklungsländer in der Weltwirtschaft. Berlin; Heidelberg: Springer, 1981.
Donges 1986: Donges, Jürgen B. Wither International Trade Policies? Worries about Continuing Protectionism. Kieler Diskussionsbeiträge, No. 125. Kiel: Institut für Weltwirtschaft, Oktober 1986.
Donges 1997: Donges, Jürgen B. Die Wirtschaftspolitik im Spannungsverhältnis zwischen Regulierung und Deregulierung. In: ORDO, Bd. 48, 1997.
Donges et al. 1973: Donges, Jürgen B., Fels, Gerhard, Neu, Axel D. Protektion und Branchenstruktur der westdeutschen Wirtschaft. Kieler Studien 123. Tübingen: Mohr, 1973.
Donges/Freytag 1998: Donges, Jürgen B, Freytag, Andreas (Hrg.). Die Rolle des Staates in einer globalisierten Wirtschaft. Stuttgart: Lucius & Lucius, 1998.
Donges/Riedel 1977: Donges, Jürgen B., Riedel, James. The Expansion of Manufactured Exports in Developing Countries: An Empirical Assessment of Supply and Demand Issues. In: Weltwirtschaftliche Archiv Bd. 113, 1977. S. 58-87.
Donges/Schatz 1980: Donges, Jürgen B., Schatz, Klaus-Werner. Muster der industriellen Arbeitsteilung im Rahmen einer erweiterten Europäischen Gemeinschaft. In: Die Weltwirtschaft, Heft 1, 1980. S. 160-186.
Dore 1997: Dore, Ronald. The Distinctiveness of Japan. In: Crouch, Colin, Streeck, Wolfgang. Political Economy of Modern Capitalism. London: Sage, 1997.
Dornbusch 1992: Dornbusch, Rudiger. Lessons from Experiences with High Inflation. In: The World Bank Economic Review, Vo. 6, No. 1, 13-31.
Dornbusch et al. 1977: Dornbusch, Rüdiger, Fischer, Stanley, Samuelson, P. A. Comparative Advantage, Trade, and the Payments in a Ricardian Model with a Continuum of Goods. In: American Economic Review, Vol. 67, No. 5, December 1997. S. 823-839.
Dornbusch/Edwards 1990: Dornbusch, Rüdiger, Edwards, Sebastian. Macroeconomic Populism. In: Journal of Development Economics, Vol. 32 (1990), pp. 247-277.
Dornbusch/Edwards 1990: Dornbusch, Rüdiger, Edwards, Sebastian. Macroeconomic Populism. In: Journal of Development Economics, Vol. 32, 1990. S. 247-277.
Dornbusch/Fischer 1992: Dornbusch, Rüdiger, Fischer, Stanley. Makroökonomik. München; Wien: Oldenbourg, 1992.
Dos Santos 2005: Dos Santos, Pablo Fonseca P. Brazil's remarkable journey. In: Finance and Development, Vol. 42, No. 2, June 2005. In: http://www.imf.org.
Dosi et al. 1990: Dosi, Giovanni, Pavitt, Keith, Soete, Luc. The Economics of Technical Change and International Trade. New York: New York University Press, 1990.
Dougherty/Jorgenson 1996: Dougherty, Chrys, Jorgenson, Dale W. International Comparisons of the Sources of Economic Growth. In: American Economic Review, Papers and Proceedings, Vol. 86, No. 2, May 1996. S. 25-29.
Drabek/Greenaway 1984: Drabek, Zdenek, Greenaway, David. Economic Integration and Intra-Industry Trade: The EEC and CMEA Compared. In: Kyklos, Vol. 37, No. 3, 1984. S. 444-469.
Dreier 1989: Dreier, Thomas. National Treatment, Reciprocity and Retorsion - The Case of Computer Programs and Integrated Circuits. In: Beier, Friedrich-Karl, Schricker, Gerhard (eds.). GATT or WIPO? New Ways in the Protection of Intellectual Property. Weinheim: Wiley-VCH, 1989.
Driffield 2001: Driffield, Nigel. Inward Investment, Industry Concentration and the Speed of Adjustment. In: Weltwirtschaftliches Archiv, Bd. 137, Heft 2, 2001. S. 193-214.

Driscoll 2005: Driscoll, Caroline Ormonde. Unforeseen Developments - An Unforeseeable Future? The Relationship Between GATT Art. XIX and the Agreement on Safeguards. In: Legal Issues of Economic Integration Vol. 32, No. 3, 2005. S. 249-258.
Droege 2001: Droege, Susanne. Ecological Labelling and the World Trade Organization. In: Aussenwirtschaft, 56 Jg., Heft I, 2001. S. 99-122.
Dryden 1995: Dryden, Steve. Trade Warriors. USTR and the American Crucade for Free Trade. New York, Oxford: Oxford University Press, 1995.
Duijm 1997: Duijm, Bernhard. Die deutsche Politik gegenüber Entwicklungsländern: Einige ordnungspolitische Anmerkungen: In: ORDO, Bd. 48, 1997.
Dunne et al. 1989: Dunne, Timothy, Roberts, Mark J., Samuelson, Larry. The Growth and Failure of U.S. Manufacturing Plants. In: Quarterly Journal of Economics, November 1989. S. 671-698.
Dunning 1993: Dunning, John H. Multinational Enterprises and the Global Economy. Harlow, England et al.: Addison-Wesley, 1993.
Dunning 1997: Dunning, John H. The European Internal Market Programme and Inbound Foreign Direct Investment. In: Journal of Common Market Studies, Vol. 35, No. 1, March 1997. S. 1-30.
Dunning 1997a: Dunning, John H. Governments and the Macro-Organization of Economic Activity: A Historical and Spatial Perspective. In: Dunning, John H. (ed.). Governments, Gobalization and International Business. Oxford: Oxford University Press, 1997.
Durling 2003: Durling, James P. Deference, but only when due: WTO review of anti-dumping measures. In: Journal of International Economic Law Vol. 6 No. 1, 2003. S. 125-153.
Dutfield 1999: Dutfield, Graham. Intellectual Property Rights, Trade and Biodiversity: The Case of Seed and Plant Varieties. IUCN Background Paper June 1999. Interessessional Meeting on the Operation of the Convention, Montreal Canada, 28-30 June 1999. In: http://www.iucn.org.
Duysters/Hagedoorn 1993: Duysters, Geert, Hagedoorn, John. Strategic Group Formation and Inter-Firm Networks in the International Information Technology Industry. MERIT, Faculty of Economics and Business Administration, Maastricht. January 1993.

E

Eaton et al. 2004: Eaton, Jonathan, Kortum, Samuel, Lerner, Josh. International Patenting and the European Patent Office: A Quantitative Assessment. In: OECD. Patents, Innovation and Economic Performance. Conference Proceedings. Paris: OECD, 2004.
Eaton/Kortum 1994: Eaton, Jonathan, Kortum, Samuel. International Patenting and Technology Diffusion. NBER Working Paper No. 4931, November 1994.
Eaton/Kortum 1995: Eaton, Jonathan, Kortum, Samuel. Trade in Ideas: Patenting and Productivity in the OECD. NBER Working Paper No. 5049, March 1995.
Eaton/Kortum 1997: Eaton, Jonathan, Kortum, Samuel. Technology and Bilateral Trade. NBER Working Paper No. 6253, November 1997.
Eatwell/Taylor 1998: Eatwell, John, Taylor, Lance. The Performance of Liberalized Capital Markets. Centre of Economic Policy Analysis. Working Paper No. 8, August 1998. In: http://www.newschool.edu/cepa.
Ebbinghaus/Hassel 1999: Ebbinghaus, Bernhard, Hassel, Anke. Striking Deals: Concertation in the Reform of Continental European Welfare States. In: MPIfG (Max Planck Institut für Gesellschaftsforschung Köln), Working Paper 99/3, December 1999. In: http://www.mpi-fg-koeln.mpg.de.
EC 2000: European Communities. The Community Budget: The Facts in Figures. Luxemburg: Office for Official Publications of the European Communities, 2000. In: http://europe.eu.int/comm//budget/financing.
ECA Economic Report on Africa. div. Jg.: ECA. Economic Report on Africa. Addis Ababa, Ethiopia: United Nations Economic Commission on Africa, div. Jg. In: http://www.uneca.org.
ECA Key Indicators 2002: UN Economic Commission for Africa. Population, Agriculture and Environment: Some Key Indicators. 09.12.2002. In: http://www.uneca.org.
Eckstein 1980: Eckstein, Wolfram. The Role of Banks in Corporate Concentration in West Germany. In: Zeitschrift für die gesamte Staatswissenschaft. Bd. 136, 1980. S. 465-482.
Edwards 1988: Edwards, Sebastian. Real And Monetary Determinants of Real Exchange Rate Behavior. In: Journal of Development Economics, Vol. 29, 1988, pp. 311-341.
Edwards 1989: Edwards, Sebastian. Real Exchange Rates, Devaluation, and Adjustment. Cambridge, Mass.: The MIT Press, 1989.
Edwards 1992: Edwards, Sebastian. Trade Orientation, Distortions and Growth in Developing Countries. In: Journal of Development Economics, Vol. 39, 1992, pp. 31-57.
Edwards 1993: Edwards, Sebastian. Exchange Rates as Nominal Anchors. In: Weltwirtschaftliches Archiv, Bd. 129, 1993, S. 1-32.
Edwards 1993a: Edwards, Sebastian. Openness, Trade Liberalization, and Growth in Developing Countries. In: Journal of Economic Literature, Vol. 31, September 1993. S. 1358-1393.
Edwards 1995: Edwards, Sebastian. Trade and Industrial Policy Reform in Latin America. In: Resende, André Lara (Moderator). Policies for Growth. The Latin American Experience. Washington: International Monetary Fund, 1995.
Edwards 1995: Edwards, Sebastian. Trade Policy, Exchange Rates, and Growth. In: Dornbusch, Rudiger, Edwards, Sebastian (eds.). Reform, Recovery, and Growth. Chicago; London: University of Chicago Press, 1995.

Edwards 1995a: Edwards, Chris. East Asia and Industrial Policy in Malaysia: Lessons für Africa? In: Stein, Howard (Hrg.). Asian Industrialization and Africa. Studies in Policy Alternatives to Structural Adjustment. London: St. Martin's Press, 1995.
Edwards 1995a: Edwards, Sebstaian. Trade Policy, Exchange Rates, and Growth. In: Dornbusch, Rudiger, Edwards, Sebastian (eds.). Reform, Recovery, and Growth. Chicago; London: University of Chicago Press, 1995.
Edwards 1998: Edwards, Sebastian. Openness, Productivity and Growth: What Do We Really Know? In: The Economic Journal, 108, March 1998. S. 383-398.
Edwards/Dornbusch 1995: Edwards, Sebastian, Dornbusch, Rudiger. Introduction. In: Dornbusch, Rudiger, Edwards, Sebastian (eds.). Reform, Recovery, and Growth. Chicago; London: University of Chicago Press, 1995.
Edwards/Lester 1997: Edwards, Robert H., Lester, Simon N. Towards a More Comprehensive World Trade Organization Agreement on Trade Related Investment Measures. In: Stanford Journal of International Law, Vol. 33, 1997. S. 169-214.
Eeckhout 2003: Eeckhout, Piet. The EC Response. In: Cottier, Thomas, Mavroidis, Petros C (eds.). The Role of the Judge in International Trade Regulation. Ann Arbor: University of Michigan Press, 2003.
Efinger et al. 1990: Efinger, Manfred, Rittberger, Volker, Wolf, Klaus Dieter, Zürn, Michael. Internationale Regime und internationale Politik. In: PVS, Jg. 31, Sonderheft 21, 1990.
Efinger/Zürn 1990: Efinger, Manfred, Zürn, Michael. Explaing conflict management in East-West relations: a quantitative test of problem-structural typologies. In: Rittberger, Volker (ed.). International Regimes in East-West Politics. London: New York: Pinter Publishers, 1990.
EGKS-Vertrag 1951: Vertrag über die Gründung der Europäischen Gemeinschaft für Kohle und Stahl. In. Europarecht. München: dtv, 1997.
Ehlermann 1997: Ehlermann, Claus Dieter. Reflections on the Process of Clarification and Improvement of the DSU. In: Ortino, Federico, Petersmann, Ernst-Ulrich (eds.). The WTO Dispute Settlement System 1995 - 2003. The Hague et al.: Kluwer Law International, 2004.
Ehlermann 2004: Ehlermann, Claus Dieter. Six years on the bench of the 'World Trade Court'. In: Ortino, Federico, Petersmann, Ernst-Ulrich (eds.). The WTO Dispute Settlement System 1995 - 2003. The Hague et al.: Kluwer Law International, 2004.
Ehlermann/Ehring 2005: Ehlermann, Claus Dieter, Ehring, Lothar. Are WTO Decision-Making Procedures Adequate for Making, Revising, and Implementing Worldwide and 'Plurilateral' Rules? In: Petersmann, Ernst-Ulrich (ed.). Reforming the World Trading System. Legitimacy, Efficiency, and Democratic Governance. Oxford: Oxford University Press, 2005.
Ehlermann/Ehring 2005a: Ehlermann, Claus Dieter, Ehring, Lothar. Can the WTO Dispute Settlement System Deal with Competition Disputes? In: Petersmann, Ernst-Ulrich (ed.). Reforming the World Trading System. Legitimacy, Efficiency, and Democratic Governance. Oxford: Oxford University Press, 2005.
Ehlermann/Lockhard 2004: Ehlermann, Claus Dieter, Lockhart, Nicolas. Standard of Review in WTO Law. In: Journal of International Economic Law, Vol. 7, No. 3, 2004. S. 491-521.
Ehring 2002: Ehring, Lothar. De Facto Discrimination in World Trade Law. National and Most-Favoured-Nation Treatment - Or Equal Treatment? In: Journal of World Trade, Vol. 36 No. 5, 2002. S. 921-977.
Eichengreen 1996: Eichengreen, Barry. Institutions and economic growth: Europa after World War II. In: Crafts, Nicolas, Toniolo, Gianni (eds.). Economic Growth in Europe since 1945. Cambridge: Cambridge University Press, 1996.
Eichengreen/Kohl 1998: Eichengreen, Barry, Kohl, Richard. The External Sector, the State and Development in Eastern Europe. In: http://brie.berkeley.edu.
Eichengreen/van der Ven 1984: Eichengreen, Barry, van der Ven, Hans. U.S. Antidumping Policies: The Case of Steel. In: Baldwin, Robert E. Krueger, Anne O. The Structure and Evolution of Recent U.S. Trade Policy. Chicago; London: The University of Chicago Press, 1984.
Eicher/Baker 1982: Eicher, Carl K., Baker, Doyle C. Research on Agricultural Development in Sub-Saharan Africa. A Critical Survey. Michigan State University, Department of Agricultural Economics, 1982. In: http://www.aec.msu.edu/agecon/pubs.htm.
Elbadawi 1992: Elbadawi, Ibrahim A. Real Overvaluation, Terms of Trade Shocks and the Cost to Agriculture in Sub-Saharan Africa: The Case of Sudan. In: Journal of African Economies, Vol. 1 No. 1, 1992. S. 59-85.
Elbadawi 2001: Elbadawi, Ibrahim A. Can Africa Export Manufactures? Endowments, Exchange Rates and Transaction Costs. In: OECD. Policies to Promote Competitiveness in Manufacturing in Sub-Saharan Africa. Development Centre Seminars within the IMF and the AERC. Kwasi Fosu, Augustin, Nsouli, Saleh M., Varoudakis, Aristomene (eds.). Paris: OECD, 2001a.
Elias 1992: Elias, Victor. Sources of Growth. A Study of Seven Latin American Economies. International Centre for Economic Growth. San Francisco, California: ICS Press, 1992.
Ellis 1992: Ellis, Frank. Agricultural Policies in Developing Countries. Cambridge: Cambridge University Press, 1992.
Elsenhans 1981: Elsenhans, Hartmut. Abhängiger Kapitalismus oder bürokratische Entwicklungsgesellschaft. Frankfurt; New York: Campus Verlag, 1981.
Elsenhans 1983: Elsenhans, Hartmut. Rising mass incomes as a condition of capitalist growth: implications for the world economy. In: IO, Vol. 37 No.1, Winter 1983. S. 1-39.
Elsenhans 1990: Elsenhans, Hartmut. Nord-Süd-Beziehungen: Theorien über die Nord-Süd-Konfliktformationen und ihre Bearbeitung. In: PVS, 31. Jg. Sonderheft 21, 1990.

Elsenhans 1996: Elsenhans, Hartmut. Gegen das Gespenst der Globalisierung. In: Jahrbuch Arbeit und Technik 1996. Bonn: Dietz, 1996.
Elzinga 1990: Elzinga, Kenneth G. The Beer Industry. In: Adams, Walter (Hrg.). The Structure of American Industry. New York: Macmillan, 1990.
Emerson et al. 1988: Emerson, Michael, Aujean, Michel, Catinat, Michel, Goybet, Philippe, Jaquemin, Alexis. Europas Zukunft - Binnenmarkt 1992. Eine Bewertung der möglichen wirtschaftlichen Auswirkungen der Vollendung des Binnenmarktes der Europäischen Gemeinschaft. In: Europäische Wirtschaft, Nummer 35, März 1988.
Emiliou/Keeffe 1996: Emiliou, Nicholas, Keeffe, David O., The European Union and World Trade Law. After the GATT Uruguay Round. Chichester et al: John Wiley, 1996.
Emmanuel 1972: Emmanuel, Arghiri. Unequal Exchange. A Study of the Imperialism of Trade. New York; London: Monthly Review Press, 1972.
Emmerich-Fritsche 2002: Emmerich-Fritsche, Angelika. Recht und Zwang im Völkerrecht, insbesondere im Welthandelsrecht. In: Schachtschneider, Karl Albrecht (Hrg.). Rechtsfragen der Weltwirtschaft. Berlin: Duncker & Humblot, 2002.
Engel 1996: Gerhard, Engel. Die Grenzen der politischen Öffentlichkeit Jürgen Habermas und die konstitutionelle Ökonomik. In: Pies, Ingo, Leschke, Martin (Hrg.). James Buchanans konstitutionelle Ökonomik. Tübingen: Mohr, 1996.
Engel/Reichert 1999: Engel, Astrid, Reichert, Tobias. Von Subsistenz bis WTO-Reform. BUKO Agrar Studien 8. Hamburg: Forum für internationale Agrarpolitik e.V., 1999.
Engels 1992: Engels, Benno (Hrg.). Weiterentwicklung des GATT durch die Uruguay Runde? Hamburg: Übersee Institut, 1992.
Engels 1996: Engels, Rainer. Nahrungsmitteldumping in Entwicklungsländern. In: BUKO Agrarkoordination (Hrg.) Welternährung. Agrar Dossier 14, Hamburg 1996.
Enos/Park 1988: Enos, J. L., Park, W. H. The Adoption and Diffusion of Imported Technology. The Case of Korea. London; New York; Sydney: Croom Helm, 1988.
Epstein/Gintis 1989: Epstein, Gerald, Gintis, Herbert. International Capital Markets and the Limits of National Economic Policy. WIDER Working Paper, Helsinki 1989.
Erber 1985: Erber, Fabio Stefano. The Development of the 'Electronics Complex' and Government Policies in Brazil. In: World Development, Vol. 13, No. 3, 1985. S. 293-309.
Ergas 1987: Ergas, Henry. Does Industrial Policy Matter? In: Audretsch, David (ed.). Industrial Policy and Competitive Advantage, Vol. I. Cheltenham, UK, Northampton, MA: Elgar, 1998.
Erhard 1957: Erhard, Ludwig. Wohlstand für Alle. Düsseldorf: Econ-Verlag, 1957.
Erlei 1993: Erlei, Mathias. Von der Steuerbarkeit des Fortschritts: eine Analyse der 'Euro-MITI'-Konzeption. In: ORDO 44, 1993. S. 169-183.
Ernst 1973: Ernst, Dieter. Wirtschaftliche Entwicklung durch Importsubsituierende Industrialisierung. In: Das Argument. Zeitschrift für Philosophie und Sozialwissenschaften. 15 Jg. Nr. 78-83, 1973. S. 332-403.
Ernst 1985: Ernst, Dieter. Automation and Worldwide Restructuring of the Electronics Industry: Strategic Implication for Developing Countries. In: World Development, Vol. 13, No. 3, 1985. S. 333-352.
Ernst 1987: Ernst, Wolfgang. Wechselwirkungen zwischen Handelspolitik und Intergration. Rückschau eines europäischen Praktikers. In: FS Hans von der Groeben. Baden-Baden: Nomos, 1987.
Ernst 1997: Ernst, Dieter. From Partial to Systemic Globalization: International Production Networks in the Electronics Industry. San Diego: Berkeley Roundtable on the International Economie (BRIE), Working Paper 98. http://brie.berkeley.edu.
Erzan et al. 1989: Erzan, Refik, Kuwahara, Kiroaki, Marchese, Serafino, Vossenar, Rene. The profile of protection in developing countries. In: UNCTAD Review, Jg. 1, No. 1, 1989. S. 29-49.
Erzan/Goto et al. 1990: Erzan, Refik, Goto, Junichi, Holmes, Paula. Effects of the Multi-Fibre Arrangement on Developing Countries' Trade: An Empirical Investigation. In: Hamilton, Carl B. Textiles Trade and the Developing Countries. Eliminating the Multi-Fibre Arrangement in the 1990s. Washington: World Bank, 1990.
Erzan/Holmes 1990: Erzan, Refik, Holmes, Paula. Phasing Out the Multi-Fibre Arrangement. In: World Economy, Vol. 13, 1990. S. 191-211.
Erzan/Karsenty 1989: Erzan, Refik, Karsenty, Guy. Products facing high tariffs in major developed market-economy countries: An area of priority for the developing countries in the Uruguay Round? In: UNCTAD Review, Jg. 1, No. 1, 1989. S. 51-73.
ESCAP 2002: United Nations Economic and Social Commission for Asia and the Pacific. Development of the Automotive Sector in Selected Countries of the ESCAP Region. UNESCAP, 2002. In: http://www.unescap.org.
ESCAP 2002a: United Nations Economic and Social Commission for Asia and the Pacific. Promotion of Interregional Trade and Investment and Economic Cooperation in the Automotive Sector, UNESCAP, 2002. In: http://www.unescap.org.
Escosura/Sanz 1996: de la Escosura, Leandro Prados, Sanz, Jorge C. Growth and macroecomomic performance in Spain 1939-93. In: Crafts, Nicolas, Toniolo, Gianni (eds.). Economic Growth in Europe since 1945. Cambridge: Cambridge University Press, 1996.
Esfahani 1991: Esfahani, Hadi Salehi. Exports, imports, and economic growth in semi-industrialized countries. In: Journal of Development Economics 35, 1991, S. 93-116.
Essar Informationen 2006: Essar Firmeninformationen 2006. In: http://www.essar.com/power/PDF/cerc/Annexure-IV.PDF.

Esser 1998: Esser, Josef. Privatization in Germay. Symbolism in a social market economy? In: Parker, David (ed.). Privatization in the European Union. Theory and Policy Perspectives. London; New York: Routledge, 1998.
Estevadeordal/Suominen 2003: Estevadeordal, Antoni, Suominen, Kati. Rules of Origin. A World Map and Trade Effects. Paper for Workshop: 'The Origin of Goods: A Conceptual and Empirical Assessment of Rules of Origin in PTAs', Paris 2003. In:
http://www.inra.fr/internet/Departements/ESR/UR/lea/actualites/ROO2003/articles/estevadeordal.pdf
Estler 1998: Estler, Otte. Der Beitrag kleiner und mittlerer Unternehmen zum Entwicklungsprozeß Thailands. Hamburg: Institut für Asienkunde, 1998.
Estrella/Horlick 2006: Estrella, Angela T., Horlick, Gary N. Mandatory Abolition of Anti-dumping, Countervailing Duties and Safeguards in Customs Unions and Free Trade Areas Constituted Between World Trade Organization Members: Revisiting a Long-standing Discussion in Light of the Appellate Body's Turkey - Textiles Ruling. In: JWT, Vol. 40, No. 5, 2006. S. 909-944.
Etcheverry 1997: Etcheverry, Raul Anibal. Settlement of Disputes in the South American Common Market (Mercosur). In: Petersmann, Ernst-Ulrich (ed.). International Trade Law and the GATT/WTO Dispute Settlement System. London, The Hague, Boston: Kluwer Law, 1997.
Ethier 1979: Ethier, Wilfred J. Internationally decreasing costs and world trade. In: Journal of International Economics, Vol. 9, 1979. S. 1-24.
Ethier 1982: Ethier, Wilfred J. National and International Returns to Scale in the Modern Theory of International Trade. In: American Economic Review, Vol. 72 No. 3, June 1982. S. 389-405.
Etukudo 2000: Etukudo, A. Issues in Privatization and Restructuring in Sub-Saharan Africa. International Labour Organization. Interdepartmental Action Programme on Privatization, Restructuring and Economic Democracy Working Paper IPPRED-5. Working Paper, 2000. In:
http://www.ilo.org/public/english/employment/ent/papers/ippred5.htm.
EU Antidumping Consolidated Version 2004: EU Antidumping Regulierung. Consolidated Version 20/03/2004. In: http://europa.eu.int/eur-lex/en/consleg/main/1996/en_1996R0384_index.html.
EU Foodlaw 2006: EU. General Food Law. Implementation Guidance Document. In:
http://ec.europa.eu/food/food/foodlaw/guidance/index_en.htm.
EU Footwear 2006: EU WTO Information. Cases involving the EU: WT/DS121 - Safeguard measures on footwear. November 2006. In: http://trade.ec.europa.eu/wtodispute/show.cfm?id=228&code=1.
EU Trade Info 2004: EU. WTO arbitrators agree on EU request for sanctions in dispute over US 1916 Anti-Dumping Act, Brussels, 24 February 2004. In: http://trade.info.cec.eu.int.
EU Wheat Gluten 2001: EU: Illegal US wheat gluten quota likely to fall: Commission welcomes "intelligent decision". Brussels, 2 June 2001. IP/01/776. In:
http://trade.ec.europa.eu/doclib/docs/2003/november/tradoc_114818.pdf
EU WTO Active Case Overview 2006: Directorate General for Trade. General Overview of Active WTO Dispute Settlement Cases Involving the EC as Complainant or Defendant and of Active Cases under the Trade Barriers Regulatoin. 13. October 2006. In: http://trade.ec.europa.eu/doclib/docs/2006/october/tradoc_129465.pdf.
Eucken 1932: Eucken, Walter. Staatliche Strukturwandlungen und die Krisis der Kapitalismus. Neuabdruck in: ORDO, Bd. 48, 1997.
Eucken 1940: Eucken, Walter. Die Grundlagen der Nationalökonomie. Berlin; Heidelberg; New York: Springer, (1940) 1989.
Eucken 1946a: Eucken, Walter. Über die Gesamtrichtung der Wirtschaftspolitik. In: Oswalt, Walter (Hrg.). Walter Eucken. Ordnungspolitik. Münster: Lit-Verlag, (1946) 1999.
Eucken 1946b: Eucken, Walter. Industrielle Konzentration. In: Oswalt, Walter (Hrg.). Walter Eucken. Ordnungspolitik. Münster: Lit-Verlag, (1946) 1999.
Eucken 1952: Eucken, Walter. Grundsätze der Wirtschaftspolitik. Tübingen: Mohr, (1952) 1975.
Euro India 2004: EuroIndia2004. Market Background Document Overview. Conference Paper, 2004. In: www.euroindia2004.org/ files/EI2004MBDOverview-101541A.pdf.
Europäische Kommission 1991: Europäische Kommission. Mitteilung der Kommission an den Rat. Die künftige Entwicklung der GAP - Grundsatzpapier der Kommission. KOM(91)100 endg. Brüssel, den 1. Februar 1991.
Europäische Kommission 1992: Europäische Kommission. Bericht des unabhängigen Sachverständigenausschusses zur Unternehmensbesteuerung. 1992. Luxemburg: Amt für amtliche Veröffentlichungen der Europäischen Gemeinschaften, 1995.
Europäische Kommission 1997: Europäische Kommission. Grünbuch über das Gemeinschaftspatent und das Patentschutzsystem in Europa. KOM(97) 314 endg. Brüssel, den 24.06.1997.
Europäische Kommission 2003: Europäische Kommission. Mitteilung der Kommission an den Rat, das Europäische Parlament, den Europäischen Wirtschafts- und Sozialausschuß und den Ausschuß der Regionen. Die Zukunft des Textil- und Bekleidungssektors in der erweiterten Europäischen Union. KOM(2003) 649 endgültig. Brüssel, den 29.10.2003. In: http://europa.eu.int.
Europäische Kommission 2004: Europäische Kommission. Mitteilung der Kommission. Den Strukturwandel begleiten: Eine Industriepolitik für die erweiterte Union. KOM (2004) 274 endgültig. Brüssel, den 20.4.2004. In: http://europa.eu.int.
Europäische Kommission 2005: EU-Handelskommissar Peter Mandelson erinnert beim Treffen mit dem Staatspräsidenten von Mali Toumani Toure an die Verpflichtungen der EU im Rahmen der Doha-Verhandlungen zum Baumwollhandel, IP/05/1443, Brüssel, den 18. November 2005. In: http://europa.eu/rapid.

Europäische Kommission 2006: Europäische Kommission. Mitteilung der Kommission. Das Globale Europa. Die handelspolitischen Schutzinstrumente der EU in einer sich wandelnden globalen Wirtschaft. KOM(2006)763 endg. 6.12.2006. http://europa.eu.int, Europäische Wirtschaft bzw. European Economic Jahreswirtschaftsbericht bzw. Annual Economic Report div. Jahrgänge: Europäische Kommission. Generaldirektion Wirtschaft und Finanzen. Europäische Wirtschaft bzw. European Economic Jahreswirtschaftsbericht bzw. Annual Economic Report. Brüssel; Luxemburg, div. Jahrgänge. In: http://europa.eu.int/comm/economy_finance/index_en.htm.
Europäische Kommission Konvergenzbericht 2000: Bericht der Kommission. Konvergenzbericht. Kom (2000) 277 endgültig. Brüssel, 3. Mai 2000. In: http://europa.eu.int/comm/economy_finance/index_en.htm
Europäische Kommission Mandarinen Schutzmaßnahmen 2004: Europäische Kommission. Verordnung (EG) Nr. 658/2004 der Kommission vom 7. April 2004 zur Einführung endgültiger Schutzmaßnahmen gegenüber den Einfuhren bestimmter zubereiteter oder haltbar gemachter Zitrusfrüchte (Mandarinen usw.). In: ABl. L 104/67, 8.4.2004.
Europäische Kommission Mandarinen Schutzmaßnahmen 2004a: Europäische Kommission. Notice regarding consultations on the application of the safeguards measures imposed on importes concerning certain prepared or preserved citrus fruits by Commission Regulation (EC) No 658/2004. In: ABl. C 322/7, 17.12.2005.
Europäische Kommission Stahl Schutzmaßnahmen 2002: Europäische Kommission. Verordnung (EG) Nr. 1694 der Kommission vom 27. September 2002 zur Einführung endgültiger Schutzmaßnahmen gegenüber den Einfuhren bestimmter Stahlerzeugnisse. In: ABl. L 261/1, 28.9.2002.
European Central Bank 2002: European Central Bank. Monthly Bulletin, August 2002. In: http://www.ecb.int.
European Commission 1991: European Commission, MONITOR/SPEAR: de la Torre, C. E. (coordinator), Hagedoorn, J., Schakenraad, J. The Economic Effects of Strategic Partnerships and Technology Cooperation. Luxemburg: September 1991.
European Commission 1994: European Economy. Reports and Studies. Toward Greater Fiscal Discipline. 1994, No. 3. Luxembourg, 1995.
European Commission 1999: Report on United States Barriers to Trade and Investment. Brussels, August 1999.
European Commission 2000: Report on United States Barriers to Trade and Investment. Brussels, July 2000. In: http://europe.eu.int/comm/trade/bilateral/usa/usa.htm.
European Commission 2003: Commission Staff Working Document. European Competitiveness Report 2003, SEC(2003)1299, Brussels, 12.11.2003. In: http://europe.eu.int.
European Commission 2004: European Commission. Directorate-General for Economic and Fiscal Affairs. Quarterly Report on the Euro Area. Vol. 3 No. 3, 2004. In: http://europe.eu.int.
European Commission 2004a: European Commission. European industry's place in the International Division of Labour: situation and prospects. Report by CEPII prepared for the Directorate-General for Trade of the European Commission, July 2004. In: http://europa.eu.int/comm/trade/.
European Commission 2004b: European Commission. Annex to the 22nd Annual Report From the Commission to the European Parliament on the Community's Anti-Dumping, Anti-Subsidy and Safeguard Activities. SEC(2004) 1707, COM (2004) 828 final. Brussels, 27.12.2004. In: http://trade.ec.europa.eu.
European Commission 2005: European Commission. Annex to the 23nd Annual Report From the Commission to the European Parliament on the Community's Anti-Dumping, Anti-Subsidy and Safeguard Activities. SEC(2005) 1038, COM (2005) 360 final. Brussels, 3.8.2005. In: http://trade.ec.europa.eu.
European Commission China Information 2006: European Commission. Bilateral Trade Relations China. In: http://europa.eu.int/comm/trade/issues/bilateral/countries/china/index_en.htm.
European Commission Electronic Sector 2006: European Commission. External Trade Information. Electronic Sector. 2006. In: http://europa.eu.int/comm/trade/issues/sectoral/industry/electro/index_en.htm.
European Commission Shipbuilding 2006: European Commission. External Trade Information. Shipbuilding. 2006. In: http://europa.eu.int/comm/trade/issues/sectoral/industry/shipbuilding/stats.htm#table1.
European Communities 1993: EC. New Location Factors for Mobile Investment in Europe. Brussels; Luxembourg: Office for Official Publications of the European Communities, 1993.
European Market Access Database div. Länder, div. Jahre: Informationen aus European Market Access Database. Div. Länderberichte und Zollinformationen. http://mkaccdb.eu.int.
Evaluation of EC TDI 2005: Mayer, Brown, Rowe & Maw LLP, Principal Author Stevenson Cliff. Evaluation of EC Trade Defence Instruments. Final Report, December 2005. In: http://trade.ec.europa.eu/.
Evans 1971: Evans, John W. The Kennedy Round in American Trade Policy. Cambridge: Harvard University Press, 1971.
Evans 1985: Evans, Peter B. Transnational Linkages and the Economic Role of the State: An Analysis of Developing and Industrialized Nations in the Post-World War II Period. In: Evans, Peter B. et al. (eds.). Bringing the State Back In. Cambridge: Cambridge University Press, 1985.
Evans 1989: Evans, David. Alternative Perspectives on Trade and Development. In: Chenery, H., Srinivasan, T.N. Handbook of Development Economics, Vol. II, Amsterdam; New York: Elsevier Science B.V., 1989.
Evans 1989a: Evans, H. David. Comparative Advantage and Growth. New York: St. Martin's Press, 1989.
Evans 1991: Evans, David. Visible and Invisible Hands in Trade Policy Reform. In: Christopher Colclough, James Manor (eds.). States or Markets? Neo-liberalism and the Development Policy Debate. Oxford. Clarendon Press, 1991.
Evans 1992: Evans, Peter B. Indian Informatics in the 1980s: The Changing Character of State Involvement. In: World Development, Vol. 20, No. 1, 1992. S. 1-18.

Evans 2000: Evans, Gail E. Lawmaking under the Trade Constitution. A Study in Legislating by the World Trade Organization. The Hague et al.: Kluwer Law International, 2000.
Evenett/Keller 1998: Evenett, Simon J., Keller, Wolfgang. On Theories Explaining the Success of the Gravity Equation. NBER Working Paper 6529, 1998.
Evenett/Primo Braga 2005: Evenett, Simon J., Primo Braga, Carlos A. WTO Accesssion: Lessons of Experience. World Bank Trade Note 22, June 6, 2005. In: http://www.worldbank.org.
Everling 1977: Everling, Ulrich. Vom Zweckverband zur Europäischen Union – Überlegungen zur Struktur der Europäischen Gemeinschaft. Gesammelte Aufsätze 1964-1984. Baden-Baden: Nomos, 1985.
Everling 1981: Everling, Ulrich. Das Europäische Gemeinschaftsrecht im Spannungfeld von Politik und Wirtschaft. Gesammelte Aufsätze 1964-1984. Baden-Baden: Nomos, 1985.
Everling 1987: Everling, Ulrich. Vertragsverhandlungen 1957 und Vertragspraxis 1987 – dargestellt an den Kapiteln Niederlassungsrecht und Dienstleistungen des EWG-Vertrags. In: FS Hans von der Groeben. Baden-Baden: Nomos, 1987.
EWG-Vertrag 1957: Die Verträge von Rom zur Gründung der Europäischen Wirtschaftsgemeinschaft (EW) und der Europäischen Atomgemeinschaft (EURATOM). Zusammengestellt von Regierungsdirektor Dr. H. von Meibom. Stuttgart: Forkel Verlag, 1957.
Ewing 1984: Ewing, A. F. Non-Tariff Barriers and Non-Adjustment or International Trade. In: JWTL, Vol. 18 No. 3, May June 1984. S. 63-80.

F

Faber 1984: Faber, Gerrit. The Economics of Stabex. In: JWT, Vol. 18 No. 1, Jan. Feb. 1984. S. 52-62.
Facchini/Willmann 1999: Facchini, Giovanni, Willmann, Gerald. Pareto Gains from Trade. Working Paper. In: http://willmann.bwl.uni-kiel.de.
Fafchamps/Minten 1998: Fafchamps, Marcel, Minten, Bart. Relationships and Traders in Madagascar. MSSD Discussion Paper No. 24, International Food Policy Institute Washington, July 1998. In: http://www.ifpri.org.
Faini et al. 1991: Faini, Riccardo, de Melo, Jaime, Senhadji, Abdelhak, Stanton, Julie. Growth-Oriented Adjustment Programs: A Statistical Analysis. In: World Development, Vol. 19, No. 8, 1991. S. 957-967.
Falke 1995: Falke, Andreas. Abkehr vom Multilateralimus? Der Kongress, die amerikanische Handelspolitik und das Welthandelssystem. Von der Reagan-Administration bis zum Abschluß der Uruguay-Runde. Habilitationsschrift Universität Göttingen, nicht verlegt, Dezember 1995.
Fanelli/Frenkel 1993: Fanelli, Jose Maria, Frenkel, Roberto. Argentina. In: Taylor, Lance (ed.). The Rocky Road to Reform. Adjustment, Income Distribution, and Growth in the Developing World. Cambridge: MIT Press, 1993.
FAO 1995: Food and Agriculture Organization of the United Nations. Dimensions of Need. An Atlas of Food and Agriculture. Rome: FAO, 1995.
FAO 1995a: FAO. Impact of the Uruguay Round on Agriculture. Rome: FAO, 1995. In: http://www.fao.org.
FAO 1996: FAO. Technical Background Documents 6-11. World Food Summit, 13-17 November 1996, Rome, Italy. FAO: Rome, 1996.
FAO 2000: FAO. Multilateral Trade Negotiations on Agriculture. A Resource Manual. FAO: Rome, 2000. In: http://www.fao.org.
FAO 2002: FAO. Agricultural Commodities: Profiles and Relevant WTO Negotiating Issues. FAO: Rome, 2002. In: http://www.fao.org.
FAO 2003: FAO. Review of Basic Food Policies. Rome: FAO, 2003. In: http://www.fao.org/es/esc/default.htm.
FAO 2003a: FAO. Synthesis of the Findings of 23 Country Case Studies. In: FAO (ed.). WTO Agreement on Agriculture: The Implementation Experience - Developing Country Case Studies. Rome: FAO, 2003. In: http://www.fao.org/trade/index_en.asp.
FAO 2003b: FAO. Trade Reform and Food Security. Conceptualizing the Linkages. FAO: Rome, 2003. In: http://www.fao.org/trade/index_en.asp.
FAO 2004: FAO. Impact of Import Surges: Country Case Study Results. Committee on Commodity Problems. Intergovernmental Group on Meat and Diary Products. Twentieth Session. CCP: ME 04/2. In: http://www.fao.org/unfao/bodies/ccp/me/04/default.htm.
FAO 2004a: FAO. Trade Policy Briefs. No. 1 Cotton. Rome: FAO, 2004. In: http://www.fao.org.
FAO 2004b: FAO. FAO Trade Backgrounder on issues related to the WTO negotiations on agriculture. No. 1 Cotton. Rome: FAO, 2004. In: http://ww.fao.org.
FAO 2004c: FAO (2004): The State of Agricultural Commodity Markets 2004. Rome: FAO, 2004. In: http://www.fao.org.
FAO div. Länder 2003a: FAO. WTO Agreement on Agriculture: The Implementation Experience - Developing Country Case Studies. Rome: FAO, 2003. In: http://www.fao.org/trade/index_en.asp.
FAO Exports: Commodities by Country, div. Länder, div. Jg.: FAO. The Statistics Division. Exports: Commodities by Country. Rome: FAO, div. Länder, div. Jg. In: http://www.fao.org/es/ess/toptrade/trade.asp.
FAO Food and Agriculture Indicators div. Countries, div. Jg.: FAO Food and Agriculture Indicators div. Countries, div. Jg. In: http://www.fao.org.
FAO State of Agricultural Commodity Markets, div. Jg.: Food and Agriculture Organization of the United Nations. State of Agricultural Commodity Markets. Rome: FAO, div. Jg. In: http://www.fao.org.
FAO State of Food and Agriculture, div. Jg.: Food and Agriculture Organization of the United Nations. The State of Food and Agriculture. Rome: FAO, div. Jg. In: http://www.fao.org.

FAO/WFP Crop and Food Supply Assessment Mission to div. Countries, div. Jg.: FAO. Special Report FAO/WFP Crop and Food Supply Assessment Mission to div. Countries, div. Jg. Rome: FAO, div. Jg. In: http://www.fao.org.

Farell 1997: Farell, Roger. Japanese Foreign Direct Investment in the World Economy 1951-1997. East Asian Bureau of Economic Research, Trade Working Papers No. 390. In: http://ideas.repec.org/p/eab/tradew/390.html.

Fassbender 1998: Fassbender, Bardo. The United Nations Charter As Constitution of the International Community. Columbia Journal of Transnational Law, 36, 1988. S. 529-619.

Fastenrath 1986: Fastenrath, Ulrich. Kompetenzverteilung im Bereich der auswärtigen Gewalt. München: C.H. Beck, 1986.

Fauchald 2003: Fauchald, Ole Kristian. Flexibility and Predictability Under the World Trade Organization's Non-Discrimination Clauses. In: JWT, Vol. 37, No. 3, 2003. S. 443-482.

Feder 1982: Feder, Gershon. On Exports and Economic Growth. In: Journal of Development Economics, Vol. 12, 1982. S. 59-73.

Feenstra 1984: Feenstra, Robert C. Voluntary Export Restraint in U.S. Autos, 1980-1981: Quality, Employment, and Welfare Effects. In: Baldwin, Robert E. Krueger, Anne O. The Structure and Evolution of Recent U.S. Trade Policy. Chicago; London: The University of Chicago Press, 1984.

Fehl/Schreiter 1997: Ordnungspolitischer Kurswechsel in der Wettbewerbspolitik. In: ORDO, Bd. 48, 1997.

Feinberg/Reynolds 2006: Feinberg, Robert M., Reynolds, Kara M. Friendly Fire? The Impact of US Antidumping Enforcement on US Exporters. American University, April 2006. In: http://darkwing.uoregon.edu/~bruceb/adpage.html.

Feinberg/Reynolds 2006a: Feinberg, Robert M., Reynolds, Kara M. The Spread of Antidumping Regimes and the Role of Retaliation in Findings, 2006. In: http://darkwing.uoregon.edu/~bruceb/adpage.html.

Feldmann 1993: Feldmann, Horst. Konzeption und Praxis der EG-Industriepolitik. In: Ordo, Bd. 44, 1993. S. 139-168.

Feldstein 1994: Feldstein, Martin. Taxes, Leverage and the National Return on Outbound Foreign Direct Investment. NBER Working Paper No. 4689, March 1994.

Feldstein 1995: Feldstein, Martin. In: Feldstein, Martin et al. (Hrsg.) The Effects of Taxation on Multinational Corporations. Chicago, London: University of Chicago Press, 1995.

Feldstein/Horioka 1980: Feldstein, Martin, Horioka, Charles. Domestic Saving and International Capital Flows. In: Economic Journal, Vol. 90, June 1980. S. 314-329.

Fels 1987: Fels, Joachim. Zur Privatisierung öffentlicher Unternehmen in Frankreich. In: Die Weltwirtschaft, Heft 1, 1987. S. 73-81.

Ferenschild/Wick 2004: Ferenschild, Sabine, Wick, Ingeborg. Globales Spiel um Kopf und Kragen. Südwind Texte 14. Siegburg/Neuwied: Südwind, 2004.

Fernandes 2003: Fernandes, Ana M. Trade Policy, Trade Volumes and Plant-Level Productivity in Colombian Manufacturing. World Bank Policy Research Working Paper No. 3064, April 2003. In: http://www.worldbank.org.

Ferrantino 1993: Ferrantino, Michael J. The Effect of Intellectual Property Rights on International Trade and Investment. In: Weltwirtschaftliches Archiv, Bd. 129, 1993. S. 300-331.

Ferrantino/Pineres 2000: Ferrantino, Michael J., Pineres, Sheila Amin Gutierrez de. Export Dynamics and Economic Growth in Latin America. A comparative perspective. Aldershot: Ashgate, 2000.

Ferraz et al. 1996: Ferraz, Joáo Carlos, Kupfer, David, Haguenauer, Lia. The competitive challenge for Brazilian industry. In: CEPAL Review 58, 1996, pp. 145- 174.

Ferreira et al. 1999: Ferreira, Francisco, Prennushi, Giovanna, Ravallion, Martin. Protecting the Poor from Macroeconomic Shocks: An Agenda for Action in a Crisis and Beyond. World Bank, Policy Research Working Paper, No. 2160, August 1999.

Feyzioglu/Willard 2006: Feyzioglu, Tarhan, Willard, Luke. Does Inflation in China Affect the United States and Japan? IMF Working Paper WP/06/36. Washington: IMF, 2996. In: http://www.imf.org.

Ffrench-Davis/Marfan 1988: Ffrench-Davis, Ricardo, Marfan, Manuel. Selective Policies under a Structural Foreign Exchange Shortage. In: Journal of Development Economics, Vol. 29, 1988. S. 347-369.

FIAN 1993: FIAN. Der subventionierte Unsinn. Das Dumping europäischer Rindfleischüberschüsse gefährdet die Viehaltung und Ernährungssituation in Westafrika. Herne: FIAN, 1993.

Fielding 1997: Fielding, David. Adjustment, trade policy and investment slumps: evidence from Africa. In: Journal of Development Economics, Vol. 52, 1997. S. 121-137.

Fikentscher/Heinemann 1994: Fikentscher, Wolfgang, Heinemann, Andreas. Der 'Draft International Antitrust Code' – Initiative für ein Weltkartellrecht im Rahmen des GATT. In: WuW 2/1994. S. 97-107.

Fikentscher/Immega 1995: Fikentscher, Wolfgang, Immaga, Ulrich. Draft International Antitrust Code. Baden-Baden: Nomos, 1995.

Findlay 1984: Findlay, Ronald. Growth and Development in Trade Models. In: Jones, R.W., Kenen, P. B. (eds.). Handbook of International Economics, Vol. I. Amsterdam: Elsevier Science, 1984.

Finger 1974: Finger, J. Michael. GATT Tariff Concessions and the Exports of Developing Countries – United States Concessions at the Dillon Round. In: Economic Journal, Vol. 84, II, September 1974, S. 566-575

Finger 1976: Finger, J. Michael. Effects of the Kennedy Round Tariff Concessions on the Exports of Developing Countries. In: Economic Journal, Vol. 86, March 1976, S. 87-95.

Finger 1981: Finger, J. M. The Industry-Country Incidence of 'Less than Fair Value' Cases in US Import Trade. In: Baer, Werner, Gillis, Malcolm (Hrg.). Export Diversification and the New Protectionism. The Experiences of

Latin America. NBER and the Bureau of Economic and Business Research University of Illinois: University of Illinois, 1981.

Finger 1991: Finger, J. Michael. The GATT as an International Discipline over Trade Restrictions: A Public Choice Approach. In: Vaubel, Roland, Willett, Thomas D. (eds.). The Political Economy of International Organizations. Boulder: Westview Press, 1991.

Finger 1992: Finger, J. Michael. Dumping and Antidumping: The Rhetoric and the Reality of Protection in Industrial Countries. In: World Bank Research Observer, Vol. 7, No. 2, July 1992. S. 121-143.

Finger 1993: Finger, J. Michael. Antidumping Is Where the Action Is. In: Finger, J. Michael. Antidumping. How It Works and Who Gets Hurt. Ann Arbor: University of Michigan Press, 1993.

Finger 1993a: Finger, J. Michael. Lessons from the Case Studies: Conclusion. In: Finger, J. Michael. Antidumping. How It Works and Who Gets Hurt. Ann Arbor: University of Michigan Press, 1993.

Finger 1998: Finger, J. Michael. GATT Experience with Safeguards: Making Economic and Political Sense of the Possibilities That the GATT Allows to Restrict Imports. World Bank, Policy Research Working Paper, No. 2000, October 1998. In: http://www.worldbank.org.

Finger 2002: Finger, J. Michael. The Doha Agenda and Development: A View from the Uruguay Round. Asien Development Bank, Economics Reserach Department Working Paper No. 21., September 2002. In: www.adb.org/Documents/ERD/Working_Papers/wp021.pdf.

Finger 2005: Finger, J. Michael. The Future of the World Trade Organization: Adressing Institutional Challenges in the New Millenium. Report by the Consultative Board to the Director General Supachai Panitchpakdi. A review. In: Journal of Wolrd Trade, Vol. 39 No. 4, 2005. S. 795-804.

Finger et al. 1982: Finger, J. Michael, Hall, H. Keith, Nelson, Douglas R. The Political Economy of Administered Protection. In: American Economic Review, Vol. 72 No. 3, June 1982. S. 452-466.

Finger et al. 1996: Finger, J. Michael. The Uruguay Round. Statistics on Tariff Concessions Given and Received. Washington: World Bank, 1996.

Finger et al. 1999: Finger, J. Michael, Reinecke, Ulrich, Castro, Adriana. Market Access Bargaining in the Uruguay Round: Rigid of Relaxed Reciprocity? World Bank, Policy Research Working Paper, No. 2258, December 1999. In: http://www.worldbank.org.

Finger et al. 2001: Finger, J. Michael, Ng, Francis, Wangchuk, Sonam, Antidumping as Safeguard Policy. World Bank Policy Research Working Paper No. 2730, December 2001. In: http://www.worldbank.org.

Finger/Fung 1994: Finger, J. Michael, Fung, K. C. Can Competition Policy Control '301'? In: Aussenwirtschaft, 49 Jg., Heft 2/3, 1994. S. 379-416.

Finger/Harrison 1994: Finger, J. Michael, Harrison, Ann. The MFA Paradox: More Protection and More Trade? NBER Working Paper No. 4751, May 1994.

Finger/Laird 1987: Finger, J. Michael. Protection in Developed and Developing Countries – An Overview. In: Journal of World Trade, Vol. 21, No. 6, 1987, S. 9-23.

Finger/Murray 1990: Finger, J. Michael, Murray, Tracy. Policing Unfair Imports: The United States Example. In: JWF, Vol. 24 No. 4, 1990. S. 39-53.

Finger/Olechowski 1987: Finger, J. Michael, Olechowski, Andrzej. Trade Barrieres: Who does what to whom? In: Giersch, Herbert (ed.). Free Trade in the World Economy. Towards the Opening of Markets. Tübingen: Mohr, 1987.

Finger/Olechowski 1987a: Finger, J. Michael, Olechowski, Andrzeij. The Uruguay Round. A Handbook on the Multilateral Trade Negotiations. Washington, D. C.: The World Bank, 1987.

Finger/Schuknecht 1999: Finger, J. Michael, Schuknecht, Ludger. Market Access Advances and Retreats Since the Uruguay Round Agreement. Paper, Annual World Bank Conference on Development Economics, Washington, 29-30 April 1999. In: http://www.worldbank.org.

Finger/Schuler 1999: Finger, J. Michael, Schuler, Philip. Implementation of Uruguay Round Commitments: The Development Challenge. World Bank, Policy Research Working Paper No. 2215, 1999. In: http://www.worldbank.org.

Finger/Yeats 1976: Finger, J. Michael, Yeats, A. J. Effective Protection by Transportation Costs and Tariffs: A Comparison of Magnitudes. In: Quarterly Journal of Economics, Vol. XC, No. 1, Feb. 1976. S. 169-176.

Fink 1989: Fink, Stefan. Ein Vergleich der Stahlindustrien der Europäischen Gemeinschaften, Japans und der Vereinigten Staaten von Amerika mit Hilfe von Wachstums-Betrachtungen. Dissertation, Aachen, 12. Januar 1989.

Finlayson/Zacher 1981: Finlayson, Jock A., Zacher, Mark W. The GATT and the regulation of trade barriers: regime dynamics and functions. In: International Organization, 35, 4, Autumn 1981.

Firmin-Sellers 1995: Firmin-Sellers, Kathryn. The Politics of Property Rights. In: American Political Science Review, Vol. 89, No. 4, December 1995. S. 867-881.

Fischer 1999: Fischer, Stanley. On the Need for an International Lender of Last Resort. Paper prepared for the American Economic Association and the American Finance Association, New York, January 3, 1999. http://www.imf.org/external/np/speeches/

Fischer et al. 1997: Fischer, Stanley, Sahay, Ratna, Végh, Carlos. How Far is Eastern Europe from Brussels? In: Siebert, Horst (ed.). Quo Vadis Europe? Tübingen: Mohr, 1997.

Fischer/Nunnenkamp et al. 1988: Fischer, Bernhard. Nunnenkamp, Peter et al. Capital-Intensive Industries in Newly Industrializing Countries. The Case of the Brazilian Automobile and Steel Industries. Kieler Studien 221. Tübingen: Mohr, 1988.

Fischer/Prusa 1999: Fischer, Ronald D., Prusa, Thomas J. Contingent Protection as Better Insurance. NBER Working Paper No. 6933, February 1999.
Flam 1996: Flam, Kenneth. Mismanaged Trade? Strategic Policy and the Semiconductor Industry. Washington: Brookings Institution, 1996.
Flam/Helpman 1987: Flam, Harry, Helpman, Elhanan. Vertical Product Differenciation and North-South Trade. In: The American Economic Review, Vol. 77, No. 5, December 1987. S. 810-822.
Foders 2001: Foders, Frederico. Die ökonomische und wirtschaftspolitische Entwicklung Lateinamerikas nach dem Zweiten Weltkrieg. Kieler Arbeitspapier Nr. 1066, Kiel: Institut für Weltwirtschaft, August 2001.
Fogel/Engerman 1969: Fogel, Robert W., Engerman, Stanley L. A Model for the Explanation of Industrial Expansion during the Nineteenth Century: With an Application to the American Iron Industry. In: Journal of Political Economy, Vol. 77, 1969. S. 309-328.
Fontagné et al. 1998: Fontagné, Lionel, Freudenberg, Michael, Péridy, Nicolas. Intra-industry Trade and the Single Market. CEPR (Centre of Economic Policy Research) Discussion Paper No. 1959, September 1998.
Footer 1997: Footer, Mary E. The Role of Consensus in GATT/WTO Decision-making. In: Northwestern Journal of International Law and Business, Vol. 17, Jg. 1996-1997. S. 653-680.
Footer 1997a: Footer, Mary E. Some Aspects of Third Party Intervention in GATT/WTO Dispute Settlement Proceedings. In: Petersmann, Ernst-Ulrich (ed.). International Trade Law and the GATT/WTO Dispute Settlement System. London, The Hague, Boston: Kluwer Law, 1997.
Footer 2001: Footer, Mary E. Developing Country Practice in the Matter of WTO Dispute Settlement. In: JWT, Vol. 35, No. 1, 2001. S. 55-98.
Foroutan 1998: Foroutan, Faezeh. Does Membership in A Regional Preference Agreement Make a Country More or Less Protectionist? World Bank, Policy Research Working Paper, No. 1898, April 1998. In: http://www.worldbank.org.
Fors 1993: Fors, Gunnar. Stainless Steel in Sweden: Antidumping Attacks Responsible International Citizenship. In: Finger, J. Michael. Antidumping. How It Works and Who Gets Hurt. Ann Arbor: University of Michigan Press, 1993.
Forster 1998: Forster, Anthony. Britain and the Negotiation of the Maastricht Treaty: A Critique of Liberal Intergovernmentalism. In: Journal of Common Market Studies, Vol. 36, No. 3, September 1998. S. 347-368.
Foster/Davidow 1996: Foster, F. David, Davidow, Joel. GATT and Reform of U.S. Section 337. In: International Lawyer, Vol. 30, No. 1, 1996. S. 97-110.
Fosu 2001: Fosu, Augustin Kwasi. A Panoramic View of Policies for Competitiveness in Manufacturing in Sub-Saharan Africa. In: OECD. Policies to Promote Competitiveness in Manufacturing in Sub-Saharan Africa. Development Centre Seminars within the IMF and the AERC. Kwasi Fosu, Augustin, Nsouli, Saleh M., Varoudakis, Aristomene (eds.). Paris: OECD, 2001a.
Fouquin et al. 1995: Fouquin, Michel, Chevallier, Agnes, Pisani-Ferry, Jean. The 'New' International Competition: Effects on Employment. In: Simai, Mihaly (ed.). Global Employment. An International Investigation into the Future of Work. Vol. 1. London: Zed Books for United Nations University/WIDER, 1995.
Fox 2000: Fox, Eleanor M. Equality, Discrimination, and Competition Law: Lessons from and for South Africa and Indonesia. In: Harvard International Law Journal, Vol. 41, Nr. 2, Spring 2000. S. 579-594.
Fox 2006: Fox, Eleanor M. The WTO's First Antitrust Case - Mexican Telecom: A Sleeping Victory for Trade and Competition. In: Journal of International Economic Law No. 9, No. 2, 2006. s. 271-292.
Franck 1911: Franck, Georg. Niederländisch-Indien. Eine Finanzquelle für das Mutterland. Stuttgart: Druck der Union deutsche Verlagsanstalt, 1911.
Franck 1988: Franck, Thomas M. Legitimacy in the International System. In: American Journal of International Law, Vol. 82, 1988. S. 705-759.
Franck 1994: Franck, Thomas M. Fairness in the International Legal and Institutional System. General Course on Public International Law. In: Recueil des Cours; Collected Courses of The Hague Academy of International Law, (1993, IV), 1994.
Francois et al. 2000: Francois, Joseph F., Bradley, McDonald, Nordström, Hakan. Assessing the Uruguay Round. In: Martin, Will, Winters, L. Alan. The Uruguay Round and the Developing Countries. World Bank Discussion Paptters 307, Washington: World Bank, 1995.
Francois et al. 2000: Francois, Joseph F., Glismann, Hans H., Spinager, Dean. The German Economy and EU Industrial Tariff Reductions: Partial and CGE Analyses of a Stillborn Millenium Round. Kiel Working Paper No. 999, September 2000.
Francois et al. 2000a: Francois, Joseph F., Glismann, Hans H., Spinager, Dean. The Cost of EU Trade Protection in Textiles and Clothing. Kieler Arbeitspapiere Nr. 997, August 2000.
Francois et al. 2006: Francois, Joseph, Martin, Will, Manole, Vlad. Formula Approaches to Liberalizing Trade in Goods: Efficiency and Market Access Considerations. In: Evenett, Simon J., Hoekman, Bernard M. Economic Development and Multilateral Trade Cooperation. Washington: World Bank/Palgrave Macmillan, 2006.
Frank et al. 1975: Frank, Charles R., Kim Kwang Suk, Westphal, Larry E. South Korea. National Bureau of Economic Research, Special Conference Series, Vol. VII. New York; London: Columbia University Press, 1975.
Frankel 2001: Frankel, Jeffrey A. Assessing the Efficiency Gains from Further Liberalization. In: Porter, Roger B., Sauvé, Pierre, Subramanian, Arvind, Zampetti, Americo Beviglia. Efficiency, Equity, Legitimacy. The Multilateral Trading System at the Millenium. Washington D.C.: Brookings Institution Press, 2001.
Frankel/Romer 1999: Frankel, Jeffrey A., Romer, David. Does Trade Cause Growth?. In: The American Economic Review, Vol. 89, No. 3, June 1999, S. 377-399.

Fransman 1984: Fransman, Martin. Technological Capability in the Third World: An Overview and Introduction to some of the Issues Raised in this Book. In: Fransman, Martin, King, Kenneth (eds.). Technology Capability in the Thirld World. London: Macmillan, 1984.
Franzmeyer et al. 1987a: Franzmeyer, Frith, Schultz, Siegfried, Seidel, Bernhard, Svindland, Eirik, Volz, Joachim. Industriepolitik im westlichen Ausland – Rahmenbedingungen, Strategien, Außenhandelsaspekte. Bd. I: Allgemeiner Teil. DIW Beiträge zur Strukturforschung, Heft 92/I. Berlin: Duncker & Humblot, 1987.
Franzmeyer et al. 1987a: Franzmeyer, Frith, Schultz, Siegfried, Seidel, Bernhard, Svindland, Eirik, Volz, Joachim. Industriepolitik im westlichen Ausland – Rahmenbedingungen, Strategien, Außenhandelsaspekte. Bd. II: Länderberichte. DIW Beiträge zur Strukturforschung, Heft 92/I. Berlin: Duncker & Humblot, 1987.
Franzmeyer et al. 1991: Franzmeyer, Fritz, Hrubesch, Peter, Seidel, Bernhard, Weise, Christian, Schweiger, Inge. Die regionalen Auswirkungen der Gemeinschaftspolitiken. Reihe Regionalpolitik und Verkehr 17. Europäisches Parlament, Generaldirektion Wissenschaft. Luxemburg. Amt für amtliche Veröffentlichungen der Europäischen Gemeinschaften, 1991.
Freeman/Hagedoorn 1992: Freeman, Chris, Hagedoorn, John. Globalization of Technology. Working paper, MERIT 92-013, Maastricht, 1992.
Freeman/Hagedoorn 1994: Freeman, Chris, Hagedoorn, John. Catching Up or Falling Behind: Patterns in International Interfirm Technology Partnering. In: World Development, Vol. 22, No. 5, 1994. S. 771-780.
French 1993: French, Richard. Produktdifferenzierung und Arbeitsteilung. Heidelberg: Physica-Verlag, 1993.
Frenkel/Menkhoff 2000: Frenkel, Michael, Menkhoff, Lukas. Stabile Weltfinanzen. Die Debatte um die neue Finanzarchitektur. Berlin: Springer, 2000.
Frey 1984: Frey, Bruno S. The Public Choice View of International Political Economy. Original 1984. In: Vaubel, Roland, Willett, Thomas D. (eds.). The Political Economy of International Organizations. Boulder: Westview Press, 1991.
Frey/Buhofer 1986: Frey, Bruno S., Buhofer, Heinz. Integration and Protectionism: A Comparative Institutional Analysis. In: Aussenwirtschaft, 41. Jg, Heft 2/3, 1986. S. 329-350.
Friedrichs 1997: Friedirchs, Jürgen. Globalisierung – Begriff und grundlegende Annahmen. In: Aus Politik und Zeitgeschichte. B 33-34/97, 8. August 1997.
Frischtak 1994: Frischtak, Claudio R. Learning and technical progress in the commuter aircraft industry: an analysis of Embraer's experience. In: Research Policy No. 23, 1994. S. 601-612.
Frischtak 1997: Frischtak, Claudio R. Latin America. In: Dunning, John H. (ed.). Governments, Gobalization and International Business. Oxford: Oxford University Press, 1997.
Frischtak et al. 1989: Frischtak, Claudio R., Hadjimichael, Bita, Zachau, Ulrich. Competition Policies for Industrializing Economies. Washington: World Bank, 1989.
Fritsch et al. 1993: Fritsch, Michael, Wein, Thomas, Ewers, Hans-Jürgen. Marktversagen und Wirtschaftspolitik. München: Verlag Franz Vahlen, 1993.
Fritsch/Franco 1992: Fritsch, Winston, Franco, Gustavo H. B. Foreign Direct Investment and Patterns of Industrialization and Trade in Developing Countries: The Brazilian Experience. In: Helleiner, Gerald K. (ed.). Trade Policy, Industrialization and Development. Study prepared for WIDER. Oxford: Clarendon Press, 1992.
Fritsch/Franco 1994: Fritsch, Winston, Franco, Gustavo H. B. Import compression, productivity slowdown and manufactured export dynamism, Brazil, 1975-90. In: Helleiner, Gerald K. (ed.). Trade Policy and Industrialization in Turbulent Times. London; New York: Routledge, 1994.
Fritz 2000: Fritz, Thomas. Market Access Problems for Developing Countries in the Agricultural Sector. Bonn: Forum Umwelt und Entwicklung, 2000.
Fröbel et al. 1977: Fröbel, Folker, Heinrichs, Jürgen, Kreye, Otto. Die neue internationale Arbeitsteilung. Reinbeck: Rowohlt, 1977.
Frost/Günter 2002: Frost, M., Günter, D. Die Bedeutung des SPS-Abkommens für ein Agrar-Exportland - Das Beispiel Thailand. In: Brockmeier, M., Isermeyer, F., von Cramon-Taubadel, S. (Hrg.). Liberalisierung des Weltagrarhandels - Strategien und Konsequenzen. Münster-Hiltrup: Landwirtschaftsverlag, 2002.
Frowein 1995: Frowein, J. A. Die Verfassung der Europäischen Union aus der Sicht der Mitgliedsstaaten. In: Europarecht. 30. Jg. Heft 4, 1995.
Frowein 1998: Frowein, J. A. Die Europäische Union im Zeichen der Globalisierung: Einbindung und Status der Europäische Union im Verfassungssystem der Staatengemeinschaft. In: http://www.rewi.hu-berlin.de/WHI/tagung98/frowein/frowein.htm.
Frowein 2000: Frowein, J. A. Konstitutionalisierung des Völkerrechts. In: Dicke, Klaus et al. Völkerrecht und Internationales Privatrecht in einem sich globalisierenden internationalen System - Auswirkungen der Entstaatlichung transnationaler Rechtsbeziehungen. Heidelberg: C.F. Müller, 2000.
FTC 2003: Federal Trade Commission To Promote Innovation: The Proper Balance of Competition and Patent Law and Policy. A Report by the Federal Trade Commission, October 2003. In: http://www.ftc.gov.
Fujita 1994: Fujita, Natsuki. Liberalization Policies and Productivity in India. In: The Developing Economies, XXXII, No. 4, December 1994. S. 509-524.
Fukunaga 2004: Fukunaga, Yuka. An 'Effect-Based' Approach to Anti-Dumping: Why Should We Introduce a 'Mandatory Lesser Duty Rule'? In: JWT, Vol. 38, No. 3, 2004. S. 491-507.

G

Gabre-Madhin et al. 2001: Gabre-Madhin, Eleni, Fafchamps, Marcel, Kachule, Richard, Soule, Bio Goura, Kahn, Zahia. Impact of Agricultural Market Reforms on Smallholder Farms in Benin and Malawi. Vol. 2. IFPRI Collaborative Research Project, February 2001. In: http://www.ifpri.org.
Gabre-Madhin et al. 2003: Gabre-Madhin, Eleni, Barret, C.B., Dorosh, P. Technological Change and Price Effects in Agriculture: Conceptual and Comparative Perspectives. MTID Discussion Paper No. 62, April 2003. In: http://www.ifpri.org.
Gabrisch 1995: Gabrisch, Hubert. Die Entwicklung der Handelsstrukturen der Transformationsländer. In: Osteuropa-Wirtschaft, 40 Jg., Heft 3, 1995. S. 211-227.
GAFTT 2005: Global Alliance for Fair Textile Trade (GAFTT). Global Alliance Presses Governments and WTO to Halt Chinese Monopolization of Global Trade in Textiles and Clothing. January 26, 2005. In: http://www.fairtextiletrade.org.
Gagne 2003: Gagne, Gilbert. The Canada-US Softwood Lumber Dispute. In: International Journal, Vol. 58, No. 3, Summer 2003. S. 335-368.
Gagne 2007: Gagne, Gilbert. Policy Diversity, State Autonomy, and the US-Canada Softwood Lumber Dispute: Philosophical and Normative Aspects. In: JWT, Vol. 41, No. 4, 2007. S. 699-730.
Gahlen et al. 1997: Gahlen, Bernhard, Hesse, Helmut, Ramser, Hans Jürgen. Finanzmärkte. Tübingen: Mohr, 1997.
Gan/Juan 1998: Gan, Vincente José Montes, Juan, Amadeo Petibò. The privatization of state enterprises in the Spanish economy. In: Parker, David (ed.). Privatization in the European Union. Theory and Policy Perspectives. London; New York: Routledge, 1998.
Ganesh-Kumar/Vaidya 1999: Ganesh-Kumar, A., Vaidya, Rajendra R. Where do India's Exports Face the Greatest Obstacles. World Bank, WTO Background Paper, December 1999. In: http://www.worldbank.org/research/trade.
Ganguli 2005: Ganguli, Bodhisattva. The Trade Effects of Indian Antidumping Actions. Rutgers University Working Paper, October 16, 2005. In: http://econweb.rutgers.edu/ganuli/Paper_AB.pdf.
Ganguly 1999: Ganguly, Samrat. The Investor-State Dispute Settlement Mechanism (ISDM) and a Sovereign's Power to Protect Public Health. In: Columbia Journal of Transnational Law, Vol. 38, 1999. S. 113-168.
Ganuza/Taylor 1998: Ganuza, Enrique, Taylor, Lance. Macroeconomic Policy, Poverty, and Equality in Latin America and the Carribbean. Centre for Economic Policy Analysis. New York. In: http://www.newschool.edu/cepa
GAO 2003: General Accounting Office. Report to the Ranking Minority Menber, Committee on Finance, U.S. Senate. World Trade Organization. Standard of Review and Impact of Trade Remedy Rulings. GAO-03-824, July 2003. In: http://www.gao.gov
GAO 2005: Government Accountability Office. Report to Congressional Requesters. International Trade. Issues and Effects of Implementing the Continued Dumping and Subsidy Offset Act. GAO-05-979, September 2005. In: http://www.gao.gov.
Garcia-Castrillón 2001: Garcia-Castrillón, Carmen Otero. Private Parties under the Present WTO (Bilaterist) Competition Regime. In: JWT, Vol. 35, No. 1, 2001. S. 99-122.
Gardner 1956: Gardner, Richard N. Sterling-Dollar Diplomacy. Oxford: Clarendon Press, 1956.
Gasiorowski 1985: Gasiorowski, Mark J. The structure of Thirld World economic interdependence. In: IO, Vol. 39 No. 2, Spring 1985. S. 331-342.
Gass et al. 1990: Gass, Liselotte, Neundörfer, Konrad, Stahr, Ernst-Heinrich. Vorwärtsstrategie für den Welttextilhandel. Schriften zur Textilpolitik Heft 8, Frankfurt am Main: Gesamttextil, 1990.
GATT 1963: GATT Programme for Expansion of International Trade. Trade in Tropical Products. Geneva: GATT, 1963.
GATT 1964: GATT. The Role of GATT in Relation to Trade and Development. Geneva: GATT, 1964.
GATT 1979: General Agreement on Tariffs and Trade. The Tokyo Round of Multilateral Trade Negotiations, Report by the Director General of GATT. Geneva: GATT, April 1979.
GATT 1980: General Agreement on Tariffs and Trade. The Tokyo Round of Multilateral Trade Negotiations, Supplementary Report by the Director General of GATT. Geneva: GATT, January 1980.
GATT Analytical Index 1995: WTO. Guide to GATT Law and Practice. Analytical Index. Updated 6th Edition. Geneva: World Trade Organization, 1995.
Gehl Sampath 2005: Gehl Sampath, Padmashree. Economic Aspects of Access to Medicines After 2005: Product Patent Protection and Emerging Firm Strategies in the Indian Industry, A Study for the World Health Organization Commission on Intellectual Property, Innovation and Health (CIPIH). United Nations University/MERIT, 2005. In: http://www.merit.unu.edu/publications/pub_search.php.
Gehring/Kerler 2007: Gehring, Thomas, Kerler, Michael A. Neue Entscheidungsverfahren in der Weltbank. In: Zeitschrift für Internationale Beziehungen, Vol. 14 No. 2, 2007. S. 217-251.
Geiger 1995: Geiger, Rudolf. EG-Vertrag. Kommentar zu dem Vertrag zur Gründung der Europäischen Gemeinschaften. München: C.H. Beck, 1995.
Geiger 2000: Geiger, Rudolf. EUV/EGV. Vertrag über die Europäische Union und Vertrag zur Gründung der Europäischen Gemeinschaft. 3. Aufl. München: C.H. Beck, 2000.
Geithmann et al. 1981: Geithmann, Frederick E., Marvel, Howard P., Weiss, Leonard W. Concentration, Price, and Critical Concentration Ratios. In: Review of Economics and Statistics, Vol. 63, 1981. S. 346-353.

Geloso Grosso 2002: Geloso Grosso, Massimo. Analysis of Non-Tariff Measures: The Case of Non-Automatic Licensing. TD/TC/WP(2002)39/Final. Working Party of the Trade Committee. Paris: OECD, 2004. In: http://www.oecd.org.
Genschel 1998: Genschel, Phillip. Markt und Staat in Europa. In: MPIfG (Max Planck Institut für Gesellschaftsforschung Köln), Working Paper 98/1, January 1998. In: http://www.mpi-fg-koeln.mpg.de.
George 1988: George, P.S. Costs and Benefits of Food Subsidies in India. In: Pinstrup-Andersen, Per (ed.) Food Subsidies in Developing Countries. Baltimore, London: John Hopkins University Press, 1988.
Gereffi 1990: Gereffi, Gary. Paths of Industrialization: An Overview. In: Gereffi, Gary, Wyman, Donald L. Manufacturing Miracles. Paths of Industrialization in Latin America and East Asia. Princeton: Princeton University Press, 1990.
Gereffi 1994: Gereffi, Gary. The Organization of Buyer-Driven Global Commodity Chains: How U.S. Retailers Shape Overseas Production Networks. In: Gereffi, Gary, Korzeniewicz, Miguel (eds.). Commodity Chains and Global Capitalism. Westport, Connecticut; London: Praeger 1994.
Gereffi et al. 1994: Gereffi, Gary, Korzeniewicz, Miguel, Korzeniewics, Roberto P. Introduction: Global Commodity Chains. In: Gereffi, Gary, Korzeniewicz, Miguel (eds.). Commodity Chains and Global Capitalism. Westport, Connecticut; London: Praeger 1994.
Gerken 1997: Gerken, Alfred. Die Außenhandelspolitik der Europäischen Union bei landwirtschaftlichen Verarbeitungsprodukten. Kiel: Wissenschaftsverlag Vauk Kiel KG, 1997.
Gerken 1999: Gerken, Lüder. Der Wettbewerb der Staaten. Walter Eucken Institut, Beiträge 1962. Tübingen: Mohr Siebek, 1999.
Gerken 1999a: Gerken, Lüder. Von Freiheit und Freihandel: Grundzüge einer ordoliberalen Außenwirtschaftstheorie. Tübingen: Mohr Siebek, 1999.
Gerken/Renner 2000: Gerken, Lüder, Renner, Andreas. Die ordnungspolitische Konzeption Walter Euckens. In: Gerken, Lüder (Hrg.). Walter Eucken und sein Werk. Rückblick auf den Vordenker der sozialen Marktwirtschaft. Tübingen: Mohr Siebek, 2000.
German 1999: German, Christiano. Der Weg Brasiliens in das Informationszeitalter. St. Augstin: Konrad-Adenauer Stiftung, 1999.
Gerosik et al. 1993: Geroski, Paul, Machin, Steve, Van Reenen, John. The Profitability of Innovating Firms. In: The Rand Journal of Economics, Vol. 24 No. 2, Summer 1993. S. 198-211.
Geroski 1989: Geroski, Paul A. Entry, Innovation and Productivity Growth. In: Review of Economics and Statistics, Vol. 71, 1989. S. 572-578.
Geroski et al. 1996: Geroski, Paul, Gregg, Paul, van Reenen, John. Market imperfections and employment. OECD Economic Studies No. 26 No. I. Paris: OECD, 1996. In: http://www.oecd.org.
Geroski/Cubbin 1987: Geroski, P., Cubbin, J. The Convergence of Profits in the Long Run: Inter-Firm and Inter-Industry Comparisons. In: Journal of Industrial Economics, Vol. XXXV, No. 4, June 1987. pp. 427-442.
Geroski/Jaquemin 1985: Geroski, Paul A., Jacquemin, Alexis. Industrial Change, barriers to mobility, and European industrial policy. In: Audretsch, David (ed.). Industrial Policy and Competitive Advantage, Vol. I. Cheltenham, UK, Northampton, MA: Elgar, 1998.
Geroski/Jaquemin 1988: Geroski, P., Jaquemin, Alexis. The Persistance of Profits: A European Perspective. In: Economic Journal, Vol. 98, June 1988. pp. 375-389.
Gerschenkron 1962: Gerschenkron, Alexander. Economic Backwardness in Historical Perspective. Cambridge, Mass.: Harvard University Press, 1962.
Gerster 1982: Gerster, Richard. Fallstricke der Verschuldung. Der Internationale Währungsfond und die Entwicklungsländer. Basel: Z-Verlag, 1982.
Gerster 1997: Gerster, Richard. Official Export Credits and Development. In: JWT, Vol. 31 No. 6, Dec. 1997. S. 123135.
Gervais 1998: Gervais, Daniel. The TRIPS Agreement: Drafting History and Analysis. London: Sweet & Maxwell, 1998.
Geue 1997: Geue, Heiko. Evolutionäre Institutionenökonomik. Stuttgart: Lucius & Lucius, 1997.
Geue/Weber 1998: Geue, Heiko, Weber, Ralf L. Arbeitsmarktverfassung und Tarifpolitik: Arbeitsmarktbeziehungen zwischen wirtschafts- und tarifpolitischer Regulierung. In: Cassel, Dieter (Hrg.). 50 Jahre Soziale Marktwirtschaft. Schriften zu Ordnungfragen der Wirtschaft, Band 57, Stuttgart, Lucius&Lucius: 1998.
Ghee/Woon 1994: Ghee, Lim Teck, Woon, Toh Kin. Industrial Restructuring and Performance in Malaysia. In: Helleiner, Gerald K. (ed.). Trade Policy and Industrialization in Turbulent Times. London; New York: Routledge, 1994.
Ghonheim 2003: Ghonheim, Ahmed Farouk. Rules of Origin and Trade Diversion: The Case of the Egyptian-European Partnership Agreement. In: JWT, Vol. 37, No. 3, 2003. S. 597-622.
Gibbs et al. 2003: Gibbs, Ryan, Gokcekus, Omer, Tower, Edward. Is Talk Cheap? Buying Congressional Testimony with Campaign Contributions. Duke University Working Paper, The Journal of Policy Reform, Vol. 5, Issue 3, 2002. S. 127-132. In: www.econ.duke.edu/Papers/Other/Tower/Talk_Cheap.pdf.
Giersch 1987: Giersch, Herbert (ed.). Free Trade in the World Economy. Towards the Opening of Markets. Tübingen: Mohr, 1987.
Gilbert 1995: Gilber, Christopher L. International Commodity Control – Retrospect and Prospect. World Bank Policy Research Working Paper No. 1545. In: http://www.worldbank.org.

Gilbert/Tom 2001: Gilbert, Richard J., Tom, Willard K. Is Innovation King at the Antitrust Agencies? The Intellectual Property Guidelines Five Years Later. In: Antitrust Law Journal, Vol. 69, 2001. S. 43-85.
Gill/Law 1988: Gill, Stephen, Law, David. The Global Political Economy. Perspectives, Problems, and Policies. New York; London: Harvester Wheatsheaf, 1988.
Gillis et al. 1996: Gillis, Malcolm, Perkins, Dwight H., Roemer, Michael, Snodgrass, Donald R. Economics of Development. Fourth Edition. New York, London: Norton, 1996.
Gilpin 1984: Gilpin, Robert G. The richness of the tradition of political realism. In: International Organization, 38, 2, Spring 1984, S. 287-304.
Gilpin 1987: Gilpin, Robert G. The political economy of international relations. Princeton: Princeton University Press, 1987.
Gilpin 2001: Gilpin, Robert. Global Political Economy. Princeton; Oxford: Princeton University Press, 2001.
Gitter/Köhler-Fleischmann 1997: Gitter, Wolfgang, Köhler-Fleischmann, Gabriele. Sozialordnung und Rechtsprechung. In: ORDO, Bd. 48, 1997.
Gleske 1987: Gleske, Leonhard. Liberalsierung des Kapitalverkehrs und Intergration der Finanzmärkte. In: FS Hans von der Groeben. Baden-Baden: Nomos, 1987.
Glismann 1996: Glismann, Hans H. Wirtschaftliche Auswirkungen mengenmäßiger Beschränkungen. Kieler Studien 279. Tübingen; Mohr, 1996.
Glismann/Horn 1988: Glismann, Hans H., Horn, Ernst-Jürgen. Zu den Produktivitätseffekten der Rüstungsausgaben in den Vereinigten Staaten. In: Die Weltwirtschaft, Heft 2, 1988. S. 146-160.
Glismann/Horn 1997: Glismann, Hans H., Horn, Ernst-Jürgen. Alterssicherung in Deutschland: Primat des Interventionismus? In: ORDO, Bd. 48, 1997.
Goco 2006: Goco, Jonell B. Non-Discrimination, 'Likeness', and Market Definition in World Trade Organization Jurisprudence. In: JWT, Vol. 40, No. 2, 2006. S. 315-340.
Global Steel Trade 2000: Global Steel Trade. Report to the President. International Trade Administration, U.S. Department of Commerce, July 2000. In: http://www.ita.doc.gov/media/steelreport726.htm.
Goddard/Wilson 1996: Goddard, J.A., Wilson, J.O.S. Persistance of Profits for UK Manufacturing and Service Sector Firms. In: The Service Industry Journal, Vol. 16, No. 2, April 1996. S. 105-117.
Goh/Ziegler 1998: Goh, Gavin, Ziegler, Andreas R. A Real World Where People Live and Work and Die. Australian SPS Measures After the WTO Appellate Body's Decision in the Hormones Case. In: JWT, Vol. 32, No. 5, 1998. S. 271-290.
Goh 2006: Goh, Gavin. Tipping the Apple Cart: The Limits of Science and Law in the SPS Agreement after Japan - Apples. In: JWT, Vol. 40, No. 4, 2006. S. 655-686.
Golan et al. 1996: Golan, Amos, Judge, George, Perloff, Jeffrey M. Estimating the Size Distribuation of Firms Using Government Summary Statistics. In: Journal of Industrial Economics, Vol. XLIV, No. 1, March 1996. S. 69-80.
Gold 1981: Gold, Bela. Changing Perspectives on Size, Scale, and Returns: An Interpretive Survey. In: Journal of Economic Literature, Vol. 19, March 1981. S. 5-33.
Goldar et al. 2004: Goldar, Arvind Virmani Bishwanath, Veeramani, Choorikkad, Bhatt, Vipul. Impact of Tariff Reforms on Indian Industry: Assessment Based on a Multi-Sector Econometric Model. Indian Council for Research on International Economic Relations, Working Paper 135, June 2004. In: http://www.icrier.res.in/.
Goldbach et al. 1997: Goldbach, Klara, Vogelsang-Wenke, Heike, Zimmer, Franz-Josef. Protection of Biotechnological Matter under European and German Law. Weinheim; New York et al.: VCH-Verlag, 1997.
Goldin et al. 1993: Goldin, Ian, Knudsen, Odin, van der Mensbrugge, Dominique. Trade Liberalization: Global Economic Implications. Paris: OECD, 1993; Washington: World Bank, 1993.
Goldin/Mensbrugghe 1995: Goldin, Ian, van der Mensbrugghe, Dominique. The Uruguay Round: An Assessment of Economywide and Agricultural Reforms. In: Martin, Will, Winters, L. Alan. The Uruguay Round and the Developing Countries. World Bank Discussion Papters 307, Washington: World Bank, 1995.
Goldstein 1988: Goldstein, Joshua S. Long Cycles. Prosperity and War in the Modern Age. New Haven; London: Yale University Press, 1988.
Goldstein 2001: Goldstein, Andrea. From National Champion to Global Player: Explaining the Success of EMBRAER. University of Oxford Centre for Brazilian Studies, Working Paper CBS-17-2001. In: http://www.brazil.ox.ac.uk/.
Goldstein et al. 2000: Goldstein, Judith, Kahler, Miles, Keohane, Robert O., Slaughter, Anne-Marie. Introduction: Legalization and World Politics. In: International Organization, Vol. 54, No. 3, Summer 2000. S. 385-399.
Goldstein/Ndungu 2001: Goldstein, Andrea, Ndungu, Njuguna S. Regional Integration Experience in the Eastern African Region. OECD Development Centre. Technical Papers No. 171. CD/DOC (2001)3. March 2001. In: http://www.oecd.org/dev/publication/tp1a.htm.
Gomes-Casseres 1993: Gomes-Casseres, Benjamin. Computers: Alliances and Industry Evolution. In: Yoffie, David B. Beyond Free Trade. Firms, Governments, and Global Competition. Boston, Mass.: Harvard Business School Press, 1993.
Gomez/Jomo 1999: Gomez, Edmund Terence, Jomo, K.S. Malaysia's Political Economy. Politics, Patronage and Proftis. Cambridge: Cambridge University Press, 1999.
Gonem 1993: Gonem, Magda Mohammed. Weizenversorgung und Ernährungsicherung in Ägypten. Aachen: Alano Verlag, Ed. Herodot, 1993.

Gordon/Bovenberg 1996: Gordon, Roger H., Bovenberg, A. Lans. Why is Capital So Immobile Internationally? Possible Explanations and Implications for Capital Income Taxation. In: The American Economic Review, Vol. 86, No. 5, December 1996, pp. 1057-1075

Gore 2000: Gore, Charles. The Rise and the Fall of the Washington Consensus as a Paradigm for Developing Countries. In: World Development, Vol. 28, No. 5, S. 789-804.

Görgens 1997: Görgens, Egon. Arbeitsmarktinstitutionen und Beschäftigung in Deutschland. In: ORDO, Bd. 48, 1997.

Goswami et al. 2002: Goswami, Omkar, Arun, A.K., Gantakolla, Srivastava, More, Vishal, Mookherjee, Arindam, Dollar, David, Mengistae, Taye, Hallward-Driemier, Mary, Iarossi, Guiseppe. Competitiveness of Indian Manufacturing. Results from a Firm-Level Survey. Washington: World Bank, January 2002. In: http://www.worldbank.org.

Goto/Suzuki 1989: Goto, Akira, Suzuki, Kazuyuki. R & D Capital, Rate of Return on R & D Investment and Spillover of R & D in Japanese Manufacturing Industries. In: Review of Economics and Statistics, Vol. 71, No. 4, November 1989. S. 555-571.

Gould/Gruben 1996: Gould, David M., Gruben, William C. The Role of Intellectual Property Rights in Economic Growth. In: Journal of Development Economics, Vol. 48, 1996. S. 323-350.

Gould/Ruffin 1995: Gould, David M., Ruffin, Joy J. Human Capital, Trade, and Economic Growth. In: Weltwirtschaftliches Archiv, Bd. 131, Heft 3, 1995. S. 425-445.

Graafsma 2001: Graafsma, Folkert. Recent WTO Jurisprudence in the Field of Antidumping. In: Legal Issues of Economic Integration, Vol. 28 No. 3, 2001. S. 337-353.

Grabowski/Vernon 1986: Grabowski, Henry, Vernon, John. Longer Patents For Lower Imitation Barriers: The 1984 Drug Act. In: American Economic Review, Vol. 76 No. 2, May 1986. S. 195-198.

Graham/Somaya 2004: Graham, Stuart, Somaya, Deepak. The Use of Patents, Copyrights and Trademarks in Software: Evidence from Litigation. In: OECD. Patents, Innovation and Economic Performance. Conference Proceedings. Paris: OECD, 2004.

Grandmont/McFadden 1972: Grandmont, J.M., McFadden, D. A Technical Not on Classical Gains from Trade. In: Journal of International Economics, Vol. 2, 1972. S. 109-125.

Grane 2001: Grane, Patricio. Remedies under WTO Law. In: Journal of International Economic Law, 2001. S. 755-772.

Granovetter 1985: Granovetter, Mark. Economic Action and Social Structure: The Problem of Embeddedness. In: American Journal of Sociology, Vol. 91, No. 3, November 1985. S. 481-510.

Grant/Keohane 2005: Grant, Ruth W., Keohane, Robert O. Accountability and Abuses of Power in World Politics. In: American Political Science Review, Vol. 99 No. 1, February 2005. S. 29-43.

Grant et al. 1987: Grant, Wyn, Paterson, William, Whitston, Colin. Government-Industry Relations in the Chemical Industry: an Anglo-German Comparison. In: Wilks, Stephen, Wright, Maurice (eds.). Comparative Government-Industry Relations. Western Europe, the United States, and Japan. Oxford: Clarendon Press, 1987.

Gray 2002: Gray, James K. The Groundnut Market in Senegal. Examination of Price and Policy Changes. Dissertation. Blacksburg, Virginia Tech, June 10, 2002. In: http://scholar.lib.vt.edu.

Graziani 1998: Graziani, Giovanni. Globalization of Production in the Textile and Clothing Industries: The Case of Italian Foreign Direct Investment and Outward Processing in Eastern Europe. BRIE-Working Paper 128, May 1998. In: http://brie.berkeley.edu.

Greaney 1996: Greaney, Theresa M. Import now! An analysis of market-share voluntary import expansions (VIEs). In: Journal of International Economics, Vol. 40, 1996. S. 149-163.

Greenaway 1992: Greenaway, David. Trade Related Investment Measures. Kyklos, Vol. 45, No. 2, 1992. S. 139-159.

Greenaway et al. 1994: Greenaway, David, Hine, Robert, Milner, Chris. Country Specific Factors and the Pattern of Horizontal and Vertical Intra-Industry Trade in the UK. In: Weltwirtschaftliches Archiv, Bd. 130, 1994. S. 77-100.

Greenaway et al. 1995: Greenaway, David, Hine, Robert, Milner, Chris. Vertical and Horizontal Intra-Industry Trade: A Cross Industry Analysis for the United Kingdom. In: Economic Journal, Vol. 105, November 1995. S. 1505-1518.

Greenaway et al. 1998: Greenaway, David, Morgan, Wyn, Wright, Peter. Trade Reform, Adjustment and Growth: What does the Evidence tell Us? In: The Economic Journal, Vol. 108, September 1998. S. 1547-1561.

Greenaway/Milner 1986: Greenaway, David, Milner, Chris. The Economics of Intra-Industry Trade. Oxford: Basil Blackwell, 1986.

Greenaway/Milner 1990: Greenaway, David, Milner, Chris. Industrial incentives, domestic resource costs and resource allocation in Madagascar. In: Applied Economics, Vol. 22, 1990. S. 805-821.

Greenaway/Sapsford 1994: Greenaway, David, Sapsford, David. What Does Liberalization Do for Exports and Growth. In: Weltwirtschaftliches Archiv, Bd. 130, Heft 1, 1994. S. 152-174.

Greenaway/Torstensson 1997: Greenaway, David, Torstensson, Johan. Back to the Future: Taking Stock on Intra-Industry Trade. In: Weltwirtschaftliches Archiv, Vol. 133 (2), 1997. S. 249-269.

Greenaway/Torstensson 1998: Greenaway, David, Torstensson, Johan. Economic Geography, Comparative Advantage and Trade Within Industries: Evidence from the OECD. CEPR (Centre of Economic Policy Research) Discussion Paper No. 1857, April 1998.

Greenpeace Informationen 2001: Greenpeace Magazin. Update. No. 6, 2001.

Grethe/Tangermann 1999: Grethe, Harald, Tangermann, Stefan. The New Euro-Meditarranean Agreements. An Analysis of Trade Preferences. Göttingen Institute for Agricultural Economics, Diskussionsbeitrag 9902, January 1999.

Grethe/Tangermann 1999a: Grethe, Harald, Tangermann, Stefan. The EU Import Regime for Fresh Fruit and Vegetables after Implementation of the Uruguay Round. Göttingen Institute for Agricultural Economics, Diskussionsbeitrag 9901, January 1999.

Grether 1997: Grether, Jean-Marie. Estimating the Pro-Competitive Gains from Trade Liberalization: An Application to Mexican Manufacturing. In: The Journal of International Trade & Economic Development, Vol. 6 No. 3, 1997. S. 393-417.

Grieco 1988: Grieco, Joseph M. Anarchy and the limits of cooperation: a realist critique of the newest liberal institutionalism. In: International Organization, Vol. 42 No. 3, Summer 1988. S. 485-507.

Grieco 1990: Grieco, Joseph M. Cooperation among Nations. Europe, America, and Non-Tariff Barriers to Trade. Itaca; London: Cornell University Press, 1990.

Grieco/Ikenberry 2003: Grieco, Joseph M., Ikenberry, G. John. State Power and World Markets. The International Political Economy. New York; London: W. W. Norton, 2003.

Griliches 1986: Grilliches, Zvi. Productivity, R&D, and Basic Research at the Firm Level in the 1970's. In: American Economic Review, Vol. 86, No. 1, March 1986. S. 141-154.

Grimm 1994: Grimm, Dieter. Der Wandel der Staatsaufgaben und die Zukunft der Verfassung. In: Grimm, Dieter (Hrg.). Staatsaufgaben. Frankfurt am Main: Surkamp, 1994.

Grinols 1989: Grinols, Earl L. Procedural Protectionism: The American Trade Bill and the New Interventionist Mode. In: Weltwirtschaftliches Archiv, Vol. 125, 1989. S. 501-521.

Groeben/Thiesing/Ehlermann 1991: von der Groeben, Hans, Thiesing, Jochen, Ehlermann, Claus-Dieter. Kommentar zum EWG-Vertrag. Baden-Baden: Nomos, 1991.

Gröhn-Wittern 1998: Gröhn-Wittern, Ursula. Nach der Saat des Hungers die Saat des Todes. BUKO Agrar Dossier 20. Stuttgart: Schmetterling Verlag,1998.

Gröner 1975: Gröner, Helmut. Die westdeutsche Außenhandelspolitik. In: Schwarz, Hans-Peter. Handbuch der deutschen Außenpolitik. München, Zürich: R. Piper und Co. Verlag, 1975.

Gröner/Schüller 1989: Gröner, Helmut, Schüller, Alfred. Grundlagen der internationalen Ordnung: GATT, IWF und EG im Wandel - Euckens Idee der Wirtschaftsverfassung des Wettbewerbs als Prüfstein. In: ORDO Bd. 40. 1989. S. 430-463.

Gros 1987: Gros, Daniel. Protectionism in a Framework with Intra-Industry Trade. In: International Monetary Fund, Staff Papers, Vol. 34, 1987. S. 86-114.

Groß 1986: Groß, Alexander. Liberalisierung der Finanzmärkte in Japan. In: Die Weltwirtschaft, Heft 1, 1986. S. 61-73.

Gross 2002: Gross, Ivo. Subventionsrecht und 'schädlicher Steuerwettbewerb': Selektivität von Steuervergünstigungen als gemeinsames Kriterium. In: Recht der Internationalen Wirtschaft, Heft 1, 2002. S. 46-55.

Grosser et al. 1998: Grosser, Dieter, Lange, Thomas, Müller-Armack, Andreas, Neuss, Beate. Soziale Marktwirtschaft. Stuttgart; Berlin; Köln: Kohlhammer, 1990.

Grossman 1986: Grossman, Gene M. Strategic Trade Promotion: A Critique. In: Krugman, Paul R. Strategic Trade Policy and the New International Economics. Cambridge, Mass.: Cambridge University Press, 1986.

Grossman/Helpman 1991: Grossman, Gene M., Helpman, Elhanan. Innovation and Growth in the Global Economy. Cambridge, Mass.; London: The MIT Press, (1991) 1997.

Grossman/Helpman 1994: Grossman, Gene M., Helpman, Elhanan. Endogenous Innovation in the Theory of Growth. In: Journal of Economic Perspectives, Vol. 8, No. 1, Winter 1994. S. 23-44.

Grossman/Stiglitz 1980: Grossman, Sanford J, Stiglitz, Joseph E. On the Impossibility of Informationally Efficient Markets. In: American Economic Review, Vol. 70 No. 3, June 1980. S. 393-408.

Grossman/Sykes 2005: Grossman, Gene M., Sykes, Alan O. A preference for development: the law and economics of GSP. In: World Trade Review Vol. 4, No. 1, 2005. S. 41-67.

Grossman/Sykes 2006: Grossman, Gene M., Sykes, Alan O. European Communities - Anti-Dumping Duties on Imports of Cotton-Type Bed Linen from India: Recourse to Article 21.5 of the DSU by India. In: World Trade Review Vol. 5 No.1, 2006. S. 133-148.

Großmann et al. 1998: Großmann, Harald, Koopmann, Georg, Borrmann, Christine, Kinne, Konstanze, Kottmann, Elke. Handel und Wettbewerb – Auswirkungen von Wettbewerbbeschränkungen zwischen Unternehmen auf die internationale Arbeitsteilung. HWWA-Institut, Nr. 47. Baden-Baden: Nomos, 1998.

Grote et al. 2002: Grote, U., Deblitz, C., Stegemann, S. Umweltstandards und internationale Wettbewerbsfähigkeit: Fallstudienergebnisse für ausgewählte Agrarhandelsprodukte aus Brasilien, Deutschland und Indonesien. In: Brockmeier, M., Isermeyer, F., von Cramon-Taubadel, S. (Hrg.). Liberalisierung des Weltagrarhandels - Strategien und Konsequenzen. Münster-Hiltrup: Landwirtschaftsverlag, 2002.

Grote et al. 2002a: Grote, Ulrike, Wobst, Peter, von Braun, Joachim. 'Development Box' and Special and Differential Treatment for Food Security of Developing Countries: Potentials, Limitations and Implementation Issues. Zentrum für Entwicklungsforschung (ZEF), Bonn. Discussion Paper on Development Policy No. 47, May 2002. In: http://www.zef.de.

Grote/Nguyen 2004: Grote, Ulrike, Nguyen, Hoa. Agricultural Policies in Vietnam: Producer Support Estimates, 1986-2002. ZEF-Discussion Papers on Development Policy No. 93, Center for Development Research (ZEF), Bonn, December 2004. In: http://www.zef.de.

Grubel/Johnson 1967: Grubel, Herbert G., Johnson, Harry G. Nominal Tariffs, Indirect Taxes and the Effective Rate of Protection: The Common Market Countries 1959. In: Economic Journal, Vol. 77, December 1967. S. 761-776.
Grubel/Lloyd 1975: Grubel, Herbert G., Lloyd, P. J. Intra-Industry Trade. The Theory and Measurement of International Trade in Differentiated Products. London; Basingstoke: Macmillan Press, 1975.
Grynberg/Qualo 2006: Grynberg, Roman, Qualo, Veniana. Labour Standards in US and EU Preferential Trading Arrangements. In: JWT, Vol. 40, No. 4, 2006. S. 619-653.
Grynberg/Rochester 2005: Grynberg, Roman, Rochester, Nathalie. The Emerging Architecture of a World Trade Organization Fisheries Subsidies Agreement and the Interests of Developing Countries Coastal States. In: JWT, Vol. 39, No. 3, 2005. S. 503-526.
GSTP Information 2005: Global System of Trade Preferences among Developing Countries. In: http://www.g77.org/gstp/.
Guasch/Hahn 1997: Guasch, J. Luis, Hahn, Robert W. The Costs and Benefits of Regulation: Some Implications for Developing Countries. World Bank, Policy Research Working Paper, No. 1772, March 1997. In: http://www.worldbank.org.
Guillaumont 1987: Guillaumont, Patrick. From Export Instability Effect to International Stabilization Policies. In: World Development, Vol. 15 No. 5, 1987. S. 633-643.
Gulati et al. 1985: Gulati, Ravi, Bose, Swadesh, Atukorala, Vimal. Exchange Rate Policies in Eastern and Southern Africa, 1965-1983. World Bank Staff Working Papers Number 720. Washington: World Bank, 1985.
Gundlach 1993: Gundlach, Erich. Empirical Evidence for Alternative Growth Models: Time Series Results. In: Weltwirtschaftliches Archiv, Vol. 129, 1993. S. 103-119.
Gundlach/Nunnenkamp 1994: Gundlach, Erich, Nunnenkamp, Peter. The European Union in the Era of Globalization. Kiel Working Paper 650, August 1994.
Gundlach/Nunnenkamp 1996: Gundlach, Erich, Nunnenkamp, Peter. Falling Behind or Catching Up? Developing Countries in the Era of Globalization. Kieler Diskussionsbeiträge, No. 263. Kiel: Institut für Weltwirtschaft, Januar 1996.
Günther 1975: Günther, Eberhard. Die geistigen Grundlagen des sogenannten Josten-Entwurfs. In: Sauermann, Heinz, Mestmäcker, Ernst-Joachim (Hrg.). Wirtschaftsordnung und Staatsverfassung. Tübingen: Mohr, 1975.
Gupta 1999: Gupta, Poonam. Why do Firms pay Antidumping Duties? IMF Working Paper WP/99/166, December 1999. In: http://www.imf.org.
Guth et al. 1995: Guth E., Ketelsen, J. V., Lambsdorff, A. Graf. Barriers to Trade and Investment in the US. Vorträge, Reden und Berichte aus dem Europa Institut Saarbrücken, Rechtswissenschaft Nr. 307, 1995.
Gutjahr 1995: Gutjahr, Lothar. Auf dem Weg zur Weltinnenpolitik? Ein Literaturüberblick. In: Bahr, Egon, Lutz, Dieter S. (Hrg.) Unsere Gemeinsame Zukunft - Globale Herausforderungen. Baden Baden: Nomos, 1995.
Gutmann 1972: Gutmann, Gernot. Individuelle Freiheit, Macht und Wirtschaftslenkung. Zur neoliberalen Konzeption einer marktwirtschaftlichen Ordnung. In: Cassel, D., Gutmann, G., Thieme, H.J. (Hrg.) 25 Jahre Marktwirtschaft in der Bundesrepublik Deutschland. Stuttgart: Gustav Fischer, 1972.
Gylfason 1998: Gylfason, Thorvaldur. Prospects for Liberalization of Trade in Agriculture. In: JWT, Vol. 32 No. 1, Feb 1998. S. 29-40.

H

Haas 1980: Haas, Ernst B. Why Collaborate? Issue-Linkage and International Regimes. In: World Politics, Vol. 32, No. 3, April 1980.
Habeler 1961: Habeler, Gottfried. Terms of Trade and Economic Development. In: Ellis, Howard S. (ed.) Economic Development for Latin America. Proceedings of a Conference held by the International Economics Association. London: Macmillan, 1961.
Haber 1958: Haber, L. F. The Chemical Industry during the Nineteenth Century. Oxford: Clarendon Press, 1958.
Häberle 1993: Häberle, Peter. Soziale Marktwirtschaft als 'Dritter Weg'. In: Zeitschrift für Rechtspolitik, Heft 10, 1993. S. 383-389.
Haberler 1948: Haberler, Gottfried. Some Economic Problems of the European Recovey Program. In: American Economic Review, Vol. 38, 1948. S. 495-525.
Habermas 1992: Habermas, Jürgen. Faktizität und Geltung. Frankfurt am Main: Surkamp, 1992.
Habermas 1996: Habermas, Jürgen. Die Einbeziehung des Anderen. Frankfurt am Main: Surkamp, 1996.
Habermas 1998: Habermas, Jürgen. Die postnationale Konstellation und die Zukunft der Demokratie. In: Habermas, Jürgen. Die postnationale Konstellation. Politische Essay. Frankfurt am Main: Surkamp, 1998.
Hachette/De la Cuadra 1991: Hachette, Dominique, de la Cuadra, Sergio. Chile. In: The Experience of Argentina, Chile and Uruguay. Liberalizing Foreign Trade Vol. 1. Oxford: World Bank/Blackwell, 1991.
Hagedoorn 1994: Hagedoorn, John. Internationalization of companies: the evolution of organizational complexity, flexibility and networks of innovation. MERIT 2/94-008. Maastricht, 1994.
Hagedoorn 1996: Hagedoorn, John. The Economics of Cooperation among High-Tech Firms – Trends and Patterns in Strategic Technology Partnering since the Early Seventies. In: Koopmann, Georg, Scharrer, Hans-Eckart (eds.). The Economics of High-Technology Competition. Baden-Baden: Nomos, 1996.
Haggard 1985: Haggard, Stephan. The politics of adjustment: lessons from the IMF's extended fund facility. In: IO, Vol. 39 No.3, Summer 1985. S. 505-534.

Hahn 1996: Hahn, Michael J. Die einseitige Aussetzung von GATT-Verpflichtungen als Repressalie. Berlin; Heidelberg; New York: Springer, 1996.
Hahn 1998: Hahn, Michael. Das neue Regime der Beihilfenkontrolle in der WTO. In: Klein, Martin, Meng, Werner, Rode, Reihnhard (Hrg.). Die Neue Welthandelsordnung der WTO. Amsterdam: Verlag Facultas/Oversees Publishers Association, 1998.
Hakura 1999: Hakura, Dalia. A Test of the General Validity of the Heckscher-Ohlin Theorem for Trade in the European Community. IMF Working Paper, VP/99/70, May 1999. In: http://www.imf.org.
Hakura/Jaumotte 2001: Hakura, Dali, Jaumotte, Florence. The Role of Trade in Technology Diffusion. In: OECD. Policies to Promote Competitiveness in Manufacturing in Sub-Saharan Africa. Development Centre Seminars within the IMF and the AERC. Kwasi Fosu, Augustin, Nsouli, Saleh M., Varoudakis, Aristomene (eds.). Paris: OECD, 2001a.
Hall et al. 2003: Hall, Bronwyn H., Stuart, J.H., Harhoff, Dietmar, Mowery, David C. Prospects for Improving U.S. Patent Quality via Post-grant Opposition University of California, Berkeley. Competition Policy Center Working Paper No. CPC 03-38. May, 2003. In: http://elsa.berkeley.edu/~bhhall/papers/BHH%20IPE%20May03WP.pdf
Hall/Jones 1996: Hall, Robert E., Jones, Charles I. The Productivity of Nations. NBER Working Paper No. 5812, November 1996.
Hall/Jones 1998: Hall, Robert E., Jones, Charles I. Why do some countries produce so much more output per worker than others? NBER Working Paper, NO. 6564, May 1998.
Hamilton 1791: Hamilton, Alexander. Report of the Secretary of the Treasury of the United States on the Subject of Manufactures. Presented to the House of Representatives, December 5, 1791.
Hamilton 1981: Hamilton, Carl. A New Approach to Estimation of the Effects of Non-Tariff Barriers to Trade: An Application to the Swedish Textile and Clothing Industry. Institute for International Economic Studies, University of Stockholm, Reprint Series (aus Weltwirtschaftliches Archiv, Heft 2, 1981), No. 160. University of Stockholm, 1981.
Hamilton 1989: Hamilton, Carl B. The Political Economy of Transient "New" Protectionism. In: Weltwirtschaftliches Archiv, Vol. 125, 1989. S. 522-546.
Hamilton/Kim 1990: Hamilton, Carl B., Kim, Chungsoo. Republic of Korea: Rapid Growth in Spite of Protectionism Abroad. In: Hamilton, Carl B. Textiles Trade and the Developing Countries. Eliminating the Multi-Fibre Arrangement in the 1990s. Washington: World Bank, 1990.
Hamm 2000: Hamm, Walter. Konstanz der Wirtschaftspolitik - Was sie bedeutet, und was sie nicht bedeutet. In: Külp, Berhard, Vanberg, Victor (Hrg.) Freiheit und wettbewerbliche Ordnung. Gedenkband zur Erinnerung und Walter Eucken. Freiburg; Berlin; München: Haufe Verlagsgruppe, 2000.
Hancher et al. 1993: Hancher, Leigh, Ottervanger, Tom, Slot, Jan Piet. EC State Aids. London: Chancery Law Publishing, 1993.
Hancher/Ruete 1987: Hancher, Leigh, Ruete, Matthias. Legal Culture, Product Licensing, and the Drug Industry. In: Wilks, Stephen, Wright, Maurice (eds.). Comparative Government-Industry Relations. Western Europe, the United States, and Japan. Oxford: Clarendon Press, 1987.
Hanrahan et al. 2006: Hanrahan, Charles, Banks, Beverly A., Canada, Carol. U.S. Agricultural Trade: Trends, Composition, Direction, and Policy. CRS Report for Congress, Updated, September 25, 2006. In: http://fpc.state.gov/fpc/c18787.htm.
Hanson 1996: Hanson, Gordon H. U.S.-Mexico Intergration and Regional Economies: Evidence form Border City Pairs. NBER Working Paper No. 5425, January 1996.
Harberger 1954: Harberger, Arnold C. Monopoly and Resource Allocation. In: American Economic Review Vol. XLIV, No. 2, May 1954. S. 77-92.
Harberger 1959: Harberger, Arnold C. Using the Resource at Hand more Effectively. In: American Economic Review, Vol. XLIX, No. 2, May 1959. S. 134-146.
Harbinson 2005: Harbinson, Stuart. The Agriculture Negotiations: The Road from Doha and How to Keep the Negotiations on a Positive Track. In: Petersmann, Ernst-Ulrich (ed.). Reforming the World Trading System. Legitimacy, Efficiency, and Democratic Governance. Oxford: Oxford University Press, 2005.
Hardin 1968: Hardin, G. The Tragedy of the Commons. In: Science 162, 1968. Hier aus: Nelissen, Nico et al. (eds.) Classics in Environmental Studies. Utrecht: International Books, 1997.
Harding et al. 2004: Harding, Alan, Söderbom, Mans, Teal, Francis. Survival among African Manufacturing Firms. WPS/2004-05. Oxford Centre for the Study of African Economies. In: http://www.csae.ox.ac.uk/workingpapers/main-wps.html.
Haritakis/Pitelis 1998: Haritakis, Nicholaos, Pitelis, Christos. Privatization in Greece. In: Parker, David (ed.). Privatization in the European Union. Theory and Policy Perspectives. London; New York: Routledge, 1998.
Harnisch 2006: Harnisch, Sandy. Die Zwanglizenz im südafrikanischen und deutschen Patentrecht. Berlin: Berliner Wissenschafts-Verlag, 2006.
Harrigan 1991: Harrigan, Jane. Malawi. In: Aid and Power. The World Bank and Policy-based Lending. Vol. 2, Case Studies. London; New York: Routledge, 1991.
Harrigan 1995: Harrigan, James. The Volume of Trade in Differentiated Intermediate Goods: Theory and Evidence. In: The Review of Economics and Statistics, Vol. 77, 1995. S. 283-293.
Harrigan 1996: Harrigan, James. Openness to trade in manufactures in the OECD. In: Journal of International Economics, Vol. 40, 1996. S. 23-39.
Harrigan 1997: Harrigan, James. Technology, Factor Supplies, and International Specialization. Estimating the Neoclassical Model. In: American Economic Review, Vol. 87 No. 4, September 1997. S. 475-494.

Harrigan/Zakrajsek 2000: Harrigan, James, Zakraysek, Egon. Factor supplies and Specialization in the World Economy. Federal Reserve Bank of New York, Staff Reports/Research Papers No. 107, August 2000. In: http://www.ny.frb.org/research/staff_reports/2000.html.

Harris 1994: Harris, Richard G. Trade and Industrial Policy for a 'Declining' Industry: The Case of the U.S. Steel Industry. In: Krugman, Paul R. Empirical Studies of Strategic Trade Policy. NBER Project Report. Chicago: Univ. of Chicago Press, 1994.

Harris/Kherfi 2001: Harris, Rirchard G., Kherfi, Samer. Productivity Growth, Converge, and Trade Specialization in Canadian Manufacturing. Canadian Institute for Advanced Research, Working Paper No. 165, January 2001. In: http://www.ciar.ca.

Harris/Lau 1998: Harris, Richard I. D., Lau, Eunice. Verdoorn's law and increasing returns to scale in the UK regions, 1968-91: some new estimates based on the cointegration approach. In: Oxford Economic Papers 50, 1998. S. 201-219.

Harrison 1994: Harrison, Ann E. An Empirical Test of the Infant Industry Argument: Comment. In: American Economic Review, Vol. 84, No. 4, September 1994, (incl. reply by Anne O. Krueger), S. 1090-1096.

Harrison 1996: Harrison, Ann. Openness and growth: A time-series, cross-country analysis for developing countries. In: Journal of Development Economics, Vol. 48, 1996. S. 419-447.

Harrison et al. 1995: Harrison, Glenn W., Rutherford, Thomas F., Tarr, David G. Quantifying the Uruguay Round. In: Martin, Will, Winters, L. Alan. The Uruguay Round and the Developing Countries. World Bank Discussion Papers 307, Washington: World Bank, 1995.

Harrison et al. 1997: Harrison, Glenn W, Rutherford, Thomas F., Tarr, David G. Quantifying the Uruguay Round. In: Economic Journal, 107, September 1997. S. 1405-1430.

Harrold 1995: Harrold, Peter. The Impact of the Uruguay Round on Africa. World Bank Discussion Papers No. 311. Washington: World Bank, 1994.

Hart 1997: Hart, Michael. The WTO and the Political Economy of Globalization. In: JWT, Vol. 31, No. 5, Oct 1997. S. 75-93.

Härtel et al. 1987: Härtel, Hans Hagen, Feldmann, Berthold, Henne, Wolfgang, Keller, Dietmar, Koopmann, Georg. Neue Industriepolitik oder Stärkung der Marktkräfte? Strukturpolitische Konzeptionen im internationalen Vergleich. Spezialuntersuchung 1 im Rahmen der HWWA-Strukturberichterstattung 1987. Hamburg: Verlag Weltarchiv, 1986.

Härtel et al. 1996: Härtel, Hans Hagen, Jungnickel, Rolf, Keller, Dietmar, Feber, Heiko, Borrmann, Christine, Winkler-Büttner, Diana, Lau, Dirk. Grenzüberschreitende Produktion und Strukturwandel - Globalsierung der deutschen Wirtschaft. Baden-Baden: Nomos, 1996.

Hartley 1981: Hartley, Keith. The aerospace industry: problems and policies. In: de Jong, H. W. (ed.). The Structure of European Industry. The Hague; Boston; London: Martinus Nijhoff, 1981.

Hartley 1993: Hartley, Keith. Aerospace: the political economy of an industry. In: de Jong, H.W. (ed.) The Structure of European Industry. Dordrecht; Boston; London: Kluwer, 1993.

Hartwich 1996a: Hartwich, Hans-Hermann. Der Sozialstaat und die Krise der Arbeitsgesellschaft. In: Gegenwartskunde, 1/1996, S. 11-25.

Hartwich 1996b: Hartwich, Hans-Hermann. Soziale Marktwirtschaft. Zur Neubestimmung des marktwirtschaftlichen Konzepts im wirtschaftlichen und sozialen Wandel. In: Gegenwartskunde, 3/1996, S. 411-448.

Hartwig 1997: Hartwig, Karl-Hans. Wirtschaftsverbände und Soziale Marktwirtschaft. In: ORDO, Bd. 48, 1997.

Hartwig 1998: Hartwig, Karl-Hans. Der Staat als Unternehmer: Zur Rolle der öffentlichen Unternehmen in der Sozialen Marktwirtschaft. In: Cassel, Dieter (Hrg.). 50 Jahre Soziale Marktwirtschaft. Schriften zu Ordnungfragen der Wirtschaft, Band 57, Stuttgart, Lucius&Lucius: 1998.

Hasenclever et al. 1996: Hasenclever, Andreas, Mayer, Peter, Rittberger, Volker. Justice, Equality, and the Robustness of International Regimes. Tübinger Arbeitspapiere zur Internationalen Politik und Friedensforschung, Nr. 25. In: http://www.

Hasenpflug 1977: Hasenpflug, Hajo. Nicht-tarifäre Handelshemmnisse. HWWA-Veröffentlichung. Hamburg: Verlag Weltarchiv, 1977.

Hasse 1997: Hasse, Rolf H. Theoretische Defizite und normative Überschüsse: Zur Analyse der Budgetkriterien des Vertrages von Maastricht. In: ORDO, Bd. 48, 1997.

Hathaway/Ingco 1995: Hathaway, Dale E., Ingco, Merlinda D. Agricultural Liberalization and the Uruguay Round. In: Martin, Will, Winters, L. Alan. The Uruguay Round and the Developing Countries. World Bank Discussion Papers 307, Washington: World Bank, 1995.

Haughton/Swaminathan 1992: Haughton, Jonathan, Swaminathan, Balu. The Employment and Welfare Effects of Quantitative Restrictions on Steel Import into the United States, 1955-1987. In: Journal of World Trade, Vol. 26, No. 2, April 1992. S. 95-118.

Hauser 1986: Hauser, Heinz. Domestic Policy Foundation and Domestic Policy Function of International Trade Rules. In: Aussenwirtschaft, 41. Jg, Heft 2/3, 1986. S. 171-184.

Hauser et al. 1988: Hauser, Heinz, Moser, Peter, Planta, Renaud, Schmid, Ruedi. Der Beitrag von Jan Tumlir zur Entwicklung einer ökonomischen Verfassungstheorie internationaler Handelsregeln. In: ORDO, Bd. 39, 1988. S. 219-237.

Hauser/Schanz 1995: Hauser, Heinz, Schanz, Kai-Uwe. Das neue GATT. Die Welthandelsordnugn nach Abschluß der Uruguay Runde. München, Wien: R. Oldenbourg, 1995.

Hay/Liu 1997: Hay, Donald A., Liu, Guy S. The Efficiency of Firms: What difference does competition make? In: Economic Journal, Vol. 107, May 1997. S. 597-617.
Hayashi 2004: Hayashi, Michiko. Trade in Textiles and Clothing. Priority Issues for Woman in the Post-ATC. Division on International Trade in Goods & Services, and Commodities. UNCTAD. In: http://www.accountability.org.uk.
Hayek 1944: Hayek, F. A. The Road to Serfdom. London: Routledge, 1944.
Hayek 1945: Hayek, F. A. The Use of Knowledge in Society. In: American Economic Review, Vol. 35 No. 4, 1945. S. 519-530.
Hayek 1960: Hayek, F. A. Wirtschaftpolitik im Rechtsstaat. In: Stützel, Wolfgang et al. (Hrg.). Grundtexte zur Sozialen Marktwirtschaft. Stuttgart: Gustav Fischer Verlag, 1981.
Hayek 1971: Hayek, F. A. Die Verfassung der Freiheit. Tübingen: Mohr, (1971) 1991.
Hayek 1974: Hayek, F. A. The Pretence of Knowledge. Nobel Memorial Lecture, Dec. 11, 1974. In: The American Economic Review, December 1989, Vol. 79, No. 6. S. 3-7.
Heath 1996: Heath, Christopher. Bedeutet TRIPS wirklich eine Schlechterstellung von Entwicklungsländern? In: GRUR Int. Heft 12, 1996. S. 1169-1185.
Heeckt/Snoek 1965: Heeckt, Hugo, Snoek, Gerd. Weltseeverkehr und Weltfrachtenmärkte. In: Die Weltwirtschaft, Heft 1, 1965. S. 32-38.
Heffernan 1999: Heffernan, William. Consolidation in the Food and Agriculture System. Report. University of Missouri, 1999. In: http://www.foodcircles.missouri.edu/consol.htm.
Heggestad 1990: Heggestad, Arnold G. The Banking Industry. In: Adams, Walter (Hrg.). The Structure of American Industry. New York: Macmillan, 1990.
Heidhues/Knerr 1994: Heidhues, Franz, Knerr, Beatrice. Food and Agricultural Policies under Structural Adjustment. Frankfurt am Main: Peter Lang, 1994.
Heilmann 2000: Heilmann, Sebastian. Die Politik der Wirtschaftsreformen in China und Rußland. Hamburg: Institut für Asienkunde, 2000.
Hein 1998: Hein, Wolfgang. Unterentwicklung und die Krise der Peripherie. Opladen: Leske & Budrich, 1998.
Heinemann 1996: Heinemann, Andreas. Antitrust Law of Intellectual Property in the TRIPS Agremment of the World Trade Organization. In: Beier, Friedrich-Karl, Schricker, Gerhard (eds.) From GATT to TRIPs. The Agreement on Trade-Related Aspects of Intellectual Property Rights. Weinheim: VHC, 1996.
Heitger 1987: Heitger, Bernhard. Import Protection and Export Performance – Their Impact on Economic Growth. In: Weltwirtschaftliches Archiv, Bd. 123, 1987, S. 249-261.
Heitger/Stehn 1988: Heitger, Bernard, Stehn, Jürgen. Protektion in Japan – Interessendruck oder gezielte Industriepolitik. In: Die Weltwirtschaft, Heft 1, 1988. S. 123-137.
Held 1995: Held, David. Democracy and the Global Order. Cambridge: Polity Press, 1995.
Helleiner 1981: Helleiner, Gerald K. The Refsnes Seminar: Economic Theory and North-South Negotiations. In: World Development, Vol. 9, No. 6, 1981. S. 539-555.
Helleiner 1989: Helleiner, Gerald K. Transnational Corporations and Direct Foreign Investment. In: Chenery, H., Srinivasan, T.N. Handbook of Development Economics, Vol. II, Amsterdam; New York: Elsevier Science B.V., 1989.
Helleiner 1990: Helleiner, Gerald K. Trade Strategy in Medium-Term Adjustment. In: World Development, Vol. 18, No. 6, 1990, pp. 879-897.
Helleiner 1992: Helleiner, Gerald K. Introduction. In: Helleiner (ed.). Trade Policy, Industrialization, and Development. New York: Oxford University Press, 1992.
Helleiner 1993: Helleiner, Gerald K. Protectionism and the developing countries. In: Salvatore, Dominick (ed.). Protectionism and World Welfare. Cambridge: Cambridge University Press, 1993.
Helleiner 1994: Helleiner, Gerald K. Introduction. In: Helleiner (ed.). Trade Policy and Industrialization in Turbulent Times. London, New York: Routledge, 1994.
Helleiner 1994a: Helleiner, Eric. States and the Emergence of Global Finance. Ithaca, London: Cornell University Press, 1994.
Helleiner 1995a: Helleiner, Gerald K. Introduction. In: Helleiner (ed.). Manufacturing for Export in the Developing World. London, New York: Routledge, 1995.
Helleiner 1995b: Helleiner, Gerald K. Trade, Trade Policy and Industrialization Reconsidered. Helsinki: UNU/World Institute for Development Economics Research, 1995.
Helpman 1999: Helpman, Elhanan. The Structure of Foreign Trade. In: Journal of Economic Perspectives, Vol. 13, No. 2, Spring 1999. S. 121-144.
Helpman 1999: Helpman, Elhanan. The Structure of Foreign Trade. NBER Working Paper, No. 6752, October 1998.
Helpman/Krugman 1985: Helpman, Elhanan, Krugman, Paul R. Market Structure and Foreign Trade. Cambridge: The MIT Press, 1985.
Hemmer 1999: Hemmer, Hans-Rimbert. Die endogene Wachstumstheorie als Reaktion auf die Erklärungsdefizite der traditionellen neoklassischen Wachstumstheorie – ein Überblick. In: Schubert, Renate (Hrg.). Neue Wachstums- und Außenhandelstheorie. Implikationen für die Entwicklungstheorie und – politik. Berlin: Duncker&Humblot, 1999.
Henkin 1968: Henkin, Louis. How Nations Behave. Law and Foreign Policy. London: Pall Mall Press, 1968.
Henkin 1995: Henkin, Louis. International Law: Politics and Values. Dordrecht: Martinus Nijhoff, 1995.

Henrekson et al. 1996: Henrekson, Magnus, Jonung, Lars, Stymne, Joakim. In: Crafts, Nicolas, Toniolo, Gianni (eds.). Economic Growth in Europe since 1945. Cambridge: Cambridge University Press, 1996.
Henrichsmeyer/Witzke 1991: Henrichsmeyer, Wilhelm, Witzke, Heinz Peter. Agarpolitik. Bd. 1 Agrarökonomische Grundlagen. Stuttgart: Eugen Ulmer, 1991.
Henrichsmeyer/Witzke 1994: Henrichsmeyer, Wilhelm, Witzke, Heinz Peter. Agarpolitik. Bd. 1 Bewertung und Willensbildung. Stuttgart: Eugen Ulmer, 1994.
Herbst 1990: Herbst, Jeffrey. The Structural Adjustment of Politics in Africa. In: World Development, Vol. 18, No. 7, 1990. S. 949-958.
Herdmann/Weiss 1985: Herdmann, Ute, Weiss, Frank D. Wirkungen von Subventionen und Quoten – Das Beispiel der EG-Stahlindustrie. In: Die Weltwirtschaft, Heft 1, 1985. S. 101-113.
Herdzina 1993: Herdzina, Klaus. Einführung in die Mikroökonomik. München: Vahlen, 1993.
Héritier 1993: Héritier, Adrienne. Einleitung Policy Analyse. Elemente der Kritik und Perspektiven der Neuorientierung. In: Héritier, Adrienne. Policy Analyse. Kritik und Neuorientierung. Opladen: Westdeutscher Verlag, 1993.
Hermanns 2001: Hermanns, Uwe. Der WTO-Beitritt Chinas mit thematischem Schwerpunkt Landwirtschaft und Subventionen. In: Nord-Süd-Aktuell, Jg. XV, Nr. 2, 2001. S. 277-300.
Hermanns 2005a: Hermanns, Uwe. Developing Countries vs. Global Competition Rules. Why? St. Augustin: Trade Focus Verlag, 2005.
Hermanns 2005b: Hermanns, Uwe. Der IMF zwischen Neoklassik und der Krise nach der Liberalisierung afrikanischer Agrarmärkte. St. Augustin: Trade Focus Verlag, 2005.
Hermanns 2005c: Hermanns, Uwe. Liberalisierung ohne Limit. Warum die NAMA Verhandlungen gefährlich für Entwicklung und Umwelt sind. St. Augustin: Trade Focus Verlag, 2005.
Hermanns 2005d: Hermanns, Uwe. Fighting Poverty after Liberalization in Africa. In: Nord-Süd-Aktuell, Jg. Nr. 2005. S. 396-414.
Herriot 1930: Herriot, Edouard. Vereinigte Staaten von Europa. Leipzig: Paul List Verlag, 1930.
Hertel et al. 1995: Hertel, Thomas, Martin, Will, Yanagishima, Koji, Dimaranan, Betina. Liberalizing Manufactures Trade in a Changing World Economy. In: Martin, Will, Winters, L. Alan. The Uruguay Round and the Developing Countries. World Bank Discussion Papters 307, Washington: World Bank, 1995.
Hertel et al. 1999: Hertel, Thomas W., Anderson, Kym, Francois, Joseph F., Martin, Will. Agriculture and Non-agricultural Liberalization in the Millenium Round. Global Trade Analysis Project, 1999. In: http://www.agecon.purdue.edu/gtap.
Hertel et al. 2000: Hertel, Thomas W., Hoekman, Bernard M., Martin, Will. Developing Countries and a New Round of WTO Negotiations. Working Paper, April 2000. Annual World Bank Conference on Development Economics. Washington: World Bank, 2000. In: http://wb.forumone.com/research/abcde/
Hertel/Reimer 2004: Hertel, Thomas W., Reimer, Jeffrey J. Predicting the Poverty Impacts of Trade Reform. World Bank, Policy Research Working Paper, No. 3444, November 2004. In: http://www.worldbank.org.
Herzog 1988: Herzog, Roman. Ziele, Vorbehalte und Grenzen der Staatstätigkeit. In: Isensee, Josef, Kirchhof, Paul (Hrg.). Handbuch des Staatsrechts (HStR). Bd. III. Heidelberg: C.F. Müller, 1987, S. 83-120.
Hesse 1999: Hesse, Konrad. Grundzüge des Verfassungsrechts der Bundesrepublik Deutschland. Heidelberg: C. F. Müller, 1999.
Heubel 1994: Heubel, Andrea. Technologietransfer durch internationale Unternehmenkooperationen. München: VVF, 1994.
Heuss 1960: Heuss, Ernst. Das Oligopol, ein determinierter Markt. In: Weltwirtschaftliches Archiv, Bd. 84 Heft 2, 1960. S. 165-190.
Heuß 1997: Heuß, Ernst. Die Deformation der Marktwirtschaft durch die Wohlfahrtspolitik. In: ORDO, Bd. 48, 1997.
Heymann 2005: Heymann, Eric. Nach dem Ende des Welttextilabkommens. China reift zur Schneiderei der Welt. Deutsche Bank Research 4. Januar 2005, Nr. 310. In: http://www.dbresearch.de.
Hickman/Schleicher 1978: Hickman, Bert G., Schleicher, Stefan. The Interdependence of National Economies and the Synchronization of Economic Fluctuations: Evidence from the LINK Project. In: Weltwirtschaftliches Archiv, Bd. 144, 1978, S. 642-708.
Hiemenz/von Rabenau 1973: Hiemenz, Ulrich, von Rabenau, Kurt. Effektive Protektion. Theorie und Berechnung für die westdeutsche Industrie. Tübingen: Mohr, 1973.
Hildebrand 2002: Hildebrand, Doris. The Role of Economic Analysis in the EC Competition Rules. The Hague: Kluwer, 2002.
Hilf 1987: Hilf, Meinhard. Solange II: Wie lange noch Solange? EuGRZ, 14. Jg., Heft 1/2, 1987. S. 1-7.
Hilf 1987a: Hilf, Meinhard. The Right to Food in National and International Law. In: Oppermann, Thomas, Petersmann, Ernst-Ulrich. Reforming the International Economic Order. Berlin: Duncker Humblot, 1987.
Hilf 1991: Hilf, Meinhard. Settlement of Disputes in International Economic Organizations: Comparative Analysis and Proposals for Strengthening the GATT Dispute Settlement Procedures. In: Hilf, Meinhard, Petersmann, Ulrich (eds.). The New GATT Round of Multilateral Trade Negotiations. Deventer, Boston: Kluwer Law and Taxation Publishers, 1991.
Hilf 1993: Hilf, Meinhard. Die Richtlinie der EG - ohne Richtung, ohne Linie. In: Europarecht, Heft 1, 1993. S. 1-22.

Hilf 1997: Hilf, Meinhard. Negotiating and Implementing the Uruguay Round: The Role of EC Member States - The Case of Germany. In: Jackson, John H., Sykes, Alan O. (eds.). Implementing the Uruguay Round. Oxford: Clarendon Press, 1997.
Hilf 1997a: Hilf, Meinhard. The Role of National Courts in International Trade Relations. In: Petersmann, Ernst-Ulrich (ed.). International Trade Law and the GATT/WTO Dispute Settlement System. London, The Hague, Boston: Kluwer Law, 1997.
Hilf 1999: Hilf, Meinhard. Freiheit des Welthandels contra Umweltschutz? Vortrag auf der Jahrestagung der Gesellschaft für Umweltrecht am 5.11.1999 in Berlin. Nicht publiziert.
Hilf 2001: Hilf, Meinhard. Power, Rules and Principles - Which Orientation for WTO/GATT Law? In: Journal of International Economic Law, 2001. S. 111-130.
Hilf 2005: Hilf, Meinhard. How Can Parliamentary Participation in WTO Rule Making and Democratic Control Be Made More Effective? The European Context. In: Petersmann, Ernst-Ulrich (ed.). Reforming the World Trading System. Legitimacy, Efficiency, and Democratic Governance. Oxford: Oxford University Press, 2005.
Hilf/Petersmann 1991: Hilf, Meinhard, Petersmann, Ulrich (eds.). The New GATT Round of Multilateral Trade Negotiations. Deventer, Boston: Kluwer Law and Taxation Publishers, 1991.
Hill 1995: Hill, Hal. Indonesia: From 'Chronic Dropout' to 'Miracle'?`In: Journal of International Development, Vol. 7, No. 5, 1995. S. 775-789.
Hillebrand/Welfens 1998: Hillebrand, Rainer, Welfens, Paul J.J. Globalisierung der Wirtschaft: Wirtschaftspolitische Konsequenzen des internationalen Standortwettbewerbs. In: Cassel, Dieter (Hrg.). 50 Jahre Soziale Marktwirtschaft. Schriften zu Ordnungfragen der Wirtschaft, Band 57, Stuttgart: Lucius&Lucius, 1998.
Hilpert 1991: Hilpert, Ulrich. Neue Weltmärkte und der Staat. Opladen: Westdeutscher Verlag, 1991.
Hilpert 1997: Hilpert, Hanns Günther. Die ostasiatische Wachstumsdebatte. In: ifo-Studien, 43 Jg. Heft 1, 1997. S. 521-548.
Hilpert et al. 1997: Hilpert, Hanns Günther, Martsch, Silvia, Heath, Christopher. Technologieschutz für deutsche Investitionen in Asien. ifo Institut für Wirtschaftsforschung München, ifo Studien zur Entwicklungsforschung 30. München: Weltforum Verlag, 1997.
Hilpold 1995: Hilpold, Peter. Die Neuregelung der Schutzmaßnahmen im GATT/WTO-Recht und ihr Einfluß auf "Grauzonenmaßnahmen". In: ZaöRV Bd. 55, 1995. S. 89-127.
Himbara 1994: Himbara, David. The Failed Industrialization of Commerce and Industry in Kenya. In: World Development, Vol. 22, No. 3, 1994. S. 469-481.
Himelfarb 1996: Himelfarb, Allison J. The International Language of Concergence: Reviving Antitrust Dialogue between the United States and the European Union with a Uniform Understanding of 'Extraterritoriality'. In: University of Pennsylvania Journal of International Economic Law, Vol. 17, No. 3, Fall 1996. S. 909-955.
Hindley 1986: Hindley, Brian. EC Imports of VCRs from Japan. A Costly Precedent. In: JWTL, Vol. 20 No. 2, March April 1986. S. 168-184.
Hines/Rice 1994: Hines, James R., Rice, Eric M. Fiscal Paradise: Foreign Tax Havens and American Business. In: Quarterly Journal of Economics, Vol. 109, Feb. 1994. S. 149-182.
Hinloopen/van Marrewijk 2001: Hinloopen, Jeroen, van Marrewijk, Charles. On the Empirical Distribution of the Balassa Index. In: Weltwirtschaftliches Archiv, Bd. 137, Heft 1, 2001. S. 1-35.
Hinze 1998: Hinze, Jörg. Aussagefähigkeit internationaler Arbeitskostenvergleiche. Baden-Baden: Nomos, 1998.
Hipple 1990: Hipple. F. Steb. The Measurement of International Trade Related to Multinational Companies. In: American Economic Review, Vol. 80 No. 5,December 1990. S. 1263-1270.
Hirsch 2002: Hirsch, Moshe. International Trade Law, Political Economy and Rules of Origin. In: JWT, Vol. 36, No. 2, 2002. S. 171-188.
Hirsch/Roth 1986: Hirsch, Joachim, Roth, Roland. Das neue Gesicht des Kapitalismus. Hamburg: VSA, 1986.
Hirsch-Kreinsen 1996: Hirsch-Kreinsen, Hartmut. Internationalisierung der Produktion. Strategien, Organisationsformen und Folgen für die Industriearbeit. In: WSI-Mitteilungen No. 1, 1996. S. 11-18.
Hirschman 1945: Hirschman, Albert O. National Power and the Structure of Foreign Trade. Berkeley, Los Angeles, London: University of California Press, 1945.
Hirschman 1967: Hirschman, Albert O. Die Strategie der wirtschaftlichen Entwicklung. Stuttgart: Gustav Fischer Verlag, 1967.
Hirschman 1968: Hirschman, Albert O. The Political Economy of Import-Substituting Industrialization in Latin America. American Economic Review, Vol. 82, No. 1, February 1968. S. 1-32.
Hirschman 1989: Hirschman, Albert O. Entwicklung, Markt und Moral. München: Carl Hanser Verlag, 1989.
Hirschman 1991: Hirschman, Albert O. Denken gegen die Zukunft. Frankfurt am Main: Fischer, (1991) 1995.
Hirst/Thompson 1996: Hirst, Paul, Thompson, Grahame. Globalization in Question. The International Economy and the Possibilities of Governance. Oxford: Polity Press, 1996.
Hobe 1998: Hobe, Stephan. Der kooperationsoffene Verfassungsstaat. In: Staat, Bd. 37, Heft 1/4, 1998. S. 521-546.
Hobsbawm 1995: Hobsbawn, Eric. Das Zeitalter der Extreme. München: Carl Hanser Verlag, 1995.
Hoda 2002: Hoda, Anwarul. Tariff Negotiations and Renegotiations under the GATT and the WTO: Procedures and Practices. Cambridge: Cambridge University Press, 2002.
Hoda/Ahuja 2005: Hoda, Anwarul, Ahuja, Rajeev. Agreement on Subsidies and Countervailing Measures: Need for Clarification and Improvement. In: JWT Vol. 39, No. 6, 2005. S. 1009-1069.
Hoekman 1995: Hoekman, Bernard M. Trade Laws and Institutions: Good Practices and the World Trade. World Bank Discussion Paper, 282. Washington: World Bank, 1995.

Hoekman 1998: Hoekman, Bernard M. Free Trade and Deep Integration: Antidumping and Antitrust in Regional Agreements. World Bank, Policy Research Working Paper No. 1950, July 1998. In: http://www.worldbank.org.

Hoekman 2004: Hoekman, Bernard M. Operationalizing the Concept of Policy Space in the WTO: Beyond Special and Differential Treatment. Working Paper, October 2004. In: http://www.gem-sciences-po.fr/content/publications/pdf/Hoekman-operationalizing_SDT.pdf.

Hoekman 2005: Hoekman, Bernard M. Operationalizing the Concept of Policy Space in the WTO: Beyond Special and Differential Treatment. In: Petersmann, Ernst-Ulrich (ed.). Reforming the World Trading System. Legitimacy, Efficiency, and Democratic Governance. Oxford: Oxford University Press, 2005.

Hoekman 2005a: Hoekman, Bernard M. Expanding WTO membership and heterogenous interests. In: World Trade Review Vol. 4, No. 3, 2005. S. 401-408.

Hoekman et al. 2002: Hoekman, Bernard M., Mattoo, Aaditya, English, Philip. Development, Trade, and the WTO. Washington: World Bank, 2002.

Hoekman et al. 2002a: Hoekman, Bernard M., Michalopoulos, Constantine, Schiff, Maurice, Tarr, David. Chapter 13. Trade Policy. In: Klugman, Jeni (ed.). A Sourcebook for Poverty Reduction Strategies. Washington: World Bank, 2002.

Hoekman/Anderson 1999: Hoekman, Bernard, Anderson, Kym. Developing Country Agriculture and the New Trade Agenda. World Bank Policy Research Working Paper No. 2125, May 1999. In: http://www.worldbank.org.

Hoekman/Holmes 1999: Hoekman, Bernard, Holmes, Peter. Competition Policy, Developing Countries and the WTO. World Bank, Policy Research Working Paper, No. 2211, October 1999.

Hoekman/Kostecki 1995: Hoekman, Bernard M., Kostecki, Michel M. The Political Economy of the World Trading System. From GATT to WTO. Oxford: Oxford University Press, 1995.

Hoekman/Kostecki 2001: Hoekman, Bernard M., Kostecki, Michel M. The Political Economy of the World Trading System. The WTO and Beyond. Oxford: Oxford University Press, 2001.

Hoekman/Leidy 1990: Hoekman, Bernard M., Leidy, Michael P. Policy Responses to Shifting Comparative Advantage: Designing a System of Emergency Protection. In: Kyklos, Vol. 43, Fasc. 1, 1990. S. 25-51.

Hoekman/Mavroidis 2003: Hoekman, Bernard M., Mavroidis, Petros C. Economic Development, Competition Policy and the World Trade Organization. In: JWT, Vol. 37, No. 1, 2003. S. 1-27.

Hoekman/Saggi 2006: Hoekman, Bernard M., Saggi, Kamal. International Cooperation on Domestic Policies. Lessons from the WTO Competition Policy Debate. In: Evenett, Simon J., Hoekman, Bernard M. Economic Development and Multilateral Trade Cooperation. Washington: World Bank/Palgrave Macmillan, 2006.

Hoelscher/Wolffgang 1998: Hoelscher, Christoph, Wolffgang, Hans-Michael. The Wassenaar-Arrangement between International Trade, Non-Proliferation, and Export Controls. In: JWT, Vol. 32 No. 1, February 1998. S. 45-63.

Höffe 1999: Höffe, Otfried. Demokratie im Zeitalter der Globalisierung. München: C. H. Beck, 1999.

Hoffmann 1995: Hoffmann, Irene. Rindfleischmärkte in Westafrika dargestellt am Beispiel der Cote d'Ivoire und Burkina Faso. In: BUKO Agrarkoordination (Hrg.). Futtermittelimporte. Hamburg: BUKO, 1995.

Hofmann 1993: Hofmann, André. Economic Development in Latin America in the 20th Century – A Comparative Perspective. In: Szirmai, Adam, van Ark, Bart, Pilat, Dirk (eds.). Explaining Economic Growth. Essays in Honour of Angus Maddison. Amsterdam: North Holland, 1993.

Hohlfeld 1995: Hohlfeld, Peter. Integration ungleich entwickelter Wirtschaftsräume – das Beispiel des EU-Beitritts Spaniens. In: RWI-Mitteilungen, Jg. 46, 1995. S. 237-255.

Höhmann-Hempler 1997: Höhmann-Hempler, Gesine. Getreidepoker. Die Rolle der Europäischen Union auf dem Weltgetreidemarkt und deren Auswirkung auf die Ernährungssicherheit in Entwicklungsländern. BUKO Agrar Studien 7. Hamburg: BUKO Agrar Koordination/Verein zur Förderung entwicklungspolitischer Zusammenarbeit, 1997.

Holland et al. 2003: Holland, David, Figueroa B., Eugenio, Alvarez, Roberto, Gilbert, John. On the Removal of Agricultural Price Bands in Chile: A General Equilibrium Analysis. Central Bank of Chile Working Papers No. 244, Diciembre 2003. In: http://www.bcentral.cl/eng/stdpub/studies/workingpaper.

Hollerman 1984: Hollerman, Leon. Japan's Direct Investment in California and the New Protectionism. In: JWTL, Vol. 18 No. 4, July August 1984. S. 309-319.

Holmer/Hippler Bello 1988: Holmer, Alan F., Hippler Bello, Judith. Section 201 of the Trade Act of 1974: The Reagan Record. In: North Carolina Journal of International Law and Commercial Regulation, Vol. 13, 1988.

Homann/Pies 1996: Homann, Karl, Pies, Ingo. Sozialpolitik für den Markt: Theoretische Positionen konstitutioneller Ökonomik. In: Pies, Ingo, Leschke, Martin (Hrg.). James Buchanans konstitutionelle Ökonomik. Tübingen: Mohr, 1996.

Homburg 1996: Homburg, Stefan. Makroökonomik. In: von Hagen, Jürgen et al. (Hrg.) Handbuch der Volkswirtschaftslehre. Berlin: Springer, 1996.

Hoppmann 1966: Hoppmann, Erich. Das Konzept der optimalen Wettbewerbsintensität. In: Jahrbücher für Nationalökonomie und Statistik, Bd. 179, 1966. S. 286-323.

Horaguchi 2004: Horaguchi, Haruo. Hollowing-out of Japanese Industries and Creation of Knowledge-Intense Clusters. Conference Paper, March 26, 2004. In: http://www.jil.go.jp/english/events_and_information/documents/keynote_report.pdf.

Horlick 1993: Horlick, Gary N. How the GATT Became Protectionist. An Analysis of the Uruguay Round Draft Final Antidumping Code. In: JWT, Vol. 27, No. 5, Oct. 1993. S. 5-17.

Horlick 2003: Horlick, Gary N. Deference - and Responsibility - by WTO 'Judges'. In: Cottier, Thomas, Mavroidis, Petros C (eds.). The Role of the Judge in International Trade Regulation. Ann Arbor: University of Michigan Press, 2003.
Horlick 2005: Horlick, Gary N. The 10 Major Problems With the Anti-Dumping Instrument in the United States. In: JWT, Vol. 39, No. 1, 2005. S. 169-179.
Horlick/Clarke 1997: Horlick, Gary N., Clarke, Peggy A. Standards for Panels Reviewing Anti-dumping Determinations under the GATT and WTO. In: Petersmann, Ernst-Ulrich (ed.). International Trade Law and the GATT/WTO Dispute Settlement System. London, The Hague, Boston: Kluwer Law, 1997.
Horlick/Shea 2005: Horlick, Gary N., Shea, Eleanor C. The World Trade Organization Antidumping Agreement. In: JWT, Vol. 29, No. 1, February 1995. S. 5-31.
Horlick/Vermulst 2005: Horlick, Gary N., Vermulst, Edwin. The 10 Major Problems With the Anti-Dumping Instrument: An Attempt at Synthesis. In: JWT, Vol. 39, No. 1, 2005. S. 67-73.
Horn 1995: Horn, Hans-Detlef. 'Grundrechtsschutz in Deutschland'- Die Hoheitsgewalt der Europäischen Gemeinschaften und die Grundrechte des Grundgesetzes nach dem Maastricht-Urteil des Bundesverfassungsgerichts. In: Deutsches Verwaltungsblatt, 15. Januar 1995. S. 89-96.
Horn 1996: Horn, Ernst-Jürgen. Considerations on International Rules for Competition Policy in the Case of High-Technology Products and Services. Kiel Working Paper No. 733, March 1996.
Horn/Mavroidis 1999: Horn, Henrik, Mavroidis, Petros C. Remedies in the WTO Dispute Settlement System and Developing Country Interests. April, 1999. In: http://www.tradeobservatory.org/library.
Horn/Mavroidis 2004: Horn, Henrik, Mavroidis, Petros C. Still Hazy after All These Years: The Interpretation of National Treatment in the GATT/WTO Case-law in Tax Discrimination. In: European Journal of International Law, Vol. 15, No. 1, 2004. S. 39-69.
Horn/Mavroidis 2004: Horn, Henrik, Mavroidis, Petros C. US - Lamb. United States - Safeguard Measures on Imports of Fresh, Chilled or Frozen Lam Meat from New Zealand and Australia: What should be required of a safeguard investigation? In: World Trade Review Vol. 2 No. 3, 2003. S. 395-430.
Horn/Mavroidis 2005: Horn, Henrik, Mavroidis, Petros C. United States - Continued Dumping and Subsidy Offset Act of 2000. In: World Trade Review Vol. 4, No. 3, 2005. S. 525-550.
Horn/Weiler 2004: Horn, Henrik, Weiler, Joseph H. H. EC-Asbestos. European Communities - Measures Affecting Asbestos and Asbestos-Containing Products. In: World Trade Review Vol. 3, No. 1, 2004. S. 129-151.
Hovenkamp 1999: Hovenkamp, Herbert. Federal Antitrust Policy. The Law of Competition and Its Practice. St. Paul, Minn.: West Group, 1999.
Howard/Mungoma 1996: Howard, Julie A., Mungoma, Catherine. Zambia's Stop- and Go- Revolution: the Impact of Policies and Organizations on the Development and Spread of Maize Technology. Michigan State University International Development Working Papers No. 61, 1996. In: http://www.aec.msu.edu/agecon/fs2/index.htm.
Howe 1996: Howe, Christoper. The Origins of Japanese Trade Supremacy. Development and Technology in Asia from 1540 to the Pacific War. London: Hurst and Company, 1996.
Howell et al. 1988: Howell, Thomas R., Noellert, William R., Kreier, Jesse G., Wolff, Alan Wm. Steel and the State. Government Intervention and Steel's Structural Crisis. Boulder; London: Westview Press, 1988.
Howell et al. 1992: Howell, Thomas R., Wolff, Alan Wm., Bartlett, Brent L., Gadbach, Michael R. Conflict among Nations. Trade Policies in the 1990s. Boulder: Westview Press, 1992.
Howells 1998: Howells, Jeremy. Innovation and Technology Transfers within Multinational Firms. In: Michie, Jonathan, Smith, John Grieve. Globalization, Growth, and Governance. Oxford: Oxford University Press, 1998.
Howse 2002: Howse, Robert. The Sardines Panel and AB Rulings - Some Preliminary Reactions. In: Legal Issues of Economic Integration, Vol. 29 No. 3, 2002. S. 247-254.
Howse 2003: Howse, Robert. The Most Dangerous Branch? WTO Appelate Body Jurisprudence on the Nature and Limits of the Judical Power. In: Cottier, Thomas, Mavroidis, Petros C (eds.). The Role of the Judge in International Trade Regulation. Ann Arbor: University of Michigan Press, 2003.
Howse/Nicolaidis 2000: Howse, Robert. Nicolaidis, Kalypso. Legitimacy and Global Governance: Why Constitutionalizing the WTO is a Step Too Far. Working Paper. Conference: Efficiency, Equity and Legitimacy: The Multilateral Trading System at the Millenium. In: http://www.ksg.harvard.edu/cbg/trade/howse.htm.
Howse/Nicolaidis 2003: Howse, Robert, Nicolaidis, Kalypso. Legitimacy through 'Higher Law'? Why Constitutionalizing the WTO is a Step Too Far. In: Cottier, Thomas, Mavroidis, Petros C (eds.). The Role of the Judge in International Trade Regulation. Ann Arbor: University of Michigan Press, 2003.
Howse/Regan 2000: Howse, Robert, Regan, Donald. The Product/Process Distinction - An Illusory Basis for Disciplining 'Unilateralism' in Trade Policy. In: European Journal of International Law, Vol. 11, No.2, 2000. S. 249-289.
Howse/Staiger 2005: Howse, Robert, Staiger, Robert W. United States - Anti-Dumping Act of 1916 (Original Complaint by the European Communities) - Recourse to arbitration by the United States under 22.6 of the DSU, WT/DS136/ARB, 24 February 2004. In: World Trade Review Vol. 4, No. 2. S. 295-316.
Huang/Rozelle 1996: Huang, Jikun, Rozelle, Scott. Technological Change: Rediscovering the engine of productivity growth in China's rural economy. In: Journal Development Economies, Vol. 49, 1996. S. 337-369.
Hudec 1970: Hudec, Robert E. The GATT Legal System: A Diplomat's Jurisprudence. In: Hudec, Robert E. Essays on the Nature of International Trade Law. London: Cameron May, 1999.
Hudec 1975: Hudec, Robert E. The GATT Legal System and World Trade Diplomacy. New York: Praeger Publishers, 1975.

Hudec 1980: Hudec. Robert E. GATT Dispute Settlement after the Tokyo Round: An Unfinished Business. In: Cornell International Law Journal, Vol. 13, No. 2, Summer 1980. S. 145-203.
Hudec 1987: Hudec, Robert E. Developing Countries in the GATT Legal System. Aldershot et al.: Gower, 1987.
Hudec 1991: Hudec, Robert E. Enforcing International Trade Law: The Evolution of the Modern GATT Legal System. New Hamphire: Butterworth Legal Publishers, 1991.
Hudec 1999: Hudec, Robert E. Essays on the Nature of International Trade Law. London: Cameron May, 1999.
Hufbauer 1986: Hufbauer, Gary Clyde, Berliner, Diane T., Elliott, Kimberly Ann. Trade Protection in the United States. In: Aussenwirtschaft, 41. Jg, Heft 2/3, 1986. S. 225-258.
Hufbauer et al. 1986: Hufbauer, Gary Clyde, Berliner, Diane T., Elliott, Kimberly Ann. Trade Protection in the United States: 31 Case Studies. Washington: Institute for International Economics, 1986.
Hufbauer/Erb 1984: Hufbauer, Gary Clyde, Erb, Joanna Shelton. Subsidies in International Trade. London: MIT-Press, 1984.
Hufbauer/Warren 1999: Hufbauer, Gary, Warren, Tony. The Globalization of Services. Institute for Internationale Economics, October 1999. In: http://www.iie.com.
Hughes 2004: Hughes, V. Arbitration within the WTO. In: Ortino, Federico, Petersmann, Ernst-Ulrich (eds.). The WTO Dispute Settlement System 1995 - 2003. The Hague et al.: Kluwer Law International, 2004.
Hughes/Krueger 1984: Hughes, Helen, Krueger, Anne O. Effects of Protection in Developed Countries on Developing Countries' Exports of Manufactures. In: Baldwin, Robert E. Krueger, Anne O. The Structure and Evolution of Recent U.S. Trade Policy. Chicago; London: The University of Chicago Press, 1984.
Hulsink/Schenk 1998: Hulsink, Willem, Schenk, Hans. Privatization and deregulation in the Netherlands. In: Parker, David (ed.). Privatization in the European Union. Theory and Policy Perspectives. London; New York: Routledge, 1998.
Hulten 1992: Hulten, Charles R. Growth Accounting When Technical Change is Emodied in Capital. In: American Economic Review, Vol. 82, No. 4, 1992. S. 964-980.
Hummels 1999: Hummels, David. Have international transportation costs declined? Manuscript. Chicago: University of Chicago, 1999. In: http://ntl.bts.gov/lib/24000/24400/24443/hummels.pdf.
Hummels et al. 2001: Hummels, David, Ishii, Jun, Yi, Kei-Mu. The nature and growth of vertical specialization in world trade. In: Journal of International Economics, Vol. 54, 2001. S. 75-96.
Hummels/Levinsohn 1993: Hummels, David, Levinsohn, James. Monopolistic Competition and International Trade: Reconsidering the Evidence. NBER Working Paper, No. 4389, June 1993.
Hummels/Levinsohn 1993a: Hummels, David, Levinsohn, James. Product Differentiation as Source of Comparativ Advantage. In: American Economic Review, Papers and Proceedings, Vol. 83, No. 2, May 1993. S.445-449.
Hummels/Levinsohn 1995: Hummels, David, Levinsohn, James. Monopolistic Competition and International Trade: Reconsidering the Evidence. In: Quarterly Journal of Economics, August 1995. S. 799-836.
Hummer/Obwexer 2000: Hummer, Waldemar, Obwexer, Walter. Die Wahrung der "Verfassungsgrundsätze der EU. In: EuZW, Heft 16/2000. 485-496.
Hummer/Weiss 1997: Hummer, Waldemar, Weiss, Friedl. Vom GATT '47 zur WTO '94. Dokumente zur alten und zur neuen Welthandelsordnung. Wien: Verlag Österreich, 1997.
Humphrey et al. 1998: Humphrey, John, Mukherjee, Avinandan, Zilbovicius, Mauro, Arbix, Glauco. Globalization, FDI and the Restructuring of Supplier Networks: The Motor Industry in Brazil and India. In: Kagami, Mitsuhiro, Humphrey, John, Piore, Michael (eds.). Learning, Liberalization and Economic Adjustment. Tokyo: Institute of Developing Economics, 1998.
Hynix Annual Report 2006: Hynix. Annual Report 2006. In: http://ww.hynix.co.kr.

I

IATRC 1994: International Agricultural Trade Research Consortium. The Uruguay Round Agreement on Agriculture: An Evaluation. Commissioned Paper No. 9, July 1994. In: http://www.iatrcweb.org.
IATRC 1997: International Agricultural Trade Research Consortium. Implementation of the Uruguay Round Agreement on Agriculture and Issues for the Next Round of Agricultural Negotiations. Commissioned Paper No. 12, October 1997. In: http://www.iatrcweb.org.
IBM Information 2006: IBM. Information. 2006. In: http://www-03.ibm.com/chips/
Ibrahim 1978: Ibrahim, Tigani E. Developing Countries and the Tokyo Round. In: JWTL, Vol. 12 No. 1. Jan. Feb. 1978. S. 1-26.
ICCA 2005: International Council of Chemical Associations. Anti Dumping in the Framework of the Doha Round. May 2005. In: http://www.icca-chem.org.
ICPAC 2000: International Competition Policy Advisory Committee to the Attorney Genery and Assistant Attorney General for Antitrust. Final Report. U.S. Department of Justice. In: http://www.usdoj.gov.
IEA 1994: IEA. The Energy Charter Treaty. A Description of Provisions. OECD, International Energy Agency. Paris: OECD, 1994.
IEG 2006: Independent Evaluation Group. Assessing World Bank Support for Trade, 1987-2006. Washington: IEC, 2006.
IFC 2000: International Finance Corporation. China's Emerging Private Enterprises. Washington: IFC, 2000. In: http://www.ifc.org.

IFC 2005: International Finance Corporation. China's Ownership Transformation. Process, Outcomes, Prospects. Washington: IFC, 2005. In: http://www.ifc.org.
Ikenberry 2001: Ikenberry, G. John. After Victory. Institutions, Strategic Restraint, and the Rebuilding of Order after Major Wars. Princeton; Oxford: Princeton University Press, 2001.
Ikenson 2004: Ikenson, Dan. Zeoring In: Antidumping's Flawed Methodology under Fire. In: Free Trade Bulletin, No. 11. Cato Institute. April 27, 2004. In: http://www.freetrade.org.
Ikenson 2004a: Ikenson, Dan. Ready to Compete. Completing the Steel Industry's Rehabilitation. In: Trade Briefing Paper No. 20. Cato Institute. June 22, 2004.
Ikenson/Lindsey 2002: Ikenson, Dan, Lindsey, Brink. Antidumping 101: The Devilish Details of 'Unfair Trade' Law. In: Trade Policy Analysis No. 20. Cato Institute. November 21, 2002. In: http://www.freetrade.org.
Ikenson/Lindsey 2002: Ikenson, Dan, Lindsey, Brink. Reforming the Antidumping Agreement. A Road Map for WTO Negotiations. In: Trade Policy Analysis No. 21. Cato Institute. December 11, 2002. In: http://www.freetrade.org.
ILEAP 2004: ILEAP. Key Issues in the Doha Round Negotiations on Non-Agricultural Market Access: An African Perspective. ILEAP Workshop Paper, Toronto 2004. In: http://www.ileapinitiative.com.
ILO div. Jg.: International Labour Organization. World Employment Report. Geneva: International Labour Office, div. Jg.
IMF 1988: IMF. Issues and Developments in International Trade Policy, Occasional Paper No. 63. Washington: IMF, 1988.
IMF 1997: IMF. Sequencing Capital Account Liberalization: Lessons from the Experiences in Chile, Indonesia, Korea and Thailand. IMF Working Paper WP/97/157. In: http://www.imf.org.
IMF 1998: IMF. External evaluation of the ESAF. Report by a group of independent experts. Washington: IMF, 1988. In: http://www.imf.org.
IMF 1998a: IMF: World Economic Outlook and International Capital Markets Interim Assessment. December 1998. Washington D.C.: International Monetary Fund, 1998.
IMF 1999: IMF. IMF-Supported Programs in Indonesia, Korea and Thailand: A Preliminary Assessment. Preliminary Copy. Washington: IMF, January 1999. In: http://www.imf.org.
IMF 1999a: IMF: World Economic Outlook. Washington D.C.: International Monetary Fund, 1999.
IMF 2000: IMF. Direction of Trade Statistics. Washington: IMF, 2000.
IMF 2004: IMF. Fund Support for Trade-Related Balance of Payments Adjustments. Prepared by the Policy Development and Review Department, approved by Mark Allen, February 27, 2004. In: http://www.imf.org/external/np/pdr/tim/2004/eng/022704.htm.
IMF 2005: IMF. World Economic Outlook. Washington: IMF, September 2005. In: http://www.imf.org.
IMF Annual Report/Jahresbericht div. Jahrgänge: IMF. Annual Report/Jahresbericht. Washington: IMF, div. Jg.
IMF Country Report div. Länder, div. Titel, Jahr: IMF Staff Country Reports. In: http://www.imf.org.
IMF Exchange Arrangements div. Jahrgänge: IMF. Annual Report on Exchange Arrangements and Exchange Restrictions. Washington: IMF, div. Jg.
Immenga 2004: Immenga, Ulrich. Internationales Wettbewerbsrecht, Unilateralismus, Bilateralismus, Multilateralismus. In: Christian Tietje et al. (Hrg.), Beiträge zum Transnationalen Wirtschaftsrecht, Heft 31, Oktober 2004. In: http://www.wirtschaftsrecht.uni-halle.de.
Immenga/Mestmäcker 1992: Immenga, Ulrich, Mestmäcker, Ernst-Joachim et al. GWB Gesetz gegen Wettbewerbsbeschränkungen. Kommentar. München: C.H. Beck, 1992.
Import Administration Antidumping Manual 1997: U.S. Department of Commerce. International Trade Administration (ITA). Import Administration Antidumping Manual. 1997. In: http://ia.ita.doc.gov/admanual/index.html.
IMS Health 2006: IMS Health. IMS Retail Drug Monitor. Tracking 13 Key Global Pharma Markets. 12 Month to August 2006. In: http://www.imshealth.de.
Inama 2003: Inama, Stefano. Trade Preferences and the World Trade Organization on Markets Access. In: JWT, Vol. 37, No. 5, 2003. S. 959-976.
Inama 2004: Inama, Stefano. Rules of Origin in International Trade. Intensive Course on Rules of Origin, Asian Development Bank, Bangkok, Thailand, 6-9 September 2004. In: http://www.adb.org.
Inama 2004a: Inama, Stefano. The Experience of Beneficiaries with GSP Rules of Origin. Intensive Course on Rules of Origin, Asian Development Bank, Bangkok, Thailand, 6-9 September 2004. In: http://www.adb.org.
Inama 2005: Inama, Stefano. The Association of South East Asian Nations - People's Republic of China Free Trade Area: Negotiating Beyond Eternity With Little Trade Liberalization? In: JWT, Vol. 39, No. 3, 2005. S. 559-579.
India Pharma Information 2006: Pharmaceutical and Drug Manufacturers. Industry Statistics. In: http://www.pharmaceutical-drug-manufacturers.com.
India Pharma Information 2006a: Boloji/Sivaprakasam, Kannan. Tale of Two Patent Regimes and the Indian Pharmaceutical Industry. In: http://www.boloji.com/health/articles/01036.htm.
Information Technology Agreement 2006: Information Technology Agreement. WTO Overview. 2006. In: http://www.wto.org/english/tratop_e/inftec_e/inftec_e.htm.
Ingco 1996: Ingco, Merlinda D. Progress in Agricultural Trade Liberalization and Welfare of Least-Developed Countries. World Bank, Working Paper, December 1996. In: http://www.worldbank.org.
Ingco 1997: Ingco, Merlinda D. Has Agricultural Trade Liberalization Improved Welfare in Least-Developed Countries. Yes. World Bank Policy Research Working Paper No. 1748, April 1997. In: http://www.worldbank.org.

Ingco/Ng 1998: Ingco, Merlinda, Ng, Francis. Distortionary Effects of State Trading in Agriculture. World Bank Policy Research Working Paper No. 1915, February 1998. In: http://www.worldbank.org.
Intel Information 2006: Intel. Informationen. 2006. In: http://www.intel.com/pressroom/kits/manufacturing/shanghai.htm.
International Intellectual Property Alliance: Copyright Industries in the US Economy, var. Reports., other Information. In: http://www.iipa.com.
International Trade Statistics Yearbook, div. Jahrgänge: International Trade Statistics Yearbook. Department of Economic and Social Development Statistical Office. New York: United Nations. div. Jahrgänge.
IPR Commission 2002: Commission on Intellectual Property Rights. Integrating Intellectual Property Rights and Development Policy. London: September, 2002. In: http://www.iprcommission.org.
Ipsen 1972: Ipsen, Hans Peter. Europäisches Gemeinschaftsrecht. Tübingen: Mohr, 1972.
Irish 2007: Irish, Maureen. GSP Tariffs and Conditionality: A Comment on EC Preferences. In: JWT, Vol. 41, No. 4, 2007. S. 683-698.
Irwin 1990: Irwin, Manley R. The Telecommunications Industry. In: Adams, Walter (Hrg.). The Structure of American Industry. New York: Macmillan, 1990.
Irwin 1994: Irwin, Douglas A. The GATT's Contribution to Economic Recovery in Post-War Europa. NBER Working Paper No. 4944, December 1994.
Irwin 2003: Irwin, Douglas, A. Causing Problems? The WTO Review of Causation and Injury Attribution in U.S. Section 201 Cases. In: World Trade Review Vol. 2 No. 3, 2003. S. 297-325.
Irwin 2003: Irwin, Douglas, A. Causing Problems? The WTO Review of Causation and Injury Attribution in U.S. Section 201 Cases. Paper prepared for the Dartmouth-Tuck Forum on International Trade and Business conference on "Managing Global Trade: The WTO, Trade Remedies and Dispute Settlement," Washington, D.C., May 16-17, 2003. In: http://www.imf.org/external/np/res/seminars/2004/mussa/pdf/irwin.pdf.
Isaac/Kerr 2003: Isaac, Grant E., Kerr, William A. Genetically Modified Organisms at the World Trade Organization: A Harvest of Trouble. In: JWT, Vol. 37, No. 6, 2003. S. 1083-1095.
Isensee 1987: Isensee, Josef. Staat und Verfassung. In: Isensee, Josef, Kirchhof, Paul (Hrg.). Handbuch des Staatsrechts. Bd. I. Heidelberg: C.F. Müller, 1987.
Isensee 1988: Isensee, Josef. Gemeinwohl und Staatsaufgaben im Verfassungsstaat. In: Isensee, Josef, Kirchhof, Paul (Hrg.). Handbuch des Staatsrechts. Bd. III. Heidelberg: C.F. Müller, 1988.
ISG 2006: International Steel Group Inc. Company Information 2006. In: http://www.intlsteel.com/.
Islam 2004: Islam, M. Rafiqul. Recent EU Trade Sanctions on the US to Induce Compliance with the WTO Ruling in the Foreign Sales Corporations Case: Its Policy Contradictions Revisited. In: JWT, Vol. 38, No. 3, 2004. S. 471-489.
Ismail 2005: Ismail, Faizel. A Development Perspective on the WTO July 2004 General Council Decision. In: Petersmann, Ernst-Ulrich (ed.). Reforming the World Trading System. Legitimacy, Efficiency, and Democratic Governance. Oxford: Oxford University Press, 2005.
Ismail 2006: Ismail, Faizel. Mainstreaming Economic Development in the Trading System. In: Evenett, Simon J., Hoekman, Bernard M. Economic Development and Multilateral Trade Cooperation. Washington: World Bank/Palgrave Macmillan, 2006.
Ismail 2006a: Ismail, Faizel. How Can Least-Developed Countries and Other Small, Weak and Vulnerable Economies Also Gain from the Doha Development Agenda on the Road to Hong Kong. In: JWT, Vol. 40, No. 1, 2006. S. 37-68.
Issing 1997: Issing, Otmar. Geldwertstabilität als ordnungspolitisches Problem. In: ORDO, Bd. 48, 1997.
ITA 2000: International Trade Administration. Report to the President. Global Steel Trade. July 2000. In: http//www.ita.doc.gov/media/steelreport726.htm.
ITA 2003: International Trade Administration. Fact Sheet. Preliminary Determination in the Countervailing Duty Investigation: Dynamic Random Access Memory Semiconductors (DRAMS) from the Republic of Korea. Undated. In: http://www.ita.doc.gov.
ITA 2004: ITA. Wooden Bedroom Furniture From China. Investigation No. 731-TA-1058 (Final), Publication 3742, December 2004. In: http://www.ita.doc.gov.
ITA 2004a: ITA. Certain Color Television Recievers from China. Investigation No. 731-TA-1034 (Final), Publication 3695, May 2004. In: http://www.ita.doc.gov.
ITA 2005: ITA. The Year in Trade 2004. Operation of the Trade Agreements Program 56th Report. Publication 3779, July 2005. In: http://www.ita.doc.gov.
ITA 2006: International Trade Administration. Continuations of AD and CVD Orders Resulting from 5-Year Sunset Reviews. Last Update 25 July 2006. In: http://ia.ita.doc.gov/sunset/ssy2kcon.html.
ITA 2006: ITA. Notice of Initiation of Administrative Reviews of the Antidumping Duty Orders on Certain Frozen Warmwater Shrimp from Brazil, Ecuador, India and Thailand. Billing Code: 3510-DS-P2006. In: http://ia.ita.doc.gov.
ITC 1999: ITC. Trade in Information Technology Products and the WTO Agreements. Current situation and views of exporters in developing countries. Geneva: International Trade Centre (ITC), 1999.
ITC Mauritius 2001: International Trade Centre. Subregional Export Expansion in Southern Africa. Mauritius Supply Survey on Textiles and Clothing, November 2001. In: http://www.intracen.org/sstp/survey/textile/mauritius.pdf.
Ito 1996: Ito, Takatoshi. Japan and the Asian Economies: A 'Miracle' in Transition. In: Brookings Papers on Economic Activity, 2, 1996. S. 205-267.

Iwasawa 1997: Iwasawa, Yuji. Constitutional problems involved in implementing the Uruguay Round in Japan. In: Jackson, John H., Sykes, Alan O. (eds.). Implementing the Uruguay Round. Oxford: Clarendon Press, 1997.
IW-Trends 3/99: IW-Trends. Aussenhandelstrends in Mittel- und Osteuropa und die Marktposition Deutschlands. 3/1999. S. 36-52.
IW-Trends Südafrika: IW-Trends. Die Reintegration Südafrikas in die Weltwirtschaft. 3/1999. S. 53-71.
IW-Trends Umsatzrendite: IW-Trends. Internationaler Vergleich der Umsatzrenditen in der Gewerblichen Wirtschaft. 4/1999. S. 28-38.

J

Jackson 1969: Jackson, John H. World Trade and the Law of the GATT. Indianapolis; Kansas City; New York: The Bobbs-Merill Company, 1969.
Jackson 1978: Jackson, John H. The Crumbling Institutions of the Liberal Trade System. In: Journal of World Trade Law, Vol. 12, 1978, S. 93-106.
Jackson 1989: Jackson, John H. The World Trading System. Law and Policy of International Economic Relations. Cambridge, Mass.: The MIT Press, 1989.
Jackson 1990: Jackson, John H. Restructuring the GATT System. London: Pinter Publishers, 1990.
Jackson 1997: Jackson, John H. The World Trading System. Law and Policy of International Economic Relations 2nd Edition. Cambridge, Mass.: The MIT Press, 1997.
Jackson et al. 1995: Jackson, John H., Davey, William J., Sykes, Alan O. Legal Problems of International Economic Relations. St. Paul, Minn.: West Publishing Co., 1995.
Jackson/Grane 2001: Jackson, John H., Grane, Patricio. The Sage Continues: An Update on the Banana Dispute and Its Procedural Offspring. In: Journal of International Economic Law, 2001. S. 581-595.
Jackson/Sykes 1997: Jackson, John H., Sykes, Alan O. (eds.). Implementing the Uruguay Round. Oxford: Clarendon Press, 1997.
Jacobitz 1995: Jacobitz, Robin. Der Niedergang institutionalisierter Kooperation. Marburg: Studien der Forschungsgruppe Europäische Gemeinschaften (FEG), 1995.
Jacobson et al. 1993: Jacobson, Louis S., LaLonde, Robert J., Sullivan, Daniel G. Earnings Losses of Displaced Workers. In: American Economic Review, Vol. 83, No. 4, September 1993.
Jacobsson 1993: Jacobsson, Staffan. The extent, nature and timing of industrial policy for infant industries. In: Brundenius, Claes, Göransson, Bo (eds.). New Technologies and Global Restructuring. The Thirld World at Crossroads. London; Los Angeles: Taylor Graham, 1993.
Jacobsson 1993: Jacobsson, Staffan. The Length of the Infant Industry Period: Evidence from the Engineering Industy in South Korea. In: World Development, Vol. 21, No. 3, 1993. S. 407-419.
Jacquemin 1994: Jacquemin, Alexis. Goals and Means of European Antitrust Policy After 1992. In: Demsetz, Harold, Jacquemin, Alexis (Hrg.). Anti-trust Economics – New challenges for competition policy. Malmö: Institute of Economic Research, 1994.
Jaeger 1992: Jaeger, William K. The Effects of Economic Policies on African Agriculture. Washington: World Bank, 1992.
Jaffe 1986: Jaffe, Adam B.. Technological Opportunity and Spillover of R & D: Evidence form Firms' Patents, Profits, and Market Value. In: American Economic Review, Vol. 76 No. 5, December 1986. S. 984-1001.
Jahrbuch der Textilindustrie, div. Jg.: Gesamtverband der Textilindustrie in der Bundesrepublik Deutschland (Gesamttextil). Jahrbuch der Textilindustrie. Eschborn/Frankfurt am Main: Textil-Service Verlags- und Zertifizierungsstelle Öko-Text GmbH, div. Jg.
Jakubson et al. 2004: Jakubson, George, Jeong, Kap-Young, Kim, DongHun, Masson, Robert T. Oligopolistic 'Agreement' and/or 'Superiority'? New Findings from New Methodologies and Data. Food Marketing Policy Centre, Research Report No. 81, June 2004. In: http://www.fmpc.uconn.edu.
James 1995: James, Jeffrex. The State, Technology and Industrialization in Africa. London: St. Martin's Press, 1995.
Janow 2003: Janow, Merit. Commentary on Nathalie McNelins Paper. In: Cottier, Thomas, Mavroidis, Petros C (eds.). The Role of the Judge in International Trade Regulation. Ann Arbor: University of Michigan Press, 2003.
Janow/Staiger 2004: Janow, Merit, Staiger, Robert W. Canada - Diary. Canada - Measures Affecting the Importation of Diary Products and the Exportation of Milk. In: World Trade Review Vol. 3 No. 2, 2004. S. 277-315.
Jans 2000: Jans, Jan H. Proportionality Revisited. In: Legal Issues of Economic Integration, Vol. 27 No. 3, 2000. S. 239-265.
Jansen 1991: Jansen, Doris J. Zambia. In: Krueger, Anne O., Schiff, Maurice, Valdes, Alberto. The Political Economy of Agricultural Pricing Policy. Vol. 3 Africa and the Mediterranean. Baltimore, London: John Hopkins University Press, 1991.
Japan Statement Ways and Means 2005: House Committee on Ways and Means. Statement of the Government of Japan. September 2, 2005. In: http://waysandmeans.house.gov.
Jaquemin 1982: Jaquemin, Alexis. Imperfect Market Structure and International Trade – Some Recent Research. In: Kyklos, Vol. 35, Heft 1, 1982. S. 75-93.
Jaquemin 1984: Jaquemin, Alexis (ed.). European Industry: Public Policy and Corporate Strategy. Oxford: Clarendon Press, 1984.
Jaquemin et al. 1980: Jaquemin, Alexis, Ghellinck, Elisabeth de, Huveneers, Christian. Concentration and profitability in a small open economy. In: Journal of Industrial Economics, Vol. XXIX, No. 2, December 1980.

Jayne 1993: Jayne, T. S. Sources and Effects of Instability in the World Rice Market. Michigan State University International Development Working Papers No. 13, 1993. In: http://www.aec.msu.edu/agecon/fs2/index.htm.
Jayne et al. 1994: Jayne, T. S., Takawarasha, T., van Zyl, Johan. Interactions between Food Market Reform and Regional Trade in Zimbabwe and South Africa: Implications for Food Security. Michigan State University International Development Working Papers No. 48, 1994. In: http://www.aec.msu.edu/agecon/fs2/index.htm.
Jayne et al. 1995: Jayne, T. S., Hajek, Milan, van Zyl, Johan. An Analysis of Alternative Maize Marketing Policies in South Africa. Michigan State University International Development Working Papers No. 50, 1995. In: http://www.aec.msu.edu/agecon/fs2/index.htm.
Jayne et al. 1996: Jayne, T. S., Mukumbu, Mulinge, Duncan, John, Staatz, John, Howard, Julie, Lundberg, Mattias, Aldridge, Kim, Nakaponda, Bethel, Ferris, Jake, Keita, Francis, Sanankoua, Abdel Kader. Trends in real food pricess in six Sub-Saharan African countries. Michigan State University International Development Working Papers No. 55, 1996. In: http://www.aec.msu.edu/agecon/fs2/index.htm.
Jayne et al. 1997: Jayne, T. S., Shaffer, James D., Staatz, John M., Reardon, Thomas. Improving the Impact of Market Reform on Agricultural Productivity in Africa: How Institutional Design makes a Difference. Michigan State University International Development Working Papers No. 66, 1997. In: http://www.aec.msu.edu/agecon/fs2/index.htm.
Jayne et al. 1998: Jayne, T.S., Negassa, Asfaw, Myers, Robert J. The Effect of Liberalization on Grain Prices and Marketing Margins in Ethiopia. Michigan State University International Development Working Papers No. 68, 1998. In: http://www.aec.msu.edu/agecon/fs2/index.htm.
Jayne et al. 2001: Jayne, T.S., Yamano, T., Nyoro, J., Awuor, T. Do Farmers Really Benefit from High Food Prices? Balancing Rural Interests in Kenya's Maize Pricing and Marketing Policy. Draft Working Paper 2 B, Tegemeo Agricultural Monitoring and Policy Analysis Project, Egerton University, University of Michigan, April 28, 2001. In: http://www.aec.msu.edu/agecon/fs2/kenya/.
Jayne et al. 2002: Jayne, T.S., Govereh, J., Mwanaumo, A., Nyoro, J.K., Chapoto, A. False Promise or False Premise? The Experience of Food and Input Market Reform in Eastern and Southern Africa. In: World Development, Vol. 30 No. 11, 2002, pp. 1967-1985.
Jayne/Jones 1997: Jayne, T. S., Jones, Stephen. Food Marketing and Pricing Policy in Eastern and Southern Africa: A Survey. In: World Development, Vol. 25 No. 9, 1997. S. 1505-1527.
Jenkins 1980: Jenkins, Glen P. Costs and Consequences of the New Protectionism. Harvard Institute for International Development. Development Discussion Paper No. 99. Cambridge: Harvard University, July 1980.
Jenkins 1995: Jenkins, Rhys. Does Trade Liberalization lead to Productivity Increases? A Case Study of Bolivean Manufacturing. In: Journal of International Development, Vol. 76, No. 4, 1995. S. 577-597.
Jenkins 2005: Jenkins, Peter T. International Law Related to Precautionary Approaches to National Regulation of Plant Imports. In: JWT, Vol. 39, No. 5, 2005. S. 895-906.
Jenkins/Lai 1991: Jenkins, Glenn P., Lai, Andrew Kwok-Kong. Malaysia. In: Krueger, Anne O., Schiff, Maurice, Valdes, Alberto. The Political Economy of Agricultural Pricing Policy. Vol. 2 Asia. Baltimore, London: John Hopkins University Press, 1991.
Jens 1981: Jens, Uwe. Möglichkeiten und Grenzen rationaler Wettbewerbspolitik in Demokratien. In: Cox, Helmut, Jens, Uwe, Markert, Kurt (Hrg.). Handbuch des Wettbewerbs. München: Vahlen, 1981.
Jensen et al. 2002: Jensen, Henning Tarp, Robinson, Sherman, Tarp, Finn. General Equilibrium Measures of Agricultural Policy Bias in Fifteen Developing Countries. TMD Discussion Paper No. 105. Trade and Macroeconomics Division, International Food Policy Research Institute. Washington: October 2002. In: http://www.cgiar.org/ifpri/divs/tmd/dp.htm.
Jerchow 1978: Jerchow, Friedrich. Deutschland in der Weltwirtschaft 1944 – 1947. Alliierte Deutschland- und Reparationspolitik und die Anfänge der westdeutschen Außenwirtschaft. Düsseldorf: Droste Verlag, 1978.
Jerger/Menkhoff 1996: Jerger, Jürgen, Menkhoff, Lukas. Der Begriff "internationale Wettbewerbsfähigkeit" im Lichte der Außenhandelstheorie. In: Wirtschaftsstudium WiSt, Heft 1, Januar 1996. S. 21- 28.
Jervis 1999: Jervis, Robert. Realism, Neoliberalism, and Cooperation. In: International Security, Vol. 24 No. 1, Summer 1999. S. 42-63.
Jessen 2004: Jessen, Henning. Zollpräferenzen für Entwicklungsländer: WTO-rechtliche Anforderungen an Selektivität und Konditionalität - Die GSP-Entscheidung des WTO Panel und Appelate Body. In: Christian Tietje et al. (Hrg.), Beiträge zum Transnationalen Wirtschaftsrecht, Heft 27, 2004. In: http://www.wirtschaftsrecht.uni-halle.de.
Jessen 2004a: Jessen, Henning. 'GSP Plus' - Zur WTO-Konformität des zukünftigen Zollpräferenzsystems der EG. Policy Paper on Transnational Economic Law, No. 9/2004. In: http://www.wirtschaftsrecht.uni-halle.de.
JETRO White Paper Foreign Direkt Investment 2002: Japan External Trade Organization. White Paper on Foreign Direct Investment. 2002. In: http://www.jetro.go.jp/en/stats/white_paper/.
JETRO White Paper Trade and Investment 2004: Japan External Trade Organization. White Paper on International Trade and Foreign Direct Investment. 2004. In: http://www.jetro.go.jp/en/stats/white_paper/.
Jha et al. 2004: Jha, Veena, Gupta, Sarika, Nedumpara, James, Karthikeyan, Kailas. Trade Liberalization and Poverty in India. Advanced/Unedited Draft. Geneva: United Nations Conference of Trade and Development, 2004. In: http://www.unctad.org.
Jimenez 2006: Jimenez, Alberto Alvarez. The WTO AB Report on Mexico - Soft Drinks, and the Limits of the WTO Dispute Settlement System. In: Legal Issues of Economic Integration Vol. 33, No. 3, 2006. S. 319-333.
Joerges 1994: Joerges, Christian. Legitimationsprobleme des Europäischen Wirtschaftsrechts und der Vertrag von Maastricht. In: Brüggemeier, Gert. Verfassungen für ein ziviles Europa. Baden-Baden: Nomos, 1994.

Joerges 2000: Joerges, Christian. Die Europäische 'Komitologie': Kafkaeske Bürokratie oder Beispiel 'deliberativen Regierens' im Binnenmarkt. In: Joerges, Christian, Falke, Josef (Hrg.). Das Ausschußwesen der Europäischen Union. Baden-Baden: Nomos, 2000.
Joerges 2001: Joerges, Christian. 'Good Governance' im Europäischen Binnenmarkt: Über die Spannungen zwischen zwei rechtswissenschaftlichen Integrationskonzepten und deren Aufhebung. European University Institute Working Paper RSC No. 2001/29.
Joerges/Neyer 1998: Joerges, Christian, Neyer, Jürgen. Von intergouvernementalem Verhandeln zur deliberativen Politik: Gründe und Chancen für eine Konstitutionalisierung der europäischen Komitologie. In: Kohler-Koch, Beate. Regieren in entgrenzten Räumen. PVS Sonderheft 29/1998. Opladen: Westdeutscher Verlag, 1998.
Johnson 1962: Johnson, Harry G. Monetary Theory and Policy. In: American Economic Review, Vol. 52, No. 3, June 1962. S. 335-384.
Johnson 1971: Johnson, Harry G. Aspects of the Theory of Tariffs. London: Allen & Unwin, 1971.
Johnson 1982: Johnson, Chalmers. MITI and the Japanese Miracle. Stanford: Stanford University Press, 1982.
Johnson 1988: Johnson, Chalmers. Introduction: The Idea of Industrial Policy. In: Audretsch, David (ed.). Industrial Policy and Competitive Advantage, Vol. I. Cheltenham, UK, Northampton, MA: Elgar, 1998.
Johnson 2002: Johnson, Daniel K.N. The OECD Technology Concordance (OTC): Patents by Industry or Manufacture and Sector of Use. OECD STI Working Paper 2002/5, DSTI/DOC(2002)5, 1 March 2002. In: http://www.wipo.int/ipstats/en/resources/studies.html.
Johnson 2004: Johnson, Richard A. Comments on Patents, Entrepreneurship and Technology Diffusion. In: OECD. Patents, Innovation and Economic Performance. Conference Proceedings. Paris: OECD, 2004.
Jomo 1993: Jomo, K.S. Malaysia. In: Taylor, Lance. The Rocky Road to Reform. Adjustment, Income Distribution, and Growth in the Developing World. Cambridge: MIT Press, 1993.
Jones 1989: Jones, Kent. Voluntary Export Restraint: Political Economy, History and the Role of the GATT. In: JWT, Vol. 23 No. 3, 1989. S. 125-140.
Jones 1995: Jones, Charles I. R & D-Based Models of Economic Growth. In: Journal of Political Economy, Vol. 103, No. 4, 1995. S. 759-784.
Jones/Williams 1997: Jones, Charles I., William, John C. Measuring the Social Return to R&D. Federal Reserve Bank, Finance and Economics Discussion Series, 2, 1997.
Jones/Womack 1985: Jones, Daniel T., Womack, James P. Developing Countries and the Future of the Automobile Industry. In: World Development, Vol. 23, No. 3, 1985. S. 393-407.
Jorge M. 1987: Technology Generation in Latin American Manufacturing Industries. London: Macmillan Press, 1987.
Jorgenson et al. 1987: Jorgenson, Dale W., Gollop, Frank M., Fraumeni, Barbara M. Productivity and U.S. Economic Growth. Cambridge, Mass.: Harvard University Press, 1987.
Jorgenson/Landau 1993: Jorgenson, Dale W., Landau, Ralph. Tax Reform and the Cost of Capital. Washington: Brookings Institution, 1993.
Jorgenson/Nishimizu 1978: Jorgenson, Dale W., Nishimizu, Meiko. U.S. and Japanese Economic Growth, 1952-1974: An International Comparison. In: The Economic Journal, Vol. 88, December 1978, S. 707-726.
Joshua 1989: Joshua, Frank T. Experience of African Regional Economic Intergration. In: UNCTAD Review, Jg. 1, No. 2, 1989. S. 59-78.
Josling 1999: Josling, Tim. Developing Countries and the New Round of Multilateral Trade Negotiations: Background Notes on Agriculture. Working Paper, 1999. In: http://www.worldbank.org/research/trade.
Josling et al. 1996: Josling, Timothy E., Tangermann, Stefan, Warley, T.K. Agriculture in the GATT. London: Macmillan Press, 1996.
Jovanovic 1997: Jovanovic, Miroslav N. European Economic Integration. Limits and Prospects. London; New York: Routledge, 1997.
Jung 2002: Jung, Youngjin. China's Agressive Legalism. China's First Safeguard Measure. In: JWT, Vol. 36, No. 6, 2002. S. 1037-1060.
Jung/Lee 2003: Jung, Youngjin, Lee, Sun Hyeong. The Legacy of the Bird Amendment Controversies: Rethinking the Principle of Good Faith. In: JWT, Vol. 37, No. 5, 2003. S. 921-958.
Jung/Marshall 1985: Jung, Woo S., Marshall, Peyton J. Exports, Growth and Causality in Developing Countries. In: Journal of Development Economics, Vol. 18, 1985. S. 1-12.
Jungnickel 1996: Jungnickel, Rolf. Globalization: Exodus of German Industry. In: Intereconomics. July/August 1996. S. 181-188.
Junne 1990: Junne, Gerd. Theorien über Konflikte und Kooperation zwischen kapitalistischen Industrieländern. In: PVS, Jg. 31, Sonderheft 21, 1990.
Jürgensen 2005: Jürgensen, Thomas. Crime and Punishment: Retaliation under the World Trade Organization Dispute Settlement System. In: JWT, Vol. 39, No. 2, 2005. S. 327-340.
Justman/Teubal 1986: Justman, Moshe, Teubal, Morris. Innovation Policy in an open economy: A normative framework for strategic and tactical issues. In: Audretsch, David (ed.). Industrial Policy and Competitive Advantage, Vol. I. Cheltenham, UK, Northampton, MA: Elgar, 1998.
Jwa 1999: Jwa, Sung-Hee. The Asian Crisis and Implications for Industrial Policies. Wien: UNIDO, 1999. In: http://www.unido.org.

K

Kabeer/Humprey 1991: Kabeer, Naila, Humprey, John. Neo-liberalism, Gender, and the Limits of the Market. In: Christopher Colclough, James Manor (eds.). States or Markets? Neo-liberalism and the Development Policy Debate. Oxford. Clarendon Press, 1991.
Kagami/Humphrey/Piore 1998: Kagami, Mitsuhiro, Humphery, John, Piore, Michael. Learning, Liberalization and Economic Adjustment. Tokyo: Institute of Developing Economics, 1998.
Kahn 1962: Kahn, Alfred E. The Role of Patents. In: Miller, John Perry. Competition Cartels and their Regulation. Amsterdam: North Holland, 1962.
Kajiwara 1994: Kajiwara, Hirokazu. The Effects of Trade and Foreign Investment Liberalization Policies on Productivity in the Philippines. In: The Developing Economies, XXXII, No. 4, December 1994. S. 492-508.
Kamin/Klau 1998: Kamin, Steven B., Klau, Marc. Some Multi-Country Evidence on the Effects of Real Exchange Rates on Output. International Finance Discussion Papers , No. 611, May 1998. In: http://www.federalreserve.gov.
Kaminiski 1995: Kaminski, Herbert. Handel und Direktinvestitionen in den japanisch-indonesischen Beziehungen. Ein Beitrag zur Entwicklung Indonesiens? Hamburg: Institut für Asienkunde, 1995.
Kanaan 2000: Kanaan, Oussama. Tanzania's Experience with Trade Liberalization. In: Finance and Development, June 2000. S. 30-33.
Kang 2005: Kang, Sungjin. Comment on Annex V of the WTO SCM Agreement Procedures in the Context of Korea - Shipbuilding Dispute. In: Legal Issues of Economic Integration Vol. 33, No. 2, 2006. S. 183-197.
Kant 1992: Kant, Immanuel. Zum Ewigen Frieden. Hamburg: Meiner, 1992.
Kantzenbach 1966: Kantzenbach, Erhard. Die Funktionsfähigkeit des Wettbewerbs. Göttingen: Vandehoeck&Ruprecht, 1966.
Kantzenbach 1994: Kantzenbach, Erhard. Unternehmenskonzentration und Wettbewerb. In: WuW, 4, 1994. S. 294-302.
Kantzenbach/Kallfass 1981: Kantzenbach, Erhard, Kallfass, Hermann H. Das Konzept des funktionsfähigen Wettbewerbs – workable competition. In: Cox, Helmut, Jens, Uwe, Markert, Kurt (Hrg.). Handbuch des Wettbewerbs. München: Vahlen, 1981.
Kantzenbach/Krüger 1990: Kantzenbach, Erhard, Krüger, Reinald. Zur Frage der richtigen Abgrenzung des sachlich relevanten Marktes bei der wettbewerbspolitischen Beurteilung von Unternehmenszusammenschlüssen. In: WuW, 6/1990. S. 472-481.
Kantzenbach/Pfister 1996: Kantzenbach, Erhard, Pfister, Marisa. National Approaches to Technology Policy in a Globalizing World Economy – The Case of Germany and the European Union. In: Koopmann, Georg, Scharrer, Hans-Eckart (eds.). The Economics of High-Technology Competition. Baden-Baden: Nomos, 1996.
Kanwar/Evenson 2001: Kanwar, Sunil, Evenson, Robert E. Does Intellectual Property Rights Spur Technological Change. Yale University, Economic Growth Center, Centre Discussion Paper No. 831, June 2001. In: http://aida.econ.yale.edu/~egcenter/
Kaosaard 1998: Kaosaard, Mingsarn. Economic Development and Institutional Failures in Thailand. TDRI Quarterly Review, Vol. 13 No. 1, March 1998. See: http://thaieconwatch.com/articles/m98_1/m98_1.htm.
Kaplan/Kaplinsky 1999: Kaplan, David, Kaplinsky, Raphael. Trade and Industrial Policy on an Uneven Playing Field: The Case of the Deciduous Fruit Canning Industry in South Africa. In: World Development, Vol. 27, No. 10, 1999, S. 1787-1801.
Kaplinsky 1991: Kaplinsky, Raphael. Industrialization in Botswana: How Getting the Prices Right Helped the Wrong People. In: Christopher Colclough, James Manor (eds.). States or Markets? Neo-liberalism and the Development Policy Debate. Oxford. Clarendon Press, 1991.
Kapoor/Saxena 1979: Kapoor, M.C., Saxena, Rajan. Taming the Multinationals in India. In: JWTL, Vol. 13 No. 2, March April 1979. S. 170-178.
Kapstein 1994: Kapstein, Ethan B. Governing the Global Economy. International Finance and the State. Cambridge, Mass.: Harvard University Press, 1994.
Kapunda 1998: Kapunda, Stephen M. The Impact of Agricultural Parastatal Reform on Agricultural Development and Food Security in Tanzania. Revised Report for the Office of the Food and Agriculture Organisation Sub-Regional Representative for East and South Africa, June 1998. In: http://www.tzonline.org.
Kapur et al. 1997: Kapur, Devesh, Lewis, John P., Webb, Richard. The World Bank. Its First Half Century. Vol. 1, Vol. 2. Washington D.C.: Brookings Institution Press, 1997.
Kapur/Patel 2004: Kapur, Devesh, Patel, Urjit R. Balance of Payments and Exchange Rate Policy in India. May, 15 2004. In: http://www.people.fas.harvard.edu/~dkapur/images/dk_balance.pdf.
Kapur/Webb 2000: Kapur, Devesh, Webb, Richard. Governance-related Conditionalities of the International Financial Institutions. UNCTAD G-24 Discussion Paper Series, UNCTAD/GDS/MDPB/G24/6, No. 6, August 2000. In: http://www.unctad.org.
Karanja et al. 1998: Karanja, Daniel D., Jayne, Thomas S., Strasberg, Paul. Maize Productivity and Impact of Market Liberalization in Kenya. Tegemeo Agricultural Monitoring and Policy Analysis Project, Egerton University, University of Michigan, April 28, 2001. In: http://www.aec.msu.edu/agecon/fs2/kenya/.
Kareseit 1998: Kareseit, Jörn Helge. Welthandelsorganisation (WTO), Allgemeines Zoll- und Handelsabkommen (GATT) 1994. Köln: Bundesstelle für Außenhandelsinformation (BfAI), 1998.
Kareseit 1998a: Kareseit, Jörn Helge. Deutschland/Europäische Union. Gewerbliche Wareneinfuhren. Zum System des Einfuhrrechts. Köln: Bundesstelle für Außenhandelsinformation (BfAI), 1998.

Karl 1998: Karl, Helmut. Ökologie, individuelle Freiheit und wirtschaftliches Wachstum: Umweltpolitik in der Marktwirtschaft. In: Cassel, Dieter (Hrg.). 50 Jahre Soziale Marktwirtschaft. Schriften zu Ordnungfragen der Wirtschaft, Band 57, Stuttgart: Lucius&Lucius, 1998.
Karmiloff 1990: Karmiloff, Igor. Zambia. In: Riddell, Roger C. (ed.). Manufacturing Africa. Performance & Prospects of Seven Countries in Sub-Saharan Africa. Overseas Development Institute. London: James Currey, 1990.
Karmiloff 1990a: Karmiloff, Igor. Cameroon. In: Riddell, Roger C. (ed.). Manufacturing Africa. Performance & Prospects of Seven Countries in Sub-Saharan Africa. Overseas Development Institute. London: James Currey, 1990.
Karns/Mingst 2004: Margaret P. Karns, Karen A. Mingst. International Organizations. The Politics and Processes of Global Governance. Boulder, London: Lynne Rienner, 2004.
Karsenty/Laird 1987: Karsenty, Guy, Laird, Sam. The GSP, Policy Options and the New Round. In: Weltwirtschaftliches Archiv, Bd. 123, 1987. S. 262-296.
Kartte 1969: Kartte, Wolfgang. Ein neues Leitbild für die Wettbewerbspolitik. Köln et al.: Carl Heymanns Verlag, 1969.
Kasteng et al. 2004: Kasteng, Jonas, Karlsson, Arne, Lindberg, Carina. Differentiation between the Developing Countries in the WTO. Swedisch Board of Agriculture, International Affairs Division, June 2004. In: http://www.sjv.se.
Kathuria et al. 2000: Kathuria, Sanjay, Martin, Will, Bhardwaj, Anjali. Implications of MFA Abolition for South Asian Countries. World Bank WTO Background Paper, December 2000. In: http://www.worldbank.org/research/trade.
Kathuria/Bhardwaj 1998: Kathuria, Sanjay, Bhardwaj, Anjali. Export quotas and policy contraints in the Indian Textiles and Garment Industries. World Bank Policy Research Working Paper, No. 2012, November 1998. In: http://www.worldbank.org.
Katics/Petersen 1994: Katics, Michelle M., Petersen, Bruce C. The Effect of Rising Import Competition on Market Power. In: Journal of Industrial Economics, Vol. XLII, No. 3, September 1994. S. 277-286.
Katrak 1997: Katrak, Homi. Developing Countries' Imports of Technology, In-House Technological Capabilities and Efforts: An Analysis of the Indian Experience. In: Journal of Development Economics, Vol. 53, 1997. S. 67-83.
Katz 1984: Katz, Jorge M. Technological Innovation, Industrial Organization and Comparative Advantages of Latin American Metalworking Industries. In: Fransman, Martin, King, Kenneth (eds.). Technology Capability in the Thirld World. London: Macmillan, 1984.
Katz 1987: Katz, Jorge M. Domestic Technology Generation in LDCs: A Review of Research Findings. In: Katz,
Katz 2000: Katz, Jorge. Structural Change and Labor Productivity Growth in Latin American Manufacturing Industries 1970-96. In: World Development, Vol. 28, No. 9, 2000, S. 1583-1596.
Katz et al. 1987: Katz, Jorge M., Gutkowsik, Mirta, Rodrigues, Mario, Goity, Gregorio. Productivity and Domestic Technological Efforts: The Growth Path of an Rayon Plant in Argentina. In: Katz, Jorge M. Technology Generation in Latin American Manufacturing Industries. London: Macmillan Press, 1987.
Katzenstein 1978: Katzenstein, Peter J. Introduction: Domestic and International Forces and Strategies of Foreign Economic Policy. In: Katzenstein, Peter J. (ed.). Between Power and Plenty. Foreign Economic Policies of Advanced Industrial States. Madison: The University of Wisconsin Press, 1978.
Kaufer 1966: Kaufer, Erich. Kantzenbachs Konzept des funktionsfähigen Wettbewerbs. Ein Kommentar. In: Jahrbücher für Nationalökonomie und Statistik, Bd. 179, 1966. S. 481-492.
Kaufer 1980: Kaufer, Erich. The Control of the Abuse of Market Power by Market-Dominant Firms Under the German Law of Against Restraints of Competition. In: Zeitschrift für die gesamte Staatswissenschaft. Bd. 136, 1980. S. 510-532.
Kaufmann 1994: Kaufmann, Franz-Xaver. Diskurse über Staatsaufgaben. In: Grimm, Dieter (Hrg.). Staatsaufgaben. Frankfurt am Main: Surkamp, 1994.
Kawahito 1982: Kawahito, Kiyoshi. Steel and the U.S. Antidumping Statutes. In: JWTL, Vol. 16 No. 2, March April, 1982. S. 152-164.
Kawai 1994: Kawai, Hiroki. International Comparative Analysis of Economic Growth: Trade Liberalization and Productivity. In: The Developing Economies, XXXII, No. 4, December 1994. S. 373-397.
Keck/Low 2006: Keck, Alexander, Low, Patrick. Special and Differential Treatment in the WTO: Why, When, and How? In: Evenett, Simon J., Hoekman, Bernard M. Economic Development and Multilateral Trade Cooperation. Washington: World Bank/Palgrave Macmillan, 2006.
Keesing 1981: Keesing, Donald B. Exports and Policy in Latin-American Countries: Prospects for the World Economy and for Latin-American Exports, 1980-90. In: Baer, Werner, Gillis, Malcolm (Hrg.). Export Diversification and the New Protectionism. The Experiences of Latin America. NBER and the Bureau of Economic and Business Research University of Illinois: University of Illinois, 1981.
Keesing/Wolf 1981: Keesing, Donald B., Wolf, Martin. Textile Quotas against Developing Countries. Trade Policy Research Centre, Thames Essay No. 23. London: Trade Policy Research Centre, 1980.
Kell/Marchese 1992: Kell, Georg, Marchese, Serafino. Developing countries' exports of textiles and metals: The question of sustainability of recent growth. In: UNCTAD Review, No. 3, 1992. S. 15-30.
Keller 1996: Keller, Wolfgang. Absorptive capacity: On the creation and acquisition of technology in development. In: Journal of Development Economics, Vol. 49, 1996. S. 199-227.

Keller/Yeaple 2003: Keller, Wolfgang, Yeaple, Stephen. Multinational Enterprises, International Trade, and Productivity Growth: Firm-Level Evidence from the United States. NBER Working Paper No. 9504, February 2003.
Kelly et al. 1996: Kelly, Valerie, Diagana, Bocar, Reardon, Thomas, Gaye, Matar, Crawford. Cash Crop and Foodgrain Productivity in Senegal: Historical View, New Survey Evidence, and Policy Implications. Michigan State University International Development Working Papers No. 20, 1996. In: http://www.aec.msu.edu/agecon/fs2/index.htm.
Kelly/Morkre 1994: Kelly, Kenneth H., Morkre, Morris E. Effects of Unfair Imports on Domestic Industries: U.S. Antidumping and Countervailing Duty Cases, 1980 to 1988. Federal Trade Commission, Bureau of Economics, 1994.
Kelly/Morkre 2002: Kelly, Kenneth H., Morkre, Morris E. Quantifying Causes of Injury to U.S. Industries Competing with Unfairly Traded Imports: 1989 to 1994. Federal Trade Commission, Bureau of Economics, December 2002. In: http://www.ftc.gov/be/economicissuespapers.htm.
Kelly/Morkre 2006: Kelly, Kenneth H., Morkre, Morris E. On Lump or Two: Unitary versus Bifurcated Measures of Injury at the USITC. Bureau of Economics, Federal Trade Commission, Working Paper No. 282, March 2006. In: http://www.ftc.gov/be/econwork.htm.
Kelly/Naseem 1999: Kelly, Valerie, Naseem, Anwar. Macro Trends and Determinants of Fertilizer Use in Sub-Saharan Africa. Michigan State University International Development Working Papers No. 73, 1999. In: http://www.aec.msu.edu/agecon/fs2/index.htm.
Kelsen 1949: Kelsen, Hans. General Theory of Law and State. Cambridge: Harvard University Press, 1949.
Kemp/Wan 1972: Kemp, Murray C., Wan, Henry Y. The Gains from Trade. In: International Economic Review, Vol. 13, No. 3, October 1972. S. 509-522.
Kemp/Wan 1986: Kemp, Murray C., Wan, Henry Y. Gains from Trade with and without Lump-Sum compensation. In: Journal of International Economics. Vol. 21, 1986. S. 99-110.
Kennedy/Jones 2003: Kennedy, Richard M., Jones, Leroy P. Reforming State-Owned Enterprises. Lessons of International Experience especially for the Least Developed Countries. Wien: UNIDO, 2003. In: http://www.unido.org.
Kennett 2005: Kennett, Maxine. The Principle Legal Obligations of Accession to the World Trade Organization. In: Kennett, Maxine, Evenett, Simon J., Gage, Jonathan. Evaluating WTO Accessions: Legal and Economic Perspectives. Draft prepared on 22 January 2005. In: http://www.worldbank.org.
Kenny/Williams 2001: Kenny, Charles, Williams, David. What Do We Know About Economic Growth? Or, Why Don't We Know Very Much? In: World Devel opment, Vol. 29, No. 1, 2001. S. 1-22.
Keohane 1984: Keohane, Robert. After Hegemony. Princeton: Princeton University Press, 1984.
Keohane 1986: Keohane, Robert O. Theory of World Politics: Structural Realism and Beyond. In: Keohane, Robert O. (Hrg.). Neorealism and its critics. New York: Columbia University Press, 1986.
Keohane/Axelrod 1985: Keohane, Robert O. Axelrod, Robert. Achieving Cooperation under Anarchy: Strategies and Institutions. In: World Politics, Vol. 38, No. 1, Oct. 1985.
Keohane/Nye 1977: Keohane, Robert. O, Nye, Joseph S. Power and Interdependence. Boston, Toronto: Little Brown, 1977.
Keohane/Nye 1987: Keohane, Robert. O, Nye, Joseph S. Power and Interdependence revisited. In: International Organization 41, 4, Autumn 1987, S. 725-753.
Keohane/Nye 2001: Keohane, Robert O., Nye, Joseph S. Jr. The Club Model of Multilateral Cooperation and Problems of Democratic Legitimacy. In: Porter, Roger B., Sauvé, Pierre, Subramanian, Arvind, Zampetti, Americo Beviglia. Efficiency, Equity, Legitimacy. The Multilateral Trading System at the Millenium. Washington D.C.: Brookings Institution Press, 2001.
Kerber 1994: Kerber, Wolfgang. Die Europäische Fusionskontrollpraxis und die Wettbewerbskonzeption der EG. Bayreuth: Verlag PCO, 1994.
Kerber 1998: Kerber, Wolfgang. Bildung, Forschung und Entwicklung: Grenzen staatlicher Politik aus der Perspektive des internationalen Wettbewerbs. In: Cassel, Dieter (Hrg.). 50 Jahre Soziale Marktwirtschaft. Schriften zu Ordnungsfragen der Wirtschaft, Band 57, Stuttgart: Lucius&Lucius, 1998.
Kersting 1994: Kersting, Wolfgang. Die Politische Philosophie des Gesellschaftsvertrags. Darmstadt: Wissenschaftliche Buchgesellschaft, 1994.
Kessie 2004: Kessie, E. The 'Early Harvest Negotiations' in 2003. In: Ortino, Federico, Petersmann, Ernst-Ulrich (eds.). The WTO Dispute Settlement System 1995 - 2003. The Hague et al.: Kluwer Law International, 2004.
Kestner 1912: Kestner, Fritz. Der Organisationszwang. Eine Untersuchung über die Kämpfe zwischen Kartellen und Außenseitern. Berlin: Carl Heymanns Verlag, 1912.
Keynes 1938: Keynes, John Maynard. The Policy of Government Storage of Foodstuffs and Raw Materials. In: Economic Journal, September 1938. S. 449-460.
Keynes 1942: Keynes, John Maynard. The International Control of Raw Materials. Abgedruckt in: Journal of Development Economics 4, 1974. S. 299-315.
Kheralla et al. 2000: Kheralla, Mylene, Delgado, Christopher, Gabre-Madhin, Eleni, Minot, Nicholas, Johnson, Michael. The Road Half Traveled: Agricultural Market Reform in Sub-Saharan Africa. Washington: International Food Policy Research Institute, October 2000. In: http://www.ifpri.org.
Kheralla et al. 2000a: Kheralla, Mylene, Löfgren, Hans, Gruhn, Peter, Reeder, Meyra M. Wheat Policy in Egypt. Adjustment of Local Markets and Options for Future Reforms. Washington: International Food Policy Research Institute, 2000.

Kheralla et al. 2001: Kheralla, Mylene, Minot, Nicholas, Kachule, Richard, Soule, Bio Goura, Berry, Philippe. Impact on Agricultural Market Reforms on Smallholder Farmers in Benin and Malawi. Vol. 1. IFPRI Collaborative Research Project, February 2001. In: http://www.ifpri.org.
Kheralla et al. 2002: Kheralla, Mylene. Delgado, Christopher, Gabre-Madhin, Eleni, Minot, Nicholas, Johnson, Michael. Reforming Agricultural Markets in Africa. Baltimore; London: John Hopkins University Press for the Interantional Food Policy Research Institute, 2002.
Kiel-Rußland 1996: Kieler Diskussionsbeiträge. Die wirtschaftliche Lage Rußlands. Januar 1997.
Kiguel/Liviatan 1995: Kiguel, Miguel A., Liviatan, Nissan. Stopping Three Big Inflations: Argentina, Brazil, Peru. In: Dornbusch, Rudiger, Edwards, Sebastian (eds.). Reform, Recovery, and Growth. Chicago; London: University of Chicago Press, 1995.
Killick 1995: Killick, Tony. IMF Programmes in Developing Countries. Design and Impact. London; New York: Routledge, 1995.
Kim 1991: Kim, Kwang Suk. Korea. In: The Experience of Korea, the Philippines, and Singapore. Liberalizing Foreign Trade Vol. 2. Oxford: World Bank/Blackwell, 1991.
Kim 1993: Kim, Kwang-Hee. Entwicklung der Automobilindustrie Südkoreas. Baden-Baden: Nomos, 1993.
Kim 1994: Kim, Kwang Suk. Trade and Industrialization Policies in Korea. In: Helleiner, Gerald K. (ed.). Trade Policy and Industrialization in Turbulent Times. London; New York: Routledge, 1994.
Kim 1995: Kim, Sukkoo. Expansion of Markets and the Geographic Distribution of Economic Activities: The Trends in U. S. Regional Manufacturung Structure, 1860 – 1987. In: Quarterly Journal of Economics, November 1995. S. 881-908.
Kim 1995a: Kim, Kwan S. The Korean Miracle (1962-80) Revisited: Myths and Realities in Strategies and Development. In: Stein, Howard (Hrg.). Asian Industrialization and Africa. Studies in Policy Alternatives to Structural Adjustment. London: St. Martin's Press, 1995.
Kim 2002: Kim, Jong Bum. Fair Price Comparison in the WTO Anti-dumping Agreement. Recent Panel Decisions against the 'Zeroing' Method. In: JWT, Vol. 36, No. 1, 2002. S. 39-56.
Kim/Lee 1994: Kim, Hyung Kook, Lee, Sun-Hoon. Commodity Chains and the Korean Automobile Industry. In: Gereffi, Gary, Korzeniewicz, Miguel (eds.). Commodity Chains and Global Capitalism. Westport, Connecticut; London: Praeger 1994.
Kim/Leipzinger 1993: Kim, Kihwan, Leipzinger, Petri, Danny M. Korea. A Case of Government-Led Development. Washington: World Bank, 1993.
Kindleberger 1986: Kindleberger, Charles P. International Public Goods without International Government. In: American Economic Review, Vol. 76, No. 1, March 1986.
Kirchhof 1988: Kirchhof, Paul. Mittel staatlichen Handels. In: Isensee, Josef, Kirchhof, Paul (Hrg.). Handbuch des Staatsrechts. Bd. III. Heidelberg: C.F. Müller, 1988.
Kirchlechner/Herz 1993: Kirchlechner, Anja-Susan, Herz, Dietmar. Rechtliche Verallgemeinerung in den internationalen Handelsbeziehungen. In: Wolf, Klaus Dieter (Hg.). Internationale Verrechtlichung. Jahresschrift für Rechtspolitologie (JfR). Pfaffenweiler: Centaurus Verlagsgesellschaft, 1993.
Kirkpatrick et al. 1984: Kirkpatrick, C. H., Lee, N., Nixon, F.I. Industrial Structure and Policy in Less Developed Countries. London: George Allen & Unwin, 1984.
Klabbers 1992: Klabbers, Jan. Jurisprudence in International Trade Law. Article XX of the GATT. In: JWT, Vol. 26, No. 2, April 1992. S. 63-94.
Klaproth 2005: Klaproth, Jesse. Decision by the Arbitrator - United States - Continued Dumping and Subsidy Offset Act of 2000. In: Tulane Journal of International and Comparative Law, Bd. 13, 2005. S. 401-420.
Kleiner 2002: Kleiner, Marc. Bananas, Airplanes and the WTO: Prohibited Export Subsidies. In: The University of Miami. International and Comparative Law Review Vol. 10, Fall 2002. S. 129-142.
Kleinert 2000: Kleinert, Jörn. Growing Trade in Intermediate Goods: Outsourcing, Global Sourcing or Increasing Importance of MNE Networks. Kiel Working Paper No. 1006, October 2000.
Kleinert/Klodt 2000: Kleinert, Jörn, Klodt, Henning. Megafusionen. Kieler Studien 302. Tübingen: Mohr Siebek, 2000.
Klepper 1985: Klepper, Gernot. Protektion und Wettbewerb der pharmazeutischen Industrie. In: Die Weltwirtschaft, Heft 1, 1985. S. 114-132.
Klepper et al. 1987: Klepper, Gernot, Weiss, Frank D. Witteler, Doris. Protection in Germay: Toward Industrial Selectivity. In: Giersch, Herbert (ed.). Free Trade in the World Economy. Towards the Opening of Markets. Tübingen: Mohr, 1987.
Kletzer 1998: Kletzer, Lori G. Trade and Job Losses in U.S. Manufacturing 1979-94. NBER Research Conference The Impact on International Trade on Wages, February 1998. In: http://www.nber.org.
Kletzer 2001: Kletzer, Lori G. Job Loss from Imports: Measuring the Costs. Washington: Institute for International Economics, September 2001.
Kletzer/Bardhan 1978: Kletzer, Kenneth, Bardhan, Pranab. Credit Markets and Patterns of International Trade. In: Journal of Developing Economics, Vol. 27, 1987, pp. 57-70.
Kley 1987: Kley, Roland. Die Theorie des Verfassungsvertrags von James Buchanan. Darstellung und Kritik. Arbeitspapier Nr. 16, Institut für Wirtschaftsethik, St. Gallen, März 1989.
Klodt 1980: Klodt, Henning. Kleine und große Unternehmen im Strukturwandel – Zur Entwicklung der sektoralen Unternehmenskonzentration. In: Die Weltwirtschaft, Heft 1, 1980. S. 79-99.
Klodt 1990: Klodt, Henning. Technologietransfer und internationale Wettbewerbsfähigkeit. In: Aussenwirtschaft, 45 Jg., Heft 1, 1990. S. 57-79.

Klodt 1992: Klodt, Henning. Theorie der strategischen Handelspolitik und neue Wachstumstheorie als Grundlage für eine Industrie- und Technologiepolitik? Arbeitspapier Nr. 533. Institut für Weltwirtschaft Kiel. Oktober 1992.
Klodt 2000: Klodt, Henning. Conflicts and Conflict Resolution in International Antitrust. Kieler Arbeitspapiere Nr. 979, May 2000.
Klodt et al. 1988: Klodt, Henning et al. Forschungspolitik unter EG-Kontrolle. Kieler Studien 220. Tübingen: Mohr, 1988.
Klodt/Stehn 1992: Klodt, Henning, Stehn, Jürgen et al. Die Strukturpolitik der EG. Kieler Studien 249. Tübingen: Mohr, 1992.
Kneen 1999: Kneen, Brewster. Cargill. Corporate Food Security? In: UK Food Group (ed.). Hungry for Power. March 1999. In: http://www.ukfg.org.uk.
Knight/Scacciavillani 1998: Knight, Malcolm, Scacialvillani, Fabio. Current Accounts: What ist their relevance for economic policymaking?. IMF Working Paper WP/98/71. Washington: IMF, 1998. In: http://www.imf.org.
Knorr 1997: Knorr, Andreas. Die Entwicklung der Umweltpolitik aus ordnungspolitischer Sicht. In: ORDO, Bd. 48, 1997.
Koch 1997a: Koch, Eckart. Internationale Wirtschaftsbeziehungen. Bd.1: Internationaler Handel. München: Vahlen, 1997.
Koch 1997b: Koch, Eckart. Internationale Wirtschaftsbeziehungen. Bd. 2: Internationale Wirtschafts- und Finanzbeziehungen. München: Vahlen, 1997.
Köddermann 1996: Köddermann, Ralf. Sind Löhne und Steuern zu hoch? In: ifo-Schnelldienst 20, 1996. S. 6-15.
Koester 1997: Koester, Ulrich. Agrarpolitik im Dauerkonflikt mit Prinzipien der Sozialen Marktwirtschaft. In: ORDO, Bd. 48, 1997.
Köhler 1998: Köhler, Claus. Währungsregime und Währungskrise. Die unterschätzte Rolle der Spekulation. In: Entwicklung und Zusammenarbeit, 39. Jg., No. 7, 1998.
Kohler/Moore 2000: Kohler, Philippe, Moore, Michael O. Injury-based protection with auditing under imperfect information. Working Paper, April 12, 2000. In: http://darkwing.uoregon.edu/~bruceb/adpage.html.
Kohler-Koch 1989: Kohler-Koch, Beate (Hrg.) Regime in den internationalen Beziehungen 1989: Baden Baden: Nomos, 1989.
Kohler-Koch 1993: Kohler-Koch, Beate. Die Welt regieren ohne Weltregierung. In: Böhret, Karl, Wewer, Göttrik (Hrg.). Regieren im 21. Jahrhundert - zwischen Globalisierung und Regionalisierung. Opladen: Leske, Budrich 1993.
Kohler-Koch 1996: Kohler-Koch, Beate. Politische Unverträglichkeiten von Globalisierung. In: Steger, Ulrich (Hrg.). Globalisierung der Wirtschaft. Berlin; Heidelberg: Springer, 1996.
Kohli 1989: Kohli, Atul. Politics of Economic Liberalization in India. In: World Development, Vol. 17 No. 3, 1989. S. 305-328.
Kokko/Blomström 1995: Kokko, Ari, Blomström, Magnus. Policies to Encourage Inflows of Technology Through Foreign Multinationals. In: World Development, Vol. 23, No. 3, 1995. S. 459-468.
Kolev/Prusa 1999: Kolev, Dobrin R., Prusa, Thomas J. Dumping and Double Crossing: The (In) Effectiveness of Cast-Based Trade Policy under Incomplete Information. NBER Working Paper No. 6986, February 1999.
Köllner 1998: Köllner, Patrick. Südkoreas technologische Abhängigkeit von Japan. Entstehung, Verlauf und Gegenstrategien. Hamburg: Institut für Asienkunde, 1998.
Komuro 1995: Komuro, Norio. The WTO Dispute Settlement Mechanism. In: JWT, Vol. 29, No. 4, August 1995. S. 5-95.
Komuro 1998: Komuro, Norio. Kodak-Fuji Film Dispute and the WTO Panel Ruling. In: JWT, Vol. 32, No. 5, 1998. S. 161-217.
Konan/Maskus 2000: Konan, Denise Eby, Maskus, Keith E. Joint Trade Liberalization and Tax Reform in a Small Open Economy: The Case of Egypt. In: Journal of Development Economics, Vol. 61, 2000, S. 365-392.
Konandreas et al. 1998: Konandreas, Panos, Greenfield, Jim, Sharma, Ramesh. The Continuation of Reform Process in Agriculture: Developing Countries Perspectives. FAO/IICA/Worldbank Seminar, Santiago, Chile, 23-24 November 1998. In: http://www.fao.org.
Konings et al. 2001: Konings, Jozef, van Cayseele, Patrick, Warzynski, Frederic. The dynamics of industrial mark-ups in two small open economies: does national competition policy matter? In: International Journal of Industrial Organization, Vol. 19, 2001. S. 841-859.
Konings et al. 2001: Konings, Jozef, Vandenbussche, Hylke, Springael, Linda. Import Diversion under European Antidumping Policy. CEPR Discussion Paper No. 2785, May 2001.
Konings/Vandenbussche 2002: Konings, Jozef, Vandenbussche, Hylke. Does Antidumping Protection Raise Market Power? Evidence from Firm Level Data. CEPR Discussion Paper No. 3571, October 2002.
Koo/Uhm 2003: Koo, Won W., Uhm, Ihn H. Trade Remedy Laws in the United States: Bilateral Grain Trade Disputes with Canada. In: North Dakota Law Review Vol. 79, No. 1, 2003. S. 921-952.
Koo/Uhm 2003: Koo, Won W., Uhm, Ihn H. Effects of Dumping vs. Anti-dumping Measures: The US Trade Remedy Laws applied to Wheat Imports from Canada. In: JWT, Vol. 41, No. 6, 2007. S. 1163-1184.
Koopmann 2001: Koopmann, Georg. Internationalisierung der Wettbewerbspolitik: Korrelat zur internationalen Handelspolitik? In: Aussenwirtschaft, 56 Jg., Heft II, 2001. S. 159-199.
Koopmans 1957: Koopmans, Tjalling C. Three Essays on the State of Economic Science. New York: McGraw-Hill Book Company, 1957.
Körner 1987: Körner, Josef. US-Steuerreform: In der Bundesrepublik nicht uneingeschränkt kopierbar. In: ifo-Schnelldient 1-2, 1987. S. 6-19.

Körner 1998: Körner, Heiko. The 'Brain Drain' from developing countries - an enduring problem. In: Intereconomics, January/February 1998. S. 26-29.
Korzeniewicz 1994: Korzeniewicz, Miguel. Commodity Chains and Marketing Strategies: Nike and the Global Athletic Footwear Industry. In: Gereffi, Gary, Korzeniewicz, Miguel (eds.). Commodity Chains and Global Capitalism. Westport, Connecticut; London: Praeger 1994.
Korzeniewicz/Martin 1994: Korzeniewicz, Roberto P., Martin, William. The Global Distribution of Commodity Chains. In: Gereffi, Gary, Korzeniewicz, Miguel (eds.). Commodity Chains and Global Capitalism. Westport, Connecticut; London: Praeger 1994.
Kosacoff 2000: Kosacoff, Bernando. Business Strategies under Stabilization and Trade Openness in the 1990s. Interamerican Development Bank, Andres Bello Auditorium, Washington D.C., September 18-19, 2000. In: http://www.iadb.org.
Kostecki/Tymowski 1985: Kostecki, M. M., Tymowski, M.J. Customs Duties versus other Import Charges in the Developing Countries. In: JWTL, Vol. 19, 1985. S. 269-286.
Kösters 1998: Kösters, Wim. Europäische Integration: Wirtschaftspolitischer Autonomieverlust durch Supranationalisierung politischer Entscheidungen. In: Cassel, Dieter (Hrg.). 50 Jahre Soziale Marktwirtschaft. Schriften zu Ordnungfragen der Wirtschaft, Band 57, Stuttgart: Lucius&Lucius, 1998.
Kowalczyk/Davis 1996: Kowolczyk, Carsten, Davis, Donald. Tariff-Phase-Outs: Theory and Evidence from GATT and NAFTA. NBER Working Paper No. 5421, January 1996.
Kozicki 1997: Kozicki, Sharon. The Productivity Growth Slowdown: Diverging Trends in the Manufacturing and Service Sectors. In: Federal Reserve Bank of Kansas Economic Review, Vol. 82, No. 1, First Quarter 1997. S. 31-46.
Krägenau 1986: Krägenau, Henry. Stahlpolitik und Strukturanpassung in der EG-Stahlindustrie. HWWA Report Nr. 72, Hamburg 1986.
Krajewski 2001: Krajewski, Markus. Verfassungsperspektiven und Legitimation des Rechts der Welthandelsorganisation (WTO). Berlin: Duncker & Humblot, 2001.
Krajewski 2001a: Krajewski, Markus. Democratic Legitimacy and Constitutional Perspectives of WTO Law. In: JWT, Vol. 35, No. 1, 2001. S. 167-186.
Krajewski 2001b: Krajewski, Markus. Public Services and the Scope of the General Agreement on Trade in Services. Centre for International Environmental Law, Research Paper, May 2001. In: http://www.ciel.org.
Kramb 2002: Kramb, M. C. Eine ökonomische Anaylse von sanitären und phytosanitären Außenhandelsmaßnahmen am Beispiel des 'Hormonstreites' zwischen den EU und den USA. In: Brockmeier, M., Isermeyer, F., von Cramon-Taubadel, S. (Hrg.). Liberalisierung des Weltagrarhandels - Strategien und Konsequenzen. Münster-Hiltrup: Landwirtschaftsverlag, 2002.
Kramer 2003: Kramer, Claire V. Dumping on Free Trade: Interests, Institutions, and the Politics of Anti-Dumping in Democracies. Draft, Conference on Politics and Varieties of Capitalism, 31 Nov./1. Sept 2003, Wissenschaftszentrum Berlin. In: http://www.wz-berlin.de.
Krancke 1999: Krancke, Jan. Liberalisierung des internationalen Dienstleistungshandels: Analyse des GATS und Perspektiven für die zukünftige Handelsliberalisierung. Kieler Arbeitspapiere Nr. 954, October 1999.
Krancke 2003: Krancke, Jan. Internationaler Handel mit Kommunikationsdienstleistungen. Anforderungen an ein multilaterales Regelwerk und die Reform des GATS. Berlin: Springer 2005.
Kranjak-Berisavljevic et al. 2001: Kranjak-Berisavljevic, G. Rice Production in Ghana. May 2001. Multi-Agency Partnerships (MAPS) for Technical Change in West African Agriculture. Phase II Ghana Report 1. In: http://www.odi.org.uk/rpeg/maps/.
Kranjak-Berisavljevic et al. 2001a: Kranjak-Berisavljevic, G. Rice Production in Ghana. May 2001. Multi-Agency Partnerships (MAPS) for Technical Change in West African Agriculture. 2001. Phase II Ghana Report 2. In: http://www.odi.org.uk/rpeg/maps/.
Kranjak-Berisavljevic et al. 2003: Kranjak-Berisavljevic, G., Blench, R.M., Chapman, R. Rice Production and Livelihoods in Ghana, 11. June 2003. Multi-Agency Partnerships (MAPS) for Technical Change in West African Agriculture. Phase I Ghana Report. In: http://www.odi.org.uk/rpeg/maps/.
Krasner 1982a: Krasner, Stephen D. Regimes and the limits of realism: regimes as autonomous variables. In: International Organization 36, 2, Spring 1982, S. 497-510.
Krasner 1982b: Krasner, Stephen D. Structural causes and regime consequences: regimes as intervening variables. In: International Organization, 36, 2, Spring 1982.
Krasner 1986: Krasner, Stephen D. Structural Conflict. The Third World against Global Liberalism. Berkely: University of California Press, 1986.
Krasner 1995: Krasner, Stephen D. Power Politics, Institutions, and Transnational Coalitions. In: Risse-Kappen, Thomas (ed.). Bringing transnational relations back in. Cambridge: Cambridge University Press, 1995.
Krauthammer 1991: Krauthammer, Charles. The Unipolar Moment. In: Foreign Affairs, Vol. 70, No. 1, 1990/91.
Kravis 1970: Kravis, Irving B. Trade as a handmaiden of growth: Similarities between the nineteenth and twentieth centuries. In: Economic Journal, Vol. 80, Dec. 1970. S. 850-872.
Kravis 1973: Kravis, Irving B. Note on 'Trade as a handmaiden of growth'. In: Economic Journal, Vol. 83, March 1973. S. 210-212.
Kravis 1976: Kravis, Irving B. A Survey of International Comparisons of Productivity. In: The Economic Journal, 86, March 1976, S. 1-44.

Kregel 1993: Kregel, Jan A. Keynesian Stabilization Policy and Post War Economic Performance. In: Szirmai, Adam, van Ark, Bart, Pilat, Dirk (eds.). Explaining Economic Growth. Essays in Honour of Angus Maddison. Amsterdam: North Holland, 1993.
Kreile 1989: Kriele, Michael. Regime und Regimewandel in den internationalen Wirtschaftsbeziehungen. In:
Kreinin 1975: Kreinin, Mordechai E. European Intergration and the Developing Countries. In: Balassa, Bela. European Economic Integration. Amsterdam; Oxford: North-Holland Publishing Company, 1975.
Kreinin/Officer 1979: Kreinin, Mordechai E., Officer, Lawrence H. Tariff Reduction under the Tokyo Round: A Review of Their Effects on Trade Flows, Employment, and Welfare. In: Weltwirtschaftliches Archiv, Bd. 115, 1979. S. 543-572.
Krieger 1980: Krieger; Christiane. Wirtschaftswachstum und Strukturwandel in den Beitrittsländern. In: Die Weltwirtschaft, Heft 1, 1980. S. 142-159.
Krieger-Boden 1995: Krieger-Boden, Christiane. Die räumliche Dimension der Wirtschaftstheorie. Kiel: Institut für Weltwirtschaft, 1995.
Krieger-Boden 2000: Krieger-Boden, Christiane. Globalization, Integration and Regional Specialization. Kiel Working Paper No. 1009, October 2000.
Krieger-Boden/Lammers 1996: Krieger-Boden, Christiane, Lammers, Konrad. Subventionsabbau in räumlicher Perspektive: Wirkungszusammenhänge und Schlußfolgerungen. Kiel Diskussion Papers No. 280, August 1996.
Kririm 1985: Kirim, Arman S. Reconsidering Patents and Economic Development: A Case Study of the Turkish Pharmaceutical Industry. In: World Development, Vol. 13, No. 2, 1985. S. 219-236.
Kririm 1990: Kirim, Arman S. Technology and Exports: The Case of the Turkish Manufacturing Industries. In: World Development, Vol. 18, No. 10, 1990. S. 1351-1362.
Krishna 1997: Krishna, Raj. Antidumping in Law and Practice. World Bank Policy Research Working Paper 1823, September 1997. In: http://www.worldbank.org.
Krishna 2000: Krishna, Sridhar. The Impact of Phasing Out of Import Licensing on Small Scale Industries. Indian Council for Research on International Economic Relations, Working Paper 60, December 2000. In: http://www.icrier.res.in/.
Krishna/Mitra 1998: Krishna, Pravin, Mitra, Devashish. Trade Liberalization, market discipline and productivity growth: new evidence from India. In: Journal of Development Economics, Vol. 56, 1998. S. 447-462.
Krishna/Morgan 1998: Krishna, Kala, Morgan, John. Implementing results-oriented trade policies: The case of the US-Japanese auto parts dispute. In: European Economic Review Vol. 42, 1998. S. 1443-1467.
Kroker 1995: Kroker, Rolf. Deutschland – Angeschlagene Standortqualität. In: WSI-Mitteilungen, 11/1995. S. 705-711.
Kromphardt 1988: Kromphardt, Jürgen. Das Verhältnis von Theorie und Empirie aus der Sicht wissenschaftstheoretischer Positionen. In: Freimann, Karsten-Dietmar, Ott, Alfred E. Theorie und Empirie in der Wirtschaftsforschung. Tübingen: Mohr, 1988.
Krueger 1974: Krueger, Anne O. The Political Economy of the Rent-Seeking Society. In: The American Economic Review, Vol. 64, No. 3, June 1974, pp. 291-303.
Krueger 1978: Krueger, Anne O. Liberalization Attempts and Consequences. National Bureau of Economic Research. Cambrigde, Mass.: Ballinger Publishing Company, 1978.
Krueger 1980: Krueger, Anne O. Trade Policy as Input to Development. In: American Economic Review, Papers and Proceedings, Vol. 70, No. 2, May 1980, S. 288-292.
Krueger 1987: Krueger, Anne O. Origins of the Developing Countries' Debt Crisis 1970 to 1982. In: Journal of Development Economics 27, 1987, S. 165-187.
Krueger 1993: Krueger, Anne O. American Bilateral Trading Arrangemets and East Asian Interest. In: Ito, Takatoshi, Krueger, Anne O. Trade and Protectionism. Chicago; London: The University of Chicago Press/NBER, 1993.
Krueger 1995: Krueger, Anne O. Policy Lessons from the Development Experience since the Second World War. In: Behrman, J. Srinivasan, T.N. (eds.) Handbook of Development Economics, Vol. III, Amsterdam; New York: Elsevier Science B.V., 1995.
Krueger 1995a: Krueger, Anne O. Trade Policies and Developing Nations. Washington, D.C.: The Brookings Institution, 1995.
Krueger 1997: Krueger, Anne O. Trade Policy and Economic Development: How We Learn. In: The American Economic Review, Vol. 87, No. 1, March 1997.
Krueger 1998: Krueger, Anne O. Why Trade Liberalization is Good for Growth. In: The Economic Journal, Vol. 108, September 1998. S. 1513-1522.
Krueger 2000: Krueger, Anne O. Why Trade Liberalization is Good for Growth. In: Dixon, Huw David. Controversies in Macroeconomics Growth, Trade and Policy. Oxford: Blackwell, 2000.
Krueger et al. 1991: Krueger, Anne O., Schiff, Maurice, Valdes, Alberto. Measuring the Effect of Intervention in Agricultural Prices. In: Krueger, Anne O., Schiff, Maurice, Valdes, Alberto. The Political Economy of Agricultural Pricing Policy. Vol. 1 Latin America. Baltimore, London: John Hopkins University Press, 1991.
Krugman 1979: Krugman, Paul. Increasing Returns, Monopolistic Competition, and International Trade. In: Journal of International Economics, Vol. 9, 1979. S. 469-479.
Krugman 1980: Krugman, Paul. Scale Economies, Product Differenciation, and the Pattern of Trade. In: American Economic Review, Vol. 70 No. 5, December 1980. S. 950-959.
Krugman 1981: Krugman, Paul. Intraindustry Specialization and Gains from Trade. In: Journal of Political Economy, No. 5, 1981. S. 959-973.

Krugman 1984: Krugman, Paul. Import Protection as Export Promotion: International Competition in the Presence of Oligopoly and Economies of Scale. In: Kierzkowski, Henryk (ed.). Monopolistic Competition and International Trade. Oxford: Clarendon Press, 1984.
Krugman 1986: Krugman, Paul R. Introduction: New Thinking about Trade Policy. In: Krugman, Paul R. Strategic Trade Policy and the New International Economics. Cambridge, Mass.: Cambridge University Press, 1986.
Krugman 1987: Krugman, Paul R. The Narrow Moving Band, The Dutch Disease, and the Competitive Consequences of Mrs. Thatcher. In: Journal of Development Economics, Vol. 27, 1987. S. 41-55.
Krugman 1991: Krugman, Paul R. Geography and Trade. Cambridge: MIT Press, 1991.
Krugman 1991a: Krugman, Paul R. History versus Expectations. In: The Quarterly Journal of Economics, Vol. 106, May 1991. S. 651-667.
Krugman 1994: Krugman, Paul R. The Myth of Asia's Miracle. In: Foreign Affairs, November/December 1994. S. 62-78.
Krugman 1995: Krugman, Paul R. Growing World Trade: Causes and Consequences. In: Brookings Papers of Economic Activity, 1, 1995. S. 327-377.
Krugman 1996: Krugman, Paul R. Wettbewerbsfähigkeit: Eine gefährliche Wahnvorstellung. In: Jahrbuch Arbeit und Technik 1996. Bonn: Dietz, 1996.
Krugman 1997: Krugman, Paul R. First: What ever happened to the Asian miracle? In: Fortune, August 18, 1997. S. 8-10.
Krugman 1997a: Krugman, Paul R. Is Capitalism too Productive?. In: Foreign Affairs, Vol. 76, No. 5, 1997. S. 79-94.
Krugman 1999: Krugman, Paul R. Was it all in Ohlin? October 1999. In: http://www.mit.edu/people/krugman.index.html
Krugman/Ostfeld 1997: Krugman, Paul R., Obstfeld, Maurice. International Economics. Theory and Policy. Reading, Mass. etc.: Addison Wesley, 1997.
Krugman/Venables 1990: Krugman, Paul R., Venables, Anthony J. Integration and the Competitiveness of Peripheral Industry. Centre of Economic Policy Research, London, Discussion Paper No. 363, January 1990.
Krugman/Venables 1995: Krugman, Paul R., Venables, Anthony J. Globalization and the Inequality of Nations. In: Quarterly Journal of Economics, November 1995. S. 857-880.
Krüsselberg 1997: Krüsselberg, Hans-Günter. Über die Bedeutung von Familienpolitik in einer Sozialen Marktwirtschaft. In: ORDO, Bd. 48, 1997.
Krüsselberg 1998: Krüsselberg, Hans-Günter. Marktwirtschaft ohne Mittelstand? Zur Rolle der unternehmerischen Selbstständigkeit in der Sozialen Marktwirtschaft. In: Cassel, Dieter (Hrg.). 50 Jahre Soziale Marktwirtschaft. Schriften zu Ordnungsfragen der Wirtschaft, Band 57, Stuttgart: Lucius&Lucius, 1998.
Küchle 1996: Küchle, Hartmut. Deutschlands Position auf dem Weltmarkt. In: WSI-Mitteilungen 5/1996. S. 295-303.
Kuilwijk 1995: Kuilwijk, Kees Jan. Castro's Cuba and the U.S. Helms-Burton Act. In: JWT, Vol. 31, No. 3, June 1997. S. 49-61.
Külp 2000: Külp, Bernhard. Walter Eucken und die soziale Frage. In: Külp, Berhard, Vanberg, Victor (Hrg.) Freiheit und wettbewerbliche Ordnung. Gedenkband zur Erinnerung and Walter Eucken. Freiburg; Berlin; München: Haufe Verlagsgruppe, 2000.
Külp/Vanberg 2000: Külp, Berhard, Vanberg, Victor (Hrg.) Freiheit und wettbewerbliche Ordnung. Gedenkband zur Erinnerung and Walter Eucken. Freiburg; Berlin; München: Haufe Verlagsgruppe, 2000.
Kumar 1990: Kumar, Nagesh. Multinational Enterprises in India. London; New York: Routledge, 1990.
Kumar 2002: Intellectual Property Rights, Technology and Economic Development, Commission on Intellectual Property Rights, Study Paper 1b, 2002. In: http://www.iprcommission.org.
Kumara 1993: Kumara, Upali Ananda. Investment, Industrialization, and TNCs in Selected Asian Countries. In: Regional Development Dialogue, Vol. 14, No. 4, Winter 1993. S. 3-22.
Kumaran 2005: Kumaran, V, Lakshmi. The 10 Major Problems With the Anti-Dumping Instrument in India. In: JWT, Vol. 39, No. 1, 2005. S. 115-124.
Kume/Piani 2005: Kume, Honorio, Piani, Guida. Antidumping and Safeguard Mechanisms: The Brazilian Experience, 1988-2003. World Bank Policy Research Working Paper 3562, April 2005. In: http://www.worldbank.org.
Kunz Hallstein 1975: Kunz Hallstein, Hans Peter. Patentschutz, Technologietransfer und Entwicklungsländer – eine Bestandsaufnahme. In: GRUR Int. Heft 8/9, August/September 1975. S. 261-322.
Kunz Hallstein 1989: Kunz Hallstein, Hans Peter. The U.S. Proposal for a GATT-Agreement on Intellectual Property and the Paris Convention for the Protection of Industrial Property. In: Beier, Friedrich-Karl, Schricker, Gerhard (eds.). GATT or WIPO? New Ways in the Protection of Intellectual Property. Weinheim: Wiley-VCH, 1989.
Kürschner-Pelkmann 2003: Kürschner-Pelkmann, Frank. Imagine - Sauberes Trinkwasser für alle. Studie: Die RWE AG am internationalen Wassermarkt. Bielefeld: Koordination Südliches Africa, 2003.
Kurtz 2002: Kurtz, Jürgen. A General Investment Agreement in the WTO? Lessons from Chapter 11 of NAFTA and the OECD Multilateral Agreement on Investment. Jean Monnet Working Paper 6/02. In: http://www.jeanmonnetprogram.org/papers/index.html.
Kuruvila 1997: Kuruvila, Pretty Elizabeth. Developing Countries and the GATT/WTO Dispute Settlement Mechanism. In: JWT, Vol. 31 No. 6, Dec. 1997. S. 171-208.

Kuschel 1995: Kuschel, Hans-Dieter. Die Bananenmarktordnung der Europäischen Union. In: Recht der Internationalen Wirtschaft (RIW), Heft 3, 1995. S. 218-222.
Kuschel 1999: Kuschel, Hans-Dieter. Auch die revidierte Bananenmarktordnung ist nicht WTO-konform. In: EuZW, Heft 3, 1999. S. 74-77.
Kuznets 1966: Kuznets, Simon. Modern Economic Growth. Rate, Structure, and Spread. New Haven; London: Yale University Press, 1966.
Kwa 2003: Kwa, Aileen. Power Politics in the WTO. Focus on the Global South. http://www.focusweb.org.
Kwa/Bello 1998: Kwa, Aileen, Bello, Walden. Guide to the Agreement on Agriculture: Technicalities and Trade Tricks Explained. In: http://www.focusweb.org/publications/1998/AOA.pdf.
Kwa/Jawara 2004: Kwa, Aileen, Jawara, Fatoumata. Behind the Scenes at the WTO. The Real World of International Trade Negotiations. The Lessons of Cancun. Updated Edition. London, New York: Zed Books, 2004.
Kwak 1994: Kwak, Hyuntai. Changing Trade Policy and Its Impact on TFP in the Republic of South Korea. In: The Developing Economies, XXXII, No. 4, December 1994. S. 398-.
Kwanashie et al. 1998: Kwanashie, Mike, Ajilima, Isaac, Garba Abdul-Ganiyu. The Nigerian Economy: Response of agriculture to adjustment policies. AERC Research Paper 78, African Economic Research Consortium, Nairobi, March 1998.
Kweka et al. 1997: Kweka, J.P., Semboja, H.H., Wangwe, S.M. Import Liberalization, Industrialization and Technological Capability in Sub-Saharan Africa: The Case of Garment and Light Engineering Industries in Tanzania. Economic and Social Sciences Foundation Tanzania. In: http://www.esrf.kabissa.org.
Kwoka 1979: Kwoka, John E. The Effect of Market Share Distribution on Industry Performance. In: Review of Economics and Statistics, Vol. 61, 1979. S. 101-109.
Kwoka 1984: Kwoka, John E. Market Power and Market Change in the U.S. Automobile Industry. In: Journal of Industrial Economicy, Vol. 32, No. 4, June 1984. S. 509-522.
Kwon 1994: Kwon, Jene. The East Asian Challenge to Neoclassical Orthodoxy. In: World Development, Vol. 22, No. 4, 1994. S. 635-644.

L

Lacarte 2005: Lacarte, Julio A. Transparency, Public Debate, and Participation by NGOs in the WTO: a WTO perspective. In: Petersmann, Ernst-Ulrich (ed.). Reforming the World Trading System. Legitimacy, Efficiency, and Democratic Governance. Oxford: Oxford University Press, 2005.
Lahiri et al. 2000: Lahiri, Sajal, Nasim, Anjum, Ghani, Jawaid. Optimal second-best tariffs on an intermediate input with particular reference to Pakistan. In: Journal of Development Economics, Vol. 61, 2000. S. 393-416.
Lal 1983: Lal, Deepak. The Poverty of 'Development Economics'. London: The Institute of Economic Affairs, 1983.
Lal/Rajapatirana 1987: Lal, Deepak, Rajapatirana, Sarath. Trade Liberalization and Economic Development. In: Giersch, Herbert (ed.). Free Trade in the World Economy. Towards the Opening of Markets. Tübingen: Mohr, 1987.
Lall 1982: Lall, Sanjaya. The Emergence of Third World Multinationals: Indian Joint Ventures Overseas. In: World Development, Vol. 10, No. 2, 1982. S. 127-146.
Lall 1984: Lall, Sanjaya. Exports of Technology by Newly-industrializing Countries: An Overview. In: World Development, Vol. 12, No. 5/6. S. 471-480.
Lall 1984a: Lall, Sanjaya. India. In: World Development, Vol. 12, No. 5/6, 1984. S. 535-565.
Lall 1984b: Lall, Sanjaya. India's Technological Capacity: Effects of Trade, Industrial Science and Technology Policies. In: Fransman, Martin, King, Kenneth (eds.). Technology Capability in the Thirld World. London: Macmillan, 1984.
Lall 1987: Lall, Sanjaya. Learning to Industrialize. The Acquisition of Technological Capability by India. London: Macmillan, 1987.
Lall 1990: Lall, Sanjaya. Building Industrial Competitiveness in Developing Countries. Paris: OECD, 1990.
Lall 1992: Lall, Sanjaya. Technological Capabilities and Industrialization. In: World Development, Vol. 20, No. 2, 1992. S. 165-186.
Lall 1993: Lall, Sanjaya. Promoting Technology Development: The Role of Technology Transfer and Indigenous Effort. In: Third World Quarterly. Vol. 14 No. 1, 1993. S. 95-108.
Lall 1994a: Lall, Sanjaya. The East Asian Miracle: Does the Bell Toll for Industrial Strategy? In: World Development, Vol. 22, No. 4, 1994. S. 645-654.
Lall 1995: Lall, Sanjaya. Malaysia: Industrial Success and the Role of Government. In: Journal of International Development, Vol. 7, No. 5, 1995. S. 759-773.
Lall 1995a: Lall, Sanjaya. Structural Adjustment and African Industry. In: World Development, Vol. 23, No. 12, 1995. S. 2019-2031.
Lall 1995b: Lall, Sanjaya. Industrial Policy Reforms: The Changing Role of Government and Private Sector Development. Global Forum on Industry, New Delhi, India, October 1995. Wien: UNIDO, 1995. In: http://www.unido.org.
Lall 1997: Lall, Sanjaya. East Asia. In: Dunning, John H. (ed.). Governments, Gobalization and International Business. Oxford: Oxford University Press, 1997.
Lall 1997a: Lall, Subir. Speculative Attacks, Forward Market Intervention and the Classic Bear Squeeze. IMF Working Paper WP/97/194. In: http://www.imf.org.

Lall 1999: Lall, Sanjaya. India's Manufactured Export: Comparative Structure and Prospects. In: World Development, Vol. 27, No. 10, 1999, S. 1769-1786.
Lall 1999a: Lall, Sanjaya. Introduction and Setting. In: In: Lall, Sanjaya (Hrg.). The Technological Response to Import Liberalization in SubSaharan Africa. United Nations University, INTECH. London: MacMillan Press, 1999.
Lall 1999b: Lall, Sanjaya. Opening Up – and Shutting Down? Synthesis, Policies and Conclusions. In: Lall, Sanjaya (Hrg.). The Technological Response to Import Liberalization in SubSaharan Africa. United Nations University, INTECH. London: MacMillan Press, 1999.
Lall 1999c: Lall, Sanjaya. Strategic Vision and Industrial Policies for the New Millenium. Asia-Pacific Forum on Industry, Bangkok, Thailand, September 1999. Wien: UNIDO, 1999. In: http://www.unido.org.
Lall 2000: Lall, Sanjaya. The Technological Structure and Performance of Developing Country Manufactured Exports, 1985-98. In: Oxford Development Studies, Vol. 28, No. 3, 2000.
Lall 2003: Lall, Sanjaya. Indicators of the Relative Importance of IPRs in Developing Countries. Issue Paper No. 3, ICTSD, UNCTAD, June 2003. In: http://www.ictsd.org.
Lall 2005: Lall, Sanjaya. Rethinking Industrial Strategy: The Role of the State in the Face of Globalization. In: Gallagher, Kevin P. Putting Development First. London, New York: Zed Books, 2005.
Lall et al. 1994: Lall, Sanjaya, Navaretti, Giorgio Barba, Teitel, Simón, Wignaraja, Ganeshan. Technology and Enterprise Development. Ghana under Structural Adjustment. New York: St. Martin's Press, 1994.
Lall/Albaladejo 2004: Lall, Sanjaya, Albaladejo, Manuel. China's Competitive Performance: A Threat to East Asian Manufactured Exports? In: World Development, Vol. 23 No. 9, 2004. S. 1441-1466.
Lall/Keesing 1992: Lall, Sanjaya, Keesing, Donald B. Marketing Manufactured Exports from Developing Countries: Learning Sequences and Public Support. In: Helleiner. G. (ed.) Trade Policy, Industrialization, and Development. New York: Oxford University Press, 1992.
Lall/Kumar 1981: Lall, Sanjaya, Kumar, Rajiv. Firm-Level Export Performance in an Inward-Looking Economy: The Indian Engineering Industry. In: World Development, Vol. 9, No. 5, 1981. S. 453-463.
Lall/Latsch 1998: Lall, Sanjaya, Latsch, Wolfram. Import Liberalization and Industrial Performance: The Conceptual Underpinnings. In: Development and Change, Vol. 29, 1998, S. 437-465.
Lall/Latsch 1999: Lall, Sanjaya, Latsch, Wolfram. Import Liberalization and Industrial Performance: Theory and Evidence. In: Lall, Sanjaya (Hrg.). The Technological Response to Import Liberalization in SubSaharan Africa. United Nations University, INTECH. London: MacMillan Press, 1999.
Lall/Wignaraja 1996: Lall, Sanjaya, Wignaraja, Ganeshan. Skills and Capabilities in Ghana's Competitiveness. In: Lall, Sanjaya. Learning from the Asian Tigers. London: Macmillan, 1996.
Lamb Proclamation 2001: President George W. Bush. To Provide for the Termination of Action Taken with Regard to Imports of Lamb Meat. November 14, 2001. In: http://www.whitehouse.gov.
LaNasa 1995: LaNasa, Joseph A. An Evaluation of the Uses and Importance of Rules of Origin, and the Effectiveness of the Uruguay Round's Agreement on Rules of Origin in Harmonizing and Regulating them. Working Paper, Jean Monnet Program, Nr. 1, 1996. In: http://www.jeanmonnetprogram.org/papers/96/9601ind.html.
Landesmann 1998: Landesmann, Michael. The Shape of the New Europe: Vertical Product Differenciation, Wage and Productivity Hierarchies. BRIE-Working Paper 104, May 1998. In: http://brie.berkeley.edu.
Landesmann/Pöschl 1995: Landesmann, Michael, Pöschl, Josef. Die Zahlungsbilanz als Begrenzungsfaktor des Wirtschaftswachstums in Ost-Mitteleuropa. In: Europa 1996 Auswirkungen einer EU-Osterweiterung. Schriftenreihe des Bundeskanzleramts. Wien: Österreichische Staatsdruckerei, 1995.
Langdon 1984: Langdon, Steven. Indigenous Technological Capability in Africa: The Case of Textiles and Wood Products in Kenya. In: Fransman, Martin, King, Kenneth (eds.). Technology Capability in the Thirld World. London: Macmillan, 1984.
Lange 1996: Lange, Peter. Patentierungsverbot für Pflanzensorten. In: GRUR Int. 1996, Heft 5. S. 586-591.
Langer 1995: Langer, Stefan. Grundlagen einer internationalen Wirtschaftsverfassung. München: C.H. Beck, 1995.
Langhammer 1980: Langhammer, Rolf J. Die Präferenzabkommen der Europäischen Gemeinschaft mit Entwickungsländern: Anpassungsprobleme in den Beitrittsländern? In: Die Weltwirtschaft, Heft 1, 1980. S. 187-203.
Langhammer 1998: Langhammer, Rolf J. Regional Integration APEC Style: Are there lessons to learn from regional intergration EU style? Kiel Working Paper No. 869, July 1998.
Langhammer 2000: Langhammer, Rolf J. Developing Countries as Exporters of Services: Looking Beyond Success Episodes. Kiel Working Paper No. 992, July 2000.
Langhammer/Menzler-Hokkanen 1994: Langhammer, Rolf J., Menzler-Hokkanen, Ingeborg. Product and Country Substitution in Imports: An Empirical Comparison of Theoretical Concepts. In: Weltwirtschaftliches Archiv, Bd. 130 Heft 2, 1994. S. 309-328.
Langhammer/Sapir 1987: Langhammer, Rolf J., Sapir, André. Economic Impact of Generalized Tariff Preferences. Adershot et al.: Gower, 1987.
Langhauser 2000: Langhauser, Simone. Marktchancenanalyse. Januar 2000. Aus: http://www.ahk-china.org.
Langille 1997: Langille, Brian A. Eight Ways to Think about International Labor Standards. In: JWT, Vol. 31, No. 4, August 1997. S. 27-53.
Lanjouw 1997: Lanjouw, Jean O. The Introduction of Pharmaceutical Patents in India: 'Heartless Exploitation of the Poor and Suffering'. Yale University, Economic Growth Centre, Centre Discussion Paper No. 775, August 1997.

Laothamatas 1992: Laothamatas, Anek. Business Associations and the New Political Economy of Thailand. Boulder: Westview Press, 1992.
Latham 1996: Latham, Scott. Market Opening or Corporate Welfare? "Results-Oriented" Trade Policy toward Japan. Cato Policy Analysis No. 252, April 15, 1996. In: www.cato.org.
Latsch/Robinson 1999: Latsch, Wolfram W., Robinson, Peter B. Technology and the Responses of Firms to Adjustment in Zimbabwe. In: Lall, Sanjaya (Hrg.). The Technological Response to Import Liberalization in SubSaharan Africa. United Nations University, INTECH. London: MacMillan Press, 1999.
Lawrence 1991: Lawrence, Robert Z. Efficient or Exclusionist? The Import Behavior of Japanese Corporate Groups. In: Brookings Papers on Economic Activity, 1, 1991. S. 311-341.
Lawrence 1992: Lawrence, Robert Z. An Analysis of Japanese Trade with Developing Countries. In: UNCTAD Review, No. 3, 1992. S. 31-52.
Lawrence 2003: Lawrence, Robert Z. Crimes and Punishments? Retaliation under the WTO. Washington: Institute for International Economics, 2003.
Leamer 1984: Leamer, Edward E. Sources of International Comparative Advantage. Cambridge: The MIT Press, 1984.
Leamer 1988: Leamer, Edward. E. Measures of Openness. In: Baldwin, Robert E. Trade Policy Issues and Empirical Analysis. Chicago; London: University of Chicago Press, 1988.
Leamer 1995: Leamer, Edward E. The Heckscher-Ohlin Model in Theory and Practice. Princeton Studies in International Finance, No. 77, February 1995.
Leamer 1998: Leamer, Edward E. In Search of Stolper-Samuelson Linkages between International Trade and Lower Wages. In: Collins, Susan M. Imports, Exports, and the American Workier. Washington: Brookings, 1998.
Leamer/Lundborg 1995: Leamer, Edward E., Lundborg, Per. A Heckscher-Ohlin View of Sweden Competing in the Global Market. NBER Working Paper No. 5114, May 1995.
Lee 1992: Lee, Chung H. The Government, Financial System, and Large Private Enterprise in the Economic Development of South Korea. In: World Development, Vol. 20, No. 2, 1992. S. 187-197.
Lee 1992a: Lee, Norman. Market Strukture and Trade in Developing Countries. In: Helleiner, Gerald K. Trade Policy, Industrialization, and Development. Oxford: Clarendon Press, 1992.
Lee 1995: Lee, Jong-Wha. Capital Goods Imports and Long-run Growth. In: Journal of Development Economics, Vol. 48, 1995. S. 91-110.
Lee 1999: Lee, Yong-Shik. Review of the First WTO Panel Case on the Agreement on Safeguards. In: JWT, Vol. 33, No. 6, 1999. 27-46.
Lee 2000: Lee, Yong-Shik. Critical Issues in the Application of the WTO Rules on Safeguards. In: JWT, Vol. 34, Vol. 2, 2000. S. 131-147.
Lee 2001: Lee, Yong-Shik. Destabilizing of the Discipline on Safeguards? JWT, Vol. 35 No. 6, 2001. S. 1235-1246.
Lee 2002: Lee, Yong-Shik. Safeguard Measures: Why are they not applied consistently with the rules? In: JWT, Vol. 36, No. 4, 2002. S. 641-673.
Lee 2002a: Lee, Yong-Shik. Revival of Grey Area Measures? The US-Canada Softwood Lumber Agreement: Conflict with the WTO Agreement on Safeguards. In: JWT, Vol. 36, No. 1, 2003. S. 155-165.
Lee 2003: Lee, Yong-Shik. Continuing Controversy on 'Unforeseen Developments' - Reviewers Note. In: JWT, Vol. 37, No. 6, 2003. S. 1153-1157.
Lee 2004: Lee, Y. S. Test of Multilateralism in International Trade: U.S. Steel Safeguards. Berkeley Electronic Press Preprint Series, Paper 253, 2004. In: http://www.law.bepress.com/expresso/eps/253.
Lee 2005: Lee, Y. S. Safeguard Measures in World Trade. The Legal Analysis. The Hague et al.: Kluwer, 2005.
Lee 2005a: Lee, Ronald D. The Dog Doesn't Bark: CFIUS, the National Security Guard Dog With Teeth. In: The M&A Lawyer, Vol. 8 No. 8. Glasser Legal Works, 2005. S. 5-11. In: http://www.arnoldporter.com/pubs/files/Article-National_Security_Guard_Dog(2-05).pdf.
Lee 2006: Lee, Y. S. Not without a clue: commentary on 'the persistent puzzles of safeguards'. In: JWT Vol. 40, No. 2, 2006. S. 385-404.
Lee/Cason 1994: Lee, Naeyoung, Cason, Jeffrey. Automobile Commodity Chains in the NICs: A Comparison of South Korea, Mexico, Brasil. In: Gereffi, Gary, Korzeniewicz, Miguel (eds.). Commodity Chains and Global Capitalism. Westport, Connecticut; London: Praeger 1994.
Leebron 1997: Leebron, David W. Implementation of the Uruguay Round results in the United States. In: Jackson, John H., Sykes, Alan O. (eds.). Implementing the Uruguay Round. Oxford: Clarendon Press, 1997.
Leff 1968: Leff, Nathaniel H. Export Stagnation and Autarkic Development in Brazil, 1947-1962. In: Quarterly Journal of Economics, Vol. 81, 1967. S. 286-301.
Lehmbruch 1986: Lehmbruch, Gerhard. Interest Groups, Government, and the Politics of Protection. In: Aussenwirtschaft, 41. Jg, Heft 2/3, 1986. S. 273-302.
Leibenstein 1957: Leibenstein, Harvey. Economic Backwardness and Economic Growth. New York: John Wiley, 1957.
Leibenstein 1966: Leibenstein, Harvey. Allocative Efficiency vs. "X-Efficiency". In: American Economic Review, Vol. 56, Nr. 1.3, 1966. S. 392-415.
Leibenstein 1989: Leibenstein, Harvey. Organizational Economics and Institutions as Missing Elements in Economic Development Analysis. In: World Development, Vol. 17, No. 9, 1989. S. 1361-1373.

Leibfried/Pierson 1995: Leibfried, Stephan, Pierson, Paul. Semisovereign Welfare States: Social Policy in a Multitiered Europe. In: Leibfried, Stephan, Pierson, Paul (eds.). European Social Policy. Between Fragmentation and Integration. Washington: Brookings Institution, 1995.
Leidy/Ibrahim 1996: Leidy, Michael, Ibrahim, Ali. Recent Trade Policies and an Approach to Further Reform in the Baltics, Russian, and Other Countries of the Former Soviet Union. IMF Working Paper WP/96/71. Washington: International Monetary Fund, July 1996.
Leier 1999: Leier, Klaus-Peter. Fortentwicklung und weitere Bewährung: Zur derzeitigen Überprüfung des Streitbeilegungsverfahrens in der WTO. In: EuZW, Heft 7, 1999. 204-211.
Leipziger/Petri 1993: Leipziger, Danny M., Petri, Peter A. Korean Industrial Policy. World Bank Discussion Papers 197. Washington: World Bank, 1993.
Leith/Malley 2003: Leith, Campbell, Malley, Jim. A Sectoral Analysis of Price-Setting Behavior in US Manufacturing Industries. CESIFO Working Paper No. 984, July 2003. In: http://www.CESifo.de.
Leither/Lester 2006: Leitner, Kara, Lester, Simon. WTO Dispute Settlement from 1995 to 2005 - A Statistical Analysis. In: Journal of International Economic Law Vol. 9, No. 1, 2006.
Lenel 1997: Lenel, Hans Otto. Ordnungspolitische Kursänderungen. In: ORDO, Bd. 48, 1997.
Lennard 2002: Lennard, Michael. Navigating by the Stars: Interpreting the WTO Agreement. In: Journal of International Economic Law, 2002. S. 17-89.
Lenovo Information 2006: Lenovo. Information. 2006: In: http://www.lenovo.com/lenovo/de/de/.
León/Soto 1995: León, Javier, Soto, Raimundo. Structural Breaks and Long-Run Trends in Commodity Prices. World Bank Policy Research Working Paper No. 1406, January 1995.
Leontief 1951: Leontief, Wassily. Input-Output Economics. In: Leontief, Wassily. Input-Output Economics. New York, Oxford: Oxford University Press, (1951) 1986.
Leontief 1956: Leontief, Wassily. Factor Proportions and the Structure of American Trade: Further Theoretical and Empirical Analysis. In: Review of Economics and Statistics, Vol. 38, 1956. S. 386-407.
Leontief 1963: Leontief, Wassily. The Structure of Development. In: Leontief, Wassily. Input-Output Economics. New York, Oxford: Oxford University Press, (1963) 1986.
Lester 1998: Lester, Simon N. Update on TRIMS. The Development of a TRIMS Jurisprudence in the WTO Panel Report on Indonesia - Certain Measures Affecting the Automobile Industry. In: World Competition, vol. 21, no. 6, 1998. S. 85-97.
Lester 2001: Lester, Simon N. WTO Panel and the Appellate Body Interpretations of the WTO Agreement in US Law. In: JWT Vol. 35, No. 3, 2001. S. 521-543.
Letzel 1999: Letzel, Hans Joachim. Streitbeilegung der Welthandelsorganisation (WTO). Münster: Aschendorff Rechtsverlag, 1999.
Levenstein 1997: Levenstein, Margaret C. Price Wars and the Stability of Collusion: A Study of the Pre-World War I Bromine Industry. In: Journal of Industrial Economics, Vol. XLV, No. 2, June 1997. S. 117-137.
Levin 2006: Levin, Carl. Statement of Senator Carl Levin at the DPC Oversight Hearing on Trade Policy and the U.S. Automobile Industry. February 17, 2006. http://levin.senate.gov/newsroom/release.cfm?id=251708.
Levin et al. 1985: Levin, Richard C., Cohen, Wesley M., Mowery, David C. R&D Appropriability, Opportunity, and Market Structure: New Evidence on Some Schumpeterian Hypotheses. In: American Economic Review, Vol. 75 No. 1, May 1985. S. 20-24.
Levin et al. 1987: Levin, Richard C., Klevorick, Alvin K., Nelson, Richard R., Winter, Sidney G. Appropriating the Returns from Industrial Research and Development. In: Brooking Papers on Economic Activity, Vol. 3, 1987. S. 783-831.
Levine/Renelt 1992: Levine, Ross, Renelt, David. A Sensitivity Analysis of Cross-Country Growth Regressions. In: American Economic Review, Vol. 82, No. 4, 1992. S. 942-963.
Levinsohn 1996: Levinsohn, James. Carwars: Trying to make sense of U.S.-Japan trade frictions in the automobile und automobile parts markets. March 25, 1996. In: http://www.econ.lsa.umich.edu/~jamesl/
Levinsohn et al. 1999: Levinsohn, James, Berry, Steven and Friedman, Jed. Impacts of the Indonesian Economic Crisis: Price Changes and the Poor. June, 1999. In: http://www.econ.lsa.umich.edu/~jamesl/.
Levy/van Wijinbergen 1992: Levy, Santiago, van Wijinbergen, Sweder. Mexican Agriculture in the Free Trade Agreement: Transition Problems in Economic Reform. Technical Paper No. 63. Paris: OECD, May 1992. In: http://www.oecd.org.
Lewis 1949: Lewis, W. A. The Principles of Economic Planning. London: Unwin University Books, (1949) 1963.
Lewis 1956: Lewis, W. A. Die Theorie wirtschaftlichen Wachstums. Tübingen: Mohr, 1956.
Lewis 1992: Lewis, Richard P. Canadian Monopolies Law: Director of Investigation and Research v. Nutra Sweet Co. Decided as First Case under Abuse-of-Dominance Provision. In: Cornell International Law Journal, Vol. 25, 1982. S. 437-480.
Leycegui/de la Torre 2005: Leycegui, Beatriz, de la Torre, Luz Elena Reynes. The 10 Major Problems With the Anti-Dumping Instrument in Mexico. In: JWT, Vol. 39, No. 1, 2005. S. 137-146.
Liapis/Britz 2001: Liapis, P., Britz, W. Modelling TQRs in Multi-Commodity Models. In: Brockmeier, M., Isermeyer, F., von Cramon-Taubadel, S. (Hrg.). Liberalisierung des Weltagrarhandels - Strategien und Konsequenzen. Münster-Hiltrup: Landwirtschaftsverlag, 2002.
Lim 1995: Lim, Linda. Foreign Investment, the State and Industrial Policy in Singapore. In: Stein, Howard (Hrg.). Asian Industrialization and Africa. Studies in Policy Alternatives to Structural Adjustment. London: St. Martin's Press, 1995.

Lim et al. 1993: Lim, Joseph Y., Montes, Manuel F., Quisumbing, Agnes R. The Philippines. In: Taylor, Lance (ed.). The Rocky Road to Reform. Adjustment, Income Distribution, and Growth in the Developing World. Cambridge: MIT Press, 1993.
Lindblom 1980: Lindblom, Charles E. Jenseits von Markt und Staat. Stuttgart: Ernst Klett, 1980.
Lindsey 1999: Lindsey, Brink. The U.S. Antidumping Law: Rhetoric versus Reality. Cato Institute, Trade Policy Analysis, August 16, 1999. In: http://www.freetrade.org.
Link 1996: Link, Thomas. Interstate Banking - Die geographische Expansion von US-Banken. Aachen: Shaker Verlag, 1996.
Link 1998: Link, Werner. Die Neuordnung der Weltpolitik. München: C.H. Beck, 1998.
Lipsey/Lancaster 1956: Lipsey, R. G., Lancaster, Kelvin. The General Theory of Second Best. In: Review of Economic Studies, Vol. 24 No. 63, 1956. S. 11-32.
Lipson 1982: Lipson, Charles. The Transformation of trade: the sources and effects of regime change. In: International Organization, 36, 2, Spring 1982.
Lipton 1991: Lipton, Michael. Market relaxation and agricultural development. In: Christopher Colclough, James Manor (eds.). States or Markets? Neo-liberalism and the Development Policy Debate. Oxford. Clarendon Press, 1991.
List 1841: List, Friedrich. Das nationale System der Politischen Ökonomie. Jena: Gustav Fischer Verlag, (1841) 1922.
List 1993: List, Martin. Recht und Moral in der Weltgesellschaft. In: Wolf, Klaus Dieter (Hg.). Internationale Verrechtlichung. Jahresschrift für Rechtspolitologie (JfR). Pfaffenweiler: Centaurus Verlagsgesellschaft, 1993.
Litman 1990: Litman, Barry R. The Motion Picture Industry. In: Adams, Walter (Hrg.). The Structure of American Industry. New York: Macmillan, 1990.
Little 1987: Little, Ian M. D. Small Manufacturing Enterprises in Developing Countries. In: The World Bank Economic Review, Vol. 1, No. 2: S. 203-235.
Little et al. 1970: Little, Ian, Scitovsky, Tibor, Scott, Maurice. Industry and Trade in Some Developing Countries. London; New York; Toronto: OECD Development Centre/Oxford University Press, 1970.
Little et al. 1987: Little, Ian M. D., Mazumdar, Dipak, Page, John M., Small Manufacturing Enterprises. A Comparative Study of India and other Economies. Oxford: Oxford University Press/World Bank, 1987.
Löbbe et al. 1993: Löbbe, Klaus, Döhrn, Roland, von Loeffelholz, Hans Dietrich (Hrg.) Strukturwandel in der Krise. Essen: RWI, 1993.
Long 1985: Long, Oliver. Law and its Limitations in the GATT Multilateral Trade System. Dordrecht, Boston: Martinus Nijhoff, 1985.
Lopez/Hathie 1998: Lopez, Rigoberto A., Hathie, Ibrahima. Structural Adjustment Programs and Peanut Market Performance in Senegal. Paper American Agricultural Association Meeting, Salt Lake City, August 2-5, 1998. IN: http://www.aaea.org.
López-Pina 1996: López-Pina, Antonio. Markt und öffentliches Interesse. Eine Sicht aus dem europäischen Süden. In: Tomuschat, Christian (Hrsg.) Eigentum im Umbruch. Berlin: Berlin Verlag Arno Spitz, 1996.
Lorz 1994: Lorz, Jens Oliver. Indikatoren zur Beurteilung der Standortqualität – Ein methodischer Überblick und neuer Ansatzpunkt am Beispiel Westdeutschlands. In: Die Weltwirtschaft, 1994. S. 448-471.
Loseby 1997: Loseby, Margaret. Vertical Coordination in the Fruit and Vegetable Sector: Implications for Existing Market Institutions and Policy Instruments. Consultant's report for OECD. Paris: OECD, 1997. In: http://www.oecd.org.
Lovewell 2002: Lovewell, Mark. Understanding Economics. A Contemporary Perspective. Internet Lecture Notes: McGrawHill, 2002. Siehe: http://highered.mcgraw-hill.com/sites/dl/free/0070916543/120413/OLCSLchap2.pdf.
Low 1982: Low, Patrick. Export Subsidies and Trade Policy: The Experience of Kenya. In: World Development. Vol. 10, No. 4, 1982. S. 293-304.
Low/Subramanian 1995: Low, Patrick, Subramanian, Arvind. TRIMs in the Uruguay Round: An Unfinished Business. In: Martin, Will, Winters, L. Alan (eds.) The Uruguay Round and the Developing Economies. World Bank Discussion Paper 307. Washington: World Bank, 1995.
Lübcke/Piazolo 1998: Lübcke, Britta, Piazolo, Daniel. Wohlfahrtseffekte einer Nordatlantischen Handelsliberalisierung. Kieler Arbeitspapiere Nr. 885, October 1998.
Lucas 1988: Lucas, Robert E. B. Demand for India's Manufactured Exports. In: Journal of Development Economics, Vol. 29, 1988. S. 63-74.
Lücke 1992: Lücke, Matthias. The Diffusion of Process Innovations in Industrialized and Developing Countries – A Case Study of the World Textile and Steel Industries. Kiel Working Paper No. 535. November 1992. Kiel: Institute of World Economics.
Lücke 1992a: Lücke, Matthias. Technical Progress and the Pattern of Specialization in World Trade in Manufactures, 1965 to 1987. Kiel Working Paper No. 534. October 1992. Kiel: Institut of World Economics.
Ludwig 1997: Ludwig, Martina. Globalisierung der Märkte. Motor oder Bremse für den Wohlstand hochentwickelter Volkswirtschaften? Frankfurt am Main et al.: Peter Lang, 1997.
Luhmann 1975: Luhmann, Niklas. Die Weltgesellschaft. In: Luhmann, Niklas. Soziologische Aufklärung 2. Opladen: Westdeutscher Verlag, 1975.
Luhmann 1995: Luhmann, Niklas. Politik und Wirtschaft. In: Merkur, Heft 7, Jg. 49, Juli 1995.
Lundvall 1992: Lundvall, Bengt-Ake. Introduction. In: Lundvall, Bengt-Ake. National Systems of Innovation. Towards a Theorey of Innovation and Interactive Learning. London; New York: Pinter, 1992.
Luttwak 1994: Luttwak, Edward N. Weltwirtschaftskrieg. Reinbeck bei Hamburg: Rowohlt, 1994.

Lutz 1994: Lutz, James M. To Import or Protect? Industrialized Countries and Manufactured Products. In: JWT, No. 4, Vol. 28, August 1994. S. 123-146.
Lyons et al. 2001: Lyons, Bruce, Matraves, Catherine, Moffatt, Peter. Industrial Concentration and Market Integration in the European Union. In: Economica, Vol. 68, 2001. S. 1-26.

M

Macario et al. 2000: Mararío, Carla, Bonelli, Regis, ten Kate, Adriaan, Niels, Gunnar. Export Growth in Latin America. Policies and Performance. Boulder; London: Lynne Rienner, 2000.
MacCormick 1995: MacCormick, Niel. Das Maastricht-Urteil: Souveränität heute. In: Juristen Zeitung, 50 Jg., 1. September 1995. S. 797-803.
MacDougall 1951: MacDougall, G. D. A. Britisch and American Exports: A Study suggested by the Theory of Comparative Costs, Part. I. In: Economic Journal, Vol. 61, December 1951. S. 697-724.
MacDougall 1952: MacDougall, G. D. A. Britisch and American Exports: A Study suggested by the Theory of Comparative Costs, Part. I. In: Economic Journal, Vol. 62, September 1952. S. 487-521.
MacDougall/Cameron 1994: MacDougall, David, Cameron, Peter. Trade in Energy and Natural Resources. Trade Related Investment Measures - Focus on Eastern Europa. In: JWT, Vol. 28, No. 3, June 1994. S. 171-180.
MacLean 1999: MacLean, Robert M. The European Community's Trade Barrier Regulation Takes Shape. In: JWT Vol. 33 No. 6, 1999. S. 69-96.
MacMillan/Turner 1987: MacMillan, Keith, Turner, Ian. The Cost-Containment Issue: a Study of Government-Industry Relations in the Pharmaceuticals Sectors of the United Kingdom and West Germany. In: Wilks, Stephen, Wright, Maurice (eds.). Comparative Government-Industry Relations. Western Europe, the United States, and Japan. Oxford: Clarendon Press, 1987.
Maddison 1987: Maddison, Angus. Growth and Slowdown in Advanced Capitalist Economies: Techniques of Quantitative Assessment. In: Journal of Economic Literature, Vol. XXV, June 1987, S. 649-698.
Maddison 1995: Maddison, Angus. Monitoring the World Economy 1820-1992. Paris: OECD, 1992.
Madison 1787: Madison, James. No. 10 The same subject continued. In: Rossiter, Clinton (ed.) The Federalist Papers. New York: Signet Classic, 1999.
Magnus 2004: Magnus, John R. World Trade Organization Subsidy Discipline: Is This the 'Retrenchment Round'? In: JWT, Vol. 38, No. 6, 2004. S. 985-1047.
Maier 1978: Maier, Charles S. The Politics of Productivity: Foundations of American International Economic Policy after World War II. In: Katzenstein, Peter J. (ed.). Between Power and Plenty. Foreign Economic Policies of Advanced Industrial States. Madison: The University of Wisconsin Press, 1978.
Maier 1987: Maier, Charles S. In Search of Stability. Explorations into historical political economy. Cambridge: Cambridge University Press, 1987.
Majmudar 1996: Majmudar, Madhavi. Trade Liberalization in Clothing: the MFA Phase-Out and the Developing Countries. In: Development Policy Review, Vol. 14, 1996. S. 5-36.
Majone 1994: Majone, Giandomenico. The European Community: An 'Independent Fourth Branch of Government'? In: Brüggemeier, Gert. Verfassungen für ein ziviles Europa. Baden-Baden: Nomos, 1994.
Majone 1996: Majone, Giandomenico. Regulating Europe. London, New York: Routledge, 1996.
Mamaty 2002: Mamaty, Isabelle. African Countries and the Agreement on Agriculture. What Scope for Sustainable Development. ICTSD Ressource Paper No. 3, March 2002. In: http://www.ictsd.org.
Mancini 1998: Mancini, G. Frederico. Europe: The Case for Statehood. In: European Law Journal, Vol. 4, No. 1, March 1998.
Mandel 1974: Mandel, Ernest. Der Spätkapitalismus. Frankfurt am Main: Surkamp, 1974.
Mandelbaum 1961: Mandelbaum, K. The Industrialization of Backward Areas. Oxford: Basil Blackwell, 1961.
Mangalo 1977: Mangalo, Nashrallah. Patentschutz und Technologietransfer im Nord-Süd-Konflikt. In: GRUR Int. Heft 10, Oktober 1977. S. 349-378.
Mangeni 2003: Mangeni, Francis. Strengthening the Special and Differential Treatment Provisions in the WTO Agreements: Some Reflection on the Stakes for African Countries. International Centre for Trade and Sustainable Development (ICTSD): Ressource Paper No. 4, 2003.
Mankiw 1995: Mankiw, N. Gregory. The Growth of Nations. In: Brookings Papers of Economic Activity, 1, 1995. S. 275-326.
Mankiw/Romer/Weil 1992: Mankiw, N. Gregory, Romer, David, Weil, David N. A Contribution to the Empirics of Economic Growth. In: The Quarterly Journal of Economics, May 1992, pp. 407-437.
Mann 1997: Mann, Catherine L. Globalization and Productivity in the United States and Germany. Federal Reserve Bank. International Finance Discussion Papers, No. 595, November 1997. In: http://www.bog.frb.fed.us.
Mann 2005: Mann, Erika. A Parliamentary Dimension to the WTO: More than just a vision? In: Petersmann, Ernst-Ulrich (ed.). Reforming the World Trading System. Legitimacy, Efficiency, and Democratic Governance. Oxford: Oxford University Press, 2005.
Mansfield 1980: Mansfield, Edwin. Basic Research and Productivity Increase in Manufacturing. In: American Economic Review, Devember 1980. S. 863-873.
Mansfield 1985: Mansfield, Edwin. How rapidly does new industrial technology leak out? In: Journal of Industrial Economics, Vol. XXXIV, No. 2, December 1985. S. 217-223.
Mansfield 1986: Mansfield, Edwin. Patents and Innovation: An Empirical Study. In: Management Science, Vol. 32 No. 2, February 1986. S. 173-181.

Mansfield 1994: Mansfield, Edwin. Intellectual Property Protection, Foreign Direct Investment, and Technology Transfer. International Finance Corporation/World Bank Discussion Paper No. 19, 1994. In: http://www.ifc.org/economics/pubs/discuss.htm.
Mansfield 1995: Mansfield, Edwin. Intellectual Property Protection, Foreign Investment, and Technology Transfer. Germany, Japan, and the United States. International Finance Corporation/World Bank Discussion Paper No. 27, Sept. 1995. In: http://www.ifc.org/economics/pubs/discuss.htm.
Mansfield et al. 1977: Mansfield, Edwin, Rapoport, John, Romeo, Anthony, Wagner, Samuel, Beardsley, George. Social and Private Returns from Industrial Innovations. In: Quarterly Journal of Economics, Vol. 91, 1977. S. 221-240.
Mansfield et al. 1981: Mansfield, Edwin, Schwartz, Mark, Wagner, Samuel. Imitation costs and patents: An empirical study. In: The Economic Journal, Vol. 91, December 1981. S. 907-918.
Mansfield et al. 1982: Mansfield, Edwin, Romeo, Anthony, Schwartz, Mark, Teece, David, Wagner, Samuel, Brach, Peter. Technology Transfer, Productivity, Economic Policy. New York, London: W. W. Norton, 1982.
Mansfield/Busch 1995: Mansfield, Edward D., Busch, Marc L. The political economy of nontariff barriers: a cross-national analysis. In: International Organization, 49, 4, Autumn 1995. S. 723-749.
Manyin 2002: Manyin, Mark E. South Korea-U.S. Economic Relations: Cooperation, Friction, and Future Prospects. Report for Congress, Congressional Research Service. Code RL30566, August 14, 2002. In: http://fpc.state.gov/c4763.htm.
Marceau 1997: Marceau, Gabrielle. The Dispute Settlement Rules of the North American Free Trade Agreement: A Thematic Comparison with the Dispute Settlement Rules of the World Trade Organization. In: Petersmann, Ernst-Ulrich (ed.). International Trade Law and the GATT/WTO Dispute Settlement System. London, The Hague, Boston: Kluwer Law, 1997.
Marceau 1998: Marceau, Gabrielle. Rules on Ethics for the New World Trade Organization Dispute Settlement Mechanism. In: JWT, Vol. 32 No. 3, June 1998. S. 57-97.
Marceau/Pedersen 1999: Marceau, Gabrielle, Pedersen, Peter N. Is the WTO Open and Transparent? In: JWT, Vol. 33 No. 1, 1999. S. 5-49.
Marceau/Trachtman 2002: Marceau, Gabrielle, Trachtman, Joel P. The Technical Barriers to Trade Agreement, the Sanitary and Phytosanitary Measures Agreement, and the General Agreement on Tariffs and Trade - A Map of the WTO Law of Domestic Regulation of Goods. In: Journal of World Trade, Vol. 36, No. 5, October 2002. S. 811-881.
Marceau/Trachtman 2004: Marceau, Gabrielle, Trachtman, Joel P. GATT, TBT and SPS: A Map of WTO Law of Domestic Regulation of Goods. In: Ortino, Federico, Petersmann, Ernst-Ulrich (eds.). The WTO Dispute Settlement System 1995 - 2003. The Hague et al.: Kluwer Law International, 2004.
Markusen 1986: Markusen, James R. Explaining the Volume of Trade. An Eclectic Approach. In: American Economic Review, Vol. 76 No. 5, December 1986. S. 1002-1011.
Markusen 1995: Markusen, James R. The Boundaries of Multinational Enterprises and the Theory of International Trade. In: Journal of Economic Perspectives, Vol. 9, No. 2, Spring 1995. S. 169-189.
Markusen et al. 1995: Markusen, James R., Melvin, James R., Kaempfer, William H., Maskus, Keith E. International Trade. Theory and Evidence. New York: McGraw Hill, 1995.
Markusen/Venables 1996: Markusen, James R., Venables, Anthony J. The Theory of Endowment, Intra-Industry, and Multinational Trade. NBER Working Paper 5529, April 1996.
Marques 1990: Marques, Jaime. Bilateral Trade Elasticities. In: Review of Economics and Statistics, Vol. 72, 1990. S. 70-77.
Marsh/Runsten 1995: Marsh, Robin, Runsten, David. The Potential for Small-Holder and Vegetable Production in Mexico: Barriers and Opportunities. North American Intergration and Development Centre (NAID), September 1995. In: http://NAID.sppsr.ucla.edu/pubs.html.
Martenczuk 1998: Martenczuk, Peter. Section 337 of the US Tariff Act and World Trade Law. Compatible at last? In: JWT, Vol. 32 No. 2, April 1998. S. 119-145.
Martin 1988: Martin, Stephen. Industrial Economics. Economic Analysis and Public Policy. New York: Macmillan, 1988.
Martin 1990: Martin, Stephen. The Petroleum Industry. In: Adams, Walter (Hrg.). The Structure of American Industry. New York: Macmillan, 1990.
Martin 1992: Martin, Lisa L. Interests, power, and multilateralism. In: IO, Vol. 46, No. 4, Autumn 1992. S. 765-792.
Martin et al. 2000: Martin, Will, Funkase, Emiko, Ianchovi, Elena. Assessing the Implications of Merchandise Trade Liberalization in China's Accession to WTO. Working Paper, World Bank Roundtables on China. In: http://www.worldbank.org/research/trade.
Martin Rodriguez 2007: Martin Rodriguez, Pablo. Safeguards in the World Trade Organization Ten Years After: A Dissociated State of the Law? In: JWT, Vol. 41, No. 1, 2007. S. 159-190.
Martinussen 1997: Martinussen, John. Society, State & Market. A Guide to Competing Theories of Development. London: Zed Books, 1997.
Marvel/Ray 1987: Marvel, Howard P., Ray, Edward John. Intraindustry Trade: Sources and Effects on Protection. In: Journal of Political Economy, Vol. 95, No. 6, 1987. S. 1278-1291.
Maskus 2000: Maskus, Keith E. Intellectual Property Rights in the Global Economy. Washington: Institute for International Economics, 2000.

Maskus et al. 1989: Maskus, Keith E., Battles, Deborah, Moffett, Michael H. Determinants of the Structure of U.S. Manufacturing Trade with Japan and Korea, 1970-1984. In: Audretsch, David B., Gordon, Michael P. (eds.) The Internationalization of U.S. Markets. New York; London: New York University Press, 1989.
Maskus/Eby 1990: Maskus, Keith E., Eby, Denise R. Developing New Rules and Disciplines on Trade-Related Investment Measures: In: World Economy, Vol. 13, No. 4, December 1990. S. 523-540.
Maskus/Penubarti 1995: Maskus, Keith E., Penunbarti, Mohan. How trade-related are intellectual property rights? In: Journal of International Economics, Vol. 39, 1995. S. 227-248.
Mason 1939: Mason, Edward S. Price and Production Policies of Large-Scale Industries. In: American Economic Review, Papers and Proceedings. Vol. 29, No. 1, March 1939. S. 61-74.
Mason 1949: Mason, Edward S. The Current Status of the Monopoly Problem in the United States: In: Harvard Law Review, Vol. 62 No. 8, June 1949. S. 1265-1285.
Mastanduno 1985: Mastanduno, Michael. Strategies of Economic Containment: U.S.-Trade Relations with the Soviet Union. In: World Politics, Vo. 37, No. 4, July 1985, S. 503-531.
Mastel 1998: Mastel, Greg. Antidumping Laws and the U.S. Economy. Armok, New York: M.E. Sharpe, 1998.
Masters 2003: Masters, William A. Policy Measurement for Trade Negotiations and Domestic Reforms. Revised 2003. In: http://www.agecon.purdue.edu/staff/masters/WillMaster-PolicyMeasurement.pdf.
Matambalya/Wolf 2001: Matambalya, Francis A.S.T., Wolf, Susanne. The Cotonou Agreement and the Challenges of Making the New EU-ACP Trade Regime WTO Compatible. In: JWT Vol. 35, No. 1, 2001. S. 123-144.
Matheny 1998: Matheny, Richard L. In the wake of the flood: 'Like products' and cultural products after the World Trade Organization's decision in Canada certain measures concerning periodicals. In: University of Pennsylvania Law Review, Vol. 147 Issue 1, November 1998. S. 245-279.
Mathis 1998: Mathis, James H. Mutual Recognition Agreements. In: JWT, Vol. 32, No. 6, 1998. S. 5-31.
Matsushita 1997: Matsushita, Mitsuo. Restrictive Business Practices and the WTO/GATT Dispute Settlement Process. In: Petersmann, Ernst-Ulrich (ed.). International Trade Law and the GATT/WTO Dispute Settlement System. London, The Hague, Boston: Kluwer Law, 1997.
Matsushita 2003: Matsushita, Mitsuo. Some Issues of the SPS Agreement. In: Cottier, Thomas, Mavroidis, Petros C (eds.). The Role of the Judge in International Trade Regulation. Ann Arbor: University of Michigan Press, 2003.
Matsushita 2004: Matsushita, Mitsuo. Appellate Body Jurisprudence on the GATS and TRIPs Agreements. In: Ortino, Federico, Petersmann, Ernst-Ulrich (eds.). The WTO Dispute Settlement System 1995 - 2003. The Hague et al.: Kluwer Law International, 2004.
Matsushita et al. 2006: Matsushita, Mitsuo, Schoenbaum, Thomas J., Mavroidis, Petros C. The World Trade Organization. Law, Practice, and Policy. Oxford: Oxford University Press, 2006.
Matto/Subramanian 2003: Mattoo, Aaditya, Subramanian, Arvind. What Would a Development-Friendly WTO Architecture Really Look Like? IMF Working Paper, WP/03/153, August 2003. In: http://www.imf.org.
Mattoo 1997: Mattoo, Aaditya. National Treatment in the GATS. Corner Stone or Pandora's Box. In: JWT, Vol. 31, No. 1, Feb. 1997. S. 107-135.
Mattoo 1998: Matto, Aaditya. Financial Services and the WTO: Liberalization in the Developing and Transition Economies. WTO 2000 Capacity Building Project. March 1998. In: http://www1.worldbank.org/wbiep/trade/wto2000_BPs.html
Mattoo 1999: Matto, Aaditya. MFN and the GATS. WTO 2000 Capacity Building Project. January 1999. In: http://www1.worldbank.org/wbiep/trade/wto2000_BPs.html.
Mattoo et al. 2002: Mattoo, Aaditya, Roy, Devesh, Subramanian, Arvind. The Africa Growth and Opportunity Act and Its Rules of Origin: Generosity Undermined? IMF Working Paper, WP/02/158. Washington: IMF, 2002. In: http://www.imf.org.
Mattoo/Mavroidis 1997: Mattoo, Aaditya, Mavroidis, Petros C. Trade, Environment and the WTO: The Dispute Settlement Practice Relating to Art. XX of GATT. In: Petersmann, Ernst-Ulrich (ed.). International Trade Law and the GATT/WTO Dispute Settlement System. London, The Hague, Boston: Kluwer Law, 1997.
Mattoo/Olarreaga 2000: Mattoo, Aaditya, Olarreaga, Marcelo. Should Credit be Given for Autonomous Liberalization in Multilateral Trade Negotiations. World Bank, Policy Research Working Paper No. 2374, June 2000. In: http://www.worldbank.org.
Matusz/Tarr 1999: Matusz, Steven J., Tarr, David. Adjusting to Trade Policy Reform. World Bank, Policy Research Working Paper No. 2142, 1999. In: http://www.worldbank.org.
Maunz/Dürig 1997: Maunz, Theodor, Dürig, Günter. Grundgesetz-Kommentar. Band 2. München: C.H. Beck, 1997.
Maurer 1993: Maurer, Rainer. Wissenstransfer, Marktexpansion und Außenhandel. Kieler Arbeitpapiere Nr. 589, Institut für Weltwirtschaft Kiel, August 1993.
Maurer 1994: Maurer, Rainer. Die Exportstärke der deutschen Industrie – Weltmarktspitze trotz technologischen Rückstands? In: Die Weltwirtschaft, 1994. S. 308-315.
Mavroidis 1992: Mavroidis, Petros C. Handelspolitische Abwehrmechanismen der EWG und der USA und ihre Vereinbarkeit mit den GATT-Regeln. Stuttgart: Blinn&Diem, Verlagsgesellschaft internationales Recht, 1993.
Mavroidis 2004: Mavroidis, Petros C. Proposals for Reform of Article 22 of the DSU: Reconsidering the 'Sequencing' Issue and Suspension of Concession. In: Ortino, Federico, Petersmann, Ernst-Ulrich (eds.). The WTO Dispute Settlement System 1995 - 2003. The Hague et al.: Kluwer Law International, 2004.

Mavroidis 2004a: Mavroidis, P.C. Development of Disputes Settlement Procedures Through Case Law. In: Ortino, Federico, Petersmann, Ernst-Ulrich (eds.). The WTO Dispute Settlement System 1995 - 2003. The Hague et al.: Kluwer Law International, 2004.
Mavroidis 2005: Mavroidis, Petros C. The General Agreement on Tariffs and Trade. A Commentary. Oxford: Oxford University Press, 2005.
Mavroidis 2005a: Mavroidis, Petros C. Come Together? Producer Welfare, Consumer Welfare, and WTO Rules. In: Petersmann, Ernst-Ulrich (ed.). Reforming the World Trading System. Legitimacy, Efficiency, and Democratic Governance. Oxford: Oxford University Press, 2005.
Mavroidis 2006: Mavroidis, Petros C. If I Don't Do It, Somebody Else Will (Or Won't). Testing the Compliance of Preferential Trade Agreements With the Multilateral Rules. In: JWT, Vol. 40, No. 1, 2006. S. 187-214.
Maxwell 1987: Maxwell, Philip. Adequate Technological Strategy in an Imperfect Economic Context: A Case-Study of the Evolution of the Acindar Steel Plant in Rosaria, Argentina. In: Katz, Jorge M. Technology Generation in Latin American Manufacturing Industries. London: Macmillan Press, 1987.
Mayer 2000: Mayer, Jörg. Globalization, Technology Transfer and Skill Accumulation in Low-Income Countries. World Bank, WTO Background Paper. In: http://www.worldbank.org/research/trade.
Mayer 2004: Mayer, Jörg. Not totally naked: Textiles and clothing in a quota free environment. UNCTAD Discussion Paper No. 176, December 2004. In: http://www.unctad.org.
Mayntz 1993: Mayntz, Renate. Policy-Netzwerke und die Logik von Verhandlungssystemen. In: Héritier, Adrienne. Policy Analyse. Kritik und Neuorientierung. Opladen: Westdeutscher Verlag, 1993.
Mazumdar 1991: Mazumdar, Dipak. Import-Substituting Industrialization and Protection of the Small-Scale: The Indian Experience in the Textile Industry. In: World Development, Vol. 19, No. 9, 1991. S. 1197-1213.
Mbilinyi/Nyoni 1997: Mbilinyi, Marjorie, Nyoni, Timothy. Agricultural and Livestock Policy 1997. Rural Food Security and Development Group (RFS), Revised Paper 2000. In: http://www.tzonline.org.
McCarthy 1998: McCarthy, C. L. Problems and Prospects of African Economic Development. In: The South African Journal of Economics. Vol. 66 No. 4, December 1998. S. 421-451.
McCarthy et al. 1987: McCarthy, F. Desmond, Taylor, Lance, Talati, Cyrus. Trade Patterns in Developing Countries. In: Journal of Developing Economics, Vol. 27, 1987. S. 5-39.
McCulloch 1981: McCulloch, Rachel. Gains to Latin America from Trade Liberalization in Developed and Developing Nations. In: Baer, Werner, Gillis, Malcolm (Hrg.). Export Diversification and the New Protectionism. The Experiences of Latin America. NBER and the Bureau of Economic and Business Research University of Illinois: University of Illinois, 1981.
McCulloch et al. 2001: McCulloch, Niel, Winters, L. Allan, Cirera, Xavier. Trade Liberalization and Poverty: A Handbook. London: Centre of Economic Policy Research, 2001.
McDonald 2005: McDonald, Jan. Domestic regulation, international standards, and technical barriers to trade. In: World Trade Review Vol. 4, No. 2, 2005. S. 249-274.
McGee 1996: McGee, Robert W. Antidumping Laws as Protectionist Trade Barriers: The Case for Repeal. Dumont Institute for Public Policy Research, Policy Analysis Working Paper, No. 14, July 1996. In: http://www.dumontinst.com.
McKibbin 1999: McKibbin, Warwick. Trade Liberalization in a Dynamic Setting. Brookings Diskussion Papers in International Economics, No. 147, September 1999. In: http://www.brookings.org.
McKinney/Rowley 1989: McKinney, Joseph, Rowley, Keith A. Voluntary Restraint Arrangements on Steel Imports: Policy Developments and Sectoral Effects. In: Journal of World Trade, Vol. 23, No. 3, 1989.
McLaren/Josling 1999: McLaren, Donald, Josling, Tim. Competition Policy and International Agricultural Trade. IATRC Working Paper 99-7. In: http://www.iatrcweb.org.
McMillan/Naughton 1992: McMillan, John, Naughton. How to Reform a Planned Economy: Lessons from China. Oxford Review of Economic Policy, Vol. 8, No. 1, 1992. S. 130-143.
McNab/Moore 1998: McNab, Robert M., Moore, Robert E. Trade Policy, export expansion, human capital and growth. In: The Journal of International Trade & Economic Development 7:2, 1998, S. 237-256.
McNelis 2001: McNelis, Natalie. The Role of the Judge in the EU and the WTO: Lessons from the BSE and Hormones Cases In: Journal of International Economic Law, 2001. S. 189-208.
McNelis 2003: McNelis, Natalie. The Role of the Judge in the EU and the WTO: Lessons from the BSE and Hormones Cases. In: Cottier, Thomas, Mavroidis, Petros C (eds.). The Role of the Judge in International Trade Regulation. Ann Arbor: University of Michigan Press, 2003.
McRae 1996: McRae, Donald M. The Contribution of International Trade Law to the Development of International Law. In: Recueil des Cours, Collected Courses of the Hague Academy of International Law, Tome 260 de la collection, 1996. The Hague/Boston/London: Martinus Nijhoff Publishers, 1997.
Meade 1955: Meade, J. E. Trade and Welfare. The Theory of International Economic Policy. Vol. II. London, New York, Oxford: Oxford University Press, 1955.
Meagher 2003: Meagher, Niall P. The Sound of Silence: Giving Meaning to Ommnissions in Provisions of World Trade Organization Agreements. A Note on the World Trade Organization Appellate Body Decision in United States - Countervailing Duties on Certain Corrosion-Resistant Carbon Steel Flat Products from Germany. In: JWT, Vol. 37, No. 2, 2003. S. 417-427.
Mecagni 1995: Mecagni, Mauro. Experience with Nominal Anchors. In: Schadler, Susan (ed.). IMF Conditionality: Experience Under Stand-By and Extended Arrangements. Part II: Background Papers. Washington: IMF, 1995.
Medick-Krakau 1995: Medick-Krakau, Monika. Amerikanische Außenhandelspolitik im Wandel. Handelsgesetzgebung und GATT 1945-1988. Berlin: Akademie Verlag, 1995.

Meier 1964: Meier, Rudolf Christoph. Bekleidungsindustrie. Strukturelle Probleme und Wachstumschancen. Berlin, München: Duncker & Humblot, 1964.
Meier 1995: Meier, Gerald M. Leading Issues in Economic Development. New York; Oxford: Oxford University Press, 1995.
Meier et al. 1989: Meier, Gerald M., Steel, William F., Carroll, Richard J. Industrial Adjustment in Sub-Saharan Africa. Oxford: Oxford University Press (Published for World Bank), 1989.
Meiklejohn 1999: Meiklejohn, R. The economics of State aid. In: State Aid and the Single Market, European Economy, Directorate-General for Economic and Financial Affairs, Reports and Studies, Number 3, 1999. In: http://europa.eu.int/comm/economy_finance/document/eerepstu/ersidxen.htm.
Meller 1994: Meller, Patricio. The Chilean Trade Liberalization and Export Expansion Process, 1974-90. In: Helleiner, Gerald K. (ed.). Trade Policy and Industrialization in Turbulent Times. London; New York: Routledge, 1994.
Meller 1995: Meller, Patricio. Chilean Export Growth, 1970-90: An Assessment. In: Helleiner (ed.). Manufacturing for Export in the Developing World. London, New York: Routledge, 1995.
Meller/Mizala 1982: Meller, Patricio, Mizala, Alejandra. US Multinationals and Latin American Manufacturing Employment Absorption. In: World Development, Vol. 10, No. 2, 1982. S. 115-126.
Mengistal/Teal 1998: Mengistal, Taye, Teal, Francis. Trade Liberalization, Regional Intergration and Firm Performance in Africa's Manufacturing Sector. Report to the European Commission: University of Oxford: Centre for the Study of African Economies, May 1998. In: http://www.csae.ox.ac.uk.
Menkhoff/Reszat 1998: Menkhoff, Lukas, Reszat, Beate (Hrg.). Asian Financial Markets – Structures, Policy Issues and Prospects. Baden-Baden: Nomos, 1998.
Menzel 1985: Menzel, Ulrich. In der Nachfolge Europas. Autozentrierte Entwicklung in den ostasiatischen Schwellenländern Südkorea und Taiwan. Münschen: Simon & Magiera, 1985.
Menzel 1988: Menzel, Ulrich. Ausweg aus der Abhängigkeit. Die entwicklungspolitische Aktualität Europas. Frankfurt am Main: Surkamp, 1988.
Menzel 1992: Menzel, Ulrich. Das Ende der Dritten Welt und das Scheitern der großen Theorie. Frankfurt am Main: Surkamp, 1992.
Menzel 1995: Menzel, Ulrich. Geschichte der Entwicklungstheorie. Einführung und systematische Bibliographie. Hamburg: Schriften des Deutschen Übersee-Instituts Hamburg, 1995.
Merril 2004: Merril, Stephen A. Improving Patent Quality: Connecting Economic Reserach and Policy. In: OECD. Patents, Innovation and Economic Performance. Conference Proceedings. Paris: OECD, 2004.
Mes 1997: Mes, Peter. Patentgesetz Gebrauchsmustergesetz. München: Beck, 1997.
Messerlin 1981: Messerlin, Patrik A. The Political Economy of Protectionism: The Bureaucratic Case. In: Weltwirtschaftliches Archiv, Bd. 117, 1981. S. 469-496.
Messerlin 1990: Messerlin, Patrik A. Anti-Dumping Regulations or Pro-Cartel Law? The EC Chemical Cases. In: World Economy, Vol. 13, No. 4, December 1990. S. 497-507.
Messerlin 1999: Messerlin, Patrik A. External Aspects of State Aids. In: State Aid and the Single Market, European Economy, Directorate-General for Economic and Financial Affairs, Reports and Studies, Number 3, 1999. In: http://europa.eu.int/comm/economy_finance/document/eerepstu/ersidxen.htm.
Messerlin 2004: Messerlin, Patrik A. China in the WTO: Antidumping and Safeguards. In: World Bank Economic Review, Vol. 18 No. 1, 2004. S. 105-130.
Messerlin 2005: Messerlin, Patrik A. Non-Discrimination, Welfare Balances, and WTO Rules: A Historical Perspective. In: Petersmann, Ernst-Ulrich (ed.). Reforming the World Trading System. Legitimacy, Efficiency, and Democratic Governance. Oxford: Oxford University Press, 2005.
Messerlin/Fridh 2006: Messerlin, Patrik A., Fridh, Hilda. The Agreement of Safeguards: Proposals for Change in the Light of the EC Steel Safeguards. In: JWT, Vol. 40, Vol. 4, 2006. S. 713-751.
Mestmäcker 1975: Mestmäcker, Ernst-Joachim. Wirtschaftsordnung und Staatsverfassung. In: Sauermann, Heinz, Mestmäcker, Ernst-Joachim (Hrg.). Wirtschaftsordnung und Staatsverfassung. FS Franz Böhm. Tübingen: Mohr, 1975.
Mestmäcker 1980: Mestmäcker, Ernst-Joachim. Competition Policy and Antitrust: Some Comparative Observations. In: Zeitschrift für die gesamte Staatswissenschaft. Bd. 136, 1980. S. 387-407.
Mestmäcker 1984: Mestmäcker, Ernst-Joachim. Recht und ökonomisches Gesetz. Baden-Baden: Nomos, 1984.
Mestmäcker 1987: Mestmäcker, Ernst-Joachim. Auf dem Wege zu einer Ordnungspolitik für Europa. In: FS Hans von der Groeben. Baden-Baden: Nomos, 1987.
Mestmäcker 1988: Mestmäcker, Ernst-Joachim. Staatliche Souveränität und offene Märkte. Konflikte bei der extraterritorialen Anwendung von Wirtschaftrecht. In: RabelsZ, 52 (1988). pp. 205-255.
Mestmäcker 1993: Mestmäcker, Ernst-Joachim. Die Wirtschaftsverfassung in der Europäischen Union. Vorträge und Berichte, Nr. 28, Zentrum für Europäisches Wirtschaftsrecht, Bonn: Friedrich-Wilhelms Universität, 1993.
Mestmäcker 1994: Mestmäcker, Ernst-Joachim. Über das Verhältnis der europäischen Wirtschaftsordnung zu den Mitgliedstaaten. In: Seifert, Gerhard (Hrg.). Vereinigtes Europa und nationale Vielfalt – Ein Gegensatz? Göttingen: Vandehoeck & Ruprecht, 1994.
Michaelowa/Naini 1995: Michaelowa, Katharina, Naini, Ahmad. Der Gemeinsame Fonds und die Speziellen Rohstoffabkommen. HWWA, Band 17. Baden-Baden: Nomos, 1995.
Michaely 1977: Michaely, Michael. Exports and Growth. An empirical investigation. In: Journal of Development Economics, Vol. 4, 1977. S. 49-53.

Michaely et al. 1991: Michaely, Michael, Papageorgiou, Demetris, Choksi, Armeane M. Liberalizing Foreign Trade. Lessons of Experience in the Developing World. In: Liberalizing Foreign Trade, Vol. 7. Oxford: World Bank/Basil Blackwell, 1991.
Michalak 1979: Michalak, Stanley J. Theoretical Perspectives for Understanding International Interdependence. In: World Politics, Vol. 32, No. 1, Oct. 1979.
Michalopoulos 1998: Michalopoulos, Constantine. WTO Accession for Countries in Transition. World Bank, Policy Research Working Paper, No. 1934, June 1998. In: http://www.worldbank.org.
Michalopoulos 1998a: Michalopoulos, Constantine. The Participation of the Developing Countries in the WTO. World Bank, Policy Research Working Paper No. 1906, March 1998. In://www.worldbank.org.
Michalopoulos 1999: Michalopoulos, Constantine. The Intergration of Transition Countries into the World Trading System. World Bank, Policy Research Working Paper, No. 2182, September 1999. In: http://www.worldbank.org.
Michalopoulos 1999a: Michalopoulos, Constantine. Trade Policy and Market Access Issues for Developing Countries. World Bank, WTO Project Working Paper. In: http://www.worldbank.org/research/trade/.
Micron Information 2005: Micron. Form 10k Information 2005. In: http://www.micron.com.
Midelfart-Knarvik et al. 2000: Midelfart-Knarvik, K. H., Overman, H. G., Redding, S. J., Venables, A. J. The Location of European Industrie. Report No. 142, European Communities, Directorate General for Economic and Financial Affairs, April 2000. In: http://europa.eu.int/comm/economy_finance/document/docum_en.htm.
Midrex Informationen 2000: MIDREX/Rob Cheeley. Combining Gasifiers with the Midrex Direct Production Process. 2000. In: http://www.midrex.com.
Mikesell 1954: Mikesell, Raymond F. Economic Doctrines Implied in the Reports of the United Nations and of the International Bank for Reconstruction and Development on Under-Developed Countries. In: American Economic Review, Vol. XLIV, Number 2, May 1954. S. 570-582.
Miksch 1947: Miksch, Leonard. Wettbewerb und Wirtschaftsverfassung. In: Stützel, Wolfgang et al. (Hrg.). Grundtexte zur Sozialen Marktwirtschaft. Stuttgart: Gustav Fischer Verlag, 1981.
Mill 1848: Mill, John Stuart. Principles of Political Economy. London: Longmans, Green, Reader, and Dyer, 1878.
Miller 1962: Miller, John Perry. Economic Goals and the Role of Competition: Introduction. In: Miller, John Perry (ed.). Competition, Cartels and Their Regulation. Amsterdam: North-Holland Publishing Company, 1962.
Millett 1999: Millett, Timothy. The Community System of Plant Variety Rights. In: European Law Review, Vol. 24, June 1999. S. 231-258.
Mills 1953: Mills, Frederic C. The Role of Productivity in Economic Growth. In: American Economic Review, Papers and Proceedings, Vol. 62, 1952. S. 545-557.
Milner 1987: Milner, Helen. Resisting the protectionist temptation: industry and the making of trade policy in France and the United States during the 1970s. In: International Organization, Vol. 41, No. 4, Autumn 1987. S. 639-665.
Milner 1988: Milner, Helen. Resisting Protectionism. Global Industries and the Politics of International Trade. Princeton: Princeton University Press, 1988.
Minasi 1998: Minasi, Nicola. The Euro-Mediterranean Free Trade Area and its Impact on the Economies Involved. Jean Monnet Working Papers 16.98, October 1998. In: http://www.fscpo.unict.it/EuroMed/cjmjmwpengl.htm.
Minot/Goletti 2000: Minot, Nicholas, Goletti, Francesco. Rice Market Liberalization and Poverty in Vietnam. IFPRI Research Report 114. Washington: International Food Policy Research Institute, 2000. In: http://www.ifpri.org.
Miranda 1991: Miranda, Casimiro V. Transnational Corporations in the Philippines. In: Regional Development Dialogue, Vol. 12, No. 1, Spring 1991. S. 139-161.
Mirowski 1989: Mirowski, Philip. More heat than light. Economics as social physics: Physics as nature's economics. Cambridge: Cambridge University Press, 1989.
Mitchell et al. 1997: Mitchell, Donald O., Ingco, Merlinda C., Duncan, Ronald C. The World Food Outlook. Cambridge: Cambridge University Press, 1997.
Miyagiwa/Ohno 1995: Miyagiwa, Kaz, Ohno, Yuka. Closing the Technology Gap under Protection. In: American Economic Review, Vol. 85, No. 4, September 1995. S. 755-770.
Mkandawire 1993: Mkandawire, Thandika. Tanzania. In: Taylor, Lance (ed.). The Rocky Road to Reform. Adjustment, Income Distribution, and Growth in the Developing World. Cambridge: MIT Press, 1993.
Mlambiti/Isinika 1999: Mlambiti, M. E., Isinika, A. C. Tanzania's Agriculture Development towards the 21th century. In: Journal of Agricultural Economics and Development, Vol. 3, June 1999. S. 3-19. In: http://www.tzonline.org.
Mlawa 1995: Mlawa, Hasa M. Technical Change and the Textiles Industry in Tanzania. In: Ogbu, Osita M., Oyeyinka, Banji O., Mlawa, Hasa M. (eds.). Technology Policy and Practice in Africa. International Development Centre (IDRC) 1995. In: http://web.idrc.ca.
Mody 1999: Mody, Ashoka. Industrial Policy after the East Asian crisis: From "outward orientation" to internationl capabilities? World Bank Policy Research Working Paper No. 2112, 1999. In: http://www.worldbank.org.
Mohr 1987: Mohr, Elske. Agrarprotektionismus - eine Sonderproblem der Handelsliberalisierung. In: IFO-Schnelldienst 9/1987. S. 6-13.
Mohr 1987a: Mohr, Elske. Agrarprotektionismus: Nicht nur Erzeugerschutz bestimmt die Wahl der Instrumente. In: IFO-Schnelldienst 10-11/1987. S. 30-38.

Mohr 1987a: Mohr, Elske. Die Agrarprotektionismussysteme der EG, der USA und Japans im Vergleich. In: Ifo-Schnelldienst 27/87. S. 3-21.
Molle 1990: Molle, Willem. The Economics of European Integration. Aldershot et al.: Dartmouth, 1990.
Molle 1993: Molle, Willem. Oil Refineries and petrochemical industries: coping with the mid-life crisis. In: de Jong, H.W. (ed.) The Structure of European Industry. Dordrecht; Boston; London: Kluwer, 1993.
Molsberger/Duijm 1997: Molsberger, Josef, Duijm, Bernhard. Deutsche Wirtschaftsordnung und internationales Handelssystem. In: ORDO, Bd. 48, 1997.
Molsberger/Kotios 1990: Molsberger, Josef, Kotios, Angelos. Ordnungspolitische Defizite des GATT. In: Ordo, Bd. 41, 1990. S. 93-115.
Monge-Gonzales/Monge-Arino 2005: Monge-Gonzales, Ricardo, Monge-Arino, Francisco. Anti-Dumping Policies and Safeguard Measures in the Context of Costa Rica's Economic Liberalization. World Bank Policy Research Working Paper 3591, May 2005. In: http://www.worldbank.org.
Mönnich 2002: Mönnich, C. Zollkontingente im Agrarsektor: Wie viel Liberalisierungsfortschritt? In: Brockmeier, M., Isermeyer, F., von Cramon-Taubadel, S. (Hrg.). Liberalisierung des Weltagrarhandels - Strategien und Konsequenzen. Münster-Hiltrup: Landwirtschaftsverlag, 2002.
Mönnich 2004: Mönnich, Christina. Tariff Rate Quotas and Their Administration. Frankfurt: Peter Lang, 2004.
Monopolkommission div. Jg.: Monopolkommission Hauptgutachten. Entweder Drucksache des Bundestags oder Baden-Baden: Nomos, div. Jg.
Mooij 1998: Mooij, Jos. Food Policy and Politics: The Political Economy of the Public Distribution System in India. In: The Journal of Peasant Studies, Vol. 25, No. 2, January 1998. S. 77-101.
Moon/Kang 1991: Moon, Pal-Yong, Kang, Bong-Soon. The Republic of Korea. In: Krueger, Anne O., Schiff, Maurice, Valdes, Alberto. The Political Economy of Agricultural Pricing Policy. Vol. 2 Asia. Baltimore, London: John Hopkins University Press, 1991.
Moore 2000: Moore, Michael O. VERs and Price Undertakings under the WTO. George Washington University, Working Paper, 2000. In: http://darkwing.uoregon.edu/~bruceb/adpage.html.
Moore 2002: Moore, Michael O. Commerce Department Antidumping Sunset Reviews: A Major Disappointment. Working Paper, April 2002. In: http://darkwing.uoregon.edu/~bruceb/adpage.html.
Moore 2002a: Moore, Michael O. Department of Commerce Administration of Antidumping Sunset Reviews: A First Assessment. In: JWT, Vol. 36, No. 4, 2002. S. 675-698, 2002.
Moore 2005: Moore, Michael O. U.S. 'facts available' antidumping decisions: An empirical analysis. Working Paper, December 2005. In: http://darkwing.uoregon.edu/~bruceb/adpage.html.
Moore 2005a: Moore, Michael O. Antidumping Reform in the Doha Round: A Pessimistic Appraisal. Working Paper, December 2005. In: http://darkwing.uoregon.edu/~bruceb/adpage.html.
Moravscsik 1991: Moravscsik, Andrew. Negotiating the Single European Act: national interests and conventional statecraft in the European Community. In: International Organization, 45, 1, Winter 1991, S. 19-56.
Moravscsik 1997: Moravscsik, Andrew. Taking Preferences Seriously: A Liberal Theory of International Politics. In: International Organization, Vol. 51 No. 4, Autumn 1997. S. 513-553.
Morawetz 1981: Morawetz, David. Why the Emperor's New Clothes Are Not Made In Columbia. A Case Study in Latin American and East Asian Manufactured Exports. Oxford: Oxford University Press/World Bank, 1981.
Morazan 1994: Morazan, Pedro. Ausgerechnet Bananen. Bilanz der EU Regelung nach einem Jahr. Materialien 3. Siegburg: Südwind e.V., 1994.
Moreira 1995: Moreira, Mauricio Mesquita. Industrialization, Trade and Market Failures. The Role of Government Intervention in Brazil and South Korea. New York: St. Martin's Press, 1995.
Moreira/Correa 1998: Moreira, Mauricio Mesquita, Correa, Paulo Guilherme. A First Look at the Impacts of Trade Liberalization on Brazilian Manufacturing Industry. In: World Development Vol. 26, No. 10, 1998. S. 1859-1874.
Moreira/Najberg 2000: Moreira, Mauricio Mesquita, Najberg, Sheila. Trade Liberalization in Brasil: Creating or Exporting Jobs. In: Journal of Development Studies Vol. 36, No. 3, February 2000. S. 78-99.
Morgan/Goh 2003: Morgan, David, Gavin, Goh. Peace in our Time? An Analysis of Article 13 of the Agreement on Agriculture. In: JWT, Vol. 37, No. 5, 2003. S. 977-992.
Morgenthau 1967: Morgenthau, Hans J. Politics among Nations. New York: Alfred A. Knopf, Inc.: 4th revised Edition 1967.
Morisset 1997: Morisset, Jaques. Unfair Trade? Empirical Evidence in World Commodity Markets over the Past 25 Years. World Bank, Policy Research Working Paper No. 1815, April 1997. In: http://www.worldbank.org.
Morrison 1997: Morrison, Peter K. WTO Dispute Settlement in Services: Procedural and Sustantive Aspects. In: Petersmann, Ernst-Ulrich (ed.). International Trade Law and the GATT/WTO Dispute Settlement System. London, The Hague, Boston: Kluwer Law, 1997.
Morrissey 1995: Morrissey, Oliver. Politics and Economic Policy Reform. Trade Liberalization in Sub-Saharan Africa. In: Journal of International Development, Vol. 7, No. 4, 1995. S. 599-618.
Morrissey/Rai 1995: Morrissey, Oliver, Rai, Yogesh. The GATT Agreement on Trade Related Investment Measures: Implications for Developing Countries and their Relationship with Transnational Corporations. In: Journal of Development Studies, Vol. 31, No. 5, June 1995, S. 702-724.
Mose 1998: Mose, Lawrence O. Factors Affecting the Distribution and Use of Fertilizer in Kenya: Preliminary Assessment. Tegemeo Agricultural Monitoring and Policy Analysis Project, Egerton University, University of Michigan, 1998. In: http://www.aec.msu.edu/agecon/fs2/kenya/.
Moser 1990: Moser, Peter. The Political Economy of the GATT. Grüsch: Verlag Rüegger, 1990.

Mosler 1992: Mosler, Hermann. Die Übertragung von Hoheitsgewalt. In: Isensee, Josef, Kirchhof, Paul (Hrg.). Handbuch des Staatsrechts. Bd. VII. Heidelberg: C.F. Müller, 1992.
Mosley 1991: Mosley, Paul. Kenya. In: Aid and Power. The World Bank and Policy-based Lending. Vol. 2, Case Studies. London; New York: Routledge, 1991.
Mosley 1995: Mosley, Paul. Development Economics and the Underdevelopment of Sub-Saharan Africa. In: Journal of International Development, Vol. 7, No. 5, 1995. S. 685-706.
Mosley et al. 1991: Mosley, Paul, Harrigan, Jane, Toye, John. Aid and Power. The World Bank and Policy-based Lending. Vol. 1, Analysis and policy proposals. London; New York: Routledge, 1991.
Mosley et al. 1995: Mosley, Paul, Subasat, Turan, Weeks, John. Assessing Adjustment in Africa. In: World Development, Vol. 23 No. 9, 1995. S. 1459-1473.
Mosoti 2003: Mosoti, Victor. Does Africa Need the WTO Dispute Settlement System? In: In: Shaffer, Gregory, Mosoti, Victor, Qureshi, Asif. Towards a development-supportive dispute settlement system in the WTO. ICTSD Resource Paper No. 5, March 2003. In: http://www.ictsd.org.
Mosoti 2006: Mosoti, Victor. Africa in the First Decade of WTO Dispute Settlement. In: Journal of International Economic Law, Vol. 9, No. 2, 2006. S. 427-453.
Motohashi 2004: Motohashi, Kazuyuki. Japan's Patent System and Business Innovation: Reassessing Pro-Patent Policies. In: OECD. Patents, Innovation and Economic Performance. Conference Proceedings. Paris: OECD, 2004.
Moulis/Gay 2005: The 10 Major Problems With the Anti-Dumping Instrument in Australia. In: JWT, Vol. 39, No. 1, 2005. S. 75-85.
Movesian 2004: Movesian, Marc L. Actions against dumping and subsidization - Antidumping and SCM Agreements - United Nations Continued Dumping and Subsidy Offset Act of 2000. In: In: American Journal of International Law, Vol. 98, 2004. S. 150-155.
Mowery/Rosenberg 1989: Mowergy, David C., Rosenberg, Nathan. Technology and the Pursuit of Economic Growth. Cambridge: Cambridge University Press, 1989.
Mozal Information 2005: Mozal Project Information, 2005. In: http://www.engineeringnews.co.za.
MSF 2005: Médecins Sans Frontières. Untangling the Web of Price Reductions, June 2005. In: http://www.accessmed-msf.org.
MSF 2005a: Médecins Sans Frontières. The Second Wave of the Drug Crisis, Briefing Note. December 2005. In: http://www.doctorswithouborders.org.
Mueller 1985: Mueller, Dennis C. Mergers and Market Share. In: The Review of Economics and Statistics, Vol. 67, 1985. S. 259-267.
Mueller 2003: Mueller, Felix. Is the General Agreement on Tariffs and Trade Article XIX 'Unforeseen Developments Clause' Still Effective under the Agreement on Safeguards? In: JWT, Vol. 37, No. 6, 2003. S. 1119-1151.
Mueller/Greer 1984: Mueller, Dennis C., Greer, Douglas F. The Effect of Market Share Distribution on Industry Performance Reexamined. In: The Review of Economics and Statistics, Vol. 66, 1984. S. 353-361.
Muendo et al. 2004: Muendo, Kavoi Mutuku, Tschirley, David, Weber, Michael T. Improving Kenya's Domestic Horticultural Production and Marketing System: Current Competitiveness, Forces of Change, and Challenges of the Future. Working Paper 08/2004. Tegemeo Institute of Agricultural Policy and Development, Egerton University. In: http://www.aec.msu.edu/agecon/fs2/kenya/.
Mulat 1997: Mulat, Teshome. Trade Liberalization and Government Tax Revenue Loss in Africa. In: JWT: Vol. 31, No. 1, Feb. 1997. S. 161-174.
Müller 1983: Müller, Ulrich. Wohlstandseffekte des internationalen Handels unter den Regeln des Allgemeinen Zoll- und Handelsabkommens. In: Willgerodt, Hans et al. (Hrg.) Institut für Wirtschaftspolitik an der Universität Köln, Untersuchungen. Köln 1983.
Müller 1994: Müller, Harald. Internationale Beziehungen und kommunikatives Handeln. In: Zeitschrift für Internationale Beziehungen, Vol. 1 No. 1, 1994. S. 15-44.
Müller 1998: Müller, Ralf. The financial system in South Korea: Intermediation Inefficiency, Crisis and Reform. In: Menkhoff, Lukas, Reszat, Beate (Eds.) Asian Financial Marktes - Structures, Policy Issues and Prospects. Baden-Baden: Nomos, 1998.
Müller/Owen 1985: Müller, Jürgen, Owen, Nicholas. The Effect of Trade on Plant Size, 1985. Reprinted in: Jaquemin, Alexis, Sapir, André (eds.) The European International Market. Selected Readings. Oxford: Oxford University Press, 1989.
Müller/Schnitzer 2005: Müller, Thomas, Schitzer, Monika. Technology Transfer and Spillovers in International Joint Ventures. GESY Discussion Paper No. 84, October 2005. In: http://www.gesy.uni-mannheim.de.
Müller-Armack 1946: Müller-Armack, Alfred. Wirtschaftslenkung und Marktwirtschaft. In: Müller-Armack, Alfred. Wirtschaftsordnung und Wirtschaftspolitik. Reihe: Tuchtfeldt, Egon (Hrg.) Beiträge zur Wirtschaftspolitik Bd. 4. Bern; Stuttgart: Verlag Paul Haupt, (1946) 1976.
Müller-Armack 1948: Müller-Armack, Alfred. Die Wirtschaftsordnungen sozial gesehen. In: Müller-Armack, Alfred. Wirtschaftsordnung und Wirtschaftspolitik. Reihe: Tuchtfeldt, Egon (Hrg.) Beiträge zur Wirtschaftspolitik Bd. 4. Bern; Stuttgart: Verlag Paul Haupt, (1948) 1976.
Müller-Armack 1956: Müller-Armack, Alfred. Soziale Marktwirtschaft. In: Müller-Armack, Alfred. Wirtschaftsordnung und Wirtschaftspolitik. Reihe: Tuchtfeldt, Egon (Hrg.) Beiträge zur Wirtschaftspolitik Bd. 4. Bern; Stuttgart: Verlag Paul Haupt, (1948) 1976.

Müller-Ohlsen 1975: Müller-Ohlsen, Lotte. Möglichkeiten und Grenzen des Industriegüterexports der Türkei. In: Die Weltwirtschaft, Heft 1, 1975. S. 114-138.
Mun/Sasaki 2001: Mun, Se-il, Sasaki, Komei. The Economic System of Small-to-Medium Sized Regions in Japan. In: Johansson, Börje, Karlsson, Charlie, Stough, Roger R. (eds.). Theories of Endogenous Regional Growth. Berlin; Heidelberg: Springer, 2001.
Murphy 1999: Murphy, Sophia. Market Power in Agricultural Markets: Some Issues for Developing Countries. South Centre Working Paper, Nov. 1999. In: http://www.southcentre.org/publications/agric/toc.htm.
Murphy 2006: Murphy, Dale D., The Tuna-Dolpin Wars. In: JWT, Vol. 40, No. 4, 2006. S. 597-617.
Murphy et al. 1989: Murphy, Kevin M., Shleifer, Andrei, Vishny, Robert W. Industrialization and the Big Push. In: Journal of Political Economy, Vol. 97, No. 5, 1989. S. 1003-1026.
Murra 1995: Murray, Tracy. Effects of the Uruguay Round Agreement on industrialization in developing countries. UNIDO, ID/WG.542/15(SPEC.), 27. September 1995. In: http://www.unido.org.
Mussa 1974: Mussa, Michael. Tariffs and the Distribution of Income: The Importance of Factor Specificity, Substitutability, and the Intensity in the Short and Long Run. In: Journal of Political Economy, Vol. 82, No. 6, 1974. S. 1191-1203.
Mutume 2002: Mutume, Gumisai. Building an efficient road network. In: Africa Renewal, Vol. 16 No. 2-3, September 2002. In: http://www.un.org/ecosocdev/geninfo/afrec/vol16no2/162reg4.htm.
Mwega 1994: Mwega, Francis M. Trade and Macroeconomic Policies and the Industrialization Experience in Kenya in the 1970 and 1980s. In: Helleiner, Gerald K. (ed.). Trade Policy and Industrialization in Turbulent Times. London; New York: Routledge, 1994.
Mwega/Ndung'u 2001: Mwega, Francis M., Ndung'u, Njuguna S. Kenya's Recent Exchange-Rate Policy and Manufactured Export Performance. In: OECD. Policies to Promote Competitiveness in Manufacturing in Sub-Saharan Africa. Development Centre Seminars within the IMF and the AERC. Kwasi Fosu, Augustin, Nsouli, Saleh M., Varoudakis, Aristomene (eds.). Paris: OECD, 2001a.
Myrdal 1959: Myrdal, Gunnar. Ökonomische Theorie und unterentwickelte Regionen. Stuttgart: Fischer Verlag, (1959) 1974.
Myrdal 1968: Myrdal, Gunnar. Asian Drama. Vol. III. New York: Pantheon, 1968.
Mytelka 1978: Mytelka, Lynn Krieger. Licensing and Technology Dependenc in the Andean Group. In: World Development, Vol. 6, 1978. S. 447-459.

N

Nackmayr 1997: Nackmayr, Jens. Globalisierungspotentiale im Maschinenbau. Berlin: IPK, 1997.
Nadvi 1995: Nadvi, Khalid. Industrial Clusters and Networks: Case Studies of SME Growth and Innovation. UNIDO Small Enterprise Programme. Wien: UNIDO, October 1995. In: http://www.unido.org.
NAFTA Investor State Arbitrations Information 2006: NAFTA Investor State Arbitrations Information 2006. In: http://www.state.gov/s/l/c3741.htm.
Nafziger 1995: Nafziger, E. Wayne. Japan's Industrial Development, 1868-1939: Lessons for Sub-Saharan Africa. In: Stein, Howard (Hrg.). Asian Industrialization and Africa. Studies in Policy Alternatives to Structural Adjustment. London: St. Martin's Press, 1995.
Nagaoka 2003: Nagaoka, Sadao. Patents and other IPRs in Use. Institution of Innovation Research, Hitotsubashi University, September 2003. In: http://www.wipo.int/ipstats/en/resources/studies.html.
Narayanan 2006: Narayanan, Prakash. Anti-Dumping in India - Present State and Future Prospects. In: JWT, Vol. 40, No. 6, 2006. S. 1081-1097.
Nam 1993: Nam, Chong-Hyun. Protectionist U.S. Trade Policy and Korean Exports. In: Ito, Takatoshi, Krueger, Anne O. Trade and Protectionism. Chicago; London: The University of Chicago Press/NBER, 1993.
Namiki 1978: Namiki, Nobuyoshi. Japanese Subsidy Policies. In: Warnecke, Steven J. (ed.). International Trade and Industrial Policies. Government Intervention and an Open World Economy. London: Macmillan Press, 1978.
Narr/Schubert 1994: Narr, Wolf-Dieter, Schubert, Alexander. Weltökonomie. Die Misere der Politik. Frankfurt am Main: Surkamp, 1994.
National Economic Accounts 2006: National Economic Accouts. GDP Data USA. In: http://www.bea.gov/bea/dn/nipaweb/TableView.asp#Mid.
Navaretti et al. 1999: Navaretti, Barba G., Falzoni, A. M., Turini, A. Italian Multinationals and De-localization of Production. Development Studies Working Papers, No. 126, June 1999, Oxord. In: http://www2.qeh.ox.ac.uk.
NCTO 2006: National Council of Textile Organizations. China versus the World. A Comprehensive Analysis of Apparel Trade in Quota-Free Categories and Quota-Restrained Categories into the United States and European Union. February 28, 2006. In: http://www.ncto.org/.
Ndulu 1993: Ndulu, Benno J. Tanzania. In: Taylor, Lance (ed.). The Rocky Road to Reform. Adjustment, Income Distribution, and Growth in the Developing World. Cambridge: MIT Press, 1993.
Ndulu/Semboja 1994: Ndulu, Benno J., Semboja, Joseph J. Trade and Industrialization in Tanzania. In: Helleiner, Gerald K. (ed.). Trade Policy and Industrialization in Turbulent Times. London; New York: Routledge, 1994.
Neckermann/Wessels 1988: Neckermann, Gerhard, Wessels, Hans. Struktur und Wettbewerbsfähigkeit der Schuhindustrie in der Bundesrepublik Deutschland. DIW Beiträge zur Strukturforschung, Heft 104. Berlin: Duncker & Humblot, 1988.

Neiss 2001: Neiss, Katharine S. The markup and inflation: evidence in OECD countries. In: Canadian Journal of Economics, Vol. 34 No. 2, May 2001. S. 570-587.
Nell 1999: Nell, Philippe G. WTO Negotiations on the Harmonization of Rules of Origin. In: JWT Vol. 33 No. 3, 1999. S. 45-71.
Nelson 1959: Nelson, Richard R. The Simple Economics of Basic Scientific Research. In: Journal of Political Economy, Vol. 67, 1959. S. 297-306.
Nelson 1981: Nelson, Richard R. Research on Productivity Growth and Productivity Differences: Dead Ends and New Departures. In: Journal of Economic Literature, Vol. 19, September 1981. S. 1029-1064.
Nelson 1986: Nelson, Richard R. Institutions Supporting Technical Advance in Industry. In: American Economic Review, Vol. 76 No. 2, May 1986. S. 186-189.
Nelson 1987: Nelson, Richard R. Innovation and Economic Development. In: Katz, Jorge M.,Technology Generation in Latin American Manufacturing Industries. London: Macmillan Press, 1987.
Nelson/Pack 1998: Nelson, Richard R., Pack, Howard. The Asian Miracle and Modern Growth Theory. World Bank, Policy Research Working Paper, No. 1881, February 1998.
Nelson/Rosenberg 1993: Nelson, Richard R., Rosenberg, Nathan. Technical Innovation and National Systems. In: Audretsch, David (ed.). Industrial Policy and Competitive Advantage, Vol. I. Cheltenham, UK, Northampton, MA: Elgar, 1998.
Nelson/Winter 1982: Nelson, Richard R., Winter, Sidney G. An Evolutionary Theory of Economic Change. Cambdrige, Mass.: The Belknap Press of Harvard University Press, 1982.
Nelson/Winter 1982a: Nelson, Richard R., Winter, Sidney G. The Schumpeterian Tradeoff Revisited. In: American Economic Review Vol. 72 No.1, May 1982. S. 114-132.
Nelson/Wright 1992: Nelson, Richard R., Wright, Gavin. The Rise and Fall of American Technological Leadership: The Postwar Era in Historical Perspective. In: Journal of Economic Literature, Vol. 30, December 1992. S. 1931-1964.
Nettesheim 1991: Nettesheim, Martin. Countervailing Duty Laws. In: Grabnitz, Eberhard, von Bogdandy, Armin (eds.). U.S. Trade Barriers: A Legal Analysis. New York; London; Rome: European Law Press Munich, Oceana Publications, 1991.
Nettesheim 1991a: Nettesheim, Martin. Sec. 337 of the Trade Act of 1974. In: Grabnitz, Eberhard, von Bogdandy, Armin (eds.). U.S. Trade Barriers: A Legal Analysis. New York; London; Rome: European Law Press Munich, Oceana Publications, 1991.
Nettesheim 1991b: Nettesheim, Martin. Sec. 301 of the Trade Act of 1974: Response to Unfair Trade Practices. In: Grabnitz, Eberhard, von Bogdandy, Armin (eds.). U.S. Trade Barriers: A Legal Analysis. New York; London; Rome: European Law Press Munich, Oceana Publications, 1991.
Nettesheim 1991c: Nettesheim, Martin. Antidumping Law. In: Grabnitz, Eberhard, von Bogdandy, Armin (eds.). U.S. Trade Barriers: A Legal Analysis. New York; London; Rome: European Law Press Munich, Oceana Publications, 1991.
Neugebauer 2000: Neugebauer, Regine. Fine-Tuning WTO Jurisprudence and the SPS Agreement: Lessons from the Beef Hormone Case. In: Law & Policy in International Business, Vol. 31, 2000. S. 1255-1284.
Neumann 1984: Neumann, Franz L. Die Wirtschaftsstruktur des Nationalsozialismus. In: Dubiel, Helmut, Söllner, Alfons (Hrg.). Wirtschaft, Recht und Staat im Nationalsozialismus. Frankfurt am Main: Surkamp, 1984.
Neumann 2002: Neumann, Jan. Die Koordination des WTO-Rechts mit anderen völkerrechtlichen Ordnungen. Berlin: Duncker & Humblot, 2002.
Neumann/Türck 2003: Neumann, Jan, Türk, Elisabeth. Necessity Revisited: Proportionality in World Trade Organization Law After Korea-Beef, EC-Asbestos and EC-Sardines. In: JWT, Vol. 37, No. 1, 2003. S. 199-233.
Neumeyer 2001: Neumeyer, Eric. Greening the WTO Agreements. Can the Treaty Establishing the European Community be of Guidance? In: JWT Vol. 35, No. 1, 2001. S. 145-166.
Neven/Mavroidis 2006: Neven, Damien, Mavroidis, Petros C. El mess in TELMEX: a comment on Mexico - measures affecting telecommunications services. In: World Trade Review Vol. 5, No. 2, 2006. S. 271-296.
Neven/Seabright 1995: Neven, Damien, Seabright, Paul. European industrial policy: the Airbus case. In: Economic Policy: a European forum. Oxford: Blackwell. October 1995. S.315-358.
Neven/Wyplosz 1996: Neven, Damien, Wyplosz, Charles. Relative Prices, Trade and Restructuring of European Industry. CEPR (Centre of Economic Policy Research) Discussion Paper No. 1451, August 1996.
Newbery/Pollitt 1997: Newbery, David M., Pollitt, Michael G. The Restructuring and Privatization of Britain's CEGB – Was it worth it? In: Journal of Industrial Economics, Vol. XLV, No. 3, September 1997. S. 269-303.
Ng/Yeats 1996: Ng, Francis, Yeats, Alexander. Open Economies Work Better! Did Africa's Protectionist Policies Cause its Marginalization in World Trade?. World Bank, Policy Research Working Paper, No. 1636, August 1996. In: http://www.worldbank.org.
Nicolaides 1987: Nicolaides, Phedon. How Fair is Fair Trade? In: JWTL, 21, 1987. S. 147-162.
Nicolaides et al. 2005: Nicolaides, Phedon, Kekelekis, Mihalis, Byskes, Philip. State Aid Policy in the European Community. The Hague: Kluwer, 2005.
Nicolaysen 1996: Nicolaysen, Gert. Europarecht II. Das Wirtschaftsrecht im Binnenmarkt. Baden-Baden: Nomos, 1996.
Niederleithinger 1985: Niederleithinger, Ernst. Gesetz gegen Wettbewerbsbeschränkungen: Freiheitsschutz oder Wirtschaftsverwaltung. In: WuW, 1984, Heft 1, 5-17.
Nieh 1998: Nieh, Yu-Hsi. Taiwan: Wirtschaftsglobalisierung und soziale Stabilität. In: Nord-Süd-Aktuell, Jahrgang XII, Nr. 3, 1988, S. 524-532.

Nilsson 1999: Nilsson, Lars. Two-Way Trade between Unequal Partners: The EU and the Developing Countries. In: Weltwirtschaftliches Archiv Vol. 135, 1, 1999. S. 102- 127.

Niosi/Rivard 1990: Niosi, Jorge, Rivard, Jaques. Canadian Technology Transfer to Developing Countries through Small and Medium-Size Enterprises. In: World Development, Vol. 18, No. 11, 1990. S. 1529-1542.

Nishimizu/Robinson 1984:

Nogués 1993: Nogués, Julio J. Social Costs and Benefits of Introducing Patent Protection for Pharmaceutical Drugs in Developing Countries. In: The Developing Economies, XXXI-1, March 1993. S. 24-53.

Nogués/Baracat 2005: Nogués, Julio J., Baracat, Elias. Political Economy of Antidumping and Safeguards in Argentina. World Bank Policy Research Working Paper 3587, May 2005. In: http://www.worldbank.org.

Nolan 2001: Nolan, Peter. China and the Global Business Revolution. New York: Palgrave, 2001.

Noland 1997: Noland, Marcus. Chasing Phantoms: The Political Economy of the USTR. In: International Organization, Vol. 51, No. 3, Summer 1997. S. 365-387.

Nolte 1990: Nolte, Dirk. Freihandel, Protektion oder 'Fair-Trade' auf den Weltautomobilmärkten? Frankfurt am Main: Harri Deutsch Verlag, 1990.

Nordas 2004: Nordas, Hildegunn Kyvik. The Global Textile and Clothing Industry post the Agreement on Textiles and Clothing. Geneva: WTO, 2004.

North 1981: North, Douglass C. Structure and Change in Economic History. New York, London: W. W. Norton, 1981.

North 1997: North, Klaus. Localizing global production. Know-how transfer in international manufacturing. Geneva: International Labour Office, 1997.

North China Pharmaceutical Information 2006: North China Pharmaceutical Huasheng Co Ltd. Information. 2006. In: http://www.ncpchs.com/en/intro.asp.

North/Wallis 1982: North, Douglass C., Wallis, John Joseph. American Government Expenditure: A historical perspective. In: American Economic Review, Vol. 72 No. 2, May 1982. S. 336-340.

Norton 1986: Norton, R. D. Industrial Policy and American Renewal. In: Audretsch, David (ed.). Industrial Policy and Competitive Advantage, Vol. I. Cheltenham, UK, Northampton, MA: Elgar, 1998.

Nouve et al. 2002: Nouve, Kofi, Staatz, John, Schweikhardt, David, and Mbaye Yade. Trading out of poverty: WTO Agreements and the West African Agriculture. Michigan State University International Development Working Papers No. 80, 2002. In: http://www.aec.msu.edu/agecon/fs2/index.htm.

Nowrot 2004: Nowrot, Karsten. Watching 'Friends of the Court' Digging their Own Grave? Policy Papers on Transnational Economic Law, No. 7/2004. In: http://www.telc.uni-halle.de.

NRW Informationen 2007: NRW Wirtschaftsministerium. Jahreswirtschaftsbericht NRW 2007. In: http://www.wirtschaft.nrw.de/.

Nsouli et al. 2001: Nsouli, Saleh M., Fosu, Augustin Kwasi, Varoudakis, Aristomene. Promoting Competitiveness in Manufacturing in Sub-Saharan Africa. In: OECD. Policies to Promote Competitiveness in Manufacturing in Sub-Saharan Africa. Development Centre Seminars within the IMF and the AERC. Kwasi Fosu, Augustin, Nsouli, Saleh M., Varoudakis, Aristomene (eds.). Paris: OECD, 2001a.

Nsouli/Varoudakis 2001: Nsouli, Saleh M., Varoudakis, Aristomene. Promoting Competitiveness in Manufacturing: A Continuing Challenge for Improving Sub-Saharan Africa's Integration into the Global Economy. In: OECD. Policies to Promote Competitiveness in Manufacturing in Sub-Saharan Africa. Development Centre Seminars within the IMF and the AERC. Kwasi Fosu, Augustin, Nsouli, Saleh M., Varoudakis, Aristomene (eds.). Paris: OECD, 2001a.

Nunnenkamp 1995: Nunnenkamp, Peter. Verschärfte Weltmarktkonkurrenz, Lohndruck und begrenzte wirtschaftspolitische Handlungsspielräume. Die Textil- und Bekleidungsindustrie im Zeitalter der Globalisierung. In: Aussenwirtschaft, 50 Jg., Heft 4, 1995. S. 545-569.

Nunnenkamp 1996: Nunnenkamp, Peter. Winners and Losers in the Global Economy. Recent Trends in the Global Division of Labour and Policy Challenges. Kiel Discussion Papers, No. 281, Institut für Weltwirtschaft Kiel, September 1996.

Nunnenkamp 1998: Nunnenkamp, Peter. Wirtschaftliche Aufholprozesse und "Globalisierungskrisen" in Entwicklungsländern. Kieler Diskussionsbeiträge, No. 328, November 1998.

Nunnenkamp 2000: Nunnenkamp, Peter. Globalisierung der Automobilindustrie: Neue Standorte auf dem Vormarsch, traditionelle Anbieter unter Druck? Kieler Arbeitspapiere Nr. 1002, September 2000.

Nunnenkamp 2002: Nunnenkamp, Peter. To what extent can foreign direct investment help achieve international development goals. Kiel Working Paper No. 1128, October 2002. Kiel: Institut für Weltwirtschaft, 2002.

Nunnenkamp et al. 1994: Nunnenkamp, Peter, Gundlach, Erich, Agarwal, Jamuna P. Globalization of Production and Markets. Kieler Studien, 262. Tübingen: Mohr, 1994.

Nunnenkamp/Agarwal 1993: Nunnenkamp, Peter, Agarwal, Jamuna P. Lateinamerika im Wettbewerb um deutsche Direktinvestitionen. Kieler Diskussionspapiere No. 215, August 1993.

Nunnenkamp/Gundlach 1995: Nunnenkamp, Peter, Gundlach, Erich. Globalization of manufacturing activity: Evidence and implications for industrialization in developing countries. UNIDO Background Paper, ID/WG.542/13 (SPEC.), 22 September 1995. Wien: UNIDO, 1995. In: http://www.unido.org.

Nurkse 1953: Nurkse, Ragnar. Problems of Capital Formation in Underdeveloped Countries. Oxford: Basil Blackwell, (First Edition 1953) 1966.

Nurkse 1961: Nurkse, Ragnar. International Trade and Development Policy. In: Ellis, Howard S. (ed.) Economic Development for Latin America. Proceedings of a Conference held by the International Economics Association. London: Macmillan, 1961.

Nutter/Einhorn 1969: Nutter, G. Warren, Einhorn, Henry Adler. Enterprise Monopoly in the United States: 1899-1958. New York, London: Columbia University Press, 1969.

Nyangito 2000: Nyangito, Hezron O. Impact of the Uruguay Agreement on Agriculture on Food Security: The Case of Kenya. In: Agricultural Trade in Times of Globalization, Workshop Proceedings Paper. BUKO Agrar Koordination. Hamburg: Forum für Internationale Agrarpolitik e.V, 2000.

Nye 1992: Nye, Joseph S. What new world order? In: Foreign Affairs, Vol. 71, No. 2, 1992.

Nyoro et al. 1999: Nyoro, J.K., Kiiru, M. W., Jayne, T.S. Evolution of Kenya's Maize Marketing Systems in the Post-Liberalization Era. Working Paper No. 2 a. Tegemeo Agricultural Monitoring and Policy Analysis Project, Egerton University, University of Michigan, June 1999. In: http://www.aec.msu.edu/agecon/fs2/kenya/.

Nyoro et al. 2001: Nyoro, J.K., Wanzala, Maria, Awour, Tom. Increasing Kenya's Agricultural Competitiveness: Farm Level Issues. Working Paper No. 4. Tegemeo Agricultural Monitoring and Policy Analysis Project, Egerton Univesity, University of Michigan, September 2001. In: http://www.aec.msu.edu/agecon/fs2/kenya/.

Nyoro et al. 2004: Nyoro, James K., Kirimi, Lilian, Jayne T.S. Competitiveness of Kenyan and Ugandan Maize Production: Challenges for the Future. Working Paper 10, 2004. In: http://www.tegemeo.org.

O

Oberender 1984: Oberender, Peter (Hrg.). Marktstruktur und Wettbewerb in der Bundesrepublik Deutschland. München: Franz Vahlen, 1984.

Oberender 1989: Oberender, Peter. Der Einfluß ordnungstheoretischer Prinzipien Walter Euckens auf die deutsche Wirtschaftspolitik nach dem Zweiten Weltkrieg: Eine ordnungspolitische Analyse. In: ORDO Bd. 40. 1989. S. 321-350.

Oberender/Okruch 1997: Oberender, Peter, Okruch, Stefan. Die Entwicklung der Sozialpolitik aus ordnungspolitischer Sicht. In: ORDO, Bd. 48, 1997.

Oberender/Rüter 1993: Oberender, Peter, Rüter, Georg. The steel industry: a crisis of adaption. In: de Jong, H.W. (ed.) The Structure of European Industry. Dordrecht; Boston; London: Kluwer, 1993.

O'Brien 2006: O'Brien, Doug. World Trade Organization and the Commodity Title of the Next Farm Bill: A Practitioner's View, April 26, 2006. In: http://www.nationalaglawcenter.org/research/#wto

Obstfeld 1996: Obstfeld, Maurice. Effectiveness of Foreign Exchange Intervention, 1985-88. In: Frenkel, Jacob A., Goldstein, Morris (eds.). Functioning of the International Monetary System. Vol. 2. Washington: IMF, 1996.

Ocampo 1994: Ocampo, José Antonio. Trade Policy and Industrialization in Columbia, 1967-91. In: Helleiner, Gerald K. (ed.). Trade Policy and Industrialization in Turbulent Times. London; New York: Routledge, 1994.

Ocampo/Taylor 1998: Ocampo, Jose Antonio, Taylor, Lance. Trade Liberalization in Developing Economies: Modest Benefits but Problems with Productivity Growth, Macro Prices, and Income Distribution. In: The Economic Journal, Vol. 108, September 1998. S. 1523-1546.

OCED 1998b: OECD. State Infrastructure and Productive Performance in Indian Manufacturing. Development Centre Technical Papers, No. 139, CD/DOC (98) 9, 14. September 1998. Paris: OECD, 1998.

OCED 1999a: OECD. Post-Uruguay Round Tariff Regimes. Achievements and Outlook. Paris, OECD, 1999.

O'Cleireacain 1978: O'Cleireacain, Seamus. Measuring the International Effect of Subsidies. In: Warnecke, Steven J. (ed.). International Trade and Industrial Policies. Government Intervention and an Open World Economy. London: Macmillan Press, 1978.

O'Connor 2003: O'Connor, Bernard. A Note on the Need for more Clarity in the World Trade Organization Agreement on Agriculture. In: JWT, Vol. 37, No. 5, 2003. S. 839-846.

Odell 1980: Odell, John S. Latin American Trade Negotiations with the United States. In: International Organization, 34, 2, Spring 1980. S. 207-228.

Odell 2005: Odell, John S. Chairing a WTO Negotiation. In: Petersmann, Ernst-Ulrich (ed.). Reforming the World Trading System. Legitimacy, Efficiency, and Democratic Governance. Oxford: Oxford University Press, 2005.

OECD 1968: OECD. Gaps in Technology. Paris: OECD, 1968.

OECD 1975: OECD. Adjustment for Trade. Paris: OECD, 1975.

OECD 1983: OECD. Textile and Clothing Industries. Paris: OECD, 1983.

OECD 1983a: OECD. The Generalized System of Preferences. Review of the First Decade. Paris: OECD, 1983.

OECD 1984: OECD. Competition and Trade Policies. Their Interaction. Paris: OECD, 1984.

OECD 1985: OECD. Cost and Benefits of Protection. Paris: OECD, 1985.

OECD 1987: OECD. National Policies and Agricultural Trade. Paris: OECD, 1987.

OECD 1987a: OECD. The Costs of Restricting Imports. The Automobile Industry. Paris: OECD, 1987.

OECD 1989: OECD. Predatory Pricing. Paris: OECD, 1989. In: http://www.oecd.org.

OECD 1989a: OECD. Competition Policy and Intellectual Property Rights. OECD: Paris, 1989. In: http://www.oecd.org.

OECD 1993: OECD. Obstacles to Trade and Competition. Paris: OECD, 1993.

OECD 1994: OECD. Agreement Respecting Normal Competitive Conditions in the Commercial Shipbuilding and Repair Industry. Paris: OECD, 1994. http://www.oecd.org//dsti/sti/industry/ship/prod/cont-e.htm

OECD 1994a: OECD. Main Science and Technology Indicators. Paris: OECD, 1994.

OECD 1995: OECD. Linkages OECD and Major Developing Economies. Paris: OECD, 1995.

OECD 1995a: OECD. Beyond the Multifibre Arrangement: Third World Competition and Restructuring Europe's Textile Industry. Developemt Centre Documents. Paris: OECD, 1995.

OECD 1995b: OECD. Kodex der Liberalisierung der laufenden unsichtbaren Operationen. Paris: OECD, 1995.

OECD 1996: OECD. Globalization of Industry. Overview and Sector Reports. Paris: OECD, 1996.
OECD 1996a: OECD. Indicators of Tariff & Non-tariff Trade Barriers. Paris: OECD, 1996.
OECD 1996b: OECD. International Direct Investment Statistics Yearbook. Paris: OECD, 1996.
OECD 1996c: OECD. Technology and Industrial Performance. Paris: OECD, 1996.
OECD 1996d: OECD. Antitrust and Market Access. The Scope and Coverage of Competition Law and Implications for Trade. Paris: OECD, 1996. In: http://www.oecd.org.
OECD 1996e: OECD. Neue Dimensionen des Marktzugangs im Zeichen der wirtschaftlichen Globalisierung. Paris: OECD, 1996.
OECD 1996f: OECD. Market Access after the Uruguay Round. Paris: OECD, 1996.
OECD 1996g: OECD. Trade and Competition: Frictions after Uruguay Round. Economics Department Working Papers No. 165. Paris: OECD, 1996.
OECD 1996h: OECD. Einführung in die OECD-Kodices der Liberalisierung des Kapitalverkehrs und der laufenden unsichtbaren Operationen. Paris: OECD, 1996.
OECD 1996i: OECD. Competition Policy and the Agro-Food Sector. Directorate for Food, Agriculture and Fisheries. Paris: OECD, 1996. In: http://www.oecd.org.
OECD 1996j: OECD. Techology, Productivity, and Job Creation. Vol. 2 Analytical Report. Paris: OECD, 1996.
OECD 1996k: OECD: Trade, Employment and Labour Standards. Paris: OECD, 1996.
OECD 1997: OECD. Proceedings of the Workshop on Steel Trade and Adjustment Issues. OECD/GD(97)158. Paris: OECD, 1997. In: http://www.oecd.org.
OECD 1997a: OECD. Market Access for the Least Developed Countries: Where are the Obstacles? OECD/GD(97)174, Paris: OECD, 1997. In: http://www.oecd.org.
OECD 1997b: OECD. Designing New Trade Policies in the Transition Economies. OECD/GD(97)199, Paris: OECD, 1997. In: http://www.oecd.org.
OECD 1997c: OECD. The Uruguay Round Agreement on Agriculture and Processed Agricultural Products. Paris: OECD, 1997.
OECD 1997d: OECD. Brazilian Agriculture: Recent Policy Changes and Trade Prospects. Directorate for Food, Agriculture and Fisheries. Paris: OECD, 1997. In: http://www.oecd.org.
OECD 1997e: Council at Ministerial Level. Economic Globalization and the Environment. C/MIN(97)13, OLIS: 6 May 1997. http://www.oecd.org.
OECD 1998: OECD Agricultural Outlook 1998-2003. Paris: OECD, 1998.
OECD 1998: OECD. Open Markets Matter. Paris: OECD, 1998.
OECD 1998a: OECD. Spotlight on Public Support to Industry. Paris: OECD, 1998.
OECD 1998a: OECD. The Multilateral Agreement on Investment. The MAI Negotiationg Text (as of 14 February 1998. Paris: OECD, 1998.
OECD 1998c: OECD. Science, Technology and Industry Outlook. Paris: OECD, 1998.
OECD 1999: OECD. National Accounts. Main Aggregates 1960-1997. Paris: OECD, 1999.
OECD 1999b: OECD. Oligopoly. DAFFE/CLP(99)25. Paris: OECD, 1999. In: http://www.oecd.org/daf/clp.
OECD 1999c: OECD. Competition Elements in International Trade Law: A Post-Uruguay Round Overview of WTO Agreements. COM/TD/DAFFE/CLP(98)26/FINAL. Paris: OECD, 1999. In: http://www.oecd.org.
OECD 1999d: OECD. Review of Tariffs. Synthesis Report. TD/TC(99)7/Final, OLIS 2 July 1999. Paris: OECD, 1999. In: http://www.oecd.org.
OECD 2000: OECD. International Strategic Alliances: Their Role in Industrial Globalization. STI Working Paper 2000/5. DSTI/DOC(2000)5. Paris: OECD, 2000. In: http://www.oecd.org/dsti/sti/prod/sti_wp.htm.
OECD 2001: OECD. The Uruguay Round Agreement on Agriculture. An Evaluation of Its Implementation in OECD Countries. Paris: OECD, 2001.
OECD 2001a: OECD. Policies to Promote Competitiveness in Manufacturing in Sub-Saharan Africa. Development Centre Seminars within the IMF and the AERC. Kwasi Fosu, Augustin, Nsouli, Saleh M., Varoudakis, Aristomene (eds.). Paris: OECD, 2001a.
OECD 2002: OECD. Forty Years of Experience with the OECD Code of Liberalization of Capital Movements. Paris: OECD, 2002.
OECD 2002a: OECD. The Relationship between Regional Trade Arrangements and Multilateral Trading System. Rules of Origin. TD/TC/WP(2002)33/Final. 2002. In: http://www.oecd.org.
OECD 2003: OECD. Trade and Competition. Paris: OECD, 2003.
OECD 2003a: OECD. Globalization, Povery and Inequality. Paris: OECD, 2003.
OECD 2003b: OECD. Regionalism and the Multilateral Trading System. Paris: OECD, 2003.
OECD 2004: OECD. African Economic Outlook 2003/2004. Paris: OECD, 2004.
OECD 2004a: OECD. Recent Steel Market Developments. Prepared for the OECD Special Meeting at High-Level on Steel Issues held on 28 June 2004. Paris: OECD, 2004. In: http://www.oecd.org.
OECD 2005: OECD. Trade and Structural Adjustment. Embracing Globalization. Paris: OECD, 2005.
OECD 2005a: OECD. China overtakes the U.S. as world's leading exporter of information technology goods. OECD Press release, 12.12.2005. In: http://www.oecd.org.
OECD 2005b: OECD. Iron and Steel Industry in 2003. Paris: OECD, 2005.
OECD 2005c: OECD. OECD Special Meeting at High-Level on Steel Issues. Capacity Expansion in the Global Steel Industry. Comment by NAFTA Industry Association. SG/STEEL(2005)31. In: http://www.oecd.org.
OECD 2005d: OECD. OECD, partner countries decide on a pause in shipbuilding subsidy talks. 19.09.2005. In: http://www.oecd.org.

OECD 2005e: OECD. Compedium of Patent Statistics. Paris: OECD, 2005. In: http:/www.oecd.org.
OECD Agricultural Policies Background Information, div. Jg.: OECD. Agricultural Policies in OECD Countries. Measurement of Support and Background Information. Paris: OECD, div. Jg.
OECD Agricultural Policies, div. Jg.: OECD. Agricultural Policies in OECD Countries. Monitoring and Evaluation. Paris: OECD, div. Jg.
OECD div. Länder 2002: OECD. Country Contributions, div. In: OECD Global Forum on Competition, 14-15 Feb. 2002. In: http://www.oecd.org.
OECD Industrial Structure, div. Jg.: OECD. Industrial Structure Statistics. Paris, OECD, div. Jg.
Oesch 2003: Oesch, Matthias. Standards of Review in WTO Dispute Settlement Resolution and the Treatment of National Law. In: Nettesheim, Martin, Sander, Gerald G. (Hrg.). WTO-Recht und Globalisierung. Berlin: Duncker&Humblot, 2003.
Ofico/Tschirley 2003: Ofico, Afonso Osorio, Tschirley, David. An Overview of the Cotton Sub-Sector in Mozambique. National Research Institute/Michigan State University, February 2003. In: http://www.imperial.ac.uk/agriculturalsciences/research/sections/aebm/projects/cotton_downloads/sysovmoz.pdf.
Ogbu et al. 1995: Ogbu, Osita M., Oyeyinka, Banji O., Mlawa, Hasa M. Technology Policy and Practice in Africa. International Development Centre (IDRC) 1995. In: http://web.idrc.ca
O'Gráda/O'Rourke 1996: O'Gráda, Cormac, O'Rourke, Kevin. Irish economic growth, 1945-88. In: Crafts, Nicolas, Toniolo, Gianni (eds.). Economic Growth in Europe since 1945. Cambridge: Cambridge University Press, 1996.
Ohlin 1978: Ohlin, Goran. Subsidies and other Industrial Aids. In: Warnecke, Steven J. (ed.). International Trade and Industrial Policies. Government Intervention and an Open World Economy. London: Macmillan Press, 1978.
Okamoto 1994: Okamoto, Yumiko. Impact of Trade and FDI Liberalization Policies on the Malaysian Economy. In: The Developing Economies, XXXII, No. 4, December 1994. S. 460-478..
Okuda 1994: Okuda, Satoru. Taiwan's Trade and FDI Policies and Their Effect On Productivity Growth. In: The Developing Economies, XXXII, No. 4, December 1994. S. 423-437.
Olivares 2001: Olivares, Gustavo. The Case for Giving Effectiveness to GATT/WTO Rules on Developing Countries and LDCs. In: JWT Vol. 35, No. 3, 2001. S. 545-551.
Oliveira Martins 1994: Oliveira Martins, Joaquim. Market Structure, Trade and Industry Wages. OECD Economic Studies No. 22. Paris: OECD, Spring 1994. In: http://ww.oecd.org.
Oliveira Martins et al. 1996: Oliveira Martins, Joaquim, Scarpetta, Stefano, Pilat, Dirk. Mark-up ratios in manufacturing industries. Estimates for 14 OECD Countries. Economics Department Working Papers No. 162, OECD/GD(96)61. Paris: OECD, 1996. In: http://www.oecd.org.
Oliveira Martins et al. 1996a: Oliveira Martins, Joaquim, Scarpetta, Stefano, Pilat, Dirk. Mark-up pricing, market structur and the business cycle. OECD Economic Studies No. 27, Vol. II.. Paris: OECD, 1996. In: http://www.oecd.org.
Oliveira Martins/Scarpetta 1999: Oliveira Martins, Joaquim, Scarpetta, Stefano. The levels and cyclical behaviour of mark-ups across countries and market structures. OECD Economics Department Working Paper No. 213, ECO/WKP(99)5. Paris: OECD, 1999. In: http://www.oecd.org.
Olson 1968: Olson, Mancur. Die Logik des kollektiven Handelns. Tübingen: Mohr, 1992.
Olson 1996: Olson, Mancur. The varieties of Eurosclerosis: the rise and decline of nations since 1982. In: Crafts, Nicolas, Toniolo, Gianni (eds.). Economic Growth in Europe since 1945. Cambridge: Cambridge University Press, 1996.
Olson 2005: Olson, Kara. M. Subsidizing Rent-Seeking: Antidumping Protection and the Byrd Amendment. American University, Working Paper, March 11, 2005. In: http://nw08.american.edu/~reynolds/.
Olten 1995: Olten, Rainer. Wettbewerbstheorie und Wettbewerbspolitik. München: Oldenbourg, 1995.
Oltersdorf/Weingärtner 1996: Oltersdorf, Ulrich, Weingärtner, Lioba. Handbuch der Welternährung. Bonn: Dietz, 1996.
Oman et al. 1997: Oman, Charles P., Brooks, DouglasH., Foy, Colm. Investing in Asia. Paris: OECD, 1997.
Onafowora/Owoye 1998: Onafowora, Olugbenga A., Owoye, Oluwole. Can Trade Liberalization Stimulate Economic Growth in Africa? In: World Development, Vol. 26, No. 3, 1998. S. 497-506.
O'Neill 1995: O'Neill, Donal. Education and Income Growth: Implications for Cross-Country Inequality. In: Journal of Political Economy, Vol. 103, No. 6, 1995. S. 1289-1301.
Onida Informationen 2004: Businessworld India/Ranju Sarkar. Onida. The return of the devil. Oct. 11, 2004. In: http://www.businessworldindia.com/oct1104/indepth04.asp.
Onyeiwu 1995: Onyeiwu, Steve. Why in Africa Research Rarely Reaches Use: A Comment on Paul B. Vitta's Article. In: Canadian Journal of Development Studies, Vol. VXI, No. 1, 1995. S. 151-160.
Oppermann 1987: Oppermann, Thomas. On the Present International Economic Order. In: Oppermann, Thomas, Petersmann, Ernst-Ulrich. Reforming the International Economic Order. Berlin: Duncker Humblot, 1987.
Oppermann 1997: Oppermann, Thomas. Dispute Settlement in the EC: Lessons for the GATT/WTO Dispute Settlement System? In: Petersmann, Ernst-Ulrich (ed.). International Trade Law and the GATT/WTO Dispute Settlement System. London, The Hague, Boston: Kluwer Law, 1997.
Oppermann/Conlan 1990: Oppermann, Thomas, Conlan, Patricia. 'Principles' - Legal Basis of Today's International Economic Order? In: ORDO, Bd. 41, 1990. S. 75-91.
O'Rourke/Williamson 1996: O'Rourke, Kevin H., Williamson, Jeffrey G. Around the European Periphery 1870-1913. Globalization, Schooling and Growth. Congress Paper, European Association of Historical Economics, Venice, 1996.

Ortino 2004: Ortino, F. WTO Jurisprudence on de jure and de facto Discrimination. In: Ortino, Federico, Petersmann, Ernst-Ulrich (eds.). The WTO Dispute Settlement System 1995 - 2003. The Hague et al.: Kluwer Law International, 2004.
Ortino/Petersmann 2004: Ortino, Federico, Petersmann, Ernst-Ulrich (eds.). The WTO Dispute Settlement System 1995 - 2003. The Hague et al.: Kluwer Law International, 2004.
Osada 1994: Osada, Hiroshi. Trade Liberalization and FDI Incentives in Indonesia: The Impact on Industrial Productivity. In: The Developing Economies, XXXII, No. 4, December 1994. S. 479-491.
Osorio-Peters et al. 1996: Osorio-Peters, Suhita, Brockmann, Karl Ludwig, Knopf, Nicole, Jäckel, Ute, Senton, Jürgen. Nord-Süd Agrarhandel unter veränderten Rahmenbedingungen. Zentrum für Europäische Wirtschaftsforschung, Mannheim, August 1996.
Osorio-Peters et al. 1997: Osorio-Peters, Suhita, Knopf, Nicole, Aslan, Hatice. Der internationale Handel mit Agrarprodukten. Umweltökonomische Aspekte des Bananenhandels. Zentrum für Europäische Wirtschaftsforschung, Mannheim, Juli 1997.
Ossenbühl 1996: Ossenbühl, Fritz. Gesetz und Recht – Die Rechtsquellen im demokratischen Rechtsstaat. In: Isensee, Josef, Kirchhof, Paul (Hrg.). Handbuch des Staatsrechts. Bd. III. 2 Aufl. Heidelberg: C.F. Müller, 1996.
Ostry 1996: Ostry, Silvia. National Technology Policies and International Cooperative Linkages among Private Firms. In: Koopmann, Georg, Scharrer, Hans-Eckart (eds.). The Economics of High-Technology Competition. Baden-Baden: Nomos, 1996.
Otsuka 1991: Otsuka, Keijiro. Determinants and consequences of land reform implementation in the Philippines. In: Journal of Development Economics, Vol. 35, 1991. S. 339-355.
Ott 1997: Ott, Andrea. GATT und WTO im Gemeinschaftsrecht. Köln et al.: Carl Heymanns, 1997.
Ott 1998: Ott, Andrea. GATT/WTO-Panels: Büchse der Pandora für die EG? In: DZWir Heft 2, 1998. S. 84-86.
Owen 1983: Owen, Nicholas. Economies of Scale, Competitiveness, and Trade Patterns within the European Community. Oxford: Clarendon Press, 1983.
Oxfam 2002: Oxfam. Cultivating Poverty. The Impact of US Cotton Subsidies on Africa. Oxfam Briefing Paper 30, 27. Dezember 2002. In: http://www.oxfam.org.
Oxfam 2002a: Oxfam. Rigged Rules and Double Standards. Trade, globalization, and the fight against poverty. 2002. In: http://www.oxfam.org.
Oyejide/Raheem 1993: Oyejide, T. Ademola, Raheem, Mufutau I. Nigeria. In: Taylor, Lance (ed.). The Rocky Road to Reform. Adjustment, Income Distribution, and Growth in the Developing World. Cambridge: MIT Press, 1993.

P

Paarlberg 1997: Paarlberg, Robert. Agricultural Policy Reform and the Uruguay Round: Synergistic Linkage in a Two-Level Game? In: International Organization Vol. 51 No. 3, Summer 1997. S. 413-444.
Paarlberg 1999: Paarlberg, Robert. Politics and Food Insecurity in Africa. In: Review of Agricultural Economics, Vol. 21 No. 2, 1999. S. 499-511.
Pack 1984: Pack, Howard. Productivity and Technical Choice. Applications to the Textile Industry. In: Journal of Development Economics, Vol. 16, 1984. S. 153-176.
Pack 1987: Pack, Howard. Productivity, Technology and Industrial Development. A Case Study in Textiles. Published for the World Bank. Oxford: Oxford University Press, 1987.
Pack 1988: Pack, Howard. Industrialization and Trade. In: Chenery, H., Srinivasan, T.N. Handbook of Development Economics. Vol. I. Amsterdam; New York: Elsevier Science Publishers, 1988.
Pack 1993: Pack, Howard. Productivity and Industrial Development in Sub-Saharan Africa. In: World Development, Vol. 21, No. 1, 1993. S. 1-16.
Pack 1994: Pack, Howard. Productivity or politics: The determinants of the Indonesian tariff structure. In: Journal of Development Economics, Vol. 44, 1994. S. 441-451.
Pack/Saggi 1999: Pack, Howard, Saggi, Kamal. Exporting, Externalities, and Technology Transfer. World Bank, Policy Research Working Paper No. 2065, February 1999.
Pack/Westphal 1986: Pack, Howard, Westphal, Larry E. Industrial Strategy and Technological Change. Theory versus Reality. In: Journal of Development Economics, Vol. 22, 1986, pp. 87-128.
Pagani 2006: Pagani, Fabrizio. Are Plurilateral Agreements Possible Outside of the World Trade Organization? At the Margins of the OECD Negotiations of Two Sectoral Subsidy Agreements. In: JWT, Vol. 40, No. 5, 2006. S. 797-812.
Page 1981: Page, Sheila. The Revival of Protectionism and its Consequences for Europe. In: Journal for Common Market Studies, Vol. XX, No. 1, September 1981. S. 17-39.
Page 1994: Page, Shiela. How Developing Countries Trade. The Institutional Constraints. London; New York: Routledge, 1994.
Page 1994a: Page, John M. The East Asian Miracle: An Introduction. In: World Development, Vol. 22, No. 4, 1994. S. 615-625.
Pallangyo 1994: Pallangyo, E. P. Food and Agricultural Policy and African Development. In: Food and Agriculture in Africa. ECA/FAO Agricultural Division, Staff Papers No. 6, 1994.
Palmeter 1996: Palmeter, David. A Commentary on the WTO Anti-Dumping Code. In: JWT, Vol. 30 No. 4, 1996. S. 43-71.

Palmeter 2003: Palmeter, David. Comment on Facial Non-Discrimination. In: Cottier, Thomas, Mavroidis, Petros C (eds.). The Role of the Judge in International Trade Regulation. Ann Arbor: University of Michigan Press, 2003.
Palmeter 2005: Palmeter, David. A note on the ethics of free trade. In: World Trade Review Vol. 4, No. 3, 2005. S. 449-467.
Palmeter/Mavroidis 2004: Palmeter, David, Mavroidis, Petros C. Dispute Settlement in the World Trade Organization. Cambridge: Cambridge University Press, 2004.
Panagariya 2000: Panagariya, Arvind. Evaluating the Case for Export Subsidies. World Bank Policy Reserach Working Paper 2276. Washington: World Bank, January 2000.
Panagariya et al. 1996: Panagariya, Arvind, Quibria, M. G., Rao, Narhari. The Emerging Global Trading Environment and Developing Asia. Asian Development Bank Staff Paper, July 1996.
Pandey 2004: Pandey, Mihir. Impact of Trade Liberalization in Manufacturing Industry in India in the 1980s and 1990s. Indian Council for Research on International Economic Relations, Working Paper 140, August 2004. In: http://www.icrier.res.in/.
Pangratis/Vermulst 1994: Pangratis, Angelos, Vermulst, Edwin. Injury in Anti-Dumping Proceedings. In: JWT, Vol. 28, No. 5, October 1994. S. 61-96.
Papageorgiou et al. 1990: Papageorgiou, Demetrios, Choksi, Armeane M., Michaely, Michael. Liberalizing Forein Trade in Developing Countries. The Lessons of Experience. Washington, D. C.: The World Bank, 1990.
Paraskewopoulos 1998: Paraskewopoulos, Spiridon. Soziale Sicherung und Umverteilung als Grundprinzipien und Gefährdungsmomente der Sozialen Marktwirtschaft. In: Cassel, Dieter (Hrg.). 50 Jahre Soziale Marktwirtschaft. Schriften zu Ordnungfragen der Wirtschaft, Band 57, Stuttgart, Lucius&Lucius: 1998.
Paredes 1994: Paredes, Carlos E. Trade Policy, Industrialization and Productivity Growth in Peru. In: Helleiner, Gerald K. (ed.). Trade Policy and Industrialization in Turbulent Times. London; New York: Routledge, 1994.
Parenti 2000: Parenti, Antonio. Accession to the World Trade Organization: A Legal Analysis. In: Legal Issues of Economic Integration, Vol. 27 No. 2, 2000. S. 141-157.
Park 2004: Park, N. Statistical Analysis of the WTO Dispute Settlement System (1995-2000). In: Ortino, Federico, Petersmann, Ernst-Ulrich (eds.). The WTO Dispute Settlement System 1995 - 2003. The Hague et al.: Kluwer Law International, 2004.
Park/Lippolt 2004: Park, Walter, Lippoldt, Douglas. International Licensing and the Strenghtening of Intellectual Property Rights in Developing Countries. TD/TC/WP(2004)31/Final. OECD Trade Policy Working Paper No. 10. Paris: OECD, 2004. In: http://www.oecd.org.
Park/Rhee 1998: Park, Daekeun, Rhee, Changyong. Currency Crisis in Korea: How was it aggravated? In: Asian Development Review, Vol. 16, No. 1, 1998. S. 149-180. In: http://www.adb.org/Documents/Periodicals/ADR/pdf/ADR-Vol16-1-Park-Rhee.pdf.
Parker 1998: Parker, David. Introduction. In: Parker, David. Privatization in the European Union. Theory and Policy Perspectives. London; New York: Routledge, 1998.
Parker et al. 1995: Parker, Ronald R., Riopelle, Randall, Steel, William F. Small Enterprises Adjusting to Liberalization in Five African Countries. World Bank Discussion Papers. Africa Technical Department Series No. 271. Washington: World Bank, 1995.
Parry 1997: Parry, Ian W. H. Agricultural Policies in the Presence of Distorting Taxes. Resources for the Future. Discussion Paper 98-05. In: http://www.rff.org.
Patel 1983: Patel, Surendra J. Editor's Introduction. In: World Development, Special Issue Health/Drug Access, Vol. 11, No. 3, 1983.
Patent Genius 2006: Patent Genius Webseite. 2006. In: http://www.patentgenius.com/.
Patnaik 1997: Patnaik, Prabhat. The context and consequences of economic liberalization in India. In: Journal of International Trade & Economic Development 6: 2, 1997. S. 165-178.
Patterson 1997: Patterson, Lee Ann. Agricultural Policy Reform in the European Community: a three-level game analysis. In: International Organization 51, 1, Winter 1997, S. 135-165.
Pauer 1984: Pauer, Erich. Technologietransfer und industrielle Revolution in Japan 1850-1920. In: Technikgeschichte Bd. 51, Nr. 1, 1984. S. 34-54.
Paus 1985: Paus, Eva. Manufactured Export Growth in Latin America in the 1970s: Reflection of improved competitiveness? Diskussionsbeiträge Nr. 37, Ibero-Amerika Institut für Wirtschaftsforschung Göttingen, July 1985.
Pauwelyn 1999: Pauwelyn, Joost. The WTO Agreement on Sanitary and Phytosanitary (SPS) Measures as Applied in the First Three SPS Disputes. In: Journal of International Economic Law, 1999. S. 641-664.
Pauwelyn 2000: Pauwelyn, Joost. Enforcement and Countermeasures at the WTO: Rules are Rules - Toward a More Collective Approach. In: American Journal of International Law, Vol. 94, 2000. S. 335-347.
Pauwelyn 2003: Pauwelyn, Joost. A Typology of Multilateral Treaty Obligations: Are WTO Obligations Bilateral or Collective in Nature? European Journal of International Law, Vol. 13, No. 5, 2003. S. 907-951.
Pauwelyn 2003a: Pauwelyn, Joost. Does the WTO Stand for 'Deferenc to' or 'Interference with' National Health Authorities When Applying the Agreement on Sanitary and Phytosanitary Measures (SPS Agreement)? In: Cottier, Thomas, Mavroidis, Petros C (eds.). The Role of the Judge in International Trade Regulation. Ann Arbor: University of Michigan Press, 2003.
Pauwelyn 2004: Pauwelyn, Joost. Proposals for Reforms of Article 21 of the DSU. In: Ortino, Federico, Petersmann, Ernst-Ulrich (eds.). The WTO Dispute Settlement System 1995 - 2003. The Hague et al.: Kluwer Law International, 2004.

Pauwelyn 2004a: Pauwelyn, Joost. Adding Sweeteners to Softwood Lumber. The WTO-NAFTA 'Spagetti Bowl' is cooking. In: Journal of International Economic Law Vol. 9 No.1, 2006. S. 197-206.
Pauwelyn 2004b: Pauwelyn, Joost. The Puzzle of WTO Safeguards and Regional Trade Agreements. In: Journal of International Economic Law, Vol. 7, No. 1, 2004. S. 109-142.
Pauwelyn 2005: Pauwelyn, Joost. Rien ne vas plus? Distinguishing domestic regulation form market access in GATT and GATS. In: World Trade Review Vol. 4, No. 2, 2005. S. 131-170.
Pavitt/Patel 1996: Pavitt, Keith, Patel, Parimal. What makes High Technology Competition different from Conventional Competition? The Central Importance of National Systems of Innovation. In: Koopmann, Georg, Scharrer, Hans-Eckart (eds.). The Economics of High-Technology Competition. Baden-Baden: Nomos, 1996.
Pay 2005: Pay, Ellen. Overview of the Sanitary and Phytosanitary Measures in Quad Countries on Tropical Fruits and Vegetables imported from Developing Countries. November 2005. In: http://www.southcentre.org.
Peacock 1993: Peacock, Alan. Liberalism and Economic Growth. In: Szirmai, Adam, van Ark, Bart, Pilat, Dirk (eds.). Explaining Economic Growth. Essays in Honour of Angus Maddison. Amsterdam: North Holland, 1993.
Pearce 2003: Pearce, Douglas. Buyer and Supplier Credit to Farmers: Do Donors have a Role to Play? Paving the Way Forward for Rural Finance, An International Conference on Best Practices, 2003. In: http://www.basis.wisc.edu/rfc/index.htm.
Pearson 1969: Pearson, Lester B and Associates. Partners in Development. Report of the Commission on International Development. New York; Washington; London: Praeger Publishers, 1969.
Pearson 1987: Pearson, Ruth. Transfer of Technology and Domestic Innovation in the Cement Industry. In: Katz, Jorge M. Technology Generation in Latin American Manufacturing Industries. London: Macmillan Press, 1987.
Peffekoven 1997: Peffekoven, Rolf. Finanzpolitik im Konflikt zwischen Effizienz und Distribution. In: ORDO, Bd. 48, 1997.
Pelzman 1983: Pelzman, Joseph. Economic Costs of Tariffs and Quotas on Textile and Apparel Products Imported into the United States: A Survey of the Literature and Implication for Policies. In: Weltwirtschaftliches Archiv, 119, 1983. S. 523- 542.
Pelzman 1984: Pelzman, Joseph. The Multifiber Arrangement and its Effect on the Profit Performance of the U.S. Textile Industry. In: Baldwin, Robert E. Krueger, Anne O. The Structure and Evolution of Recent U.S. Trade Policy. Chicago; London: The University of Chicago Press, 1984.
Pérez/Pérez y Peniche 1987: Pérez, Luis Alberto, Pérez y Peniche, José de Jesús. A Summary of the Principal Findings of the Case-Study on the Technological Behavior of the Mexican Steel Firm Altos Hornos de Mexico. In: Katz, Jorge M. Technology Generation in Latin American Manufacturing Industries. London: Macmillan Press, 1987.
Perini 2003: Perini, Federico Gonzales. Patents vs. Trade? The Issue of Patent Rights Exhaustion. In: Legal Issues of Economic Integration, Vol. 30 No. 2, 2003. S. 133-156.
Perkins 1994: Perkins, Dwight H. There Are At Least Three Models of East Asian Development. In: World Development, Vol. 22, No. 4, 1994. S. 655-661.
Perlitz 2005: Perlitz, Uwe. Chemical Industry in China: Overtaking the competition. Deutsche Bank Research, China Special, Current Issues. October 25, 2005. In: http://www.dbresearch.com.
Perlitz 2006: Perlitz, Uwe. World steel market: Asia forging ahead. Deutsche Bank Research, International Topics, Current Issues. January 10, 2006. In: http://www.dbresearch.com.
Perotti 1992: Perotti, Roberto. Income Distribution, Politics, and Growth. In: American Economic Review, Papers and Proceedings, Vol. 82, No. 2, May 1992.
Perotti/Whalley 1994: Perotti, Carlo, Whalley, John. The New Regionalism: Trade Liberalization or Insurance? NBER Working Paper No. 4626, January 1994.
Persson/Tabellini 1994: Persson, Torsten, Tabellini, Guido. Is Inequality Harmful for Growth? In: American Economic Review, Vol. 84, No. 3, June 1994.
Pestieau 1978: Pestieau, Caroline. Revising the GATT Approach to Subsidies: A Canadian View. In: Warnecke, Steven J. (ed.). International Trade and Industrial Policies. Government Intervention and an Open World Economy. London: Macmillan Press, 1978.
Petersmann 1980: Petersmann, Ernst-Ulrich. Dreißig Jahre Allgemeines Zoll- und Handelsabkommen. In: Archiv des Völkerrechts, 19 Bd., 1. Heft, 1980. S. 23-80.
Petersmann 1986: Petersmann, Ernst-Ulrich. Trade Policy as a Constitutional Problem. On the 'Domestic Policy Functions' of International Trade Rules. In: Aussenwirtschaft, 41. Jg, Heft 2/3, 1986. S. 405-439.
Petersmann 1987: Petersmann, Ernst-Ulrich. International Trade Order and International Trade Law. Economic and Legal Issues of Integrating Developing Countries into the Multilateral Trading System. In: Oppermann, Thomas, Petersmann, Ernst-Ulrich. Reforming the International Economic Order. Berlin: Duncker Humblot, 1987.
Petersmann 1988: Petersmann, Ernst-Ulrich. Handelspolitik als Verfassungsproblem. In: ORDO, Bd. 39, 1988. S. 239-254.
Petersmann 1988a: Petersmann, Ernst-Ulrich. Grey Area Trade Policy and the Rule of Law. In: JWT, Vol. 22, No. 2, 1988. S. 23-44.
Petersmann 1989: Petersmann, Ernst-Ulrich. Wie kann Handelspolitik konstitutionalisiert werden? In: Europa-Archiv, Folge 2, 1989. S. 55-64.
Petersmann 1990: Petersmann, Ernst-Ulrich. Need for Reforming Antidumping Rules and Practices. In: Aussenwirtschaft, 45. Jg. (1990), Heft II. S. 179-198.
Petersmann 1993: Petersmann, Ernst-Ulrich. Freier Warenverkehr und nationaler Umweltschutz in EWG und EWR. In: Aussenwirtschaft, 48 Jg., Heft I, S. 95-128.

Petersmann 1997: Petersmann, Ernst-Ulrich. The GATT/WTO Dispute Settlement System. London, The Hague, Boston: Kluwer Law, 1997.
Petersmann 1997a: Petersmann, Ernst-Ulrich. Darf die EG das Völkerrecht ignorieren. In: EuZW, Heft 11, 1997. S. 325-331.
Petersmann 1997b: Petersmann, Ernst-Ulrich (ed.). International Trade Law and the GATT/WTO Dispute Settlement System. London, The Hague, Boston: Kluwer Law, 1997.
Petersmann 1997c: Petersmann, Ernst-Ulrich (ed.). International Trade Law and the GATT/WTO Dispute Settlement System 1948-1996: An Introduction. In: Petersmann, Ernst-Ulrich (ed.). International Trade Law and the GATT/WTO Dispute Settlement System. London, The Hague, Boston: Kluwer Law, 1997.
Petersmann 2001: Petersmann, Ernst-Ulrich. Time for Integrating Human Rights into the Law of Worldwide Organizations. Lessons from European Integration Law for Global Integration Law. Jean Monnet Working Paper 7/2001. In: http://www.jeanmonnetprogram.org/papers/index.html
Petersmann 2003: Petersmann, Ernst-Ulrich. Theories of Justice, Human Rights and the Constitution of International Markets. European University Institute, Florence, EUI Working Paper LAW No. 2003/17. In: http://hdl.handle.net/1814/1880.
Petersmann 2003a: Petersmann, Ernst-Ulrich. Human rights and liberalization of markets: the social responsibility of international organisations to make market competition and social rights mutually consistent. In: Council of Europe. The state and new social responsibilities in a globalising world. Trends in social cohesion, No. 6. Strasbourg: Council of Europe, June 2003. In: http://www.coe.int/T/E/social_cohesion/social_policies/
Petersmann 2003b: Petersmann, Ernst-Ulrich. Constitutional Economics, Human rights and the Future of the WTO. In: Aussenwirtschaft, 58 Jg., Heft 1, 2003. S. 49-91.
Petersmann 2003c: Petersmann, Ernst-Ulrich. Limits of WTO Jurisprudence: Comments from and International Law and Human Rights Perspective. In: Cottier, Thomas, Mavroidis, Petros C (eds.). The Role of the Judge in International Trade Regulation. Ann Arbor: University of Michigan Press, 2003.
Petersmann 2004: Petersmann, Ernst-Ulrich. The Doha Development Round Negotiations on Improvements and Clarification of the Dispute Settlement Understanding 2001-2003: An Overview. In: Ortino, Federico, Petersmann, Ernst-Ulrich (eds.). The WTO Dispute Settlement System 1995 - 2003. The Hague et al.: Kluwer Law International, 2004.
Petersmann 2004a: Petersmann, Ernst-Ulrich. Additional Negotiation Proposals on Improvements and Clarifications for the DSU. In: Ortino, Federico, Petersmann, Ernst-Ulrich (eds.). The WTO Dispute Settlement System 1995 - 2003. The Hague et al.: Kluwer Law International, 2004.
Petersmann 2005: Petersmann, Ernst-Ulrich (ed.). Reforming the World Trading System. Legitimacy, Efficiency, and Democratic Governance. Oxford: Oxford University Press, 2005.
Petersmann 2005a: Petersmann, Ernst-Ulrich. WTO Negotiatiors and Academics Analyse the Doha Development Round of the WTO: Overview and Summary of the Book. In: Petersmann, Ernst-Ulrich (ed.). Reforming the World Trading System. Legitimacy, Efficiency, and Democratic Governance. Oxford: Oxford University Press, 2005.
Petersmann 2005b: Petersmann, Ernst-Ulrich. Strategic Use of WTO Dispute Settlement Proceedings for Advancing WTO Negotiations on Agriculture. In: Petersmann, Ernst-Ulrich (ed.). Reforming the World Trading System. Legitimacy, Efficiency, and Democratic Governance. Oxford: Oxford University Press, 2005.
Petersmann 2005c: Petersmann, Ernst-Ulrich. The 'Human Rights Approach' Advocated by the UN High Commissioner for Human Rights and by the International Labor Organization: Is it relevant for WTO Law and Policy? In: Petersmann, Ernst-Ulrich (ed.). Reforming the World Trading System. Legitimacy, Efficiency, and Democratic Governance. Oxford: Oxford University Press, 2005.
Pfetsch 1994: Pfetsch, Frank R. Internationale Politik. Stuttgart; Berlin; Köln: Kohlhammer, 1994.
Phelps 2004: Phelps, David H. US Steel Trade Policy, the US Steel Industry, and the Importance of Free Trade for Economic Growth. Speech, February 2004. In: http://www.aiis.org/speeches/speech93.htm.
Piazolo 1994: Piazolo, Marc. Bestimmungsfaktoren des wirtschaftlichen Wachstums von Entwicklungsländern. Berlin: Duncker & Humblot, 1994.
Pieper 2000: Pieper, Ute. Deindustrialization and the Social and Economic Sustainability Nexus in Developing Countries: Cross-Country Evidence on Productivity and Employment. In: Journal of Development Studies, Vol. 36, No. 4, April 2000. S. 66-99.
Pieper/Taylor 1998: Pieper, Ute, Taylor, Lance. The Revival of the Liberal Creed: The IMF, the World Bank, and the Inequality in a Globalized Economy. Center for Economic Policy Analysis, Working Paper Series, No. 4, January 1998. In: http://www.newschool.edu/cepa.
Pierce 2000: Pierce, Richard J. Antidumping Law as a Means of Facilitating Cartelization. In: Antitrust Law Journal. Vol. 67, 2000. pp. 725-745.
Piermartini/Teh 2005: Piermartini, Roberta, Teh, Robert. Demystifying Modelling Methods for Trade Policy. Discussion Paper No. 10. Geneva: World Trade Organization, 2005. In: http://www.wto.org.
Pies 1996: Pies, Ingo. Theoretische Grundlagen demokratischer Wirtschafts- und Gesellschaftspolitik – Der Beitrag James Buchanans. In: Pies, Ingo, Leschke, Martin (Hrg.). James Buchanans konstitutionelle Ökonomik. Tübingen: Mohr, 1996.
Pies 1998: Pies, Ingo. Theoretische Grundlagen einer Konzeption der 'sozialen Marktwirtschaft': Normative Institutionenökonomik als Renaissance der klassischen Ordnungstheorie. In: Cassel, Dieter (Hrg.). 50 Jahre Soziale Marktwirtschaft. Schriften zu Ordnungfragen der Wirtschaft, Band 57, Stuttgart, Lucius&Lucius: 1998.

Pietrobelli 1994: Pietrobelli, Carlo. Technological Capabilities at the National Level: An International Comparison of Manufacturing Export Performance. In: Development Policy Review Vol. 12, 1994, S. 115-148.
Pilat 1996: Pilat, Dirk. Competition, Productivity and Efficiency. OECD Economic Studies No. 27 Vol. II. Paris: OECD, 1996. In: http://www.oecd.org.
Pincus 1975: Pincus, J. J. Pressure Groups and the Pattern of Tariffs. In: Journal of Political Economy, Vo. 83, No. 4, 1975. S. 757-778.
Pindyck/Solimano 1993: Pindyck, Robert S., Solimano, Andrés. Economic Instabilty and Aggregate Investment. NBER Macroeconomics Annual 1993. S. 259-317.
Pineres/Ferrantino 1997: Pineres, Sheila Amin Gutierrez de, Ferrantino, Michael. Export diversification and structural dynamics in the growth process: The case of Chile. In: Journal of Development Economics, Vol. 52, 1997. S. 375-391.
Pinheiro/Giambiagi 1994: Pinheiro, Armando Castelar, Giambiagi, Fabio. In: World Development, Vol. 22, No. 5, 1994. S. 737-753.
Pinheiro/Moreira 2000: Pinheiro, Armando Castelar, Moreira, Mauricio Mesquita. The Profile of Brazil's Manufacturing Exporters in the Nineties. Banco Nacional de Desenvolvimento Econômico e Social (BNDES), Textos para Discussao 80, June, 2000. In: http://www.bndes.gov.br/english/studies.asp.
Pinstrup-Andersen 1988: Pinstrup-Andersen, Per. The Social and Economic Effects of Consumer-Oriented Food Subsidies: A Summary of Current Evidence. In: Pinstrup-Andersen, Per (ed.) Food Subsidies in Developing Countries. Baltimore, London: John Hopkins University Press, 1988.
Pitcher 1996: Pitcher, M. Anne. Recreating Colonialism or Reconstructing the State? Privatization and Politics in Mozambique. In: Journal of Southern African Studies, Vol. 22 No. 1, March 1996. S. 49-74.
Pitcher 1998: Pitcher, M. Anne. Disruption Without Transformation: Agrarian Relations and Livelihoods in Nampula Province, Mozambique 1975-1995. In: Journal of Southern African Studies, Vol. 24 No. 1, March 1998. S. 115-140.
Pitt 1991: Pitt, Mark M. Indonesia. In: The Experience of Indonesia, Pakistan, and Sri Lanka. Oxford: World Bank/Blackwell, 1991. Szirmai, Adam, van Ark, Bart, Pilat, Dirk (eds.). Explaining Economic Growth. Essays in Honour of Angus Maddison. Amsterdam: North Holland, 1993.
Pohl 1989: Pohl, Hans. Aufbruch der Weltwirtschaft. Stuttgart: Franz Steiner Verlag, 1989.
Poire/Ruiz Durán 1998: Piore, Michael, Ruiz Durán, Clemente. Industrial Development as a Learning Process: Mexican Manufacturing and the Opening to Trade. In: Kagami, Mitsuhiro, Humphrey, John, Piore, Michael (eds.). Learning, Liberalization and Economic Adjustment. Tokyo: Institute of Developing Economics, 1998.
Poirson 2000: Poirson, Helene. Factor Reallocation and Growth in Developing Countries. IMF Working Paper, WP/00/94, In: http://www.imf.org.
Polak 1991: Polak, Jacques. The Changing Nature of IMF Conditionality. OECD/GD(91)152, Technical Papers No. 41. Paris: OECD, 1991.
Polak 1997: Polak, Jaques. The IMF Monetary Model. In: Finance and Development, December 1997. Washington: IMF, 1997. In: http://www.imf.org.
Pöland 2005: Pöland, Jens. Free Trade vs. Protectionism: What Impact did Section 201 Steel Safeguard Measures have on the US & Global Steel Markets, and What Lessons can be Learned. In: Legal Issues of Economic Integration Vol. 32, No. 3, 2005. S. 235-247.
Polanyi 1995: Polanyi, Karl. The Great Transformation. Frankfurt am Main: Surkamp, 1995.
Pomerleano 1998: Pomerleano, Michael. The East Asia Crisis and Corporate Finances. World Bank, Policy Research Working Paper, No. 1990, October 1998. In: http://www.worldbank.org.
Pomerleano et al. 2005: Pomerleano, Michael, Shaw, William. World Bank. Corporate Restructuring. Lessons of Experience. Washington, D.C., World Bank, 2005.
Pomfret 1988: Pomfret, Richard. World Steel Trade at Crossroads. In: JWTL, Vol. 22, No. 1, 1988. S. 81-89.
Porges/Trachtman 2003: Porges, Amelia, Trachtman, Joel P. Robert Hudec and Domestic Regulation: The Resurrection of Aim and Effects. In: JWT, Vol. 37, No. 4, 2003. S. 783-799.
Porter 1993: Porter, Michael E. Nationale Wettbewerbsvorteile. Wien: Ueberreuter, 1993.
Porter 2001: Porter, Roger B. Efficiency, Equity, and Legitimacy: The Global Trading System in the Twenty-First Century. In: Porter, Roger B., Sauvé, Pierre, Subramanian, Arvind, Zampetti, Americo Beviglia. Efficiency, Equity, Legitimacy. The Multilateral Trading System at the Millenium. Washington D.C.: Brookings Institution Press, 2001.
Porter Liebeskind et al. 1996: Porter Liebeskind, Julia, Opler, Tim C, Hatfield, Donald E. Corporate Restructuring and the Consolidation of U.S. Industry. In: Journal of Industrial Economics, Vol. XLIV, No. 2, March 1996. S. 53-68.
Porter/van Opstal 2001: Porter, Michael E., van Opstal, Debra. U.S. Competitiveness 2001: Strengths, Vulnerablities and Long-Term Priorities. Council on Competitiveness, January 2001. In: http://www.compete.org.
POSCO Informationen 2006: POSCO. POSCO India Project. 2006. In: http://www.posco-india.com/india/app/india/project.htm.
Posner 1975: Posner, Richard A. The Social costs of Monopoly and Regulation. In: Journal of Political Economy Vol 83, No. 4, 1975. S. 807-827.
Posner 1979: Posner, Richard A. The Chicago School of Antitrust Analysis. In: University of Pennsylvania Law Review, Vol. 127, 1979. S. 925-948.
Potratz/Widmaier 1996: Potratz, Wolfgang, Widmaier, Brigitta. Industrie und Innovation in Europa: Verlust von Wettbewerbsfähigkeit durch Spezialisierung? In: WSI-Mitteilungen, 49 Jg. Januar 1996. S. 1-10.

Poulton et al. 1998: Poulton, Colin, Dorward, Andrew, Kydd, Jonathan. The Revival of Smallholder Cash Crops in Africa: Public and Private Roles in the Provision of Finance. In: Journal of International Development, Vol. 10 No. 1, 1998. S. 85-103.
PPI Fact Letter 2005: Progressive Policy Institute. Tariffs on Cars are 2.5 Percent, But on Pickup Trucks 25 Percent. May, 11, 2005. In: In: http://www.ppionline.org.
Prais 1986: Prais, S. J. Some International Comparisons of the Age of Capital Stock. In: Journal of Industrial Economics, Vol. XXXIV, No. 3, March 1986. S. 261-277.
Prall 1998: Prall, Ursula. Saatgut und internationale Vorgaben des gewerblichen Rechtsschutzes. In: Saatgut. BUKO Agrar Dossier 20. Stuttgart: Schmetterling Verlag,1998.
Pratten 1988: Pratten, Cliff. A Survey of the Economies of Scale. Economic Papers. No. 67, II/290/88-EN. Directorate-General for Economic and Financial Affairs. Brussels: Commission of the European Communities, October 1988.
Prebisch 1950: Prebisch, Raúl. The Economic Development of Latin America and its Principal Problems. In: United Nations. Economic Bulletin for Latin America, Published by the Secretariat of the Economic Commission for Latin America. United Nations Document E/CN.12/89. Vol. VII, No. 1, February 1962 (printed as mimeo May 1950). S. 1-22.
Prebisch 1959: Prebisch, Raúl. Commercial Policy in the Underdeveloped Countries. In: American Economic Review, Vol 49, 1959. S. 251-273.
Prebisch 1984: Prebisch, Raúl. Five Stages in My Thinking on Development. In: Meier, Gerald M., Seers, Dudley. Pioneers in Development. Oxford: Oxford University Press, 1984.
Preeg 1970: Preeg, Ernest H. Traders and Diplomats. Washington: Brookings Institution, 1970.
Preeg 1995: Preeg, Ernest H. Traders in a Brave New World. The Uruguay Round and the Future of the International Trading System. Chicago, London: University of Chicago Press, 1995.
Press Release Shelby 2004: Press Release, U.S. Senator Richard C. Shelby. Shelby helps to protect Alabama sock producers. November 19, 2004. In: http://shelby.senate.gov.
Preuße 2000: Preuße, Heinz Gert. Sechs Jahre Nordamerikanisches Freihandelsabkommen (NAFTA). Wirtschaftswissenschaftliches Seminar, Tübinger Diskusssionbeitrag Nr. 183, März 2000. In: http://www.uni-tuebingen.de.
Prévost 2000: Prévost, Denise. WTO Subsidies Agreement and Privatized Companies. In: Legal Issues of Economic Integration, Vol. 27 No. 3, 2000. S. 279-294.
Prévost/Matthee 2002: Prévost, Denise, Matthee, Marielle. The SPS Agreement as a Bottleneck in Agricultural Trade betweeen the European Union and Developing Countries: How to Solve the Conflict. In: Legal Issues of Economic Integration, Vol. 29 No. 1, 2002. S. 43-59.
Primary Commodities, 1900-1982: The Controversy and Its Origins. In: Economic Development and Cultural Change, 1991. S. 231-251.
Primo Braga 1995: Primo Braga, Carlos A. Trade-Related Intellectual Property Issues: The Uruguay Round Agreements and Its Economic Implications. In: Martin, Will, Winters, L. Alan (eds.). The Uruguay Round and the Developing Countries. World Bank Discussion Patpers 307, Washington: World Bank, 1995.
Primo Braga/Davi Siber 1993: Primo Braga, Carlos Alberto, Davi Silber, Simao. Brazilian Frozen Concentrated Orange Juice: The Folly of Unfair Trade Cases. In: Finger, J. Michael. Antidumping. How It Works and Who Gets Hurt. Ann Arbor: University of Michigan Press, 1993.
Pritchett 1996: Pritchett, Lant. Measuring outward orientation in LDCs: Can it be done? In: Journal of Development Economics, Vol. 49, 1996, pp. 307-335.
Prusa 1996: Prusa, Thomas J. The Trade Effects of U.S. Antidumping Actions. NBER Working Paper No. 5440, January 2996.
Prusa 1997: Prusa, Thomas J. The Trade Effects of U.S. Antidumping Actions. In: Feenstra, Robert C. (ed.). The Effects of U.S. Trade Protection and Promotion Policies. Chicago, London: University of Chicago Press, 1997.
Prusa 1999: Prusa, Thomas J. On the Spread and Impact of Antidumping. NBER Working Paper, No. 7404. October 1999.
Prusa 2001: Prusa, Thomas J. On the Spread and Impact of Antidumping. Canadian Journal of Economics, Vol. 24 No. 3, August 2001. S. 591-611.
Prusa/Skeath 2001: Prusa, Thomas J., Skeath, Susan. The Economic and Strategic Motives for Antidumping Filings. NBER Working Paper No. 8424, August 2001.
Przyblyla/Roma 2005: Pryzyblyla, Marcin, Roma, Moreno. Does Product Market Competition Reduce Inflation. European Central Bank Working Paper No. 453, March 2005. In: http://www.ecb.int/pub/pdf/scpwps/ecbwp453.pdf.
Psacharopoulos 1994: Psacharopoulos, George. Returns to Investment in Education: A Global Update. In: World Development, Vol. 22, No. 9, 1994. S. 1325-1343.
PSIA Mongolia 2003: World Bank. Analysis of Mongolia's Cashmere Sector. 2003. In: http://www.worldbank.org/psia.
Pugel 1980: Pugel, Thomas A. Foreign Trade and US Market Performance. In: Journal of Industrial Economics, Vol. XXIX, No. 2, December 1980. S. 119-129.
Puri 2005: Puri, Lakshmi. Towards a New Trade 'Marshall Plan' for Least Developed Countries. UNCTAD/DITC/TAB/POV/2005/1, United Nations: New York and Geneva, 2005. In: http://www.unctad.org.

Pursell/Gupta 1998: Pursell, Garry, Gupta, Anju. Trade Policy and Incentives in Indian Agriculture. Methodology, Background Statistics and Protection and Incentive Indicators, 1965-95. World Bank Policy Research Working Paper No. 1953, August 1998. In: http://www.worldbank.org.
Putterman 1995: Putterman, Louis. Economic Reform and Smallholder Agriculture in Tanzania: A Discussion of Recent Market Liberalization, Road Rehabilitation, and Technology Dissemination Efforts. In: World Development, Vol. 23, No. 2, 1995. S. 311-326.
Puzier 1987: Puzier, Eckard. Die Ermächtigungen des Außenwirtschaftsgesetzes. Stuttgart: Schäffer Verlag, 1987.

Q

Qureshi 2003: Qureshi, Asif H. Interpreting World Trade Organization Agreements for the Development Objective. In: JWT, Vol. 37, No. 5, 2003. S. 847-882.
Qureshi 2003a: Qureshi, Asif H. Interpreting World Trade Organization Agreements for the Development Objective. In: Shaffer, Gregory, Mosoti, Victor, Qureshi, Asif. Towards a development-supportive dispute settlement system in the WTO. ICTSD Resource Paper No. 5, March 2003. In: http://www.ictsd.org.
Qureshi 2004: Qureshi, Asif H. Participation of Developing Countries in the WTO Dispute Settlement System. In: Ortino, Federico, Petersmann, Ernst-Ulrich (eds.). The WTO Dispute Settlement System 1995 - 2003. The Hague et al.: Kluwer Law International, 2004.

R

Raaflaub 1994: Raaflaub, Patrick. Subventionsregeln der EU und des GATT. Chur; Zürich: Verlag Rüegger, 1994.
Radice 1995: Radice, Hugo. Großbritannien in der Weltwirtschaft: Niedergang der Nation, Erfolg des Kapitalismus? In: PROKLA, Zeitschrift für kritische Sozialwissenschaft, Heft 101, Jg. 25, Nr. 4, S. 565-585.
Raghavan 1990: Raghavan, Chakravarthi. Recolonization. GATT, the Uruguay Round & the Third World. Penang, Malaysia: Third World Network, 1990.
Raghavan 2000: Raghavan, Chakravarthi. Recolonization. BOP, as special and differential right in the WTO without substance? Malaysia: Third World Network, 2000. In: http://www.twnside.org.sg.
Rahman 1994: Rahman, Sultan Hafeez. Trade and Industrialization in Bangladesh. An assessment. In: Helleiner, Gerald K. (ed.). Trade Policy and Industrialization in Turbulent Times. London; New York: Routledge, 1994.
Raikes 1997: Raikes, Philip. Structural Adjustment and agriculture in Africa. In: Spoor, Max (ed.). The 'Market Panacea'. Agrarian transformation in developing countries and former transition economies. London: Intermediate Technology Publications, 1997.
Raiser 1997: Raiser, Martin. Soft Budget Constraints and the Fate of Economic Reforms in Transition Economies and Developing Countries. Tübingen: Mohr, 1997.
Raiser/Nunnenkamp 1997: Raiser, Martin, Nunnenkamp, Peter. Die andere Seite Chinas. Strukturprobleme, Reformdefizite und verzögerte Aufholprozesse im chinesischen Binnenland. Kiel Working Paper No. 794, February 1997. Kiel: Institut für Weltwirtschaft, 1997.
Rajapatirana 1995: Rajapatirana, Sarath. Post Liberalization Policy and Institutional Challenges in Latin America and the Caribbean. World Bank, Policy Research Working Paper, No. 1465, May 1995.
Ram 1986: Ram, Rati. Government Size and Economic Growth: A New Framework and Some Evidence form Cross-Section and Times-Series Data. In: The American Economic Review, , Vol. 76, No. 1, March 1986, S. 191-203.
Rama 2003: Rama, Martin. Globalization and Workers in Developing Countries. World Bank Policy Research Working Paper No. 2958, January 2003. In: http://www.worldbank.org.
Ramos 1997: Ramos, Joseph. Neo-liberal structural reforms in Latin America: The current situation. In: CEPAL Review 62, August 1997. S. 15-39.
Ramser 1992: Ramser, Hans Jürgen. Grundlagen der 'neuen' Wachstumstheorie. Diskussionsbeiträge Nr. 261, Fakultät für Wirtschaftswissenschaften und Statistik, Universität Konstanz, September 1992.
Rangnekar 2005: Rangnekar, Dwijen. No Pills for Poor People? Understanding the Disembowelment of India's Patent Regime. University of Warwick, CSGR Working Paper Series No. 176/05, October 2005. In: http://www2.warwick.ac.uk.
Rankin 2002: Rankin, Niel. The Export Behavior of South African Manufacturing Firms. TIPS Working Paper 5, 2002. In: http://www.tips.org.za/research/papers/.
Rankin et al. 2000: Rankin, Niel, Söderbom, Mans, Teal, Francis. The Ghanaian Manufacturing Enterprise Survey 2000. University of Oxford: Centre for the Study of African Economies, November 2002. In: http://www.csae.ox.ac.uk.
Rankin et al. 2002: Rankin, Niel, Harding, Alan, Kahyarara, Godius. Firm Growth, Productivity and Earnings in Tanzanian Manufacturing 1992-1999. University of Oxford: Centre for the Study of African Economies, November 2002. In: http://www.csae.ox.ac.uk.
Rao 1986: Rao, J. Mohan. Agriculture in Recent Development Theory. In: Journal of Development Economics Vol. 22, 1986. S. 41-86.
Rao/Sastry 1989: Rao, Krishna P. V., Sastry, K. P. Restrictive Trade Practices Policy in India. In: Journal of Industrial Economics, Vol. XXXVII, No. 4, June 1989. S. 427-435.

Rashid 1995: Rashid, Aneesa Ismail. Trade, Growth, and Liberalization. The Indian Experience 1977-1989. In: The Journal of Developing Areas, 29, April 1995, pp. 355-370.
Rath 1990: Rath, Amitav. Science, Technology, and Policy in the Periphery: A Perspective from the Centre. In: World Development, Vol. 18, No. 11, 1990. S. 1429-1443.
Raut 1995: Raut, Lakshmi K. R & D spillover and productivity growth: Evidence from Indian private firms. In: Journal of Development Economics, Vol. 48, 1995. S. 1-23.
Ravallion 2004: Ravallion, Martin. Looking Beyond Averages in the Trade and Poverty Debate. World Bank, Policy Research Working Paper, No. 3461, November 2004. In: http://www.worldbank.org.
Ravenscraft 1983: Ravenscraft, David J. Structure-Profit Relationsships at the Line of Business and Industry Level. In: Review of Economics and Statistics, Vol. 65, 1983. S. 22-31.
Ravenscraft/Scherer 1987: Ravenscraft, David J., Scherer, F.M. Life after Takeover. In: Journal of Industrial Economics, Vol. 36 No. 2, December 1987. S. 147-156.
Rawls 1994: Rawls, John. Eine Theorie der Gerechtigkeit. Frankfurt: Surkamp, 1994.
Raynolds 1994: Raynolds, Laura T. Institutionalizing Flexibility: A Comparative Analysis of Fordist and Post-Fordist Models of Third World Argo-Export Production. In: Gereffi, Gary, Korzeniewicz, Miguel (eds.). Commodity Chains and Global Capitalism. Westport, Connecticut; London: Praeger 1994.
Reagan 1981: Reagan, Ronald. Remarks at a Luncheon of the World Affairs Council of Philadelphia in Philadelphia, Pennsylvania, October 15, 1981. In: http://www.reagan.utexas.edu/.
Reardon 1993: Reardon, Thomas. Cereals Demand in the Sahel und Potential Impacts of Regional Cereals Protection. In: World Development, Vol. 21 No.1, 1993. S. 17-35.
Rebelo 1991: Rebelo, Sergio. Long-Run Policy Analysis and Long-Run Growth. In: Journal of Political Economy, Vol. 99, No. 3, 1991, S. 500-521.
Reblin 1993: Reblin, Jörg. Das GATT und der Weltagrarhandel. Hamburg: Kovac, 1993.
Redding/Tam 1995: Redding, S. Gordon, Tam, Simon. Colonialism and Entrepreneurship in Africa and Hong Kong: A Comparative Perspective. In: Stein, Howard (Hrg.). Asian Industrialization and Africa. Studies in Policy Alternatives to Structural Adjustment. London: St. Martin's Press, 1995.
Reddy 1997: Reddy, Prasada. New Trends in Globalization of Corporate R&D and Implications for Innovation Capability in Host Countries: A Survey from India. In: World Development, Vol. 25 No. 11, 1997. S. 1821-1837.
Regan 2003: Regan, Donald H. Further Thoughts on the Role of Regulatory Purpose Under Article III of the General Agreement on Tariffs and Trade. In: JWT, Vol. 37, No. 4, 2003. S. 737-760.
Regan 2003a: Regan, Donald H. The Dormant Commerce Clause and the Hormones Problem. In: Cottier, Thomas, Mavroidis, Petros C (eds.). The Role of the Judge in International Trade Regulation. Ann Arbor: University of Michigan Press, 2003.
Regini 1997: Regini, Marino. Social Institutions and Production Structure: The Italian Variety of Capitalism in the 1980s. In: Crouch, Colin, Streeck, Wolfgang. Political Economy of Modern Capitalism. London: Sage, 1997.
Regmi 2001: Regmi, Anita. Changing Structure of Global Food Consumption and Trade: An Introduction. In: Regmi, Anita. Changing Structure of Global Food Consumption and Trade. WRS-01-1. U.S. Department of Agriculture. May, 2001. In: http://www.
Reichert 1999: Reichert, Tobias. Das Agrarabkommen der WTO und seine Auswirkungen auf die Ernährungssouveränität. In: Agrarbündnis (Hrg.). Der Kritische Agrarbericht. Kassel; Rheda-Wiedenbrück: ABL Bauernblatt Verlag, 1999.
Reina/Zuluaga 2005: Reina, Mauricio, Zuluaga, Sandra. Application of Safeguards and Anti-Dumping Duties in Columbia. World Bank Policy Research Working Paper 3608, May 2005. In: http://www.worldbank.org.
Reiser 1995: Reiser, Fritz. Futtermittel und Agrarreform. In: BUKO Agrarkoordination (Hrg.). Futtermittelimporte. Hamburg: BUKO, 1995.
Reitz 1996: Reitz, Curtiz. Enforcement of the General Agreement on Tariffs and Trade. In: University of Pennsylvania Journal of International Economic Law, Vol. 17, No. 2, Summer 1996. S. 555-603.
Rensman/Kuper 1999: Rensman, Marieke, Kuper, Gerard H. Do Technology Spillovers Matter for Growth? In: CCSO Quarterly Journal, Vol. 1, No. 3, Sept. 1999. In: http://www.eco.rug.nl/ccso/quarterly/qarchive.html.
Resnick 1975: Resnick, Stephen A. State of Development Economics. In: American Economic Review, Papers and Proceedings, Vol. 65, No. 2, 1975. S. 317-322.
Rettberg 1983: Rettberg, Jürgen. Weltwährungsfond mit Weltbankgruppe und UNCTAD als Bezugspunkte der internationalen Handels- und Entwicklungspolitik. Köln; Berlin; Bonn; München: Heymanns Verlag, 1983.
Reus-Smit 1997: Reus-Smit, Christian. The Constitutional Structure of International Society and the Nature of Fundamental Institutions. In: IO, 51, 4, Autumn 1997. S. 555-589.
Reuter 1975: Reuter, Dieter. Die Arbeitskampffreiheit in der Verfassungs- und Rechtsordnung der BRD. In: Sauermann, Heinz, Mestmäcker, Ernst-Joachim (Hrg.). Wirtschaftsordnung und Staatsverfassung. FS Franz Böhm. Tübingen: Mohr, 1975.
Reuter 1997: Reuter, Dieter. Die Praxis des Arbeitsrechts – eine Achillesferse der Sozialen Marktwirtschaft. In: ORDO, Bd. 48, 1997.
Revenga 1992: Revenga, Ana L. Exporting Jobs? In: Quarterly Journal of Economics, Vol. 107, Feb. 1992. S. 255-283.
Reynolds 2005: Reynolds, Kara M. Dumping on U.S. Farmers. Are there biases in global antidumping regulations? American University Working Paper, October 20, 2005. In: http://nw08.american.edu/~reynolds/.
Rhodes 1993: Rhodes, Carolyn. Reciprocity, U.S. Trade Policy, and the GATT Regime. Itaca; London: Cornell University Press, 1993.

Ricardo 1817: Ricardo, David. The Principles of Political Economy and Taxation. London: Dent&Sons Ltd., 1911.
Richardson 1960: Richardson, G.B. Information and Investment. A Study in the Working of the Competitive Economy. Oxford: Clarendon Press, (Original 1960) 1990.
Richter 1994: Richter, Reiner. Die philippinische Bekleidungsindustrie. Entwicklungspolitische Wirkungen der exportorientierten Industriealisierung. Hamburg: Institut für Asienkunde, 1994.
Riddell 1990: Riddell, Roger C. (ed.). Manufacturing Africa. Performance & Prospects of Seven Countries in Sub-Saharan Africa. Overseas Development Institute. London: James Currey, 1990.
Riddell 1990a: Riddell, Roger C. Cote d'Ivoire. In: Riddell, Roger C. (ed.). Manufacturing Africa. Performance & Prospects of Seven Countries in Sub-Saharan Africa. Overseas Development Institute. London: James Currey, 1990.
Ridler 1988: Ridler, Niel B. The Caisse de Stabilisation in the Coffee Sector of the Ivory Coast. In: World Development, Vol. 16 No. 12, 1988. S. 1521-1526.
Rieble 2000: Rieble, Volker. Walter Euken und die Frage nach der Arbeitsmarktordnung. In: Külp, Bernhard, Vanberg, Victor (Hrg.). Freiheit und wettbewerbliche Ordnung. Gedenkband zur Erinnerung an Walter Euken. Freiburg, Berlin, München: Haufe Verlag, 2000.
Riedel 1975: Riedel, James. Wirtschaftspolitik und Exportentwicklung in Taiwan. In: Die Weltwirtschaft, Heft 1, 1975. S. 100-114.
Riedel 1977: Riedel, James. Tariff Concessions in the Kennedy Round and the Structure of Protection in West Germany. In: Journal of International Economics Vol. 7, 1977. S. 133-143.
Riedel 1984: Riedel, James. Trade as Engine of Growth in Developing Countries Revisited. In: Economic Journal, Vol. 94, March 1984. S. 56-73.
Rijnsburger/Wijers 1995: Rijnsburger, W., Wijers, K.H. The Impact of the GATT-Uruguay Round on agriculture in the Asia-Pacific region. Part 4 Taiwan, Japan, South Korea. Rabobank Nederland, Agribusiness Research, 1995. Erhältlich in der Bibiothek des Instituts für Agrarökonomie, Universität Göttingen.
Rill/Goldman 1997: Rill, James F., Goldman, Calvin S. Confidentiality in the Era of Increased Cooperation between Antitrust Authorities. In: Waverman, Leonard, Comanor, William S., Goto, Akira (Hrg.). Competition Policy in the Global Economy. Routledge: London and New York, 1997.
Risse-Kappen 1995: Risse-Kappen, Thomas. Structures of Governance and Transnational Relations: what have we learned? In: Risse-Kappen, Thomas (ed.). Bringing transnational relations back in. Cambridge: Cambridge University Press, 1995.
Rittberger 1995: Rittberger, Volker. Internationale Organisationen. Politik und Geschichte. Opladen: Leske und Budrich, 1995.
Rittberger et al. 1997: Rittberger, Volker, Hasenclever, Andreas, Mayer, Peter. Theories of international Regimes. Cambridge: Cambridge University Press, 1997.
Rittberger/Hummel 1990: Rittberger, Volker, Hummel, Hartwig. Die Disziplin 'Internationale Beziehungen' im deutschsprachigen Raum auf der Suche nach ihrer Identität. Entwicklung und Perspektiven. In: PVS, 31. Jg., Sonderheft 21, 1990. S. 17-47.
Ritter 1979: Ritter, Ernst-Hasso. Der kooperative Staat. In: Archiv des öffentlichen Rechts. Bd. 104, 1979. S. 389-413.
Roberts 2005: Roberts, I. WTO Agreement on Agriculture: The Blue Box in the July 2004 Framework Agreement. ABARE eReport 054. Canberra: Australian Bureau of Agricultural and Resource Economics, March 2005. In: http://www.abareonlineshop.com.
Roberts/Thoburn 2002: Roberts, Simon, Thoburn, John. Globalization and the South African Textiles Industry. Discussion Paper 9. GAP Projekt. In: http://www.gapresearch.org/production/globprodpov.html.
Roberts/Unnevehr 2005: Roberts, Donna, Unnevehr, Laurian. Resolving trade disputes arising from trends in food safety regulation: the role of the multilateral governance framework. In: World Trade Review Vol. 4 No. 3, 2005. S. 469-497.
Rock 1995: Rock, Michael T. Thai Industrial Policy: How irrelevant was it to export success. In: Journal of International Development, Vol. 7, No. 5, 1995. S.745-757.
Rock 1999: Rock, Michael T. Reassessing the Effectiveness of Industrial Policy in Indonesia: Can the Neoliberals be Wrong? World Development Vol. 27, No. 4, 1999. S. 691-704.
Rodino 1994: Rodino, JR., Peter W. The future of antitrust: ideology vs. legislative intent. In: Kovaleff, Theodore P. The Antitrust Impulse. Vol. 2. New York, London: M.E. Sharpe, 1994.
Rodrik 1988: Rodrik, Dani. Imperfect Competition, Scale Economies, and Trade Policy in Developing Countries. In: Baldwin, Robert E. Trade Policy Issues and Empirical Analysis. Chicago; London: University of Chicago Press, 1988.
Rodrik 1990: Rodrik, Dani. How Should Structural Adjustment Programs be Designed? In: World Development, Vol. 18, No. 7, pp. 933-947.
Rodrik 1992: Rodrik, Dani. Closing the Productivity Gap: Does Trade Liberalization Really Help?. In: Helleiner. G. (ed.) Trade Policy, Industrialization, and Development. New York: Oxford University Press, 1992.
Rodrik 1994: Rodrik, Dani. King Kong meets Godzilla: The World Bank und The East Asian Miracle. Discussion Paper, No. 944. Centre for Economic Policy Research, London, April 1994.
Rodrik 1994a: Rodrik, Dani. Industrial Organization and Product Quality: Evidence from South Korean and Taiwanese Exports. In: Krugman, Paul R. Empirical Studies of Strategic Trade Policy. NBER Project Report. Chicago: Univ. of Chicago Press, 1994.

Rodrik 1995: Rodrik, Dani. Trade and Industrial Policy Reform. In: Behrman, J. Srinivasan, T.N. (eds.) Handbook of Development Economics, Vol. III, Amsterdam; New York: Elsevier Science B.V., 1995.
Rodrik 1996: Rodrik, Dani. Coordination Failures and Government Policy: A model with applications to East Asia and Eastern Europe. In: Journal of Development Economics, Vol. 40, 1996. S. 1-22.
Rodrik 1997: Rodrik, Dani. Has Globalization Gone Too Far? In: California Management Review, Vol. 39, No. 3, Spring 1997. S. 29-53.
Rodrik 1997a: Rodrik, Dani. TFPG Controversies, Institutions, and Economic Performance. NBER Working Paper 5914, February 1997.
Rodrik 1998: Rodrik, Dani. Why Do More Open Economies Have Bigger Governments? In: Journal of Political Economy, Vol. 106, No. 5, 1998.
Rodrik 1998a: Rodrik, Dani. Trade Policy and Economic Performance in Sub-Saharan Africa. NBER Working Paper No. 6562, May 1998.
Rodrik 2000: Rodrik, Dani. Development Strategies for the Next Century. Working Paper. Annual World Bank Conference on Development Economics. Washington: World Bank, 2000. In: http://wb.forumone.com/research/abcde/.
Rodrik 2001: Rodrik, Dani. The Global Governance of Trade. As if development really mattered. United Nations Development Programme, October 2001. In: http://www.undp.org/bdp.
Rodrik 2004: Rodrik, Dani. Industrial Policy for the Twenty First Century. September 2004. In: http://ksghome.harvard.edu/~drodrik/.
Rodrik et al. 2005: Rodrik, Dani, Birdsall, Nancy, Subramanian, Arvind. If Rich Governments Really Cared About Development. 2005. In: http://www.ictsd.org/issarea/S&DT/resources/index.htm
Rodrigues/Rodrik 1999: Rodrigues, Francisco, Rodrik, Dani. Trade Policy and Economic Growth: A Sceptic's Guide to the Cross National Evidence. NBER Working Paper 7081, 1999.
Rodrik/Subramanian 2004: Rodrik, Dani, Subramanian, Arvind. From Hindu Growth to Productivity Surge: The Mystery of the Indian Growth Transition, February 2004. In: http://ksghome.harvard.edu/~drodrik/papers.html.
Roessler 1978: Roessler, Frieder. The Rationale for Reciprocity in Trade Negotiations under Floating Currencies. In: Kyklos, Vol. 31, No. 2, 1978. S. 258-274.
Roessler 1997: Roessler, Frieder. The Concept of Nullification and Impairment in the Legal System of the World Trade Organization. In: Petersmann, Ernst-Ulrich (ed.). International Trade Law and the GATT/WTO Dispute Settlement System. London, The Hague, Boston: Kluwer Law, 1997.
Roessler 2001: Roessler, Frieder. Are the Judical Organs of the World Trade Organization Overburdened. In: Porter, Roger B., Sauvé, Pierre, Subramanian, Arvind, Zampetti, Americo Beviglia. Efficiency, Equity, Legitimacy. The Multilateral Trading System at the Millenium. Washington D.C.: Brookings Institution Press, 2001.
Roessler 2004: Roessler, Frieder. Special and Differential Treatment of Developing Countries under the WTO Dispute Settlement System. In: Ortino, Federico, Petersmann, Ernst-Ulrich (eds.). The WTO Dispute Settlement System 1995 - 2003. The Hague et al.: Kluwer Law International, 2004.
Rogers 1988: Rogers, Beatrice Lorge. Pakistan's Ration System: Distribution of Costs and Benefits. In: Pinstrup-Andersen, Per (ed.) Food Subsidies in Developing Countries. Baltimore, London: John Hopkins University Press, 1988.
Röhl 1996: Röhl, Klaus F. Die Rolle des Rechts im Prozeß der Globalisierung. In: Zeitschrift für Rechtssoziologie, Jg. 17, Heft 1, August 1996. S. 1-57.
Romer 1986: Romer, Paul M. Increasing Returns and Long Run Growth. In: Journal of Political Economy, Vol. 94, No. 5, 1986. S. 1002-1037.
Romer 1993: Romer, David. Openness and Inflation: Theory and Evidence. In: Quarterly Journal of Economics, Vol. CVIII, Issue 4, November 1993. S. 869-903.
Romer 1994: Romer, Paul M. The Origins of Endogenous Growth. In: Journal of Economic Perspectives, Vol. 8, No. 1, Winter 1994, S. 3-22.
Roningen/Yeats 1976: Roningen, Vernon, Yeats, Alexander. Nontariff Distortions of International Trade: Some Preliminary Empirical Evidence. In: Weltwirtschaftliches Archiv, Bd. 112, 1976, S. 613-625.
Ronning 1996: Ronning, Gerd. Ökonometrie. In: von Hagen, Jürgen et al. (Hrg.) Handbuch der Volkswirtschaftslehre. Berlin: Springer, 1996.
Roobeek/Broeders 1993: Roobeek, Annemarie, Broeders, Jeroen. Telecommunications: global restructuring at full speed. In: de Jong, H.W. (ed.) The Structure of European Industry. Dordrecht; Boston; London: Kluwer, 1993.
Röpke 1944: Röpke, Wilhelm. Richtpunkte des liberalen Gesamtprogramms. In: Stützel, Wolfgang et al. (Hrg.). Grundtexte zur Sozialen Marktwirtschaft. Stuttgart: Gustav Fischer Verlag, 1981.
Röpke 1950: Röpke, Wilhelm. Ist die deutsche Wirtschaftspolitik richtig? In: Stützel, Wolfgang et al. (Hrg.). Grundtexte zur Sozialen Marktwirtschaft. Stuttgart: Gustav Fischer Verlag, 1981.
Röpke 1953: Röpke, Wilhelm. Kernfragen der Wirtschaftsordnung. Neuabdruck in: ORDO, Bd. 48, 1997.
Röpke 1966: Röpke, Wilhelm. Nation und Weltwirtschaft. In: ORDO, Bd. 17, 1966. S. 37-56.
Ros 1994: Ros, Jaime. Mexico's Trade and Industrialization Experience since 1960. In: Helleiner (ed.)
Rosas 2001: Rosas, Allan. Implementation and Enforcement of WTO Dispute Settlement Findings: An EU Perspective. In: Journal of International Economic Law, 2001. S. 131-144.
Rose 1981: Rose, Klaus. Theorie der Außenwirtschaft. München: Vahlen, 1981.
Rose 1995: Rose, Klaus. Grundlagen der Wachstumstheorie. Göttingen: Vandenhoeck und Ruprecht, (1973) 1995.

Rose/Sauernheimer 1999: Rose, Klaus, Sauernheimer, Karlhans. Theorie der Außenwirtschaft. München: Vahlen, 1999.
Rosecrance 1987: Rosecrance, Richard. Der neue Handelsstaat. Frankfurt am Main: Campus, 1987.
Rosenberg 1976: Rosenberg, Nathan. Perspectives on Technology. Cambridge: Cambridge University Press, 1976.
Rosenberg 1982: Rosenberg, Nathan. Inside the Black Box. Technology and Economicy. Cambridge: Cambridge University Press, 1982.
Rosenstein-Rodan 1943: Rosenstein-Rodan, P. N. Problems of Industrialization of Eastern and South-Eastern Countries. In: Economic Journal, June-Sept. 1943, S. 202-211.
Rosenstein-Rodan 1961: Rosenstein-Rodan, P. N. Notes on the Theory of the 'Big Push'. In: Ellis, Howard S. (ed.) Economic Development for Latin America. Proceedings of a Conference held by the International Economics Association. London: Macmillan, 1961.
Rosenstein-Rodan 1984: Rosenstein-Rodan, P. T. Natura Facit Saltum: Analysis of the Disequilibrium Growth Process. In: Meier, Gerald M., Seers, Dudley. Pioneers in Development. Oxford: Oxford University Press, 1984.
Rosenstock 1995: Rosenstock, Manfred. Die Kontrolle und Harmonisierung nationaler Beihilfen durch die Kommission der Europäischen Gemeinschaften. Frankfurt am Main: Peter Lang, 1995.
Rosset 1999: Rosset, Peter M. The Multiple Functions and Benefits of Small Farm Agriculture. Food First, Policy Brief No. 4, September 1999. In: http://www.foodfirst.org.
Rossi/Toniolo 1996: Rossi, Nicola, Toniolo, Gianni. Italy. In: Crafts, Nicolas, Toniolo, Gianni (eds.). Economic Growth in Europe since 1945. Cambridge: Cambridge University Press, 1996.
Rostow 1956: Rostow, W. W. The Take-Off into Self-Sustained Growth. In: Economic Journal, Vol. LXVI, March 1956.
Rostow 1960: Rostow, W. W. The Process of Economic Growth. Oxford: Clarendon Press, 1960.
Rothbard 1973: Rothbard, Murray N. Eine neue Freiheit. Das libertäre Manifest. Berlin: S. Kopp Verlag, (1973) 1999.
Rowley/Tollison 1986: Rowley, Charles K., Tollison, Robert D. Rent-Seeking and Trade Protection. In: Aussenwirtschaft, 41. Jg, Heft 2/3, 1986. S. 303-328.
Rowthorn/Ramaswamy 1998: Rowthorn, Robert, Ramaswamy, Ramana. Growth, Trade, and Industrialization. IMF Working Paper, WP/98/60. Washington: IMF, 1998. In: http://www.imf.org.
Royall 1995: Royall, Sean. Symposion: Post-Chicago Economics. Editor's Note. In: Antitrust Law Journal, Vol. 63, 1995. S. 445-454.
Ruffert 2001: Ruffert, Matthias. Der Entscheidungsmaßstab im WTO-Streitbeilegungsverfahren - Prozessuale Relativierung materieller Verpflichtungen? In: Zeitschrift für vergleichende Rechtswissenschaft, Vol. 100, 2001. S. 304-321.
Ruffin 1984: Ruffin, Roy J. International Factor Movements. In: Jones, R.W., Kenen, P. B. (eds.). Handbook of International Economics, Vol. I. Amsterdam: Elsevier Science, 1984.
Ruggie 1975: Ruggie, John Gerard. International Responses to Technologie: Concepts and Trends. In: International Organization, Vol. 29, No. 3, Summer 1975. S. 557-583.
Ruggie 1982: Ruggie, John Gerard. International Regimes, transactions, and change: embedded liberalism in the postwar economic order. In: International Organization, 36, 2, Spring 1982.
Ruggie 1993: Ruggie, John Gerard. Territoriality and beyond: problemizing modernity in international relations. In: International Organization, Vol. 47, 1, Winter 1993.
Ruggie 1997: Ruggie, John Gerard. Globalization and the Embedded Liberalism Compromise: The End of an Era? In: MFIfG (Max Planck Institut für Gesellschaftsforschung Köln), Working Paper 97/1, January 1997. In: http://www.mpi-fg-koeln.mpg.de.
Ruggie/John Gerard 1992g: Multilateralism. the anatomy of an institution. In: IO, Vol. 46, No. 3, Summer 1992. S. 561-598.
Ruiz 1997: Ruiz, Ricardo M. The Restructuring of the Brazilian Industrial Groups between 1980 and 1993. In: CEPAL Review 61, April 1997. S. 167-185.
Rukstad 1993: Rukstad, Michael G. Construction Equipment: From Dominance to Duopoly. In: Yoffie, David B. Beyond Free Trade. Firms, Governments, and Global Competition. Boston, Mass.: Harvard Business School Press, 1993.
Rupp 1987: Rupp, Hans Heinrich. Die Unterscheidung zwischen Staat und Gesellschaft. In: Isensee, Josef, Kirchhof, Paul (Hrg.). Handbuch des Staatsrechts. Bd. I. Heidelberg: C.F. Müller, 1987
Russet 1985: Russet, Bruce. The mysterious case of vanishing hegemony; or, Is Mark Twain really dead? In: International Organization 36, Spring 1985, S. 207-231.
Ryan 2003: Ryan, P. Is China Exporting Globally, Hollowing Out Japan. Marubeni Research Institute, March 2003. In: http://www.marubeni.co.jp.
Rydelski 1998: Rydelski, Michael Sanchez. The Future of the Lome Convention and its WTO compatibility. In: EuZW, Heft 13/1998. S. 398-401.
Rydelski 1999: Rydelksi, Michael Sanchez. The WTO and EC Law on Safeguard Measures. In: EuZW, Heft 21, 1999. S. 654-659.

Sacerdoti 1997: Sacerdoti, Giorgio. Bilateral Treaties and Multilateral Instruments on Investment Protection. IN: Recueil der Cours. Collected Courses of the Hague Academy of International Law. The Hague; London; Boston: Martinus Nijhoff, 1998.

Sacerdoti 1997a: Sacerdoti, Giorgio. Appeal and Judical Review in International Arbitration and Adjudication: The Case of the WTO Appellate Review. In: Petersmann, Ernst-Ulrich (ed.). International Trade Law and the GATT/WTO Dispute Settlement System. London, The Hague, Boston: Kluwer Law, 1997.

Sachs/Shatz 1996: Sachs, Jeffrey D., Shatz, Howard J. U.S. Trade with Developing Countries and Wage Inequality. In: American Economic Review, Vol. 86 No. 2, May 1996. S. 234-239.

Sachs/Warner 1995: Sachs, Jeffrey J., Warner, Andrew. Economic Reform and the Process of Global Integration. In: Brookings Papers on Economic Activity 1: 1995. S. 1-118.

Sachs/Warner 1995a: Sachs, Jeffrey J., Warner, Andrew. Economic Convergence and Economic Policies. NBER Working Paper No. 5039, February 1995.

Sachverständigenrat 1969: Sachveständigenrat zur Begutachtung der gesamtwirtschaftlichen Entwicklung. Jahresgutachten. Bundestag, Drucksache VI/100, Bonn 1. Dezember 1969.

Sachverständigenrat 1972: Sachveständigenrat zur Begutachtung der gesamtwirtschaftlichen Entwicklung. Jahresgutachten. Bundesrat, Drucksache 612/72, Bonn 6. Dezember 1972.

Sadni-Jallab et al. 2005: Sadni-Jallab, Mustapha, Sandretto, Rene, Feinberg, Robert M. An Empirical Analysis of US and EU Antidumping Initiation and Decision. Working Paper, March 2005. In: http://darkwing.uoregon.edu/~bruceb/adpage.html.

Saez 2005: Saez, Sebastian. Keeping Animal Spirits Asleep: The Case of Chile. World Bank Policy Research Working Paper 3615, May 2005. In: http://www.worldbank.org.

Safadi/Laird 1996: Safadi, Raed, Laird, Sam. The Uruguay Round Agreement: Impact on Developing Countries. In: World Development, Vol. 24, No. 7, 1996. S. 1223-1242.

Sahn 1992: Sahn, David E. Public Expenditures in Sub-Saharan Africa During a Period of Economic Reforms. In: World Development, Vol. 20, No. 5, 1992. S. 673-693.

Sahn et al. 1997: Sahn, David E., Dorosh, Paul A., Younger, Stephen D. Structural Adjustment Reconsidered. Economic Policy and Poverty in Africa. Cambridge: Cambridge University Press, 1997.

Sala-i-Martin 1997: Sala-i-Martin, Xavier. I Just Run Two Million Regressions. In: American Economic Review, Vol. 87, No. 2, 1997. S. 178-183.

Sala-I-Martin, Xavier 2000: Sala-i-Martin, Xavier. The Classical Approach to Convergence Analysis. In: Dixon, Huw David. Controversies in Macroeconomics Growth, Trade and Policy. Oxford: Blackwell, 2000.

Salleh 1991: Salleh, Halim. State Capitalism in Malaysian Agriculture. In: Journal of Contemporary Asia, Vol. 21 No. 3, 1991. S. 327-343.

Salvatore 1993: Salvatore, Dominick (ed.). Protectionism and World Welfare. Cambridge: Cambridge University Press, 1993.

Sampson 2005: Sampson, Gary P. Is There a Need for Restructuring the Collaboration among the WTO and UN Agencies so as to Harness their Complementarities? In: Petersmann, Ernst-Ulrich (ed.). Reforming the World Trading System. Legitimacy, Efficiency, and Democratic Governance. Oxford: Oxford University Press, 2005.

Samuelson 1948: Samuelson, Paul A. International Trade and the Equalization of Factor Prices. In: Economic Journal, June 1948, S. 163-184.

Sander/Inotai 1996: Sander, Harald, Inotai, András. World Trade after the Uruguay Round. London, New York: Routledge, 1996.

Sapir/Lundberg 1984: Sapir, André, Lundberg, Lars. The U.S. Generalized System of Preferences and Its Impacts. In: Baldwin, Robert E. Krueger, Anne O. The Structure and Evolution of Recent U.S. Trade Policy. Chicago; London: The University of Chicago Press, 1984.

SAPRIN 2002: Structural Adjustment Participatory Review International Network. The Policy Roots of Economic Crisis and Poverty. A Multi-Country Participatory Assessment of Structural Adjustment. World Bank/SAPRIN, April 2002. In: http://www.saprin.org.

Saric 2005: Saric, M.G. Softwood Lumber IV: 'As it pertains to Countervailing Duties'. In: Legal Issues of Economic Integration Vol. 32, No. 3, 2005. S. 313-324.

Sasdi 2003: Sasdi, Andreas. Das Panelverfahren 'Canada - Patent Protection of Pharmaceutical and Agrochemical Products. In: Nettesheim, Martin, Sander, Gerald G. (Hrg.). WTO-Recht und Globalisierung. Berlin: Duncker&Humblot, 2003.

Sathirathai/Siamwalla 1987: Sathirathai, Surakiart, Siamwalla, Ammar. GATT Law, Agricultural Trade, and Developing Countries: Lessons from two Case Studies. In: World Bank Economic Review Vol. 1 No. 4, 1987. S. 595-618.

Sauernheimer 2004: Sauernheimer, Karlhans. Nicht-Tarifäre Handelshemmnisse: Analyse der Auswirkungen auf den Außenhandel. Uni-Skript, hier datiert auf das Jahr 2002. In: http://www.aussenwirtschaft.vwl.uni-mainz.de.

Saunders/Klau 1985: Saunders, Peter, Klau, Friedrich. The Role of the Public Sector. Causes and Consequences of the Growth of Government. OECD Economic Studies No. 4, Spring 1985. Paris: OECD, 1985.

Sauner-Leroy 2003: Sauner-Leroy, Jacques Bernard. The impact of the implementation of the Single Market Programme on productive efficiency and on mark-ups in the European Union manufacturing industry. European Economy Economic Papers No. 192, September 2003. In: http://europa.eu.int/comm/economy_finance.

Sawhney 2004: Sawhney, Aparna. WTO-Related Matters in Trade and Environment. Relationship between WTO Rules and MEAs. ICRIER WTO Research Series No. 5, 2004. In: http://www.icrier.org/pdf/WTO-5.pdf.
Schachter/Hellawell 1981: Schachter, Oscar, Hellawell, Robert. Competition in International Business. Law and Policy on Restrictive Practices. New York: Columbia University Press, 1981.
Schadler et al. 1993: Schadler, Susan, Rozwadowski, Franek, Tiwari, Siddharth, Robinson, David O. Economic Adjustment in Low-Income Countries. Experience under the Enhanced Structural Adjustment Facility. Occasional Paper No. 106. Washington: IMF, 1993.
Schadler et al. 1995: Schadler, Susan, Bennett, Adam, Carkovic, Maria, Dicks-Mireaux, Louis, Mecagni, Mauro, Morsink, James H. J., Savastano, Miguel A. IMF Conditionality: Experience under Stand-by and Extended Arrangements. Part I, Key Issues and Findings. Occasional Paper 128. Washington: IMF, 1995.
Schadler et al. 1995a: Schadler, Susan, Bennet, Adam, Carkovic, Maria, Dicks-Mireaux, Louis, Mecagni, Mauro, Morsink, James H. J., Savastano, Miguel. IMF Conditionality: Experience under Stand-by and Extended Arrangements. Part II: Background Papers. Occasional Paper 129. Washington: IMF, 1995.
Schäfer 1996: Schäfer, Claus. Mit falschen Verteilungs-"Götzen" zu echten Standortproblemen. In: WSI-Mitteilungen 49 Jg. 10/1996. S. 597-629.
Schäfers/Schennen 1992: Schäfers, Alfons, Schennen, Detlef. Die Lissaboner Konferenz über das Gemeinschaftspatent 1992. In: GRUR, Int. 1992, Heft 8-9. S. 638-653.
Scharpf 1992: Scharpf, Fritz W. Die Handlungsfähigkeit des Staates am Ende des Zwanzigsten Jahrhunderts. In: Kohler-Koch, Beate (Hrg.). Staat und Demokratie in Europa. 18. Wiss. Kongreß der Dt. Vereinigung für Politikwissenschaft. Opladen: Leske & Budrich, 1992.
Scharpf 1993: Scharpf, Fritz W. Legitimationsprobleme der Globalisierung, Regieren in Verhandlungssystemen. In: Böhret, Karl, Wewer, Göttrik (Hrg.). Regieren im 21. Jahrhundert - zwischen Globalisierung und Regionalisierung. Opladen: Leske, Budrich 1993.
Scharpf 1996: Scharpf, Fritz W. Politisch Optionen im vollendeten Binnenmarkt. In: Kohler-Koch, Beate, Jachtenfuchs, Markus. Europäische Integration. Opladen: Leske & Budrich, 1996.
Scharpf 1997: Scharpf, Fritz W. Konsequenzen der Globalisierung für die nationale Politik. In: Internationale Politik und Gesellschaft, 2/1997. S. 184-192.
Scharpf 1997a: Scharpf, Fritz W. Globalisierung als Beschränkung der Handlungsmöglichkeiten nationalstaatlicher Politik. Max-Planck-Institut für Gesellschaftsforschung Discussion Paper 97/1, November 1997.
Scharpf 1998: Scharpf, Fritz W. Die Problemlösungsfähigkeit der Mehrebenenpolitik in Europa. In: PVS, Sonderheft 29/1998. S. 121-144.
Scharrer 1972: Scharrer, Eva-Maria. Die Chancen der Textil- und Bekleidungsindustrie in hochentwickelten Ländern – Ein empirischer Beitrag zu kontroversen Fragen der Standortwohl beider Industriezweige. Kieler Diskussionsbeiträge, No. 26. Kiel: Kieler Diskussionsbeiträge, Dezember 1972.
Schatz 1997: Schatz, Ulrich. Zur Patentierbarkeit gentechnischer Erfindungen in der Praxis des Europäischen Patentamts. In: GRUR Int. 1997, Heft 7. S. 588-595.
Schatz 2004: Schatz, Ulrich. Recent Changes and Expected Developments in Patent Regimes: A European Perspective. In: OECD. Patents, Innovation and Economic Performance. Conference Proceedings. Paris: OECD, 2004.
Schätzl 1996: Schätzl, Ludwig. Wirtschaftsgeographie 1. Theorie. Paderborn: Schöningh, 1996.
Schätzl 1996a: Schätzl, Ludwig. Wirtschaftsgeographie 2. Empirie. Paderborn: Schöningh, 1996.
Scherer 1970: Scherer, Josef. Die Wirtschaftsverfassung der EWG. Dissertation Würzburg. Baden-Baden: Nomos, 1970.
Scherer 1973: Scherer, F. M. The Determinants of Industrial Plant Sizes in Six Nations. In: Review of Economics and Statistics, Vol. 55, No. 2, 1973. S. 135-145.
Scherer 1974: Scherer, F. M. Economies of Scale and Industrial Concentration. In: Goldschmid, Harvey J., Mann, Michael H., West, Fred J. Industrial Concentration: The New Learning. Boston, Toronto: Little, Brown and Company, 1974.
Scherer 1977: Scherer, F. M. The Economic Effects of Compulsory Patent Licensing. New York University, Graduate School of Business Administration, Monograph 1977.
Scherer 1980: Scherer, F. M. Industrial market structure and economic performance. Second Edition. Chicago: Rand McNally, 1980.
Scherer 1982: Scherer, F. M. Inter-Industry Technology Flows and Productivity Growth. In: The Review of Economics and Statistics, Vol. 64, 1982. S. 627-634.
Scherer 1982a: Scherer, F. M. Inter-Industry Technology Flows in the United States. In: Research Policy, Vol. 11, 1982, 227-245.
Scherer 1992: Scherer, F.M. International High-Technology Competition. Cambridge: Harvard University Press, 1992.
Scherer 1994: Scherer, F. M. Competition Policies for an Integrated World Economy. Washington: Brookings Institution, 1994.
Scherer 1996: Scherer, F. M. Industry Structure, Strategy, and Public Policy. New York: HarperCollins, 1996.
Scherer 1998: Scherer, F. M. Comment. In: Anderson, Robert D., Gallini, Nancy T. Competition Policy and Intellectual Property Rights in the Knowledge-Based Economy. Calgary: University of Calgary Press, 1998.
Scherer 1999: Scherer, F.M. Retail Distribution Channel Barriers to International Trade. In: Antitrust Law Journal, Vol. 67, 1999. S. 77-112.

Scherer 2001: Scherer, F.M. Part Two Summary. In: Porter, Roger B., Sauvé, Pierre, Subramanian, Arvind, Zampetti, Americo Beviglia. Efficiency, Equity, Legitimacy. The Multilateral Trading System at the Millenium. Washington D.C.: Brookings Institution Press, 2001.
Scherer 2003: Scherer, F.M. The Economics of Compulsory Drug Patent Licensing. In: Workshop on Key Issues in Improving the Accessability to Drugs in Developing Countries, June 2, 2003. World Bank. In: http://www.cptech.org.
Scherer et al. 1975: Scherer, F. M., Beckenstein, Alan, Kaufer, Erich, Murphy, R. Dennis. The Economics of Multi-Plant Operation. Cambridge, Mass.: Harvard University Press, 1975.
Scherer/Ross 1990: Scherer, F. M., Ross, David. Industrial market structure and economic performance. Third Edition. Boston: Houghton Mifflin, 1990.
Scherer/Watal 2001: Scherer, F.M., Watal, Jayashree. Post-Trips Options for Access to Patented Medicines in Developing Countries. WHO Commission on Macroeconomics and Health Working Paper Series Paper No. WG4: 1. Geneva: WHO, 2001.
Scherrer 1992: Scherrer, Christoph. Im Bann des Fordismus. Die Auto- und Stahlindustrie der USA im internationalen Konkurrenzkampf. Berlin: Ed. Sigma Bohn, 1992.
Scherrer 1999: Scherrer, Christoph. Globalisierung wider Willen? Die Durchsetzung liberaler Außenwirtschaftspolitik in den USA. Berlin: Edition Sigma, 1999.
Scherrer 2000: Scherrer, Christoph. Global Governance: Vom fordistischen Trilateralismus zum neoliberalen Konstitutionalismus. In: Prokla, 30 Jg., Heft 118, März 2000.
Scherrer et al. 1998: Scherrer, Christoph, Greven, Thomas, Frank, Volker. Sozialklauseln: Arbeiterrechte im Welthandel. Münster: Westfälisches Dampfboot, 1998.
Schiff 1971: Schiff, Eric. Industrialization without National Patents. The Netherlands, 1969-1912, Switzerland, 1850-1907. Princeton: Princeton University Press, 1971.
Schiff/Valdes 1992: Schiff, Maurice, Valdes, Alberto. A Synthesis of the Economics in Developing Countries. The Political Economy of Agricultural Pricing Policy, Vol. 4, Baltimore, London: John Hopkings University Press for the World Bank, 1992.
Schiffer 1981: Schiffer, Jonathan. The Changing Post-war Pattern of Development: The Accumulated Wisdom of Samir Amin. In: World Development, Vol. 9, No. 5, 1981. S. 515-537.
Schilder 1999: Schilder, Klaus. Background Paper on the Ongoing ACP-EU Negotiations on the Future of the Lomé Convention. WEED. In: http://www.weedbonn.org.
Schink 1999: Schink, Alexander. Beinträchtigung der Umwelt in Deutschland durch landwirtschaftliche Produktion. In: Umwelt und Planungsrecht, Januar 1999. S. 8-17.
Schmalensee 1987: Schmalensee, Richard. Intra-Industry Profitability Differences in US Manufacturing 1053-1983. In: Journal of Industrial Economics, Vol. XXXVII, No. 4, June 1989. S. 337-357.
Schmidt 1990: Schmidt, Reiner. Öffentliches Wirtschaftsrecht. Allgemeiner Teil. Berlin: Springer Verlag, 1990.
Schmidt 1995: Schmidt, Klaus-Dieter. Motives of Large Multinationals Investing in Small Transition Countries. Kiel Working Paper No. 668, January 1995.
Schmidt 1995a: Schmidt, Manfred G. Demokratietheorien. Opladen: Leske & Budrich, 1995.
Schmidt 1996: Schmidt, Manfred G. Staat und Markt in den demokratischen Industrieländern. In: Spektrum der Wissenschaft, November 1996. S. 36-44.
Schmidt 1996a: Schmidt, Ingo. Wettbewerbspolitik und Kartellrecht. Stuttgart: Lucius&Lucius, 1996.
Schmidt 2005: Schmidt, Christian. Lizenzverweigerung als Missbrauch einer marktbeherrschenden Stellung. Berlin: Wissenschaftlicher Verlag Berlin, 2005.
Schmidt/Binder 1996: Schmidt, Ingo, Binder, Steffen. Wettbewerbspolitik im internationalen Vergleich. Heidelberg: Verlag Recht und Wirtschaft, 1996.
Schmitz/Hewitt 1991: Schmitz, Hubert, Hewitt, Tom. Learning to Raise Infants: A Case-study in Industrial Policy. In: Christopher Colclough, James Manor (eds.). States or Markets? Neo-liberalism and the Development Policy Debate. Oxford. Clarendon Press, 1991.
Schnepf 2004: Schnepf, Randy. U.S.-Canada Wheat Trade Dispute. CRS Report for Congress, RL32426, Updated, June 14, 2004. In: http://www.fpc.state.gov/c4763.htm.
Schnepf 2006: Schnepf, Randy. U.S. Agricultural Policy Response to WTO Cotton Decision. CRS Report for Congress, RS22187, Updated, September 8, 2006. In: http://fpc.state.gov/fpc/c18787.htm.
Schoch 1994: Schoch, Frank. Unbestimmte Rechtsbegriffe im Rahmen des GATT. Eine Untersuchung anhand der Regelungen über Dumping und Subventionen. Frankfurt am Main: Peter Lang, 1994.
Schoenbaum 1994: Schoenbaum, Thomas J. The International Trade Laws and the New Protectionism: The Need for a Synthesis with Antitrust. In: North Carolina Journal of International Law and Commercial Regulation. Vol. 19, 1994. S. 393-439.
Schoneveld 1992: Schoneveld, Frank. The European Community Reaction to the 'Illicit' Commercial Trade Practices of Other Countries. In: JWT, Vol. 26, No. 2, April 1992. S. 17-33.
Schott 2001: Schott, Peter K. One Size Fits All? Heckscher-Ohlin Specialization in Global Production. NBER Working Paper No. 8244, April 2001.
Schreiber 1997: Schreiber, Sebastian. Freihandel und Gerechtigkeit. Frankfurt am Main et al.: Lang, 1997.
Schröder 1995: Schröder, Meinhard. Die Berücksichtigung des Umweltschutzes in der gemeinsamen Agrarpolitik der Euopäischen Union. In: Natur und Recht, Heft 3, 1995. S. 117-123.
Schröder 1999: Schröder, Christoph. Produktivität und Lohnstückkosten im internationalen Vergleich. In: iw-Trend, 3, 1999. S. 19-35.

Schröter 1999: Schröter, Helmuth. Einführung Art. 85. In: In: Groeben, Hans von, Thiesing, Jochen, Ehlermann, Claus-Dieter (Hrg.). Kommentar zum EU-/EG-Vertrag. Fünfte Auflage. Baden-Baden: Nomos, 1999.
Schuknecht 1992: Schuknecht, Ludger. Trade Protection in the European Community. Chur; Reading; Paris: Harwood Academic Publishers, 1992.
Schuknecht/Kono 1998: Schuknecht, Ludger, Kono, Masamichi. Financial Services Trade, Capital Flows, and Financial Stability. WTO Staff Working Paper ERAD-98-12, November 1998. In: http://www.wto.org.
Schüler 1991: Schüler, Jeannette. Voluntary Export Restraints. In: Grabnitz, Eberhard, von Bogdandy, Armin (eds.). U.S. Trade Barriers: A Legal Analysis. New York; London; Rome: European Law Press Munich, Oceana Publications, 1991.
Schüler 1991a: Schüler, Jeannette. The Political System Governing Foreign Trade in the United States. In: Grabnitz, Eberhard, von Bogdandy, Armin (eds.). U.S. Trade Barriers: A Legal Analysis. New York; London; Rome: European Law Press Munich, Oceana Publications, 1991.
Schüller 2000: Schüller, Margot. Die Volksrepublik China 1949 bis 2000: Vom sozialistischen Entwicklungsland zur wirtschaftlichen Großmacht. In: Nord-Süd-Aktuell, Jahrgang XIV, Nr. 4, 2000. S. 671-687.
Schultz 1961: Schultz, Theodore W. Economic Prospects of Primary Products. In: Ellis, Howard S. (ed.) Economic Development for Latin America. Proceedings of a Conference held by the International Economics Association. London: Macmillan, 1961.
Schultz 1978: Schultz, Theodore W. On Economics and Politics of Agriculture. In: Schultz, Theodore William. Distortions of Agricultural Incentives. Bloomington; London: Indiana University Press, 1978.
Schulz-Nieswandt 1994: Schulz-Nieswandt, Frank. Zur Theorie der Transformation. Weiden, Regensburg: eurotrans-Verlag, 1994.
Schumpeter 1946: Schumpeter, Joseph A. Kapitalismus, Sozialismus und Demokratie. Tübingen: Mohr, 1993.
Schwarz 1994: Schwarz, Karl. Car Wars. Die Automobilindustrie im globalen Wettbewerb. Frankfurt am Main: Peter Lang, 1994.
Schwarz 2004: Mathias, Schwarz. Theorie internationaler Handelsbeziehungen. Uni-Skript. Lehrstuhl Karlhans Sauernheimer. In: http://www.aussenwirtschaft.vwl.uni-mainz.de.
Schwering 1996: Schwering, Heinz-Jürgen. Kommentar zu G. Engel. In: Pies, Ingo, Leschke, Martin (Hrg.). James Buchanans konstitutionelle Ökonomik. Tübingen: Mohr, 1996.
Schwintowski 1996: Schwintowski, Hans-Peter. Recht und Gerechtigkeit. Eine Einführung in Grundfragen des Rechts. Berlin: Springer, 1996.
Schwintowski 2000: Schwintowsik, Hans-Peter. Freier Warenverkehr im europäischen Binnenmarkt. In: RabelsZ VI. 64, 2000. S. 38-59.
Scitovsky 1954: Scitovsky, Tibor. Two Concepts of External Economies. In: Journal of Political Economy, Vol. 62, 1954. S. 142-151.
Scott 1993: Scott, John T. Purposive Diversitfication and Economic Performance. Cambridge: Cambrigde University Press, 1993.
Scott 1999: Scott, Robert E. Exported to Death. The Failure of Agricultural Deregulation. Economic Policy Institute, Briefing Paper. July 1999. In: http://epinet.org.
Scott 2005: Scott, Robert E. U.S.-China Trade, 1989-2003. Impact on jobs and industries, nationally and state-by-state. EPI Working Paper 270, January 2005. In: http://www.epi.org.
SCVPH 2002: Scientific Committee on Veterinary Measures Relating to Public Health. Opionion on Review of previous SCVPH opinions of 30 April 1999 and 3 May 2000 on the potential risks for human health from hormone residues in bovine meat and meat products, adopted on 10 April 2002. European Commission. Health & Consumer Protection Directorate General. In:
http://ec.europa.eu/food/food/chemicalsafety/contaminants/hormones/index_en.htm.
Seidel 1996: Seidel, Gerd. Handbuch der Grund- und Menschenrechte auf staatlicher, europäischer und universeller Ebene. Baden-Baden: Nomos, 1996.
Seidl-Hohenveldern 1986: Seidl-Hohenveldern, I. International Economic Law. General Course on Public International Law. In: Recueil des Cours, 1986 III. Dordrecht: Martinus Nijhoff, 1987.
Seiler/Dutfield 2001: Seiler, Achim, Dutfield, Graham. Regulating Access and Benefit Sharing: Basic Issues, legal instruments, policy proposals. Study commissioned by the Federal Republic of Germany in preparation for the 1st meeting of the Ad Hoc Working Group on Access and Benefit Sharing in Bonn, October 2001. Berlin: Wissenschaftszentrum Berlin für Sozialforschung (WZB), 2001.
Seitz 1994: Seitz, Konrad. Deutschland und Europa in der Weltwirtschaft von morgen. In: Merkur, 1994. S. 828-849.
Seitz 1999: Seitz, Helmut. Subnational Government Bailouts in Germany. ZEI-Working Paper B-20, 1999. In: http://www.zei.de.
Seliger 1999: Seliger, Bernhard. "Big Deals" – Wettbewerbspolitik als Antwort auf die Krise in Südkorea. In: Wirtschaft und Wettbewerb, 6/1999. pp. 574-581.
Sell 1995: Sell, Susan K. Intellectual property protection and antitrust in the developing world: crisis, coercion, and choice. In: International Organization, Vo. 49, No. 2, Spring 1995: S. 315-349.
Sell 1998: Sell, Friedrich J. Max Weber - der Nationalökonom. Zur Neuinterpretation seines Werkes durch Wilhelm Hennis. In: ORDO, Bs. 49, 1998.
Selzer 1995: Selzer, Andrew J. The Political Economy of the Fair Labor Standards Act of 1938. In: Journal of Political Economy, Vol. 103, No. 6, 1995. S. 1302-1342.

Semiconductor Agreement U.S. Japan 1986: Agreement on Semiconductor Trade, Japan-United States, September 2, 1986. In: 25 I.L.M. 1408, 1986. Sowie: EU-Challenge : In: 25 I.L.M. 1621, 1986.
Semiconductor Agreement U.S. Japan 1996: Joint Statement by the Government of the United States and the Governenment of Japan concerning Semiconductors, August 2, 1996. Expired July 31, 1999. In: http://www.mac.doc.gov/japan/source/ menu/semiconductors/semis.html.
Sen 1970: Sen, Amartya. The Impossibility of a Paretian Liberal. In: Arrow, Kenneth J., Debreu, Gérard (eds.). Landmark Papers in General Equilibrium Theory, Social Choice and Welfare. Cheltenham: Edgar Elgar, 2001.
Sen 1988: Sen, Amartya. The Concept of Development. In: Chenery, H., Srinivasan, T.N. Handbook of Development Economics. Vol. I. Amsterdam; New York: Elsevier Science Publishers, 1988.
Sen 1990: Sen, Amartya. Food, Economics and Entitlements. In: Drèze, Jean, Sen, Amartya. The Political Economy of Hunger. WIDER Studies, United Nations University. New York: Oxford University Press, 1990.
Sen 1999: Sen, Amartya. Development as Freedom. New York: Anchor Books, 1999.
Sen 2002: Sen, Kunal. Globalization and Employment in Bangladesh and Kenya. Discussion Paper 7. GAP Projekt. In: http://www.gapresearch.org/production/globprodpov.html.
Sen 2006: Sen, Rahul. 'New Regionalism' in Asia: A Comparative Analysis of Emerging Regional and Bilateral Trading Agreements involving ASEAN, China and India. In: JWT, Vol. 40, No. 4, 2006. S. 553-596.
Senghaas 1977: Senghaas, Dieter. Weltwirtschaftsordnung und Entwicklungspolitik. Plädoyer für Dissoziation. Frankfurt am Main: Surkamp, 1977.
Senses 1989: Senses, Fikret. The Nature and Main Characteristics of Recent Turkish Growth in Export of Manufactures. In: The Developing Economies, Vol. XXVII, No. 1, March 1989. S. 19-33.
Senti 1986: Senti, Richard. Erscheinungsformen und Ursachen des neuen Protektionismus im Außenhandel. In: ORDO, 37, 1986. S. 217-234.
Senti 1986a: Senti, Richard. GATT Allgemeines Zoll- und Handelsabkommen als System der Welthandelsordnung. Zürich: Schulthess Polygraphischer Verlag, 1986.
Senti 1994: Senti, Richard. GATT-WTO. Die neue Welthandelsordnung nach der Uruguay Runde. Zürich: Institut für Wirtschaftsforschung, ETH, 1994.
Senti 1996: Senti, Richard. NAFTA. Die Nordamerikanische Freihandelszone. Zürich: Schulthess Polygraphischer Verlag, 1996.
Sercovich 1984: Sercovich, Franciso Colman. Brazil. In: World Development, Vol. 12, No. 5/6, 1984. S. 575-599.
Serletis 1992: Serletis, Apostolos. Export growth and Canadian economic development. In: Journal of Development Economics, Vol. 38, 1992. S. 133-145.
Seung 1996: Seung, Jung-Hun. Die sektorale Wirtschaftsstruktur Südkoreas - bisherige Entwicklung und zukünftige Perspektiven. Münster: LIT, 1996.
Shackle 1950: Shackle, G. L. S. On Optimum Tariff Structures. In: Review of Economic Studies, Vol. 17 No. 42, 1949-1950. S. 47-59.
Shaffer 2003: Shaffer, Gregory. How to make the WTO Dispute Settlement System Work for Developing countries: Some Proactive Developing Country Strategies. In: Shaffer, Gregory, Mosoti, Victor, Qureshi, Asif. Towards a development-supportive dispute settlement system in the WTO. ICTSD Resource Paper No. 5, March 2003. In: http://www.ictsd.org.
Shaffer 2003a: Shaffer, Gregory. Defending Interests. Public-Private Partnerships in WTO Litigation. Washington: Brookings Institution, 2003.
Shaffer 2005: Shaffer, Gregory. Can WTO Technical Assistance and Capacity-Building Serve Developing Countries? In: Petersmann, Ernst-Ulrich (ed.). Reforming the World Trading System. Legitimacy, Efficiency, and Democratic Governance. Oxford: Oxford University Press, 2005.
Shaffer 2005a: Shaffer, Gregory. Parliamentary Oversight of WTO Rule-Making: the Political, Normative, and Practical Contexts. In: Petersmann, Ernst-Ulrich (ed.). Reforming the World Trading System. Legitimacy, Efficiency, and Democratic Governance. Oxford: Oxford University Press, 2005.
Shaffer/Apea 2005: Shaffer, Gregory, Apea, Yvonne. Institutional Choice in the Generalized System of Preferences Case: Who Decides the Conditions for Trade Preferences? The Law and Politics of Rights. In: JWT, Vol. 39, No. 6, 2005. S. 977-1008.
Shaked/Sutton 1984: Shaked, Avner, Sutton, John. Natural Oligopolies and International Trade. In: Kierzkowski, Henryk (ed.). Monopolistic Competition and International Trade. Oxford: Clarendon Press, 1984.
Shallue 2001: Shallue, James Joseph. An Analysis of Foreign Sales Corporations and the European Communities' Four Billion-Dollar Retaliation. In: Denver Journal of International Law and Policy, Vol. 30, No. 1, Winter 2001. S. 179-221.
Shank 1996: Shank, Robert D. The Justice Department's Recent Antitrust Enforcement Policy: Toward a 'Positive Comity' Solution to International Competition Problems. In: Vanderbilt Journal of Transnational Law, Vol. 29, 1996. S. 155-189.
Shao 2002: Shao, John R. Agriculture and Market Liberalization in Tanzania: Problems of Cotton Production and Marketing in the Bunda District. Tanzania Development Research Group, Tanzania Agriculture Situation Analysis, November 2002. In: http://www.tzonline.org.
Shapiro 1990: Shapiro, Helen. Rent Seeking or Rent Distribution? Automobile Firms and the Brazilian State 1956-68. In: McCarthy, Desmond F. (Hg.). Problems of Developing Countries in the 1990s. Washington: World Bank, 1990.
Shapiro 2001: Shapiro, Carl. Navigating the Patent Thicket: Cross Licenses, Patent Pools, and Standard-Setting. University of California at Berkeley, March 2001. In: http://faculty.haas.berkeley.edu/shapiro/thicket.pdf

Shapiro/Taylor 1990: Shapiro, Helen, Taylor, Lance. The State and Industrial Strategy. In: World Development, Vol. 18, No. 6, 1990. S. 861-878.
Sharer et al. 1998: Sharer, Robert, Sorsa, Piritta, Calika, Nur, Ross, Paul, Shiells, Clinton, Dorsey, Thomas. Trade Liberalization in IMF-Supported Programs. Washington: IMF, 1998.
Sharma 2000: Sharma, Kishor. Liberalization and Structural Change: Evidence from Nepalese Manufacturing. Yale University, Economic Growth Center, Centre Discussion Paper No. 812, April 2000. In: http://aida.econ.yale.edu/~egcenter/.
Sharpley/Lewis 1990: Sharley, Jennifer, Lewis, Stephen. Kenya. In: Riddell, Roger C. (ed.). Manufacturing Africa. Performance & Prospects of Seven Countries in Sub-Saharan Africa. Overseas Development Institute. London: James Currey, 1990.
Shaw/Schwartz 2002: Shaw, Sabrina, Schwartz, Risa. Trade and Environment in the WTO. In: JWT, Vol. 36, No. 1, 2002. S. 129-154.
Sheehey 1990: Sheehey, Edmund J. Exports and Growth: A flawed framework. In: The Journal of Development Studies, Vol. 27, No. 1, October 1990. S. 111-116.
Shelton 1994: Shelton, Dinah. The Participation of Nongovernmental Organizations in International Judicial Proceedings. In: AJIL, Vol. 88, 1994, S. 611-642.
Shen 1984: Shen, T. Y. The Estimation of X-Inefficiency in Eighteen Countries. In: The Review of Economics and Statistics. Vol. 66, 1984. S. 98-103.
Shepherd 1981: Shepherd, William G. Public Enterprises in Western Europe and the United States. In: de Jong, H. W. (ed.). The Structure of European Industry. The Hague; Boston; London: Martinus Nijhoff, 1981.
Shepherd 1982: Shepherd, William G. Causes of Increased Competition in the U.S.-Economy, 1939-1980. In: The Review of Economics and Statistics, Vol. 64, 1982. S. 613-626.
Shepherd 1984: Shepherd, Willam G. 'Contestability' vs. Competition. In: American Economic Review, Vol. 74 No. 4, September 1984. S. 572-587.
Shepherd 1990: Shepherd, William G. The Airline Industry. In: Adams, Walter (Hrg.). The Structure of American Industry. New York: Macmillan, 1990.
Shepherd/Alburo 1991: Shepherd, Geoffrey, Alburo, Florian. The Philippines. In: The Experience of Korea, the Philippines, and Singapore. Liberalizing Foreign Trade Vol. 2. Oxford: World Bank/Blackwell, 1991.
Sherman/Kaen 1997: Sherman, Heidemarie C., Kaen, Fred R. Die deutschen Banken und ihre Einfluß auf Unternehmensentscheidungen. In: ifo-Schnelldienst, 23/1997. S. 3-20.
Sherwood 1990: Sherwood, Robert M. Intellectual Property and Economic Development. Boulder: Westview Press, 1990.
Shihepo 1999: Shihepo, Gabriel. The Impact of EU Beef Dumping on Namibia's Beef Market. In: Farewell to Lomé? The Impact of Neo-liberal EU Policies on ACP Countries. WEED, terre des hommes, KOSA. Bonn, July 1999.
Shin 1994: Shin, Ja Hyun. Census and Analysis of Antidumping Actions in the United States. OECD Committee on Competition Law and Policy, Working Paper No. 1 on Competition and International Trade. DAFFE/CLP/WP1(94)12. Paris: OECD, 1994. In: http://ftc.gov.
Shiva/Holla-Bar 1993: Shiva, Vandana, Holla-Bar, Radha. Intellectual Piracy and the Neem Tree. In: The Ecologist, Vol. 23 No. 6, November/December 1993. S. 223-227.
Short 1984: Short, R. P. The Role of Public Enterprises: An International Statistical Comparison. In: Floyd, Robert H., Gray, Clive S., Short, R. P. Public Enterprise in Mixed Economies. Washington: International Monetary Fund, 1984.
SIA Information 2006: Semiconductor Industry Information. Industry Facts and Figures. 2006. In: http://www.sia-online.org.
SIA Information 2006a: Semiconductor Industry Information. Papers and Publications. Total Semiconductor World Market Sales & Shares 1994-2004. 2006. In: http://www.sia-online.org.
SIA Information 2006b: Semiconductor Industry Information. Keeping Semiconductor Leadership in the U.S.. 2006. In: http://www.sia-online.org.
Sicsic/Wyplosz 1996: Sicsic, Pierre, Wyplosz, Charles. France, 1945-92. In: Crafts, Nicolas, Toniolo, Gianni (eds.). Economic Growth in Europe since 1945. Cambridge: Cambridge University Press, 1996.
Siebe 1997: Siebe, Thomas. Ökonomische Aufholprozesse: Was erklären 'weiche' Faktoren. In: RWI-Mitteilungen, Jg. 47, 1997, S. 95-114.
Siebert 1997: Siebert, Horst. An Institutional Order for a Globalizing World Economy. Kiel Working Paper No. 807, April 1997.
Siebert 1999: Siebert, Horst. Mit dem Verursacherprinzip gegen Währungskrisen. In: Frankfurter Allgemeine Zeitung, Donnerstag, 18. Februar 1999, Nr. 41, S. 19.
Siebert/Klodt 1998: Siebert, Horst, Klodt, Henning. Towards Global Competition: Catalysts and Constraints. Kiel Working Paper No. 897, December 1998.
Siegel 2002: Siegel, Deborah E. Legal Aspects of the IMF/WTO Relationship: The Fund's Articles of Agreement and the WTO Agreements. IMF Seminar on Current Developments in Monetary and Financial Law, May 7-17, 2002, Washington D.C. In: http://www.imf.org.
Sievers 2001: Sievers, Sara E. Competitiveness and Foreign Direct Investment in Africa. In: OECD. Policies to Promote Competitiveness in Manufacturing in Sub-Saharan Africa. Development Centre Seminars within the IMF and the AERC. Kwasi Fosu, Augustin, Nsouli, Saleh M., Varoudakis, Aristomene (eds.). Paris: OECD, 2001a.

Simma 1972: Simma, Bruno. Das Reziprozitätselement im Zustandekommen völkerrechtlicher Verträge. Berlin: Duncker & Humblot, 1972.
Simon 1995: Simon, David. The Demise of 'Socialist' State forms in Africa: An Overview. In: Journal of International Development, Vol. 7, No. 5, 1995. S. 707-739.
Singer 1950: Singer, H. W. The Distribution of Gains between Investing and Borrowing Countries. In: American Economic Review, Bd. 40, 1950, S. 473-485.
Singh 1993: Singh, Ajit. The Stock-market and economic development: Should developing countries encourage stock markets? In: UNCTAD Review, No. 4, 1993. S. 1-18.
Singh 2005: Singh, Ajit. Special and Differential Treatment: The Multilateral Trading System and Economic Development in the Twenty-first Century. In: Gallagher, Kevin P. Putting Development First. London, New York: Zed Books, 2005.
Singh et al. 1999: Singh, Harsha Vardhana, Soni, Anita, Kathuria Rajat. Telecom Policy Reform in India. Working Paper, World Bank, 1999. In: http://www.worldbank.org/research/trade.
Singh et al. 2003: Singgh, R.B., Kumar, P., Woodhead, T. Smallholder Farmers in India: Food Security and Agricultural Policy. FAO Regional Office for Asia and the Pacific. Bangkok, Thailand: FAO, 2002. In: http://www.fao.org.
Singh/Dhumale 1999: Singh, Ajit. Competition Policy, Development and Developing Countries. South Centre Working Paper, Nov. 1999. In: http://ww.southcentre.org.
Singh/Zammit 1998: Singh, Ajit, Zammit, Ann. Foreign Direct Investment: Towards Co-operative Institutional Arrangements between the North and the South. In: Michie, Jonathan, Smith, John Grieve. Globalization, Growth, and Governance. Oxford: Oxford University Press, 1998.
SITC Rev. 3 Vereinte Nationen 2004: Vereinte Nationen. Standard International Trade Classification, Revision 3. In: http://unstats.un.org/.
Skaggs 2005: Skaggs, David E. How Can Parliamentary Participation in the WTO Rule-Making and Democratic Control be Made More Effective in the WTO? A United States Congressional Perspective. In: Petersmann, Ernst-Ulrich (ed.). Reforming the World Trading System. Legitimacy, Efficiency, and Democratic Governance. Oxford: Oxford University Press, 2005.
Sklair 1995: Sklair, Leslie The Sociology of the Global System. Baltimore, Maryland: John Hobkins University Press, 1995.
Skocpol 1985: Skocpol, Theda. Bringing the State Back In: Strategies of Analysis in Current Research. In: Evans, Peter B. et al. (eds.). Bringing the State Back In. Cambridge: Cambridge University Press, 1985.
Skully 1999: Skully, David W. The Economics of TRQ Administration. IATRC Working Paper No. 6, 1999. In: http://www.iatrcweb.org.
Slaugher 2000: Slaughter, Anne-Marie. International Law and International Relations. In: Recueil des Cours 285, 2000. Collected Courses of The Hague Academy of International Law. The Hague: Martinus Nijhoff, 2001.
Slaughter 1997: Slaughter, Matthew J. Per Capita Income Convergence and the Role of International Trade. In: American Economic Review, Vol. 87, No. 2, 1997. S. 194-204.
Slaughter 1998: Slaughter, Matthew J. International Trade and Per Capita Income Convergence: A Difference-In-Differences Analysis. NBER Working Paper 6557, May 1998.
Slonina 2003: Slonina, Michael. Durchbruch im Spannungsverhältnis TRIPS and Health: Die WTO-Entscheidung zu Exporten unter Zwangslinzenzen. In: Tietje, Christian (et al.). Beiträge zum Transnationalen Wirtschaftsrecht. Heft 20, September 2003. In: http://www.wirtschaftsrecht.uni-halle.de/.
Slotboom 2001: Slotboom, Marco M. Do Different Treaty Purposes Matter for Treaty Interpretation? The Elimination of Discriminatory Internal Taxes in EC and WTO Law. In: Journal of International Economic Law, 2001. S. 557-579.
Slotboom 2002: Slotboom, Marco M. Subsidies in WTO Law and in EC Law. In: JWT, Vol. 36, No. 3, 2002. S. 517-542.
Slotboom 2003: Slotboom, Marco M. Do Public Health Measure Recieve Similar Treatment in the European Community and World Trade Organization Law? In: JWT, Vol. 37, No. 3, 2003. S. 553-596.
SME India 2005: Webseite: http://www.smeindia.com/ssivariousstates.asp.
Smeets 1996: Smeets, Heinz-Dieter. Grundlagen der regionalen Integration: Von der Zollunion zum Binnenmarkt. In: Ohr, Renate (Hrg.). Europäische Integration. Stuttgart; Berlin; Köln: Kohlhammer, 1996.
Smeets 1997: Smeets, Heinz-Dieter. Internationales Währungssystem und deutsche Wirtschaftspolitik. In: ORDO, Bd. 48, 1997.
Smith 1776: Smith, Adam. Der Wohlstand der Nationen. (Hrg.) Recktenwald, Horst Claus. München: dtv, 1974 (1999).
Smith 1984: Smith, Alasdair. Capital Theory and Trade Theory. In: Jones, R.W., Kenen, P. B. (eds.). Handbook of International Economics, Vol. I. Amsterdam: Elsevier Science, 1984.
Smith 1994: Smith, Alasdair. Strategic Trade Policy in the European Car Market. In: Krugman, Paul R. Empirical Studies of Strategic Trade Policy. NBER Project Report. Chicago: Univ. of Chicago Press, 1994.
Smith 1997: Smith, Stephen C. Case Studies in Economic Development. Reading, Mass.: Addison-Wesley, 1997.
Smith 1997a: Smith, Vincent H. NAFTA, GATT, and Agriculture in the Northern Rockies and Great Plains. Special Report March 1997. Nothern Plains and Rockies Centre for the Study of Western Hemisphre Trade. In: http://www.agecon.lib.umn.edu.

Smith 1998: Smith, Heather. The Determinants of Manufacturing Protection in Taiwan. In: The Developing Economies, XXXVI-3, September 1998: 305-331.
Smith/Urey 2002: Smith, L.E.D, Urey, I. Agricultural Growth and Poverty Reduction: A Review of Lessons from the Post-Independence and Green Revolution Experience in India. October 2002. In: www.imperial.ac.uk/agriculturalsciences
Söderbom 2001: Söderbom, Mans. Contraints and Opportunities in Kenyan Manufacturing: Report on the Kenyan Manufacturing Enterprise Survey 2000. CSAE Working Paper September 2001. In: http://www.csae.ox.ac.uk/.
Söderbom/Teal 2000: Söderbom, Mans, Teal, Francis. Skills, Investment and Exports from Manufacturing Firms in Africa. CSAE Working Paper WPS/2000.8, 2000. In: http://www.csae.ox.ac.uk/.
Söderbom/Teal 2001: Söderbom, Mans, Teal, Francis. Can African manufacturing firms become successful exporters? UNIDO Working Paper. In: http://www.unido.org/.
Söderbom/Teal 2001a: Söderbom, Mans, Teal, Francis. Are African Manufacturing Firms Really Inefficient? Evidence from Firm-Level Panel Data. CSAE Working Paper WPS/01.14, 2001. In: http://www.csae.ox.ac.uk/.
Söderbom/Teal 2002: Söderbom, Mans, Teal, Francis. Are Manufacturing Exports the Key to Economic Success in Africa. CSAE Working Paper November 2002. In: http://www.csae.ox.ac.uk/.
Söderling 1999: Söderling, Ludvig. Structural Policies for International Competitiveness in Manufacturing: The Case of Cameroon. OECD Development Centre, Working Paper No. 146, CD/DOC(99)3, March 1999. In: http://www.oecd.org.
Soete/Verspagen 1993: Soete, Luc, Verspagen, Bart. Technology and Growth: The Complex Dynamics of Catching Up, Falling Behind and Taking Over. In: Szirmai, Adam, van Ark, Bart, Pilat, Dirk (eds.). Explaining Economic Growth. Essays in Honour of Angus Maddison. Amsterdam: North Holland, 1993.
Sohmen 1959: Sohmen, Egon. Competition and Growth: The Lesson of West Germany. In: American Economic Review, Vol. 49, 1959. S. 986-1003.
Soifer 1984: Soifer, Ricardo J. Argentina. In: World Development, Vol. 12, No. 5/6, 1984. S. 625-644.
Solimano 1993: Solimano, Andres. Chile. In: Taylor, Lance. The Rocky Road to Reform. Adjustment, Income Distribution, and Growth in the Developing World. Cambridge: MIT Press, 1993.
Söllner 1999: Söllner, Fritz. Die Geschichte ökonomischen Denkens. Berlin et al.: Springer, 1999.
Solow 1956: Solow, Robert M. A Contribution to the Theory of Economic Growth. In: Quarterly Journal of Economics, Vol. 70, 1956. S. 65-94.
Solow 1957: Solow, Robert M. Technical Change and the Aggregate Production Function. In: The Review of Economics and Statistics, Vol. XXXIX, No. 3, August 1957, pp. 312-320.
Solow/Baily 2001: Solow, Robert M., Baily, Martin Niel. International Productivity Comparisons Built from the Firm Level. In: Journal of Economic Perspectives, Vol. 15, No. 3. Summer 2001. S. 151-172.
Soltwedel et al. 1988: Soltwedel, Rüdiger. Subventionssysteme und Wettbewerbsbedingungen in der EG. Kiel: Institut für Weltwirtschaft, 1988.
South Africa Customs Information 2004: South Africa Customs Information. In: http://rapidttp.com/tariff/.
South Centre 1996: South Centre. International Commodity Problems and Policies. The Key Issues for Developing Countries. Geneva: South Centre, 1996.
South Centre 2005: South Centre. Observations on the Proposal for a New Peace Clause. SC/TADP/TA/AG/1, November 2005. In: http://www.southcentre.org.
Souty 2005: Souty, Francois. Is there the need for additional WTO competitions rules promoting non-discriminatory competitions laws and competition institutions in WTO Members? In: Petersmann, Ernst-Ulrich (ed.). Reforming the World Trading System. Legitimacy, Efficiency, and Democratic Governance. Oxford: Oxford University Press, 2005.
Spamann 2004: Spamann, Holger. Standard of Review for World Trade Organization Panels in Trade Remedy Cases: a Critical Analysis. In: JWT, Vol. 38, No. 3, 2004. S. 509-555.
Spamann 2006: Spamann, Holger. The Myth of 'Rebalancing' Retaliation in WTO Dispute Settlement Practice. In: Journal of International Economic Law Vol. 9, No. 1, 2006. S. 31-79.
Spatz/Nunnenkamp 2002: Spatz, Julius, Nunnenkamp, Peter. Globalization of the Automobile Industry - Traditional Locations under Pressure? Kiel Working Paper No. 1093, Kiel: Institut für Weltwirtschaft, January 2002.
Spero/Hart 1997: Spero, Joan E., Hart, Jeffrey A. The Politics of International Economic Relations. New York: St. Martin's Press, 1997.
Spinanger 1985: Spinanger, Dean. Protektion im internationalen Handel mit Textilien und Bekleidung – Auswirkungen des Multifaserabkommens. In: Die Weltwirtschaft, Heft 1, 1985. S. 133-145.
Spinanger 2000: Spinanger, Dean. Faking Liberalization and Finagling Protectionism: The ACT at Its Best. World Bank, WTO Background Paper, June 2000. In: http://www.worldbank.org/research/trade.
Spoor 1997: Spoor, Max. Agrarian Transformation in Nicaragua: market liberalization and peasant rationality. In: Spoor, Max (ed.). The 'Market Panacea'. Agrarian transformation in developing countries and former transition economies. London: Intermediate Technology Publications, 1997.
Spoor 2000: Spoor, Max. Two Decades of Adjustment and Agricultural Development in Latin America and the Caribbean. Serie Reformas Economicas No. 56, Comisión Económica para América Latina y el Caribe. In: http://www.eclac.cl/publicationes/.
Srinivasan 1994: Srinivasan, T. N. Data base for development analysis: An overview. In: Journal of Development Economics, Vol. 44, 1994. S. 3-27.

Srinivasan 1994a: Srinivasan, T. N. Indian Agriculture: Policies and Performance. In: Srinivasan, T.N. (ed.). Agriculture and Trade in China and India. San Francisco: ICS Press, 1994.
Srinivasan 2001: Srinivasan, T. N. India's Reform of External Sector Policies and Future Multilateral Trade Negotiations. Yale University, Economic Growth Center, Centre Discussion Paper No. 830, June 2001. In: http://aida.econ.yale.edu/~egcenter/.
Srinivasan 2004: Srinivasan, T.N. Comments on Dani Rodrik and Arvind Subramanian, "From 'Hindu Growth' to Productivity Surge: The Mystery of the Indian Growth Transition." IMF Jaques Polak Annual Research Conference, 4-5 November 2004. In: www.imf.org/external/pubs/ ft/staffp/2004/00-00/sriniv.pdf
Srinivasan/Bhagwati 1978: Srinivasan, T.N., Bhagwati, Jagdish. Shadow Prices for Project Selection in the Presence of Distortions: Effective Rates of Protection and Domestic Resource Costs. In: Journal of Political Economy, Vol. 86 No. 1, 1978. S. 97-116.
Srinivasan/Bhagwati 1999: Srinivasan, T. N., Bhagwati, Jagdish. Outward-Orientation and Development: Are Revisionists Right? Yale University, Economic Growth Center, Centre Discussion Paper No. 806, September 1999. In: http://aida.econ.yale.edu/~egcenter/ oder http://www.columbia.edu/~jb38.
Srivastava/Ahuja 2002: Srivatava, Jayati, Ahuja, Rajeev. Mainstreaming Environment through Jurisprudence. Indian Council for Research on International Economic Relations (ICRIER), Working Paper No. 78, April 2002. In: http://www.icrier.org.
Staehelin 1997: Staehelin, Alesch. Das TRIPs-Abkommen. Immaterialgüterrechte im Licht der globalisierten Handelspolitik. Bern: Stämpfli Verlag AG, 1997.
Stallings 1990: Stallings, Barbara. The Role of Foreign Capital in Economic Development. In: Gereffi, Gary, Wyman, Donald L. Manufacturing Miracles. Paths of Industrialization in Latin America and East Asia. Princeton: Princeton University Press, 1990.
Stansel/Moore 1997: Stansel, Dean, Moore, Stephen. Federal Aid to Dependent Corporations: Clinton and Congress Fail to Eliminate Business Subsidies. In: The Cato Institute, Briefing Papers, 1997. In: http://www.cato.org.
Starbatty/Vetterlein 1994: Starbatty, Joachim, Vetterlein, Uwe. Forschungs- und Technologiepolitik der Europäischen Union. Diskussionsbeitrag Nr. 39, Wirtschaftswissenschaftliche Fakultät Tübingen, November 1994.
Starck 1987: Starck, Christian. § 29, Grundrechtliche und demokratische Freiheitsidee. In: Handbuch des Staatsrechts, Bd. II. Heidelberg: C. F. Müller, 1987. S. 3-27.
Stead et al. 1996: Stead, Richard, Curwen, Peter, Lawler, Kevin. Industrial Economics. Theory, Application and Policy. London: McGraw-Hill, 1996.
Steel 201 Reports 2001: U.S. Imports of Steel Products: Overall Trends by Source Country Quantity. In: http://www.usitc.gov.
Steel Proclamation 2003: President George W. Bush. To Provide for the Termination of Action Taken with Regard to Imports of Certain Steel Products by the President of the United States of America a Proclamation. Office of the Press Secretary, December 4, 2003. In: http://www.whitehouse.gov.
Steel Technology Informationen 2006: Steel Technology Website. Projects Overview. In: http://www.steel-technology.com.
Stegemann 1998: Stegemann, Klaus. The Integration of Intellectual Property Rights into the WTO System. Diskussionsbeitrag 10-98. Max Planck Institute for Research into Economic Systems. Jena: 1998.
Steger 2004: Steger, D.P. Improvements and Reforms of the WTO Appellate Body. In: Ortino, Federico, Petersmann, Ernst-Ulrich (eds.). The WTO Dispute Settlement System 1995 - 2003. The Hague et al.: Kluwer Law International, 2004.
Stehmann 1999: Stehmann, Oliver. Export Subsidies in the Regional Aircraft Sector. The Impact of Two WTO Panel Rulings against Canada and Brazil. In: JWT, Vol. 33 No. 6, 1999. S. 97-120.
Stehmann 2000: Stehmann, Oliver. Foreign Sales Corporations under the WTO. The Panel Ruling on US Export Subsidies. In: JWT, Vol. 34, No. 3, 2000. S. 127-156.
Stein 1995: Stein, Howard. Policy Alternatives to Structural Adjustment in Africa: An Introduction. In: Stein, Howard (Hrg.). Asian Industrialization and Africa. Studies in Policy Alternatives to Structural Adjustment. London: St. Martin's Press, 1995.
Stein 1995a: Stein, Howard. The World Bank, Neo-Classical Economics and the Application of Asian Industrial Policy to Africa. In: Stein, Howard (Hrg.). Asian Industrialization and Africa. Studies in Policy Alternatives to Structural Adjustment. London: St. Martin's Press, 1995.
Steinberger 1992: Steinberger, Helmut. Allgemeine Regeln des Völkerrechts. In: Isensee, Josef, Kirchhof, Paul (Hrg.). Handbuch des Staatsrechts. Bd. VII. Heidelberg: C.F. Müller, 1992.
Stern 1977: Stern, Klaus. Das Staatsrecht der Bundesrepublik Deutschland. Band 1. Grundbegriffe und Grundlagen des Staatsrechts, Strukturprinzipien der Verfassung. Münschen: C.H. Beck, 1977.
Stern 1990: Stern, Robert M. Symposion on TRIPs and TRIMs in the Uruguay Round: Analytical and Negotiating Issues: Introduction. In: World Economy, Vol. 13, No. 4, December 1990. S. 493-496.
Stern 1997: Stern, Brigitte. Can the United States set Rules for the World? In: JWT, Vol. 31, No. 4, August 1997. S. 6-26.
Stern/Maskus 1981: Stern, Robert M., Maskus, Keith E. Determinants of the Structure of U.S. Foreign Trade. In: Journal of International Economics, Vol. 11, 1981. S. 207-224.
Sternberger 1979: Sternberger, Dolf. Verfassungspatriotismus. In: Sternberger, Dolf. Schriften X. Frankfurt am Main: Insel Verlag, 1990.

Stevens 1990: Stevens, Christopher. Nigeria. In: Riddell, Roger C. (ed.). Manufacturing Africa. Performance & Prospects of Seven Countries in Sub-Saharan Africa. Overseas Development Institute. London: James Currey, 1990.

Stevens 2002: Stevens, Christopher. The Future of Special and Differential Treatment (SDT) for Developing Countries in the WTO. IDS Working Paper 163. Institute of Development Studies, Brighton, Sussex: 2002. In: www.ids.ac.uk/ids/bookshop/.

Stevens/Kennan 1995: Stevens, Christoper, Kennan, Jane. How will the EU's Response to the GATT Round affect Developing Countries? In: Nord-Süd Aktuell, Heft 3, 1995. S. 395-415.

Stevenson 2004: Stevenson, Cliff. Are World Trade Organization Members Correctly Applying World Trade Organization Rules in Safeguard Determinations? In: JWT Vol. 38, No. 2, 2004. S. 307-329.

Stewart 1984: Stewart, Frances P. Facilitating Indigenous Technical Change in Thirld World Countries. In: Fransman, Martin, King, Kenneth (eds.). Technology Capability in the Thirld World. London: Macmillan, 1984.

Stewart 1993: Stewart, Terence P. (ed.). The GATT Uruguay Round. A Negotiating History (1986-1994). Vol. I Commentary. Deventer, Boston: Kluwer Law and Taxation Publishers 1993.

Stewart 1994a: Stewart, Frances P. Recent Theories of International Trade. Some Implications for the South. In: Kierzkowski, Henryk (ed.). Monopolistic Competition and International Trade. Oxford: Clarendon Press, 1984.

Stewart 1999: Stewart, Terence P. (ed.). The GATT Uruguay Round. A Negotiating History (1986-1994). Volume IV: The End Game (Part I). The Hague; London; Boston: Kluwer Law International, 1999.

Stewart 2005: Stewart, Terence P. Statement of Terence P. Stewart, Esq. Stewart and Stewart. House Committee on Ways and Means. Hearings. May 17, 2005. In: http://waysandmeans.house.gov.

Stewart/Dwyer 1998: Stewart, Terence P., Dwyer, Amy S. Sunset Reviews of Antidumping and Countervailing Duty Measures. US Implementation of the Uruguay Round Commitments. In: Journal of World Trade, Vol. 32, Heft 5, 1998. S. 101-135.

Stewart/Dwyer 1998a: Stewart, Terence P., Dwyer, Amy S. WTO Antidumping and Subsidy Agreements. A Practitioner's Guide to 'Sunset' Reviews in Australia, Canada, the European Union, and the United States. The Hague et al.: Kluwer, 1998.

Stewart/Ghani 1992: Stewart, Frances, Ghani, Ejaz. Externalities, Development and Trade. In: Helleiner (ed.). Trade Policy, Industrialization, and Development. New York: Oxford University Press, 1992.

Stigler 1975: Sigler, George W. The Citizen and the State. Chicago, London: University of Chicago Press, 1975.

Stiglitz 1986: Stiglitz, Joseph E., Greenwald, Bruce E. Externalities in Economies with Imperfect Information and Incomplete Markets. In: Quarterly Journal of Economics, Vol. 101, 1986. S. 229-264.

Stiglitz 1987: Stiglitz, Joseph E. On the Microeconomics of Technical Progress. In: Katz, Jorge M., Technology Generation in Latin American Manufacturing Industries. London: Macmillan Press, 1987.

Stiglitz 1987a: Stiglitz, Joseph E. Technological Change, Sunk Costs, and Competition. In: Brookings Papers on Economic Activity, Vol. 3, 1987. S. 883-947.

Stiglitz 1989: Stiglitz, Joseph E. Market, Market Failures, and Development. In: American Economic Review, Papers and Proceedings, Vol. 79, No. 2, May 1989, S. 197-203.

Stiglitz 1994: Stiglitz, Joseph E. Wither Socialism? Cambridge, Mass.: The MIT-Press, 1994.

Stiglitz 1998: Stiglitz, Joseph E. The East Asian Crisis and Its Implications for India. Golden Jubilee Year Celebration of the Industrial Finance Corporation of India, Lecture, May 19, 1998. In: http://www.worldbank.org.

Stiglitz 1998a: Stiglitz, Joseph E. More Instruments and Broader Goals: Moving Toward the Post-Washington Consenus. WIDER-Annual Lectures 2. http://www.worldbank.org.

Stiglitz 1998b: Stiglitz, Joseph E. Towards a New Paradigm for Development: Strategies, Policies, and Process. Prebisch Lecture, UNCTAD Geneva, October 19, 1998. http://www.worldbank.org

Stiglitz 1999: Stiglitz, Joseph E. Wither Reform. Ten Years of the Transition. Word Bank Annual Conference on Development Economics. http://www.worldbank.org.

Stiglitz 2002: Stiglitz, Joseph E. Die Schatten der Globalisierung. Bonn: Bundeszentrale für politische Bildung, 2002.

Stiglitz 2005: Stiglitz, Joseph E. Development Policies in a World of Globalization. In: Gallagher, Kevin P. Putting Development First. London, New York: Zed Books, 2005.

Stiglitz 2006: Stiglitz, Joseph E. Making Globalization Work. London: Penguin Books, 2006.

Stiglitz/Charlton 2005: Stiglitz, Joseph E., Charlton, Andrew. Fair Trade for All. Oxford: Oxford University Press, 2005.

Stigum/Stigum 1968: Stigum, Bernt P., Stigum, Marcia L. Economics. Reading, Mass.: Addison-Wesley, 1968.

Stikova/Maug 2004: Stikova, Jana, Maug, Ernst. Acerlor: The Creation of a European Steel Company. Revised: April 14, 2004. In: http://www.konzern-management.de/Lehre/KMII/Seminar/arcelor.htm.

Stiles 1990: Stiles, Kendall W. IMF Conditionality: Coercion or Compromise? In: World Development, Vol. 18, No. 7, 1990. S. 959-974.

Stirling/Yochelson 1985: Stirling, Catherine, Yochelson, John H. Under Pressure. U.S. Industry and the Challenges of Structural Adjustment. Boulder, London: Westview Press, 1985.

Stobaugh/Wells 1984: Stobaugh, Robert, Wells, Louis T. Technology Crossing Borders. The Choice, Transfer, and Management of International Technology Flows. Boston, Mass.: Harvard Business School Press, 1984.

Stockey 1988: Stockey, Nancy L. Learning by Doing and the Introduction of New Goods. In: Journal of Political Economy, Vol. 96, No. 4, 1988. S. 701-717.

Stockings/Watkins 1947: Stocking, George W., Watkins, Myron W. Cartels in Action. Case Studies in International Business Diplomacy. New York: The Twentieth Century Fund, 1947.

Stoll 1994: Stoll, Peter-Tobias. Technologietransfer. Internationalisierungs- und Nationalisierungstendenzen. Berlin etc.: Springer Verlag, 1994.
Stoll 1994a: Stoll, Peter-Tobias. Die WTO: Neue Welthandelsorganisation, neue Welthandelsordnung. Ergebnisse der Uruguay-Runde des GATT. In: ZaöRV, Band 54, 1994. S. 241-339.
Stoll 1997: Stoll, Peter-Tobias. Freihandel und Verfassung. Einzelstaatliche Gewährleistung und die konstitutionelle Funktion der Welthandelsordnung (GATT/WTO). In: ZaöRV, 57/1, 1997. S. 83-146.
Stoll/Schorkopf 2002: Stoll, Peter-Tobias, Schorkopf, Frank. WTO - Welthandelsordnung und Welthandelsrecht. Köln et al.: Carl Heymanns, 2002.
Stolper/Samuelson 1941/1942: Stolper, Wolfgang F., Samuelson, Paul A. Protection and Real Wages. In: Review of Economic Studies, Vol. IX, 1941-1942. S. 58-73.
Stone 1994: Stone, Andrew. Complex Transactions under Uncertainty. Brazil's Machine Tool Industry. World Bank Policy Reserach Working Paper 1247. Washington: World Bank, January 1994.
Stone/Lee 1995: Stone, Joe A., Lee, Hyun-Hoon. Determinants of Intra-Industy Trade: A Longitudinal, Cross-Country Analysis. In: Weltwirtschafliches Archiv, Bd. 131, Heft 1, 1995. S. 67-85.
Storm 1997: Storm, Servaas. Agriculture under Trade Policy Reform: A Quantitative Assessment for India. In: World Development, Vol. 25 No. 3, 1997. S. 425-436.
Storper et al. 2000: Storper, Michael, Chen, Yun-chung, De Paolis, Fernando. The Effects of Globalization on the Location of Industries in the OECD and European Union. DRUID Working Paper No. 00-7. February 2000. In: http://www.business.auc.dk/druid.
Strange 1982: Strange, Susan. Cave! hic dragones: a critique of regime analysis. In: Krasner, Stephen D. (Hrg.) International Regimes. Ithaca, London: Cornell University Press, 1982 (1983).
Strange 1985: Strange, Susan. Protectionism and World Politics. In: International Organization, 39, 2, Spring 1985. S. 233-259.
Strange 1987: Strange, Susan. The persistent myth of lost hegemony. In: International Organization, 41, 4, Autumn 1987. S. 551-574.
Strange 1994: Strange, Susan. States and Markets. London, Washington: Pinter, 1994.
Strange 1995: Strange, Susan. The Limits of Politics. In: Government & Opposition, Vol. 30, No. 3, 1995. S. 291-311.
Strange 1996: Strange, Susan. The Retreat of the State. Cambridge: Cambridge University Press, 1996.
Strange 1997: Strange, Susan. An International Political Economy Perspective. In: Dunning, John H. (ed.). Governments, Gobalization and International Business. Oxford: Oxford University Press, 1997.
Strasberg et al. 1999: Strasberg, Paul J., Jayne, T. S., Yamano, Takashi, Nyoro, James, Karanja, Daniel, Strauss, John. Effects of Agricultural Commercialization on Food Crop Inputs Use and Productivity in Kenya. Michigan State University International Development Working Papers No. 71, 1999. In: http://www.aec.msu.edu/agecon/fs2/index.htm.
Strasberg/Kloeck-Jenson 2002: Strasberg, Paul J., Kloeck-Jenson, Scott. Challenging Conventional Wisdom: Smallholder Perceptions and Experience of Land Access and Tenure Security in the Cotton Belt of Northern Mozambique. Working Paper No. 48 Mozambique Series, Land Tenure Centre, University of Wisconsin-Madison, April 2002. In: http://www.wisc.edu/ltc.
Strauß 1996: Strauß, Joseph. Implications of the TRIPS Agreement in the Field of Patent Law. In: Beier, Friedrich-Karl, Schricker, Gerhard (eds.) From GATT to TRIPs. The Agreement on Trade-Related Aspects of Intellectual Property Rights. Weinheim: VHC, 1996.
Streeck 1997: Streek, Wolfgang. German Capitalism: Does it exist? Can it survive?. In: Crouch, Colin, Streeck, Wolfgang. Political Economy of Modern Capitalism. London: Sage, 1997.
Streeten 1989: Streeten, Paul P. International Cooperation. In: Chenery, H., Srinivasan, T.N. Handbook of Development Economics, Vol. I, Amsterdam; New York: Elsevier Science B.V., 1989.
Streit 1986: Streit, Joachim. Zur Liberalisierung des Finanzsektors in der Bundesrepublik Deutschland. In: Die Weltwirtschaft, Heft 1, 1986. S. 55-73.
Streit 1988: Streit, Manfred E. Freiheit und Gerechtigkeit. Ordnungspolitische Aspekte zweier gesellschaftlicher Grundwerte. In: ORDO, Bd. 39, 1988.
Streit 1991: Streit, Manfred E. Theorie der Wirtschaftspolitik. Düsseldorf: Werner, 1991.
Streit 1995: Streit, Manfred E. Ordnungsökonomik. Versuch einer Standortbestimmung. Max-Planck-Institut zur Erforschung von Wirtschaftssystemen, Diskussionsbeitrag 04/95. Jena, 1995.
Streit 1998: Streit, Manfred E. Soziale Marktwirtschaft im europäischen Integrationsprozeß: Befund und Perspektiven. In: Cassel, Dieter (Hrg.). 50 Jahre Soziale Marktwirtschaft. Schriften zu Ordnungsfragen der Wirtschaft. Bd. 57, Stuttgart: Lucius&Lucius, 1998.
Streit/Wohlgemuth 1999: Streit, Manfred E., Wohlgemuth, Michael. Walter Eucken und Friedrich A. Hayek. Initiatoren der Ordnungsökonomik. Max-Planck-Institut zur Erforschung von Wirtschaftssystemen, Diskussionsbeitrag 11-99. Jena, 1999.
Struck 1995: Struck, Hans-Joachim. Die Automobilindustrie in den Entwicklungsländern - dargestellt am Beispiel 'Nigeria'. Münster: Lit-Verlag, 1995.
Stryker 1991: Stryker, J. Dirck. Ghana. In: Krueger, Anne O., Schiff, Maurice, Valdes, Alberto. The Political Economy of Agricultural Pricing Policy. Vol. 3 Africa and the Mediterranean. Baltimore, London: John Hopkins University Press, 1991.
Subrahmanian 1993: Subrahmanian, K. K. India. In: Patel, Surendra J. Technological Transformation in the Thirld World. Aldershot: Avebury/UNU/WIDER, 1993.

Subramanian /Roy 2001: Subramania, Arvind, Roy, Devesh. Who Can Explain the Mauritian Miracle: Meade, Romer, Sachs, or Rodrik? IMF Working Paper, 01/116, 2001. In: http://www.imf.org.
Subramanian 1990: Subramanian, Arvind. TRIPs and the Paradigm of the GATT: a Tropical, Temperate View. In: World Economy, Vol. 13, No. 4, December 1990. S. 509-521.
Subramanian 1991: Subramanian, Arvind. The International Economics of Intellectual Property Right Protection: A Welfare-Theoretic Trade Policy Analysis. In: World Development, Vol. 19, No. 8, 1991. S. 945-956.
Subramanyam 2006: Subramanyam, BVR. Investment Incentives and Multilateral Disciplines. In: Evenett, Simon J., Hoekman, Bernard M. Economic Development and Multilateral Trade Cooperation. Washington: World Bank/Palgrave Macmillan, 2006.
Subramanian/Tamirisa 2001: Subramanian, Arvind, Tamarisa, Nathalie. Africa's Trade Revisited. IMF Working Paper WP/01/33. Washington: IMF, March 2001.
Subramanian/Wei 2003: Subramanian, Arvind, Wei, Shang-Jin. The WTO Promotes Trade, Strongly but Unevenly. IMF Working Paper, WP/03/185. September 2003. In: http://www.imf.org.
Suits 1990: Suits, Daniel B. Agriculture. In: Adams, Walter (Hrg.). The Structure of American Industry. New York: Macmillan, 1990.
Sun 1998: Sun, Haishun. Foreign Investment and Economic Development in China: 1979-1996. Adershot: Ashgate, 1998.
Sun 2003: Sun, Haochen. Reshaping the TRIPs Agreement Concerning Public Health: Two Critical Issues. In: JWT, Vol. 37, No. 1, 2003. S. 163-197.
Suphachalasai 1990: Suphachalasai, Suphat. Export Growth of Thai clothing and textiles. In: World Economy, Vol. 13. S. 51-73.
Sutham et al. 2005: Sutham, Apisith John, Attavipach, Parate, Eiamchinda, Patamaporn. The 10 Major Problems With the Anti-Dumping Instrument in Thailand. In: JWT, Vol. 39, No. 1, 2005. S. 159-168.
Sutherland 2005: Sutherland, Peter. The Doha Development Agenda: Political Challenges to the World Trading System - a Cosmopolitan Perspective. In: Petersmann, Ernst-Ulrich (ed.). Reforming the World Trading System. Legitimacy, Efficiency, and Democratic Governance. Oxford: Oxford University Press, 2005.
Sutherland et al. 2005: Sutherland, Peter, Bhagwati, Jagdish, Botchwey, Kwesi, Fitzgerald, Niall, Hamada, Koichi, Jackson, John H., Lafer, Celso, de Montbrial, Thierry. The Future of the WTO. Adressing institutional challenges in the new millenium. Geneva: WTO, 2005.
Sutton 1991: Sutton, John. Sunk Costs and Market Structure. Price Competition, Advertising, and the Evoluation of Concentration. Cambridge: MIT Press, 1991.
Sutton 1998: Sutton, John. Technology and Market Structure. Theory and History. Cambridge: MIT Press, 1998.
Sykes 2001: Sykes, Alan O. 'Efficient Protection' through WTO rulemaking. In: Porter, Roger B., Sauvé, Pierre, Subramanian, Arvind, Zampetti, Americo Beviglia. Efficiency, Equity, Legitimacy. The Multilateral Trading System at the Millenium. Washington D.C.: Brookings Institution Press, 2001.
Sykes 2003: Sykes, Alan O. The safeguards mess: A critique of WTO jurisprudence. In: World Trade Review Vol. 2 No. 3, 2003. S. 261-295.
Sykes 2004: Sykes, Alan O. The Persistant Puzzles of Safeguards: Lessons from the Steel Dispute. In: Journal of International Economic Law, Vol. 7, No. 3, 2004. S. 523-564.
Sykes 2006: Sykes, Alan O. The WTO Agreement on Safeguards. Oxford: Oxford University Press, 2006.
Sykes 2006a: Sykes, Alan O. The Fundamental Deficiencies of the Agreement on Safeguards: A Reply to Professor Lee. In: JWT, Vol. 40, No. 5, 2006. S. 979-996.
Symeonidis 1996: Symeonidis, George. Innovation, Firms Size and Market Structure: Schumpeterian Hyptheses and Some New Themes. OECD/GD(96)58. Paris: OECD, 1996.
Syrquin 1994: Syrquin, Moshe. Growth and Industrialization since 1965. In: Helleiner, Gerald K. (ed.). Trade Policy and Industrialization in Turbulent Times. London; New York: Routledge, 1994.
Szepesi 2003: Szepesi, Stefan. Preparing for the Inevitable? The African, Caribeean and Pacific Countries and Trade Negotiations with the European Union. Master Thesis, Maastricht University. In: http://www.acp-eu-trade.org/biblio_acpeutraderelations.php.
Szirmai 1993: Szirmai, Adam. Comparative Productivity in Manufacturing: A Case Study for Indonesia. In: Szirmai, Adam, van Ark, Bart, Pilat, Dirk (eds.). Explaining Economic Growth. Essays in Honour of Angus Maddison. Amsterdam: North Holland, 1993.
Szirmai 1994: Szirmai, Adam. Real Output and Labour Productivity in Indonesian Manufacturing, 1975-90. In: Bulletin of Indonesian Economic Studies, Vol. 30, No. 2, August 1994. S. 49-90.
Szirmai et al. 2005: Szirmai, Adam, Ren, Ruoen, Bai, Manyin. Chinese Manufacturing Performance in Comparative Perspective, 1980-2002. Economic Growth Center, Yale University, Center Discussion Paper No. 920, July 2005. In: http://www.econ.yale.edu/~egcenter/.

T

TAFTA 2005: Thailand Austrialia Free Trade Agreement. Text of the Agreement. Entry into Force: 1 January 2005. In: http://www.dfat.gov.au/trade/negotiations/aust-thai/.
Taiwan Zölle 1998: Customs Import Tariff and Classification of Import & Export Commodities of the Republic of China, June 1998, Rev. Edition. Published by the Directorate General of Customs, M.O.F, Board of Foreign Trade, M.O.E.A, 1998.

Takeda 1996: Takeda, Yasutsugu. National Technolgy Policies and International Cooperative Linkages among Private Firms – Perspective from a Japanes Private Firm. In: Koopmann, Georg, Scharrer, Hans-Eckart (eds.). The Economics of High-Technology Competition. Baden-Baden: Nomos, 1996.
Takenaka 1995: Takenaka, Toshiko. Interpreting Patent Claims: The United States, Germany and Japan. Weinheim: VCH, 1995.
Takigawa 1998: Takigawa, Toshiaki. The Impact of the WTO Telecommunications Agreement on US and Japanese Telecommunications Regulations. In: JWT, Vol. 32, No. 6, 1998. S. 33-55.
Tangermann 1994: Tangermann, Stefan. An Assessment of the Uruguay Round on Agriculture. Paper prepared for OECD Food Agriculture and Fisheries Directorate and Trade Directorate. Standord, June 1994.
Tangermann 1995: Tangermann, Stefan. Implementation of the Uruguay Round Agreements on Agriculture by Major Developed Countries. United Nations Conference on Trade and Development. UNCTAD/ITD/16, 3 October. Geneva: UNCTAD, 1995.
Tangermann 1996: Tangermann, Stefan. Implementation of the Uruguay Round Agreement on Agriculture: Issues and Prospects. In: Journal of Agricultural Economics Vol. 47 No. 3, 1996. S. 315-337.
Tangermann 1997: Tangermann, Stefan. Reforming the CAP: A Prerequisite for Eastern Enlargement. In: Siebert, Horst (ed.). Quo Vadis Europe? Tübingen: Mohr, 1997.
Tangermann 1997a: Tangermann, Stefan. Reformbedarf in der EU-Agrarpolitik und die Agenda 2000. Expertise für den Sachverständigenrat zur Begutachtung der gesamtwirtschaftlichen Entwicklung. Institut für Agrarökonomie Universität Göttingen, September 1997. In: http://wwwuser.gwdg.de/~uaao/welcome.htm.
Tangermann 2001: Tangermann, Stefan. Auswirkungen der WTO-Verhandlungen auf die deutsche Landwirtschaft. Vortrag auf der RKL-Tagung in Neumünster, 4.1.2001. In: http://wwwuser.gwdg.de/~uaao/welcome.htm.
Tangermann 2001a: Tangermann, Stefan. The Future of Preferential Trade Arrangements for Developing Countries and the Current Round of WTO Negotiations on Agriculture. Paper Prepared for FAO/ESCP, April 2001. In: http://wwwuser.gwdg.de/~uaao/welcome.htm.
Tangermann 2004: Tangermann, Stefan, Agricultural Policies in OECD Countries Ten Years After the Uruguay Round: How much progress? In: Anania, Giovanni et al. (Hrg.). Agricultural Policy Reform and the WTO. Cheltenham: Edward Elgar, 2004.
Tangermann 2005: Tangermann, Stefan. How to Forge a Compromise in the Agriculture Negotiations. In: Petersmann, Ernst-Ulrich (ed.). Reforming the World Trading System. Legitimacy, Efficiency, and Democratic Governance. Oxford: Oxford University Press, 2005.
Tangermann/Hartwig 1987: Tangermann, Stefan, Hartwig, Bettina. Legal Aspects of Restricting Manioc Trade between Thailand and the EEC. Kiel: Wissenschaftsverlag Vauk, 1987.
Tangermann/Josling 1999: Tangermann, Stefan, Josling, Tim. The Interests of Developing Countries in the Next Round of WTO Agricultural Negotiations. Workshop Paper for UNCTAD, June/July 1999. In: http://www.unctad.org/en/posagen/agricult/document.htm.
Taplin 1994: Taplin, Ian M. Strategic Reorientation of U.S. Apparel Firms. In: Gereffi, Gary, Korzeniewicz, Miguel (eds.). Commodity Chains and Global Capitalism. Westport, Connecticut; London: Praeger 1994.
Tarr 1979: Tarr, David G. Cyclical Dumping. The Case of Steel Products. In: Journal of International Economics, 9, 1979. S. 57-63.
Tarullo 2002: Tarullo, Daniel K. The Hidden Costs of International Dispute Settlement: WTO Review of Domestic Anti-Dumping Decisions. In: Georgetown University Law Centre, Working Paper Series No. 351080. In: http://papers.ssrn.com/.
Taube 2001: Taube, Markus. Japanese Influences on Industrializaton in China. Duisburger Arbeitspapier zur Ostasienwirtschaft, No. 58, 2001. In: http://www.uni-duisburg.de/FB5/VWL/OAWI/ARBEITSPAPIERE/main.html
Taylor 1983: Taylor, Lance. Structuralist Macroeconomics. Applicable Models for the Third World. New York: Basic Books, 1983.
Taylor 1988: Taylor, Lance. Varieties of Stabilization Experience. Towards Sensible Macroeconomics in the Third World. Oxford: Clarendon Press, 1988.
Taylor 1991: Taylor, Lance. Foreign Resource Flows and Developing Country Growth. WIDER, March 1991.
Taylor 1993: Taylor, Charles. Multikulturalismus und die Politik der Anerkennung. Frankfurt am Main: Fischer, 1993.
Taylor 1993a: Taylor, Lance. Stabilization, Adjustment and Reform. In: Taylor, Lance (ed.). The Rocky Road to Reform. Adjustment, Income Distribution, and Growth in the Developing World. Cambridge: MIT Press, 1993.
Taylor 2001: Taylor, Christopher T. The Economic Effects of Withdrawn Antidumping Investigations: Is the Evidence of Collusive Settlements? Federal Trade Commission, Bureau of Economics, Working Paper, August 2001. In: http://www.ftc.gov/be/econwork.htm.
Taylor 2006: Taylor, Martyn D. International Competition Law. A New Dimension for the WTO? Cambridge: Cambridge University Press, 2006.
Taylor/Silberston 1973: Taylor, C.T., Silberston, Z.A. The Economic Impact of the Patent System. A Study of the British Experience. Cambridge: At the University Press, 1973.
Teal 1999: Teal, Francis. Why can Mauritius export manufactures and Ghana not? WPS/99-10. Oxford Centre for the Study of African Economies. In: http://www.csae.ox.ac.uk/workingpapers/main-wps.html.
Teal 2000: Teal, Francis. Real Wages and the demand for skilled and unskilled male labour in Ghana's manufacturing sector. In: Journal of Development Economics, Vol. 61, 2000. S. 447-461.

Teal/Vigneri 2004: Teal, Francis, Vigneri, Marcella. Production Changes in Ghana Cocoa Farming Households under Market Reforms. WPS/2004-16. Oxford Centre for the Study of African Economies. In: http://www.csae.ox.ac.uk/workingpapers/main-wps.html.
Tecson 1989: Tecson, Gwendolyn R. Structural Changen and Barriers to Philippine Manufactured Exports. In: The Developing Economies, XXVII, Bd. 1, March 1989. S. 34-59.
Teitel 1987: Teitel, Simón. Science and Technology Indicators, Country Size and Economic Development: In International Comparison. In: World Development, Vol. 15, No. 9, 1987. S. 1225-1235.
Teitel/Sercovich 1984: Teitel, Simón, Sercovich, Francisco Colman. Latin America. In: World Development, Vol. 12, No. 5/6, 1984. S. 645-660.
Teitel/Thoumi 1986: Teitel, Simón, Thoumi, Francisco E. From Import Substitution to Exports: The Manufacturing Exports Experience of Argentina and Brazil. In: Economic Development and Cultural Change, Vol. 34, 1986. S. 455-490.
Tekere 1999: Tekere, Moses. Farewell to Lomé – Implications of Trade Liberalization on Zimbabwe's Textile and Clothing Industry with Emphasis on the Position of Workers. In: Farewell to Lomé? The Impact of Neo-liberal EU Policies on ACP Countries. WEED, terre des hommes, KOSA. Bonn, July 1999.
Ten Kate 1992: Ten Kate, Adriaan. Trade Liberalization and Economic Stabilization in Mexico: Lessons of Experience. In: World Development, Vol. 20, No. 5, 1992. S. 659-672.
Tendenzen der Bundesrepublik in der Textilhandelspolitik der EG: In: ORDO Bd. 41, 1990. S. 117-130.
Terra 1998: Terra, Cristina T. Openness and Inflation: A New Assessment. In: Quarterly Journal of Economics, Vol. CXIII, Issue 3, August 1998. S. 641-652.
Tetzlaff 1995: Tetzlaff, Rainer. Die neue deutsche Außenpolitik zwischen überholter Selbstbeschränkung und unerprobter Interventionspolitik: Erste Gehversuche mit politischer Konditionalität. In: Bahr, Egon, Lutz, Dieter S. (Hrg.) Unsere Gemeinsame Zukunft - Globale Herausforderungen. Baden Baden: Nomos, 1995.
Teubal/Steimueller 1982: Teubal, Morris, Steimmueller, Edward. Government Policy, Innovation and Economic Growth. In: Research Policy, Vol. 11, 1982. S. 271-287.
Thai Automotive Institute 2006: Thai Automotive Institute. Statistical Information. 2006. In: http://www.thaiauto.or.th/index_eng.asp.
Tharakan 1986: Tharakan, P. K. Mathew. The Intra-Industry Trade of Benelux with the Developing World. In: Weltwirtschaftliches Archiv, Bd. 122, 1986, S. 131-149.
Tharakan/Kerstens 1995: Tharakan, P. K. Mathew, Kerstens, Birgit. Does North-South Horizontal Intra-Industry Trade Really Exist? An Analysis of the Toy Industry. In: Weltwirtschaftliches Archiv, Bd. 131, Heft 1, 1995. S. 86-105.
Theron 1998: Theron, Nicola. Anti-Dumping Procedures: Lessons for Developing Countries with Special Emphasis on the South African Experience. In: http://www.sba.muohio.edu/ABAS/1998/anti-dumping.pdf.
Thiesenhusen/Melmed-Sanjak 1990: Thiesenhusen, William C., Melmed-Sanjak, Jolyne. Brazil's Agrarian Structure: Changes from 1970 through 1980. In: World Development Vol. 18 No. 3, 1990. S. 393-415.
Thoburn 2000: Thoburn, John. Finding the Right Track for Industry in Africa - Some Policy Issues and Options. Discussion Paper. Wien: UNIDO, 2000. In: http://www.unido.org.
Thoburn et al. 2002: Thoburn, John, Nguyen, Thi Thanh Ha, Nguyen Thi Hoa. Globalization and the textile industry in Vietnam. Discussion Paper 10. GAP Project. http://www.gapresearch.org/production/globprodpov.html.
Thomas 1991: Thomas, Heike. A. Increased Import Competition - Section 201 of the Trade Act of 1974 (The Escape Clause). In: Grabnitz, Eberhard, von Bogdandy, Armin (eds.). U.S. Trade Barriers: A Legal Analysis. New York; London; Rome: European Law Press Munich, Oceana Publications, 1991.
Thomas 1991: Thomas, Heike. Underlying Policy of Fair Trade Remedies. In: Grabnitz, Eberhard, von Bogdandy, Armin (eds.). U.S. Trade Barriers: A Legal Analysis. New York; London; Rome: European Law Press Munich, Oceana Publications, 1991.
Thomas 2000: Thomas, Chantal. Balance-of-Payments Crises in the Developing World: Balancing Trade, Finance and Development in the New Economic Order. In: American University International Law Review, Vol. 15, 2000. S. 1249-1277.
Thomas/Wang 1996: Thomas, Vinod, Wang, Yan. Distortions, Interventions, and Productivity Growth: Is East Asia Different? In: Economic Development and Cultural Change, Vol. 44, 1995/96. S. 265-288.
Thomas-Emeagwali 1991: Thomas-Emeagwali, Gloria. Technology Transfer: Explaining the Japanese Success Story. In: Journal of Contemporary Asia, Vol. 21 No. 4, 1991. S. 504-512.
Thompson 2001: Thompson, Aileen J. Import Competition and Market Power: Canadian Evidence. Washington: Federal Trade Commission, Bureau of Economics, Working Papers, January 2001. In: www.ftc.gov/be/econwork.htm
Thorpe 1997: Thorpe, Andy. Structural Adjustment and the agrarian sector in Latin America. In: Spoor, Max (ed.). The 'Market Panacea'. Agrarian transformation in developing countries and former transition economies. London: Intermediate Technology Publications, 1997.
Thrupp et al. 1995: Thrupp, Lori Ann, Bergeron, Gilles, Waters, William F. Bittersweet Harvests for Global Supermarktes: Challenges in Latin America's Agricultural Export Boom. World Resources Institute, August 1995.
Thuy 1998: Thuy, Peter. 50 Jahre Soziale Marktwirtschaft: Anspruch und Wirklichkeit einer ordnungspolitischen Konzeption. In: ORDO, Bd. 49, 1998.
Tiefer 2001: Tiefer, Charles. Sino 301: How Congress can effectively review relations with China after WTO accession. In: Cornell International Law Journal, 55, 201. S. 55-93.

Timberg 1981: Timberg, Sigmund. Restrictive Business Practices in the International Transfer of Technology. In: Schachter/Hellawell 1981: Schachter, Oscar, Hellawell, Robert. Competition in International Business. Law and Policy on Restrictive Practices. New York: Columbia University Press, 1981.
Timmer 2000: Timmer, Marcel P. Reconciling Accumulationists and Assimilationists. A new framework for measuring technology assimilation in East-Asian manufacturing.
Timmer/van Ark 2001: Timmer, Marcel, van Ark, Bart. PPPs and international productivity comparisons: bottlenecks and new directions. OECD, World Bank. 2001. In: http://www.oecd.org/catch_404/?404; http://www.oecd.org/std/ppp/MTG2001/vanark8.pdf
TIPS Report Employment 2004: Trade and Industrial Policy Strategies (TIPS), South Africa. Snapshot of Industry-Wide Trends in Employment, 1991-2002. In: http://www.tips.org.za.
TIPS Report Imports 2004: Trade and Industrial Policy Strategies (TIPS), South Africa. Snapshot of Industry-Wide Trends in Imports, 1991-2002. In: http://www.tips.org.za.
Tkacik 2002: Tkacik, John J. Strategic Risks for East Asia in Economic Integration with China. The Heritage Foundation. Web Memo 171, November 12, 2002. In: http://www.heritage.org.
Todaro 1997: Todaro, Michael P. Economic Development. London; New York: Longman, 1997.
Tom et al. 2000: Tom, Willard K., Balto, David A., Averitt, Niel W. Anticompetitive Aspects of Market-Share Discounts and other Incentives to Exclusive Dealing. In: Antitrust Law Journal, Vol. 67, 2000. S. 615-639.
Tomar 1999: Tomar, David K. A Look into the WTO Pharmaceutical Patent Dispute Between the United States and India. In: Wisconsin International Law Journal, Vol. 17, No. 3, 1999. S. 579-603.
Tomuschat 1973: Tomuschat, Christian. Repressalie und Retorsion. Zu einigen Aspekten ihrer innerstaatlichen Durchführung. In: ZaöRV, Bd. 33, Nr. 1, März 1973. S. 179-222.
Tomuschat 1976: Tomuschat, Christian. Die Charta der wirtschaftlichen Rechte und Pflichten der Staaten. Zur Gestaltungskraft von Deklarationen der UN-Generalversammlung. In: ZaöRV, Vol. 36, 1976. S. 444-491.
Tomuschat 1978: Tomuschat, Christian. Der Verfassungsstaat im Geflecht internationaler Beziehungen. In: Veröffentlichungen der Vereinigung der Deutschen Staatsrechtslehrer, Bd. 36, 1978.
Tomuschat 1992: Tomuschat, Christian. Die staatsrechtliche Entscheidung für internationale Offenheit. In: Isensee, Josef, Kirchhof, Paul (Hrg.). Handbuch des Staatsrechts. Bd. VII. Heidelberg: C.F. Müller, 1992.
Tomuschat 1992a: Tomuschat, Christian. Menschenrechte. Eine Sammlung internationaler Dokumente zum Menschenrechtsschutz. Bonn: Deutsche Gesellschaft für die Vereinten Nationen, 1992.
Tomuschat 1993: Tomuschat, Christian. Die Europäische Union unter Aufsicht des Bundesverfassungsgerichts. In: EuGRZ, 20. Jg., Heft 20-21, S. 489-496.
Tomuschat 1994: Tomuschat, Christian. Obligations Arising for States Without or Against Their Will. In: Recueil des Cours; Collected Courses of The Hague Academy of International Law, (1993, IV), 1994.
Tomuschat 1995: Tomuschat, Christian. Die internationale Gemeinschaft. In: Archiv des Völkerrechts, Bd. 33, 1995. S. 1-20.
Tönnies Evers/von Wogau 1973: Tönnies Evers, Tilman, von Wogau, Peter. "dependencia": lateinamerikanische Beiträge zur Theorie der Unterentwicklung. In: Das Argument. Zeitschrift für Philosophie und Sozialwissenschaften. 15 Jg. Nr. 78-83, 1973. S. 332-403.
Tornell/Esquivel 1995: Tornell, Aaron, Esquivel, Gerardo. The Political Economy of Mexico's Entry to NAFTA. NBER Working Paper No. 5322, October 1995.
Townsend 1999: Townsend, Robert F. Agricultural Incentives in Sub-Saharan Africa. World Bank Technical Paper No. 444. Washington: World Bank, 1999.
Toye 1991: Toye, John. Ghana. In: Mosley, Paul, Harrigan, Jane, Toye, John (eds.). Aid and Power. The World Bank and Policy-based Lending. Vol. 2, Case Studies. London; New York: Routledge, 1991.
Toye 1991a: Toye, John. Is There a New Political Economy of Development? In: Christopher Colclough, James Manor (eds.). States or Markets? Neo-liberalism and the Development Policy Debate. Oxford. Clarendon Press, 1991.
Trachtman 2003: Trachtman, Joel P. The Agency Model of Judging in Economic Integration: Balancing Responsibilities. In: Cottier, Thomas, Mavroidis, Petros C (eds.). The Role of the Judge in International Trade Regulation. Ann Arbor: University of Michigan Press, 2003.
Trachtman 2005: Trachtman, Joel P. Negotiations on Domestic Regulation and Trade in Services (GATS Article VI): A legal analysis of selected current issues. In: Petersmann, Ernst-Ulrich (ed.). Reforming the World Trading System. Legitimacy, Efficiency, and Democratic Governance. Oxford: Oxford University Press, 2005.
Trade Policy Review div. Länder, div. Jahre: GATT bzw. WTO. Trade Policy Review of GATT/WTO Members. Geneva: WTO.
Trebilcock/Howse 2005: Trebilcock, Michael J., Howse, Robert. The Regulation of International Trade. Third Edition. London, New York: Routledge, 2005 (2007).
Trefler 1993: Trefler, Daniel. International Factor Price Differences: Leontief was right! Journal of Political Economy, Vol. 101, No. 6, 1993. S. 961-987.
Trefler 1995: Trefler, Daniel. The Case of the Missing Trade and Other Mysteries. In: American Economic Review, Vol. 85 No. 5, December 1995. S. 1029-1046.
Truman 1975: Truman, Edwin M. The Effects of European Economic Integration on the Production and Trade of Manufactured Products. In: Balassa, Bela. European Economic Integration. Amsterdam; Oxford: North-Holland Publishing Company, 1975.

Tschirley 2002: Tschirley, David L. Some Characteristics of Pro-Poor Growth, and Policy Implications for Mozambique. Policy Department Flash No. 29 E, February 25, 2002. In: http://www.aec.msu.edu/agecon/fs2/mozambique/flash29e.pdf.
Tsie 1996: Tsie, Balefi. The Political Context of Botswana's Development Performance. In: Journal of Southern African Studies, Vol. 22 No. 4, December 1996. S. 599-616.
Tuchtfeldt 1973: Tuchtfeldt, Egon. Soziale Marktwirtschaft und Globalsteuerung. In: Stützel, Wolfgang et al. (Hrg.). Grundtexte zur Sozialen Marktwirtschaft. Stuttgart: Gustav Fischer Verlag, 1981.
Tudyka 1989: Tudyka, Kurt. 'Weltgesellschaft' - Unbegriff und Phantom. In. PVS, Jg. 30, Heft 3, 1989. S. 503-508.
Tudyka 1990: Tudyka, Kurt. Politische Ökonomie in den internationalen Beziehungen. In: PVS, Jg. 31, Sonderheft 21, 1990.
Tullock 1959: Tullok, Gordon. Problems of Majority Voting. In: Journal of Political Economy, Vol. 67, 1959. S. 571-579.
Tullock 1967: Tullock, Gordon. The Welfare Costs of Tariffs, Monopolies and Theft. In: Buchanan, James M., Tollison, Robert D., Tullock, Gorbon (eds.). Toward a Theory of the Rent-Seeking Society. College Station: Texas A&M University Press, 1980.
Tullock 1980: Tullock, Gordon. Efficient Rent Seeking. In: Buchanan, James M., Tollison, Robert D., Tullock, Gorbon (eds.). Toward a Theory of the Rent-Seeking Society. College Station: Texas A&M University Press, 1980.
Tumlir 1980: Tumlir, Jan. National Souvereinty, Power and Interest. In: ORDO, Bd. 31, 1980. S. 25.
Tumlir 1983: Tumlir, Jan. International Economic Order and Democratic Constitutionalism. In: ORDO, Bd. 34, 1983. S. 71-83.
Tumlir 1985: Tumlir, Jan. Trade Policy in Democratic Societies. Washington: American Enterprise Institute, 1985.
Tybout 1992: Tybout, James R. Linking Trade and Productivity: New Research Dimensions. In: The World Bank Economic Review, Vol. 6, No. 2, 1992, pp. 189-211.
Tybout 1993: Tybout, James R. Internal Returns to Scale as a Source of Comparative Advantage. In: American Economic Review, Papers and Proceedings, Vol. 83, No. 2, May 1993. S. 440-444.
Tybout 1996: Tybout, James R. Chile, 1979-86: Trade Liberalization and Its Aftermath. In: Roberts, Mark J., Tybout, James R. Industrial Evolutions in Developing Countries. Micro Patterns of Turnover, Productivity, and Market Structure. Oxford: Oxford University Press (Published for World Bank), 1996.
Tybout 1998: Tybout, James. Manufacturing Firms in Developing Countries: How Well Do They Do, and Why? World Bank Policy Research Working Paper No. 1965, August 1998. In: http://wbln0018.worldbank.org/research/workpapers.nsf/policyresearch?openform
Tybout et al. 1991: Tybout, James, Melo, Jamie de, Corbo, Vittorio. The Effects of Trade Reforms on Scale and Technical Efficieny. In: Journal of International Economics, Vol. 31, 1991. S. 231-250.
Tybout/Westbrook 1996: Tybout, James R., Westbrook, Daniel M. Scale Economies as a Source of Efficiency Gains. In: Roberts, Mark J., Tybout, James R. Industrial Evolutions in Developing Countries. Micro Patterns of Turnover, Productivity, and Market Structure. Oxford: Oxford University Press (Published for World Bank), 1996.
Tudyka 1990: Tudyka, Kurt. Politische Ökonomie der internationalen Beziehungen. In: Politische Vierteljahresschrift, Vol. 31, Sonderheft 21. Opladen: Westdeutscher Verlag, 1990.
Tyler 1976: Tyler, William G. Manufactured Export Expansion and Industrialization in Brazil. Kieler Studien 134, Tübingen: Mohr, 1976.
Tyler 1985: Tyler, William G. Effective Incentives for Domestic Market Sales and Exports. A View of Anti-Export Biases and Commercial Policy in Brazil, 1980-81. In: Journal of Development Economics, Vol. 18, 1985. S. 219-242.
Tyson/Yoffie 1993: Tyson, Laura D'Andrea, Yoffie, David B. Semiconductors: From Manipulated to Managed Trade. In: Yoffie, David B. Beyond Free Trade. Firms, Governments, and Global Competition. Boston, Mass.: Harvard Business School Press, 1993.

U

U.S. Bureau of Census 1997: U.S. Bureau of Census. 1997 Economic Census. Manufacturing Subject Series. Issued 2001. In: http://www.census.gov/epcd/www/econ97.html.
U.S. Bureau of Census 1999: U.S. Bureau of Census, Economics and Statistics Administration. United States Department of Commerce News. A Profile of U.S Exporting Companies 1996-97. CR-99-76. In: http://www.cache.census.gov.
U.S. Bureau of Census 2002: U.S. Bureau of Census. 2002 Economic Census. Manufacturing Subject Series. Issued October 2005. In: http://www.census.gov/econ/census02/.
U.S. Bureau of Census Foreign Trade Statistics div. Länder 2006: U.S. Bureau of Census. Foreign Trade Statistics. U.S. Imports from all countries from 2001 to 2005. By 5-digit End-Use Code In: http://www.census.gov/foreign-trade/statistics/product/enduse/imports/index.html#C.
U.S. Bureau of Economic Analysis 1995: U.S. Bureau of Economic Analysis. Statistics on U.S. Multinational Companies. 1995. In: http://www.esa.doc.gov.
U.S. China Accession Tariffs 2000: Schedule CLII - People's Republic of China. Die verbindlichen MFN Industriegüterzölle Chinas. Veröffentlicht, aber nicht mehr zugänglich in U.S. China Business Council, 2000. In: http://www.uschina.org.

U.S. China Economic and Security Review Commission 2005: U.S. China Economic and Security Review Commission. 2005 Report to Congress. Washington: Government Printing Office, 2005. In: http://www.uscc.gov.
U.S. China Memorandum of Understanding 2005: Memorandum of Understanding Between the Governments of the United States of America and the People's Republic of China Concerning Trade in Textile and Apparel, Nov. 2005. In: http://otexa.ita.doc.gov.
U.S. Committee on Ways and Means Oversight Report 2005: Report on the Legislative and Oversight Activities of the Committee on Ways and Means during the 108th Congress. 3. January 2005. In: http://waysandmeans.house.gov/media/pdf/108thLegandOversReport.pdf.
U.S. Council of Economic Advisors 1999: Council of Economic Advisors. America's Interest in the World Trade Organization: An Economic Assessment. November 16, 1999. In: http://www.whitehouse, gov/WH/EOP/CEA.html.
U.S. Department of Commerce Manufacturing in America 2004: U.S. Department of Commerce Manufacturing in America. 2004. In: http://www.ita.doc.gov/media/Publications/pdf/manuam0104final.pdf.
U.S. Exports and Imports by Harmonized Commodity Annual 1996: U. S. Census Bureau. U. S. Exports and Imports by Harmonized Commodity, 1996 Annual. In: http://www.cache.census.gov.
U.S. GAO Textile Safeguards 2005: United States Government Accountability Office. U.S. China Trade Textile Safeguards Should Be Improved. GAO-05-296. April 2005. In: http://www.gao.gov/new.items/d05296.pdf.
U.S. Industry and Trade Outlook div. Chap. 2000: International Trade Administration. U.S. Industry and Trade Outlook. 2000. In: http://www.ita.doc.gov/td/industry/otea/outlook/ Oder: http://www.industrypro.com/reports.
U.S. Manufacturing 2004: Department of Commerce. Manufacturing in America. 2004. In: http://www.manufacturing.gov.
U.S. Mexico Agreement on Cement 2006: United States Trade Representative/Department of Commerce. Agreement between the Office of the United States Trade Representative and the Department of Commerce of the United States of America and the Ministry of Economy of the United Mexican States (Secretaria de Economia) on Trade in Cement. In: http://www.ustr.gov.
U.S. National Science Foundation R&D Data: U.S. National Science Foundation. Data Bank on National R&D Expenditures var. Years. In: http://www.nsf.gov/sbe/srs/.
U.S. Rules of Origin 2004: U.S. Customs and Border Protection. Rules of Origin. Informed Compliance Publications. Revised 2004. In: http://www.cbp.gov/xp/cgov/toolbox/legal/informed_compliance_pubs/.
U.S. Trade Stats Express 2006: TradeStats Express. Trade Data. 2006. In: http://tse.export.gov.
Ullrich 1989: Ullrich, Hanns. GATT: Industrial Property Protection, Fair Trade and Development. In: Beier, Friedrich-Karl, Schricker, Gerhard (eds.). GATT or WIPO? New Ways in the Protection of Intellectual Property. Weinheim: Wiley-VCH, 1989.
Ulrich 1989: Ulrich, Peter. Diskursethik und Politische Ökonomie. Arbeitspapier Nr. 28, Institut für Wirtschaftsethik, St. Gallen, März 1989.
Ulrich 1990: Ulrich, Peter. Der kritische Adam Smith – im Spannungsfeld zwischen sittlichem Gefühl und ethischer Vernunft. Arbeitspapier Nr. 40, Institut für Wirtschaftsethik, St. Gallen, März 1990.
Umbadda 1985: Umbadda, Siddiq. Domestic Resource Costs for Sudanese Manufacturing Industry: A preliminary analysis. In: Development and Change, Vol. 16, 1985. S. 149-158.
UN 1966: United Nation. Economic Commission for Asia and the Far East. Industrial Developments in Asia and the Far East. New York: United Nations, 1966.
UN International Trade Statistics Yearbook, div. Jahrgänge. United Nations. International Trade Statistics Yearbook, New York: UN, div. Jahrgänge.
UNCTAD 1985: UNCTAD. The history of UNCTAD 1964-1984. New York: United Nations, 1985.
UNCTAD 1989: UNCTAD. Uruguay Round. Papers on Selected Issues. New York: United Nations, 1989.
UNCTAD 1991: UNCTAD. The Impact of Trade-related Investment Measures on Trade and Development. United Nations: New York, 1991.
UNCTAD 1994: UNCTAD. Handbook of International Trade and Development Statistics, 1994. New York; Geneva: United Nations, 1995.
UNCTAD 1996/1997: UNCTAD. Handbook of International Trade and Development Statistics, 1996/1997. New York; Geneva: United Nations, 1999.
UNCTAD 1996: UNCTAD. Strengthening the Participation of Developing Countries in World Trade and the Multilateral Trading System. TD/375/Rev.1. New York; Geneva: United Nations, 1996.
UNCTAD 1996a: UNCTAD. Emerging Forms of Technology Cooperation: The Case for Technology Partnership. United Nations: New York and Geneva, 1996.
UNCTAD 1996b: UNCTAD. Fostering Technological Dynamism: Evoluation of Thought on Technological Development Processes and Competitiveness: A Review of the Literature. United Nations: New York and Geneva, 1996.
UNCTAD 1996c: UNCTAD. Incentives and Foreign Direct Investment. UNCTAD/DCTI/28, Current Studies, Series A, No. 20. New York and Geneva: United Nations, 1996.
UNCTAD 1997: UNCTAD/UN. International Monetary and Financial Issues for the 1990s. Research Papers for the Group of Twenty-Four, Vol. VIII. United Nations: New York and Geneva, 1997.
UNCTAD 1997a: UNCTAD. Opportunities for Vertical Diversification in the Food Processing Sector in Developing Countries. TD/B/COM.1/EM.2/2, 23 June 1997, Geneva.

UNCTAD 1998: UNCTAD. Ways and Means of Enhancing the Utilization of Trade Preferences by Developing Countries, in particular LDCs, as well as further ways of Expanding Preferences. Report by the UNCTAD Secretariat, TD/B/COM.1/20, TD/B/COM.1/20/Add.1, 21 July 1998, Geneva.
UNCTAD 1998a: UNCTAD. Anti-Dumping and Safeguards in the Euro-Mediterranean Assocication Agreements. Technical Cooperation Project INT/93/A24, UNCTAD/ITCD/TSB/Misc.10, 3 April 1998.
UNCTAD 1999: UNCTAD. Improvement of Transit Transport Systems in Landlocked and Transit Developing Countries: Issues for Consideration. TD/B/LDC/AC.1/13, 14. May 1999.
UNCTAD 1999a: UNCTAD. The World Commodity Economy: Revent Evoluation, Financial Crises, and Changing Market Structures. TD/B/COM.1/27, 16 July 1999. Geneva.
UNCTAD 1999b: UNCTAD. Examining Trade in the Agricultural Sector, with a View to Expanding the Agricultural Exports of the Developing Countries, and to Assisting Them in better Understanding the Issues at Stake in the Upcoming Agricultural Negotiations. TB/B/COM.1/EM.8/2, 23 February 1999. Geneva, UNCTAD, 1999. In: http://www.unctad.org.
UNCTAD 2000: UNCTAD. Impact of Anti-Dumping and Countervailing Duty Actions. TD/B/COM.1/EM.14/2, 24 October 2000. In: http://www.unctad.org.
UNCTAD 2000a: UNCTAD. Competition Policy and the Exercise of Intellectual Property Rights. TD/RBP/CONF.5/6, 11. August 2000. In: http://www.unctad.org/en/subsites/cpolicy.
UNCTAD 2001: UNCTAD. FDI in Least Developed Countries at a Glance. Geneva: UNCTAD, 2001. In: http://www.unctad.org.
UNCTAD 2001a: UNCTAD. Improving Market Access for Least Developed Countries. UNCTAD/DITC/TNCD/4, United Nations, 2 May 2001. In: http://www.unctad.org.
UNCTAD 2001b: UNCTAD. Duty and Quota Free Market Access for LDCs: An Analysis of Quad Initiatives. New York and Geneva: UNCTAD and The Commonwealth Secretariat, 2001. In: http://ww.unctad.org.
UNCTAD 2001c: UNCTAD. Economic Development in Africa: Performance, Prospects and Policy Issues. New York, Geneva: UNCTAD, 2001. In: http://www.unctad.org.
UNCTAD 2002: UNCTAD. Trade and Development Report, 2002. New York, Geneva: United Nations, 2002.
UNCTAD 2003: UNCTAD. Economic Development in Africa. Trade Performance and Commodity Dependence. New York, Geneva: United Nations, 2003. In: http://www.unctad.org.
UNCTAD 2004: UNCTAD. Development and Globalization. Facts and Figures. New York, Geneva: United Nations, 2004. In: http://www.unctad.org.
UNCTAD 2005: UNCTAD. Trade Adjustment Study India. United National Conference on Trade and Development. Trade Analysis Branch. Non-Agricultural Market Access (NAMA) Negotiations. Adjusting to Trade Reforms: What are the Major Challenges for Developing Countries? 18 - 19 January 2005 Geneva, Switzerland. In: http://192.91.247.38/tab/namameeting/nama.asp#NAMADocs.
UNCTAD 2005a: UNCTAD. Policy Reforms and Trade Liberalization in Bangladesh. United National Conference on Trade and Development. Trade Analysis Branch. Non-Agricultural Market Access (NAMA) Negotiations. Adjusting to Trade Reforms: What are the Major Challenges for Developing Countries? 18 - 19 January 2005 Geneva, Switzerland. In: http://192.91.247.38/tab/namameeting/nama.asp#NAMADocs.
UNCTAD EU GSP Handbook 2002: UNCTAD. Handbook on the Scheme of the European Community. UNCTAD/ITCD/TSB/Misc.25/Rev. 2. New York, Geneva: United Nations, 2002. In: http://www.unctad.org.
UNCTAD Handbook of Statistics On-Line 2006: UNCTAD. Handbook of Statistics On-Line 2005. In: http://www.unctad.org.
UNCTAD LDC Report 2004: UNCTAD. The Least Developed Countries Report 2004. United Nations, 2004. in: http://www.unctad.org.
UNCTAD USA GSP Handbook 2000: UNCTAD. Handbook on the Scheme of the United States of America. UNCTAD/ITCD/TSB/Misc. 58. New York, Geneva: United Nations, 2000. In: http://www.unctad.org.
UNCTAD/WTO 2000: UNCTAD/WTO. The Post-Uruguay Round Environment for Developing Country Exports: Tariff Peaks and Tariff Escalation. TB/B/COM.1/14/Rev.1, 25 January 2000. Geneva: UNCTAD, 2000.
UNCTC 1992: United Nations Conference on Transnational Corporations. Foreign Direct Investment and Technology Transfer in India. New York: United Nations, 1992.
UNDP 2003: UNDP. Making Global Trade Work for People. New York: UNDP, 2003.
UNESCO 2001: UNECSO. Universal Declaration on Cultural Diversity. 2001. In: http://www.unesco.org.
UNESCO 2005: UNESCO. UNESCO Science Repo rt 2005. Paris: UNESCO, 2005. In: http://www.unesco.org.
UNHCR 2000: UNHCR. State of World's Refugees. Fifty Years of Humanitarian Action. Geneva: UNHCR, 2000. In: http://www.unhcr.org.
UNIDO 1995: UNIDO Secretariat. Industrial Policy Reforms: The Changing Role of Governments and private sector development. Issue Paper. ID/WG.542/21 (SPEC.), 29. September 1995. In: http://www.unido.org.
UNIDO 1997: UNIDO Secretariat. Progress and Prospects for Industrial Development in Least Developed Countries (LDCs) – Towards the 21st Century. 19. November 1997. In: http://www.unido.org.
UNIDO 2004: UNIDO. Industrialization, Environment and the Millenium Development Goals in Sub-Saharan Africa. Wien: UNIDO, 2004. In: http://www.unido.org.
UNIDO Apparal 2003: UNIDO. The Global Apparale Value Chain. What Prospects for Upgrading by Developing Countries. Wien: UNIDO, 2003. In: http://www.unido.org.
UNIDO Industrial Development Report var. Years: UNIDO. Industrial Development Report. var. Year. In: http://www.unido.org.

UNIDO Industry and Development Report var. Years: UNIDO. Industry and Development. Global Report. var. Years. In: http://www.unido.org.
UNIDO Leather 2004: UNIDO. A Blueprint for the African Leather Industry. Wien: UNIDO, 2004. In: http://www.unido.org.
UNIDO var. Countries, var. Years: UNIDO. Industrial Development Review Series. Published for UNIDO by: London: The Economist Intelligence Unit, var. Countries, var. Years.
UNIDO Wood Furniture 2003: UNIDO. The Global Wood Furniture Value Chain: What Prospect for Upgrading by Developing Countries. The Case of South Africa. Wien: UNIDO, 2003. In: http://www.unido.org.
UNTCAD ICTSD 2005: UNCTAD-ICTSD. Resource Book on TRIPS and Development. UNCTAD, 2005. In: http://www.unctad.org.
Upham 1996: Upham, Frank K. Retail Convergence: The Structural Impediments Initiative and the Regulation of the Japanese Retail Industry. In: Berger, Suzanne, Dore, Ronald (ed.). National Diversity and Global Capitalism. Ithaca, London: Cornell University Press, 1996.
UPOV 1978: UPOV. Gesetz zu der in Genf am 23. Oktober 1978 unterzeichneten Fassung des Internationalen Übereinkommens zum Schutz von Pflanzenzüchtungen. BGBl. Teil II, 1984 Nr. 29.
UPOV 1991: UPOV. Internationales Übereinkommen zum Schutz von Pflanzenzüchtungen. In: Gewerblicher Urheberrechtsschutz International (GRUR Int.) 1991, Heft 7. S. 538-545.
Urata/Kawai 1998: Urata, Shujiro, Kawai, Hiroki. Intra-Firm Technology Transfer by Japanese Manufacturing Firms in Asia. NBER Working Paper , 1998. NBER Conference The Role of Foreign Investment in Economic Development. East Asian Seminar on Economics Vol. 9. In: http://www.nber.org.
Urata/Yokota 1994: Urata, Shujiro, Yokota, Kazuhiko. Trade Liberalization and Productivity Growth in Thailand. In: The Developing Economies, XXXII, No. 4, December 1994. S. 444-459.
Urban 2000: Urban, Dieter M. Neoclassical Growth, Manufacturing Agglometration and Terms of Trade. Development Studies Working Papers, No. 136, March 2000, University of Oxford. http://www2.qeh.ox.ac.uk.
Urquidi 1993: Urquidi, Victor L. The Developmentalist View. In: Szirmai, Adam, van Ark, Bart, Pilat, Dirk (eds.). Explaining Economic Growth. Essays in Honour of Angus Maddison. Amsterdam: North Holland, 1993.
USA Zolltarif 2004: United States International Trade Commisssion. Harmonized Tariff Schedule of the United States (2004). USITC Publication 3653. Washington: USTR, 2004. In: http://www.usitc.gov.
USDA 1996: United States Department of Agriculture. Globalization of Processed Food Markets. Agricultural Economic Report No. 742, September 1996. In: http://www.usda.gov.
USDA 1998: United States Department of Agriculture. Agriculture in the WTO. Situation and Outlook Series. WRS-98-4, December 1998. In: http://www.usda.gov.
USDA 1998a: United States Department of Agriculture. Uruguay Round Agreement on Agriculture: The Record to Date. Special Article. Agricultural Outlook/December 1998. In: http://www.usda.gov.
USDA 1999: United States Department of Agriculture. In Introduction into State Trading in Agriculture. Agricultural Economic Report No. 783, September 1996. In: http://www.usda.gov.
USDA Agriculture Fact Book div. Jg.: United States Department of Agriculture. Agriculture Fact Book, div. Jg. http://www.usda.gov.
USITC 1988: United States International Trade Commission. Economic Effects of Intellectual Property Right Infringement. Investigation 332-245. In: JWT, Vol. 22 No. 2, 1988. S. 101-114.
USITC 1994: United States International Trade Commission. Potential Impact on the U.S. Economy and Industries of the GATT Uruguay Round Agreements. Publication 2790. In: World Trade and Arbitration Materials, Vol. 6, No. 5, Sept. 1994. In: http://www.usitc.gov.
USITC 1997: United States International Trade Commission. The Dynamic Effects of Trade Liberalization: An Empirical Analysis, Publication 3069, October 1997. In: http://www.usitc.gov.
USITC 1997a: United States International Trade Commission. Section 337 Investigations at the U.S. International Trade Commission: Answers to Frequently Asked Questions. USITC Publication 3027, March 1997. In: http://www.usitc.gov.
USITC 1997b: United States International Trade Commission. Production Sharing: Use of U.S. Components and Materials in Foreign Assembly Operations, 1993-1996. Investigation No. 332-237, USITC Publication 3077, December 1997. In: http://www.usitc.gov.
USITC 1998: United States International Trade Commission. Market Developments in Mercosur Countries Affecting Leading U.S. Exporters. Staff Issue Paper, Publication 3117, July 1998. In: http://www.usitc.gov.
USITC 1998a: United States International Trade Commission. U.S.-Africa Trade Flows and Effects of the Uruguay Round Agreements and U.S. Trade and Development Policy. Investigation No. 332-362. Publication 3139. 1998. In: http://www.usitc.gov.
USITC 2001: United States International Trade Commission. Steel. Vol. I. Investigation No. TA-201-73. Publication 3479. December 2001. In: http://www.usitc.gov.
USITC 2001a: United States International Trade Commission. Year in Review. Fiscal Year 2001. In: http://www.usitc.gov.
USITC 2002: United States International Trade Commission. Factors affecting U.S. trade and shipments of information technology products: Computer equipment, telecommunications equipment, and semiconductors. Office of Industries Working Paper, February 2002. In: http://www.usitc.gov.
USITC 2002a: United States International Trade Commission. Softwood Lumber from Canada. Investigation Nos. 701-TA-414, 731-TA-928 (Final). USITC Pub. 3509, May 2002. In: http://www.usitc.gov.

USITC 2003: United States International Trade Commission. The Impact of Trade Agreements: Effect of the Tokyo Round, U.S.-Israel FTA, U.S.-Canada FTA, NAFTA, and the Uruguay Round on the U.S. Economy. Investigation No. TA-2111-1, Publication 3621, August 2003. In: http://www.usitc.gov.
USITC 2003a: United States International Trade Commission. DRAMs and DRAM Modules from Korea. Investigation No. 701-TA-431 (Final). Publication 3616, August 2003. In: http://www.usitc.gov.
USITC 2003b: United States International Trade Commission. Certain Color Television Recievers from China and Malaysia. Investigations Nos. 731-TA-1034 and 1035 (Preliminary), USITC Publication No. 3607, June 2003. In: http://www.usitc.gov.
USITC 2004: United States International Trade Commission. Textiles and Apparel: Assessment of the Competitiveness of Certain Foreign Suppliers to the U.S. Market, Investigation No. 332-448, Publication 3671, January 2004. In: http://www.usitc.gov.
USITC 2004a: United States International Trade Commission/William Greene. The Liberalization of India's Telecommunications Sector: Implications for Trade and Investment. Office of Economics Working Paper No. 2004-09-B, September 2004. In: http://www.usitc.gov.
USITC 2004b: United States International Trade Commission. Softwood Lumber from Canada. Investigation Nos. 701-TA-414, 731-TA-928 Section 129 Consistency Determination. USITC Pub. 3740, November 2004. In: http://www.usitc.gov.
USITC 2005: United States International Trade Commission. Sec 337 Cases. March, 2005. In: http://www.usitc.gov.
USITC 2005a: United States International Trade Commission. Import Injury Investigations Case Statistics (FY 1980 - 2004). Public Version. Washington D.C., October 2005. In: http://www.usitc.gov.
USITC 2005b: United States International Trade Commission. Antidumping and Countervailing Duty Handbook, Eleventh Edition, Publication 3750, January 2005. In: http://www.usitc.gov.
USITC 2005c: United States International Trade Commission. Certain Hot-Rolled Flat-Rolled Carbon-Quality Steel Products from Brazil, Japan, and Russia. 701-TA-384, 731-TA-806-808 (Review), Pub. 3767. Washington: ITC, April 2005.
USITC 2006: United States International Trade Commission. Antidumping and Countervailing Duty Orders in Place, February 16, 2006, by Country. In: http://www.usitc.gov/trade_remedy/731_ad_701_cvd/investigations/antidump_countervailing/index.htm.
USITC 2006a: United States International Trade Commission. DRAMs and DRAM Modules from Korea. Investigation No. 701-TA-431 (Section 129 Consistency Determination), Publication 3839, February 2006. In: http://www.usitc.gov.
USITC 2006b: United States International Trade Commission. Antidumping and Countervailing Duty Orders in Place, Last Update 10.07.2006. In: http://info.usitc.gov/oinv/sunset.nsf/ALLDocID/.
USITC 2006c: United States International Trade Commission. Certain Orange Juice From Brazil Investigation No. 731-TA-1089 (Final), Publication 3838, March 2006. In: http://www.usitc.gov.
USITC Line Pipe 1999: United States International Trade Commission. Circular Welded Carbon Line Pipe. Investigation No. TA-201-70. Publication 3261. December 1999. In: http://www.usitc.gov.
USITC Tradeshifts, div. Titel, 2004: United States International Trade Commission. Shifts in U.S. Merchandize Trade. Diverse spezielle Titel dieser Untersuchung. Investigation No. 332-345, 2004. In: http://www.usitc.gov/tradeshifts/default.htm.
USITC Wheat Gluten 1998: United States International Trade Commission. Views of the Commission on Injury. Investigation No. TA-201-67. Publication 3088. March 1998. In: http://www.usitc.gov.
USITC Wheat Gluten 2001: United States International Trade Commission. Determination and Views of the Commission. Investigation No. TA-201-67. Publication 3423. May 2001. In: http://www.usitc.gov.
USTR 1999: USTR. The Economic Effects of Significant U.S. Import Restrictions. Publication 3201. May 1999. In: http://www.ustr.gov.
USTR 2006: USTR. The Office of the United States Trade Representative. Press Release. U.S., Canada Reach Final Agreement on Lumber Dispute. 07/06/2006. In: http://www.ustr.gov.
USTR Sec. 301 Fallübersicht: The Office of the United States Trade Representative. Sec. 301 Table of Cases. In: http://www.ustr.gov/Trade_Agreements/Monitoring_Enforcement/Section_Index.html.

V

Vainio 1996: Vainio, Matti. Quantifiable Impact of the Uruguay Round on Poverty. In: Development Policy Review, Vol. 14, 1996. S. 37-49.
Valavanis-Vail 1955: Valavanis-Vail, Stefan. An Econometric Model of Growth U.S.A. 1869-1953. In: American Economic Review, Papers and Proceedings, Vol. 45, No. 2, 1955. S. 208-227.
Valdes 1987: Valdes, Alberto. Agriculture in the Uruguay Round: Interests of Deleloping Countries. The World BanK Economic Review, Vol. 1 No. 4, 1987. S. 571-593.
Valdes/Zietz 1987: Valdes, Alberto, Zietz, Joachim. Export Subsidies and Minimum Access Guarantees in Agricultural Trade: A Developing Country Perspective. In: World Development, Vol. 15 No. 5, 1987. S. 673-683.
Valdes/Zietz 1995: Valdes, Alberto, Zietz, Joachim. Distortions in World Food Markets in the Wake of the GATT: Evidence and Policy Implications. In: World Development, Vol. 23 No. 6, 1995. S. 913-926.

van Ark 1993: van Ark, Bart. International comparisons of output and productivity. Manufacturing productivity performance of ten countries from 1950 to 1990. University of Groningen: Groningen Growth and Development Centre, 1993. In: http://www.tm.tue.nl/ecis/teg/.
van Ark 1993a: van Ark, Bart. The ICOP Approach – Its Implications and Applicability. In: Szirmai, Adam, van Ark, Bart, Pilat, Dirk (eds.). Explaining Economic Growth. Essays in Honour of Angus Maddison. Amsterdam: North Holland, 1993.
van Ark 1996: van Ark, Bart. Convergence and divergence in the European periphery: productivity in Eastern and Southern Europe in retrospect. In: van Ark, Bart, Crafts, Nicholas (eds.). Quantitative aspects of post-war European economic growth. Cambridge: Cambridge University Press, 1996.
van Ark 1999: van Ark, Bart. Economic Growth and Labour Productivity in Europe: Half a Century of East-West Comparisons. Groningen Growth and Development Centre. September 1999. In: http://www.econ.rug.nl/ggdc.
van Ark/Timmer 2000: van Ark, Bart, Timmer, Marcel. Asia's Productivity Performance at the Turn of the Century: An International Perspective. University of Groningen, March 2000. In: http://www.eco.rug.nl/medewerk/ark/ark.htm.
van Bergeijk 1993: van Bergeijk, Peter A. G., Kabel, Dick L. Strategic Trade Theories and Trade Policy. In: Journal of World Trade, Vol. 27, 1993. S. 175-186.
van den Bossche 1997: Van den Bossche, Peter L. H. The Europan Community and the Uruguay Round Agreement. In: Jackson, John H., Sykes, Alan O. (eds.). Implementing the Uruguay Round. Oxford: Clarendon Press, 1997.
van den Bossche 2005: Van den Bossche, Peter L. H. The Law and Policy of the World Trade Organization. Text, Cases and Materials. Cambridge: Cambridge University Press, 2005.
van Paridon 1995: von Paridon, C. W. A. M. European Economic Integration: Did it Matter in the Past, Will it Matter in the Future. In: Tilly, Richard, Welfens, Paul J.J. (eds.) European Economic Intergration as a Challenge to Industry and Government. Berlin: Springer, 1995.
van Zyl et al. 1998: van Zyl, Johan, Vink, Nick, Townsend, Rob, Kirsten, Johann. Agricultural Market Liberalization: A Case Study of the Western Cape Province in South Africa. In: Journal of International Development, Vol. 10 No. 1, 1998. S. 75-84.
Vanberg 1988: Vanberg, Victor. 'Ordnungstheorie' as Constitutional Economics – the German Conception of 'Social Market Economy'. In: ORDO, Bd. 39, 1988. S. 17-31.
Vanberg 1992: Vanberg, Victor. A Constitutional Political Economy Perspective on International Trade. In: ORDO, Bd. 43, S. 375-392.
Vanberg 1997: Vanberg, Victor. Die normativen Grundlagen der Ordnungspolitik. In: ORDO, Bd. 48, 1997.
Vandenbussche et al. 1999: Vandenbussche, Hylke, Veugelers, Reinhilde, Beldersbos, Rene. Undertakings and Antidumping Jumping FDI in Europe. CEPR Discussion Paper No. 2320, December 1999.
Vandenbussche et al. 1999a: Vandenbussche, Hylke, Konings, Jozef, Springdael, Linda. Import Diversion under European Antidumping Policy. NBER Working Paper No. 7340, September 1999.
Vandenbussche/Wauthy 2000: Vandenbussche, Hylke, Wauthy, Xavier. European Antidumping Policy and Firms's Strategic Choice of Quality. CEPR Discussion Paper No. 2624, November 2000.
Vandenbussche/Zanardi 2006: Vandenbussche, Hylke, Zanardi, Maurizio. The Global Chilling Effects of Antidumping Proliferation. CEPR Discussion Paper No. 5597, April 2006.
Vandevelde 1988: Vandevelde, Kenneth J. The Bilateral Investment Treaty Program of the United States. In: Cornell International Law Journal, Vol. 21, No. 2, Summer 1988. S. 202-203.
Vandevelde 2000: Vandevelde, Kenneth J. The Economics of Bilateral Investment Treates. In: Harvard International Law Journal, Vol. 41, No.2 Spring 2000. S. 489-502.
VanDuzer 2005: VanDuzer, Anthony J. Navigating between the Poles: Unpacking the Debate on the Implications for Development of GATS Obligations to Health and Education Services. In: Petersmann, Ernst-Ulrich (ed.). Reforming the World Trading System. Legitimacy, Efficiency, and Democratic Governance. Oxford: Oxford University Press, 2005.
VanGrasstek Communications 1990: VanGrasstek Communications. Trade-Related Intellectual Property Rights: United States Trade Policy, Developing Countries and the Uruguay Round. In: UNCTAD. Uruguay Round: Further Papers on Selected Issues. UNCTAD/ITP/42. New York: United Nations, 1990.
Vanzetti et al. 2005: Vanzetti, David, McGuire, Greg, in collaboration with Prawobo. Trade Policy at the Crossroads - the Indonesian Story. United Nations Conference on Trade and Development. Trade Analysis Branch. Policy Issues in International Trade and Commodities Study Series No. 28. United Nations: New York and Geneva, 2005. In: http://192.91.247.38/tab/Default.asp.
Varian 2001: Varian, Hal R. Grundzüge der Mikroökonomik. München; Wien: R. Oldenbourg Verlag, 2001.
Vaubel 1986: Vaubel, Roland. A Public Choice View of International Organization. Original 1986. In: Vaubel, Roland, Willett, Thomas D. (eds.). The Political Economy of International Organizations. Boulder: Westview Press, 1991.
Vautier et al. 1999: Vautier, Kerrin, Lloyd, Peter John, Tsai, Ing-Wen. Competition Policy, Developing Countries, and the WTO. World Bank: Washington. http://www1.worldbank.org/wbiep/trade/manila/compet_DC_WTO.pdf
Venables 1999: Venables, Anthony J. Regional Integration Agreements: a force for convergence or divergence? World Bank Conference on Development Economics, Paris, June 1999. In: http://www.worldbank.org.
Verbruggen 1989: Verbruggen, Harmen. GSTP, the structure of protection and South-South Trade in manufactures. In: UNCTAD Review, Jg. 1, No. 2, 1989. S. 23-40.

Verdross/Simma 1984: Verdross, Alfred, Simma, Bruno. Universelles Völkerrecht. Berlin: Duncker und Humblot, 1984.
Verhoosel 2002: Verhoosel, Gaetan. National Treatment and WTO Dispute Settlement. Adjudicating the Boundaries of Regulatory Autonomy. Oxford, Portland: Hart Publishing, 2002.
Vermulst 1997: Vermulst, Edwin. Adopting and Implementing Anti-Dumping Laws. In: JWT, Vol. 31, No. 2, April 1997. S. 5-23.
Vermulst 2000: Vermulst, Edwin. EC Countervailing Practice after the Uruguay Round Revisited. In: Legal Issues of Economic Integration, Vol. 27, No. 3, 2000. S. 217-238.
Vermulst 2004: Vermulst, Edwin. Keynote Speech for the ADB Intensive Course on Rules of Origin. Intensive Course on Rules of Origin, Asian Development Bank, Bangkok, Thailand, 6-9 September 2004. In: http://www.adb.org.
Vermulst 2005: Vermulst, Edwin. The WTO Anti-Dumping Agreement. A Commentary. Oxford: Oxford University Press, 2005.
Vermulst 2005a: Vermulst, Edwin. The 10 Major Problems With the Antidumping Instrument in the European Community. In: JWT, Vol. 39, No. 1, 2005. S. 105-113.
Vermulst et al. 2004: Vermulst, Pernaute, Marta, Lucenti, Krista. Recent European Community Safeguards Policy: 'Kill Them All and Let God Sort Them Out'? In: JWT, Vol. 38, No. 6, 2004. S. 955-984.
Vermulst/Dacko 2004: Vermulst, Edwin, Dacko, Carolina. Rules of Origin in the European Union: Practical Aspects. Intensive Course on Rules of Origin, Asian Development Bank, Bangkok, Thailand, 6-9 September 2004. In: http://www.adb.org.
Vermulst/Driessen 1997: Vermulst, Edwin, Driessen, Bart. New Battle Lines in the Anti-Dumping War. In: JWT, Vol. 31, No. 3, June 1997. S. 135-157.
Vermulst/Graafsma 2001: Vermulst, Edwin, Graafsma, Folkert. WTO Dispute Settlement with Respect to Trade Contingency Measures. In: JWT Vol. 35, No. 2, 2001. S. 209-228.
Vermulst/Komuro 1997: Vermulst, Edwin, Komuro, Norio. Anti-Dumping Disputes in the GATT/WTO. In: JWT, Vol. 31, No. 1, Feb. 1997. S. 5-43.
Vermust/Waer 1991: Vermulst, Edwin, Waer, Paul. The Calculation of Injury Margins in EC Anti-Dumping Procceedings. In: JWT Vol. 25, No. 6, 1991. S. 5-42.
Vernon 1966: Vernon, Raymond. International Investment and International Trade in the Product Cycle. In: Quarterly Journal of Economics, Vol. 80, No. 319, No. 2, May 1966. S. 190-207.
Vernon 1981: Vernon, Raymond. State-Owned Enterprises in Latin American Exports. In: Baer, Werner, Gillis, Malcolm (Hrg.). Export Diversification and the New Protectionism. The Experiences of Latin America. NBER and the Bureau of Economic and Business Research University of Illinois: University of Illinois, 1981.
Verspagen 1996: Verspagen, Bart. Technology indicators and economic growth in the European area: some empirical evidence. In: van Ark, Bart, Crafts, Nicholas (eds.). Quantitative aspects of post-war European economic growth. Cambridge: Cambridge University Press, 1996.
Verspagen 1997: Verspagen, Bart. Estimating International Technology Spillovers Using Technology Flow Matrices. In: Weltwirtschaftliches Archiv, Vol. 133, No. 3, 1997. S. 226-248.
Vertrag von Amsterdam 1997: Vertrag vom Amsterdam. Text und konsolidierte Fassungen des EU- und EG-Vertragas. Baden-Baden: Nomos, 1997.
Vestal 1989: Vestal, James E. Evidence on the Determinants and Factor Content Characteristics of Japanese Technology Trade 1977-1981. In: Review of Economics and Statistics, Vol. 71, No. 4, November 1989. S. 565-571.
Vickery 1988: Vickery, Graham. A Survey on International Technology Licensing. In: STI-Review, No. 4, Paris: OECD, December 1988. pp. 7-49.
Videocon Information 2006: Videocon. Company Information. 2006. In: http://www.videoconworld.com.
Vietor/Yoffie 1993: Vietor, Richard H., Yoffie, David B. Telecommunications: Deregulation and Globalization. In: Yoffie, David B. Beyond Free Trade. Firms, Governments, and Global Competition. Boston, Mass.: Harvard Business School Press, 1993.
Vieweg 1993: Vieweg, H. G. Maschinenbau: Vorübergehende Schwäche oder existentielle Krise?. In: ifo-Schnelldienst 46 Jg. 7. April 10/1993. S. 11-21.
Vieweg 1997: Vieweg, H. G. Der europäische Maschinenbau im internationalen Wettbewerb. In: ifo-Schnelldienst 29 Jg. 1997. S. 3-13.
Vieweg/Hilpert 1993: Vieweg, Hans-Günter, Hilpert, Hanns Günther. Japans Herausforderung an den deutschen Maschinenbau. Berlin, München: Duncker & Humblot, 1993.
Villarreal 1990: Villareal, René. The Latin American Strategy of Import Substitution: Failure or Paradigm for the Region. In: Gereffi, Gary, Wyman, Donald L. Manufacturing Miracles. Paths of Industrialization in Latin America and East Asia. Princeton: Princeton University Press, 1990.
Viner 1923: Viner, Jacob. Dumping: A Problem in International Trade. Chicago: University of Chicago Press, 1923.
Viner 1953: Viner, Jacob. International Trade and Economic Development. Oxford: Clarendon Press, (First Edition 1953) 1964.
VN-Charta Kommentar 1991: Simma, Bruno et al. (Hrg.) Charta der Vereinten Nationen: Kommentar. München: C.H. Beck, 1991.

Vogel 1987: Vogel, David. Government-Industry Relations in the United States: an Overview. In: Wilks, Stephen, Wright, Maurice (eds.). Comparative Government-Industry Relations. Western Europe, the United States, and Japan. Oxford: Clarendon Press, 1987.
Voigt 1962: Voigt, Fritz. German Experience with Cartels and their Control during the Pre-War and Post-War Periods. In: Miller, John Perry (ed.). Competition, Cartels and Their Regulation. Amsterdam: North-Holland Publishing Company, 1962.
Volke 1997: Volke, Matthias. Investment Implications of Selected WTO Agreements and the Proposed Multilateral Agreement on Investment. IMF Working Paper WP/97/60, May 1997. In: http://www.imf.org.
Vollmer 1998: Vollmer, Uwe. Finanzmärkte, Bankenstruktur und Regulierungen: Unternehmensfinanzierung und Unternehmenskontrolle in einer offenen Marktwirtschaft. In: Cassel, Dieter (Hrg.). 50 Jahre Soziale Marktwirtschaft. Schriften zu Ordnungfragen der Wirtschaft, Band 57, Stuttgart: Lucius&Lucius, 1998.
von Braun 1988: von Braun, Joachim. Food Subsidies in Egypt: Implications for the Agricultural Sector. In: Pinstrup-Andersen, Per (ed.) Food Subsidies in Developing Countries. Baltimore, London: John Hopkins University Press, 1988.
von der Groeben 1985: von der Groeben, Hans. The European Community. The formative years. Luxembourg: Office for Official Publications of the European Communities, 1987.
von Hauff 1994: von Hauff, Michael, Kruse, Beate, de Haan, Arjan. Die Systemtransformation in Indien unter Berücksichtigung ordnungspolitischer und soziokultureller Faktoren. Arbeitspapier Nr. 66, Institut für Wirtschaftsethik, St. Gallen, September 1994.
von Hippel 1988: von Hippel, Eric. The Sources of Innovation. New York, Oxford: Oxford University Press, 1988.
Voon/Yanovich 2006: Voon, Tania, Yanovich, Alan. The Facts Aside: The Limitations of WTO Appeals to Issues of Law. In: JWT, Vol. 40, No. 2, 2006. S. 239-258.
VR-Verträge 1995: Randelzhofer, Albrecht (Hrg.). Völkerrechtliche Verträge. Nördlingen: C.H. Beck (und dtv), 1995.

W

Wacziarg 1998: Wacziarg, Romain. Measuring the Dynamic Gains from Trade. World Bank, Policy Research Working Paper, No. 2001. November 1998.
Wade 1990: Wade, Robert. Governing the Market. Economic Theory and the Role of Government in East Asian Industrialization. Princeton: Princeton University Press, 1990.
Wade 1990a: Wade, Robert. Industrial Policy in East Asia: Does it lead or follow the market? In: Gereffi, Gary,
Waelbroeck 1984: Waelbroeck, Jean. The Logic of EC Commercial and Industrial Policy Making. In: Jaquemin, Alexis (ed.). European Industry: Public Policy and Corporate Strategy. Oxford: Clarendon Press, 1984.
Waelbroeck 2003: Waelbroeck, Michel. To What Extent Is the Description of the U.S. Law Made by Professor D.H. Regan Applicable in EC Context? In: Cottier, Thomas, Mavroidis, Petros C (eds.). The Role of the Judge in International Trade Regulation. Ann Arbor: University of Michigan Press, 2003.
Waelde 1995: Waelde, Thomas W. International Investment under the 1994 Energy Charter Treaty. In: JWT, Vol. 29, No. 5, October 1995. S. 5-75.
Waer 1993: Waer, Paul. Constructed Normal Values in EU Dumping Margin Calculations. Fiction, or Realistic Approach? JWT Vol. 27, No. 4, 1993. S. 47-80.
Waer/Driessen 1995: Waer, Paul, Driessen, Bart. The New European Union Generalized System of Preferences. In: JWT, Vol. 29, No. 4, August 1995. S. 97-124.
Waer/Vermulst 1999: Waer, Paul, Vermulst, Edwin. EC Anti-Subsidy Law and Practice After the Uruguay. In: JWT, Vol. 33, No. 3, 1999. S. 19-43.
Wagacha 2000: Wagacha, Mbui. Analysis of Liberalization of the Trade and Exchange Regime in Kenya since 1980. DP No. 023/2000. May 2000. In: http://www.ipar.or.ke.
Wagner 1988: Wagner, R. Harrison. Economic interdependence, bargaining power, and political influence. In: IO, 42, 3, Summer 1988. S. 461-483.
Wagner 1997: Wagner, Helmut. Wachstum und Entwicklung. Theorie der Entwicklungspolitik. München; Wien: Oldenbourg Verlag, 1997.
Wakelin 1997: Wakelin, Katharine. Trade and Innovation. Theory and Evidence. Cheltenham, UK, Northampton, USA: Edward Elgar, 1997.
Wälde 1994: Wälde, Klaus. Trade pattern reversal: The role of technological change, factor accumulation and government intervention. Kiel Discussion Paper No. 100, January 1994. Kiel: Institut für Weltwirtschaft, 1994.
Wälde 1995: Wälde, Thomas W. A Requiem for the "New International Economic Order" – The Rise and Fall of Paradigms in International Economic Law. In: Al-Nauimi, Najeeb, Meese, Richard (eds.). International Legal Issues Arising Under The United Nations Decade of International Law. The Hague: Martinus Nijhoff, 1995.
Walerius/Wang 2004: Walerius, Randolph, Wang, Michael. Europe's Steel Juggernaut. In: Wall Street Journal Europe, Friday, March 12, 2004.
Walker 1981: Walker, William N. Private Initiative to Thwart the Trade in Counterfeit Goods. In: The World Economy, Vol. 4 No. 1, March 1981. S. 29-48.
Wallerstein 1986: Wallerstein, Immanuel. Das moderne Weltsystem: Kapitalistische Landwirtschaft und die Entstehung der europäischen Weltwirtschaft im 16 Jhd. Frankfurt am Main: Syndikat, 1986.
Wallsten 1999: Wallsten, Scott J. An Empirical Analysis of Competition, Privatization, and Regulation in Africa and Latin America. World Bank, Policy Research Working Papers, No. 2136. June 1999.

Walter 1971: Walter, Ingo. Nontariff Barriers and the Export Performance of Developing Economies. In: American Economic Review, Vol. 61, 1971. S. 195-210.
Walter 2000: Walter, Christian. Die Folgen der Globalisierung für die Europäische Verfassungsdiskussion. In: Deutsches Verwaltungsblatt, Heft 1, 115 Jg., 2000, S. 1-13.
Waltz 1954: Walth, Kenneth. Man, the State and War. New York: Columbia University Press, (1959) 1954.
Waltz 1979: Waltz, Kenneth. Theory of International Politics. New York etc.: McGraw-Hill, 1979.
Walz 1997: Walz, Uwe. Innovation, Foreign Direct Investment and Growth. In: Economica, Vol. 64, February 1997. S. 63-79.
Walz 1999: Walz, Uwe. Wissenakkumulation, endogenes Wachstum und Implikationen für die Entwicklungstheorie und –politik. In: Schubert, Renate (Hrg.). Neue Wachstums- und Außenhandelstheorie. Implikationen für die Entwicklungstheorie und – politik. Berlin: Duncker&Humblot, 1999.
Wang 1994: Wang, Lei. Non-Application Issues in the GATT and the WTO. In: JWT Vol. 28, No. 2, 1994. S. 49-74.
Wang 2003: Wang, Yongjian. WTO - Chile Price Band System. In: Legal Issues of Economic Integration, Vol. 30 No. 3, 2003. S. 279-290.
Wang 2004: Wang, Tao. China: Sources of Real Exchange Rate Fluctuations. IMF Working Paper WP 04/18. Washington: IMF, 2004. In: http://www.imf.org.
Wang/Winters 1997: Wang, Zehn Kun, Winters, L. Alan. Africa's Role in Multilateral Trade Negotiations: Past and Future. World Bank Policy Research Working Paper, No. 1846, 1997. In: http://www.worldbank.org.
Wangwe 1995: Wangwe, Samuel M. Exporting Africa: Technology, Trade and Industrialization in Sub-Saharahn Africa. London, New York: The United Nations University/Institute for New Technologies, 1995. In: http://www.unu.edu/unupress/unupbooks/uu34ee/uu34ee00.htm.
Warnecke 1978: Warnecke, Steven J. The European Community and National Subsidy Policies. In: Warnecke, Steven J. (ed.). International Trade and Industrial Policies. Government Intervention and an Open World Economy. London: Macmillan Press, 1978.
Warwick Commission 2007: The First Warwick Commission. The Multilateral Trading System: Which Way Forward. 2007. http://www2.warwick.ac.uk/newsandevents/pressreleases/wcreport.
Watal/Mathai 1995: Watal, Jayashree, Mathai, Anu P. Sectoral impact of the Uruguay Round Agreements on developing countries: Pharmaceutical industry. UNIDO Background Paper. ID/WG.542/20 (SPEC.) 27. September 1995. In: http://www.unido.org.
Watanabe 1996: Watanabe, Chihiro. National Approaches to Technology Policy in a Globalizing World Economy – The Case of Japan. In: Koopmann, Georg, Scharrer, Hans-Eckart (eds.). The Economics of High-Technology Competition. Baden-Baden: Nomos, 1996.
Watanabe 2004: Watanabe, Osamu. Three Myths and Three Truths About the Japanese Economy. Speech by Chairman and CEO of JETRO, Churchill College, Cambridge University, January 20, 2004. In: http://www.jetro.go.jp.
WDI: World Bank: World Development Indicators. Online Datenbank der Weltbank. In: http://devdata.worldbank.org/data-query/.
Webb et al. 2005: Webb, Richard, Camminati, Josefina, Thorne, Raul Leon. Antidumping Mechanism and Safeguards in Peru. World Bank Policy Research Working Paper 3658, July 2005. In: http://www.worldbank.org.
Webber 1998: Webber, Douglas. The Hard Core: The Franco-German Relationship and Agricultural Crisis Politics in the European Union. European University Institute, Working Paper RSC No. 98/46. In: http://www.iue.it/PUB/rsc_fm.html.
Weber 1988: Weber, Max. Gesammelte Aufsätze zur Wissenschaftslehre. Tübingen: Mohr, 1988.
Weber 1995: Weber, Eberhard. Globalisierung und Politische Ökonomie der Armut in Indien. Limbach: Selbstverlag, 1997.
Weeks 1999: Weeks, John. Trade Liberalization, Market Deregulation and Agricultural Performance in Central America. In: Journal of Development Studies, Vol. 35 No. 5, June 1999. S. 48-75.
Weidenbaum 1993: Weidenbaum, Murray. A New Technology Policy for the United States. In: Regulation (Zeitschrift des Cato-Instituts), Vol. 16, No. 4. In: http://www.cato.org.
Weiler 1997: Weiler, Joseph H. H. The Reformation of European Constitutionalism. In: Journal of Common Market Studies, Vol. 35, No. 1, March 1997, S. 97-131.
Weiler 1998: Weiler, Joseph. H.H. The Case Against the Case for Statehood. In: European Law Journal, Vol. 4, No. 1, March 1998, S. 43-62.
Weiler 1999: Weiler, Joseph H.H. The Constitution of Europe. Cambridge: Cambridge University Press, 1999.
Weiler 2001: Weiler, Joseph H.H. The Rule of Lawyers and the Ethos of Diplomats. Reflections on WTO Dispute Settlement. In: Porter, Roger B., Sauvé, Pierre, Subramanian, Arvind, Zampetti, Americo Beviglia. Efficiency, Equity, Legitimacy. The Multilateral Trading System at the Millenium. Washington D.C.: Brookings Institution Press, 2001.
Weir/Skocpol 1985: Weir, Margaret. State Structure and the Possibilities for "Keynesian" Responses to the Great Depression in Sweden, Britain, and the United States. In: Evans, Peter B. et al. (eds.). Bringing the State Back In. Cambridge: Cambridge University Press, 1985.
Weisburd 1999: Weisburd, A. M. Implications of International Relations Theory for the International Law of Human Rights. Columbia Journal of Transnational Law, 38; 45, 1999. S. 45-112.

Weise et al. 1997: Weise, Christian, Brückner, Herbert, Franzmeyer, Fritz, Lodahl, Maria, Möbius, Uta, Schultz, Siegfried, Schumacher, Dieter, Trabold, Harald. Ostmitteleuropa auf dem Weg in die EU – Transformation, Verflechtung, Reformbedarf. DIW Beiträge zur Strukturforschung, Heft 167. Berlin: Duncker & Humblot, 1997.
Weiss 1974: Weiss, Leonard W. The Concentration-Profits Relation and Antitrust. In: Goldschmid, Harvey J., Mann, Michael H., West, Fred J. Industrial Concentration: The New Learning. Boston, Toronto: Little, Brown and Company, 1974.
Weiss 1992: Weiss, John. Trade Liberalization in Mexico in the 1980s: Concepts, Measures and Short-Run Effects. In: Weltwirtschaftliches Archiv, Vol. 128, 1992. S. 711-725.
Weiß 1996: Weiß, Jörg Peter. Maschinenbau: Bedeutung für den deutschen Außenhandel. Wochenbericht des DIW Berlin 5/03. In: http://www.diw.de.
Weiss 1997: Weiss, Friedl. Dispute Settlement under the 'Plurilateral Trade Agreements': The Case of the Agreement on Government Procurement. In: Petersmann, Ernst-Ulrich (ed.). International Trade Law and the GATT/WTO Dispute Settlement System. London, The Hague, Boston: Kluwer Law, 1997.
Weiss 1997: Weiss, Peter. Techno-Globalism and Industrial Policy Responses in the USA and Europe. In: Intereconomics, March/April 1997. S. 74-85.
Weiß 1998: Weiß, Thomas. Has the Decline in the Productivity of Capital Been Halted. In: Intereconomics, March/April 1998. S. 86-135.
Weiss 2004: Weiss, Friedl. Inherent Powers of National and International Courts. In: Ortino, Federico, Petersmann, Ernst-Ulrich (eds.). The WTO Dispute Settlement System 1995 - 2003. The Hague et al.: Kluwer Law International, 2004.
Weiss et al. 1988: Weiss, Frank D., Heitger, Berhard, Jüttemeier, Karl Heinz, Kirkpatrick, Grant, Klepper, Gernot. Trade Policy in West Germany. Kieler Studien No. 217. Tübingen: Mohr, 1988.
Weissmann 1996: Weissmann, Robert. A Long, Strange TRIPS: The Pharmaceutical Industy Drive to Harmonize Global Intellectual Property Rules, and the Remaining WTO Legal Alternatives Available to Third World Countries. In: University of Pennsylvania Journal of International Law, Vol. 17, No. 4 Winter 1996. S. 1069-1125.
Weitzel 1996: Weitzel, G. Utz. Unternehmensdynamik und globaler Innovationswettbewerb. Wiesbaden: Gabler, 1996.
Weller 1999: Weller, Christian. Financial Liberalization, Multinational Banks and Credit Supply: The Case of Poland. ZEI-Policy Working Paper, B10-1999. In: http://www.zei.de/
Weller/Scher 1999: Weller, Christian, Scher, Mark J. Multinational Banks and Development Finance. ZEI-Policy Working Paper, B 16-1999. In: http://www.zei.de/
Weltentwicklungsbericht bzw. World Development Report, div. Ausgaben: Weltbank/World Bank. Weltentwicklungsbericht bzw. World Development Report. Washington: World Bank.
Wellmer 2003: Wellmer, Christoph. Die Welt, der Diskurs und Global Governance. In: Zeitschrift für Internationale Beziehungen, Vol. 10 No. 2, 2003. S. 365-382.
Wells 1993: Wells, Louis T. Jr. Minerals: Eroding Oligopolies. In: Yoffie, David B. Beyond Free Trade. Firms, Governments, and Global Competition. Boston, Mass.: Harvard Business School Press, 1993.
Wells 2002: Wells, Wyatt. Antitrust and the Formation of the Postwar World. New York: Columbia University Press, 2002.
Welzmüller 1997: Welzmüller, Rudolf. Zu den Folgen der Globalisierung für die nationalen Güter-, Finanz- und Arbeitsmärkte. In: Aus Politik und Zeitgeschichte, B 33-34, 8. August 1997.
Wendt 1999: Wendt, Alexander. Social Theory of International Politics. Cambridge: Cambridge University Press, 1999.
Wenig 2005: Wenig, Harald. The European Community's Anti-dumping System: Salient Features. In: JWT, Vol. 39, No. 4, 2005. S. 787-794.
Werden 2001: Werden, Gregory J. Network Effects and Conditions of Entry: Lessons from the Microsoft Case. In: Antitrust Law Journal, Vol. 69, 2001. S. 87-111.
Wergo 1928: Wergo, Herbert. Freihandel und Schutzzoll als Mittel staatlicher Machtentfaltung. Schriften des Instituts für Weltwirtschaft und Seeverkehr der Universität Kiel. Jena: Gustav Fischer, 1928.
Werner/Willms 1984: Werner, Horst, Willms, Dorit. Zollstruktur und Effektivzölle nach der Tokio-Runde. Die Auswirkungen der Tokio-Runde auf die Tarifeskalation und die Effektivzölle der Bundesrepublik Deutschland und der EG. Köln: Institut für Wirtschaftspolitik, 1984.
Wessels 1999: Wessels, Bernhard. Political Representation and Political Integration in Europe: Is it possible to square the circle? In: European Integration Online Papers: http://eiop.or.at/eiop/texte/1999/-009.htm.
Westphal 1981: Westphal, Larry E. Empirical Justification for Infant Industry Protection. World Bank, Staff Working Paper No. 445, March 1981. Washington: World Bank, 1981.
Westphal 1990: Westphal, Larry E. Industrial Policy in an Export-Propelled Economy: Lessons from South Korea's Experience. In: Journal of Economic Perspectives, Vol. 4, No. 3, Summer 1990. pp. 41-59.
Westphal et al. 1981: Westphal, Larry E., Rhee, Yung W., Pursell, Garry. Korean Industrial Competence: Where it came from. World Bank Staff Working Paper No. 469, July 1981. Washington: World Bank, 1981.
Westphal et al. 1984: Westphal, Larry E., Kim, Linsu, Amsden, Alice H. Republic of Korea. In: World Development, Vol. 12, No. 5/6, 1984. S. 505-533.
Westphal et al. 1984a: Westphal. Larry E., Yung, W. Rhee, Pursell, Gary. Sources of Technological Capability in South Korea. In: Fransman, Martin, King, Kenneth (eds.). Technology Capability in the Thirld World. London: Macmillan, 1984.

Whalley 1989: Whalley, John. The Uruguay Round an Beyond. The Final Report from the Ford Foundation Supported Project on Developing Countries and the Global Trading System. London: Macmillan, 1989.
Whalley 1990: Whalley, John. Non-Discriminatory Discrimination: Special and Differential Treatment under the GATT for Developing Countries. The Economic Journal, Vol. 100, December 1990. S. 1318-1328.
Whalley 1999: Whalley, John. Notes on Textiles and Apparel in the Next Trade Round. World Bank, WTO Background Paper, October 1999. In: http://www.worldbank.org/research/trade.
Wienert 1995: Wienert, Helmut. Marktstrukturelle Veränderungen in der europäischen Stahlindustrie. In: RWI-Mitteilungen, Jg. 46, 1995. S. 297-315.
Wienert 1995a: Wienert, Helmut. Stahlbericht 1995. RWI-Mitteilungen, Jg. 46, 1995, S. 69-92.
Wienert 1996: Wienert, Helmut. Technischer und wirtschaftlicher Wandel in der Stahlindustrie seit den sechziger Jahren unter besonderer Berücksichtigung Nordrhein-Westfalens. Untersuchungen des Rheinisch-Westfälischen Instituts für Wirtschaftsforschung, H. 20. Essen: RWI, 1996.
Wiese 2002: Wiese, Harald. Mikroökonomik. Berlin: Springer, 2002.
Wiggerthale 1999: Wiggerthale, Marita. Europäische Agrarumweltpolitik in den Grenze der WTO. Magisterarbeit. Unveröffentlicht. Uni-Oldenburg, 1999.
Wiggerthale 2004: Wiggerthale, Marita. Entwicklung statt Freihandel: Zeit für eine Kehrtwende!. Eine Zwischenbilanz der WTO Agrarverhandlungen. Oktober 2004. In: http://www.fairer-agrarhandel.de.
Wignaraja 1994: Wignaraja, Ganeshan. Trade and Industrial Policies in Sri Lanka. In: Helleiner, Gerald K. (ed.). Trade Policy and Industrialization in Turbulent Times. London; New York: Routledge, 1994.
Wignaraja/Ikiara 1999: Wignaraja, Ganeshan, Ikiara, Gerrishon. Adjustment, Technological Capabilities and Enterprise Dynamics in Kenya. In: Lall, Sanjaya (Hrg.). The Technological Response to Import Liberalization in SubSaharan Africa. United Nations University, INTECH. London: MacMillan Press, 1999.
Wilcox 1940: Wilcox, Clair. Competition and Monopoly in American Industry, Monograph 21, Temporary National Economic Committee. Investigation of Concentration of Economic Power. United States: Government Printing Office, 1940.
Wilcox 1949: Wilcox, Clair. A Charter for World Trade. New York: The Macmillan Company, 1949.
Wilcox 1950: Wilcox, Clair. An the Alleged Ubiquity of Oligopoly. In: American Economic Review, Vol. XL No. 2, May 1950. S. 67-73.
Wilcox 1953: Wilcox, Clair. Trade Policies for the Fifties. American Economic Review, Vol. 43, No. 2, Paper und Proceedings, 1953. S. 61-70.
Wilks/Wright 1987: Wilks, Stephen, Wright, Maurice. Conclusion: Comparing Government-Industry Relations: States, Sectors, and Networks. In: Wilks, Stephen, Wright, Maurice (eds.). Comparative Government-Industry Relations. Western Europe, the United States, and Japan. Oxford: Clarendon Press, 1987.
Willgerodt 1989: Willgerodt, Hans. Staatliche Souveränität und die Ordnung der Weltwirtschaft. In: ORDO Bd. 40. 1989. S. 401-427.
Willgerodt 1998: Willgerodt, Hans. Die Liberalen und ihr Staat - Gesellschaftspolitik zwischen Laissez-faire und Diktator. In: ORDO, Bd. 49, 1998.
Williamson 1985: Williamson, Oliver E. The Economic Institutions of Capitalism. New York: The Free Press, 1985.
Williamson 1990: Williamson, John. What Washington Means by Policy Reform. In: Williamson (ed.). Latin American Adjustment: How much has happened? Washington: Institute for International Economics, 1990.
Williamson 1990a: Williamson, John. The Progress of Policy Reform in Latin America. In: Williamson (ed.). Latin American Adjustment: How much has happened? Washington: Institute for International Economics, 1990.
Willmann 2000: Willmann, Gerald. Essays on Trade Policy and Pareto Gains from Trade. Dissertation Stanford University, May 2000. In: http://willmann.bwl.uni-kiel.de/.
Wilmes 1996: Wilmes, Bodo. Deutschland und Japan im globalen Wettbewerb. Erfolgsfaktoren, empirische Befunde, strategische Empfehlungen. Heidelberg: Physica-Verlag, 1996.
Windfuhr 1996: Windfuhr, Michael. Zum Beispiel Rohstoffe. Göttingen: Lamuv Verlag, 1996.
Windfuhr/Braßel 1995: Windfuhr, Michael, Braßel, Frank. Welthandel und Menschenrechte. Bonn: Dietz, 1995.
Winham 1986: Winham, Gilbert R. International Trade and the Tokyo Round Negotiation. Princeton: Princeton University Press, 1986.
Winter 1994: Winter, Helen. Interdependenzen zwischen Industriepolitik und Handelspolitik der Europäischen Gemeinschaften. Baden-Baden: Nomos, 1994.
Winters 1990: Winters, L. Alan. The Road to Uruguay. In: Economic Journal, Vol. 100, Dec. 1990. S. 1288-1303.
Winters 1994: Winters, L. Alan. Import Surveillance as an Strategic Trade Policy. In: Krugman, Paul R. Empirical Studies of Strategic Trade Policy. NBER Project Report. Chicago: Univ. of Chicago Press, 1994.
Winters 2005: Wintes, L. Alan. Developing Country Proposals for the Liberalization of Movements of Natural Service Suppliers. In: Petersmann, Ernst-Ulrich (ed.). Reforming the World Trading System. Legitimacy, Efficiency, and Democratic Governance. Oxford: Oxford University Press, 2005.
Winters/Chang 1997: Winters, L. Alan, Chang, Won. Regional Integration and the Prices of Imports: An Empirical Investigation. World Bank, Policy Research Working Paper, No. 1782, June 1997. In: http://www.worldbank.org.
WIPO 2005: World Intellectual Property Organization. The International Patent System in 2005. Geneva: WIPO, 2005. In: http://www.wipo.int.
WIPO 2006: World Intellectual Property Organization. WIPO Patent Report 2006. Statistics on Worldwide Patent Activity. Geneva: WIPO, 2006. In: http://www.wipo.int.

Wissenschaftlicher Beirat 1979: Wissenschaftlicher Beirat beim Bundesministerium für Wirtschaft. Staatliche Interventionen in einer Marktwirtschaft. In: Stützel, Wolfgang et al. (Hrg.). Grundtexte zur Sozialen Marktwirtschaft. Stuttgart: Gustav Fischer Verlag, 1981.
Witteler 1986: Witteler, Doris. Tarifäre und nichttarifäre Handelshemmnisse in der Bundesrepublik Deutschland – Ausmaß und Ursachen. In: Die Weltwirtschaft, Heft 1, 1986. S. 136-155.
Wogart 1975: Wogart, Jan Peter. Erfahrungen mit der exportorientierten Industrialisierungstrategie in Kolumbien. In: Die Weltwirtschaft, Heft 1, 1975. S. 69-79.
Wolf 1986: Wolf, Martin. Discussion to Section I: Industrial and Trade Policy. In: Aussenwirtschaft, 41. Jg, Heft 2/3, 1986. S. 259-269.
Wolf 1987: Wolf, Manfred. Handmaiden unter Harrassment: The Multi-Fibre Arrangement as an Obstacle to Development. In: Giersch, Herbert (ed.). Free Trade in the World Economy. Towards the Opening of Markets. Tübingen: Mohr, 1987.
Wolf 1994: Wolf, Klaus Dieter. Normen und Institutionen im internationalen System. In: Alemann, Ulrich von et al. (Hrg.) Politik. Eine Einführung. Opladen: Westdeutscher Verlag, 1994.
Wolf et al. 1984: Wolf, Dieter, Glismann, Hans Hinrich, Pelzman, Joseph, Spinanger, Dean. Costs of Protecting Jobs in Textiles and Clothing. Thames Essay No. 37, London: Trade Policy Research Centre, 1984.
Wolf/Zürn 1993: Wolf, Klaus Dieter, Zürn Michael. Macht Recht einen Unterschied? Implikationen und Bedingungen internationaler Verrechtlichung im Gegensatz zu weniger bindenden Formen internationaler Verregelung. In: Wolf, Klaus Dieter (Hg.). Internationale Verrechtlichung. Jahresschrift für Rechtspolitologie (JfR). Pfaffenweiler: Centaurus Verlagsgesellschaft, 1993.
Wolfe 2004: Wolfe, Robert. Informal ministerial meetings and the WTO: multilateralism with large and small numbers, revisited. Annual Meeting of the International Studies Association, Montreal, March 17-20, 2004. In: http://www.allacademic.com/meta/p72232_index.html.
Wolff 1996: Wolff, Edward N. The Productivity Slowdown: The Culprit at Last. Follow up on Hulten and Wolff. In: American Economic Review, Vol. 86, No. 5. December 1996. S. 1237-1252.
Wolff 1996a: Wolff, Alan Wm. Probleme des Marktzugangs in der globalen Wirtschaft: Handels- und Wettbewerbspolitik. In: OCED. Neue Dimensionen des Marktzugangs im Zeichen wirtschaftlicher Globalisierung. Paris: OECD, 1996.
Wolff/Gittleman 1993: Wolff, Edward N., Gittleman, Maury. The Role in Education in Productivity Performance: Does Higher Education Matter? In: Szirmai, Adam, van Ark, Bart, Pilat, Dirk (eds.). Explaining Economic Growth. Essays in Honour of Angus Maddison. Amsterdam: North Holland, 1993.
Woll 1998: Woll, Artur. Adam Smith - Gründe für ein erneutes Studium seiner Werke. In: ORDO, Bd. 49, 1998.
Womack et al. 1994: Womack, James P, Jones, Daniel T., Roos, Daniel. Die zweite Revolution in der Autoindustrie. Frankfurt; New York: Campus Verlag, 1994.
Wood 1994: Wood, Adrian. North-South Trade, Employment and Inequality. Oxford: Clarendon Press, 1994.
Wood 1994a: Wood, Adrian. Give Heckscher and Ohlin a Chance! In: Weltwirtschaftliches Archiv, Bd. 130, Heft 1, 1994. S. 20-49.
Wood 2003: Wood, Diane P. A U.S. Perspective on Ducks. In: Cottier, Thomas, Mavroidis, Petros C (eds.). The Role of the Judge in International Trade Regulation. Ann Arbor: University of Michigan Press, 2003.
Working Group on Globalization 2006: Pascal Morand (chair). Report of the International Working Group on Globalization. 2007. In: http://www.lamondialisation.fr/.
World Bank 1981: World Bank. Accelerated Development in Sub-Saharan Africa. An Agenda for Action. Washington: World Bank, 1981.
World Bank 1993: World Bank. The East Asian Miracle. New York: Oxford University Press, 1993 (1996).
World Bank 1994: World Bank. Adjustment in Africa. Washington: World Bank, 1994.
World Bank 1994a: World Bank. Benin. Toward A Poverty Alleviation Strategy, Report No. 12706-BEN, August 5, 1994 Washington: World Bank, 1994.
World Bank 1995: World Bank. Findings. Africa Region. Number 42, June 1995. In: http://www.worldbank.org/afr/findings/english/find42.htm.
World Bank 1998: World Bank. Development and Human Rights: The Role of the World Bank. Washington: World Bank, 1998. In: http://www.worldbank.org.
World Bank 1999: World Bank. Accelerating China's Rural Development. Washington: World Bank, 1999.
World Bank 2000: World Bank. World Development Report 2000/1, Attacking Poverty, Consultation Draft, January 17, 2000. In: http://www.worldbank.org/poverty/wdrpoverty.
World Bank 2000a: World Bank. Agriculture in Tanzania Since 1986: Leader or Follower of Growth. World Bank Country Study, June 2000. In: http://www.worldbank.org.
World Bank 2002: World Bank. Globalization, Growth, and Poverty. Washington: World Bank, 2002. In: http://www.worldbank.org.
World Bank 2002a: World Bank. Global Economic Prospects and the Developing Countries. Washington: World Bank, 2002. In: http://www.worldbank.org.
World Bank 2004: World Bank. Global Development Finance. Washington: World Bank, 2004. In: http://www.worldbank.org.
World Bank 2005: World Bank. Global Economic Prospects. Trade, Regionalism and Development. Washington: World Bank, 2005.
World Bank 2005a: World Bank. DR-CAFTA. Challenges and Opportunities for Central America. Central America Department. Washington: World Bank, 2005. In: http://www.worldbank.org.

World Bank 2005b: World Bank. Prospects for the Global Economy. Commodity Prices. Published November 16, 2005. In: http://www.worldban.org.
World Bank 2005c: DR-CAFTA. Challenges and Opportunities for Central America. Central America Department., Washington: World Bank, 2005. In: http://www.worldbank.org.
World Bank Brazil 2006: World Bank. Brazil at a Glance. 14.03.2006. In: http://www.worldbank.org.
World Bank Data Profile, var. Countries, var. Dates: World Bank Data Profile. In: http://www.worldbank.org.
World Bank India 2000: World Bank. India. Reducing Poverty, Accelerating Development. Oxford: University Press, 2000.
World Bank Tanzania 2002: World Bank. Tanzania at the Turn of the Century. Background Papers and Statistics. Washington: World Bank, 2002.
World Investment Report div. Jahrgänge: UNCTAD. World Investment Report. United Nations: New York and Geneva, 1998.
World Rainforest Movement Bulletin 2001: World Rainforest Movement Bulletin. Cote d'Ivoire: Increasing Conflict between smallholders and oil palm estates. Bulletin No. 47, June 2001. In: http://www.wrm.org.uy/bulletin/47/CoteIvoire.html.
World Tables div. Jg.: World Bank. World Tables. Washington: World Bank, div. Jg.
WTO 1995: World Trade Organization. The Results of the Uruguay Round of Multilateral Trade Negotiations. Geneva: WTO, 1995.
WTO 1998: Benedek, Wolfgang (Hrsg.) Die Welthandelsorganisation (WTO). München: C.H. Beck, 1998.
WTO 1998a: WTO. Electronic Commerce and the Role of the WTO. Special Studies 2. Geneva: WTO, 1998.
WTO 1999: Ben-David, David, Nordström, Hakan, Winters, L. Alan. Trade, Income Disparity and Poverty. Special Studies 5. Geneva: WTO, 1999.
WTO 1999a: Finger, J. Michael, Schuknecht, Ludger. Trade Finance and Financial Crises. Special Studies 3. Geneva: WTO, 1999.
WTO 2000: WTO Secretariat. International Trade Statistics 2000. Geneva: WTO, 2000. In: http://www.wto.org.
WTO 2001: WTO Secretariat. International Trade Statistics 2001. Geneva: WTO, 2004. In: http://www.wto.org.
WTO 2001a: WTO. Market Access. Unfinished Business. Special Studies 6. Geneva: WTO, 2001. In: http://www.wto.org.
WTO 2001b: WTO. WTO Ministerial Conference approves China's accession, Press/252, 10 November 2001. In: http://www.wto.org.
WTO 2001c: WTO. Doha Declarations. 2001. In: http://www.wto.org.
WTO 2003: WTO. World Trade Report 2003. Trade and development, the Doha Development Agenda. Geneva: WTO, 2003. In: http://www.wto.org.
WTO 2004: WTO Secretariat. A Handbook on the WTO Dispute Settlement System. Geneva: WTO, 2004.
WTO 2004a: WTO Secretariat. International Trade Statistics 2004. Geneva: WTO, 2004. In: http://www.wto.org.
WTO 2005: WTO. World Trade Report 2005. Exploring the links between trade, standards and the WTO. Geneva: WTO, 2005. In: http://www.wto.org.
WTO 2006: WTO. World Trade Report 2006. Exploring the links between subsidies, trade and the WTO. Geneva: WTO, 2006. In: http//www.wto.org.
WTO Analytical Index 2003: WTO. Analytical Index. Geneva: WTO, 2003.
WTO Focus, div. Jg., div. Monate, div. Jahre: WTO Focus. Newsletter. Geneva: WTO, div. Jg, div. Jahre.
WTO/WHO 2002: WTO/WHO. WTO Agreements & Public Health. A Joint Study by the WHO and the WTO Secretariat. Geneva: WTO/WHO, 2002.
Wyman, Donald 1990: L. Manufacturing Miracles. Paths of Industrialization in Latin America and East Asia. Princeton: Princeton University Press, 1990.

Y

Yamamoto 1994: Yamamoto, Takehiko. The US-Japan Structural Impediments Initiative: A Model for Reducing Trade Frictions. In: Waldenberger, Franz (ed.). The Political Economy of Trade Conflicts. Heidelberg et al.: Springer Verlag, 1994.
Yanagihara 1994: Yanagihara, Toru. Anything New in the Miracle Report? Yes and No. In: World Development, Vol. 22, No. 4, 1994.S. 663-670.
Yang 1993: Yang, Ya-Hwei. Government Policy and Strategic Industries in Taiwan. In: Ito, Takatoshi, Krueger, Anne O. Trade and Protectionism. Chicago; London: The University of Chicago Press/NBER, 1993.
Yang 2002: Yang, Jijian. Market Power in China: Manifestations, Effects and Legislation. In: Review of Industrial Organization 21, 2002. S. 167-183.
Yap 1991: Yap, C.L. A comparison of the cost of producing rice in selected countries. FAO Economic and Social Development Paper No. 101. Rome: FAO, 1991.
Yeats 1989: Yeats, Alexander. Developing Coutries' Exports of Manufacturers: Past and Future Implications of Shifting Patterns of Comparative Advantage. In: The Developing Economies. Vol. 27, No. 2, June 1989,S. 109-145.
Yeats 1998: Yeats, Alexander. Just How Big Is Global Production Sharing? World Bank, Policy Research Working Papers, No. 1871, January 1998. In: http://www.worldbank.org.
Yeats 1998a: Yeats, Alexander. What can be expected from African regional trade arrangements? World Bank, Policy Research Working Paper, No. 2004, November 1998. In: http://www.worldbank.org.

Yeats/Amjadi 1995: Yeats, Alexander, Amjadi, Azita. Have Transport Costs Contributed to the Relative Decline of Sub-Saharan African Exports? Some Preliminary Empirical Evidence. World Bank, Policy Research Working Paper No. 1559, December 1995. In: http://www.worldbank.org.
Yeboah 1993: Yeboah, Dickson. Intra-African Food Trade: An Empirical Investigation. In: The Developing Economies, Vol. 31, No.1, March 1993.
Yenkong 2006: Yenkong, Ngangjoh H. World Trade Organization Dispute Settlement Retaliatory Regime at the Tenth Anniversary of the Organization: Reshaping the 'Last Resort' Against Non-compliance. In: JWT, Vol. 40, No. 2, 2006. S. 365-384.
Yi 2001: Yi, Kei-Mu. Can Vertical Specialization Explain the Growth of World Trade. Working Paper, Federal Reserve Bank of New York. In: http://www.newyorkfed.org.
Yoffie 1993: Yoffie, David B. Introduction: From Comparative Advantage to Regulated Competition. In: Yoffie, David B. Beyond Free Trade. Firms, Governments, and Global Competition. Boston, Mass.: Harvard Business School Press, 1993.
Yokoyama et al. 1989: Yokoyama, Hisashi, Ohno, Koichi, Itoga, Shigeru, Imaoka, Hideki. Factor Abundance in East and Southeast Asian Countries: An Empirical Study with Leontief's and Leamer's Formulas. The Developing Economies, Vol. XXVII-4, December 1989. S. 398-406.
Yoo 1993: Yoo, Jung-ho. The Political Economy of Protection Structure in Korea. In: Ito, Takatoshi, Krueger, Anne O. Trade and Protectionism. Chicago; London: The University of Chicago Press/NBER, 1993.
Yoshino/Rangan 1995: Yoshino, Michael Y., Rangan, U. Srinivasa. Stategic Alliances. An Entrepreneurial Approach to Globalization. Boston, Mass.: Harvard Business School Press, 1995.
Young 1980: Young, Oran R. International Regimes: Problems of Concept Formation. In: World Politics, Vol. 32, No. 3, April 1980, S. 331-356.
Young 1991: Young, Alwyn. Learing by Doing and the Dynamik Effects of International Trade. In: The Quarterly Journal of Economics, May 1991. S. 369-405.
Young 1995: Young, Alwyn. The Tyranny of Numbers: Confronting the Statistical Realities of the East Asian Growth Experience. In: The Quarterly Journal of Economics, August 1995, pp. 641- 680.
Yu 2005: Yu, Tian. The 10 Major Problems With the Anti-Dumping Instrument in China. In: JWT, Vol. 39, No. 1, 2005. S. 97-103.
Yu 2006: Yu, Yanning. Circumvention and Anti-Circumvention in Anti-Dumping Practice: A New Problem in China's Outbound Trade. In: JWT, Vol. 41, No. 5, 2007. S. 1015-1041.

Z

Zacher 1975: Zacher, Hans F. Gewerkschaften in der rechtsstaatlichen Demokratie einer Arbeitsnehmergesellschaft. In: Sauermann, Heinz, Mestmäcker, Ernst-Joachim (Hrg.). Wirtschaftsordnung und Staatsverfassung. FS Franz Böhm. Tübingen: Mohr, 1975.
Zacher 1987: Zacher, Hans F. Das soziale Staatsziel. In: Isensee, Josef, Kirchhof, Paul (Hrg.). Handbuch des Staatsrechts. Bd. I. Heidelberg: C.F. Müller, 1987.
Zakariya 1978: Zakariya, Hasan S. State Petroleum Companies. In: Journal of World Trade Law, Vol. 12, 1978. S. 481-501.
Zampetti 1995: Zampetti, Americo Beviglia. The Uruguay Round Agreement on Subsidies. In: JWT, Vol. 29, No. 6, December 1995. S. 5-29.
Zanardi 2000: Zanardi, Maurizio. Antidumping Law as Collusive Device. Working Paper, November 2000. In: http://darkwing.uoregon.edu/~bruceb/adpage.html.
Zanardi 2005: Zanardi, Maurizio. Antidumping: A Problem in International Trade. University of Tilburg Working Paper, June 2005. In: http://darkwing.uoregon.edu/~bruceb/adpage.html.
Zanardi/Anderson 2004: Zanardi, Maurizio, Anderson, James E. Political Pressure Deflection. NBER Working Paper No. 10439, April 2004.
Zangl 2001: Zangl, Bernhard. Bringing Courts Back In: Normdurchsetzung im GATT, in der WTO und der EG. In: Swiss Political Science Review, Vol. 7 Heft 2, 2001. S. 49-80.
Zangl/Zürn 1996: Zangl, Bernhard, Zürn, Michael. Argumentatives Handeln bei internationalen Verhandlungen. In: Zeitschrift für Internationale Beziehungen, Vol. 3 No. 2, 1996. S. 341-366.
Zangl/Zürn 2004a: Zangl, Bernhard, Zürn, Michael. Make Law, Not War: Internationale und transnationale Verrechtlichung als Baustein für Global Governance. In: Zürn, Michael, Zangl, Bernhard (Hrg.). Verrechtlichung - Baustein für Global Governance. Bonn: Dietz, 2004.
Zangl/Zürn 2004b: Zangl, Bernhard, Zürn, Michael. Verrechtlichung jenseits des Staates - Zwischen Hegemonie und Globalisierung. In: Zürn, Michael, Zangl, Bernhard (Hrg.). Verrechtlichung - Baustein für Global Governance. Bonn: Dietz, 2004.
Zangl 2005: Zangl, Bernhard. Is there an emerging international rule of law? In: European Review, Vol. 13, Supp. No. 1, 2005. S. 73-91.
Zangl 2006: Zangl, Bernhard. Die Internationalisierung der Rechtsstaatlichkeit. Frankfurt/New York: Campus, 2006.
Zavatta 1993: Zavatta, Roberto. The pulp and paper industry. In: de Jong, H.W. (ed.) The Structure of European Industry. Dordrecht; Boston; London: Kluwer, 1993.
Zavlaris 1970: Zavlaris, Démètre. Die Subventionen in der Bundesrepublik Deutschland seit 1951. DIW, Beiträge zur Strukturforschung, Heft 14, Berlin: Duncker&Humblot, 1970.

Zdouc 2004: Zdouc, W. WTO Dispute Settlement Practice Relating to the General Agreement on Trade in Services. In: Ortino, Federico, Petersmann, Ernst-Ulrich (eds.). The WTO Dispute Settlement System 1995 - 2003. The Hague et al.: Kluwer Law International, 2004.
Zedalis 2001: Zedalis, Rex J. Labeling of Genetically Modified Foods. In: JWT Vol. 35, No. 2, 2001. S. 301-347.
Zedillo et al. 2005: Zedillo, Ernesto, Messerlin, Patrick, Nielson, Julia. Trade for Development. UN Millenium Project. Directed by Jeffrey D. Sachs. London: Earthscan, 2005
Zeiler 1999: Zeiler, Thomas W. Free Trade Free World. The Advent of GATT. Chapel Hill, London: The University of North Carolina Press, 1999.
Zeitler 2005: Zeitler, Helge Elisabeth. 'Good Faith' in the WTO Jurisprudence. In: Journal of International Economic Law Vol. 8, No. 3, 2005. S. 721-758.
Zeppernick 1987: Zeppernick, Ralf. Zur Rolle des Staates in der Sozialen Marktwirtschaft. Walter Eucken Institut, Vorträge und Aufsätze 113. Tübingen: Mohr, 1987.
Zhang/Assuncao 2001: Zhang, ZongXiang, Assuncao, Lucas. Domestic Climate Policies and the WTO. Unctad, Honolulu East West Centre, 2001.
Zhang/Zou 1995: Zhang, Xiaoming, Zou, Heng-fu. Foreign Technology Imports and Economic Growth in Developing Countries. World Bank, Policy Research Working Paper No. 1412, January 1995.
Zhao 1997: Zhao, Haiying. Foreign Trade in the People's Republic of China: Past Performance and Future Challenges. In: Asian Development Review, Vol. 15, No. 1, 1997. S. 88-110.
Ziegler 1996: Ziegler, Andreas R. Erste Erfahrungen mit der Beufungsinstanz der WTO. Anmerkungen zum WTO-Streitschlichtungsverfahren 'United States - Standards for Reformulated and Conventional Gasoline'. Aussen, 51. Jahrgang, Heft III, 1996. S. 417-432.
Zietz 1985: Zietz, Joachim. Nichttarifäre Handelshemmnisse in der EG – Der Bereich der Telekommunikation. In: Die Weltwirtschaft, Heft 2, 1985. S. 149-165.
Zietz 1987: Zietz, Joachim. Der Agrarsektor in den GATT-Verhandlungen. In: Die Weltwirtschaft, Heft 1, 1987. S. 200-211.
Zietz/Valdés 1986: Zietz, Joachim, Valdés, Alberto. The Costs of Protectionism to Developing Countries. An Analysis for Selected Agricultural Products. World Bank Staff Working Papers Number 769. Washington: The World Bank, 1986.
Zietz/Valdés 1986: Zietz, Joachim, Valdés, Alberto. The Potential Benefits to LDCs of Trade Liberalization in Beef and Sugar by Industrialized Countries. In: Weltwirtschaftliches Archiv, Bd. 122, 1986. S. 93-112.
Zinn 1978: Zinn, Karl Georg. Preissystem und Staatsinterventionismus. Geschichte und Theorie der privaten Preisadministration und der Preiskontrolle in Großbritannien und den USA. Köln: Bund-Verlag, 1978.
Zinn 1992: Zinn, Karl Georg. Soziale Marktwirtschaft. Idee, Entwicklung und Politik der bundesdeutschen Wirtschaftsordnung. Mannheim: B.I.-Taschenbuchverlag, 1992.
Zolltarif EU 1999: Europäische Union (EU). Jahrgang 1998-99. 14. Heft (21. Ausgabe) Internationales Büro für Zolltarife. Brüssel.
Zolltarif EWG 1973: EWG-Zolltarif vom 1. Januar 1973. In: ABl. Nr. L 1/3. S. 330-331. Anhang von Verordnung EWG Nr. 1/73 des Rates vom 19. Dezember 1972
Zolltarif EWG 1987: EU-Zolltarif vom 7. September 1987, in ABl. L 256. Anhang von Verordnung EWG Nr. 2658/87 des Rates vom 23. Juli 1987.
Zürn 1989: Zürn, Michael. Das CoCom-Regime. Zum Erklärungswert rationalistischer Theorien. In: Kohler-Koch, Beate (Hrg.). Regime in den internationalen Beziehungen. Baden Baden: Nomos, 1989.
Zürn 1992: Zürn, Michael. Jenseits der Staatlichkeit: Über die Folgen der ungleichzeitigen Denationalisierung. In: Leviathan, Heft 4, 1992, Opladen: Westdeutscher Verlag.
Zürn 1998: Zürn, Michael. Regieren jenseits des Nationalstaates. Frankfurt am Main: Surkamp, 1998.
Zürn 1998a: Zürn, Michael. Gesellschaftliche Denationalisierung und Regieren in der OECD-Welt. In: PVS, Sonderheft 29/1998. S. 91-120.
Zürn/Wolf/Efinger 1990: Zürn, Michael, Wolf, Klaus Dieter, Efinger, Manfred. Problemfelder und Situationsstrukturen in der Analyse internationaler Politik. Eine Brücke zwischen den Polen? In: PVS, 31. Jg. Sonderheft 21, 1990.
Zweifel/Heller 1997: Zweifel, Peter, Heller, Robert H. Internationaler Handel. Theorie und Empirie. Heidelberg: Physica-Verlag, 1997.

N Tabellen

- Tabellen 1542

N Tabellen

Tabelle 1: Exclusions from Patent Protection. Aus: GATT Document. Group on Negotiations on Goods. MTN.GNG/N11/W/24/Rev. 1, 15. September 1988: 47-49.
Erwähnung in: Abschnitt 'B', 84; Abschnitt 'H', 707, Abschnitt 'J', 1292.

Exclusions from Patent Protection

(i) Pharmaceutical Procucts (49): Argentina, Australia (where the Commissioner *can* refuse to grant a patent therefor where the product is a mere mixture of known ingredients), Bolivia, Brazil, Canada (unless produced by processes also claimed or their equivalents), Chad, China (if obtained by chemical processes), Columbia, Cuba, Czechoslovakia, Ecuador, Egypt (as regards chemical inventions), Finland, German Democratic Republic, Ghana, Greece, Hungary, Iceland, India, Iran (Islamic Republic of), Iraq, Lebanon, Libya (as regards chemical inventions), Malawi, Mexico, Monaco, Mongolia, Morocco, New Zealand (where the Commissioner *can* refuse to grant a patent therefor where the product is a mere mixture of known ingredients), Norway, Pakistan, Peru, Poland, Portugal, Republic of Korea, Romania, Soviet Union, Spain (until 1992), Syria, Thailand, Tunisia, Turkey, Uruguay, Venezuela, Viet Nam, Yugoslaviw, Zambia (where the Registrar *can* refuse to grant a patent therefor where the product is a mere mixture of known ingredients), Zimbabwe (where the Registrar *can* refuse to grant a patent therefor where the product is a mere mixture of known ingredients);

(ii) Animal Varieties (45): Algeria, Austria, Bahamas, Barbados, Belgium, Brazil, Bulgaria, Canada, China, Columbia, Cuba, Cyprus, Denmark, Ecuador, EPC (European Patent Cooperation Treaty), Finland, France, German Democratic Republic, Germany (Federal Republic of), Ghana, Israel, Italy (In this memorandum, the information on Italy also applies on the Holy See and San Marino), Kenya, Luxembourg, Malaysia, Mexico, Netherlands, Nigeria, Norway, OAPI (Benin, Burkina Faso, Cameroon, Central African Republic, Congo, Cote d'Ivoire, Gabon, Mali, Mauritania, Niger, Senegal, Togo. Chad is Member of OAPI but is Member of the Libreville Agreement which, in Article 3 of its Annex I, only excludes pharmaceutical compositions and remedies from patent protection), Peru, Poland, Romania, South Africa, Soviet Union, Spain, Sri Lanka, Sweden, Switzerland (In this memorandum, the information on Switzerland also applies to Liechtenstein), Uganda, United Kingdom, United Republic of Tanzania, Viet Nam, Yugoslavia;

(iii) Methods for Treatment of Human or Animal Body (44): Austria, Barbados, Belgium, Brazil, Bulgaria, Canada, China, Columbia, Cuba, Cyprus, Denmark, Ecuador, EPC, Finland, France, German Democratic Republic (except for apparatuses), Germay (Federal Republic of), Ghana, Hungary, India, Israel, Italy, Japan, Kenya, Malaysia, Mexico, Mongolia, Netherlands, Norway, OAPI, Peru, Poland, Romania, South Africa, Soviet Union, Spain, Sri Lanka, Sweden, Switzerland, Uganda, United Kingdom, United Republic of Tanzania, Viet Nam, Yugoslavia;

(iv) Plant Varieties (44): Algeria, Austria, Bahamas, Barbados, Belgiuim, Brazil, Bulgaria, Canada, China (except of relevant processes), Colombia, Cuba, Cyprus, Denmark, Ecuador, EPC, Finland, France, German Democratic Republic, Germay (Federal Republic of), Ghana, Israel, Kenya, Luxembourg, Malaysia, Mexico, Netherlands, Nigeria, Norway, OAPI, Peru, Poland, Portugal, Romania, South Africa, Soviet Union, Spain, Sri Lanka, Sweden, Switzerland, Thailand, Uganda, United Kingdom, United Republic of Tanzania, Yugoslavia;

(v) Biological Processes for Producing Animal or Plant Varieties (42): Algeria, Austria, Bahamas, Barbados, Belgium, Brazil, Canada, Colombia, Cuba, Cyprus, Denmark, Ecuador, EPC, Finland, France, German Democratic Republic, Germay (Federal Republic of), Ghana, Israel, Italy, Kenya, Luxembourg, Malaysia, Mexico, Mongolia, Netherlands, Nigeria, Norway, OAPI, Peru, Poland, Portugal, South Africa, Spain, Sri Lanka, Sweden, Switzerland, Thailand, Uganda, United Kingdom, United Republic of Tanzania, Yugoslavia;

(vi) Food Products (35): Australia (where the Commissioner *can* refuse to grant a patent therefor where the product is a mere mexture of known ingredients), Bolivia, Brazil, Bulgaria, Canada (unless produced by processes also claimed or their equivalents), China, Czechosloviakia, Columbia, Cuba, Denmark, Ecuador, Egypt (as regards chemical inventions), Finland, German Democratic Republic, Hunagry, Iceland, India, Libya (as regards chemical inventions), Malawi, Mexico, New Zealand (where the Commissioner *can* refuse a patent therefor), Norway, Peru, Poland, Portugal, Republic of Korea, Romania, Thailand, Tunisia, Venezuela, Viet Nam, Yugoslavia, Zambia (where the Registrar *can* refurs a patent therefor where the product is a mere mixture of known ingredients), Zimbabwe where the Registrar *can* refurs a patent therefor where the product is a mere mixture of known ingredients);

(vii) Computer Programs (32): Australia, Austria, Belgium, Brazil, Canada, Cyprus, Denmark, EPC, Finland, France, German Democratic Republic, Germany (Federal Republic of), Ghana, Hungary, Israel, Italy, Japan, Kenya, Mexico, Norway, OAPI, Poland, Portugal, South Africa, Spain, Sweden, Switzerland, Thailand, Uganda, United Kingdom, United Republic of Tanzania, Yugoslavia;

(viii) Chemical Products (22): Bolivia, Brazil, Bulgaria, China, Cuba, Czechoslovakia, German Democratic Republic, Hungary, India, Mexico, Mongolia, Morocco (but only in the former zone of Tangier), Poland, Portugal, Republic of Korea, Romania, Soviet Union, Spain (until 1992), Uruguay, Venezuela, Viet Nam, Yugoslavia;

(ix) Nuclear Inventions (14): Brazil, Bulgaria, China, Cuba, Czechoslovakia, German Democratic Republic, India, Japan, Mexico, Poland, Republic of Korea, Romania, United States of America, Yugoslavia;

(x) Pharmaceutical Processes (10): Australia (where the Commissioner *can* refuse to grant a patent therefor where the process produces a mere mixture of known ingredients by mere admixture), Brazil, Colombia (unless exploited in Colombia), Malawi, Mexico, New Zealand (where the Commissioner *can* refuse to grant a patent therefor where the process produces a mere mixture of known ingredients by mere admixture), Republic of Korea, Turkey, Zambia (where the Registrar *can* refuse to grant a patent therefor where the process produces a mere mixture of known ingredients by mere admixture), Zimbabwe (where the Commissioner *can* refuse to grant a patent therefor where the process produces a mere mixture of known ingredients by mere admixture).

(xi) Food Processes (9): Australia (where the Commissioner *can* refuse to grant a patent therefor where the process produces a mere mixture of known ingredients by mere admixture), Brazil, Colombia (unless exploited in Colombia), Denmark, Malawi, Mexico, New Zealand (where the Commissioner *can* refuse to grant a patent therefor where the process produces a mere mixture of known ingredients by mere admixture), Zambia (where the Registrar *can* refuse to grant a patent therefor where the process produces a mere mixture of known ingredients by mere admixture), Zimbabwe (where the Registrar *can* refuse to grant a patent therefor where the process produces a mere mixture of known ingredients by mere admixture);

(xii) Microorganisms (9): Brazil, Cuba, Czechoslovakia (if used in industrial manufacture), German Democratic Republic, Hungary, Malaysia (except for man-made living microorganisms), Spain, Romania, Yugoslavia;

(xiii) Substances Obtained by Microbiological Processes (7): Czecholovakia, Brazil, German Democratic Republic, Malaysia, Romania, Spain (until 1992), Yugoslavia;

(xiv) Cosmetics (2): Bulgaria, Republic of Korea;

(xv): Fertilizers (2): Mexico, Yugoslavia;

(xvi) Mixture of Metals and Alloys (2): Mexico, Yugoslavia;

(xvii) Agricultural Machines (1): Thailand;

(xviii) Anticontaminants (1): Yugoslavia;

(xix) Methods of Agriculture or Horticulture (1): India.

Tabelle 2: Ausmaß von Betriebsgrößenvorteilen und Anbieterkonzentration in 18 Branchen.
Aus: Monopolkommission, 6. Hauptgutachten, 1984/1985: 231-269. In: Schmidt 1996a: 87.
Erwähnung in: Abschnitt 'C', 123.

Produktgruppe	Mindestoptimale Betriebsgröße (MOTB) Produktionmenge/Jahr	Herstellstück-kostennachteil bei einem Drittel des MOTB	Technisch bedingte Konzentration		Tatsächliche Konzentration: Anteil der drei größten Anbieter	
			Anteil eines MOTB-Anbieters 1984 (%)	Anteil von drei MOTB-Anbieter 1984 in %	am Produktionswert der Güterklasse 1984 (%)	an der Produktionsmenge der Produktgruppe 1984 (%)
PKW	500 Tsd. Einheiten/Jahr	hoch	14	42	64,2	64,8
LKW	200 Tsd. Einheiten/Jahr	hoch	100	>100	91,3-97,6	97,9
Ackerschlepper	100-120 Tsd. Einheiten/Jahr	hoch	>100	>100	69,9	-
Mähdrescher	20 Tsd. Einheiten/Jahr	mittel	>100	>100	-	100
Motorräder	200 Tsd. Einheiten/Jahr	-	>100	>100	-	100
Kühl-/Gefrierschränke	1,5 Mill. Einheiten/Jahr	hoch	56	>100	69,5	-
Reifen	9 Mio. Stück/Jahr	mittel	25	75	60,5	-
Unterhaltungselektronik -Farbfernsehgeräte	1,3-2,2 Mio. Stück/Jahr	gering	33-56	100	38,2	-
-Videorecorder	0,8-1,0 Mio. Stück/Jahr	-	62-77	>100	-	-
Digitale Telefonvermittlungseinrichtungen	0,4-0,5 Mio. Anschlußeinheiten/Jahr	mittel	11-17	33-51	69,7	-
Elektronische Schreibmaschinen	500 Tsd. Stück/Jahr	mittel	70	>100	99,0	100
Mineralölprodukte	10 Mio. t/Jahr	gering	14	42	43,6-61,7	-
Chemische Grundstoffe -Äthylen	0,5 Mio. t/Jahr	mittel	16	48	46,0	-
-Ammoniak	0,55 Mio. t/Jahr	mittel	28	87	89,0	-
-Schwefelsäure	0,35 Mio. t/Jahr	mittel	12	36	45,8	-
Stahl -intergriertes Hüttenwerk	9,6-12 Mio. t/Jahr	hoch	31	93	47,9-62,5	-
-Ministahlwerk	0,7-0,8 Mio. t/Jahr	hoch	2	6	-	-
Zement	1,3 Mio. t/Jahr	hoch	5	15	47,6	-
Bier	2,8 Mio. hl/Jahr	mittel	3	9	11,5	-
Zigaretten	70 Mrd. Stück/Jahr	gering	44	>100	62,0	-
Tiefdruckerzeugnisse	-	gering	-	-	-	-
Regionale Abonnementstageszeitungen	150-180 Tsd. Exemplare/Tag	hoch	-	-	-	-

Der Herstellstückkostennachteil wird als gering, mittel bzw. hoch bezeichnet, wenn er unter 5 %, zwischen 5 und 10 % bzw. über 10 % liegt.

Tabelle 3: Scale Ecomomies for Plants. Modified, food products excluded, because there scale economies do not lead to substantial concentration. In: Pratten 1988: 76-80.
Erwähnung: Abschnitt 'C', 123, Abschnitt 'E', 358, 361.

NACE 3 Number	Industry	MES Scale	Percentage increase in costs at less than MES (3)		Output measure	Output circa 1983 (1)		MES as % of output		Size of the industry: percentage of employment in UK manufacturing industry
			total unit costs	value added per unit		UK	EC	UK	EC	
14	Oil refineries	200,000 barrels a day	4 (1/3)		m tons a year	75	406	14	2.6	0.3
221	Integrated steel plants	4 m tons a year	11 (1/3)		m tons a year	15	110	27	3.6	(0.8)
	- ditto	9.6-12 m tons a year	> 10 (1/3)					72	9.8	
	-ditto for flat rolled products	10 m tons a year	-					67	9	
	Mini steelworks	0.7-0.8 m tons a year	> 10 (1/3)					5	0.7	
2245	Rolled aluminium semi manufactures	200,000 tons a year	-		th tons a year	175		114	(15)	(0.1)
223	Barbed wire fencing	0.76 m pounds sales per	-					(10)	(2)	(0.04)

		year in 1986						(20)	(4)	
	Wire netting	4 m pounds sales per year	-							
241	Bricks - non flettons	25 m bricks a year (at least)	25 (1/2)	30 (1/2)	th m a year	3.4	14	1	0.2	0.4
242	Cement	1.3 m tons a year	26 (1/3)		m tons a year	13	133	10	1.0	0.2
	- ditto	-ditto	> 10 (1/3)							
243	Plasterboard	18-20 sq mtrs a year	-		m sq mtrs	121		16	(3)	(0.1)
247	Glass bottles	133,000 tons a year	11 (1/3)					(5)	(0.5)	(0.1)
248	Pottery	small relative to UK capacity						(2)	(0.2)	1.1
251	Petrochemicals	500,000 tons a year	19 (1/3)		m tons all plastics a year	2.2	18	23 (2)	2.8 (2)	(0.2)
	Sulphuric acid	1 m tons a year	1 (1/2)	19 (1/2)	m tons a year	2.6	18	38	5.6	(0.01)
	- ditto	0.35 m tons a year	5-10 (1/3)					13	2.0	
251	Titanium Oxides	130,000 tons a year	8-16 (1/2)		th tons a year	206	262	63	50	(0.01)
	Synthetic rubber	60.000 tons a year	15 (1/2)		m tons a year	0.25	1.7	24	3.5	(0.01)
255	Paint	10 m galls. a year	4.4 (1/3)		m tons	0.7	3.0	7	2	0.6
256	Fertilizers	300.000-350.000 tons a year	-		m tons a year	1.4	8	23	4.1	(0.1)
258	Detergents	70,000 tons a year	2 1/2 (1/2)	20 1/2				207	(3)	
	Soap	10,000 tons a year	-					(4)	(1)	(0.2)

26	Synthetic fibres	50 m lbs. a year	12 (1/2)		th tons of the synthetic fibre	530	1,901	4 (2)	1 (2)	0.2
	Nylon	42.4 m lbs. a year	9.5 (1/2)		"			4	1 (2)	
	Acrylic	40 m lbs. a year	10 (1/2)		"			3 (2)	1 (2)	
	Polyester	100,000 tons a year	2.6 (1/2)		"			18	5 (2)	
	Cellulosic fibres	70 m lbs a year	5 (1/2)		th tons a year	25	188	125	16	
	Rayon staple	125 m lbs a year	5 (1/2)		"	128	246	40	23	
311	Foundries									
	Cylinder blocks	50,000 tons a year	10 (1/2)	15 (1/2)	th tons of all iron castings		1,435	3	0.3	1.0
	Small engineering castings	10,000 tons a year	5 (1/2)	10 (1/2)				0.7	0.1	
322	Machine tools	Small relative to UK capacity						(1)	(0.2)	1.2
326	Ball bearings	800 employee	8-10 (1/3)					(20)	(2)	(0.15)
342	Large turbo generators	6,000 MW	15 (1/2)	20 (1/2)				(50)	(10)	(0.1)
	Electric motors	60 % of UK market 1970						(60)	(6)	(0.2)
343	Auto batteries	1m units a year	4.6 (1/3)		m units a year	4.5	25	(22)	(4)	(>0.1)
344	Public switches	4-500,000 lines a year	5-10 (1/3)		m units a year	(2.0)		(25)	(4)	(0.4)

	-ditto	500,000 lines a year	4.5 (1/2)					
	TV sets	1.1-1.2 m units a year	15 (1/3)		2.9	12.4	(40)	(9)	(0.2)
	Videos	0.8-1 m units a year	-					(20)	(<0.1)
346	Refrigerator factory	1.0 - 1.2 m units a year	6.5 (1/3)	m units a year	1.3	9.7	(85)	11	0.3
	Washing machine factory	800.000 units a year	7.5 (1/3)		1.4	8.0	57	10	0.3
361	Marine diesels	100,000 hp a year	8 (1/2)	10 (1/2)			(30)	(5)	(<0.1)
363	Bicycles	100,000 units per year	-	m units a year	(1.0)	10.3	(10)	1	(0.1)
427	Beer	4.5 m barrels a year	5 (1/3)	m barrels a year	37	143	12	3	0.7
		3 m	7 (1/2)	"					
		2-3 m	5-10 (1/3)						
429	Cigarettes	36 bill cigarettes a year	2.2 (1/3)	bill a year	149	566	24	6	0.5
431	Wool industry	Small relative to UK capacity	-				(1)	(less than 1)	0.8
432	Cotton spinning	Small relative to UK capacity	-				(1)	(less than 1)	0.6
	Integrated cotton spinning	1.5 % of US capacity c 1975	-				(5)	(1)	0.6
	Weaving cotton	300 looms	-	th looms installed	18.7	142	2	0.2	0.6
438	Tufted carpets	64,000 sq. ft. a week	10 (1/2)	m sq. mtrs	114		0.3	(0.04)	(0.2)

451	Footwear factory	4,000 pairs a week	1.5 (1/3)	m pairs a year	58		0.3	(0.04)	1.0
471	Linerboard	850 tons	8 (1/2)	total output of paper excl. newsprint m tons			10 (2)	1.3 (2)	0.6
	Kraft paper	986 tons	13 (1/2)		3.1	23.2	11 (2)	1.4 (2)	0.6
	Printing paper	567 tons	9 (1/2)				7 (2)	0.9 (2)	0.6
472	Disposable diapers	3 % of US capacity	-				(10)	(2)	(>0.1)
481	Tyres	16,500 tyres a day	5 (1/2)	m a year	24	136	17	3	(0.4)

(1) The figures in brackets are guess estimates. In most cases they provide reasonable orders of magnitude.

(2) For many trades, and particularly those referred to footnote (2) the MES sould be related to a more narrowly defined output. This would have the effect of increasing the MES as a percentage of output.

(3) The figure shown in brackets indicates the proportion of the MES to which the percentage refers.

Tabelle 4: Economies of scale in U.K. manufacturing industry. Source: Pratten (1971) in Shaw/Sutton 1976: 17.
Erwähnung in: Abschnitt 'C', 123, Abschnitt 'E', 358.

Industry/Product	Minimum efficient scale as a proportion of U.K. output in 1969	Percentage increase in unit costs at 50 per cent of m.e.s. compared with the m.e.s. level
Aircraft	> 100	> 20
Machine tools	> 100	5
Diesel engines	> 100	4
Dyes	100	22
Newspapers (single class)	100	>20
Computers (a)	100	10
Turbo-generators	100	5
Steel rollling	80	8
Synthetic fibres polymer manufacture (nylon)	66	5
Electric motors (a)	60	15
Domestic electrical appliances (a) (refrigerators, washing machines)	50	8
Cars (a)	50	6
Cement	40 R	9
Oil refineries	40 R	5
Bread	33 R	15
Bulk steel	33	5-10
Synthetic fibres polymer extrusion (nylon)	33	7
Cylinder blocks for cars	30	10
Sulpuric acid	30	1
Ethylene	25	9
Detergents	20	2-5
Bicycles (a)	10	Small
Beer	6 R	9
Bricks	5 R	25
Warp knitting	3	Small
Book printing	2	Small
Cotton textiles spinning	<2	Small
weaving	<2	Small
Plastics	<1	Small

R - The letter R indicates those cases where a regional market has been used rather than the whole of the United Kingdom. (a) The estimates relate to a range of models or products.

Tabelle 5: 1982 Concentration Ratios for Representative Industries. Aus: Scherer/Ross 1990: 77.
Erwähnt in Abschnitt 'C', 127, 136; Abschnitt 'E', 358.

S.I.C. Code	Industry Description	4-firm ratio	8-firm ratio	Number of Firms	HHI-Index (a)
3711	Passenger cars (five-digit)	97	99	n.a.	n.a.
2067	Chewing gum	95	n.a.	9	n.a.
3632	Household refrigerators and freezers	94	98	39	2745
33310	Primary copper (five-digit)	92	100	7	2483
3641	Electric lamps	91	96	113	n.a.
21110	Cigarettes (five-digit)	90	n.a.	8	n.a.
2043	Cereal breakfast goods	86	n.a.	32	n.a.
3211	Flat glass	85	n.a.	49	2032
3511	Turbines and turbine generators	84	92	71	2602
2082	Beer and malt beverages	77	94	67	2089
39641	Zippers (five-digit)	70	81	n.a.	1452
36512	Household television recievers (five-digit)	67	90	n.a.	1351
3011	Tires and inner tubes	66	86	108	1591
3721	Aircraft	64	81	139	1358
3334	Primary aluminium	64	88	15	1704
2841	Soap and detergents	60	63	642	1306
3691	Storage batteries	56	79	129	989
3523	Farm machinery and equipment	53	63	1787	1468
3221	Glass containers	50	73	41	966
3411	Metal cans	50	68	168	790
2822	Synthetic rubber	49	74	63	935
3562	Ball and roller bearings	47	65	109	724
3312	Blast furnaces and steel mills	42	64	211	650
2211	Cotton weaving firms	41	65	209	645
2041	Flour and other grain mills	40	60	251	551
3674	Semiconductors	40	57	685	597
3144	Women's footwear, except athletic	38	47	209	492
3621	Motors and generators	36	50	349	476
2051	Bread, cake, and related products	34	47	1869	410
2873	Nitrogenous fertilizers	32	57	109	515
3241	Portland cement	31	52	119	469
3541	Metal-cutting machine tools	30	44	865	351
2911	Petroleum refining	28	48	282	380
2834	Pharmaceutical preparations	26	42	584	318
2851	Paints and allied products	24	36	1170	2222
2651	Folding paperboard boxes	22	35	457	212
2711	Newspapers	22	34	7520	193
3552	Textile machinery	22	32	511	200
2421	Sawmills and planing mills	17	23	5810	113
2026	Fluid milk	16	27	853	151
2086	Bottled and canned soft drinks	14	23	1236	109
3451	Screw machine products	8	11	1744	30
2335	Woman's and misses's dresses	6	10	5489	24
3273	Ready-mix concrete	6	9	4161	18

(a) Hirschfeld/Herfindal-Index. With the underlying market shares measured in percentage terms, the maximum possible value is 10.000. Values not available are in all cases relatively high.

Tabelle 6: The most concentrated and least concentrated industries.
In: Davies/Lyons 1996: 52.
Erwähnung in Abschnitt 'C', 127, 129, 136.

Industry	C5EU (a)	HEU (b)	NEU (c)	Type (d)
(i) The 20 most concentrated (C5EU>33.3%)				
Optical instruments	73.1	0.135	7	2AR
Computers/Office machinery	71.2	0.203	5	2R
Electric lamps & lighting, etc.	64.7	0.189	5	2R
Motor vehicles	62.9	0.104	10	2AR
Domestic & office chemicals	62.9	0.118	9	2R
Man-made fibres	62.6	0.105	10	2R
Aerospace	57.0	0.087	12	2R
Tobacco	56.1	0.074	14	2A
Rubber	48.7	0.080	12	2R
Domestic electrical appliances	46.4	0.060	17	2AR
Confectionary	43.7	0.050	20	2A
Steel tubes	40.5	0.044	23	1
Iron & steel	40.2	0.041	25	1
Rails stock	40.1	0.043	23	2R
Cycles & motorcycles	39.3	0.046	22	2R
Glass	37.8	0.048	21	1
Radio & TV	37.2	0.045	22	2AR
Abrasives	36.4	0.036	28	1
Paint & ink	35.8	0.038	26	2AR
Soaps & detergents	34.8	0.034	29	2AR
(ii) The 25 least concentrated (C5EU<10%)				
Household textiles	9.6	0.004	276	1
Leather products	9.4	0.004	258	1
Printinig & publishing	9.3	0.004	270	1
Wood-sawing	8.9	0.004	257	1
Forging	8.5	0.002	470	1
Cotton-weaving	8.2	0.003	375	1
Jewellery	8.1	0.004	255	1
Stone products	7.8	0.003	382	1
Boilers & containers	7.4	0.002	438	1
Wool	7.2	0.003	348	1
Leather-tanning	6.5	0.002	484	1
Knitting	6.4	0.002	544	1
Fur	5.9	0.002	582	1
Footwear	5.8	0.002	515	1
Tools and cans	5.7	0.002	588	1
Metal structures	5.7	0.002	589	1
Meat products	5.7	0.002	535	1
Plastics	5.6	0.002	479	1
Wooden structures	5.5	0.002	596	1
Silk	5.3	0.001	712	1

Clothing	4.3	0.001	1,000	1
Wooden containers	4.1	0.001	957	1
Metal treatment	3.8	0.001	1,111	1
Other wood products	3.2	0.001	1,390	1
Wooden furniture	3.1	0.001	1,289	1

(a) Shares of the 5 most important firms, (b) Herfindal Index of concentration, summing up the square production shares of all firm in industry, advantage is that all firms are included. Lower bound tends towards zero, with n industries, upper bound tends towards unity, this designated a monopoly, (c) Number equivalent form the the Herfindal Index. Nummerically it is the reciprocal of the Herfindal value, it identifies the number of hypothetical equal-sized firms which would be required to generate the Hefindal value. If a given industrie records H = 0.01, the number equivalent is 100, since this number of equal sized firms it needed to record that Herfindal value, (d) 2A advertising intensive, but not R&D intensive; 2 R R&D intensive but not advertizing intensive; 2 AR both intensities are there; 1 neither nor. Davies/Lyons 1998: 250-251, 272-273.

Tabelle 7: Estimated sectoral mark-ups for G-7 countries: Roeger's method (1) (period 1980-92). In: Oliveira Martins et al. 1996: 20.
Erwähnung in Abschnitt 'C', 129, 132.

Sector (by market structure type and ISIC classification)	United States	Japan	Germany	France	Italy	United Kingdom	Canada
Food products	1.07	1.35	1.10	1.10	.	1.19	1.10
Textiles	1.09	1.17	1.13	1.10	1.18	1.03	1.23
Wearing apparel	1.11	.	1.08	1.14	1.16	1.03	1.11
Leather products	1.10	.	1.14	1.11	1.17	1.04	1.15
Footwear	1.10	.	1.04	1.10	1.15	.	1.08
Wood products	1.23	.	1.17	1.14	1.18	1.17	1.24
Furniture	1.05	1.18	1.13	1.19	1.21	1.15	1.14
Printing & Publishing	1.22	.	1.15	1.16	1.19	1.07	1.17
Plastic products	1.06	1.15	.	.	1.05	.	1.15
Non-metal mineral products	1.19	1.30	1.28	1.19	1.31	1.20	1.31
Metal products	1.10	1.12	1.20	1.17	1.42	1.03	1.14
Chemical products	1.26	1.37	1.29	1.19	.	1.05	1.21
Machinery and equipment	.	1.14	.	1.12	1.18	.	1.16
Motorcycles and bicycles	1.09	.	1.34	.	.	.	.
Professional goods	1.07	1.27	1.77	.	1.24	1.28	.
Other manufacturing	1.08	1.47	1.25	.	1.10	.	.
Beverages	1.04	1.09	1.31	1.64	.	1.54	1.22
Paper products & pulp	1.12	1.23	1.23	1.11	1.15	1.04	1.37
Petroleum and coal products.	1.12	1.15	1.08	.	.	1.08	1.25
Rubber products	.	1.10	.	1.16	1.12	.	.
Pottery & china	1.10	1.15	1.26	1.19	1.31	.	1.44
Glass products	1.17	1.72	1.27	1.23	1.31	1.08	1.30
Iron & steel	1.10	1.43	1.18	1.11	1.14	.	1.26
Non-ferrous metals	1.12	1.21	1.09	1.25	1.11	1.05	1.18
Shipbuilding & repair	.	1.29	.	.	.	.	1.19
Other transport equipment	.	.	.	.	1.05	.	.
Tobacco products	1.73	.	1.60	3.17	.	1.67	1.12
Petroleum refineries	1.05	.	.	1.16	.	1.07	.
Industrial chemicals	1.22	1.27	1.40	1.21	1.17	1.05	1.50
Drugs & medicines	1.45	1.75	1.49	.	.	1.11	1.27
Office & computing equipment	1.39	1.32	.	1.18	1.65	1.43	1.14
Radio, TV & comm. equipment	1.38	1.15	1.28	1.11	1.19	1.28	.
Electrical apparatus	.	.	.	1.27	1.08	.	1.14
Railroad equipment	.	.	.	1.70	.	.	1.13
Motor vehicles	1.06	1.18	1.13	1.13	1.02	.	1.14
Aircraft	.	.	.	1.19	1.11	.	.

Tabelle 8: Breakdown of industries according to market structure characteristics. In: Oliveira Martins et al. 1996: 23.
Erwähnt in Abschnitt 'C', 129, 132.

ISIC	Sectors (ordered by research intensity)	Establishment size (1)	R&D intensity by establishment (2)	R&D / output intensity (3)	R&D stock /output intensity (4)
	Fragmented, low-differentiation				
3320	Furnitures and fixtures	62	3	8	7
3310	Wood products	61	3	7	5
3230	Leather products	56	4	13	15
3220	Wearing apparel	72	4	16	19
3210	Textiles	98	7	11	9
3240	Footwear	109	7	14	13
3420	Printing and publishing	68	9	17	11
3810	Metal products	71	17	35	22
3690	Non-metal products, nec	65	23	39	30
3112	Food products	101	25	15	12
3560	Plastic products	75	30	57	33
	Fragmented, high-differentiation				
3900	Other manufacturing, nec	84	74	111	58
3829	Machinery & equipment, nec	96	84	105	67
3844	Motorcycles & bicycles	98	112	116	138
3850	Professional goods	106	197	276	167
3529	Chemical products, nec	123	212	141	112
	Segmented, low-differentiation				
3610	Pottery, china etc.	152	33	50	39
3410	Paper products & pulp	195	46	12	8
3620	Glass products	171	65	43	32
3550	Rubber products	179	74	66	39
3841	Shipbuilding & repair	153	75	69	63
3130	Beverages	193	92	29	20
3849	Transport equipment, nec	176	95	111	100
3540	Petroleum & coal products	156	134	123	86
3710	Iron & steel	336	156	40	26
3720	Non-ferrous metals	233	199	54	35
3140	Tobacco products	696	379	30	22
3530	Petroleum refineries	654	2400	36	32
	Segmented, high-				

	differentiation				
3842	Railroad equipment	466	327	117	136
3843	Motor vehicles	255	445	136	95
3839	Electrical apparatus, nec	151	492	154	260
3510	Industrial chemicals	268	730	131	120
3825	Office & computing equipment	271	935	488	316
3832	Radio, TV & comm. equipment	242	1123	589	602
3522	Drugs & medicines	272	2178	612	417
3845	Aircraft	568	3207	604	433

(1) Average employment per establishment normalized by the total manufacturing average in each country. (2) R&D expenses by establishment normalized by the total manufacturing average in each country. (3) R&D / expenditure gross output ratio normalized by the total manufacturing average in each country. (4) R&D stock / gross output ratio normalized by the total manufacturing average in each country. R&D stocks are calculated as cumulated R&D expenditures, using an annual depreciation rate of 15 %. Sources: Calculations based on OECD-STAN database (OECD, 1995), OECD-ISIS data bases (OECD 1995a), for establishment size data and OECD-ANBERD (OECDb) for data on R&D expenditure.

Tabelle 9: Comparative price level indices for selected product categories in 2000 (household final consumption expenditure) (euro average = 100)
Erwähnung in Abschnitt 'C', 132.

Product category	Highest	Lowest	Coefficient of variation (1)
Food and non-alcoholic beverages	115 (Finland)	87 (Spain)	9.2
Recreation and culture	122 (Finland)	87 (Greece)	9.6
Clothing and footwear	117 (Luxembourg)	79 (Portugal)	9.9
Furnishings, household equipment	115 (Netherlands)	78 (Portugal)	10.6
Restaurant and hotels	126 (Finland)	84 (Portugal)	11.9
Transport	129 (Finland)	75 (Greece)	13.9
Electricity, gas and other fuels	132 (Netherlands)	66 (Greece)	16.3
Health	137 (Finland)	62 (Greece)	18.8
Education	169 (Luxembourg)	63 (Portugal)	29.4
Communications	159 (Finland)	68 (Greece)	29.7
Alcoholic beverages, tobacco	175 (Ireland)	72 (Spain)	30.2
Rentals for housing	141 (Ireland)	33 (Portugal)	30.9

Sources: Eurostat and ECB calculations.
(1) The coefficient of variation is used to show relative dispersion, i.e. the spread around its mean value. It is defined as the ratio of the standard deviation to the sample mean. The higher the value, the higher the degree of price level dispersion between countries.

Tabelle 10: Four-Firm Concentration Ratios by Country and Industry Type. In: Lyons et al. 2001: 12.
Erwähnt in Abschnitt 'C', 136.

Sample/Country	Mean CR 4	S.D.	Min.	Max.	Cases
All industries					
USA	31.4	16.4	7.0	87.4	96
EU	20.1	15.2	2.7	66.3	96
Big 4	33.3	19.0	3.4	100	393
G		35.9	20.8	7.8	91.3	98
Fr		34.9	23.5	3.5	99.9	99
It		31.6	22.3	3.4	100	100
UK		39.5	22.3	7.8	98.0	96
Type 1					
USA	25.4	12.8	7.0	74.0	45
EU	12.2	8.6	2.7	37.0	45
Big 4	28.0	18.9	3.4	100	186
G		30.9	19.4	7.8	91.3	47
Fr		28.9	22.9	3.5	94.8	47
It		26.2	22.7	3.4	100	48
UK		35.7	23.1	7.8	98.0	44
Type 2A					
USA	33.0	18.6	14.0	76.4	16
EU	18.0	11.9	3.8	46.4	16
Big 4	34.1	18.7	4.0	99.9	68
G		33.9	19.7	9.9	88.9	17
Fr		33.8	24.4	4.5	99.9	17
It		33.6	20.7	4.0	87.4	17
UK		45.8	23.1	13.4	94.4	17
Type 2R					
USA	36.7	15.9	12.4	73.5	26
EU	28.3	15.3	9.2	64.0	26
Big 4	38.9	16.4	7.9	93.4	103
G		42.4	21.8	7.9	85.3	25
Fr		44.4	20.5	11.0	93.4	26
It		35.1	17.9	8.3	71.4	26
UK		39.3	21.5	8.8	86.3	26
Type 2AR					
USA	43.8	19.3	23.6	87.4	9
EU	40.0	18.1	16.9	66.3	9
Big 4	44.4	20.6	10.8	92.4	36
G		48.1	20.3	22.9	75.3	9
Fr		40.9	26.0	10.8	85.1	9
It		46.6	28.2	17.0	92.4	9
UK		46.9	17.2	32.0	85.6	9

Tabelle 11: 4-firm and 4-plant concentration ratios, UK, Germany and France, 1963. In: George/Ward 1975: 46.
Erwähnt in Abschnitt 'C', 136.

Industry	4-firm concentration ratio			4-plant concentration ratio		
	UK	WG	France	UK	WG	France
Sugar	95	41	42	42	15	22
Tobacco	88	34	100	33	13	18
Watches and clocks	66	29	24	46	23	20
Aircraft	65	59	57	18	42	20
Motor cycles	65	25	43	45	21	27
Alcohol	58	13	13	31	11	9
Office machinery	54	53	67	31	35	43
Grain milling	51	10	10	16	9	7
Bread, biscuits	48	4	15	6	3	10
Glass	48	21	39	18	14	15
Confectionary	47	25	15	32	19	12
Textile machinery	45	28	23	25	24	23
General chemicals	44	38	35	13	33	11
Beer and Malt	41	7	24	9	5	15
Domestic electr. app.	40	28	25	27	21	16
Autos and parts	40	39	50	16	28	38
Soft drinks	40	15	22	14	-	9
Games, toys	38	18	11	17	16	9
Canned frozen food	35	12	15	15	8	9
Paper and board	35	25	26	11	11	12
Rubber and asbestos	35	34	50	18	31	32
Electronic apparatus	33	37	43	11	13	11
Jewellery, etc.	27	11	9	12	8	8
Textile finishing	24	15	37	6	13	15
Metal working tools	22	8	13	11	8	7
Scientific instruments	21	17	22	11	15	18
Mattresses and bedding	21	18	25	10	13	14
Fur	21	8	15	16	8	8
Paper and board products	17	12	5	7	5	4
Wool	16	14	14	5	-	13
Footwear	16	19	13	6	11	7
Hosiery	16	10	7	5	4	5
Printing and publishing	16	6	7	5	5	5
Mining machinery	15	21	14	12	14	8
Wood furniture	15	4	3	6	3	2
Clay and pottery	13	18	14	6	-	7
Leather and tanning	12	39	16	6	34	11
Leather products	12	5	6	9	5	5
Plastic	11	10	6	6	7	6
Clothing	9	4	2	4	1	1
Timber	6	4	3	4	2	1

Tabelle 12: Shares of products in world exports, 1985 and 1998 (%). In: Lall 2000: 344.
Erwähnung in Abschnitt 'D', 157, 171, 216, 217, 250, 251.

	All products	Primary	All manufactures	RB	LT	MT	HT
	Shares in products in world exports, 1985 and 1998 (%)						
1985	100	21.7	73.8	21.1	13.7	30.2	12.4
1998	100	11.5	84.2	14.5	15.8	32.8	21.1
	Shares of developing countries in world exports, 1985 and 1998 (%)						
1985	24.3	52.1	16.4	26.3	26.7	8.3	10.7
1998	25.0	39.7	23.3	23.7	34.5	15.3	27.0

Note: Other transactions are not shown here, and account for differences between total exports and primary plus manufactured exports. RB - resource based manufactures; LT - low-technology manufactures; MT medium-technology manufactures, and HT, high-technology manufactures.

Tabelle 13: Growth rates and shares of manufactured exports by technological categories, 1980-1996 (%). In: Lall 1999: 1775.
Erwähnung in Abschnitt 'D', 157, Abschnitt 'G', 586.

	Growth rates (% p.a.)				Developing country shares (%)		
	World	Industrialized countries	Developing countries	Developing less industrialized	1980	1996	Change in share
Total	8.1	6.6	14.0	7.4	9.8	23.0	13.3
Ressoure-based	5.7	5.2	7.4	2.2	17.9	23.1	5.2
Low-technology	6.9	5.9	12.6	6.7	15.0	34.4	19.4
Medium-technology	7.8	7.2	17.4	10.2	3.0	11.5	8.6
High-technology	11.6	9.8	21.1	11.3	8.1	29.8	21.7

Tabelle 14: Die 50 deutschen Branchen mit dem wertmäßig höchsten Export, 1985. In: Porter 1990: 777-778.
Erwähnung in Abschnitt 'D', 157.

Branche	Anteil am ges. Weltexport	Exportwert (Mio. $)	Importwert (Mio. $)	Anteil am ges. deutsch. Export
PKWs	23,1	19,118,000	4,344,396	10,42
Autokarosserien, - teile, -zubehör	15,5	6,341,841	2,134,554	3,46
Meß-, Steuergeräte	15,8	2,484,492	1,382,339	1,35
Schaltvorrichtungen	21,4	2,427,723	984,522	1,32
Flugzeuge über 15000 kg	38,1	2,377,571	2,362,416	1,30
LKWs	9,9	2,089,820	449,741	1,14
Verschiedene chemische Produkte	24,5	1,997,810	964,465	1,09
Spezialmaschinen	18,9	1,781,181	637,921	0,97
Teile für Büro-, ADV-Geräte	7,9	1,661,001	2,063,364	0,91
ADV-Peripheriegeräte	15,3	1,443,513	1,499,948	0,79
Kunststoffartikel	19,8	1,274,569	653,337	0,69
Medikamente mit Hormonen	16,1	1,258,621	678,727	0,69
Kolbenmotoranteile	14,5	1,207,932	296,223	0,66
Erzeugnisse aus unedlem Metall	16,4	1,163,157	586,727	0,63
Hähne, Ventile	21,1	1,156,869	487,103	0,63
Nahtlose Eisen-, und Stahlrohre	19,9	1,145,710	176,128	0,62
Funktelefone, TV-Kameras, Teile	8,0	1,109,642	807,689	0,61
Kondensationsprodukte	25,9	1,094,911	505,275	0,60
Andere Haushaltsgeräte	15,8	1,012,347	474,679	0,55
Straßenwalzen/Tiefbaumaschinen	10,4	1,010,463	287,696	0,55
Wellen, Kurbeln, Rollen	29,9	960,332	294,859	0,52
Gasgeneratoren, Ofenbrenner	22,2	927,559	218,586	0,51
Rotationsmaschinen	51,1	923,218	50,671	0,50
Erdölgase	8,1	922,456	5,914,597	0,50
Dünnblech aus Eisen, einfachem Stahl	16,7	896,142	514,027	0,49
KFZ-Kolbenmotoren	14,5	872,278	754,087	0,48
Medizinische Geräte	20,9	859,792	343,001	0,47
Synthetische organische Farbstoffe	32,4	849,848	153,271	0,46
Gummi-, kunststoffverarbeitende Maschinen	35,5	849,798	107,651	0,46
Metallbearbeitungsmaschinen	24,6	815,380	267,162	0,44
Flugzeugteile	8,1	811,723	1,177,712	0,44
Radschlepper	23,5	810,339	94,275	0,44

Verpackungs-, Flaschenfüllmaschinen	34,1	802,409	125,408	0,44
Holzmöbel	19,8	797,212	526,253	0,43
Kugel-, Rollenlager	24,3	782,989	417,090	0,43
Artikel aus vorgeschnittenem Papier	19,6	774,632	387,527	0,42
Andere Hub-, Verladegeräte	19,2	731,961	135,819	0,40
Elektrische Mikroschaltungen	5,9	720,432	1,323,628	0,39
Azyklische Alkohole	21,5	713,425	381,830	0,39
Heterozyklische Verbindungen	14,3	712,932	496,440	0,39
Textil-, Ledermaschinen	30,4	695,938	106,064	0,38
Gewebte Baumwolle, gebleicht	15,5	681,016	355,560	0,37
Polymerisationsprodukte	16,2	679,882	352,908	0,37
Blätter, Werkzeugspitzen	19,9	677,492	404,001	0,37
Rindfleisch mit Knochen	22,3	672,096	222,944	0,37
Eisen-, Stahlblech	13,6	658,354	279,951	0,36
Alubleche, -bänder	20,1	654,541	317,370	0,36
Elektromaschinen	13,0	653,247	434,304	0,36
Schlosserwaren	26,0	646,838	204,307	0,35
Isolierdraht,-kabel	12,2	646,668	377,144	0,35
Gesamt				41,62

Tabelle 15: Die 50 japanischen Branchen mit dem wertmäßig höchsten Export, 1985. In: Porter 1990: 780-781.
Erwähnung in Abschnitt 'D', 157.

Branche	Anteil am ges. Weltexport	Exportwert (Mio. $)	Importwert (Mio $)	Anteil am ges. jap. Export
PKWs	30,8	25.402,210	538,683	14,46
LKWs, Sattelschlepper	37,5	7.956,271	16,969	4,53
Videorecorder, Tonaufnahmegeräte	80,7	6.622,119	9,924	3,77
KFZ-Karosserien,-Teile,-Zubehör	12,8	5.227,670	187,706	2,98
Andere Frachtschiffe	35,7	4.399,729	216,601	2,50
Funktelefone, TV-Kameras, Teile	28,6	3.945,888	302,334	2,25
ADV-Peripheriegeräte	37,9	3.571,949	427,126	2,03
Farbfernsehgeräte	49,5	2.691,101	6,899	1,53
Elektronische Mikroschaltungen	19,9	2.415,252	699,618	1,37
Nahtlose Eisen-, Stahlrohre	38,7	2.227,632	6,587	1,27
ADV-Geräteteile	10,0	2.105,665	501,908	1,20
Motorräder	82,0	2.092,416	16,684	1,19
Fotoapparate, Thermokopierer	65,9	2.032,389	6,055	1,16
Gewalzte Dünnbleche aus Eisen und einfachem Stahl	35,2	1.893,459	84,656	1,08
Schaltvorrichtungen	16,5	1.877,891	34,619	1,07
Diktiergeräte	71,7	1.817,413	15,194	1,03
Einzelbildkameras, Blitzgeräte	62,2	1.608,936	82,174	0,92
Bespielte Tonträger	41,5	1.589,513	96,184	0,90
Meß-, Steuergeräte	9,3	1.459,409	924,601	0,83
Synthetische Kontinuegewebe ohne Flor	34,7	1.456,391	31,808	0,83
Rohre, Leitungen aus Eisen, Stahl	30,6	1.437,337	17,006	0,82
Universalbleche aus Eisen, Stahl	29,3	1.419,903	11,577	0,81
Andere Haushaltsgeräte	21,8	1.401,394	72,247	0,80
Schnurtelefone	26,2	1.378,545	57,018	0,78
Spezialmaschinen	14,3	1.349,143	290,643	0,77
Kolbenmotorteile	15,9	1.320,517	45,806	0,75
Kofferradios	48,4	1.171,209	31,718	0,67
Andere Elektrogeräte	20,3	1.014,478	427,359	0,58
Werkzeugmaschinen für Metall	36,5	1.009,629	111,274	0,57
Armbanduhren	24,0	997,512	160,139	0,57
Mikrofone, Lautsprecher, Verstärker	55,7	981,176	51,602	0,56
Selbstfahrende Löffelbagger	38,4	964,624	-	0,55
Autoradios	42,5	908,083	3,051	0,52

LKW-Reifen	39,1	860,530	4,411	0,49
Piezoelektrische Kristalle	14,0	835,800	43,896	0,48
KFZ-Kolbenmotoren	13,5	813,915	25,749	0,46
Stabstahl, andere Stahlträger	24,1	811,754	-	0,46
Tankschiffe	31,7	767,626	13,116	0,44
Straßenwalzen/Tiefbaumaschinen	7,8	754,372	56,111	0,43
Motoradteile,-zubehör	53,4	747,246	13,370	0,43
TV-Bildröhren	42,2	709,509	35,503	0,40
Isolierdraht, -kabel	13,3	700,607	58,412	0,40
Eisen-, einfache Stahlcoils	18,5	695,106	337,018	0,40
Gasgeneratoren, Ofenbrenner	16,7	694,773	107,846	0,40
Fernseh-, Rundfunkgeräte	29,8	692,249	14,810	0,39
Klaviere, Musikinstrumente, Teile	51,0	687,841	47,188	0,39
Gaspumpen	24,1	686,437	63,585	0,39
Webwaren aus Kunstfasern	16,0	668,946	77,921	0,38
Rechenmaschinen	69,7	660,432	11,294	0,38
Gewalztes Grobblech aus Eisen und einfachem Stahl	25,1	653,184	210,305	0,37
Gesamt				62,74

Anmerkung: Importwerte sind nicht angegeben, wenn der Importwert unter 0,3 Prozent des Gesamthandels für 1985 liegt.

Tabelle 16: Die 50 U.S.-Branchen mit dem wertmäßig höchsten Export, 1985. In: Porter 1990: 792-793.
Erwähnung in Abschnitt 'D', 157, 217.

Branche	Anteil am ges.Weltexport	Exportwert (Mio. $)	Importwert (Mio $)	Anteil am ges. amerik. Export
KFZ-Karosserien,-Teile,-Zubehör	25,6	10,476,330	9,669,742	4,92
Geschäftsflugzeuge und -hubschrauber	79,4	8,823,833	1,806,783	4,14
Büro- und ADV-Geräteteile	37,1	7,816,542	5,326,652	3,67
PKWs	7,5	6,153,623	39,088,930	2,89
Flugzeugteile	56,6	5,674,001	1,793,513	2,66
Unverarbeiteter Mais	69,5	5,335,039	20,588	2,50
Meß-, Steuergeräte	28,1	4,422,593	1,883,423	2,07
Kohle, Braunkohle und Torf	64,4	4,399,776	135,986	2,06
Analog-, Hybridrechner, Speichereinheiten	64,3	4,091,920	4,116,526	0,20
Straßenwalzen/Tiefbaumaschinen	41,6	3,749,941	193,708	0,19
Sojabohnen	67,1	3,019,250	976	1,76
Piezoelektrische Kristalle	50,7	2,888,887	1,100,923	1,42
Waffen, Munition	62,7	2,451,731	203,863	1,36
Flugzeugtriebwerke und Motorenteile	41,6	2,121,790	1,202,089	1,15
Spezialmaschinen	22,5	2,069,649	1,681,149	1,00
Kolbenmotorteile	24,9	2,069,200	1,431,972	0.97
LKWs	9,8	2,066,605	7,489,290	0,97
Funktelefone, TV-Kameras, Teile	15,0	1,889,673	4,647,997	0,97
Heizöl	7,2	1,775,540	7,652,369	0,89
Schaltvorrichtungen	15,6	1,678,027	1,794,662	0,83
Elektronische Mikroschaltungen	13,8	1,634,779	4,421,879	0,79
Rohbaumwolle	34,2	1,548,476	15,773	0,77
Digitale Zentralrechner	30,4	1,519,395	-	0,73
Digitalcomputer	35,8	1,322,441	-	0,71
Nichtmonetäres Gold	17,4	1,298,038	2,690,974	0,62
Elektromaschinen	25,9	1,272,439	1,641,469	0,61
Andere Kunstdünger	69,6	1,229,403	992	0,60
Gasturbinen	62,8	1,209,376	1,254,813	0,58
KFZ-Kolbenmotoren	20,1	1,183,792	1,904,359	0,57
Zigaretten	36,6	1,170,516	21,863	0,56
Grobes Sägefurnier, Funierstämme	75,8	1,155,456	17,408	0,55
Verschiedene chemische Produkte	14,2	1,021,116	395,435	0,54

Rinder-, Pferdehäute, ungegerbt	45,3	997,437	30,670	0,48
Hormonhaltige Medikamente	12,7	980,118	816,088	0,47
Radioaktive Stoffe	57,1	962,927	1,399,330	0,46
Kunststoffartikel	14,9	937,298	1,670,496	0,45
Gebleichter nichtlöslicher Zellstoff	17,8	906,005	1,225,127	0,44
Schnurtelefonanlagen	17,2	904,765	2,099,325	0,43
Andere organische Chemikalien	30,4	885,712	341,823	0,42
Fotofilme, nicht belichtet, nicht entwickelt	81,9	870,651	630,695	0,42
Ölkuchen und Sojarückstände	21,7	865,609	-	0,41
Elektromedizinische Geräte	46,6	828,165	524,326	0,41
Medizinische Geräte	20,1	820,142	524,589	0,39
Isolierdraht,- kabel	15,5	806,956	1,420,983	0,38
Pharmazeutische Artikel ohne Medikamente	41,8	788,551	52,058	0,38
Fungizide, Desinfektionsmittel	40,3	769,266	116,851	0,37
Sorghum, unverarbeitet	65,8	761,027	13	0,36
Flüssigkeitspumpen	25,9	760,981	625,712	0,36
Petrolkoks	80,3	760,081	19,522	0,36
Klimaanlagen	35,4	751,041	309,924	0,35
Gesamt				51,59

Anmerkung: Importwerte sind nicht angegeben, wenn der Importwert unter 0,3 Prozent des Gesamthandels für 1985 liegt.

Tabelle 17: Die 50 koreanischen Branchen mit dem wertmäßig höchsten Export, 1985. In: Porter 1990: 786-787.
Erwähnung in Abschnitt 'D', 157.

Branchen	Anteil am ges. Weltexport	Exportwert (Mio. $)	Importwert (Mio. $)	Anteil am ges. korean. Export
Andere Frachtschiffe	36,9	4.545,449	3.296,174	15,01
Lederschuhe	14,3	1.436,334	-	4,74
Synthetische Kontinuegewebe ohne Flor	21,1	885,906	69,888	2,93
Elektronische Mikroschaltungen	6,3	760,213	261,271	2,51
Eisen-, Stahlkonstruktionen, Teile	14,4	700,826	28,280	2,31
Lederbekleidung, Zubehör	26,7	518,789	862	1,78
PKWs	0,6	475,254	-	1,71
Spielzeug, Synthetik	10,8	448,201	7,283	1,57
Sweater aus synthetischen Fasern	24,2	417,910	-	1,48
Herrenjacketts, -blazer	39,4	381,006	233	1,38
Rohre, Leitungen aus Eisen, Stahl	8,1	376,049	40,035	1,26
Farbfernsehgeräte	6,9	342,319	5,626	1,24
Tankschiffe	14,1	337,005	17,381	1,13
Reiseartikel,- taschen	24,6		1,274	1,11
Heizöl	1,1	300,988	271,955	0,99
Baumwollsweater	11,4	299,388	512	0,99
Eisen-, einfache Stahlcoils	7,8	293,666	280,343	0,97
Herrenhemden aus Kunstfasern	40,9	292,283	-	0,97
Unterwäsche aus Wolle, Fasern	13,7	283,956	677	0,94
Container, auch für Straße und Schiene	32,2	279,768	11,815	0,92
Herrenmäntel,-oberbekleidung	11,9	261,603	160	0,86
Tiefkühlfisch, ohne Filets	15,7	260,784	58,225	0,86
Flugzeug, Motoradreifen	9,6	249,212	3,175	0,82
Düsentreibstoff	2,0	242,708	158,076	0,80
Off-line Datenverarbeitungsgeräte	41,8	238,310	73,350	0,79
Spülmaschinen, Rasierapparate, Haushaltsgeräte	3,6	233,057	16,371	0,77
Bespielte Tonträger	6,0	231,939	20,412	0,77
Frische, tiefgekühlte Schalentiere	4,4	223,669	17,582	0,74
Synthetische Webwaren	5,3	219,732	119,297	0,73
Flugzeuge über 15000 kg	3,5	215,745	204,617	0,71
Schwarzweiß- Fernsehgeräte	52,4	215,941	347	0,71

Damenmäntel, Jacketts aus Kunstfaser	31,8	212,399	-	0,70
Herrenhemden aus Baumwolle	15,0	211,624	-	0,70
Eisenträger, anderer Stabstahl	6,3	210,964	-	0,70
Telekommunikationsgeräte, Teile	1,5	209,727	368,652	0,69
Videorecorder, Tonaufnahmegeräte	2,5	206,562	12,745	0,68
Gewalztes Dünnblech aus Eisen und einfachem Stahl	3,8	202,556	49,701	0,67
Kinderwagen, Teile	7,3	188,476	50,826	0,62
Textilien	11,2	186,546	2,054	0,62
Nichtelektrische Öfen, Heizgeräte	9,8	185,942	12,278	0,61
Autoradios	8,6	182,887	5,368	0,60
Kofferradios	7,2	174,489	1,023	0,58
Fernsehbildröhren	9,7	162,286	41,177	0,54
Pelzartikel	14,7	161,287	994	0,53
ADV-Geräteteile	0,7	157,694	133,357	0,52
Dioden, Transistoren	5,2	154,821	74,388	0,51
Damenblusen aus synthetischen Fasern	16,4	149,778	-	0,49
Gewalztes Grobblech aus Eisen und einfachem Stahl	5,5	144,248	140,708	0,48
Andere Radiogeräte	11,9	142,529	9,432	0,47
Gasöle	0,8	139,262	-	0,46
Gesamt				65,67

Anmerkung: Importwerte sind nicht angegeben, wenn der Importwert unter 0,3 Prozent des Gesamthandels für 1985 liegt.

Tabelle 18: Import structure by origin and by major commodity groups. Manufactured Goods (SITC 5 to 8 less 68) In: UNCTAD 1994: 88-89.
Erwähnung in Abschnitt 'D', 158.

Origin	1970	1980	1992
Share in total trade	100.0	100.0	100.0
All food items (SITC 0 + 1 + 22 +4)	14.7	11.1	9.7
Agricultural raw materials (SITC 2 - 22-27-28)	5.8	3.7	2.7
Ores and Metals (SITC 27 + 28 + 68)	7.3	4.7	3.1
Fuels (SITC 3)	9.2	24.0	8.7
Manufactured goods (SITC 5 to 8 less 68)	60.9	54.2	73.5
World	100.0	100.0	100.0
- Developed Market Economies	84.4	82.2	77.7
- Developing countries and territories			
Total	5.5	9.7	18.2
OPEC	0.2	0.5	1.0
Other	5.3	9.2	17.1
- Countries in Eastern Europe			
Total	9.5	7.2	1.6
USSR (former)	2.6	1.7	0.5
- Developed Market Economies			
-- Europe			
Total	54.6	54.1	49.6
EU	45.8	46.6	43.0
EFTA	8.1	7.5	6.6
-- USA	15.0	12.8	12.0
-- Canada	4.3	2.8	2.9
-- Japan	9.4	11.3	12.0
-- Australia, New Zealand	0.5	0.4	0.4
-- South Africa	0.4	0.5	0.3
- Developing countries and territories by region			
-- America			
Total	1.0	1.5	1.8
LAIA	0.6	1.3	1.6
-- Africa	0.4	0.4	0.4
-- Asia			
West Asia	0.2	0.6	0.8
South and Southeast Asia	3.3	6.6	14.7
China	0.6	0.9	2.5
Oceania	0.0	0.0	0.0

Tabelle 19: R & D Expenditure of the Top 300 Companies World-wide, 1995 and 1998 ($ billion). In: Nolan 2001: 766.
Erwähnung in Abschnitt 'D', 158, Abschnitt 'J', 1288, 1337.

Sector	No. of Companies (1998)	of which: USA	1995	1998	% increase/decrease in R & D expenditure (1995-98)
Total	300	129	176.6	253.7	44
of which:					
IT hardware	55	36	41.8	70.0	68
Software/IT Services	17	16	3.3	7.5	127
Telecoms services	9	1	9.0	9.8	9
Autos	25	5	31.2	43.4	39
Pharmaceuticals	35	13	22.4	33.1	48
Electronic/electricals	28	7	22.3	26.6	19
Chemicals	31	9	14.5	20.7	43
Aerospace/defence	11	7	5.7	6.9	21
Engineering/machinery	21	8	4.8	6.5	35
Oil/gas	11	6	4.0	5.1	28
Steel/metals	9	0	1.2	1.1	-7

Tabelle 20: Japanese consumer electronics manufacturers' share of world production and ratio of domestic production, 2000, 2003. In: JETRO White Paper Trade Investment 2004: 22.
Erwähnung in Abschnitt 'D', 158, 278, 280, 303.

Ratio of domestic production of Japanese manufacturers (%):	2000		
50-100	Desktop PCs 52,5 % and one other product	TFT liquid crystal 100 %, LCD monitors 100 %, PDAs 100 %, Cordless phones 92,2 %, Notebook PCs 65,6 %, Washing machines 64,0 %, Vaccum cleaners 58,1 %	Car navigation systems 100,0 %, VTR cameras 87,2 %, Digital cameras 81,2 %, DVD Roms, etc. 73,2 %
10-50		Refrigerators 48,7 %, Room air conditioners 44,5 %, Cellular phones (CDMA) 37,6 %, CRT monitors 35,5 %, Hard disk drives 23,9 %, Microwave ovens 18,8 %, CRT TVs 11,7 %, and four other products	Optical pickups 37,5 %, DVD players 35,1 %, Portable CD players 25,1 %, Fax machines 23,2 %, Copiers 22,5 %, Car audio equipment 22,2 %, Inkjet printers 20,5 %, Laser printers 17,5 %, VTRs 10,4 %
0-10	Scanners 8,2 %, Cellular phones (GSM) 8,5 %	Radio-cassette players 7,2 %, Keyboards 1,9 %	Stereo systems 4,6 %, Floppy disk drives 2,0 %
World share of Japanese manufactures (%):	0-10	10-50	50-100

Ratio of domestic production of Japanese manufacturers (%):	2003		
50-100	Digital audio equipment 66,7 %, LDC monitors 51,1 %	PDAs 100,0 %, TFT liquid crystal 91,7 %, PDP TVs 88,5 %, Notebook PCs 66,0 %	Car navigation systems 99,7 %, PDPs 99,1 %, VTR cameras 84,6 %, LCD TVs 81,5 %, Compact/Small and medium liquid crystal parts 78,1 %, DVD recorders 65,4 %, Digital cameras 57,7 %
10-50	Desktop PCs 39,4 % CRT monitors 25,7 %	Washing machines 47,0 %, Cellular phones (CDMA) 45,5 %, Room air conditioners 39,2 %, Refrigerators 33,8 %, Home game consoles, 31,0 %, Vaccuum cleaners 24,9 %, Microwave ovens 14,1 %, and four other products	Combo drives 24,8 %, Copiers 19,6 %, Optical pickups 17,0 %, Car audio equipment 13,8 %, Laser printers 10,0 %
0-10	Cellular phones (GSM) 5,0 %, and one other products	Radio-cassette players 9,6 %, Keyboards, 1,7 %, CRT TVs 1,5 %, DVD players, 0,8 %, Hard disk drives 0,0 %, Scanners 0,0 %, and three other products	Fax machines 9,1 %, DVD ROMs, etc. 4,9 %, Inkjet printers MFP 2,9 %, VTRs 2,0 %, Rear projection TVs 0,8 %, Floppy disk drives 0,6 %, Inkjet printers SFP 0,2 %
World share of Japanese manufactures (%):	0-10	10-50	50-100

Figures indicate the ratio of domestic production by Japanese manufacturers (%).

Tabelle 21: Global market share of Top 10 companies in knowledge-intense industries, 1998. In: Nolan 2001: 768.
Erwähnung in Abschnitt 'D', 158, Abschnitt 'J', 1337.

Sector	US$ billion	Global Market Share (%)
Commercial seeds	7,4	32
Pharmaceuticals	104,0	35
Veterinary medicine	10,2	60
Computers	233,8	70
Pesticides	26,4	85
Telecommunications	225,3	86

Tabelle 22: Technological classification of exports. In: Lall 2000: 341.
Erwähnung in Abschnitt 'D', 159, 160, 250, Abschnitt 'F', 443.

Classification	Examples
Primary products	Fresh fruit, meal, rice, cocoa, tea, coffee, wood, coal, crude petroleum, gaz
Manufactured products	
Agro/forest-based products	Prepared meats/fruits, beverages, wood products, vegetable oils
Other resource-based products	Ore concentrates, petroleum/rubber products, cement, cut gems, glass
Low-technology manufactures	
Textile/fashion cluster	Textile fabrics, clothing, headgear, footwear, leather, manufactures, travel goods
Other low technology	Pottery, simple metal parts/structures, furniture, jewellery, toys, plastic products
Medium-technology manufactures	
Automotive products	Passenger vehicles and parts, commercial vehicles, motorcycles and parts
Medium technology process industries	Synthetic fibres, chemicals and paints, fertilizers, plastics, iron, pipes/tubes
Medium technology engineering industries	Engines, motors, industrial machinery, pumps, switchgear, ships, watches
High-technology manufactures	
Electronics and electrical products	Office/data processing/telecommications equipment, TVs, transistors, turbines, power-generating equipment
Other high technology	Pharmaceuticals, aerospace, optical/measuring instruments, cameras
Other transactions	Electricity, cinema film, printed matter, "special transactions", gold, art, coins, pets

Tabelle 23: Trend movements of relative prices, nominal exchange rates, real effective exchange rate, and terms of trade for different regions (Cumulative percentage change). In: Aghevli/Montiel 1996: 622.
Erwähnt in Abschnitt 'D', 165, 166.

		1978-81	1982-85	1986-89	1978-89
Industrial countries					
	Relative prices	-4.9	-7.1	-1.8	-13.7
	Nominal effective exchange rate	-5.9	-9.2	1.5	-13.6
	Real effective exchange rate	-1.1	-2.1	3.3	0.1
	Terms of trade	-0.7	2.3	9.8	5.1
Developing countries					
	Relative prices	-20.1	-30.9	-54.8	-105.8
	Nominal effective exchange rate	-15.6	-34.1	-74.7	-124.4
	Real effective exchange rate	4.5	-3.2	-19.9	-18.6
	Terms of trade	-12.4	2.1	-21.0	-31.4
Africa					
	Relative prices	-19.2	-21.8	-26.6	-67.6
	Nominal effective exchange rate	-8.3	-32.2	-56.4	-96.9
	Real effective exchange rate	10.8	-10.4	-29.8	-29.4
	Terms of trade	-22.4	9.1	-27.4	-41.0
Asia					
	Relative prices	-5.9	-8.2	-6.2	-20.2
	Nominal effective exchange rate	-12.8	-8.1	-27.4	-48.2
	Real effective exchange rate	-6.9	0.1	-21.2	-28.0
	Terms of trade	-7.0	8.4	-5.3	-3.9
Europe					
	Relative prices	-27.6	-30.1	-85.0	-142.8
	Nominal effective exchange rate	-27.9	-38.1	-90.1	-156.0
	Real effective exchange rate	-0.2	-8.0	-5.1	-13.3
	Terms of trade	-19.7	1.7	2.7	-15.2
Middle East					
	Relative prices	-16.8	-33.5	-49.1	-99.4
	Nominal effective exchange rate	-19.7	-19.2	-65.5	-104.4
	Real effective exchange rate	-3.0	14.3	-16.4	-5.1
	Terms of trade	20.7	-7.8	-58.9	-46.1
Western Hemisphere					
	Relative prices	-31.9	-58.9	-126.4	-217.2
	Nominal effective exchange rate	-22.8	-62.8	-136.6	-222.3
	Real effective exchange rate	9.0	-3.9	-10.3	-5.1
	Terms of trade	-18.8	-6.9	-7.1	-32.9

Tabelle 24: Bedeutung der Landwirtschaft in ausgewählten AKP-Ländern (1990):
Brockmann 1996: 9.
Erwähnung in Abschnitt 'D', 168.

Länder	Anteil der Landwirtschaft am BIP in %	Agrarhandel Importanteil	Agrarhandel Anteil an den Exporten	Anteil (%) der Erwerbstätigen in der Landwirtschaft
Äthiopien	52,1	22,7	88,2	74,5
Benin	36,1			61,4
Burkina Faso	31,8	18.8	76,5	84,4
Burundi	55,9			91,3
Cote d'Ivoire	46,7	19,1	51,8	55,6
Ghana	51,1	14,7	43,9	50,0
Guinea Bissau	46,3			78,6
Kamerun	26,6	16,7	27,7	61,0
Kenia	28,6	9,7	62,8	77,0
Madagaskar	32,3	13,1	56,9	76,6
Malawi	33,3	11,3	91,6	75,2
Mali	45,9	18,8	75,1	80.9
Mosambik	64,6			81,6
Ruanda	38,1			91,3
Senegal	20.5	34,5	29.4	78,4
Sierra Leone	31,7	68,1	12,2	62,3
Simbabwe	12,9	4,4	43,4	68,1
Sudan	30,3	29,4		60,2
Swasiland	18,2			66,3
Tansania	59,0	5,2	68,9	80.8
Togo	32,9	20,0	44,6	69,6
Tschad	35,1	8,8	69,8	74,6
Uganda	53,3	4,5	92,1	80,9
Zaire	29,0	25,9	14,2	65,8
Zentralafrikanische Republik	42,6	26,8	37,6	62,6
Dominikanische Republik	17,4	15,8	49,3	35,8
Haiti	32,2	72,9	19,1	63,7
Fidschi	20,2	12,1	37,0	39,2
Papua Neuguinea	28,4	14,9	18,7	67,1

Tabelle 25: Structure of merchandise exports: Selected Developing Countries, 1965 and 1990. In: Borensztein et al. 1994: 3.
Erwähnung in Abschnitt 'D', 168.

	1965			1990		
Country	Fuels, minerals and metals	Other primary commodities	Manufactures	Fuels, minerals and metals	Other primary commodities	Manufactures
Africa						
Burundi	0	94	6	0	98	2
Cote d' Ivoire	2	93	5	10	80	10
Kenya	13	77	10	19	70	11
Mauritania	94	5	1	81	13	6
Senegal	9	88	3	22	56	22
Tanzania	1	86	13	5	84	11
Asia						
Malaysia	34	60	6	19	37	44
Pakistan	2	62	36	1	29	70
Philippines	11	84	5	12	26	62
Sri Lanka	0	99	1	6	47	47
Thailand	11	86	3	2	34	64
Latin America						
Argentina	1	93	6	6	59	35
Bolivia	93	4	4	69	27	14
Brazil	9	83	8	16	31	53
Colombia	18	75	7	32	42	26
Mexico	22	62	16	43	13	54
Uruguay	0	95	5	0	60	40

Tabelle 26: Countries dependent on a single primary commodity for export earnings (annual average of export data, U.S. dollars, 1992-1997). In: Cashin et al. 2000: 179-181.
Erwähnung in Abschnitt 'D', 168.

	For 50 per cent or more of export earnings	For 20-49 per cent of export earnings	For 10-19 per cent of export earnings
Countries in Middle East			
Crude Petroleum	Bahrain, Iran, Islamic Rep., Irak, Kuwait, Libya, Oman, Quatar, Saudi Arabia, Yemen, Rep.	Syria, Arab Rep., United Arab Emirates	Egypt
Aluminium			Bahrain
Countries in Africa			
Crude Petroleum	Angola, Congo, Rep., Gabon, Nigeria	Cameroon, Equatorial Guinea	Algeria
Natural gas		Algeria	
Bauxite and alumina	Guinea		
Iron ore		Mauritania	
Rutile			Sierra Leone
Copper	Zambia		Congo, Dem. Rep.
Cobalt			Congo, Dem. Rep., Zambia
Gold		Ghana, South Africa	Mali, Zimbabwe
Diamonds	Botswana	Central African Rep., Namibia, Sierra Leone	Congo, Dem. Rep.
Uranium	Niger		
Timber (African hardwood)		Equatorial Guinea	Central African Rep. Gabon, Ghana, Swaziland
Cotton		Benin, Chad, Mali, Sudan	Burkina Faso
Tobacco	Malawi	Zimbabwe	
Arabica coffee	Burundi, Ethiopia	Rwanda	
Robusta coffee	Uganda		Cameroon
Cocoa	Sao Tome and Principe	Cote d' Ivoire, Ghana	Cameroon
Tea			Kenya, Rwanda
Vanilla		Comoros	
Sugar		Mauritius	Swaziland
Cashew nuts	Guinea Bissau		
Livestock		Mali	Niger, Sudan
Fish	Mauritania	Mozambique	Senegal, Namibia
Oilseeds			Sudan
Countries in the Western Hemisphere			
Crude petroleum	Venezuala	Equador, Trinidad and Tobago	Colombia, Mexico
Bauxite and alumina		Jamaica, Surinam	Guyana
Copper		Chile	Peru
Gold			Guyana
Cotton			Paraguay
Arabica coffee			Columbia, El Salvador, Guatemala, Honduras, Nicaragua
Sugar		Guyana, St. Kitts and Nevis	Belize
Bananas		St. Vincent, Honduras	St. Lucia, Costa Rica
Livestock			Nicaragua
Fish			Ecuador
Fishmeal			Peru
Rice			Guyana
Countries in Europe, Asia and the Pacific			
Crude Petroleum		Azerbaijan, Brunei Darussalem, Norway, Papua New Guinea, Russia	Indonesia, Kazakhstan, Vietnam
Natural Gas	Turkmenistan		
Aluminium		Tajikistan	
Copper		Mongolia	Kazakhstan, Papua New Guinea
Gold		Papua New Guinea	Uzbekistan
Timber (Asian hardwood)		Lao P.D.R, Solomon Islands	Cambodia, Indonesia, Myanmar, Papua New Guinea
Timber (softwood)			Latvia, New Zealand
Cotton		Pakistan, Uzbekistan	Azerbaijan, Turkmenistan, Tajikistan
Jute			Bangladesh
Livestock			New Zealand
Fish			Maldives, Solomon Islands
Copra and coconut oil	Kiribati		

Note: Trade data denominated in local currency was converted to U.S. dollars using the period-average exchange rate.

Tabelle 27: Exports form developing countries by main commodity group, 1980-1991. In: South Centre 1996: 94.
Erwähnt in Abschnitt 'D', 171, 181.

	Value		Indices for 1991				
	1980	1991	Value	Unit value	Volume	Real commodity prices (a)	Purchasing power (b)
	($ billion)		(1980 = 100)				
Food, drink and tobacco	64.9	86.1	133	82	162	59	96
Tropical beverages	17.4	11.4	66	50	131	37	48
Oilseeds, oil and fats	9.0	12.3	137	71	192	53	102
Other	38.5	62.4	162	96	169	71	120
Industrial raw materials	44.1	47.4	107	90	120	67	80
Agricultural	18.4	18.5	100	91	110	67	74
Minerals and metals	25.7	28.9	112	89	126	66	83
Total	109.0	133.5	122	85	145	63	91
Memo item: Commodity exports from developed market economy countries	241.5	356.7	148	92	161	68	109

(a) Unit value of commodity exports deflated by U.N. index of unit value of manufactures exported by developed market-economy countries. This latter index was 135 for 1991 (1980 = 100).
(b) Volume index multiplied by index of real commodity prices.

Tabelle 28: Percentage change in primary commodity world prices, 1980-1998. In: Kheralla et al. 2002: 5.
Erwähnt in Abschnitt 'D', 182.

	Period		
	1980-90	1990-98	1980-98
Cotton	-36	-24	-51
Cocoa	-65	27	-55
Coffee robusta	-74	48	-61
Palm oil	-64	123	-20

Tabelle 29: Price Indices of Selected African Commodity Exports, 1980-2002 (1980=100).
In: UNCTAD 2003: 17.
Erwähnt in Abschnitt 'D', 182.

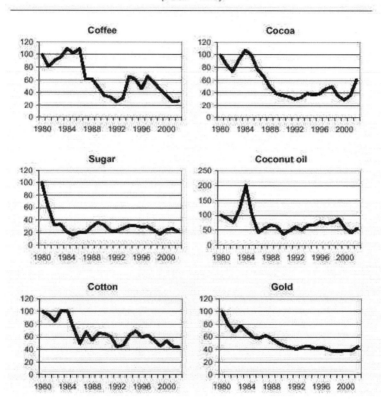

Tabelle 30: Mais-, Weizen- und Reisweltmarktpreise ($/t). Daten: HWWA. *Erwähnung in Abschnitt 'D', 182, 183.*

	Mais $/t	Weizen $/t	Reis $/t
Jan 80	108,40	161,96	365,0
Feb 80	107,01	161,20	379,0
Mrz 80	103,47	155,51	397,1
Apr 80	105,49	145,28	415,0
Mai 80	107,95	154,27	418,6
Jun 80	109,82	150,38	422,3
Jul 80	122,73	159,64	433,3
Aug 80	134,73	161,88	442,0
Sep 80	138,82	175,60	442,0
Okt 80	142,11	182,50	442,0
Nov 80	150,16	181,92	442,0
Dez 80	145,64	173,80	442,0
Jan 81	146,29	172,75	462,8
Feb 81	142,21	164,52	470,0
Mrz 81	139,50	161,10	470,0
Apr 81	143,30	163,14	470,0
Mai 81	136,98	160,27	470,0
Jun 81	134,19	155,64	504,8
Jul 81	133,80	163,66	510,0
Aug 81	122,46	154,36	516,7
Sep 81	112,15	158,06	516,7
Okt 81	114,47	164,75	535,0
Nov 81	109,03	162,06	494,5
Dez 81	102,23	157,39	487,0
Jan 82	107,39	153,17	428,0
Feb 82	105,60	150,64	378,6
Mrz 82	103,45	145,16	357,7
Apr 82	109,50	148,06	325,6
Mai 82	103,01	138,49	323,8
Jun 82	107,49	133,81	320,0
Jul 82	102,72	134,40	305,7
Aug 82	91,79	133,60	291,0
Sep 82	87,92	139,78	287,3
Okt 82	86,51	131,30	287,2
Nov 82	91,47	135,68	275,8
Dez 82	93,60	138,57	257,0
Jan 83	100,36	138,94	254,8
Feb 83	107,71	143,17	266,0
Mrz 83	114,19	142,98	262,2
Apr 83	123,00	144,90	269,5
Mai 83	121,56	135,27	276,3
Jun 83	122,54	131,60	282,0
Jul 83	128,23	132,63	280,1
Aug 83	138,99	141,89	280,0
Sep 83	139,95	150,44	261,3
Okt 83	137,14	139,29	261,3
Nov 83	137,26	136,78	298,8
Dez 83	131,73	136,18	289,7
Jan 84	130,02	135,72	285,2
Feb 84	127,78	132,83	273,0
Mrz 84	136,45	135,99	258,7
Apr 84	139,20	138,80	247,4
Mai 84	138,18	133,91	247,4
Jun 84	137,51	134,17	253,5
Jul 84	130,71	132,91	255,0
Aug 84	117,01	135,50	255,0
Sep 84	117,07	136,70	266,1
Okt 84	109,58	138,15	266,5
Nov 84	107,48	136,38	255,2
Dez 84	102,54	131,40	251,0
Jan 85	106,63	129,56	231,0
Feb 85	105,71	129,62	224,1
Mrz 85	107,52	126,77	228,2
Apr 85	111,51	127,75	230,0
Mai 85	109,20	118,00	220,1
Jun 85	108,45	117,72	222,0
Jul 85	103,33	113,67	222,0
Aug 85	90,51	108,25	223,4
Sep 85	88,82	112,72	210,0
Okt 85	87,97	115,00	210,0
Nov 85	93,86	120,26	210,0
Dez 85	97,29	123,84	210,0
Jan 86	97,10	118,45	210,0
Feb 86	94,01	116,22	217,5
Mrz 86	91,47	104,90	240,0
Apr 86	90,71	100,15	233,5
Mai 86	95,64	95,24	218,1
Jun 86	91,48	89,48	207,3
Jul 86	76,96	89,83	200,7
Aug 86	63,44	91,60	204,1
Sep 86	63,24	91,82	206,0
Okt 86	66,64	92,82	213,1
Nov 86	66,92	93,95	207,0
Dez 86	62,95	93,39	206,1
Jan 87	61,97	94,54	204,3
Feb 87	58,74	99,26	197,5
Mrz 87	62,44	98,95	200,8
Apr 87	66,20	99,23	206,2
Mai 87	73,47	105,52	210,8
Jun 87	74,12	97,11	213,0
Jul 87	65,18	94,99	213,0
Aug 87	61,93	98,04	212,2
Sep 87	67,03	105,54	243,1
Okt 87	72,04	108,23	285,4
Nov 87	72,26	105,49	253,2

Dez 87	73,26	112,36	307,4	Feb 92	104,12	160,11	293,8
Jan 88	77,21	116,04	275,5	Mrz 92	105,30	149,15	292,6
Feb 88	79,11	118,23	268,8	Apr 92	99,95	135,44	290,0
Mrz 88	79,71	112,09	272,3	Mai 92	102,48	132,70	290,2
Apr 88	80,35	114,36	307,4	Jun 92	100,34	132,02	291,8
Mai 88	82,16	116,52	301,1	Jul 92	93,01	122,18	291,7
Jun 88	113,73	139,34	302,6	Aug 92	86,35	113,05	294,0
Jul 88	122,97	139,66	297,5	Sep 92	90,13	121,53	295,0
Aug 88	113,90	140,21	301,0	Okt 92	82,17	124,73	292,7
Sep 88	112,47	147,95	306,7	Nov 92	83,20	130,92	287,6
Okt 88	113,63	152,58	305,0	Dez 92	84,59	130,58	278,2
Nov 88	105,97	151,68	305,0	Jan 93	85,69	132,44	275,0
Dez 88	105,85	153,33	305,0	Feb 93	83,58	128,31	276,0
Jan 89	109,39	159,34	300,4	Mrz 93	88,19	129,64	279,7
Feb 89	106,09	156,23	290,5	Apr 93	89,95	121,06	278,8
Mrz 89	108,50	160,13	278,8	Mai 93	92,36	119,00	266,0
Apr 89	105,67	155,05	275,5	Jun 93	85,85	105,51	248,2
Mai 89	107,47	158,62	282,6	Jul 93	94,21	113,48	228,8
Jun 89	102,54	152,11	296,3	Aug 93	93,44	113,88	228,4
Jul 89	98,53	150,28	315,0	Sep 93	94,10	117,12	230,0
Aug 89	90,40	147,83	329,3	Okt 93	97,87	120,99	230,0
Sep 89	91,90	146,64	362,1	Nov 93	107,59	131,87	237,4
Okt 89	94,15	147,35	367,0	Dez 93	109,70	141,41	280,0
Nov 89	93,63	150,33	350,0	Jan 94	118,90	138,57	352,5
Dez 89	92,76	151,55	350,0	Feb 94	114,52	133,04	376,7
Jan 90	94,40	146,71	316,3	Mrz 94	109,68	126,83	414,3
Feb 90	94,98	141,19	315,5	Apr 94	104,78	122,06	441,5
Mrz 90	98,89	137,28	315,0	Mai 94	103,80	121,77	418,6
Apr 90	107,28	134,51	315,0	Jun 94	105,40	123,64	402,1
Mai 90	111,98	131,65	315,0	Jul 94	94,04	123,15	369,3
Jun 90	112,05	120,81	302,0	Aug 94	86,77	130,89	334,6
Jul 90	107,89	110,68	292,6	Sep 94	90,13	142,10	315,0
Aug 90	98,65	101,83	277,8	Okt 94	85,01	150,30	312,8
Sep 90	92,73	99,30	271,1	Nov 94	84,79	143,31	304,6
Okt 90	90,40	99,99	273,7	Dez 94	87,28	147,58	300,0
Nov 90	88,92	96,35	271,3	Jan 95	91,49	139,78	295,9
Dez 90	89,51	96,52	277,3	Feb 95	91,88	137,73	290,2
Jan 91	93,47	95,20	276,5	Mrz 95	95,19	136,22	283,5
Feb 91	94,60	96,93	275,1	Apr 95	97,97	131,22	283,8
Mrz 91	97,77	103,47	275,0	Mai 95	101,27	144,73	284,2
Apr 91	100,54	105,48	275,0	Jun 95	107,46	155,88	285,0
Mai 91	96,14	106,59	275,0	Jul 95	112,65	175,91	304,0
Jun 91	94,20	105,02	275,0	Aug 95	111,34	167,95	331,7
Jul 91	93,95	101,59	275,0	Sep 95	119,24	175,36	343,6
Aug 91	98,30	110,30	275,0	Okt 95	127,26	186,75	348,3
Sep 91	97,91	118,38	305,5	Nov 95	129,08	185,94	375,0
Okt 91	98,71	130,79	315,0	Dez 95	136,62	189,64	383,8
Nov 91	95,85	133,87	313,0	Jan 96	142,62	184,22	380,6
Dez 91	96,99	143,81	305,0	Feb 96	147,62	197,23	375,0
Jan 92	101,56	152,81	302,5	Mrz 96	153,68	193,38	373,5

Apr 96	177,70	227,48	370,5	Jun 00	81,94	111,26	204,4
Mai 96	183,86	239,96	358,2	Jul 00	71,59	104,03	198,5
Jun 96	152,73	211,56	350,8	Aug 00	70,06	102,81	190,7
Jul 96	152,49	189,17	352,8	Sep 00	73,01	108,40	186,0
Aug 96	140,62	175,98	366,8	Okt 00	78,67	115,58	180,9
Sep 96	126,54	163,65	371,2	Nov 00	82,37	114,40	183,0
Okt 96	111,65	158,20	345,2	Dez 00	83,77	115,21	184,7
Nov 96	105,71	156,92	324,2	Jan 01	85,12	121,21	183,4
Dez 96	104,09	160,00	312,3	Feb 01	83,03	114,22	183,7
Jan 97	105,61	151,64	314,9	Mrz 01	83,21	114,88	182,2
Feb 97	110,35	154,10	323,3	Apr 01	80,84	115,89	170,6
Mrz 97	119,63	158,58	350,3	Mai 01	77,18	118,05	171,3
Apr 97	117,80	166,25	336,0	Jun 01	75,78	113,25	173,0
Mai 97	109,89	158,18	310,8	Jul 01	82,62	112,15	176,9
Jun 97	104,73	133,88	304,5	Aug 01	85,30	109,66	173,9
Jul 97	98,66	126,92	323,9	Sep 01	84,36	107,11	176,5
Aug 97	103,45	137,42	321,3	Okt 01	80,22	106,79	173,5
Sep 97	104,37	137,18	301,6	Nov 01	80,28	105,85	173,8
Okt 97	111,84	137,91	275,3	Dez 01	82,26	103,09	184,2
Nov 97	110,29	132,05	270,6	Jan 02	81,69	106,65	192,4
Dez 97	108,03	127,61	264,3	Feb 02	80,59	104,36	200,4
Jan 98	106,69	125,87	260,7	Mrz 02	80,11	103,59	197,6
Feb 98	106,39	126,57	269,7	Apr 02	78,80	104,55	194,0
Mrz 98	106,52	126,36	293,1	Mai 02	81,66	102,74	199,9
Apr 98	99,02	118,22	297,3	Jun 02	83,15	113,41	207,5
Mai 98	97,87	117,07	289,1	Jul 02	90,91	129,43	211,0
Jun 98	97,20	111,60	305,8	Aug 02	102,20	143,44	196,7
Jul 98	91,89	105,81	318,3	Sep 02	105,91	168,46	192,4
Aug 98	84,44	101,05	321,7	Okt 02	99,34	172,67	191,1
Sep 98	82,18	104,56	321,9	Nov 02	95,51	159,80	191,3
Okt 98	86,14	118,66	321,5	Dez 02	94,12	145,66	187,6
Nov 98	89,47	117,58	306,9	Jan 03	92,69	129,38	202,5
Dez 98	87,38	112,65	295,3	Feb 03	93,06	130,78	200,0
Jan 99	85,35	115,10	284,2	Mrz 03	91,85	124,55	199,2
Feb 99	84,50	107,38	307,2	Apr 03	93,87	117,86	198,0
Mrz 99	87,59	109,03	284,9	Mai 03	96,61	126,09	200,4
Apr 99	87,71	105,08	259,8	Jun 03	94,33	115,15	206,2
Mai 99	86,68	101,71	244,7	Jul 03	83,77	115,55	206,3
Jun 99	85,58	104,22	233,0	Aug 03	86,78	132,98	198,1
Jul 99	75,82	98,31	253,4	Sep 03	91,15	130,42	199,0
Aug 99	84,07	107,43	258,1	Okt 03	88,84	128,43	199,1
Sep 99	81,45	107,07	246,0	Nov 03	93,42	140,18	196,7
Okt 99	79,20	102,71	237,8	Dez 03	97,99	144,90	199,3
Nov 99	77,02	99,92	222,0	Jan 04	105,11	146,47	214,9
Dez 99	76,28	96,47	227,0	Feb 04	111,39	141,96	221,3
Jan 00	85,06	105,13	232,3	Mrz 04	120,18	144,55	234,2
Feb 00	86,46	106,20	223,5	Apr 04	124,10	147,66	243,0
Mrz 00	89,39	103,39	245,1	Mai 04	119,15	146,33	234,8
Apr 00	89,76	102,40	222,0	Jun 04	112,67	138,40	229,3
Mai 00	93,03	108,36	219,0	Jul 04	93,85	132,53	230,9

Aug 04	88,50	120,82	237,5
Sep 04	85,82	128,29	235,7
Okt 04	80,69	124,82	242,1
Nov 04	78,30	127,77	255,5
Dez 04	80,72	123,38	277,1
Jan 05	78,73	122,73	288,2
Feb 05	78,86	122,62	291,4
Mrz 05	85,63	129,37	292,9
Apr 05	81,84	120,23	297,3
Mai 05	83,88	119,41	299,2
Jun 05	87,33	120,65	289,9
Jul 05	94,24	125,31	282,7
Aug 05	84,70	126,01	285,8
Sep 05	83,48	131,20	287,1

Tabelle 31: Number of commodities exported and indices of export commodity concentration in SSA adjusters: 1980 and 1990. In: Brownbridge/Harrigan 1996: 418.
Erwähnung in Abschnitt 'D', 187.

Country	No. of commodities exported		Commodity concentr. index	
	1980	1990	1980	1990
Benin	30	29	0.415	0.482
Burkina Faso	43	23	0.476	0.481
Burundi	26	7	0.594	0.744
Cameroon	90	103	0.409	0.311
Central African Republic	15	25	0.415	0.588
Chad	15	17	0.794	0.688
Congo	29	34	0.890	0.797
Cote d'Ivoire	154	106	0.383	0.0345
Gabon	46	45	0.763	0.812
The Gambia	23	22	0.418	0.353
Ghana	55	54	0.729	0.450
Guinea	23	28	0.905	0.840
Guinea-Bissau	22	n.a.	0.331	n.a.
Kenya	143	183	0.383	0.239
Madagascar	53	70	0.501	0.309
Malawi	47	35	0.409	0.656
Mali	40	41	0.477	0.565
Mauritania	24	20	0.661	0.621
Mozambique	n.a.		n.a.	
Niger	39	44	0.821	0.767
Nigeria	147	102	0.948	0.959
Rwanda	13	16	0.668	0.552
Senegal	113	106	0.271	0.251
Sierra Leone	39	16	0.444	0.458
Tanzania	83	66	0.286	0.250
Togo	51	47	0.468	0.468
Uganda	22	13	0.950	0.868
Zambia	49	33	0.717	0.931
Zimbabwe	87	170	0.257	0.245

Notes: n.a. not available. The number of commodities exported refers to products at the three digit SITC level, the value of which was greater than $ 50.0000 in 1980 or $ 100.000 in 1990 or was more than 0.3 % of the country's total exports. The export concentration index is a Hirschmann index which takes values between 0 and 1. Higher values of the index denote a greater commodity concentration of exports: i.e., a single commodity or a few commodities account for a larger proportion of total exports. Data Source: UNCTAD.

Tabelle 32: Verarbeitung der Hauptmineralrohstoffe in Subäquatorial-Afrika (Mengenangaben in t). Quelle: US Bureau of Mines 1991. In: Barth/Kürsten 1996: 38. Erwähnung in Abschnitt 'D', 187.

	Namibia	Ruanda	Südafrika	Zaire	Sambia	Simbabwe	Region, gesamt	Welt, gesamt	Welt, gesamt (%)
Kobaltmetall				520	10139	5025	15684	26900	58
Kupfermetall:									
Rohkupfer	42163		180600	436200	459000	27500	1145463	8800000	13
Raffinadekupfer			13944	202800	422252	27500	791952	10800000	7
Roheisen			6700			550	7250	538500	1
Stahlblöcke und Gußstücke			8645			600	9245	776000	1
Ferrolegierungen:									
Ferrochrom			1000000			180000	1180000	320000	37
Ferrosilicochrom			21000			29000	50000	n.a.	n.a.
Ferromangan			300000			200	3020000	6500000	5
Ferrosilicomangan			320000				3200000	n.a.	n.a.
Ferrosilizium			87000				87000	3200000	3
andere Eisenlegierungen			1000				1000	n.a.	n.a.
Siliziummetall			39000				39000	636000	6
Raffinadeblei	44447		362000		6385		87032	5700000	2
Hüttenzinn	1187	168	1377	1943		855	5530	205000	3
Hüttenzink			844000	61086	20220		165706	7100000	2

Tabelle 33: Anteile afrikanischer Länder an der Welt-Bergwerksförderung mineralischer Rohstoffe 1994 (> 0,1 %). In: Barth/Kürsten 1996: 9. Erwähnung in Abschnitt 'D', 187.

Land	Platin	PT-Metalle	Vanadium	Rutil	Palladium	Chromit	Kobalt	Gold	Ilmenit	Mangan	Bauxit	Kupfer	Nickel	Blei	Eisen	Zink	Zinn	Diamanten	Phosphat
Ägypten															0,2				0,4
Algerien															0,2	0,1			0,6
Äthiopien																			
Botsuana								0,2											
Burkina Faso							1,2												
Cote d'Ivoire								0,1											
Gabun								0,1		6,9									
Ghana								2,0		1,1	0,4								
Guinea								0,1											
Madagaskar						0,9													
Mali								0,1											
Marokko							1,9			0,1		0,2		2,9		1,0			17,1
Mauretanien															1,4				
Namibia								0,1				0,3		0,5		0,5		1,5	
Nigeria								0,1											
Südafrika	80,3	68,2	48,5	18,3	44,4	37,5	1,0	26,6	22,5	13,7		2,0	3,4	3,6	3,9	1,1		12,1	2,5
Ruanda																			
Sambia							14,5					4,1							
Senegal																			1,5
Sierra Leone				27,1					0,9		0,6							3,0	

	C1	C2	C3	C4	C5	C6	C7	C8	C9	C10	C11	C12	C13	C14	C15	C16	C17	C18	C19
Simbabwe						5,4	0,3	0,9				0,1	1,6					0,2	0,1
Sudan						0,1		0,1											
Tansania								0,1											
Togo																			
Tunesien														0,1		0,1			
Zaire							13,2					0,4				0,1	0,4	18,1	
Zentr. Afri. Rep.																		0,6	
Afrika, gesamt	80,3	68,2	48,5	45,4	44,4	43,9	32,1	30,9	23,4	21,9	16,7	7,3	7,2	7,1	5,7	2,9	1,0	50,8	28,5

Tabelle 34: Comparative international wage rates (United States = 100). In: Krugman/Obstfeld 1997: 79.
Erwähnung in Abschnitt 'D', 194.

Country	Hourly wage rate in 1992
United States	100
Germany	160
Japan	100
Spain	83
Greece	44
Hong Kong	24
Taiwan	32
Korea	30
Mexico	15

Tabelle 35: Mark-up & Costs in US Manufacturing Industries. In: Leith/Malley 2003: 4. *Erwähnung in Abschnitt 'D', 195, 208.*

Industry	Production worker wages costs / variable costs	Production worker wage / gross output	Material costs / gross output	Markup (1)
Agg. manufacturing	0.169	0.115	0.682	0.319
Food and kindred products	0.085	0.063	0.673	0.265
Tobacco products	0.090	0.071	0.717	0.234
Textile mill products	0.205	0.115	0.598	0.246
Apparel & other finished products made from fabrics	0.261	0.185	0.519	0.304
Lumber & wood products (exc. furniture)	0.221	0.168	0.590	0.251
Furniture & fixtures	0.279	0.187	0.482	0.333
Paper & allied products	0.178	0.121	0.557	0.317
Printing, publishing & allied industries	0.302	0.154	0.350	0.500
Chemicals & allied products	0.116	0.064	0.485	0.450
Petroleum refining & related industries	0.029	0.025	0.831	0.141
Rubber & plastics products	0.235	0.152	0.493	0.355
Leather & leather products	0.259	0.180	0.512	0.306
Stone, clay, glass & concrete products	0.266	0.163	0.450	0.384
Primary metal industries	0.172	0.128	0.617	0.247
Fabricated metal products, exc. machinery & transportation equipment	0.248	0.165	0.499	0.334
Industrial & commercial machinery & computer equipment	0.242	0.145	0.462	0.388
Transportation equipment	0.160	0.114	0.595	0.287
Miscellaneous manufacturing industries	0.247	0.154	0.465	0.386

(1) Value added - production worker payroll / value added + cost of materials

Tabelle 36: Import Penetration by industry in the G7 group of countries. Imports as a percentage of total domestic demand. Not all data shown. OECD 1996: 27.
Erwähnung in Abschnitt 'D', 197.

	USA		Japan		France		Germany		UK		Italy	
	1980	1991	1980	1991	1980	1991	1980	1991	1980	1991	1980	1991
Total manuf.	8.9	14.6	5.3	5.9	21.3	30.4	19.6	27.1	23.4	32.8	20.0	21.9
High wage	10.4	18.6	7.3	7.3	24.3	38.0	22.3	32.3	28.0	43.4	35.2	50.1
Medium wage	8.9	14.0	3.6	4.8	22.4	29.5	17.0	22.9	21.8	31.0	18.9	19.1
Low wage	7.4	11.6	5.7	6.3	17.7	24.7	19.8	26.9	21.8	26.9	12.9	15.7
High tech	10.3	22.0	6.0	6.1	25.4	40.4	24.9	39.0	34.0	50.9	23.4	36.0
Medium tech	13.4	19.6	4.5	5.2	30.5	39.8	21.3	28.1	31.9	41.1	31.2	36.1
Low tech	6.3	8.7	5.4	6.4	15.8	21.5	17.2	21.9	16.6	21.8	14.1	14.3

Tabelle 37: FDI inward stock, by host region and economy, 1980, 1985, 1990, 1995, 2002 (Millions of Dollars). (a) In: World Investment Report 2004: 376-380.
Erwähnung in Abschnitt 'D', 200, Abschnitt 'F', 446, 457, Abschnitt 'G', 500, 542, 552, 555.

Countries	1980	1985	1990	1995	2002	Share 2002 (%) (b)
USA	83 046	184 615	394 911	535 553	1 505 171	42,7 %
Germany	36 630	36 926	119 618	192 898	531 738	15,0 %
Hongkong	177 755	183 219	201 652	227 532	366 278	10,0 %
Singapore	6 203	13 016	30 468	65 644	135 890	3,0 %
China	1 077	6063	20 694	134 869	447 966	12,7 %
Mexico	8 0105	18 797	22 424	41 130	155 121	4,4 %
Brazil	17 480	25 664	37 143	41 696	100 847	2,8 %
Indien	452	747	1 657	5 641	25 408	0,7 %
Korea	1 327	2 160	5 186	9 451	43 713	0,1 %
Taiwan	2 405	2 930	9 735	15 736	33 478	0,09 %
Malaysia	5 169	7 388	10 318	28 731	56 505	1,5 %
Thailand	981	1 999	8 242	17 684	35 108	0,09 %
Indonesia	10 274	24 971	38 883	50 601	57 806	1,6 %
South Africa	16 519	9 024	9 221	15 016	29 611	0,08 %

(a) See World Investment Report for comments on data.
(b) Divided by the total of the investment sums presented here.

Tabelle 38: Shares of FFEs (foreign-funded enterprises) and DOEs (domestically owned enterprises) in manufacturing by industries (end 1995). In: Chunlai 1997. Calculation based on total assets, China Statistical Yearbook.
Erwähnung in Abschnitt 'D', 200.

Industries	Shares of FFEs (%)	Shares of DOEs (%)
Clothing & other fibre products	47,91	52,09
Leather & fur products	46,45	53,55
Electronics & telecom equipment	44,49	55,51
Cultural, education & sports goods	42,93	57,07
Plastic products	37,11	62,89
Furniture	35,46	64,54
Others	33,99	66,01
Food manufacturing	32,19	67,81
Timber processing	31,42	68,48
Metal products	29,35	70,65
Beverage manufacturing	25,31	74,69
Rubber products	25,08	74,92
Instruments & meters	23,87	76,13
Electrical machinery & equipment	22,44	77,56
Printing	21,74	78,26
Food processing	20,50	79,50
Transport equipment	20,09	79,91
Paper & paper products	19,89	80,11
Medical & pharmaceutical products	19,49	80,51
Textile	18,81	81,19
Non-metal mineral products	16,40	83,60
Chemical fibre	15,06	84,94
General machinery	13,34	86,66
Chemical materials & products	12,58	87,42
Non-ferrous metal smelting & pressing	11,30	88,70
Special machinery	8,21	91,79
Ferrous metal smelting & pressing	4,59	95,41
Petroleum refining & coking	1,64	98,36
Tobacco processing	0,95	99,05
Total	19,09	80,91

Tabelle 39: Chinas Exporte und Importe gegliedert nach dem SITC-System in zweistelliger Aufgliederung, für 2000. In tausend Dollar. Quelle: Bfai.
Erwähnung in Abschnitt 'D', 201.

SITC Code	Warenbeschreibung	Exporte	Importe	Export-anstieg in %	Import-anstieg in %
	Total	249,211,619	225,069,566	27.8	35,8
	Subtotal 0-4	<u>25,457,590</u>	<u>46,739,878</u>	27,7	74,1
0	**Food And Live Animals**	12,281,531	4,758,296	17,4	31,5
00	Live Animals Other Than Fish, Crustaceans, Molluscs And Aquatic Invertebrates	384,808	52,284	-0,1	-20,3
01	Meat And Meat Preparations	1,253,403	651,026	17,7	27,2
02	Dairy Products And Birds' Eggs	86,024	216,460	14,2	34,6
03	Fish (Not Marine Mammals), Crustaceans, Molluscs And Aquatic Invertebrates	3,651,730	1,210,283	23,5	37,4
04	Cereals And Cereal Preparations	1,816,887	613,261	42,4	13,1
05	Vegetables And Fruit	3,299,052	524,410	6,3	33,3
06	Sugars, Sugar Preparations And Honey	316,951	178,103	22,1	-3,1
07	Coffee, Tea, Cocoa, Spices And Manufactures Thereof	554,910	94,846	0,1	29,4
08	Feeding Stuff For Animals (Not Including Unmilled Cereals)	303,048	907,808	26,7	46,6
09	Miscellaneous Edible Products And Preparations	614,720	309,816	13,5	64,6
1	**Beverages And Tobacco**	744,835	364,258	-3,4	75,2
11	Beverages	442,940	159,812	1,8	32,8
12	Tobacco And Tobacco Manufactures	301,895	204,445	-10,2	133,5
2	**Crude Materials, Inedible, Except Fuels**	4,463,660	20,004,066	13,8	57,0
21	Hides, Skins And Furskins, Raw	11,488	638,081	-10,6	56,4
22	Oil Seeds And Oleaginous Fruits	416,675	2,943,593	11,9	92,2
23	Crude Rubber (Including Synthetic And Reclaimed)	53,850	1,320,529	42,4	46,9
24	Cork And Wood	456,160	2,658,585	22,0	37,1
25	Pulp And Waste Paper	10,587	2,677,913	207,6	61,6
26	Textile Fibers (Other Than Wool Tops And Other Combed Wool) And Their Wastes (Not Manufactured Into Yarn Or Fabric)	1,085,564	2,846,376	10,8	46,8
27	Crude Fertilizers (Imports Only), Except Those Of Division 56, And Crude Minerals (Excluding Coal, Petroleum And Precious Stones)	1,103,397	728,088	17,4	57,5
28	Metalliferous Ores And Metal Scrap	113,668	5,828,786	-10,0	61,3
29	Crude Animal And Vegetable Materials, N.E.S.	1,212,271	362,115	12,9	25,4
3	**Mineral Fuels, Lubricants And Related Materials**	7,851,392	20,636,868	68,5	131,6
32	Coal, Coke And Briquettes	2,378,858	70,094	45,2	14,5
33	Petroleum, Petroleum Products And Related	4,661,996	18,929,583	108,0	148,1

	Materials				
34	Gas, Natural And Manufactured	221,465	1,540,924	-3,1	28,6
35	Electric Current	589,072	96,267	6,9	354,4
4	**Animal And Vegetable Oils, Fats And Waxes**	116,171	976,390	-11,7	-28,6
41	Animal Oils And Fats	8,734	143,841	321,1	13,0
42	Fixed Vegetable Fats And Oils, Crude, Refined Or Fractionated	95,740	754,865	-13,9	-36,1
43	Animal Or Vegetable Fats And Oils Processed; Waxes And Inedible Mixtures Or Preparations Of Animal Or Vegetable Fats Or Oils, N.E.S.	11,697	77,685	-36,1	33,4
	Subtotal 5-9	223,754,029	178,356,687	27,9	28,4
5	**Chemicals And Related Products**	12,098,421	30,212,548	16,6	25,7
51	Organic Chemicals	3,113,428	8,301,086	19,9	53,2
52	Inorganic Chemicals	2,619,405	891,336	15,3	35,1
53	Dyeing, Tanning And Coloring Materials	1,146,722	1,714,889	18,1	27,2
54	Medicinal And Pharmaceutical Products	1,788,365	952,531	6,5	16,1
55	Essential Oils And Resinoids And Perfume Materials; Toilet, Polishing And Cleansing Preparations	462,887	401,310	20,9	20,2
56	Fertilizers (Exports Include Group 272; Imports Exclude Group 272)	313,448	1,725,085	42,5	-23,1
57	Plastics In Primary Forms	586,689	11,450,223	43,5	26,1
58	Plastics In Nonprimary Forms	523,931	1,886,699	20,5	16,6
59	Chemical Materials And Products, N.E.S.	1,543,546	2,889,390	9,6	15,1
6	**Manufactured Goods Classified Chiefly By Material**	42,549,926	41,806,841	27,9	21,8
61	Leather, Leather Manufactures, N.E.S., And Dressed Furskins	837,203	2,493,972	48,7	21,0
62	Rubber Manufactures, N.E.S.	1,438,379	577,201	32,8	2,2
63	Cork And Wood Manufactures Other Than Furniture	1,655,516	1,074,340	23,7	7,8
64	Paper, Paperboard, And Articles Of Paper Pulp, Paper Or Paper Board	1,354,852	3,745,603	52,9	-0,9
65	Textile Yarn, Fabrics, Made-Up Articles, N.E.S., And Related Products	16,135,031	12,832,319	23,7	15,8
66	Nonmetallic Mineral Manufactures, N.E.S.	4,700,656	2,401,316	18,5	40,0
67	Iron And Steel	4,390,878	9,689,600	65,1	29,3
68	Nonferrous Metals	3,362,932	6,745,916	22,5	43,1
69	Manufactures Of Metals, N.E.S.	8,674,479	2,246,575	24,4	17,7
7	**Machinery And Transport Equipment**	82,601,844	91,934,116	40,4	32,4
71	Power Generating Machinery And Equipment	2,996,089	5,232,452	31,8	14,5
72	Machinery Specialized For Particular Industries	1,946,206	10,704,518	41,8	27,8
73	Metalworking Machinery	719,572	3,000,163	60,2	15,1

74	General Industrial Machinery And Equipment, N.E.S., And Machine Parts, N.E.S.	5,851,361	7,749,737	39,6	10,8
75	Office Machines And Automatic Data Processing Machines	18,638,072	10,858,173	39,4	40,4
76	Telecommunications And Sound Recording And Reproducing Apparatus And Equipment	19,508,304	12,416,470	49,4	32,6
77	Electrical Machinery, Apparatus And Appliances, N.E.S., And Electrical Parts Thereof (Including Nonelectrical Counterparts Of Household Type, N.E.S.)	24,023,389	35,632,797	34,5	49,3
78	Road Vehicles (Including Air-Cushion Vehicles)	6,566,545	3,583,102	66,5	54,9
79	Transport Equipment, N.E.S.	2,352,304	2,756,703	1,6	-24,1
8	**Miscellaneous Manufactured Articles**	86,282,515	12,750,485	19,0	31,4
81	Prefabricated Buildings; Sanitary, Plumbing, Heating And Lighting Fixtures And Fittings, N.E.S	2,187,587	128,239	31,0	19,4
82	Furniture And Parts Thereof; Bedding, Mattresses, Mattress Supports, Cushions And Similar Stuffed Furnishings	4,582,060	170,496	32,5	60,9
83	Travel Goods, Handbags And Similar Containers	3,881,816	32,852	13,6	28,7
84	Articles Of Apparel And Clothing Accessories	36,072,461	1,191,978	19,9	8,2
85	Footwear	9,852,584	320,472	13,5	4,7
87	Professional, Scientific And Controlling Instruments And Apparatus, N.E.S.	2,604,791	4,433,912	39,1	48,8
88	Photographic Apparatus, Equipment And Supplies And Optical Goods, N.E.S.; Watches And Clocks	4,620,042	2,903,755	18,8	30,4
89	Miscellaneous Manufactured Articles, N.E.S.	22,481,173	3,568,782	15,6	25,3
9	**Commodities And Transactions Not Classified Elsewhere In The SITC**	221,323	1,652,698	2346,5	22,2

Tabelle 40: Growing chemicals consumption. EUR bn. In: Perlitz 2005: 2.
Erwähnung in Abschnitt 'D', 203.

	China	Germany	EU-25	World
1994	50	90	343	1,147
1995	58	93	363	1,190
1996	67	89	366	1,219
1997	81	93	389	1,282
1998	81	95	394	1,344
1999	93	100	409	1,453
2000	129	111	467	1,788
2001	139	110	479	1,802
2002	149	109	480	1,786
2003	157	109	486	1,697
2004	162	110	514	1,766

Source: VCI.

Tabelle 41: Manufactured exports by technological sub-categories. In: Lall 2000: 345. *Erwähnt in Abschnitt 'D', 217, 250, 251, 252, 285, Abschnitt 'G', 586.*

Technological classification	Growth rates 1985-1998 (% per annum)			Developing world shares (%) (a)		Value of developing country manu-factured exports (current US$ billion)	
	World	Developed	Developing	1985	1998	1985	1998
All manufactures	9.7	8.8	12.5	16.4	23.3	210.2	997.0
Ressource based (RB)	7.0	7.0	6.0	**26.3**	**23.7**	80.0	175.1
RB 1: Agro based: prepared foods, vegetable oils	8.8	8.4	9.1	19.9	20.6	24.3	77.4
RB 2: Other RB: petroleum products, ore concentrates, cement, glass	5.5	5.7	4.2	31.8	26.8	55.6	97.7
Low technology (LT)	9.7	8.5	11.7	**26.7**	**34.5**	63.8	277.4
LT 1: Textile/fashion cluster	9.6	8.0	11.1	41.1	<u>49.1</u>	42.2	170.0
LT 2: Other low technology: furniture, plastic products	9.8	8.8	12.8	16.9	24.1	21.6	107.4
Medium Technology (MT)	9.3	8.5	14.3	**8.3**	**15.3**	43.4	254.3
MT1: Automotive products and parts	9.3	8.4	20.2	3.0	10.5	4.4	51.5
MT2: Process industries: chemicals, basic metals, plastics, synthetic fibres	8.9	7.8	13.4	11.9	<u>20.1</u>	14.0	<u>75.5</u>
MT3: Engineering products: engines, motors, industrial machinery, ships, watches	9.5	9.0	13.2	10.5	<u>16.3</u>	24.9	<u>127.2</u>
High-technology (HT)	13.1	11.3	21.4	**10.7**	**27.0**	23.0	290.1
HT1: Electronic, electrical: TV, office machinery, power generating equipment	14.1	11.7	22.1	14.0	<u>34.2</u>	19.4	<u>265.1</u>
HT2: Other high tech: pharma, aerospace, optical and measuring instruments	11.0	10.7	16.1	4.8	8.6	3.6	25.0

(a) It follows that total world trade has the value of US$ 4278,9 bill.

The technological categories are exemplified by examples, the products listed are not exhaustive. See for more details of the techological categories Lall 2000: 341.

Tabelle 42: Regional shares of developing countries' manufactured exports (% of developing world total). In: Lall 2000: 347.
Erwähnt in Abschnitt 'D', 217, 250, 251, 252, 253, 285, 306, Abschnitt 'G', 586.

	Year	East Asia	South Asia	MENA	LAC1 (incl. Mexico)	LAC2 (excl. Mexico)	Mexico	SSA 1 (incl. South Africa)	SSA 2 (excl. South Africa)
All manufactures	1985	56.9	4.5	12.9	23.1	16.9	6.2	-	2.6
	1998	**69.0**	**3.8**	**6.0**	**19.3**	**8.9**	**10.4**	**1.8**	**0.8**
Ressource based	1985	34.6	3.8	23.8	32.9	30.7	2.2	-	4.9
	1998	**47.5**	**4.7**	**15.0**	**28.0**	**24.0**	**4.0**	**4.8**	**1.4**
RB1: Agro based	1985	55.1	2.2	4.5	32.0	30.4	1.6	-	6.2
	1998	55.1	1.7	4.9	33.1	28.3	4.6	5.3	2.4
RB2: Other RB	1985	25.6	4.5	32.3	33.3	30.8	2.5	-	4.3
	1998	41.4	7.2	23.1	23.1	20.6	2.5	4.4	0.6
Low technolgy	1985	71.1	8.3	7.3	11.9	10.2	1.7	-	1.8
	1998	**70.2**	**8.5**	**7.2**	**12.6**	**5.4**	**7.2**	**1.5**	**0.2**
LT1: Textile	1985	69.9	11.6	8.1	9.5	8.5	1.0	-	0.9
	1998	67.3	12.1	9.1	10.4	4.9	5.5	1.1	0.8
LT2: Other	1985	75.2	1.7	5.7	16.6	13.5	3.1	-	0.8
	1998	74.9	2.9	4.2	16.0	6.3	9.7	2.0	0.3
Medium Technolgy	1985	63.4	2.0	7.1	25.8	17.5	8.3	-	1.8
	1998	**63.8**	**1.8**	**4.4**	**28.1**	**10.2**	**17.9**	**1.9**	**0.2**
MT1: Automobile	1985	40.6	2.7	5.9	50.3	32.9	17.4	-	0.4
	1998	39.8	1.4	2.9	54.2	16.9	37.3	1.7	0.1
MT2: Process	1985	53.4	2.3	13.8	28.2	25.2	3.0	-	2.3
	1998	65.6	3.3	8.4	19.9	13.0	6.9	2.8	0.5
MT3: Engineering	1985	73.0	1.7	3.5	20.1	10.4	9.7	-	1.7
	1998	72.5	1.1	2.6	22.4	5.8	16.6	1.3	0.1
High Technolgy	1985	81.0	1.1	1.8	14.8	6.6	8.2	-	1.3
	1998	**85.5**	**0.6**	**0.7**	**12.9**	**2.1**	**10.8**	**0.4**	**0.0**
HT1: Electronic	1985	84.7	0.5	0.7	14.0	5.1	8.9	-	0.1
	1998	87.2	0.3	0.6	11.8	1.2	10.6	0.2	0.1
HT2: Other high tech	1985 (a)	60.3	4.5	8.2	19.2	15.2	4.0	-	7.8
	1998	66.9	4.5	1.9	25.0	12.2	12.8	0.0	0.3

'East Asia' includes all countries in Asia east of Myanmar, including Myanmar and Vietnam (but not Laos or Cambodia for lack of reported data) and China, and excludes Japan and Central Asian transition countries. 'South Asia' comprises India, Pakistan, Bangladesh, Sri Lanka, Maldives, Nepal and Bhutan. 'MENA' (Middle East and North Africa) includes Afghanistan and Turkey as well as all Arab countries (Sudan is counted under SSA). 'SSA' (Sub-Saharan Africa) includes South Africa (SSA1) unless specified (SSA2). 'LAC' (Latin America and the Caribbean) includes Mexico (LAC1) and excludes it (LAC2) when specified.

(a) Total value of developing countries HT product in 1985 was only US$ 3.6 billion until it increased to US$ 25.0 billion in 1998. Lall 2000: 345.

Tabelle 43: Change in the Share of Intra-Industry Trade between 1970 and 1980 (percentage units) In: Culem/Lundberg 1986: 117.
Erwähnt in Abschnitt 'D', 219.

Country	Trade with							
	World	South Europe	Asian NICs	Latin America	other LDCs	all LDCs	all DCs	CPEs
Australia	5,4	-0,7	-8,3	2,8	3,8	0,1	4,2	-10,6
Belgium	4,1	15,3	10,7	-1,1	17,1	16,3	5,2	-17,7
Canada	-3,4	19,6	7,9	13,0	-8,4	11,6	-5,4	-6,5
France	3,6	29,4	9,2	1,5	11,0	19,0	6,4	4,0
Germany	6,6	14,5	7,5	4,9	14,1	15,1	7,4	-4,2
Italy	6,6	26,8	1,1	9,3	7,5	20,5	0,3	8,7
Japan	-7,3	7,3	10,3	2,9	-2,5	1,9	-4,6	-21,5
Netherlands	5,5	7,8	11,3	-9,1	-1,2	7,0	5,7	-18,8
Sweden	4,1	9,3	9,0	2,7	-1,2	4,8	5,8	-0,6
U.K.	18,3	21,1	-0,8	7,3	12,7	12,8	12,3	-3,4
USA	1,4	8,1	2,4	6,3	1,1	4,3	5,8	6,9

Definitions: South Europe: Greece, Portugal, Spain, Cyprus, Gibraltar, Israel, Malta, Turkey, Yugoslavia. Asien NICs: Hongkong, Macao, Singapore, Taiwan, South Korea. CPEs: European centrally planned economies.

Tabelle 44: Shares of Intra-Industry Trade in Total Trade and in Trade with Certain Groups of Countries in 1980. In: Culem/Lundberg 1986: 116.
Erwähnt in Abschnitt 'D', 219.

Country	Trade with							
	World	South Europe	Asian NICs	Latin America	other LDCs	all LDCs	all DCs	CPEs
Australia	35,8	16,3	26,9	19,4	22,9	29,2	22,7	5,5
Belgium	79,7	54,1	29,8	11,4	33,4	40,1	77,6	29,0
Canada	58,5	30,6	15,7	25,0	11,0	33,0	56,7	18,1
France	80,4	64,4	29,7	16,3	31,4	44,2	79,2	40,0
Germany	65,4	42,3	24,4	13,0	28,9	34,6	74,1	31,6
Italy	65,4	55,1	36,0	19,8	28,1	44,3	59,8	40,2
Japan	28,8	14,8	27,2	10,6	10,1	17,6	33,6	11,8
Netherlands	74,2	43,0	24,8	17,7	35,5	45,5	70,3	22,6
Sweden	66,5	29,2	15,1	7,6	8,8	17,4	72,5	30,7
U.K.	79,1	50,7	27,4	24,0	38,6	44,2	77,5	30,9
USA	60,7	33,8	26,5	29,6	25,8	35,0	66,7	37,9

Definitions: South Europe: Greece, Portugal, Spain, Cyprus, Gibraltar, Israel, Malta, Turkey, Yugoslavia. Asien NICs: Hongkong, Macao, Singapore, Taiwan, South Korea. CPEs: European centrally planned economies.

Tabelle 45: Indexes of Intraindustry Trade for U.S. Industries, 1993. In: Krugman/Obstfeld 1997: 140.
Erwähnt in Abschnitt 'D', 220.

Inorganic chemicals	0.99
Power-generating equipment	0.97
Electrical machinery	0.96
Organic chemicals	0.91
Medical and pharmaceuticals	0.86
Office machinery	0.81
Telecommunications equipment	0.69
Road vehicles	0.65
Iron and steel	0.43
Clothing and apparel	0.27
Footwear	0.20

Tabelle 46: Ranking of industries by percentage of Intra-Industry Trade.
In: Grubel/Lloyd 1975: 37.
Erwähnt in Abschnitt 'D', 220.

Rank	SITC Class	Description	Percentage
1	5	Chemicals	66
2	7	Machinery and transport equipment	59
3	9	Commodities and transactions, n.e.s	55
4	8	Miscellaneous manufactured articles	52
5	6	Manufactured goods classified by material	49
6	1	Beverages and tobacco	40
7	4	Animal and vegetable oil and fats	37
8	0	Food and live animals	30
9	2	Crude materials, inedible, except fuels	30
10	3	Mineral fuels, lubricants and related materials	30

Tabelle 47: World merchandise exports, production and gross domestic product, 1950-03 (Annual percentage change). WTO 2004a. Erwähnt in Abschnitt 'D', 233, 242.

	Value				Volume							
	Exports				Exports				Production			World GDP
	Total	Agriculture products	Mining products	Manufactures	Total	Agriculture products	Mining products	Manu-factures	Total	Agriculture products	Mining products	Manu-facturing	
1951	31,1	28,6	33,3	39,1	9,5	4,8	4,3	18,8	8,8	1,7	10,5	11,5	7,9
1952	-1,3	-13,9	16,7	6,3	4,3	0,0	16,7	0,0	2,7	3,4	2,4	3,4	2,4
1953	2,5	0,0	0,0	2,9	8,3	2,3	7,1	10,5	7,9	3,3	2,3	10,0	7,1
1954	4,9	3,2	7,1	5,7	7,7	0,0	6,7	9,5	0,0	1,6	0,0	0,0	2,2
1955	9,4	3,1	13,3	13,5	10,7	11,1	9,4	8,7	9,8	3,1	11,4	15,2	6,5
1956	8,6	3,0	11,8	14,3	6,5	2,0	5,7	8,0	4,4	4,5	6,1	5,3	4,1
1957	7,9	8,8	5,3	8,3	9,1	9,8	8,1	11,1	2,1	0,0	1,9	2,5	3,9
1958	-3,7	-5,4	-5,0	-1,9	-2,8	1,8	-5,0	0,0	0,0	7,2	-1,9	-2,4	0,0
1959	8,6	8,6	5,3	9,8	11,4	12,3	7,9	10,0	8,3	2,7	3,8	12,5	5,7
1960	13,2	5,3	5,0	14,3	12,8	6,3	22,0	12,1	7,7	2,6	9,3	8,9	5,4
1961	3,9	2,5	9,5	6,3	4,5	5,9	4,0	5,4	3,6	1,3	6,8	6,1	5,1
1962	6,0	0,0	4,3	7,4	6,5	0,0	3,8	7,7	8,6	3,8	6,3	9,6	6,5
1963	9,2	9,8	8,3	11,0	12,2	2,8	5,6	11,9	4,8	2,4	4,5	5,3	4,5
1964	11,6	6,7	11,5	14,8	10,9	5,4	8,8	14,9	9,1	4,8	8,6	10,0	7,2
1965	8,1	4,2	6,9	10,8	6,6	5,1	3,2	7,4	5,6	0,0	3,9	9,1	4,1
1966	9,1	4,0	9,7	10,7	7,7	3,7	6,2	10,3	6,6	3,4	5,1	8,3	6,5
1967	5,4	0,0	5,9	7,9	5,7	2,4	10,3	4,7	4,9	3,3	2,4	5,1	3,7
1968	10,7	3,8	13,9	14,6	10,8	5,7	12,0	17,9	5,9	3,2	7,1	7,3	5,9
1969	14,7	7,4	9,8	17,0	12,2	5,4	6,0	16,5	5,6	0,0	2,2	8,0	6,7
1970	14,3	10,3	13,3	15,2	8,7	3,1	12,4	8,7	5,3	3,1	7,5	5,3	5,1

Year												
1971	12,2	7,8	11,8	14,2	7,0	2,0	1,0	9,0	5,0	3,0	4,0	5,0	4,4
1972	18,3	20,3	14,0	19,4	8,4	6,9	6,9	10,1	4,8	0,0	2,9	6,7	5,6
1973	38,6	45,8	47,7	34,4	12,1	0,9	10,2	14,2	8,2	4,9	6,5	9,8	6,9
1974	45,6	22,3	124,0	31,9	5,4	-4,5	-1,7	8,8	2,5	1,9	1,8	3,3	2,1
1975	4,7	1,4	-3,7	9,2	-7,3	1,0	-12,0	-4,0	-1,6	3,6	-6,0	-3,9	1,4
1976	13,3	10,7	16,4	13,0	11,8	7,5	6,8	12,6	6,7	0,9	8,3	8,2	5,1
1977	13,5	13,3	10,4	14,5	4,2	3,5	2,7	5,0	3,9	2,6	3,4	4,5	4,2
1978	15,8	13,3	3,8	21,6	4,7	6,8	5,3	5,9	4,5	3,4	0,8	5,1	4,6
1979	25,5	23,0	45,3	19,9	5,2	4,8	5,9	5,0	3,6	0,8	8,9	4,1	4,0
1980	21,4	13,8	41,8	15,9	3,0	6,8	-6,3	5,9	1,1	0,8	-2,2	1,2	2,9
1981	-1,2	-1,9	-3,2	-0,7	-0,6	5,0	-9,9	4,0	-0,4	3,6	-7,9	0,2	2,0
1982	-6,4	-7,5	-10,6	-3,6	-2,2	-2,0	-5,8	-2,1	-1,4	3,2	-6,9	-1,4	0,8
1983	-2,0	-1,4	-8,0	0,5	2,7	0,2	-0,9	5,1	2,0	0,1	-0,9	3,1	2,9
1984	5,9	5,3	-0,9	8,1	8,5	2,8	4,8	10,8	6,3	5,3	3,8	7,2	4,6
1985	-0,3	-5,7	-3,2	3,8	2,6	-1,2	-1,2	4,8	2,5	2,4	-1,1	3,4	3,5
1986	9,4	11,1	-23,8	20,3	4,0	-1,7	9,1	4,1	2,8	1,8	3,0	3,1	3,4
1987	17,5	14,9	11,0	19,7	5,5	5,6	1,7	6,3	3,3	1,0	1,3	4,4	3,7
1988	13,7	13,1	0,9	16,1	8,5	2,7	5,6	9,5	4,9	1,7	5,3	5,7	4,5
1989	7,8	4,3	15,5	6,9	6,4	3,1	4,4	7,8	3,6	3,4	4,5	3,4	3,8
1990	12,9	4,7	15,3	14,7	3,8	1,0	3,2	6,1	1,3	2,5	1,0	1,0	2,5
1991	1,5	0,8	-6,2	3,3	3,7	3,3	3,4	3,6	-0,4	0,4	-0,5	-0,6	0,8
1992	6,4	7,1	-0,9	8,0	4,5	6,0	4,4	4,7	0,2	2,3	0,8	-0,5	1,1
1993	-0,2	-4,1	-3,5	0,0	4,2	1,0	3,7	4,1	0,0	0,6	2,0	-0,6	0,9
1994	13,6	15,8	5,1	15,6	9,2	8,7	6,8	11,1	2,7	2,9	1,6	2,9	2,2
1995	19,4	17,3	15,5	20,0	7,4	4,4	4,1	9,0	4,1	2,1	1,9	5,1	2,3
1996	4,3	2,9	13,6	3,5	4,9	4,4	3,4	5,3	3,6	4,3	2,7	3,5	3,2

1997	3,4	-1,3	2,7	4,6	10,1	5,7	7,4	11,0	4,9	2,3	3,3	5,7	3,5
1998	-1,3	-4,7	-20,5	2,3	4,7	1,7	2,9	4,8	2,2	1,7	1,1	2,4	2,2
1999	3,9	-3,7	15,6	3,3	4,6	1,0	-0,5	5,1	3,2	3,3	-1,3	3,6	2,9
2000	12,8	0,7	47,0	10,2	10,5	3,7	4,0	13,0	5,1	2,0	3,7	5,9	4,0
2001	-3,8	0,3	-8,0	-3,8	-0,4	2,6	0,9	-1,2	-0,7	1,3	-0,3	-1,2	1,2
2002	4,5	5,6	-0,5	5,2	3,1	3,3	0,4	3,9	0,8	1,5	-0,4	0,8	1,7
2003	15,8	15,4	21,4	14,5	4,5	3,0	2,7	4,8	2,8	2,0	3,7	2,9	2,3
Durchschnitt	9,8	6,6	10,8	11,2	6,2	3,6	4,3	7,6	3,8	2,4	2,8	4,6	3,8

(a) Includes unspecified products.
Note: World merchandise production differs from world GDP in that it excludes services and construction. For sources and methods, see WTO Technical Notes.

Tabelle 48: FDI inward stock, by host region and economy, 1980, 1985, 1990, 1995, 2002 (Millions of Dollars). (a) In: World Investment Report 2004: 376-380.
Erwähnt in Abschnitt 'D', 233, 235, 312.

Countries	1980	1985	1990	1995	2002	Share 2002 (%) (b)
USA	83 046	184 615	394 911	535 553	1 505 171	42,7 %
Germany	36 630	36 926	119 618	192 898	531 738	15,0 %
Hongkong	177 755	183 219	201 652	227 532	366 278	10,0 %
Singapore	6 203	13 016	30 468	65 644	135 890	3,0 %
China	1 077	6063	20 694	134 869	447 966	12,7 %
Mexico	8 0105	18 797	22 424	41 130	155 121	4,4 %
Brazil	17 480	25 664	37 143	41 696	100 847	2,8 %
Indien	452	747	1 657	5 641	25 408	0,7 %
Korea	1 327	2 160	5 186	9 451	43 713	0,1 %
Taiwan	2 405	2 930	9 735	15 736	33 478	0,09 %
Malaysia	5 169	7 388	10 318	28 731	56 505	1,5 %
Thailand	981	1 999	8 242	17 684	35 108	0,09 %
Indonesia	10 274	24 971	38 883	50 601	57 806	1,6 %
South Africa	16 519	9 024	9 221	15 016	29 611	0,08 %

(a) See World Investment Report for comments on data.
(b) Divided by the total of the investment sums presented here.

Tabelle 49: Inward and Outward FDI Stock as a Percentage of Gross Domestic Product, by Region and Economy, 1975, 1985, 1995. Daten für 1975 aus World Investment Report 1992: 326-329; Daten für 1985 und 1995 in World Investment Report 1997: 339-352.
Erwähnt in Abschnitt 'D', 233, Abschnitt 'F', 457,Abschnitt 'G', 555, Abschnitt 'J', 1336.

Country	1975	1985	1995
World			
- inward	-	6,4	10,1
- outward	-	8,1	9,9
Developed coutries			
- inward	-	6,0	9,1
- outward	-	7,5	11,5
Developing countries			
- inward	-	8,1	15,4
- outward	-	1,0	4,5
Developed Countries			
United States			
- inward	1,7	4,6	7,7
- outward	-	6,2	9,8
Japan			
- inward	0,3	0,4	0,3
- outward		3,3	6,0
Great Britan	-	14,0	28,5
Germany	-	6,0	6,9
France	1,5	6,4	9,6
Italy	5,0	4,5	5,7
Spain	2,4	5,4	17,6
Portugal	3,5	6,5	7,4
Developing Europe			
Turkey	-	0,7	3,9
Developing Countries			
Africa			
insgesamt	-	6,4	13,3
South Africa	-	19,1	7,8
Egypt	-	12,0	23,3
Morocco	2,5	3,4	9,2
Tunisia	-	22,0	22,8
Nigeria	9,7	5,5	22,7
Kenya	-	7,1	7,7
Ghana	-	4,3	15,8
Gambia	-	9,4	26,8
Zaire	-	11,8	3,6
Latin America and the Carribean			
insgesamt	-	8,9	14,3
Brasil	5,9	11,3	17,8
Argentina	-	7,4	8,7
Mexico	-	10,2	25,6
Asia			
insgesamt	-	7,3	14,2
China	-	3,6	18,2
Taiwan	-	4,7	7,3
Südkorea	-	2,3	2,3
Malaysia	-	27,2	52,1
Thailand	3,5	5,1	10,3
Indonesia	7,5	28,6	25,2
Philippines	2,4	4,2	9,2
India	1,3	0,5	1,9
Bangladesh	-	0,7	0,6
LDCs			
LDCs insgesamt (a)	-	3,4	5,2
LDCs Africa	-	4,7	9,8
LDCs Latin America Caribbean	-	5,6	5,7
LDCs Asia	-	0,8	2,3

(a) Siehe die LDC-Liste im Annex.

Tabelle 50: Share of (gross) output in selected host countries accounted for by foreign affiliates. Aus: Dunning 1993: 38-39.
Erwähnt in Abschnitt 'D', 233, Abschnitt 'G', 500, 555, Abschnitt 'J', 1336.

Part I Industrialized Countries

	Australia 1983	Belgium 1975	Canada 1986 (1)	France 1982	Germany 1982 (2)	Italy 1985 (2)	Japan 1986	Netherlands 1987 (2)	Portugal 1978	Spain 1977 (2)	UK 1988	US 1987 (2)
Primary												
Agriculture	na	3,1	nsa	na	0,5	nsa	nsa	na	1,2	17,0	na	1,0
Mining and quarrying	33,6	nsa	40,5	na	10,1	2,2	nsa	30,0	31,0	48,0	na	8,4
Petroleum	na	77,7	nsa	51,4	25,0	1,7	nsa	na			na	na
Secondary	21,6	44,0	49,0	25,3 (2)	15,8	na	2,2	14,0	19,6	46,6	20,7	7,3
Food and drink products	25,6	22,5	29,4	nsa	17,7	12,8	0,5	18,0	15,8	52,0	14,6	8,8
Chemical and allied products	65,7	55,6	75,8	40,0	21,8	62,4	3,4	nsa	31,0	77,0	33,0	23,5
Metals	30,7	16,1	17,5	15,0	30,4	5,6	0,2	8,0	22,6	28,0	8,5	6,7
Mechanical engineering	32,9	57,7	50,2	nsa	16,3	12,6	2,2	nsa	14,1	45,0	22,7	5,8
Electrical and electronic goods	43,3	87,3	60,6	34,0	18,8	44,4	3,0	23,0	67,3	82,0	21,2	9,3
Motor vehicles	61,9	54,7	87,2	14,9	18,9	9,2	0,4	nsa	51,3	99,0	69,2	6,5
Textiles, clothing and leather goods	22,3	11,3	50,0 (5)	7,2	4,8	1,9	0,1	9,0	9,3	na	4,2	3,2
Paper products	15,6	30,4	25,9	24,1	7,6	4,0	0,3	19,0	25,4	na	4,2	3,2
Rubber products	41,1	59,8	88,2	24,8	24,4	16,6	nsa	nsa	46,2	63,0	22,2	6,6
Coal and petroleum products	59,0	nsa	66,7	nsa	61,0	nsa	29,0	nsa	26,0	12,0	nsa	39,5
Tertiary	na	na	na	na	na	na	na	4,0	na	na	na	na
Construction			5,7		1,8		nsa	2,0	9,8	22,0		0,8
Transport and communication			na		6,3		nsa	1,0	4,4	39,0		2,6
Trade and distribution			24,6 (6)		3,5		0,6	3,0	12,5	33,0		3,6
Real estate			na		nsa		nsa	nsa	nsa	nsa		2,3
Finance and insurance			na		6,3		nsa	8,0	8,1	93,0		4,4
Other services			na		2,6		0,3	13,0	2,1	nsa		1,2
Total	na	na	33,0	na	na	11,8	na	na	na	46,6	na	na

Part II Developing Countries

	Brazil 1987	Hong Kong 1987	Mexico (2) 1985	Morocco 1987	Singapore 1975 (1)	Taiwan 1981	Thailand 1986
Primary							74,8
Agriculture	22,8	na	3,8	na	neg	na	6,5
Mining and quarrying	2,7	na	0,1	na		na	93,6
Petroleum	34,0	na	6,5	na		na	21,5
Secondary	34,2	17,3	20,2	14,0 (7)	62,9 (8)	16,7 (2)	43,2
Food and drink products	17,7	28,9	6,5	9,9	67,3	6,8	22,0
Chemical and allied products	38,9 (4)	50,8	44,7	10,1	97,2	28,8	72,0
Metals	34,1	12,9	10,6	3,5	96,7	4,4	60,8
Mechanical engineering	46,4	8,2	32,1	20,8		24,5	80,3
Electrical and electronic goods	50,9	48,2	45,6	27,7	88,7	48,6	89,4
Motor vehicles	80,6	nsa	96,4	25,5		nsa	59,8
Textiles, clothing and leather goods	11,7	6,3	nsa	14,1	98,0 (4)	nsa	nsa
Paper products	19,4	12,4	nsa	22,4	45,4	6,5	nsa
Rubber products	44,7	8,8	nsa	12,1	70,5	7,9	30,5
Coal and petroleum products	nsa	nsa	nsa	22,0	100,0	nsa	77,7
Tertiary	8,3	na	na	na	18,1 (8)	na	30,3
Construction	5,1		nsa				30,4
Transport and communication	2,0		nsa		10,1		52,4
Trade and distribution	11,2		2,3		25,5		37,6
Real estate	9,2		nsa		17,9 (8)		4,8
Finance and insurance	8,5		nsa		14,5		10,8
Other services	9,6		3,2				37,5
Total	17,1		10,9		na		39,3

na not available
nsa not seperately available

(1) Share of assets
(2) Share of employment
(3) Food only
(4) Chemicals only
(5) Textiles only
(6) Wholesale trade only
(7) Share of assets in 1982
(8) Excluding construction
(9) Including business services

Tabelle 51: Motivations for FDI by region 1989 (multiple answers).
In: Farell 1997: 37.
Erwähnt in Abschnitt 'D', 233.

	North America	Europe	Oceania	Asia	Latin America
Access to local market	80.4	79.8	63.9	61.2	62.1
Export to Japan	10.0	3.7	14.8	18.2	6.2
Access to other markets	12.5	36.8	25.3	25.3	13.0
Collection of information	26.2	19.9	13.1	6.7	5.6
'Trade friction'	16.4	16.3	1.6	1.8	0.6
Official incentives	9.4	20.2	23.0	32.8	37.9
Dividends reinvested	9.2	4.3	14.8	9.8	11.9
Supply of labour	14.6	20.9	16.4	64.3	48.0
Supply of raw material	8.9	1.8	23.0	6.5	14.1

Tabelle 52: Motivations for FDI by region 1997 (multiple answers). In: Farell 1997: 40.
Erwähnt in Abschnitt 'D', 233, 302.

	NIEs	China	ASEAN	Other Asia	US/Canada	EU
Maintain market share	73.5	63.5	65.7	46.5	76.8	71.8
Develop new market	27.9	54.8	37.1	62.0	22.2	33.8
Export to Japan	19.1	31.0	25.0	7.0	9.1	5.6
Export to third countries	35.3	31.0	45.0	15.5	8.1	21.1
Spread production overseas	29.4	27.8	35.7	21.1	31.3	23.9
Inexpensive labour	11.8	33.3	30.0	31.0	2.0	1.4
Supply parts	14.7	9.5	20.7	14.1	19.2	21.1
Reduce foreign exchange risk	11.8	6.3	16.4	7.0	20.2	16.9

Tabelle 53: The 1995 Value and Share of OECD Imports of Parts and Components Identified in the SITC Rev. 2 System. (a) In: Yeats 1998: 5-6.
Erwähnt in Abschnitt 'D', 237.

SITC Rev. 2 - Description	Trade balance (%) (b)	1995 Value of Imports ($ million)	Share of total (%)
711.9 Parts of steam boilers and auxiliary plants	66.5	464.2	0.13
713.19 Parts of aircraft internal combustion engines	21.4	281.5	0.08
713.9 Parts of aircraft internal combustion engines nes	27.2	13,142.2	3.59
714.9 Parts of engines and motors nes	14.8	12,343.5	3.37
716.9 Parts of rotating electric motors	39.3	2,315.1	0.63
718.89 Parts of water turbines and hydraulic motors	69.4	126.1	0.03
721.19 Parts of cultivating equipment	-16.3	563.8	0.15
721.29 Parts of harvesting machinery	-10.3	1,054.2	0.29
721.39 Parts of dairy machinery	7.1	459.0	0.13
721.98 Parts of wine making machinery	50.0	14.8	0.00
721.99 Parts of other agricultural machinery nes	26.1	310.6	0.08
723.9 Parts of construction machinery	75.2	1,440.2	0.39
724.49 Parts of spinning and extruding machinery	45.8	921.2	0.25
724.69 Parts of looms and knitting machinery	29.0	1,245	0.34
724.29 Parts of spinning and extruding machinery	24.3	576.4	0.16
724.69 Parts of looms and knitting machinery	34.2	1,917.6	0.52
724.79 Parts of textile machinery nes	-4.0	182.1	0.05
725.9 Parts of paper making machinery	20.8	1,710.2	0.47
726.89 Parts of bookbinding machinery	37.2	117.7	0.03
726.9 Parts of printing and typesetting machinery	-300.0	32.2	0.01
727.19 Parts of grain milling machinery	22.5	695.7	0.19
727.29 Parts of food processing machinery	48.2	995.2	0.27
728.19 Parts of machine tools for special industries	38.1	6,078	1.66
728.39 Parts of mineral working industry	26.2	3,084.8	0.84
728.48 Parts of machiney for special industries nes	39.6	391.8	0.11
736.9 Parts of machine tools for metal working	19.8	1,425.4	0.39
737.19 Parts of foundry equipment	13.5	3,423.0	0.94
741.49 Parts of refrigerating equipment	23.9	4,851.9	1.33
742.9 Parts of pumps for liquids	53.3	70.3	0.02
743.9 Parts of centrifuges and filters	22.6	9,025.7	2.47
744.19 Parts of fork lift tractors	-5.3	516.2	0.14
744.9 Parts of lifting and loading machines	49.9	1,694.4	0.46
745.19 Parts of power hand tools			
749.99 Parts of non electric machinery nes			

759 Parts of office and adding machinery	-12.7	68,964.4	18.85
764 Parts of telecommunications equipment	19.0	64,874.2	17.73
711.29 Parts of electric power machinery	47.1	1,388.1	0.38
772 Parts of switchgear	23.0	37,822.1	10.34
775.79 Parts of domestic electrical equipment	1.2	641.0	0.18
778.29 Parts of electric lamps and bulbs	30.9	399.6	0.11
778.89 Parts of electric machinery nes	24.4	3,624.8	0.99
784 Parts of motor vehicles and accessories	16.7	91,611.0	25.04
785.39 Parts of carriages and cycles	2.3	3,625.7	0.99
786.89 Parts of trailers and nonmotor vehicles	-4.8	1,867.3	0.51
791.99 Parts of railroad equipment and vehicles	16.2	1,860.1	0.51
792.9 Parts of aircraft and helicopters	27.1	17,656.3	4.83
All above items	17.2	365,806.0	100.0

(a) The table is as far as possible corrected using comments of the author.

(b) Trade balance: Export of the item less imports divided by exports and multiplied by 100.

Tabelle 54: North-South distribution of vertical specialization (VS). Modified. In: Hummels et al. 2001: 93.
Erwähnt in Abschnitt 'D', 238.

Country	Partner VS as % of total VS Origin-destination			
	N-N	N-S	S-N	S-S
1972				
Australia	47.4	26.3	17.3	9.0
Canada	87.5	6.6	5.3	0.6
Denmark	64.6	15.3	17.3	2.8
France	50.5	21.6	20.0	7.9
Germany	59.1	18.2	17.2	5.5
Italy	50.1	19.0	22.8	8.1
Japan	29.2	28.5	20.9	21.3
Netherlands	67.0	14.3	15.6	3.1
United Kingdom	48.5	24.5	18.2	8.9
United States	48.8	25.1	17.2	8.8
1990				
Australia	43.1	27.5	17.0	12.4
Canada	86.0	5.5	7.9	0.6
Denmark	72.4	12.6	12.9	2.1
France	62.1	17.3	16.2	4.4
Germany	61.4	15.8	17.9	4.9
Italy	56.3	16.9	20.5	6.2
Japan	29.8	24.9	23.2	22.2
Netherlands	69.5	9.7	18.5	2.3
United Kingdom	66.1	17.2	13.3	3.4
United States	40.7	22.6	22.6	14.2

Tabelle 55: Merchandise Exports as Per Cent of GDP in Sample Countries (exports and GDP at 1990 prices) Aus: Maddison 1992: 38.
Erwähnt in Abschnitt 'D', 242, Abschnitt 'F', 446, Abschnitt 'G', 565, 589.

	1820	1870	1913	1929	1950	1973	1992
France	1,3	4,9	8,2	8,6	7,7	15,4	22,9
Germany	n.a.	9,5	15,6	12,8	6,2	23,8	32,6
Netherlands	n.a.	17,5	17,8	17,2	12,5	41,7	55,3
UK	3,1	12,0	17,7	13,3	11,4	14,0	21,4
Total Western Europe	n.a	10,0	16,3	13,3	9,4	20,9	29,7
Spain	1,1	3,8	8,1	5,0	1,6	5,0	13,4
USSR/Russia	n.a.	n.a.	2,9	1,6	1,3	3,8	5,1
Australia	n.a.	7,4	12,8	11,2	9,1	11,2	16,9
Canada	n.a.	12,0	12,2	15,8	13,0	19,9	27,2
USA	2,0	2,5	3,7	3,6	3,0	5,0	8,2
Argentina	n.a.	9,4	6,8	6,1	2,4	2,1	4,3
Brazil	n.a.	11,8	9,5	7,1	4,0	2,6	4,7
Mexico	n.a.	3,7	10,8	14,8	3,5	2,2	6,4
Total Latin America	n.a.	9,0	9,5	9,7	6,2	4,6	6,2
China	n.a.	0,7	1,4	1,7	1,9	1,1	2,3
India	n.a.	2,5	4,7	3,7	2,6	2,0	1,7
Indonesia	n.a.	0,9	2,2	3,6	3,3	5,0	7,4
Japan	n.a.	0,2	2,4	3,5	2,3	7,9	12,4
Korea	0,0	0,0	1,0	4,5	1,0	8,2	17,8
Taiwan	-	-	2,5	5,2	2,5	10,2	34,4
Thailand	n.a.	2,1	6,7	6,6	7,0	4,5	11,4
Total Asia	n.a.	1,3	8,7	2,8	2,3	4,4	7,2
World	1,0	5,0		9,0	7,0	11,2	13,5

Tabelle 56: Import Penetration by industry in the G7 group of countries. Imports as a percentage of total domestic demand. Not all data shown. OECD 1996: 27.
Erwähnt in Abschnitt 'D', 242.

	USA		Japan		France		Germany		UK		Italy	
	1980	1991	1980	1991	1980	1991	1980	1991	1980	1991	1980	1991
Total manuf.	8.9	14.6	5.3	5.9	21.3	30.4	19.6	27.1	23.4	32.8	20.0	21.9
High wage	10.4	18.6	7.3	7.3	24.3	38.0	22.3	32.3	28.0	43.4	35.2	50.1
Medium wage	8.9	14.0	3.6	4.8	22.4	29.5	17.0	22.9	21.8	31.0	18.9	19.1
Low wage	7.4	11.6	5.7	6.3	17.7	24.7	19.8	26.9	21.8	26.9	12.9	15.7
High tech	10.3	22.0	6.0	6.1	25.4	40.4	24.9	39.0	34.0	50.9	23.4	36.0
Medium tech	13.4	19.6	4.5	5.2	30.5	39.8	21.3	28.1	31.9	41.1	31.2	36.1
Low tech	6.3	8.7	5.4	6.4	15.8	21.5	17.2	21.9	16.6	21.8	14.1	14.3

Tabelle 57: World merchandise exports by region, 2003. In: WTO 2004a: 37.
Erwähnt in Abschnitt 'D', 244.

World merchandise exports by region, 2003
(Billion dollars and percentage)

	Value	Share			Annual percentage change			
	2003	1990	1995	2000	1995-00	2001	2002	2003
World	7294	100,0	100,0	100,0	5	-4	5	16
North America	997	15,4	15,5	16,9	6	-6	-4	5
United States	724	11,6	11,7	12,5	6	-6	-5	4
Latin America	378	4,3	4,6	5,8	10	-3	0	9
Mexico	165	1,2	1,6	2,7	16	-5	1	3
Western Europe	3145	48,3	44,8	40,0	2	0	6	18
European Union (15)	2901	44,4	41,5	37,0	2	0	6	18
C./E. Europe/Baltic States/CIS	401	3,1	3,9	4,3	7	5	10	28
Central and Eastern Europe	192	1,4	1,6	1,9	8	12	15	30
Russian Federation	134	...	1,6	1,7	5	-2	4	25
Africa	173	3,1	2,2	2,3	6	-6	2	23
South Africa	36	0,7	0,6	0,5	1	-2	2	23
Middle East	299	4,1	3,0	4,3	12	-8	2	19
Asia	1901	21,8	26,0	26,4	5	-9	8	17
Japan	472	8,5	8,8	7,6	2	-16	3	13
China	438	1,8	3,0	4,0	11	7	22	34
Six East Asian traders	688	7,9	10,3	10,4	5	-12	6	14
Memorandum item:								
NAFTA (3)	1162	16,6	17,1	19,5	7	-6	-4	5
MERCOSUR (4)	106	1,4	1,4	1,4	4	4	1	19
ASEAN (10)	451	4,2	6,4	6,8	6	-10	5	11

Tabelle 58: Merchandise exports of Western Europe by product, 2003. In: WTO 2004a: 60. *Erwähnt in Abschnitt 'D', 244.*

(Billion dollars and percentage)	Value	Share in exports of Western Europe		Share in world exports		Annual percentage change			
	2003	1995	2003	1995	2003	1995-00	2001	2002	2003
Total merchandise exports	3145	100,0	100,0	44,8	43,1	2	0	6	18
Agricultural products	301	11,3	9,6	43,1	44,6	-2	0	9	19
Food	255	9,4	8,1	46,8	46,8	-2	2	9	19
Raw materials	46	1,9	1,5	30,8	35,5	-1	-8	9	18
Mining products	222	6,0	7,1	24,8	23,1	7	-7	2	20
Ores and other minerals	21	0,8	0,7	28,7	26,3	-1	-5	8	22
Fuels	152	3,4	4,8	20,1	20,1	12	-7	3	22
Non-ferrous metals	49	1,9	1,6	39,1	38,8	2	-6	-2	13
Manufactures	2528	79,3	80,4	48,0	46,5	3	1	7	16
Iron and steel	83	3,5	2,6	50,8	45,8	-3	-4	7	24
Chemicals	484	12,9	15,4	59,7	61,0	3	6	15	19
Other semi-manufactures	268	9,7	8,5	55,1	50,7	0	-2	7	15
Machinery and transport equipment	1256	38,1	39,9	44,2	43,4	4	0	3	15
Automotive products	380	10,6	12,1	51,9	52,5	3	2	12	21
Office and telecom equipment	252	7,5	8,0	27,7	27,0	10	-7	-4	3
Other machinery and transport equipment	624	20,1	19,8	51,5	50,4	2	3	3	17
Textiles	67	3,0	2,1	44,5	39,3	-3	-2	3	12
Clothing	72	2,5	2,3	36,0	32,1	0	2	9	17
Other consumer goods	298	9,5	9,5	49,6	46,2	2	2	7	16

Tabelle 59: Merchandise trade of the European Union (15) by region and economy, 2003. In: WTO 2004a: Erwähnt in Abschnitt 'D', 245.

Exports Destination (Billion dollars and percentage)	Value	Share		Annual percentage change	
	2003	1995	2003	2002	2003
Region					
World	2900,7	####	####	6	18
Western Europe	1966,7	69,7	67,8	6	18
North America	272,3	7,1	9,4	6	9
Asia	227,2	9,3	7,8	6	19
C./E. Europe/Baltic States/CIS	199,9	4,3	6,9	13	27
Africa	75,6	2,8	2,6	5	21
Middle East	73,9	2,4	2,5	7	21
Latin America	53,7	2,2	1,9	-6	5
Economies					
European Union (15)	1795,4	64,0	61,9	6	18
United States	247,1	6,4	8,5	7	9
Switzerland	77,1	3,2	2,7	0	16
China	44,9	0,9	1,5	20	40
Japan	44,4	2,0	1,5	1	12
Above 5	2209,0	77,4	76,2	6	17
Poland	42,8	1,0	1,5	11	23
Russian Federation	36,9	1,0	1,3	16	30
Czech Republic	33,6	0,7	1,2	12	25
Turkey	31,2	0,8	1,1	27	38

Imports Origin	Value	Share		Annual percentage change	
	2003	1995	2003	2002	2003
Region					
World	2919,6	####	####	4	19
Western Europe	1956,7	69,3	67,0	6	18
Asia	350,0	10,9	12,0	4	24
C./E. Europe/Baltic States/CIS	199,3	4,2	6,8	12	29
North America	187,8	7,6	6,4	-6	4
Africa	86,9	3,0	3,0	-2	22
Latin America	58,5	2,2	2,0	5	18
Middle East	44,1	1,6	1,5	-5	18
Economies					
European Union (15)	1800,6	65,2	61,7	6	18
United States	169,5	6,8	5,8	-5	3
China	107,8	1,8	3,7	14	39
Japan	75,2	3,6	2,6	-5	17
Switzerland	64,4	2,7	2,2	2	15
Above 5	2217,5	83,0	76,0	5	17
Russian Federation	48,6	1,3	1,7	8	30
Norway	46,0	1,6	1,6	4	22
Poland	35,3	0,8	1,2	12	33
Czech Republic	33,6	0,6	1,1	16	29

Hungary	29,3	0,5	1,0	11	25
Norway	28,7	1,1	1,0	7	16
Canada	23,5	0,6	0,8	8	12
Hong Kong, China	20,1	1,0	0,7	-2	8
Australia	19,3	0,7	0,7	13	24
Korea, Republic of	18,0	0,8	0,6	17	12
United Arab Emirates	17,5	0,4	0,6	9	33
India	15,8	0,6	0,5	11	30
Mexico	15,8	0,3	0,5	6	12
Singapore	15,3	0,7	0,5	3	15
Saudi Arabia	14,9	0,5	0,5	13	13
South Africa	14,8	0,5	0,5	3	31
Romania	14,3	0,2	0,5	15	33
Brazil	13,5	0,7	0,5	-11	-6
Israel	12,6	0,6	0,4	-7	7
Taipei, Chinese	12,0	0,6	0,4	-4	11
Slovak Republic	11,3	0,2	0,4	16	38
Iran, Islamic Rep. of	10,8	0,2	0,4	28	45
Slovenia	10,0	0,3	0,3	8	24
Morocco	9,0	0,3	0,3	9	25
Malaysia	8,9	0,5	0,3	-6	15
Above 30	2688,7	92,4	92,7	-	-
Memorandum item:					
EU new member States (10)	144,7	3,2	5,0	12	25

Hungary	29,4	0,5	1,0	7	23
Turkey	27,0	0,6	0,9	15	30
Korea, Republic of	26,3	0,7	0,9	9	25
Taipei, Chinese	22,9	0,8	0,8	-6	15
Brazil	20,2	0,7	0,7	0	24
Canada	17,2	0,8	0,6	-7	15
South Africa	16,4	0,5	0,6	0	17
Malaysia	15,8	0,6	0,5	10	16
Singapore	15,3	0,6	0,5	9	24
India	15,1	0,5	0,5	6	23
Saudi Arabia	14,6	0,6	0,5	-1	25
Slovak Republic	13,9	0,2	0,5	26	51
Algeria	12,8	0,3	0,4	0	20
Romania	12,7	0,2	0,4	17	29
Thailand	12,4	0,4	0,4	-1	17
Libyan Arab Jamahiriya	12,4	0,4	0,4	-13	38
Indonesia	11,0	0,4	0,4	0	13
Hong Kong, China	10,5	0,5	0,4	1	16
Australia	9,9	0,3	0,3	0	19
Israel	8,3	0,3	0,3	-7	5
Slovenia	8,1	0,3	0,3	10	26
Above 30	2713,2	97,6	92,9	-	-
Memorandum item:					
EU new member States (10)	131,7	2,7	4,5	12	30

Tabelle 60: Merchandise imports of the United States, the European Union (15) and Japan from China by major product, 2003. Modified. In: WTO 2004a: 89.
Erwähnt in Abschnitt 'D', 245.

(Billion dollars and percentage)	Value	Share in economy's total merchandise imports		Share in economy's total imports by product group		Annual percentage change			
	2003	1995	2003	1995	2003	1995-00	2001	2002	2003
United States Memo item: GDP 2003 10.9 Trillion (a); Exports US$ 723 Mrd.; Imports US$ 1303 Mrd. (b)									
Total merchandise imports	163,2	100,0	100,0	6,3	12,5	17	2	22	22
Agricultural products	2,8	1,8	1,7	1,7	3,7	13	7	27	32
Food	2,3	1,4	1,4	1,8	3,7	12	11	30	33
Mining products	1,1	1,8	0,7	1,1	0,6	10	-28	-6	12
Manufactures	157,5	95,6	96,5	7,6	15,9	17	2	22	22
Chemicals	3,3	1,9	2,0	2,2	3,2	16	13	17	26
Other semi-manufactures	13,6	6,1	8,3	5,5	14,9	24	8	23	20
Machinery and transport equipment	63,5	25,8	38,9	3,5	11,9	24	0	32	32
Office and telecom equipment	42,7	15,7	26,2	5,4	23,7	24	-1	40	37
Electrical machinery and apparatus	11,5	6,2	7,0	9,0	20,9	24	1	12	17
Textiles	3,6	2,5	2,2	11,6	19,8	10	2	35	35
Clothing	12,0	12,7	7,4	14,9	16,9	8	4	9	19
Other consumer goods	61,0	46,0	37,4	25,5	38,7	15	2	17	14
Toys and games	17,8	15,0	10,9	52,3	76,9	14	-3	16	11
Footwear	11,1	12,7	6,8	48,4	67,9	10	6	5	4
Travel goods	3,7	3,5	2,3	47,4	69,7	7	-2	32	20
Furniture	10,2	2,1	6,3	11,2	38,2	39	11	37	28
European Union 15 Memo item: GDP 2003 US$ 8.2 Trillion (a); Imports 2003: ECU 988 Mrd.; Exports ECU 976Mrd. (c)									
Total merchandise imports	107,8	100,0	100,0	1,8	3,7	13	5	14	39
Agricultural products	2,7	5,5	2,5	0,7	0,9	4	4	-11	27
Food	1,9	3,4	1,8	0,6	0,7	4	12	-11	33
Mining products	1,7	3,1	1,6	0,5	0,5	3	16	-12	42
Manufactures	103,2	91,3	95,7	2,2	4,7	14	5	16	40
Chemicals	3,9	5,7	3,7	0,9	1,1	4	9	11	36
Other semi-manufactures	8,0	7,3	7,4	1,5	3,6	15	6	13	31
Machinery and transport equipment	47,3	24,2	43,8	1,2	4,3	23	8	20	53
Office and telecom equipment	30,2	13,8	28,0	2,5	10,0	23	13	25	60
Electrical machinery and apparatus	9,9	6,6	9,1	2,8	8,4	24	-7	17	36

Textiles	2,8	3,9	2,6	2,5	5,3	7	0	15	31
Clothing	12,4	16,3	11,5	7,9	12,2	8	4	15	26
Other consumer goods	28,5	32,9	26,4	6,4	10,4	11	0	12	30
Toys and games	8,3	10,1	7,7	26,0	39,8	11	-2	15	27
Footwear	2,6	3,2	2,4	6,7	11,0	9	6	9	33
Travel goods	3,0	5,2	2,8	40,4	44,3	8	-2	2	17
Furniture	2,5	1,2	2,3	2,0	7,7	24	5	33	56
Japan Memo item GDP US$ 4.3 Trillion (a); Exports US$ 471 Mrd.; Imports US$ 382 Mrd. (d)									
Total merchandise imports	75,4	100,0	100,0	10,7	19,7	9	5	7	22
Agricultural products	7,1	16,0	9,5	7,7	12,2	4	-1	-1	4
Food	6,2	13,4	8,2	8,9	13,1	4	1	-1	4
Mining products	3,8	8,8	5,0	4,2	3,8	0	-10	-2	33
Manufactures	63,9	74,8	84,8	15,1	29,3	11	7	9	24
Chemicals	2,2	3,5	2,9	5,3	7,5	5	6	3	27
Other semi-manufactures	4,3	4,3	5,7	9,5	25,8	12	11	13	23
Machinery and transport equipment	25,7	12,9	34,0	6,1	24,3	23	16	26	35
Office and telecom equipment	15,3	6,0	20,2	5,8	28,0	24	27	35	39
Electrical machinery and apparatus	6,2	3,9	8,3	15,6	39,9	24	1	15	29
Textiles	2,4	5,2	3,2	31,3	48,3	2	5	1	13
Clothing	15,6	29,5	20,7	56,6	80,0	7	1	-7	13
Other consumer goods	13,1	16,1	17,3	18,7	33,6	11	7	7	18
Toys and games	2,4	2,6	3,2	26,4	67,6	14	7	8	14
Footwear	2,1	3,9	2,8	47,3	68,2	7	4	-2	6
Travel goods	1,4	2,7	1,9	32,9	45,2	5	4	-2	10
Furniture	1,8	1,8	2,3	20,8	42,0	11	23	11	20

(a) Source: World Bank Country Datasheets. (b) WTO 2004a: 48. (c) Eurostat. (d) WTO 2004a: 33.

Tabelle 61: Indikatoren für die Entwicklung in einzelnen Industriebranchen 1979-2001.
In: Europäische Kommission 2004: 47.
Erwähnt in Abschnitt 'D', 246, Abschnitt 'K', 1341.

Industriebereich	Entwicklung von Wertschöpfung, Beschäftigung und Arbeitsproduktivität (durchschnittliche jährliche Veränderungsrate 1979-2001)			Anteil am verarbeitenden Gewerbe (in % der Wertschöpfung zu Preisen von 1995)		Handelsbilanz von EU-15 (Mrd. Euro)	
	Wertschöpfung (Preise von 1995)	Beschäftigung	Arbeitsproduktivität	1979	2001	1989	2001
Elektronische Bauelemente	8,5	-0,1	8,6	0,2	1,0	n.v.	n.v.
Telekommunikationsgeräte	7,3	-1,2	8,6	0,4	1,6	n.v.	n.v.
Büromaschinen	7,4	-0,6	8,0	0,3	1,2	-16,3	-33,5
Radio- und Fernsehgeräte	3,9	-2,3	6,3	0,3	0,6	-11,9	-17,7
Chemische Erzeugnisse	3,4	-1,3	4,7	4,7	7,5	14,0	53,5
Sonstige Apparate und Geräte	2,5	-1,8	4,4	0,4	0,5	n.v.	n.v.
Metallerzeugung und -bearbeitung	0,7	-3,1	3,7	2,9	2,6	-5,1	-15,6
Geräte der Elektrizitätserzeugung, -verteilung u.ä.	2,5	-0,7	3,2	2,4	3,2	3,5	4,6
Papier, Pappe und Waren daraus	2,0	-1,0	3,0	1,8	2,1	0,8	5,3
Luft- und Raumfahrzeuge	2,1	-0,6	2,7	0,9	1,1	n.v.	n.v.
Wissenschaftliche Instrumente	2,4	-0,2	2,6	1,1	1,4	-1,6	0,8
Glas- und Glaswaren, Keramik, Verarbeitung von Steinen und Erden	1,1	-1,3	2,3	3,6	3,4	5,4	7,6
Kraftwagen	1,6	-0,7	2,3	4,5	4,8	16,7	43,3
Holz sowie Holz- und Korkwaren	1,1	-1,0	2,1	1,7	1,6	-4,4	-4,8
Elektrokabel, -leitungen und -drähte	1,1	-1,0	2,1	0,3	0,3	n.v.	n.v.
Gummi und Kunststoff	2,4	0,6	1,8	2,7	3,5	2,5	4,4
Nahrungsmittel, Getränke und Tabak	1,1	-0,6	1,7	7,1	6,9	2,3	7,0
Verlags- und Druckerzeugnisse	1,6	-0,1	1,7	3,7	4,0	1,7	3,1
Maschinenbau	0,6	-1,1	1,7	7,7	6,7	n.v.	n.v.
Metallerzeugnisse	0,8	-0,8	1,6	6,7	6,1	2,0	-6,9
Möbel, verschiedene Waren, Recycling	0,4	-0,7	1,1	3,2	2,7	2,0	-6,2
Bekleidung	-0,2	-3,4	3,2	2,2	1,6	-9,1	-29,1
Schiffs-, Boots- und Jachtbau	-0,2	-3,4	3,2	2,2	1,6	n.v.	n.v.
Textilien	-0,8	-3,2	2,3	3,7	2,3	-0,2	-0,8
Leder- und Lederwaren	-1,1	-3,3	2,2	1,4	0,9	0,9	-3
Kokerei, Mineralölverarbeitung, Herstellung und Verarbeitung von Spalt- und Brutstoffen	-3,6	-2	-1,7	2,8	0,9	-7,5	-6,7

Tabelle 62: Industrial production Euroland. In: Deutsche Bank Research 2001: 1.
Erwähnt in Abschnitt 'D', 246.

	92	93	94	95	96	97	98	99	00	01 (2)	02 (2)	Shares 00
	% yoy (1)											%
Automobile ind.	-0.1	-16.4	12.9	4.4	2.4	8.2	12.0	3.5	9.0	4.0	5.0	9.0
Mech. engineering	-5.3	-7.5	3.7	6.9	1.5	3.9	3.4	-1.1	6.0	5.0	4.0	9.2
Electr. engineering	-2.3	-3.4	5.8	2.2	0.3	5.4	6.2	6.4	9.0	6.0	7.0	10.0
IT, office equipment	-10.3	-10.4	7.6	15.8	14.6	10.9	15.1	3.2	21.0	15.0	15.0	2.1
Chemicals	1.5	-1.3	6.6	2.2	2.7	5.8	1.6	2.4	3.5	3.0	3.5	10.4
Textiles & Clothing	-4.0	-5.2	3.2	-0.8	-3.6	1.9	-1.6	-5.0	-1.0	1.0	1.5	10.0
Food	-0.3	0.7	1.6	2.1	0.7	3.1	1.5	2.1	2.0	1.0	2.0	13.0
Total	-1.9	-4.9	4.9	3.1	0.1	4.7	4.2	2.4	5.0	3.5	4.0	100.0
Construction	0.4	-2.9	2.7	1.5	-0.9	0.7	2.1	4.0	3.0	2.0	2.5	-

(1) yoy = year on year .. percentage
(2) estimated numbers

Tabelle 63: Exports 1950-2000. Billions of dollar f.o.b. UNCTAD 2000: 2-8.
Erwähnt in Abschnitt 'D', 246, Abschnitt 'G', 501, 561.

	1950	1960	1970	1980	1990	1999
World total	61,9	129,9	314,6	2022.4	3483,3	5620,6
Developed market economies	37,5	85,6	224,9	1285,3	2489,2	3769,8
Developing countries	20,4	31,0	59,3	586,8	823,4	1648,7
Countries						
United States	9,9	19,6	42,6	225,5	393,5	695,2
Japan	0,8	4,0	19,3	130,4	287,5	419,3
Germany	1,9	11,4	34,2	192,8	410,1	541,0
Korea	0,02	0,03	0,8	17,5	65,0	144,7
Taiwan	0,07	0,1	1,4	19,8	67,2	121,5
Thailand	0,3	0,4	0,7	6,5	23,0	58,3
Indonesia	0,8	0,8	1,1	21,9	25,6	48,6
China	0,5	2,5	2,3	18,0	61,2	195,1 (b)
India	1,1	1,3	2,0	8,5	17,9	36,5
Brazil	1,3	1,2	2,7	20,1	31,4	48,0
Nigeria	0,2	0,4	1,2	25,9	13,6	12,9
South Africa	1,1	1,9	3,3	25,5	23,5	26,6
Regional groupings						
South America	5,0	6,6	11,6	66,3	86,7	134,1 (c)
Other Asia (a)	7,3	10,6	16,9	161,4	449,7	1045,1
Africa	3,2	5,3	12,7	93,8	79,7	87,4

(a) Other Asia: Afghanistan, Bangladesh, Brunei Darussalam, Cambodia, China, Hong Kong, India, Indonesia, Korea, Rep. of, Lao People's Dem. Rep., Macau, Malaysia, Maldives, Mongolia, Myanmar, Nepal, Pakistan, Philippines, Singapore, Sri Lanka, Taiwan, Thailand, Viet Nam. (b) Hongkong, China 173,8 billion US $, 152,0 re-exports, the biggest part of which stems from China. GATT International Trade 2000. (c) Excluding among others Mexico's exports of 136,7 billion US $).

Tabelle 64: Ländervergleich Exporte. Aus: UNCTAD 1994: 224-275.
Erwähnt in Abschnitt 'D', 246.

Land/Region	1970	1975	1980	1985	1990	1993
Südamerika	16449	42572	105401	103850	132061	141345
-Argentinien	1773	2961	8021	8396	12354	13117
-Chile	1113	1590	4705	3804	8310	9202
-Brasilien	2739	8492	20132	25634	31408	38783
Other Africa (a)	7644	20734	51025	35095	45197	39047
-Ghana	427	801	1103	632	890	986
-Kenya	285	633	1261	943	1010	1185
-Tanzania	245	372	582	328	407	462
- Zambia	942	803	1457	797	1254	-
- Zimbabwe	-	-	1445	1120	1748	1609
- Cote d'Ivoire	497	1238	3012	2761	3027	2734
- Mauritius	69	303	430	440	1205	1304
Andere Länder:						
Korea	882	5003	17214	26442	63123	80950
Taiwan	1469	5321	19575	30469	66823	84155
Thailand	686	2177	6449	7059	22811	36410
Philippines	1064	2263	5788	4629	8186	11375
Indonesia	1173	6888	21795	18527	26807	36607
India	1879	4666	8303	9465	18286	-
China	-	25108	-	-	51519	75659
Türkei	588	1401	2910	8255	13026	15610

(a) Angola, Benin, Botswana, Burkina Faso, Burundi, Cameroon, Cape Verde, Central African Republic, Chad, Comoros, Congo, Cote d'Ivoire, Djibuti, Equatorial Guinea, Ethiopia, Gabon, Gambia, Ghana, Guinea, Guinea-Bissau, Kenya, Lesotho, Liberia, Madagascar, Malawi, Mali, Mauritania, Mauritius, Mozambique, Namibia, Niger, Nigeria, Rwanda, Sao Tome and Principe, Senegal, Seychelles, Sierra Leone, Somalia, Swaziland, Togo, Uganda, Tanzania, Zaire, Zambia, Zimbabwe.

Zahlen hinter der Kommastelle sind hier nicht gerundet, sondern einfach weggelassen.

Tabelle 65: Changes in the international distribution in MVA for selected branches.
In: UNIDO 2004: 34.
Erwähnt in Abschnitt 'D', 246.

Branch	Year	World share (percent)		Gain/loss for developing countries (percent	Regional shares (percent) in 1990 and 2001		
		Developed countries	Developing countries		Sub-Saharan Africa	Latin America	Southeast Asia
Food and beverages	1990	82.6	17.4		6.5	45.7	31.7
	2001	79.2	20.8	3.4	6.5	43.5	37.0
Textile	1990	74.9	25.1		3.8	23.1	54.2
	2001	67.0	33.0	7.9	3.9	19.5	60.6
Apparel, leather, fur, foodwear	1990	75.3	24.7		2.4	34.3	43.4
	2001	72.2	27.8	3.1	3.4	33.3	44.9
Wood and cork products	1990	88.1	11.9		6.2	20.9	55.2
	2001	87.9	12.1	0.2	6.0	24.0	55.3
Paper and paper products	1990	89.6	10.4		2.0	46.3	37.9
	2001	87.2	12.8	2.4	1.4	43.5	45.4
Printing and publishing	1990	93.8	6.2		3.0	41.3	42.9
	2001	92.8	7.2	1.0	2.7	42.4	47.0
Industrial chemicals	1990	84.7	15.3		1.7	47.1	36.3
	2001	81.3	18.7	3.4	1.3	39.9	48.9
Petroleum and coal products	1990	64.4	35.6		1.8	33.8	33.8
	2001	56.8	43.2	7.6	1.4	27.1	44.2
Rubber and plastic products	1990	85.9	14.1		2.0	33.4	54.4
	2001	84.0	16.0	1.9	1.8	31.9	55.5
Non-metal mineral products	1990	83.3	16.7		2.4	33.0	40.2
	2001	77.4	22.6	5.9	2.1	27.9	49.8
Basic metals	1990	83.4	16.6		1.0	39.0	45.0
	2001	76.6	23.4	6.8	1.3	27.9	54.9
Metal products	1990	90.7	9.3		2.5	34.3	45.7
	2001	89.5	10.5	1.2	2.1	35.5	50.2
Non-electric machinery	1990	93.3	6.7		2.5	34.3	45.7
	2001	95.3	4.7	-2.0	2.1	35.5	50.2
Electrical machinery	1990	88.7	11.3		0.6	29.0	60.1
	2001	89.2	10.8	-5.0	0.3	18.4	75.5
Transport equipment	1990	89.6	10.4		1.3	40.9	47.2
	2001	82.2	17.8	7.4	0.5	30.6	64.7

Tabelle 66: Production, investment and employment: textiles and apparel, 1960-86.
Gekürzt, aus Cline 1987: 27.
Erwähnt in Abschnitt 'D', 247.

	Textiles				Apparel			
Year	Production	Production at constant 1982 prices	Investment (mill. $)	Employment (thousand workers)	Production	Production at constant 1982 prices	Investment (mill. $)	Employment (thousand workers)
1960	12,629	21,103	417	874,6	12,999	30,867	86	1,234
1965	17,080	33,634	618	893,2	16,426	36,271	168	1,335
1970	21,112	38,110	811	924,5	20,394	34,765	299	1,341
1975	29,208	41,832	997	835,1	27,098	40,270	381	1,214
1980	44,774	49,423	1,487	817,5	40,293	45,742	608	1,307
1983	50,147	48,498	n.a.	670,2	50,784	48,551	n.a.	1,142
1986	51,917	49,210	n.a.	668,9	53,323	49,548	n.a.	1,133

Tabelle 67: Indicators of Overall Market Penetration by Manufactured Products from Developing Countries into Seven Industrial Countries, 1976, percent. Cline 1984: 150.
Erwähnt in Abschnitt 'D', 248.

	Import-penetration ratios (four-digit ISIC number)		Percentage of gross industrial output in sectors with 7 percent or higher import penetration
Importing country	Average (a)	Median	
United States	1.91	0.85	1.6 (4.9 (b))
Canada	1.44	0.77	3.6
West Germany	1.98	0.65	8.4
France	1.57	0.38	1.4
Italy	2.12	0.49	6.1
United Kingdom	2.58	0.98	9.8
Japan	2.31	0.74	8.8

Tabelle 68: Southern import penetration ratios (%). In: Wood 1994: 97.
Erwähnt in Abschnitt 'D', 248, 249, Abschnitt 'K', 1353.

	1959-69	1969-70	1980-81	1984-85	1988-89
Primary products (UNCTAD)	11.6	12.9	26.5	20.5	16.7
Manufactures (including processed primary products)					
UNCTAD estimates	1.2	1.4	2.0	2.9	3.3
OECD estimates		1.7	3.2	3.7	
Hughes and Waelbroeck estimates		1.7	3.4		

Notes: The Southern import penetration ratio is calculated as the share of imports from developing countries in total developed-country apparent consumption of the goods concerned. Apparent consumption is output plus imports minus exports.

Tabelle 69: Developing country imports penetration of manufactured goods markets in OECD countries (Measure by import - domestic sales ratio (MDS). In: Athukorala/Hazari 1988: 59.
Erwähnt in Abschnitt 'D', 248, Abschnitt 'K', 1353.

		OECD		
ISIC code	Product group	1970	1975	1983
321	Textiles	2.1	3.1	4.8
322	Wearing apparel	3.7	9.2	17.5
323	Leather products	5.2	9.1	18.1
324	Leather footwear	1.3	5.7	19.0
331	Wood products	3.6	2.7	2.4
332	Furniture	0.4	0.7	2.5
341	Paper	0.2	0.7	0.5
342	Printing and publishing	0.1	0.1	0.6
351	Industrial chemicals	0.8	1.1	2.2
352	Other chemicals	0.4	0.4	0.5
355	Rubber products	0.4	0.7	2.2
356	Plastic products	1.4	1.6	2.1
361	Ceramics	0.2	1.1	4.7
362	Glass	0.3	0.5	1.3
369	Other non-metallic minerals	0.4	0.2	0.4
381	Metal products	0.1	0.3	1.1
382	Non-electrical machinery	0.1	0.5	1.5
383	Electrical machinery	0.7	2.1	5.1
384	Transport equipment	0.1	0.3	1.0
385	Measuring and control equipment	0.3	1.5	2.8
390	Other	4.3	6.0	12.6
Total		1.1	2.2	3.2

Tabelle 70: Import Penetration from All Sources into Seven Industrial Countries, Three-Digit Estimates (per cent), of manufacturing output, 1978. In: Cline 1984: 154-155.
Erwähnung Abschnitt 'D', 248.

ISIC Number	Product sector	United States	Canada	West Germany	France	Italy	United Kingdom	Japan
311	Food products	5.3	11.4	20.0	16.4	28.7	21.7	12.0
312	Food products, diverse	3.0	8.6	14.6	7.8	12.0	14.2	3.2
313	Beverages	7.7	10.7	8.1	10.1	9.1	4.9	2.3
314	Tobacco	5.7	2.0	11.2	8.1	26.2	31.6	4.3
321	Textiles	5.1	23.4	34.3	26.1	25.1	24.3	8.6
322	Apparel	15.3	18.4	48.6	0.0 (a)	34.5	31.9	10.4
323	Leather products (except footwear)	14.3	33.4	39.2	22.9	29.7	22.5	11.3
324	Footwear	29.3	30.0	37.6	0.0 (b)	1.9	22.4	7.4
331	Wood products	11.5	9.9	17.7	14.5	74.2	29.4	5.2
332	Furniture	6.8	15.8	0.0 (c)	0.0 (c)	15.3	13.8	2.5
341	Paper	6.8	7.8	23.1	20.4	19.2	24.5	3.0
342	Printing	2.0	18.7	13.4	13.2	8.3	7.6	1.2
351	Industrial chemicals	8.4	42.0	17.2	38.6	23.9	22.3	6.6
352	Other chemical products	3.2	16.5	0.0 (d)	15.5	0.0 (d)	15.3	5.5
353	Petroleum refineries	9.7	4.1	28.5	10.2	26.9	19.2	15.0
354	Petroleum and coal products	1.5	18.8	0.0 (e)	0.0 (e)	0.0 (e)	6.6	0.8
355	Rubber products	11.4	22.3	23.2	32.2	17.3	14.4	2.3
356	Plastic products	9.2	47.9	29.5	0.0 (f)	43.7	33.8	2.4
361	Pottery, china, and earthenware	34.1	69.6	41.2	12.6	12.4	12.0	1.8
362	Glass products	7.1	46.9	23.8	24.4	0.0 (g)	22.3	2.1
369	Other nonmetallic minerals	3.9	11.3	13.2	0.0 (g)	0.0 (g)	7.3	1.9
371	Iron and steel	11.7		21.0	32.6	16.1	16.1	0.9
372	Nonferrous metals	12.5	23.4	33.2	29.4	58.9	32.6	12.8
381	Fabricated metal products	4.0	19.3	14.1	14.3	16.0	9.5	1.1
382	Machinery (nonelectrical)	7.3	15.4	18.9	41.2	37.2	26.4	3.2
383	Electrical machinery and equipment	10.5	36.0	13.6	16.8	18.8	16.6	1.9
384	Transport equipment	12.6	45.5	22.7	19.7	26.7	32.8	2.6
385	Technical instruments	11.1	60.2	51.3	0.0 (h)	37.6	45.8	12.8
390	Manufactures not elsewhere classified	23.0	25.1	61.2	0.0 (c)	53.7	n.a.	11.9

n.a. not available (a) included in 321, (b) included in 323, (c) included in 331, (d) included in 351, (e) included in 553, (f) included in 355, (g) included in 361, (h) included in 382.

Tabelle 71: Market Penetration of Manufactured Goods Imports (a) in OECD Countries: Basic Indicators, 1970, 1975 and 1983. Aus: Athukorala/Hazari 1988: 58.
Erwähnt in Abschnitt 'D', 248.

		Import-Domestic Sales Ratio (%) (MDS)		Import-Domestic Output Ratio (%) (MDP)		DC share in total imports (%) (MSH)
		(1)	(2)	(3)	(3)	(4)
		Total imports	DC Imports	Total Imports	DC Imports	
Australia	1970	24,3	1,5	32,6	2,0	6,1
	1975	25,1	2,9	33,2	3,5	10,6
	1983	28,9	4,4	36,8	5,6	15,2
Canada	1970	35,8	1,4	39,8	1,5	3,8
	1975	37,9	1,5	42,5	1,7	4,1
	1983	38,2	2,0	39,2	2,1	5,3
EEC(b)	1970	19,8	1,1	18,7	1,1	5,8
	1975	26,8	1,7	23,8	1,5	6,3
	1983	41,3	4,2	43,2	4,4	10,2
Japan	1970	6,8	1,2	6,1	1,1	17,4
	1975	6,6	1,4	5,6	1,2	21,4
	1983	4,5	1,0	3,9	0,9	23,3
Sweden	1970	32,0	1,3	29,5	1,6	4,2
	1975	35,8	1,5	32,8	1,4	4,3
	1983	51,5	2,8	43,2	2,4	4,5
United States	1970	10,3	1,6	5,8	0,9	15,2
	1975	7,2	1,4	6,8	1,3	19,0
	1983	11,3	3,3	11,5	1,0	29,4
Other (c)	1970	n.a.	n.a.	n.a.	n.a.	n.a.
	1975	33,3	2,1	38,1	2,3	6,2
	1983	55,8	3,1	48,1	2,6	5,4
TotalOECD(d)	1970	13,2	1,3	12,5	1,3	10,2
	1975	16,1	1,8	15,0	1,7	11,1
	1983	19,2	2,6	18,3	2,5	13,7

Notes: (a) SITC 3 less 311 (food), 313 (beverages), 314 (tobacco), 353 (petroleum), 371 (iron and steel) and 372 (non-ferrous metal).
(b) Excluding Greece, Ireland and Spain.
(c) Norway and Finland.
(d) Only the countries listed above.
DC = Developing countries

Tabelle 72: Import Penetration by Developing Countries into Seven Industrial Countries, Three-Digit Estimates (per cent) of manufacturing output, 1978. In: Cline 1984: 152-153. *Erwähnt in Abschnitt 'D', 248.*

ISIC Number	Product sector	United States	Canada	West Germany	France	Italy	United Kingdom	Japan
311	Food products	2.3	1.8	3.8	4.4	4.2	4.6	5.0
312	Food products, diverse	2.0	1.6	3.4	1.4	1.0	4.0	1.6
313	Beverages	0.2	0.7	0.2	0.9	0.0	0.2	0.1
314	Tobacco	3.9	0.3	3.4	2.3	1.3	10.4	0.8
321	Textiles	2.3	3.4	7.7	4.4	7.7	5.6	5.2
322	Apparel	12.5	10.9	13.9	0.0 (a)	7.2	15.2	7.8
323	Leather products (except footwear)	10.3	9.5	8.5	5.2	15.0	9.4	7.1
324	Footwear	14.0	9.8	2.4	0.0 (b)	0.5	4.9	5.8
331	Wood products	2.6	1.7	1.9	1.7	8.6	5.4	1.3
332	Furniture	2.3	1.1	0.0 (c)	0.0 (c)	0.9	0.7	1.4
341	Paper	0.1	0.0	0.3	0.3	0.2	0.2	0.1
342	Printing	0.8	0.7	0.9	0.3	0.6	0.9	0.2
351	Industrial chemicals	1.2	1.7	0.4	1.1	0.9	1.1	0.8
352	Other chemical products	0.5	0.2	0.0 (d)	0.7	0.2	0.7	0.7
353	Petroleum refineries	6.1	1.4	2.1	1.0	7.6	2.2	13.1
354	Petroleum and coal products	0.1	1.0	0.0 (e)	0.0 (e)	0.0 (e)	0.6	0.2
355	Rubber products	3.2	1.1	0.7	1.0	0.8	1.2	0.7
356	Plastic products	4.2	2.1	1.1	0.0 (f)	1.4	2.3	0.5
361	Pottery, china, and earthenware	6.1	6.0	2.3	0.4	0.5	1.6	0.4
362	Glass products	0.8	0.7	0.5	0.2	0.0 (g)	0.3	0.3
369	Other nonmetallic minerals	0.8	0.5	0.5	0.0 (g)	0.0 (g)	0.4	0.7
371	Iron and steel	1.2	0.5	0.4	0.6	0.4	0.4	0.3
372	Nonferrous metals	4.0	1.4	6.1	5.6	14.4	5.3	5.6
381	Fabricated metal products	1.0	0.6	0.5	0.2	0.4	0.5	0.1
382	Machinery (nonelectrical)	0.6	0.5	0.3	0.5	0.5	0.4	0.2
383	Electrical machinery and equipment	4.1	1.6	1.1	0.8	1.2	1.4	0.5
384	Transport equipment	0.3	0.1	0.6	0.2	0.6	2.9	0.1
385	Technical instruments	2.0	2.1	3.6	0.0 (h)	0.9	4.4	1.4
390	Manufactures not elsewhere classified	9.3	4.7	12.8	0.0	9.9	4.6	6.8

n.a. not available (a) included in 321, (b) included in 323, (c) included in 331, (d) included in 351, (e) included in 553, (f) included in 355, (g) included in 361, (h) included in 382.

Tabelle 73: Exports of Manufactures, Shares in Market Growth, and Growth Rates by Area and Sector, 1973 and 1985. Aus. IMF 1988: 128 (Aus GATT, International Trade, var. issues).
Erwähnt in Abschnitt 'D', 248.

	1973	1985	Increase	Share of increase	Growth rate
	(In millions of U.S. dollars)			(In percent)	
Total exports of manufactures					
World	347.50	1,190.75	843.25	100.0	10.8
Industrial countries	285.60	940.35	654.75	77.6	10.4
Developing countries	24.10	144.70	120.60	14.3	14.4
Clothing					
World	12.59	48.65	36.06	100.0	11.9
Industrial countries	6.92	21.20	14.28	39.6	9.8
Developing countries	3.82	21.05	17.23	47.8	15.3
Textiles					
World	23.35	54.55	31.20	100.0	7.3
Industrial countries	17.12	35.30	18.18	58.3	6.2
Developing countries	4.05	13.45	9.40	30.1	10.5
Other consumer goods					
World	24.26	91.25	66.99	100.0	11.7
Industrial countries	18.43	64.60	46.17	68.9	11.0
Developing countries	3.18	19.95	16.77	25.0	16.5
Other semimanufactures					
World	28.95	84.30	55.35	100.0	9.3
Industrial countries	23.31	67.60	44.29	80.0	9.3
Developing countries	3.39	12.20	8.81	15.9	11.3
Iron and steel					
World	28.46	69.20	40.74	100.0	7.7
Industrial countries	23.78	54.75	30.97	76.0	7.2
Developing countries	0.95	6.75	5.80	14.2	17.8
Chemicals					
World	41.87	163.05	121.18	100.0	12.0
Industrial countries	36.46	136.90	100.44	82.9	11.7
Developing countries	1.83	13.35	11.52	9.5	18.0
Engineering products					
World	187.97	679.75	419.78	100.0	11.3
Industrial countries	159.60	560.00	400.40	81.4	11.0
Developing countries	5.91	57.95	52.04	10.6	21.0

Tabelle 74: Developed market economy countries selected industry sectors with higher than average export dependence on developing countries markets measured as a share of production and as a share of exports to world market, by industrial sector for 1985, and its increment in the 1975-1985 period. In: De Castro 1989: 16.
Erwähnt in Abschnitt 'D', 249.

ISIC	Description	Exports to developing countries				
		(A) Value of exports 1985 (US$ Million)	(B) as a % of production 1985 (%)	(C) increment of (B) 1975-85 (%)	(D) as a % of exports to world 1985 (%)	(E) increment of (D) 1975-85 (%)
		United States				
3232	Fur, dressing & dying ind.	20.2	17.1	7.7	29.5	11.2
3821	Engines & turbines	974.1	12.4	4.6	38.4	2.8
3512	Fertilizer & pesticides	1,653.4	12.1	-6.2	48.6	-23.4
3824	Spec. industrial machinery	4,031.3	11.3	-2.5	47.9	-0.9
3231	Tanneries & leather finishing	175.2	8.6	4.9	62.8	38.1
3845	Aircraft	5,308.2	8.2	-1.4	32.2	-0.3
3825	Office, computing, acc. machinery	3,268.5	6.4	2.2	22.3	5.5
3832	Radio, TV, telecommuncation equip.	6,096.1	5.9	0.3	55.7	7.4
3851	Prof., scientific, measuring equip.	1,827.4	5.6	0.1	28.7	2.5
3842	Railroad equip.	233.4	5.5	-2.0	64.7	-11.1
3831	Electrical industrial machinery	1,500.4	4.7	-0.9	43.4	8.9
3513	Synth. resins, plastics	1,888.1	4.6	0.7	43.4	8.9
3511	Basic industrial chemicals	3,456.5	4.5	-0.6	35.7	-0.2
3829	Machinery and equipment (excl. electric)	3,072.4	3.6	-4.4	29.8	-8.5
3843	Motor vehicles	3,486.9	2.0	-2.1	16.8	-12.7
		EEC				
3901	Jewellery and related art	2,428.2	...	...	...	...
3232	Fur dressing & dying ind.	96.9	26.8	20.4	54.5	33.8
3824	Spec. indust. machinery	6,288.3	22.9	-0.4	43.3	-9.7
3851	Prof., scientific, measuring equip.	2,535.2	19.3	6.7	39.4	-1.1
3842	Railroad equip.	588.1	18.7	6.5	66.3	16.3
3821	Engines and turbines	901.5	15.9	4.3	51.5	-7.1
3841	Shipbuilding and repairing (a)	1,478.4	15.4	-5.0	56.8	-3,4
3852	Photographic & optical goods	510.8	15.0	6.5	24.6	1.4
3845	Aircraft	2,508.3	14.9	-0.1	29.0	-22.4
3839	Electr. appl. & supplies NEC	1,832.5	14.1	2.5	43.5	-6.3
3829	Machinery & equipment NEC	7,438.1	14.0	0.4	46.4	-2.0
3511	Basic industrial	5,718.4	11.3	3.8	36.3	0.4

	chemicals					
3832	Radio, TV, telecommuncations equipment	4,301.2	10.8	3.9	43.7	9.2
3513	Synth. resins, plastics etc.	2,933.8	9.4	2.7	36.4	-0.8
3843	Motor vehicles	8,512.5	7.8	-4.3	30.8	-14.9
						Japan
3841	Shipbuilding and repairs (a)	5,085.2	42.7	-5.7	71.2	-7.5
3231	Tanneries and leather finishing	212.1	23.9	4.4	81.8	3.5
3853	Watches & Clocks	981.7	23.0	3.7	56.8	-6.7
3824	Spec. industr. machinery	3,154.8	17.6	0.1	50.4	-18.0
3211	Spinning, weaving & finishing textiles	3,014.9	17.3	2.3	69.2	-2,6
3551	Tyres & tubes industries	701.2	16.9	-5.5	45.4	-21.7
3839	Electr. appl. supplies NEC	1,673.4	15.5	6.0	50.2	-9.2
3842	Railroad equipment	194.0	14.4	-2.6	36.0	-13.6
3710	Iron & Steel basic industries	9,062.2	12.6	-4.5	65.3	6.3
3829	Machinery & equip. excl. electr.	5,166.1	11.9	3.9	52.9	-3.8
3832	Radio, TV, telecommunications equipment	8,648.7	11.7	3.2	30.6	-0.8
3831	Electrical industrial machinery & app.	2,652.6	11.4	3.4	56.4	-6.6
3513	Synthetic resins, plastics etc.	2,001.8	11.4	-4,8	64.8	-5.0
3843	Motor vehicles	8,943.9	7.8	0.2	21.8	-12.8
3511	Basic industrial chemicals	2,112.3	6.5	-2.6	52.0	-7.9

Source: UNCTAD secretariat calculations from OECD compatible trade and production database, COMTAP tapes, 1975 and 1985.
(a) High export values in this particular sector should however be analysed with great care since their magnitude may be the reflection, for a large part, of ships and boats with flags of convenience (Panama, Liberia).

Tabelle 75: Penetration rates. Proportion of domestic demand accounted for by imports (as percentages). Total Industry. Buigues/Goybet 1985: 230.
Erwähnt in Abschnitt 'D', 249.

	1973	1979	1980	1981	1982	1983	1984	1985	Difference 1979-73	Difference 1985-79
EUR7	8.7	10.4	11.1	11.3	11.4	11.9	13.1	13.1	+ 1.7	+ 2.7
USA	6.3	8.7	9.3	9.5	9.6	10.0	11.7	12.3	+ 2.4	+3.6
Japan	4.9	5.1	5.2	4.9	5.2	4.9	5.1	4.8	+ 0.2	- 0.3

Tabelle 76: Leading exporters of manufactures in 1998, values of export in 1985 and 1998 (US million). In: Lall 2000: 368. Erwähnt in Abschnitt 'D', 250, 252, 253, Abschnitt 'F', 443, Abschnitt 'G', 586.

	Total manufactures	RB total	RB1	RB2	LT total	LT 1	LT 2	MT total	MT 1	MT 2	MT 3	HT total	HT 1	HT 2
1985														
China	6049.2	2349.7	677.7	1672.0	2645.2	2217.4	427.8	738.9	28.6	589.5	120.8	315.4	38.6	276.8
Korea	29025.0	2493.6	1016.7	1477.0	12017.6	7892.5	4125.1	10807.1	678.6	3020.4	7108.1	3706.7	3287.7	419.0
Taiwan	29092.5	2883.2	1690.3	1192.9	15381.6	8597.1	6784.5	6124.1	865.6	1668.5	3590.4	4703.6	4430.0	272.6
Mexico	8336.3	1761.4	401.4	1360.0	1097.2	429.3	667.8	3600.7	766.1	415.6	2419.0	1877.0	1736.4	140.5
Singapore	19014.0	8266.6	1527.8	6738.7	1640.2	764.7	875.5	4445.2	146.4	1066.3	3232.4	4662.1	3916.9	745.3
Malaysia	8626.5	4632.1	3998.9	633.3	692.4	466.6	225.8	982.1	20.5	262.9	698.7	2319.9	2167.4	152.5
Thailand	3657.6	1386.5	1029.8	356.6	1295.1	981.8	313.3	803.8	13.9	289.0	501.0	172.2	147.7	24.5
Brazil	17616.8	7744.6	3563.2	4181.4	3757.2	2042.9	1714.4	5249.6	1287.2	2079.7	1882.7	865.4	578.4	287.1
Philippines	2428.7	1359.1	1047.0	312.0	585.7	352.3	233.4	217.8	21.1	163.5	33.3	266.1	256.5	9.6
Indonesia	3856.4	2899.3	1690.4	1208.9	596.2	505.1	91.1	246.1	0.9	222.2	23.0	114.8	80.9	33.9
India	6208.9	2518.8	255.1	2263.8	2813.2	2542.2	270.9	624.7	118.9	171.5	334.4	252.1	97.4	154.8
Hong Kong	15979.5	504.2	278.1	226.1	10063.3	7045.7	3017.6	3050.2	1.9	196.4	2851.8	2361.8	2163.1	198.7
Turkey	5790.4	1263.4	590.3	673.1	3075.5	2138.6	936.9	1359.6	102.8	752.4	504.3	91.9	64.7	27.2
Total above	155681.5	37568.9	17766.8	22295.8	43642.7	35976.2	19684.1	27442.7	4052.1	10897.8	23299.8	18002.2	18965.5	2743.4
Developing world	210244.6	79986.4	24308.2	55678.2	63839.8	42194.1	21645.7	43369.6	4380.5	14040.5	24948.6	23048.7	19490.7	3558.0
%	74.0 %	47.0 %	73.1 %	40.0 %	68.4 %	85.3 %	90.9 %	63.3 %	92.5 %	77.6 %	93.4 %	78.1 %	97.3 %	77.1 %
1998														
China	167681.1	16551.3	7155.4	9395.8	83803.2	52814.7	30988.5	33853.9	1864.5	10556.4	21433.4	33472.8	28605.5	4867.3
Korea	120700.3	12914.5	4739.6	8175.0	25325.3	13673.1	11652.2	46443.7	11354.5	14998.0	20091.3	36016.7	32800.6	3216.2
Taiwan	105553.7	5811.3	2761.3	3050.1	32100.7	14291.0	17809.7	29044.5	4256.5	9644.3	15143.6	38597.2	37259.0	1338.2
Mexico	103681.3	6977.1	3743.6	3233.5	19848.6	9358.2	10490.4	45598.6	19200.6	5264.1	21133.9	31257.0	28055.0	3202.0
Singapore	103488.5	14588.6	3471.0	11117.6	7254.0	2226.8	5027.2	19326.6	861.8	5091.1	13373.0	62319.7	59674.4	2645.2
Malaysia	65940.5	11004.8	9543.2	1461.7	7245.9	3301.7	3944.3	13360.2	455.2	3107.9	9797.0	34329.6	32276.3	2053.3
Thailand	44759.5	8657.7	5532.4	3125.3	11345.3	6798.2	4547.1	9165.0	1014.8	2438.8	5711.5	15591.5	14593.9	997.5
Brazil	38881.6	15424.7	9319.0	6105.7	5900.6	3158.6	2742.1	14363.8	4770.0	4563.9	5029.9	3192.5	1476.4	1716.0
Philippines	28118,8	2022.3	1548.6	473.7	4074.3	2988.2	1086.1	3058.9	382.2	346.8	2329.9	18963.3	18673.5	289.8
Indonesia	26894.8	10447.6	7154.9	3292.7	8868.8	5511.1	3357.7	4972.1	310.0	2647.5	2014.6	2606.3	2381.3	225.0
India	25855.1	7801.8	847.5	6954.3	12583.4	9977.4	2606.0	3763.5	735.2	1820.4	1208.0	1706.3	708.5	997.8
Hong Kong	23136.7	1041.7	661.4	380.3	13034.7	11049.2	1985.5	3044.5	0.7	717.9	2325.9	6015.8	4920.1	1095.7
Turkey	22885.2	3339.9	2204.1	1135.8	13236.9	10276.1	2960.8	4870.8	761.5	1992.9	2116.4	1437.7	1156.3	281.3
Total above	877577.3	116583.5	58681.9	57901.6	244621.8	145424.2	99197.6	230865.8	45967.0	63.190.3	121708.5	285506.2	262580.8	22925.4
Developing world	996967.5	175130.4	77385.7	97744.7	277435.3	169990.4	107444.9	254289.1	51537.3	75515.3	127236.4	290112.8	265114.5	24998.3
%	88.0 %	66.6 %	75.8 %	59.2 %	88.2 %	85.5 %	92.3 %	90.8 %	89.2 %	83.7 %	95.7 %	98.4 %	99.0 %	91.7 %

Tabelle 77: Die 10 bedeutendsten Exportwaren Südkoreas, 1961-1992. In: Seung 1996: 71. *Erwähnt in Abschnitt 'D', 252.*

1961		1970		1975	
1. Eisenerz	13,0	Textilien, Bekleidung	40,8	Textilien, Bekleidung	36,2
2. Wolfram	12,6	Sperrholz	11,0	Elektronische Produkte	8,9
3. Rohseide	6,7	Perücken	10,8	Stahlprodukte	4,6
4. Anthrazit	5,8	Eisenerz	5,9	Sperrholz	4,1
5. Tintenfisch	5,5	Elektronische Produkte	3,5	Schuhwerk	3,8
6. Sonst. lebende Fische	4,5	Süßwaren	2,3	Fische	2,7
7. Graphit	4,2	Schuhwerk	2,1	Schiffe	2,4
8. Sperrholz	3,3	Tabak und Tabakwaren	1,6	Metallprodukte	2,4
9. Getreide	3,3	Stahlprodukte	1,5	Petro-Produkte	1,9
10. Schweinehaare	3,0	Metallprodukte	1,5	Synthetische Harze	1,7
Zusammen	62,0		77,1		69,9
1980		1985		1992	
1. Textilien, Bekleidung	28,6	Textilien, Bekleidung	23,4	Elektronische Produkte	28,2
2. Elektronische Produkte	11,4	Schiffe	16,6	Textilien, Bekleidung	20,5
3. Stahlprodukte	10,6	Elektronische Produkte	14,1	Stahlprodukte	7,0
4. Schuhwerk	5,2	Stahlprodukte	8,1	Chemische Produkte	5,5
5. Schiffe	3,5	Schuhwerk	5,2	Schiffe	5,4
6. Synthetische Harze	3,3	Petro-Produkte	3,0	Schuhwerk	4,2
7. Metallprodukte	2,5	Synthetische Harze	2,4	Automobile	3,7
8. Sperrholz	2,0	Elektrische Produkte	2,0	Maschinen	3,2
9. Fische	2,0	Automobile	1,9	Petro-Produkte	2,2
10. Elektrische Produkte	1,9	Metallprodukte	1,7	Fischprodukte	2,0
Zusammen	71,0		78,5		81,8

Tabelle 78: Manufactured trade balance by main category. In: UNCTAD 2004: 91.
Erwähnt in Abschnitt 'D', 253, 306.

Regions	1980-1984				1997-2001			
	Chemicals	Machinery and transport equipment less electronic	Electronics	Other manu-factured goods	Chemicals	Machinery and transport equipment less electronic	Electronics	Other manu-factured goods
World	-1.0	11.7	0.4	-0.3	-8.4	1.1	-9.0	-8.9
Developing countries	-71.5	-81.9	-46.2	-25.9	-53.2	-50.8	-3.8	4.7
Africa	-76.4	-97.5	-97.5	-74.8	-62.5	-84.2	-83.6	-27.8
- North Africa	-66.3	-99.1	-98.2	-88.0	-53.6	-97.2	-74.2	-45.8
- Sub-Saharan Africa	-82.2	-96.5	-97.0	-63.5	-67.9	-75.6	-89.3	-13.1
America	-60.7	-68.8	-41.4	-33.9	-64.8	-38.4	-26.9	-33.9
- Central America and the Caribbean	-47.5	-66.0	29.2	-53.1	-63.9	-19.1	5.0	-37.5
- South America	-67.7	-70.1	-76.8	-14.1	-65.3	-58.6	-86.0	-26.5
Asia	-73.9	-78.9	-34.8	-6.8	-47.7	-51.2	4.6	19.9
- West Asia	-87.9	-95.0	-97.9	-87.7	-52.1	-85.3	-81.7	-40.0
- Central Asia	..	..	..	..	-62.1	-84.8	-90.8	-46.4
- South, East, and South East Asia	-68.0	-66.0	-2.4	61.4	-46.7	-40.8	9.7	30.2
-- South, East, and South East Asia less China	-78.5	-68.4	-5.1	53.3	-43.7	-38.0	8.8	2.9
Oceania	-97.8	-96.4	-98.4	-73.9	-94.5	-88.2	-89.4	-3.1
Countries in Central and Eastern Europe	11.4	104.4	73.5	142.2	-37.4	-26.8	-35.5	9.8
Developed Countries	27.8	48.0	16.8	5.6	14.8	20.8	-10.7	-15.3
- North America	67.9	3.8	-12.8	-43.6	3.7	-15.8	-38.9	-49.0
- Europe	26.3	45.6	-5.6	13.6	20.1	24.4	-8.4	3.0
- Others	-16.7	332.5	345.8	118.4	4.6	204.9	72.9	-8.9
Memorandum								
Developing countries less China	-75.5	-82.6	-47.5	-28.6	-52.8	-50.8	-6.0	-13.6
Least developed countries	-86.3	-98.6	-96.2	-73.5	-88.4	-96.2	-95.9	-24.5

Siehe für die Definitionen der Ländergruppen die Originalpublikation: Die meisten Definitionen erklären sich selbst, deshalb sei hier nur die Definition von Asien näher erklärt: South, East and South-East Asia: Afghanistan, Bangladesh, Bhutan, Brunei Darussalam, Cambodia, China, China, Hong Kong SAR, China, Macao SAR, China, Taiwan Province of, India, Indonesia, Korea, Democratic People's Rep. of, Korea, Republic of Lao People's Democratic Republic, Malaysia, Maldives, Mongolia, Myanmar, Nepal, Pakistan, Philippines, Singapore, Sri Lanka, Thailand, Timor-Leste, Viet Nam.

Tabelle 79: Top Automobile Manufactures. Daten aus CCFA 2006.
Erwähnt in Abschnitt 'D', 254, 255.

Produzenten	Rang	Alle Fahrzeuge Tausend	Automobile	Pickups u.a.	Lkw	Busse
General Motors Opel Vauxhall	1	8.067	4.503	3.531	33	-
Toyota	2	6.815	5.870	676	231	38
Ford Jaguar Volvo	3	6.644	3.497	3.072	74	1
Volkswagen	4	5.095	4.893	169	29	5
DaimlerChrysler	5	4.628	1.914	2.368	299	47
PSA Peugeot Citroen	6	3.405	3.005	401	-	-
Honda	7	3.237	3.183	54	-	-
Nissan	8	3.190	2.424	616	146	4
Hyundai Kia	9	2.766	2.378	147	129	113
Renault Dacia Samsung	10	2.472	2.164	308	-	-
Fiat Iveco Irisbus	11	2.120	1.584	385	120	31
Suzuki Maruti	12	1.977	1.639	337	-	-
Mitsubishi	13	1.429	1.111	311	7	-
Mazda	14	1.275	1.043	228	4	-
BMW Mini	15	1.250	1.259	-	-	-
Daihatsu	16	965	785	173	7	-
GM Daewoo u. DIMC	17	899	869	15	4	11
AUTOVAZ	18	718	718	-	-	-
FUJI (Subaru)	19	601	513	88	-	-
FAW Gruppe (u.a. VW, Toyota, Mazda)	20	587	50	403	125	9
Beijing AIG	21	539	-	539	-	-
ISUZU	22	500	15	50	433	3
Dongfeng (Citroen)	23	442	-	252	180	10
Chana Automobile Liability	24	419	-	419	-	-
TATA (Telco)	25	379	179	131	10	59
SAIC (GM und VW)	26	309	-	309	-	-
GAZ	27	214	66	149	-	-
Harbin Hafei Automobile	28	206	-	206	-	-
Volvo Renault Trucks, Mack	29	191	-	8	175	8
Manhindra & Mahindra	30	185	79	67	36	3
Ssangyong	31	144	132	4	-	9
Anhui Jianghuai Auto	32	131	-	119	-	12
Navistar	33	126	-	-	110	16
PACCAR-DAF	34	125	-	-	125	-
Jinbei Auto Holding	35	111	-	111	-	-
MG Rover	36	106	106	0	-	-
Change Aircraft Industry	37	104	-	104	-	-
Ljmach Avto	38	96	83	14	-	-
Hino	39	95	-	5	84	6
Nanjing Auto	40	95	95	-	-	5
Zhejiang Geely	41	92	-	92	-	-
Porsche	42	84	84	-	-	-
Chery Auto	43	80	80	-	-	-
MAN ERF Neoman Bus	44	70	-	-	64	6
KAMAZ	45	70	41	-	29	-
UAZ	46	67	31	36	-	-
SCANIA	47	59	-	-	53	6
Southeast Auto Industrial	48	58	-	58	-	-
Great Wall Motor	49	55	55	-	-	-
Nissan Diesel	50	40	-	1	38	2
Evobus	-	8	-	-	-	8
Irisbus	-	6	-	-	-	6
erwähnte Produzenten total		63 329	44.435	15.953	2.545	396
andere Produzenten (China, Rußland, Türkei)		836				
Total 2004		64 165				

Tabelle 80: Global furniture trade - top 15 net exporting countries (US$ million). (a). In: UNIDO Wood Furniture 2003: 2.
Erwähnt in Abschnitt 'D', 286.

Country	Gross exports 2000	Net exports 1995	Net exports 2000	Net exports percentage change 1995-2000
Italy	8,359	7,595	7,395	-3
China	4,582	1,671	4,412	164
Canada	5,179	685	2,044	198
Poland	2,191	1,180	1,815	54
Indonesia	1,518	819	1,498	83
Malaysia	1,596	826	1,491	80
Denmark	1,900	1,687	1,209	-28
Mexico	3,315	468	1,273	151
Thailand	949	712	909	28
Spain	1,453	523	531	2
Slovenia	586	409	461	13
Czech Republic	780	148	445	201
Romania	445	472	377	-20
Sweden	1,298	510	338	-34
Brazil	496	212	333	57
Total of the rest	22,742			
Total (b)	57,388			

Source: ITC (www.intracen.org)
Notes: (a) Standard international trade classification SItC 821, Furniture and stuffed furnishings and includes wood, metal and plastic items; (b) Statistically speaking, total net exports should equal zero (total gross exports equal total gross imports). Accounting practices vary among statistical units responsible for totalling trade flows so any figure (other than the statistical zero) is nonsensical.

Tabelle 81: World Largest Automobile Companies, 1998.
In: Nolan 2001: 533.
Erwähnt in Abschnitt 'D', 255, Abschnitt 'J', 1335.

Company	Output (million)	% World total	Revenues ($ billion)	Profits ($ billion)	R&D Expenditure ($ billion)
General Motors	7.55	14.8	161.3	2.96	7834
Ford/Volvo*	7.21	14.1	171.2	23.16	7485
Daimler/Chrysler*	5.08	9.9	154.6	5.66	5788
Volkswagen	4.69	9.2	76.3	1.26	3501
Renault/Nissan*	4.57	8.9	92.9	1.28	1604**
Toyota	4.48	8.8	99.7	2.78	3907
Fiat	2.50	4.9	51.0	0.69	1356
Honda	2.39	4.6	48.7	2.39	2513
Peugeot	2.25	4.4	37.5	0.54	1531
Mitsubishi	1.52	3.0	27.5	0.04	766
Other	8.92	17.4	-	-	-
World	51.16	100.0	-	-	-

* pro forma
** Renault only

Tabelle 82: Leading Global Auto Components Companies, 1998.
In: Nolan 2001: 522.
Erwähnt in Abschnitt 'D', 255.

Company	Revenues ($ billion)	Profits ($ billion)	R&D ($ billion)
Robert Bosch	28.6	446	2071
Delphi	28.8	-	-
Denso	13.8	461	1384
Michelin	13.3	-	-
Dana	12.8	534	272
Johnson Controls	12.6	338	244
TRW	11.9	477	-
Lear	9.1	116	-
Goodyear	12.5	1114 *	417
Valeo	6.0	401 *	365
Pioneer	4.9	193 *	272
Pirelli	6.8	520 *	213
Autoliv	3.5	365 *	175
GKN	4.9	1191 *	144

* before tax and dividends.

Tabelle 83: Leading exporters and importers of automotive products, 2003.
In: OECD 2005: 54.
Erwähnt in Abschnitt 'D', 257.

	Value	Share in world exports/imports				Annual percentage change			
	2003	1980	1990	2000	2003	1995-00	2001	2002	2003
	Exporters								
European Union (15)	371.11	52.8	53.8	46.8	51.3	3	2	12	20
Extra EU 15 exports	124.97	19.5	14.3	14.5	17.3	4	5	17	22
Japan	102.73	19.8	20.8	15.3	14.2	2	-9	15	11
USA	69.25	11.9	10.2	11.7	9.6	5	-6	6	3
Canada	56.95	6.9	8.9	10.5	7.9	7	-9	2	1
Mexico (1)	30.13	0.3	1.5	5.3	4.2	17	0	1	-3
Korea (2)	22.36	0.1	0.7	2.6	3.1	11	2	10	31
Czech Republic	7.87	-	-	0.8	1.1	...	19	16	23
Hungary	7.21	0.6	0.2	0.8	1.0	...	12	12	20
Poland	7.12	0.6	0.1	0.7	1.0	...	6	23	37
Brazil	6.53	1.1	0.6	0.8	0.9	10	3	2	33
Slovak Republic	5.91	-	-	0.4	0.8	...	-5	23	111
Turkey	4.90	0.0	0.0	0.3	0.7	19	54	35	55
Thailand (2)	3.97	0.0	0.0	0.4	0.5	38	11	8	38
China	3.57	0.0	0.1	0.3	0.5	21	20	41	33
Chinese Taipei	3.05	...	0.3	0.4	0.4	6	-2	14	23
Above 15	702.67	94.3	97.3	97.1	97.1	-	-	-	-
									Importers
European Union (15)	312.66	37.5	47.0	39.3	42.6	4	1	10	22
Extra EU 15 imports	66.52	5.3	7.3	7.6	9.1	10	2	12	30
USA	181.28	20.3	24.7	28.9	24.7	10	-3	7	3
Canada (3)	49.00	8.7	7.7	7.9	6.7	7	9	11	5
Mexico (1,3)	20.19	1.8	1.6	3.4	2.7	35	-2	9	-5
China (1)	12.78	0.6	0.6	0.6	1.7	8	29	42	84
Japan	11.13	0.5	2.3	1.7	1.5	-4	-7	7	13
Australia	11.10	1.3	1.2	1.5	1.5	7	-15	18	30
Switzerland	7.15	1.8	1.9	1.1	1.0	0	3	-1	11
Poland	6.83	0.9	0.1	0.7	0.9	...	7	8	35
Turkey	6.19	...	0.4	1.0	0.8	28	-64	31	122
Saudi Arabia	6.05	2.7	0.9	0.6	0.8	12	36	5	11
Russian Federation (2)	5.97	-	-	0.4	0.8	...	57	19	27
Czech Republic (1,3)	4.97	-	-	0.4	0.7	...	23	19	26
Hungary (1)	3.94	0.4	0.2	0.4	0.5	...	2	22	27
Slovak Republic	3.64	-	-	0.2	0.5	...	25	25	66
Above 15	642.71	76.3	88.5	88.2	87.5	-	-	-	-

Tabelle 84: Einfuhr, Wert 1000 US$, Stück. Personen – und Kombinationskraftwagen. Teilweise SITC Rev.2, Umrechung der ausländischer Währungen meist für 1990, siehe (11)(12). Daten: Auto International in Zahlen, div. Jahrgänge.
Erwähnt in Abschnitt 'D', 257, Abschnitt 'E', 367, Abschnitt 'I', 836, 843, 850.

	1983	1985	1989	1994	1998
USA					
Einfuhr Wert	23.874.885 (1)	31.470.987 (1)	44.441.479 (2)	53.454,937 (3)	73.063.638 (3)
Einfuhr Stück	3.621.122 (1)	4.443.818 (1)	4.050.147 (2)	3.811.513 (3)	- (15)
Produktion - Personenkfz - Nutzkraftwagen insgesamt:	6.781.184 3.148.217 (4) 9.929.401	8.184.821 3.463.406 11.648.227	6.823.097 4.024.530 10.847.627	6.613.983 5.648.767 12.262.750	5.637.089 6.959.027 12.596.116
- davon japanische Werke	55.335 (5)	189.147 (6)	694.359 (7)	1.511.732 (8)	1.673.120 plus 432.882 (9)
Ausfuhr -davon Kanada -übrige Welt	560.022 522.802 37.220	707.247 676.180 31.067	929.519 569.893 359.623	1.052.690 487.667 565.023	905.410 (15) 583.999
Japan					
Einfuhr Wert (10)	623.056	921.631	3.654.500	7.219.035	5.206.423
Einfuhr Stück	37.478	52.673	195.312	295,476	268,795
Produktion	7.073.173	7.646.816	9.052.406	7,801,317	8.100.169
Ausfuhr	3.946.975	4.887.985	4.776.658	3.572.772	4.101.097
Frankreich					
Einfuhr Wert (10)	5.173.673	6.051.036	11.180.019	12.605.537	14.414.815
Einfuhr Stück	995.519	1.020.957	1.382.747	1.230.776	1.393.833
Produktion	2.960.823	2.632.366	3.409.017	3.175.213	2.784.469
Ausfuhr	1.248.708	1.251.518	1.513.287	1.415.977	1.971.030
England					
Einfuhr Wert (10)	5.935.501 (11)	8.021.858 (12)	14.297.368	17.751.078 (11)	22.568.800
Einfuhr Stück	1.077.792	1.070.873	1.416.694	1.133.667	1.601.176
Produktion	1.044.597	1.047.973	1.299.082	1,475,549	1.786.623
Ausfuhr	279.296	249.880	394.969	640.085	1.028.742
Italien					
Einfuhr Wert (10)	3.818.364	6.099.142	11.278.499	15.082.312	14.770.763 (13)
Einfuhr Stück	660.041	869.225	1.197.133	1.133.667	1.673.603
Produktion	1.395.531	1.389.156	1.971.969	1.340.878	1.378.106
Ausfuhr	486.299	467.550	1.752.041	771.771	733.974
Deutschland					
Einfuhr Wert (10)	7.366.332	8.146.174	13.093.448	18.879.016	20.041.018 (13)
Einfuhr Stück	1.072.303	1.084.398	1.361.631	1.623.015	2.016.041
Produktion	3.877.641	4.166.686	4.563.673	4.093.685	5.348.115
Ausfuhr	2.606.530	2.914.225	2.987.574	2.492.988	3.543.679

(1) Abgrenzung SITC Rev. 2, 781.0 – 0.10, 020, 030, 040. (2) Abgrenzung HS, (3) Wieder SITC, diesmal Rev. 3, Abgrenzung für Personenwagen 7812-0. (4) Nutzkraftwagen werden hier zusätzlich aufgeführt, weil in dieser Sparte Jeeps und Pickups enthalten sein dürften, die als Personenkraftwagen genutzt werden. (5) Im Jahre 1983 produziert allein Honda Personenkraftwaren. Nissan wird mit 19.979 Einheiten in der Sparte der Nutzfahrzeuge erstmals geführt. (6) Honda und Nissan. (7) Zahl für Honda, Nissan, Mazda ohne die beiden Toyota/GM-Joint Ventures, die 343.390 Einheiten herstellen. (8) Diesmal Honda, Nissan, Toyota, Auto Alliance (Mazda/Ford), Subaru, ohne Toyota/GM mit 114.576 Einheiten. (9) Honda, Mitsubishi, Nissan, Toyota, SIA (Subaru/Isuzu), ohne

Joint Veture von Toyota/GM mit 160.144 Einheiten. Die zusätzliche Zahl bezieht die japanische Produktion von Nutzfahrzeugen, diesmal als Light Trucks bezeichnet mit ein. (11) Währungsumrechnungzahlen von 1991, 19 August. (12) Währungsumrechungszahlen von 1992, 19 August. Umrechungen nach: http://www.oanda.com/converter/classic (13) Euro 2001, 19 August. (15) U.S.-Daten für 1999.

	1983	1985	1989	1994	1998
Spanien					
Einfuhr Stück	69.584	44.923	379.984	519.722	871.841
Produktion	1.414.581	1.230.071	1.638.615	1.821.696	2.216.386
Ausfuhr	703.167	707.510	958.178	1.649.325	1.919.387
Portugal					
Einfuhr Stück	97.777	103.948 (4)	162.147	216.023	278.574
Produktion	65.903 (1)	60.975	73.181 (3)	37.754	181.388 (2)
Ausfuhr	16.061	16.344	45.124	29.498	176.606
Brasilien					
Einfuhr Stück	-		-	-	-
Produktion	774.012	776.890	730.992	1.248.773	1.254.016
Ausfuhr	-		-	-	-
Korea					
Einfuhr Stück	-	-	-	8.643	-
Produktion	121.987	264.458	871.898	1.805.895	1.625.125
Ausfuhr	-	-	-	342.294	1.228.144
Indien					
Einfuhr Stück	-	-	-	-	-
Produktion	66.575	129.332	214.993	298.044	457.819
Ausfuhr	-	-	-	-	-

(1) Eingetragen als Montage. (2) Autoeuropa VW und Ford; Citroen, Renault seit 1996 Produktion; Opel, Montage.
(3) Auf und Ab liegt an Renault und seiner Montage. (4) Zahlen für 1985.

Tabelle 85: Die Weltproduktion von Automobilen und Lkw nach Regionen 2004. Daten CCFA 2006.
Erwähnt in Abschnitt 'D', 258.

Zonen	Nord-amerika	Südamerika	EU-15	Europa andere u.a. Türkei	Japan	Korea	andere Länder: Asien, Afrika	Total
Produzenten	Tausend							
Europäische Produzenten	3.267	1.376	11.697	1.671	119	81	1.272	19.483
Anteil der gesamten Produktion	17 %	7 %	60 %	9 %	1 %	0 %	7 %	100 %
BMW	143		1.063				44	1.250
FIAT-IVECO Irisbus		444	1119	452			105	2.120
Irisbus			4	2				6
MAN			68	2				70
Daimler-chrysler	2.834	68	1.543	12	119		53	4.628
Porsche			84					84
PSA Peugeot Citroen		118	2.871	17			399	3405
Renault Dacia Samsung	12	120	1.829	424		81	6	2.472
MG Rover			106					106
Scania	1	14	44					59
VW	225	603	2.842	761			664	5.095
Volvo	52	9	129	1				191
Amerikanische Produzenten	8.857	965	3.927	401	0	0	811	14.962
Anteil der gesamten Produktion	59 %	6 %	26 %	3 %	0 %	0 %	5 %	100 %
FORD	3.522	346	2.207	230			338	6.644
GM	5.134	619	1.670	171			473	8.067
Navistar	126							126
PACCAR	75		50					125
Japanische Produzenten	4.191	185	1.216	231	10.390	1	3.911	20.124
Anteil der gesamten Produktion	21 %	1 %	6 %	1 %	52 %	0 %	19 %	100 %
DAIHATSU			7		679		279	965
FUJI HEAVY (Subaru)	109				492		1	601
Hino				1	94			95
HONDA	1.235	62	191	16	1.243		491	3237
ISUZU	17	14		4	218		247	500
MAZDA	97	6			819	1	353	1.275
MITSUBISHI	104	21	88		640		575	1.429
NISSAN	1.080		463		1.439		209	3.190
NISSAN Diesel					40			40
Susuki - Maruti	5		16	73	1.046		837	1.977
Toyota	1.544	82	451	137	3.681		919	6.815
Koreanische Produzenten	0	32	0	247	0	3200	330	3.810
Anteil der gesamten Produktion	0 %	1 %	0 %	6 %	0 %	84 %	9 %	100 %
GM DAEWOO		24		155		555	165	899
Hyundai-Kia		8		92		2506	160	2.766
Ssangyong		0	0			139	5	144
Alle Produzenten	16.265	2.562	16.854	3.975	10.512	3.469	10.528	64.165
Anteil an der gesamten Produktion	25 %	4 %	26 %	6 %	16 %	5 %	16 %	100 %

Tabelle 86: Minimum Efficient Scale in Different Parts of the Auto Industry.
In: Nolan 2001: 503.
Erwähnt in Abschnitt 'D', 258.

Acitivty	Volume required to achieve minimum unit costs
Casting engine blocks	1 million
Casting other parts	100 000 - 750 000
Power train machining/assembly	600 000
Axle making/assembly	500 000
Pressing various panels	1- 2 million
Painting	250 000
Final assembly	250 000
Advertising	1 million
Finance	2-5 million
R & D	5 million

Tabelle 87: Ausmaß von Betriebsgrößenvorteilen und Anbieterkonzentration in 18 Branchen. Aus: Monopolkommission, 6. Hauptgutachten, 1984/1985: 231-269. In: Schmidt 1996a: 87.
Erwähnt in Abschnitt 'D', 258, Abschnitt E', 358.

Produktgruppe	Mindestoptimale Betriebsgröße (MOTB) Produktionmenge/Jahr	Herstellstückkostennachteil bei einem Drittel des MOTB	Technisch bedingte Konzentration		Tatsächliche Konzentration: Anteil der drei größten Anbieter	
			Anteil eines MOTB-Anbieters 1984 (%)	Anteil von drei MOTB-Anbieter 1984 in %	am Produktionswert der Güterklasse 1984 (%)	an der Produktionsmenge der Produktgruppe 1984 (%)
PKW	500 Tsd. Einheiten/Jahr	hoch	14	42	64,2	64,8
LKW	200 Tsd. Einheiten/Jahr	hoch	100	>100	91,3-97,6	97,9
Ackerschlepper	100-120 Tsd. Einheiten/Jahr	hoch	>100	>100	69,9	-
Mähdrescher	20 Tsd. Einheiten/Jahr	mittel	>100	>100	-	100
Motorräder	200 Tsd. Einheiten/Jahr	-	>100	>100	-	100
Kühl-/Gefrierschränke	1,5 Mill. Einheiten/Jahr	hoch	56	>100	69,5	-
Reifen	9 Mio. Stück/Jahr	mittel	25	75	60,5	-
Unterhaltungselektronik						
-Farbfernsehgeräte	1,3-2,2 Mio. Stück/Jahr	gering	33-56	100	38,2	-
-Videorecorder	0,8-1,0 Mio. Stück/Jahr	-	62-77	>100	-	-
Digitale Telefonvermittlungseinrichtungen	0,4-0,5 Mio. Anschlußeinheiten/Jahr	mittel	11-17	33-51	69,7	-
Elektronische Schreibmaschinen	500 Tsd. Stück/Jahr	mittel	70	>100	99,0	100
Mineralölprodukte	10 Mio. t/Jahr	gering	14	42	43,6-61,7	-
Chemische Grundstoffe						
-Äthylen	0,5 Mio. t/Jahr	mittel	16	48	46,0	-
-Ammoniak	0,55 Mio. t/Jahr	mittel	28	87	89,0	-
-Schwefelsäure	0,35 Mio. t/Jahr	mittel	12	36	45,8	-
Stahl						
-intergriertes Hüttenwerk	9,6-12 Mio. t/Jahr	hoch	31	93	47,9-62,5	-
-Ministahlwerk	0,7-0,8 Mio. t/Jahr	hoch	2	6	-	-

Zement	1,3 Mio. t/Jahr	hoch	5	15	47,6	-
Bier	2,8 Mio. hl/Jahr	mittel	3	9	11,5	-
Zigaretten	70 Mrd. Stück/Jahr	gering	44	>100	62,0	-
Tiefdruck-erzeugnisse	-	gering	-	-	-	-
Regionale Abonnementstages-zeitungen	150-180 Tsd. Exemplare/Tag	hoch	-	-	-	-

Der Herstellstückkostennachteil wird als gering, mittel bzw. hoch bezeichnet, wenn er unter 5 %, zwischen 5 und 10 % bzw. über 10 % liegt.

Tabelle 88: Growing chemicals consumption. EUR bn.
In: Perlitz 2005: 2.
Erwähnt in Abschnitt 'D', 262.

	China	Germany	EU-25	World
1994	50	90	343	1,147
1995	58	93	363	1,190
1996	67	89	366	1,219
1997	81	93	389	1,282
1998	81	95	394	1,344
1999	93	100	409	1,453
2000	129	111	467	1,788
2001	139	110	479	1,802
2002	149	109	480	1,786
2003	157	109	486	1,697
2004	162	110	514	1,766

Source: VCI.

Tabelle 89: The 30 Top Chemical companies in the world, share in sales.
In: CEFIC 1998: 13.
Erwähnt in Abschnitt 'D', 263.

		Worldwide sales		Share of world chemicals sales
Based in	Number	In bn ECU	In %	
EU	15	189	54%	15%
other w. Europe	3	36	10%	3&
USA	8	94	27%	8%
Japan	3	26	7%	2%
other	1	6	2%	0%
Total	**30**	**351**	**100%**	**29%**

Tabelle 90: The 30 Top Chemical companies in the world. In: CEFIC 1998: 14. *Erwähnt in Abschnitt 'D', 263.*

	Company	1997 worldwide sales	
		In mio ECU	In mio USD
1.	**BASF**	**28 360**	**32 169**
2.	**Bayer**	**27 966**	**31 722**
3.	**Hoechst**	**26 489**	**30 046**
4.	Du Pont	21 237	24 089
5.	Merck	20 838	23 637
6.	**Novartis**	**18 957**	**21 503**
7.	Dow	17 648	20 018
8.	**ICI**	**15 961**	**18 105**
9.	**Rhône-Poulenc**	**13 587**	**15 412**
10.	Mitsubishi Chem	12 630	14 326
11.	**Shell**	**12 556**	**14 242**
12.	**Roche**	**11 410**	**12 942**
13.	**Akzo Nobel**	**10 869**	**12 328**
14.	Exxon	10 751	12 195
15.	**Elf Atochem**	**8 760**	**9 936**
16.	**Solvay**	**7 666**	**8 696**
17.	**Zeneca**	**7 494**	**8 501**
18.	Sumitomo Chem	7 434	8 433
19.	Monsanto	6 624	7 514
20.	**Henkel**	**6 212**	**7 046**
21.	**Norsk Hydro**	**5 986**	**6 790**
22.	**Huls**	**5 953**	**6 752**
23.	General Electric	5 881	6 671
24.	Showa Denko	5 812	6 593
25.	**Air Liquide**	**5 797**	**6 576**
26.	Union Carbide	5 732	6 502
27.	**BOC**	**5 719**	**6 487**
28.	SABIC	5 647	6 405
29.	**DSM**	**5 606**	**6 358**
30.	Amoco	5 238	5 941

Sources: Chemical Insight & CEFIC-Ecostat analysis.
 List of 30 top chemical companies reproduced with the kind permission of Reed Business Publishing - Chemical Insight, but adjusted by using average rather than year end exchange rates.

Tabelle 91: Geographic breakdown of world chemicals production. In: CEFIC 1998: 1.
Erwähnt in Abschnitt 'D', 263.

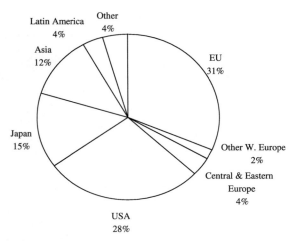

Production 1997: 1223 bn ECU

Sources: ESCIMO, UNIDO Industrial Statistics & CEFIC-Ecostat analysis.
Notes: Estimated world production; estimates for all regions except EU, USA & Japan.
Other = Africa, Oceania, Canada, Turkey, Malta & other Balkan States.
(*) Strictly speaking, value of production sold, augmented by value of sales of products purchased and resold in their original condition.

Tabelle 92: World Production of Ethylene, Selected Countries, 1989-1996 (millions tons). In: Nolan 2001: 451.
Erwähnt in Abschnitt 'D', 263.

Country	1989	1996	Increase 1989-96	(%)
USA	15.9	22.3	6.4	(40)
Japan	5.6	7.2	1.6	(29)
Germany	3.0	3.8	0.8	(27)
Korea	0.7	4.0	3.3	(571)
France	2.5	2.7	0.2	(8)
Canada	2.3	3.2	0.9	(39)
China	1.4	3.0	1.6	(114)

Tabelle 93: Synthetic Fibre Production Capacity, Selected Countries, 1989-96 (million tons). In: Nolan 2001: 451.
Erwähnt in Abschnitt 'D', 263.

Country	1989	1996	Increase 1989-96	(%)
World	18.0	24.2	6.2	(34)
USA	3.5	3.7 (1995)	0.2	(6)
Japan	1.8	1.9	0.1	(6)
Korea	1.2	2.0	0.8	(67)
Taiwan	1.7	2.5	0.8	(47)
China	1.3	3.2	1.9	(146)

Tabelle 94: World Production of Plastics, Selected Countries, 1989-96 (million tons). In: Nolan 2001: 451.
Erwähnt in Abschnitt 'D', 263.

Country	1989	1996	Increase 1989-96	(%)
World	95.2	129.4	34.2	(36)
USA	26.5	38.6	12.1	(46)
Japan	11.9	14.7	2.8	(24)
Germany	9.1	10.9	1.8	(20)
Korea	2.5	7.7	5.2	(208)
Taiwan	2.5	4.6	2.1	(84)
Netherlands	3.3	4.2	0.9	(27)
Belgium	2.8	4.6	1.8	(64)
France	4.3	5.2	0.9	(21)
China	2.2	3.6	1.4	(64)

Tabelle 95: World network of major chemicals trade flows. In: CEFIC 1998: 2.
Erwähnt in Abschnitt 'D', 263.

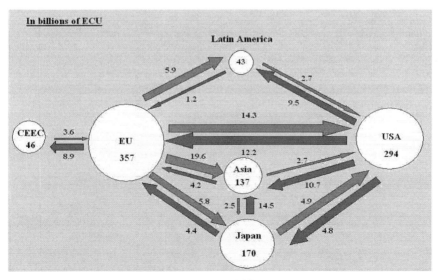

Tabelle 96: Recent Steel Market Statistics and Outlook. Crude Steel Production, Million tonnes. In: OECD 2004a: 6.
Erwähnt in Abschnitt 'D', 264, 265.

	1998	1999	2000	2001	2002	2003	2004	2005
USA	98.7	97.4	101.8	90.1	92.2	90.4	91.0	95.5
Canada	15.8	16.1	16.5	15.2	15.9	15.8	16.1	16.3
Mexico	14.2	15.3	15.6	13.3	14.1	15.2	14.7	14.8
EU 15	159.9	155.2	163.4	158.5	158.7	160.3	163.2	166.5
other Europe	39.1	36.6	39.9	39.3	41.0	44.3	47.4	47.6
Japan	93.6	94.2	106.4	102.9	107.8	110.5	109.8	108.0
Korea	39.9	41.0	43.1	43.9	45.4	46.3	47.3	49.2
Australia and N-Z	9.7	9.0	7.8	7.9	8.3	8.4	8.9	8.9
North America	128.7	128.9	133.9	118.6	122.2	121.4	121.8	126.6
Europe	199.0	191.8	203.3	197.8	199.7	204.7	210.6	214.1
Pacific Area	143.2	144.2	157.4	154.6	161.4	165.2	166.1	166.2
Total OECD	470.8	464.9	494.5	471.0	483.3	491.2	498.5	506.8
Brazil	25.8	25.0	27.9	26.7	29.6	31.2	32.2	31.5
other Latin America	11.5	10.7	12.6	11.8	12.6	13.3	13.4	13.4
Latin America	37.2	35.7	40.5	38.6	42.2	44.4	45.7	44.9
India	23.5	24.3	26.9	27.3	28.8	31.8	32.8	33.9
ASEAN (5)	7.8	8.3	9.6	9.9	10.6	11.2	12.0	12.7
Other Asia	18.2	16.7	18.2	18.8	19.7	20.3	19.2	19.5
total other Asia	49.5	49.3	54.8	56.0	59.1	63.3	64.0	66.1
Middle East	13.1	13.7	14.7	16.3	17.7	18.6	19.4	20.4
Other Africa	1.1	1.4	1.4	1.4	1.5	1.4	1.3	1.4
South Africa	8.0	7.9	8.5	8.8	9.1	9.5	9.3	9.5
Total Africa	9.1	9.2	9.9	10.2	10.6	10.9	10.6	10.9
Non-OECD economies	108.9	107.9	119.8	121.1	129.6	137.1	139.7	142.3
CEEC (2)	8.6	6.2	6.8	7.0	7.4	7.6	7.9	8.0
Russia	43.8	51.5	59.4	59.0	59.8	62.7	64.6	67.2
Ukraine	24.5	27.5	31.8	33.1	34.1	36.9	39.3	39.9
Other NIS	6.2	7.2	8.1	8.1	7.8	8.4	10.7	12.5
N.I.S.	74.4	86.1	99.3	100.1	101.6	108.0	114.6	119.5
NIS & CEEC	83.0	92.4	106.1	107.1	109.0	115.6	122.5	127.5
China	114.6	124.0	127.2	150.9	181.6	220.1	255.0	288.7
World	777.4	789.1	847.6	850.0	903.4	964.1	1015.6	1065.4

Tabelle 97: Total Exports and Imports of Steel 2003. Thousand tonnes. Modifiziert aus: OECD 2005b: 24-25.
Erwähnt in Abschnitt 'D', 264.

Countries	Exports	Imports
Germany	24430	17840
Austria	5652	3259
Belgium	16023	10532
Denmark	1102	2867
Spain	6733	12185
Finland	3696	1337
France	17343	14858
Greece	727	2584
Ireland	80	1033
Italy	11707	17654
Luxembourg	4479	2565
Netherlands	8400	6115
Portugal	954	3075
United Kingdom	7326	8191
Sweden	4352	3303
EU (15) total	113205	107930
Norway	914	1305
Switzerland	1190	2075
Turkey	..	..
Hungary	..	..
Poland	3666	3482
Czech Republic	4042	1046
Slovac Republic	4572	3028
Other OECD Europe total	14384	10936
OECD Europe total	127589	118866
Canada	5103	6578
Mexico	5141	6256
United States	7620	21443
Japan	34461	5954
Australia	2831	1657
Korea	14118	15583
OECD total	196863	176337
Brazil	12985	550
Bulgaria	1707	646
India	4252	1460
Romania	3273	1178
Russia	33169	3717
Ukraine	...	...

Tabelle 98: Steel: World Exports, Imports, and Trade Balance. 1980-88 (In million of ingot tons equivalent). Aus: IMF 1988: 159.
Erwähnt in Abschnitt 'D', 264.

	1980	1982	1983	1984	1985	1986	1987	1988 (1)
Exports								
OECD	103.0	96.7	101.2	111.7	115.4	100.4	98.1	...
United States	4.8	2.3	1.5	1.1	1.1	1.2	1.4	1.5
European Community (10)	36.6	33.9	34.5	40.1	...	...	...	...
European Community (12)	...	...	...	...	50.0	39.7	39.9	40.0
Japan	38.6	37.2	40.1	41.2	41.0	37.3	32.8	31.8
Canada	...	4.6	3.5	4.0	4.1	4.5	5.2	...
Australia. New Zealand	...	1.8	1.7	1.3	2.0	2.0	2.1	...
Other OECD	23.0	16.9	19.9	24.0	17.2	15.7	16.7	...
Developing countries	36.9	19.4	23.2	23.3	25.3	24.3	26.2	...
Others (2)	...	23.2	27.4	28.3	33.1	35.8	34.2	...
World	139.9	139.3	151.8	163.3	173.8	160.4	158.5	...
Imports								
OECD	52.4	52.6	53.7	68.0	63.7	61.1	65.2	...
United States	17.9	19.3	19.7	30.3	28.1	23.9	23.5	24.0
European Community (10)	13.5	13.0	13.0	12.5	...	...	...	...
European Community (12)	...	...	...	...	12.1	14.2	13.7	14.2
Japan	1.5	2.6	3.6	5.2	3.8	4.3	6.5	7.5
Canada	...	1.4	1.6	2.5	3.1	2.8	3.9	...
Australia. New Zealand	...	1.7	1.4	1.8	1.7	1.6	1.8	...
Other OECD	19.5	14.5	14.4	15.7	14.9	14.3	15.8	...
Developing countries	84.9	57.2	54.6	51.4	52.6	45.6	46.7	...
Others (2)	...	30.0	39.4	41.3	56.6	52.7	44.7	...
World	137.3	139.8	147.7	160.7	172.8	159.4	156.6	...
Net exports								
OECD	50.6	44.1	47.5	43.7	51.7	39.3	32.9	31.5
United States	-13.1	-17.0	-18.2	-29.2	-0.27	-22.1	-22.1	-22.5
European Community (10)	23.1	20.9	21.5	27.6	-	-	....	-
European Community (12)	...	...	...	...	38.0	25.5	26.2	25.8
Japan	37.1	34.6	36.5	36.0	37.2	33.0	26.3	24.3
Canada	-	3.2	1.9	1.5	1.0	1.7	1.3	1.3
Australia. New Zealand	-	0.1	0.3	-0.5	0.3	0.4	0.3	0.4
Other OECD	3.5	2.4	5.5	8.3	2.3	1.4	0.9	2.2
Developing countries	-40.6	-37.8	-31.4	-28.1	-27.3	-21.3	-20.5	-18.4
Others (2) (3)	-10.0	-6.3	-12.0	-13.0	-23.5	-17.0	-10.5	-11.1

(1) OECD Projections
(2) Includes South Africa. U.S.S.R. other East European Countries. China. and the Democratic Peoples's Republic of Korea (North Korea).
(3) Includes small amounts from unspecified sources for 1980 and 1982.

Tabelle 99: Top Ten World Steel Producers in 2001. In: Stikova/Maug 2004: Exibit 2. Erwähnt in Abschnitt 'D', 264, 265.

Rang	Group	Production (mt)	Market Share (%)	Country
1	Acerlor	45	5,3	France/Lux./Spain
2	Posco	29	3,4	South Korea
3	Nippon Steel	29	3,4	Japan
4	NKK/Kawasaki	24	2,8	Japan
5	LNM	22	2,6	Great Britan
6	Corus	18	2,1	Great Britan
7	Thyssen Krupp	18	2,1	Germany
8	Shanghai Baosteel	20	2,4	China
9	Riva	16	1,9	Italy
10	US Steel	11	1,3	United States
		232	27,3	

Tabelle 100: Evolution of 3-firm concentration ratios, 1962-1990. Aus: De Jong 1993: 10-11. Erwähnt in Abschnitt 'D', 264.

	Industry	Number of firms (a)	1962	1967	1972	1977	1982	1989	1990	Industry growth
1	Aerospace	15	42,7	40,7	35,5	39,4	37,3	36,6	41,1	strong
2	Electronics	20	41,8	38,2	35,2	35,4	28,8	32,0	30,2	very strong
3	Pharmaceuticals	20	48,6	35,2	30,2	32,8	31,8	27,5	30,9	very strong
4	Chemicals	20	32,7	29,1	24,8	26,4	27,7	31,8	33,8	slow since 70s
5	Motorvehicles (incl. components)	20	66,7	63,2	56,2	50,5	41,3	43,2	40,3	very slow in 80s
6	Industrial & farm equipment	20	34,7	32,2	32,1	29,6	24,0	32,7	34,0	stagnant, decline
7	Metalproducts & manufacturing	20	31,7	29,1	27,1	27,3	31,4	35,4	35,5	average growth
8	Paper & wood products	19	29,5	27,1	26,6	28,6	26,3	25,8	30,0	below average
9	Food	20	38,8	36,3	34,6	34,9	35,1	37,8	41,7	below average since 70s
10	Drinks	9	50,0	47,3	52,0	52,8	53,2	51,6	54,4	below average since 70s
11	Tobacco	9	58,2	57,0	56.2	59,8	68,9	74,0	75,0	decline, stagnant

(a) Bezug ist hier nicht etwa der weltweite Output in diesen Bereichen oder der Konsum, sondern es geht um die Anteile der 3 größten Firmen innerhalb der Gruppe größerer Firmen, deren Anzahl in dieser Spalte angegeben ist.

Tabelle 101: Production Costs of Boninas Laminada a Frio, Selected Countries, April 2001 (US$/dispatched tons). In: Ferraz et al. 2003: 27.
Erwähnt in Abschnitt 'D', 266.

	USA	Japan	Germany	UK	S. Korea	China	Brazil
Raw materials	115	106	109	105	112	118	103
Coal	27	27	26	24	28	28	37
Iron ore	55	56	62	58	59	75	40
Scrap / DRI	33	26	21	23	25	15	26
Other raw materials	172	150	148	153	134	152	135
Labour costs	154	142	136	113	62	26	57
Hourly wage	38	36	34	27,6	13	1,25	10,5
Total operational costs	441	398	392	371	308	297	295
Financial costs	39	60	40	46	42	50	67
Depreciation	29	40	30	26	30	30	32
Interest	10	20	10	20	12	10	35
Total cost	480	458	432	417	350	297	362

Tabelle 102: Ausfuhr von Maschinenbauerzeugnissen ausgewählter Länder.
In: Weiß 2005: 10.
Erwähnt in Abschnitt 'D', 267.

	In Mill. US$ zu jeweiligen Preise und Wechselkursen			Welthandelsanteil in %			Jährliche Veränderung in %		
	1991	1995	2000	1991	1995	2000	1991-1995	1995-2000	1991-2000
EU-Länder	181 403	236 754	234 754	57,7	55,7	50,8	5,5	-0,2	4,1
Belgien/ Luxemburg	6 346	10 157	13 094	2,0	2,4	2,8	11,4	5,7	9,1
Dänemark	4 824	6 445	5 467	1,5	1,5	1,2	5,5	-3,2	1,9
Deutschland	67 906	83 546	77 865	21,6	19,6	16,9	3,7	-1,1	2,7
Griechenland	110	299	372	0,0	0,1	0,1	28,2	3,9	14,9
Spanien	4 492	6 460	7 573	1,4	1,5	1,6	7,6	3,0	7,8
Frankreich	18 941	25 927	24 723	6,0	6,1	5,4	6,6	-0,3	4,3
Irland	1 261	1 545	1 532	0,4	0,4	0,3	4,3	-0,4	4,0
Italien	33 109	45 568	46 063	10,5	10,7	10,0	7,4	-0,6	5,0
Niederlande	8 456	9 534	9 432	2,7	2,2	2,0	1,5	-0,7	1,5
Österreich	6 494	8 199	8 084	2,1	1,9	1,8	4,6	0,5	3,2
Portugal	675	963	1 296	0,2	0,2	0,3	6,7	6,4	8,3
Finnland	2 573	4 599	4 697	0,8	1,1	1,0	15,0	-0,5	8,4
Schweden	7 121	9 403	10 041	2,3	2,2	2,2	6,4	1,0	5,2
Großbritannien	19 097	24 110	24 145	6,1	5,7	5,2	5,1	-0,2	4,7
USA	45 055	64 376	86 108	14,3	15,1	18,7	9,3	4,8	7,7
Japan	44 381	68 036	67 341	14,1	16,0	14,6	11,0	-1,9	3,3
Summe	270 840	369 166	387 833	86,1	86,8	84,1	7,1	0,5	4,7
OECD	291 110	399 689	421 710	92,6	94,0	91,4	7,3	0,6	4,8
Welt (1)	314 503	425 404	461 288	100,0	100,0	100,0	6,9	1,1	5,0

(1) Berechnet als Importe der OECD aus allen Ländern plus Exporte der OECD Länder in die Nicht-OECD Länder (OECD nach dem Stand von 1993). Quelle: DIW Außenhandelsdaten.

Tabelle 103: U.S. imports for consumption, by principal source, 1991 and 2000 (in thousand dollars). In: USITC 2002: 20.
Erwähnt in Abschnitt 'D', 271.

Country	1991	Country	2000
Japan	1,845,190	Canada	9,065,413
Canada	694,421	Mexico	5,863,411
Malaysia	506,944	Japan	3,646,647
China	487,895	China	3,312,227
Singapore	280,556	Korea	3,182,509
Taiwan	273,796	Malaysia	2,019,019
Korea	271,263	Taiwan	1,891,293
Thailand	225,416	United Kingdom	914,119
Sweden	181,298	Israel	889,332
Hong Kong	176,646	Sweden	663,644
Israel	127,690	Thailand	487,402
Mexico	124,785	France	379,414
France	105,170	Germany	379,030
United Kingdom	101,471	Brazil	342,667
Philippines	93,678	Singapore	336,729
All other	250,709	All other	1,095,508
Total	5,746,928	Total	34,468,392
EU 15	554,461	EU 15	2,858,934

Tabelle 104: Semiconductors: U.S. imports for consumption, by principal source, 1991 and 2000 (in thousand dollars). In: USITC 2002: 34.
Erwähnt in Abschnitt 'D', 271.

Country	1991	Country	2000
Japan	3,574,552	Japan	8,044,785
Korea	1,778,542	Korea	7,478,707
Malaysia	1,584,345	Malaysia	6,296,658
Canada	1,419,743	Philippines	5,531,519
Singapore	1,172,933	Taiwan	5,073,665
Taiwan	672,819	Singapore	3,316,451
Philippines	650,286	Canada	2,110,235
Thailand	382,477	Mexico	1,511,219
Mexico	333,612	Thailand	1,394,727
Hong Kong	276,253	Hong Kong	1,275,654
Germany	253,775	Germany	798,504
United Kingdom	228,211	China	716,081
Israel	143,980	France	572,080
France	117,215	Israel	497,653
Ireland	74,516	United Kingdom	480,285
All other	264,881	All other	2,449,499
Total	12,928,139	Total	47,447,721
EU 15	838,603	EU 15	3,030,507

Tabelle 105: Trade in Computers, selected countries, 2004. Source: UN Comtrade Database. Computers are SITC Rev. 2 - 752, including peripherals, data for Taiwan not available.
Erwähnt in Abschnitt 'D', 273, 277.

Countries	Exports (US$ Mill.) Value	Share	Imports (US$ Mill.) Value	Share
China	59 991	24 %	14 456	5 %
USA	24 048	9 %	60 782	23 %
Germany	18 434	7 %	21 263	8 %
Singapore	15 859	6 %	4 984	1 %
Malaysia	12 080	4 %	2 220	> 1
Mexico	10 882	4%	6 240	2 %
Korea	10 148	4 %	3 445	1 %
United Kingdom	9 465	3 %	17 904	6 %
Japan	8 453	3 %	17 617	6 %
China Hongkong	6 872	2 %	7 441	2 %
France	5 085	2 %	11 428	4 %
Indonesia	1 517	> 1	291	> 1
Brazil	237	> 1	763	> 1
Israel	206	> 1	906	> 1
Indien	126	> 1	1 471	> 1
Argentine	10	> 1	509	> 1
Total	244 631		258 991	

Tabelle 106: Computer Equipment: U.S. Imports for Consumption, by principal source 1991 and 2000 (thousand dollars). In: USITC 2002: 14.
Erwähnt in Abschnitt 'D', 275, 276.

Country	1991	Country	2000
Japan	9,497,727	Japan	14,502,522
Singapore	4,493,528	Taiwan	10,682,035
Taiwan	3,587,818	China	10,618,332
Canada	2,140,485	Singapore	10,092,690
Korea	1,203,008	Mexico	9,042,814
United Kingdom	912,292	Malaysia	8,149,368
Hong Kong	690,904	Korea	7,769,765
Mexico	655,360	Canada	3,741,679
Germany	557,466	Philippines	2,917,725
Thailand	534,229	Thailand	2,738,624
Malaysia	409,375	United Kingdom	2,100,670
Ireland	400,566	Ireland	1,458,084
France	241,975	Hungary	1,262,752
China	193,969	Costa Rica	835,842
Isreal	118,299	Germany	747.822
All other	634,827	All other	3,603,374
Total	26,271,428	Total	90,264,419
EU 15	2,488,420	EU 15	5,986,205

Tabelle 107: Budget authority for R&D by function and character of work: Anticipated levels for FY 1998. Aus: http://www.nsf.gov/sbe/srs/.
Erwähnt in Abschnitt 'D', 283.

Budge Function	Basic research	Applied research	Development	R&D total
		Millions of dollar		
Total	15,710	15,570	42,359	73,639
National Defense	1,099	4,308	34,463	39,871
Nondefense (total)	14,611	11,261	7,895	33,768
Health	7,361	4,618	1,578	13,557
Space research and technology	1,658	1,591	5,015	8,265
Energy	257	370	516	1,143
General science	3,944	266	0	4,210
National resources and environment	156	1,667	191	2,015
Transportation	459	1,258	203	1,920
Agriculture	560	589	94	1,243
All other	216	902	297	1,415

Tabelle 108: Preliminary federal obligation for research and development and for R&D plant, by agency, category, and performer: FY 2000. Aus: http://www.nsf.gov/sbe/srs/
Erwähnt in Abschnitt 'D', 283.

Agency and category	Performer							
	Total performers	Federal intramural	Federal extramural					
			Industrial firms	Universities and colleges	All FFRDCs	Other nonprofits	State and local governments	Foreign
Agency	(In millions of current dollars)							
Total	77,186	18,118	32,157	15,339	7,407	3,483	422	260
DoD	34,475	7,906	24,254	1,383	670	134	4	123
HHS	16,361	3,406	885	9,208	256	2,386	172	49
NASA	9,695	2,356	4,735	787	1,389	370	13	47
DOE	7,458	667	1,226	648	4,868	46	3	1
NSF	2,890	23	158	2,329	189	175	4	11
USDA	1,709	1,211	11	475	0	7	1	4
All other	4,597	2,549	888	509	36	366	224	25
Category								
Development	77,186	18,118	32,157	15,339	7,407	3,483	422	260
Total research	40,425	8,866	26,930	1,769	1,935	711	75	138
Basic research	34,680	8,776	4,710	13,422	4,543	2,762	346	122
Applied research	18,209	3,336	1,440	9,227	2,437	1,624	88	58
R&D plant	16,470	5,440	3,270	4,195	2,106	1,138	258	64
	2,081	477	517	147	929	10	1	0

FFRDCs: Federally Funded Reseach and Development Centers; DoD: Department of Defense; HHS: U.S. Department of Health and Human Services; NASA: National Aeronautics and Space Agency; DOE: Department of the Environment; NSF: National Science Foundation; USDA: United States Department of Agriculture.

Tabelle 109: Textiles MFA quota shares US. Aus: Erzan/Holmes 1990: 198, 209.
Erwähnt in Abschnitt 'D', 288, Abschnitt 'F', 448, Abschnitt 'G', 547, 553, 561, 584, 629, Abschnitt 'I', 886.

Exporter	1986-88 average quota growth rate	1986-88 average quota growth rate	1988 actual quota share
Argentina	n.a.	n.a.	n.a.
Bangladesh	93,9	15,8	1,29
Brasil	60,6	9,8	2,35
China	94,6	9,3	11,72
Egypt	93,7	18,5	2,11
Hong Kong	93,3	3,0	11,21
India	96,1	13,6	2,34
Indonesia	94,7	-16,7	1,62
Korea, Rep. of	86,5	4,9	11,39
Macao	72,7	5,0	1,50
Malaysia	60,7	32,1	3,66
Mauritius	80,2	13,2	0,41
Mexico	55,3	10,0	6,65
Nepal	49,8	6,0	0,17
Pakistan	82,3	-1,3	3,81
Peru	19,0	1,9	1,06
Philippines	79,4	10,2	3,63
Romania	43,9	0,2	1,53
Singapore	67,0	1,8	2,98
Sri Lanka	92,4	-24,8	0,82
Taiwan (China)	82,0	5,2	13,39
Thailand	78,4	6,5	2,86
Turkey	95,4	4,7	0,69
Uruguay	77,9	-5,1	0,06
Yugoslavia	87,4	2,1	0,65
Guam			0,05
Trinidad & Tobago			0,31
Poland			1,29
Panama			0,05
Japan			5,63
Burma			0,05
Haiti			0,74
Jamaica			1,52
Columbia			0,05
Pakistan			3,81
Hungary			0,32
El Salvador			0,35
Germany, E.			0,01
Costa Rica			0,19
United Arab Emirates			0,08
Dominican Republic			0,61
Guatemala			0,05
All the countries above			100,0

Tabelle 110: Applied tariffs on selected product groups, simple averages by importer, 2003.
In: Mayer 2004: 6.
Erwähnt in Abschnitt 'D', 290.

	Manufactures		Textiles		Clothing	
	Simple averages	Share of tariff lines above 15 %	Simple averages	Share of tariff lines above 15 %	Simple average	Share of tariff lines above 5 %
Developed countries						
Australia (2004)	5.6	6.7	10.1	4.0	19.7	68.0
Canada	4.2	7.8	8.5	7.9	14.3	65.4
European Union (2002)	1.3	0.6	2.8	0.0	3.8	0.0
Japan	3.2	10.1	5.6	3.9	12.1	37.6
United States (2004)	3.3	4.2	6.9	4.4	10.3	20.6
Developing countries						
Brazil	14.71	45.0	17.1	86.7	20.0	100.0
China (2004)	9.7	15.1	11.4	11.4	17.0	89.7
India (2001)	30.8	93.5	29.3	98.3	34.0	95.9
Malaysia (2002)	8.0	30.3	14.3	57.0	14.6	53.1
Mexico	18.5	51.3	21.5	87.4	34.3	98.2
Republic of Korea	7.8	0.4	9.5	0.0	12.5	0.0
Taiwan Province of China	5.7	3.4	8.8	3.4	11.9	14.3
Thailand (2001)	14.6	51.6	17.0	70.1	35.3	84.4
Tunisia	24.5	65.8	31.3	83.7	41.3	96.0
Turkey	1.7	0.6	2.9	0.0	5.4	0.0
Countries in Central and Eastern Europe						
Czech Republic	5.0	1.4	6.5	2.9	8.4	1.6
Poland	2.4	3.5	2.4	3.7	8.2	46.7
Romania (2001)	10.7	22.1	14.9	41.6	21.9	63.6

Tabelle 111: Leading exporters and importers of clothing, 2003.
In: WTO 2004a: 152.
Erwähnt in Abschnitt 'D', 291.

(Billion dollars and percentage)	Value	Share in world exports/imports				Annual percentage change			
	2003	1980	1990	2000	2003	1995-00	2001	2002	2003
Exporters									
European Union (15)	59,95	42,0	37,7	24,1	26,5	0	2	7	15
Extra-EU (15) exports	19,04	10,4	10,5	7,4	8,4	0	7	5	15
China a	52,06	4,0	8,9	18,3	23,0	8	2	13	26
Hong Kong, China	23,15	-	-	-	-	3	-3	-5	4
domestic exports	8,20	11,5	8,6	5,0	3,6	1	-7	-10	-1
re-exports	14,95	-	-	-	-	4	-1	-1	7
Turkey	9,94	0,3	3,1	3,3	4,4	1	2	21	23
Mexico a	7,34	0,0	0,5	4,4	3,2	26	-7	-3	-5
India b	6,46	1,7	2,3	3,1	2,9	8	-11	10	7
United States	5,54	3,1	2,4	4,4	2,5	5	-19	-14	-8
Bangladesh b	4,36	0,0	0,6	2,1	1,9	16	2	-6	8
Indonesia	4,11	0,2	1,5	2,4	1,8	7	-4	-13	4
Romania	4,07	...	0,3	1,2	1,8	11	19	17	25
Thailand b	3,62	0,7	2,6	1,9	1,6	-6	-5	-6	7
Korea, Republic of b	3,61	7,3	7,3	2,5	1,6	0	-14	-9	-8
Viet Nam b	3,56	...	...	0,9	1,6	-	3	41	35
Morocco a, b	2,83	0,3	0,7	1,2	1,3	-	-2	4	16
Pakistan	2,71	0,3	0,9	1,1	1,2	6	0	4	22
Above 15	178,34	71,3	77,5	75,9	78,6	-	-	-	-
Importers									
European Union (15)	101,29	54,3	50,6	38,7	42,9	2	1	7	17
Extra-EU (15) imports	60,39	23,0	25,2	22,9	25,6	3	2	6	18
United States	71,28	16,4	24,0	32,4	30,2	10	-1	1	7
Japan	19,49	3,6	7,8	9,5	8,3	1	-3	-8	11
Hong Kong, China	15,95	-	-	-	-	5	1	-3	2
retained imports	0,99	0,9	0,7	0,8	0,4	14	11	-16	-38
Canada c	4,50	1,7	2,1	1,8	1,9	7	6	2	12
Switzerland	3,93	3,4	3,1	1,6	1,7	-3	0	7	14
Russian Federation b	3,71	-	-	1,3	1,6	...	13	27	-4
Mexico a, c	3,03	0,3	0,5	1,7	1,3	14	-3	-5	-9
Korea, Republic of b	2,50	0,0	0,1	0,6	1,1	4	25	38	11
Australia c	2,19	0,8	0,6	0,9	0,9	8	-12	11	20
Singapore	1,94	0,3	0,8	0,9	0,8	3	-10	7	7
retained imports	0,53	0,2	0,3	0,3	0,2	-6	-18	18	-2
United Arab Emirates b, d	1,78	0,6	0,5	0,7	0,8	1	9	15	..
Norway	1,52	1,7	1,1	0,6	0,6	-2	-4	10	12
China a	1,42	0,1	0,0	0,6	0,6	4	7	6	5
Saudi Arabia	1,03	1,6	0,7	0,4	0,4	-2	6	6	13
Above 15	220,60	85,8	92,8	92,6	93,5	-	-	-	-

a Includes significant shipments through processing zones.
b Includes Secretariat estimates.
c Imports are valued f.o.b.
d 2002 instead of 2003.

Tabelle 112: Clothing and Textile imports of selected economies by region and supplier, 1996. Value Mill. US$ (in parantheses selected textile values). In WTO Annual Report 1997: 108-109.
Erwähnt in Abschnitt 'D', 291, Abschnitt 'F', 448, Abschnitt 'G', 618, Abschnitt 'I', 888, 889.

United States	Value Mill. US$	EU (15)	Value (Mill. US$)	Japan	Value (Mill. US$)
Region		**Region**		**Region**	
World	43317 (10702)	World	78753 (54228) ohne EU 15 43664 (17025)	World	19672 (6075)
Asia	26436 (5105)	Western Europe	41825 (40572)	Asia	15836 (4243)
Latin America	10784 (1225)	Asia	21759 (7755)	Western Europe	2645 (1312)
Western Europe	2988 (2669)	C.E.Europe/Baltic States	7021 (1740)	North America	1092 (401)
North America	1095 (1300)	Africa	5878 (804)	Latin America	55 (46)
Middle East	857 (152)	North America	901 (1713)	C.E.Europe/Baltic States	25 (12)
Africa	709 (102)	Middle East	848 (814)	Africa	10 (13)
C.E.Europe/Baltic States	449 (148)	Latin America	346 (396)	Middle East	10 (48)
Suppliers		**Suppliers**		**Suppliers**	
China	6615 (1097)	European Union (15)	35071 (37203)	China	11687 (1948)
Hong Kong, China	4194 (180)	China	6059 (1330)	European Union (15)	2600 (1236)
Mexico	3886 (887)	Turkey	4836	Korea, Rep. of	1359 (597)
European Union (15)	2237 (2374)	Hong Kong, China	4414 (136)	United States	1052 (388)
Taipei, Chinese	2167 (701)	India	2608 (1836)	Thailand	493 (137)
Above 5	19099	Above 5	52988	Above 5	17191
Dominican Republic	1812	Tunisia	2582 (128)	Viet Nam	489 (71)
Philippines	1612	Morocco	2265 (101)	Indonesia	398 (321)
Korea, Rep. of	1594 (732)	Poland	2225 (342)	Hong Kong, China	384 (21)
Indonesia	1530	Romania	1563	Taipei, Chinese	290 (379)
India	1468 (682)	Bangladesh	1509 (122)	Philippines	199 (20)
Malaysia	1295	Indonesia	1389 (734)	Malaysia	154 (88)
Thailand	1280	Hungary	1106 (222)	India	137 (172)
Honduras	1268	United States	894	Korea, Peoples R	124
Bangladesh	1195	Pakistan	890 (1036)	Canada	40 (13)
Sri Lanka	1116	Thailand	877 (413)	Switzerland	28

Canada	1095 (1300)	Malaysia	818 (172)	Sri Lanka	27
Guatemala	832	Sri Lanka	692	Macau	19
Macau	797	Mauritius	655	Bangladesh	15 (14)
El Salvador	740	Czech Rep.	642	Singapore	11
Costa Rica	722	Korea, Rep. of	637 (601)	Mexico	11
Pakistan	678	Slovenia	575 (218)	Pakistan	10 (445)
Turkey	629	Croatia	560	Hungary	9
Jamaica	515	Macau	551	Turkey	9
Singapore	341	Viet Nam	518	Australia	8
Colombia	325	Taipei, Chinese	472 (420)	Peru	7
Israel	312	Switzerland	436	Israel	5
Egypt	270	Slovak Rep.	428	New Zealand	5
United Arab Emirates	220	Philippines	379	Poland	5
Mauritius	175	Bulgaria	373	Slovenia	5
Peru	154	Israel	332	Jamaica	5

Tabelle 113: Survey of engineering estimates of the economies of scale. Gekürzt, ohne Lebensmittelprodukte und die im Text präsentierten Beispiele: Automobile, Lkw, Stahl, Reifen, Petrochemie, Chemikalien, Zement, TV-/Video, Bier siehe Text. In: Pratten 1988: 42-54. Erwähnt in *Abschnitt 'E'*, 358.

NACE 3 No./Industry	Source/Country for which estimate is made	M.E.S. Dimension of Scale – M.E.S. Scale for that dimension	Increases in unit costs below M.E.S. Scale	Main dimension of scale to which economies relate	Comments	Representativeness of the estimates for UK industry
NACE 224: Non-ferrous metals industry Primary and secondary aluminium: NACE 2245: Aluminium Semi manufactures	L. Wagner, UK	Works making rolled products – 200.000 t per annum		Size of works – no estimate; Production runs – significant; Products – significant R&D- significant	Scale economies much smaller for making extrude products	Aluminium processing is probably representative. There are significant economies for large outputs and production runs. The MES varies according to the process uses and the market often limits the scale of production in practice
NACE 241: Manufacture of clay products for construction purposes: Bricks	Pratten 1971; UK	Non-fletton brickworks 25 mill. bricks at least Size of company manufacturing non-flettons	25 % at half MES Slight if any advantage for multi-works firm	Size of works – substantial	The MES for fletton brickworks is higher	The estimates for non-fletton bricks are representative for much of the industry, but economies of scale for flettons are greater. Also there are niches where small establishments can compete: for example making bricks which match bricks used in existing buildings and which are no longer made on large scale
NACE 243: Building products of concrete, cement and plaster: Plasterboard	L. Wagner 1981; UK	Works, 18-20 sq. mtrs. a year				Plasterboard is not typical for this industry which includes ready mixed concrete and concrete products which are constly to transport and are made at many sites to minimize transport costs
NACE 247 Manufacture of glass and glassware: Glass bottles	Scherer 1975; UK Monopolies commission report: International	Factories 133.000 tons a year or 1000 employees	11 % at 1/3 MES	Size of works – moderate; Production runs – some benefits	There are scale economies for large outputs of specialized products e.g. pharmaceutical bottles	Glass bottles are not typical for this industry. It includes flat glass for which there are large economies of scale and ornamental and scientific glassware for which there may be large economies for some products but product markets are so limited that small establishments are competitive
NACE 249: Manufacture of ceramic goods: Pottery	P.W. Gay and R.L. Smyth, 1974; UK	Tableware: Factories – the MES is small in relation to UK output	No estimate	Specialization and production runs – moderate	There are economies of scale for firms based on marketing, commercial and financial economies. The economies of scale may be larger for industrial	The estimate that the MES for establishments is small is representative for the industry. Also the economies of specialization and production runs apply in much of the industry. In segments, for example fine china, there are economies of scale for marketing

Industry	Source	Plant/Works size	MES estimate	Other economies	Comments
NACE 25 Chemical industry: NACE 255: Paint	Scherer 1975: International	Works for producing paint – 10 mill. US galls a year/600 employes	4,4 % at 1/3rd MES	Production runs – moderate. Products – moderate. Works – moderate. R&D significant in certain segments of the trade	Paint is representative for the other products included in this trade, varnishes and printing ink
				ceramics: There is scope for specialization in the industry and for small firms to be competitive for some products	
NACE 256: Manufacture of other chemical products: Fertilizers	L. Wagner 1976; International	Ammoia plants – 300.000 - 350.000 tons		Output of plants – large	NACE 256 includes a wide range of products. Generally there are large economies of scale for production of each of these products, but must of them are made in much smaller plants (measured in tons of capacity) than those used for fertilizers
NACE 257: Manufacture of Pharmaceutical products: Pharmaceuticals	Reckie 1975: UK	Works for producing drugs – no estimate but production cost generally a small party of total product costs		Production runs and works – scale economies for these dimensions swamped by other factors affecting costs R&D – large for new drugs. Marketing – large for such of the industry's output	NACE 257 is limited to pharmaceutical products
NACE 258: Manufacture of Soap and Synthetic detergents	Pratten 1971: UK	Plant – 70.000 tons; Plant – at least 10.000 tons.	2 1/2 at half MES, no estimate	Marketing - large	NACE 258 includes perfums, cosmetics and toilet preparations for which production costs generally represent a small part of the prices charged to consumers. Economies of scale for production are not very significant for these products and so estimates of economies of scale for detergents and soap are not representative for this heading.
NACE 76: Man-made Fibres:					
Nylon, acrylic and polyester fibres	Scherer 1980, Weiss 1976, R.W. & S.A. Shaw: USA, UK	Works – Nylon – 50mill. lbs a year, Acrylic - 42,4 mill. lbs a year, Polyester – 40,0 mill. lbs, Polyester – 100.00 tons per year	12 % at 1/2 MES 9,5 % at 1/2 MES 10 % at 1/2 MES 2,6 % at 1/2 MES	Products – moderate Production runs – moderate R&D – moderate	NACE 26 is confined to man-made fibres for which the estimates are representative
Cellulosic fibres	Scherer 1980 Weiss 1976: USA	Works - Filament 70 mill. lbs a year -Rayan staple – 125 mill. lbs a year	5 % at 1/2 MES 5 % at 1/2 MES		
NACE 322: Manufacture	Boston consulting				.

of machine tools				
Standard conventional machine tools	group 1985, International, Pratten 1971, UK	Firm – output at one factory – no estimate given	3-5 % if output halved	Output of model – moderate
Sophisticated machine tools made in volume		Firm – output at one factory at least 400 mil. t a year		Productions runs – moderate
Specialized machine tools		Firm – output at one factory – small firms can be competitive if the market for their specialized tools is small		Output at factory - moderate R&D – large for some types of products
NACE 326: Ball Bearings	Müller, Owen 1983, Germany, Scherer 1975, international, authors knowledge	Factory – about 800 employees Firm – say 10 % of world market	8-10 % at 1/3 of MES; no estimate but large economies by concentrating production of different types and sizes of bearings	Output of products (types and sizes) – large Productions runs – moderate Output of factories (including economies of output of products) – large R&D – large for some products	Factories with less than MES may not have significantly higher costs if they specialise	NACE 326 includes a wide range of products such as chains, gears and gear boxes. Rather large economies of scale apply to many, but not to all products. Difficult to measure the representativeness of ball bearings
NACE 328: Manufacture of other machinery and equipment						NACE 328 is a residual heading und includes a wide range of machinery such as compressors, refrigerating machinery, pumps and valves. The MES scale for firms and factories at which these products are made must vary considerably with th complexity of the products and the markets for them. Generally there would be large economies of scale for products.
Diesel engine	Weiss 1976, USA, Pratten 1971, UK	Firm output of diesels – 5 % of US shipments in 1967. 100.000 units of a design	10 % at 1/2 MES 4 % at 1/2 MES	Outputs of desigens – moderate Production runs – moderate Factories - moderate		
Chain saw	Porter 1983, USA	Firm making petrol chain-saws 150.000 units a year	No estimate	Insufficient information to complete this section		
NACE 33: Manufacture of office machinery and data processing equipment	L. Wagner 1981, UK Johnson 1980, P.L. Stoneman 'Computers', UK					Again NACE 33 includes a wide range of products for which the MES must vary. For most products there are large economies of scale.
Electronic calculators		Firm output of calculators – 3-4 Mill. a year	No estimate			
Computers, mainframes		Firm output of computers	No estimate	Output of mainframes – large; Output of computers for specialized		

1663

		- a large share of world market		users - large		
NACE 34: Electrical engineering: NACE 342 Manufacture of electrical machinery					-	-
Transformers, Distribution transformers, Small power transformers, Large power transformers	Weiss 1976, USA	Firms – 2 % of US output in 1967, 6,9 % of US output in 1967, 7,1 % of US output in 1967	7 % at 1/2 MES 7 % at 1/2 MES 10 % at 1/2 MES	Insufficient information to complete this section		
Large turbo generators	Pratten 1971, UK, Porter 1983, USA, et al.	A design - at least four units. Factories – output at least 6,000 MW a year	5 % at 1/2 MES No estimate	Designs – large Factories – large R&D – large		
Electric motors	Pratten 1971	Factories make a range of products	15 % at 1/2 MES	Production runs - large, factories - large		
NACE 343: Electrical equipment for industrial use, and batteries and accumulators	Scherer 1975, International	Factory – 1 mill. units a year	4,6 % at 1/3 MES	Factories - moderate		Information on batteries is not representative for this heterogenous NACE heading
Auto batteries						
NACE 344: Manufacture of telecommunication equipment	F. Malerbs, The semi-conductor business, London 1985, USA	Production of types of microprocessors by a firm – no estimate of MES, probably greater than in the UK market in 1975	No estimate but large	R%D - large	Scope for smaller scale production of devices with special applications	The estimates are representative in showing large economies of scale for products. The MES scale of factories and firms varies for the wide range of equipment made by the industry.
Microprocessors						
NACE 36: Manufacture of other means of transport:	Daniel Todd, The World Shipbuilding Industry, London 1985, UK	Shipyards – no estimate		Series of ships – large		NACE 361 includes the building of yachts, ship repairing and breaking for which the economies of scale differ from those for major ship construction. The latter represent less than half of the industry.
NACE 361: Shipbuilding						
Marine Diesels	Pratten 1971, UK.	Factory – at least 100.00 h.p. a year	8 % at 1/2 MES	Designs of engines – moderate Factories - moderate		
NACE 363: Manufacture of cycles						-
Bicycles	Pratten 1971, UK	Factory assembling range of bicycles – less than 100,000 a year	No estimate but small – the difference in costs depends upon the range of operations performed in-house	Products – slight Production runs – slight Factories - slight	Firms with small output can limit their disadvantage by importing components	
NACE 364: Aeroplanes	Pratten 1971, UK	Firms making commercial	20 % at 1/2 MES	Models – large		Apart from commercial aircraft, the

Industry	Source	Estimate	R&D/Firm	Comments
NACE 37: Instrument engineering: NACE 371: Instruments		airoplanes – more than 50 of any model		industry develops and manufactures defence equipment. The estimate of large economies of scale for products attributable to spreading large development costs is representative for the industry
	Luc Soete et al., UK	No estimates		Generally there are economies of scale for products
NACE 429: Cigarettes	Scherer 1975, International, Müller et al. 1985	Factories – 36 billion cigarettes a year, companies 1-2 factories Factories 70 billion cigarettes a year	Products – large R&D - large	-
		2,2 % at 1/3 MES less than 5 % at 1/3 MES	Factories – slight to moderate Marketing – slight to moderate	For the textile, clothing and footwear industries the estimates are representative of the bulk of the industries, but there are segments of these industries for which the economies of scale are larger than indicated
NACE 43: Textile industry				
NACE: 431: Wool Industry	C.F. Rainie, 1965, UK	-	-	There is an "absence over a large part of the industry of any significant economies of scale"
NACE 432: Cotton Industry	B. Toyne et al., Scherer 1975, International	Mill – 1,5 % of US capacity in 1975	-	
Integrated weaving		Mill – little evidence of economies of scale		
Spinning-ring		Mill – 5000 –6000 rotas	Significant economies of scale	
Spinning-open-end weaving		Mill – 300 looms	No estimate	
NACE: 436: Knitting Industry	C. Gulvin, UK	-	-	"The advantages of large firms in the knitwear trade seem to have increased but there is still scope for very small firms to set up"
NACE 438: Manufacture of carpets	Weiss 1976, USA, author's knowledge of the industry, Uk	Factory 64.000 square feet a week	10 % at 50 % MES	Production runs - large	The economies of scale of Axminster carpets are much lower than for tufted carpets

NACE 45: Footwear and clothing industries: NACE 451: Manufacture of Mass-produced footwear and leather shoes	Müller & Owen 1983, Germany; Scherer 1975, International, and author's knowledge of the industry	Factory – 4000 pairs	1,5 % at 1/3 MES Production runs – moderate Factories - slight	Products – moderate Advantages of large firms generally slight	-
NACE 471: Processing of paper and board	Weiss 1976, USA			-	The estimates are representative
Linerboard		Mill – 850 tons a day	8 % at 50 % of MES		
Kraft paper		Mill – 896 tons a day	13 % at 50 % of MES		
Printing paper		Mill – 567 tons a day	9 % at 50 % of MES		
NACE 472: Conversion of Paper and Board Disposable Papers	Porter 1983, USA	Factory – 3-4 machines about 3 % of US capacity	No estimate	Factories - moderate/large R&D – moderate/large	The industry makes a wide range of products. the estimate for disposable papers is not representative
NACE 473: Printing and Allied Industries Bookprinting	Pratten 1971, UK	Titles – Hardback – 10.000 Paperback – 100.000 Firm 2 % of UK industry in 1971	36 % at 50 % of MES 20 % at 50 % of MES		The industry includes publishing. The estimates are represrentative in showing large economies of scale for products attributable to spreading first copy costs.
NACE 48 Processing of rubber and plastics: NACE 483: Moulded plastic products	Pratten 1971, UK	-	-	Products – slight to large economies of scale, Factories – small factories can be competitive in this trade	The estimates are representative

Tabelle 114: Minimum Efficient Scale in Different Parts of the Auto Industry. In: Nolan 2001: 503.
Erwähnt in Abschnitt 'E', 358, 359.

Acitivity	Volume required to achieve minimum unit costs
Casting engine blocks	1 million
Casting other parts	100 000 - 750 000
Power train machining/assembly	600 000
Axle making/assembly	500 000
Pressing various panels	1- 2 million
Painting	250 000
Final assembly	250 000
Advertising	1 million
Finance	2-5 million
R & D	5 million

Tabelle 115: Concentration ratios in manufacturing. Aus: World Bank 1993: 93. Siehe Amsden 1989: 116-125.
Erwähnt in Abschnitt 'E', 365, 374.

Economy	Share
Three firm concentration ratios	
Japan, 1980	56
Korea, Rep. of, 1981	62
Taiwan, 1981	49
Four-firm concentration ratios	
Argentina, 1984	43
Brazil, 1980	51
Chile, 1979	50
India, 1984	46
Indonesia, 1985	56
Mexico, 1980	48
Pakistan, 1985	68
Turkey, 1976	67
United States, 1972	40

Tabelle 116: Comparison of Seller Concentration in Selected Industries, Pakistan and United States, 1967/8, and Malaysia and United Kingdom, 1972. In: Kirkpatrick et al. 1984: 71.
Erwähnt in Abschnitt 'E', 365, 374.

Four-firm seller concentration ratio			Four-firm seller concentration ratio		
Industry	Pakistan (%)	United States (%)	Industry	Malaysia (%)	United Kingdom (%)
Fertilizer	100	33	Soap	94	52
Sulphuric Acid	100	54	Ice-cream	87	73
Paper	100	26	Tobacco	76	23
Nylon yarn	100	91	Bicycles	72	61
Cigarettes	92	81	Cement	69	48
Cement	86	28	Chemical fertilizer	63	38
Jute Textiles	37	70	Printing	19	4
Cotton Textiles	25	30	Plastic products	18	3
Dyeing, bleaching and finishing	10	42	Furniture	18	10
Unweighted average (51 industries)	66	49	Unweighted average (28 industries)	35	24

Tabelle 117: The Scale of Production of Passenger Cars and Light Multiple-Usage Vehicles at the Firm and Model Level in Selected Countries, 1984. In: Fischer/Nunnenkamp et al. 1988: 77.
Erwähnt in Abschnitt 'E', 367, 374.

	Total passenger car production	Mass produced cars (a)			Basic models per firm	Average volume of production per firm	Average volume of production per basic model
		firms	mass-produced basic models	volume of mass production			
	1000 units	number		1000 units	average number	1000 Units	
Brasil	679	4	21	676	5.3	169	32
Mexico	232	6	17	216	2.8	36	13
South Korea	159	2	4	156	2.0	78	39
India	86	4	4	85	1.0	21	21
Spain	1225	6	n.a.	1254	n.a.	209	n.a.
United States	7952	4	64	7742	16.0	1935	121
West Germany	3754	4	24	2819	6.0	705	117
Japan	7771	5	n.a.	7071	18.0	1414	134

(a) Hier werden nur die wichtigsten Hersteller in den jeweiligen Ländern einbezogen. Siehe für weitere Anmerkungen: Fischer/Nunnenkamp et al. 1988: 77.

Tabelle 118: The Automobile Industry in Developing Countries (1986).
In: Rodrik 1988: 116.
Erwähnt in Abschnitt 'E', 367, 374.

Country	Number of Firms	Number of Basic Models	Average Output per Model per Year
Argentina	4	6	20,357
Brazil	4	4	182,539
Chile	2	5	1,872
India	4	4	20,807
South Korea	3	3	70,494
Taiwan	6	6	19,783
Turkey	3	3	19,123
Venezuela	4	4	17,731

Source: Automobile International 1986.

Tabelle 119: Structure of Manufacturing Output. In: Pandey 2004: 33.
Erwähnt in Abschnitt 'E', 387.

Classification	1980-81	1988-89	1996-97
Labor Intensive	20.3	17.8	17.4
Resource Intensive	33.8	34.2	29.1
Scale Intensive	33.1	35.4	41
Specialized Supplier Industries	12.8	12.7	12.5

Tabelle 120: Production, Trade, and Apparent consumption of Rolled Steel Products (a), Brazil, 1925-1985. In: Fischer/Nunnenkamp et al. 1988: 168.
Erwähnt in Abschnitt 'E', 395, Abschnitt 'G', 569, Abschnitt 'I', 866.

	Production	Imports	Exports	Apparent consumption (b)	Share of exports in production	Share of imports in apparent consumption
	1000 tons				per cent	
Five-year annual averages						
1925-1929	18	403	-	421	-	95,8
1930-1934	33	205	-	238	-	86,1
1935-1939	75	330	-	405	-	81,5
1940-1944	153	232	12	373	7,9	62,2
1945-1949	302	336	13	625	4,4	53,8
1950-1954	717	383	2 (c)	1099	0,2	34,8
1955-1959	1186	325	4 (d)	1508	0,3	21,5
1960	1712	435	19	2128	1,0	20,4
1961	1932	334	8	2258	0,4	14,8
1962	1999	282	6	2276	0,3	12,4
1963	2140	474	1	2614	0,0	18,1
1964	2213	303	43	2473	1,9	12,2
1965	2164	254	167	2252	7,7	11,3
1966	2795	318	109	3005	3,9	10,6
1967	2748	340	286	2802	10,4	12,1
1968	3399	348	191	3556	5,6	9,8
1969	3781	391	218	3954	5,8	9,9
1970	4091	543	405	4230	9,9	12,8
1971	4661	849	172	5339	3,7	15,9
1972	5276	699	365	5610	6,9	12,5
1973	5870	1424	227	7066	3,9	20,1
1974	6127	3851	137	9842	2,2	39,1
1975	6866	2193	127	8932	1,8	24,6
1976	7362	1059	140	8281	1,9	12,8
1977	8799	805	218	9387	2,5	8,6
1978	9834	565	530	9869	5,4	5,7
1979	11217	367	867	10717	7,7	3,4
1980	12745	435	1006	12174	7,9	3,6
1981	10870	479	1499	9851	13,8	4,9
1982	11194	156	2072	9278	18,5	1,7
1983	12428	79	4854	7652	39,1	1,0
1984	13649	95	4520	9224	33,1	1,0
1985	14593	89	4395	10288	30,1	0,9

Tabelle 121: Percentage distribution of firms, by average number of month (after development) before the nature and operation of a new product or process are reported to be known to the firm's rivals, 10 industries, United States. Mansfield 1985: 220.
Erwähnt in Abschnitt 'E', 399, 400.

Industry	Products (Average Number of Month)					Processes (Average Number of Month)				
	Less than 6	6 to 12	12 to 18	18 and more	Total	Less than 6	6 to 12	12 to 18	18 and more	Total
	Percentage of Firms									
Chemicals	18	36	9	36	100	0	0	10	90	100
Pharmaceuticals	57	14	29	0	100	0	33	0	67	100
Petroleum	22	33	22	22	100	10	50	10	30	100
Primary Metals	40	20	0	40	100	40	40	0	20	100
Electrical Equipment	38	50	12	0	100	14	14	57	14	100
Machinery	31	31	31	8	100	10	20	30	40	100
Transportation Equipment	25	50	0	25	100	0	67	0	33	100
Instruments	50	38	12	0	100	33	33	33	0	100
Stone, Glass and Clay	40	60	0	0	100	0	20	20	60	100
Other (b)	31	15	15	38	100	27	0	36	36	100
Average	35	35	13	17	100	13	28	20	39	100

Tabelle 122: Export Specialization by type of industry. (1) In: OECD 1996c: 181. Erwähnt in Abschnitt 'E', 402.

		High-tech	Medium-tech	Low-tech	High-wage	Medium-wage	Low-wage	Resource-intensive	Labour-intensive	Scale-intensive	Specialized-supplier	Science-based
USA	1970	159	110	64	136	95	64	77	48	89	123	206
	1993	144	93	73	115	97	82	83	65	84	114	166
Canada	1970	55	125	92	126	100	68	140	26	145	50	63
	1993	52	120	114	126	87	83	153	37	151	47	54
Japan	1970	124	78	114	64	122	102	40	139	123	105	66
	1993	142	114	47	107	122	56	21	50	117	152	103
Austria	1970	70	73	142	33	118	146	104	173	91	99	27
	1993	71	98	126	62	128	112	87	152	100	116	43
Belgium	1970	44	95	128	87	106	105	130	133	119	52	27
	1993	42	121	121	109	74	130	133	167	124	47	39
Denmark	1970	73	62	151	43	78	208	234	88	49	97	65
	1993	70	58	184	48	94	191	249	106	54	84	74
Finland	1970	20	36	200	17	143	117	134	68	152	44	5
	1993	64	56	192	42	168	80	115	61	137	92	36
France	1970	86	94	110	103	87	118	103	116	106	97	89
	1993	94	96	112	108	84	116	123	99	105	75	105
Germany (2)	1970	97	125	76	116	107	70	57	95	109	132	84
	1993	83	120	84	103	105	84	72	95	113	111	77
Greece	1970	15	60	177	48	87	188	227	154	93	10	10
	1993	22	37	255	44	59	260	275	327	35	25	14
Ireland	1970	72	22	192	31	42	286	303	150	25	26	90
	1993	168	57	104	120	59	139	170	55	59	68	222
Italy	1970	78	99	111	92	88	135	86	195	70	117	72
	1993	59	90	149	57	105	159	106	244	67	104	53

Netherlands	1970	98	63	139	103	70	153	193	101	76	72	72
	1993	89	74	143	102	75	135	201	85	83	65	99
Portugal	1970	46	37	189	41	48	267	199	268	46	34	26
	1993	48	39	229	42	62	257	137	377	56	59	15
Spain	1970	37	63	166	61	78	189	208	143	76	56	26
	1993	55	197	129	112	88	102	130	110	131	60	49
Sweden	1970	74	84	129	66	140	67	74	59	136	109	56
	1993	85	88	127	82	137	65	90	58	122	107	75
UK	1970	105	117	82	109	98	95	87	123	89	112	114
	1993	126	93	88	115	95	85	96	90	88	97	149

(1) The export specialization of a particular industry (or industry group) is defined as the ratio of the share of the country's exports in that industry in its total manufacturing exports to the share of total exports by that industry (or industry group) in total OECD manufacturing exports. With exports denoted by X, for a country k, the index of an industry i is given by 100 [X (i, k) / X+, k)] / [X (i, +) / X (+,+)]. A value of 100 indicates the same export specialization as the OECD average.

(2) Figures for Germany up to and including 1990 refer to the western part of Germany only; from 1991 onwards they refer to the whole of Germany.

Source: OECD, STAN Database (STI/EAS Division)

Tabelle 123: Production, Trade, and Apparent consumption of Rolled Steel Products (a), Brazil, 1925-1985. In: Fischer/Nunnenkamp et al. 1988: 168.
Erwähnt in Abschnitt 'F', 436.

	Production	Imports	Exports	Apparent consumption (b)	Share of exports in production	Share of imports in apparent consumption
	1000 tons				per cent	
Five-year annual averages						
1925-1929	18	403	-	421	-	95,8
1930-1934	33	205	-	238	-	86,1
1935-1939	75	330	-	405	-	81,5
1940-1944	153	232	12	373	7,9	62,2
1945-1949	302	336	13	625	4,4	53,8
1950-1954	717	383	2 (c)	1099	0,2	34,8
1955-1959	1186	325	4 (d)	1508	0,3	21,5
1960	1712	435	19	2128	1,0	20,4
1961	1932	334	8	2258	0,4	14,8
1962	1999	282	6	2276	0,3	12,4
1963	2140	474	1	2614	0,0	18,1
1964	2213	303	43	2473	1,9	12,2
1965	2164	254	167	2252	7,7	11,3
1966	2795	318	109	3005	3,9	10,6
1967	2748	340	286	2802	10,4	12,1
1968	3399	348	191	3556	5,6	9,8
1969	3781	391	218	3954	5,8	9,9
1970	4091	543	405	4230	9,9	12,8
1971	4661	849	172	5339	3,7	15,9
1972	5276	699	365	5610	6,9	12,5
1973	5870	1424	227	7066	3,9	20,1
1974	6127	3851	137	9842	2,2	39,1
1975	6866	2193	127	8932	1,8	24,6
1976	7362	1059	140	8281	1,9	12,8
1977	8799	805	218	9387	2,5	8,6
1978	9834	565	530	9869	5,4	5,7
1979	11217	367	867	10717	7,7	3,4
1980	12745	435	1006	12174	7,9	3,6
1981	10870	479	1499	9851	13,8	4,9
1982	11194	156	2072	9278	18,5	1,7
1983	12428	79	4854	7652	39,1	1,0
1984	13649	95	4520	9224	33,1	1,0
1985	14593	89	4395	10288	30,1	0,9

Tabelle 124: Marktgröße in ausgewählten Entwicklungs- und Industrieländern. Bruttosozialprodukt und Pro-Kopf-Einkommen 1970, 1980, 1990. Aus: Für 1970 Weltentwicklungsbericht 1993: 294-295, Pro-Kopf-Einkommen aus World Tables 1990. Für 1980 Weltentwicklungsbericht 1982: 118-123. Für 1990 in $ 1990 Weltentwicklungsbericht 1992: 250, 254.
Erwähnt in Abschnitt 'F', 442, Abschnitt 'G', 541, 561.

Länder	1970		1980		1990	
	BSP Mrd. US$	Pro-Kopf US$	BSP Mrd. US$	Pro-Kopf US$	BSP Mrd. US$	Pro-Kopf US$
China	93	120	252	290	365	370
Indien	52	110	142	240	254	350
Mexiko	38	710	166	2090	238	2490
Brasilien	35	450	237	2050	414	2680
Argentinien	20	910	130	2390	93	2370
Nigeria	12	150	91	1010	34	290
Türkei	11	400	53	1470	96	1630
Indonesien	9	80	69	430	107	570
Korea	8	270	58	1520	236	5400
Thailand	7	210	33	670	80	1420
Kolumbien	7	349	29	1180	41	1260
Malaysia	4	390	23	1620	42	2320
Portugal	6	700	21	2370	57	4900
Spanien	37	-	198	5400	491	11020
Deutschland	184	-	819	13590	1488	22320
USA	1011	-	2587	11360	5392	21790

Kommentar: Teils sinkende BSP Werte wie für Nigeria oder Argentinien können durch die Berechnungsmethode der Weltbank erklärt werden, die auch Wechselkursveränderungen einbezieht, welche dann das Einkommensniveau beeinflussen. Hier geht es nur darum, ungefähre Anhaltspunkte zu gewinnen. Siehe z.B. die Erläuterung der Atlas-Berechnungsmethode in Weltentwicklungsbericht 1993: 360.

Tabelle 125: Exportvergleich verschiedener Länder: Aus: UNCTAD 1994: 224-275.
Erwähnt in Abschnitt 'F', 443.

Land/Region	1970	1975	1980	1985	1990	1993
Südamerika	16449	42572	105401	103850	132061	141345
-Argentinien	1773	2961	8021	8396	12354	13117
-Chile	1113	1590	4705	3804	8310	9202
-Brasilien	2739	8492	20132	25634	31408	38783
Other Africa (a)	7644	20734	51025	35095	45197	39047
-Ghana	427	801	1103	632	890	986
-Kenya	285	633	1261	943	1010	1185
-Tanzania	245	372	582	328	407	462
- Zambia	942	803	1457	797	1254	-
- Zimbabwe	-	-	1445	1120	1748	1609
- Cote d'Ivoire	497	1238	3012	2761	3027	2734
- Mauritius	69	303	430	440	1205	1304
Andere Länder:						
Korea	882	5003	17214	26442	63123	80950
Taiwan	1469	5321	19575	30469	66823	84155
Thailand	686	2177	6449	7059	22811	36410
Philippines	1064	2263	5788	4629	8186	11375
Indonesia	1173	6888	21795	18527	26807	36607
India	1879	4666	8303	9465	18286	-
China	-	25108	-	-	51519	75659
Türkei	588	1401	2910	8255	13026	15610

(a) Angola, Benin, Botswana, Burkina Faso, Burundi, Cameroon, Cape Verde, Central African Republic, Chad, Comoros, Congo, Cote d'Ivoire, Djibuti, Equatorial Guinea, Ethiopia, Gabon, Gambia, Ghana, Guinea, Guinea-Bissau, Kenya, Lesotho, Liberia, Madagascar, Malawi, Mali, Mauritania, Mauritius, Mozambique, Namibia, Niger, Nigeria, Rwanda, Sao Tome and Principe, Senegal, Seychelles, Sierra Leone, Somalia, Swaziland, Togo, Uganda, Tanzania, Zaire, Zambia, Zimbabwe.

Zahlen hinter der Kommastelle sind hier nicht gerundet, sondern einfach weggelassen.

Tabelle 126: Exports by group of products, 1997-01 (US$ million and per cent). In: Trade Policy Review India 2002: 146.
Erwähnt in Abschnitt 'F', 443.

	1997/98	1998/99	1999/00	2000/01
Total exports (US$ million)	34,933.9	33,120.6	36,698.0	44,560.3
	(Per cent)			
Total	100.0	100.0	100.0	100.0
Total primary products	23.9	21.7	18.7	21.4
Agriculture	19.7	18.8	15.9	14.2
Food	17.7	17.2	14.5	12.9
030613 Shrimps and prawns, frozen	2.2	2.2	2.1	2.0
100630 Rice, wholly milled or semi-milled	2.6	4.5	1.9	1.4
Agricultural raw material	2.0	1.7	1.4	1.2
Mining	4.2	2.9	2.8	7.2
Ores and other minerals	2.4	2.1	1.8	2.0
Non-ferrous metals	0.7	0.4	0.7	0.9
Fuels	1.1	0.4	0.2	4.3
271000 Petroleum, other than crude	1.0	0.3	0.1	4.2
Manufactures	74.2	75.9	79.1	76.4
Iron and steel	3.3	2.4	2.8	2.9
Chemicals	9.8	9.4	10.0	10.4
Other semi-manufactures	18.5	20.8	24.2	21.1
710239 Diamonds, excl. industrial	12.3	14.3	17.6	13.9
Machinery and transport equipment	8.0	7.1	6.9	7.9
Power generating machines	0.2	0.3	0.2	0.3
Other non-electrical machinery	2.1	2.3	1.9	2.2
Office machines & telecommunication equipment	1.3	0.7	0.8	1.1
Other electrical machines	1.3	1.2	1.4	1.6
Automotive products	1.7	1.4	1.3	1.4
Other transport equipment	1.3	1.2	1.4	1.4
Textiles	15.1	13.8	13.9	13.3
Clothing	12.4	14.4	14.1	13.7
Other consumer goods	7.1	8.1	7.3	7.2
711319 Articles of jewellery, other than silver	2.3	2.6	2.2	2.0
Other	1.9	2.3	2.2	2.2
Special transactions n.e.s.	1.9	2.3	2.2	2.2

Tabelle 127: Structure of Exports and Imports, selected years. In: UNIDO India 1995: 55. *Erwähnt in Abschnitt 'F', 443.*

	1960/61	1970/71	1980/81	1993/94
A. Exports				
Agricultural products	44.2	31.7	30.6	18.0
Iron ore	2.6	7.6	4.5	1.9
Petroleum products	0.6	0.3	0.1	1.8
Manufactured goods	45.3	50.3	55.8	75.7
- Gems and jewellery	0.1	2.8	9.6	17.6
- Ready-made garments	0.1	1.9	8.4	11.3
- Engineering goods	2.0	12.0	13.0	11.7
- Chemicals and products	1.1	2.3	3.5	11.0
- Leather and products	3.9	4.7	5.0	5.8
- Jute manufactures	21.0	12.3	4.9	0.5
- Other manufactures	17.0	14.2	11.3	17.8
Other	7.2	10.0	8.9	2.6
Total Exports	100.0	100.0	100.0	100.0
B. Imports				
Petroleum	6.1	8.3	41.9	24.8
Fertilizers	1.1	5.1	5.2	3.6
Cereal	16.1	13.0	0.8	0.4
Edible oils	0.3	1.4	5.4	0.2
Capital goods	31.7	24.7	15.2	26.0
Other (mostly intermediate)	44.6	47.4	31.4	45.0
Total imports	100.0	100.0	100.0	100.0

Tabelle 128: Coverage Ratio for Non-Tariff Barriers on Indian Imports. In: World Bank India 2000: 163.
Erwähnt in Abschnitt 'F', 445.

	1988-9	1995-6		1999-2000	
	Method 2	Method 1	Method 2	Method 1	Method 2
Average all sectors	91.63	44.47	50.31	28.31	31.60
Activity based		44.63	54.32	41.64	44.07
1 Primary	99.79	44.40	48.43	22.05	27.23
2 Secondary	89.37				
Industry based					
1 Food, beverages, and tobacco	100.00	74.46	74.76	42.90	44.57
2 Textiles and leather	100.00	52.88	61.46	39.99	49.18
3 Wood, cork and products	100.00	55.81	55.81	5.42	10.85
4 Paper and printing	100.00	39.58	42.50	16.77	20.58
5 Chemicals, petrol, and coal	95.54	35.33	42.77	11.27	14.55
6 Non-metallic minerals	98.81	76.35	47.03	11.16	15.33
7 Basic metal industries	53.74	16.13	16.55	7.79	9.23
8 Metal products and machinery	80.83	35.59	37.81	18.63	23.12
9 Other manufacturing	78.49	45.39	51.64	19.80	26.48
10 Agriculture	100.00	60.15	74.43	58.05	61.62
11 Mining	99.38	13.60	14.10	8.84	8.97
Use based					
1 Consumer non-durables	100.00	58.60	68.05	45.27	49.59
2 Consumer durables	88.20	45.29	56.19	26.68	34.19
3 Intermediate goods	96.84	38.45	35.67	14.35	18.50
4 Basic goods	79.44	30.52	34.88	11.41	15.31
5 Capital goods	75.19	26.52	28.28	13.61	16.17

Notes: 1. In Method 1, Special Import License (SILs) have been given a weight of 50 per cent, and all other non-tariff barriers a weight of 100 per cent.
2. In Method 2, all non-tariff barriers have been assigned an equal weight of 100 per cent.

Tabelle 129: Percent of developed or commerically introduced inventions that would not have been developed or commerically introduced if patent protection could not have been obtained, twelve industries, 1981-1983. In: Mansfield 1986: 175.
Erwähnt in Abschnitt 'E', 400.

Industry	Percent that would not have been introduced	Percent that would not have been developed
Pharmaceuticals	65	60
Chemicals	30	38
Petroleum	18	25
Machinery	15	17
Fabricated metal products	12	12
Primary metals	8	1
Electrical equipment	4	11
Instruments	1	1
Office equipment	0	0
Motor vehicles	0	0
Rubber	0	0
Textiles	0	0

Tabelle 130: The Growth of Outputs, Inputs, and Total Factor Productivity (percent). Aus: Chenery et al.:1986: 20-22.
Erwähnt in Abschnitt 'F', 451, Abschnitt 'G', 565.

Economy	Years	Growth of value added (G_V)	TFP Growth rate (G_A)	Share	Total Factor input Growth rate	(G_F) Share	Growth of capital input (G_K)	Growth of labor input (G_L)	Capital income share (β_K)	Labour income share (β_L)
Developed										
Belgium	1949-59	2,95	2,05	69,5	0,90	30,5	2,55	0,25	30,0	70,0
Canada	1947-60	5,20	3,50	32,5	1,70	67,6	6,80	1,10	42,0	58,0
	1960-73	5,10	1,80	35,3	3,30	64,7	4,90	2,00	44,9	55,1
Denmark	1950-62	3,51	1,64	46,7	1,87	53,3	3,84	1,21	25,0	75,0
France	1950-60	4,90	2,90	59,5	2,00	40,4	4,70	0,30	38.2	61,8
	1960-73	5,90	3,00	50,8	2,90	49,2	6,30	0,40	41,7	58,3
F.R.Germany	1950-60	8,20	3,60	56,8	4,70	43,0	6,90	1,60	36,7	63,3
	1960-73	5,40	3,00	55,6	2,40	44,4	7,00	-0,70	40,1	59,9
Italy	1952-60	6,00	3,80	62,7	2,30	37,5	3,30	1,60	40,5	59,5
	1960-73	4,80	3,10	64,6	1,60	35,4	5,40	-0,70	38,3	61,7
Japan	1960-73	10,90	4,50	41,3	6,40	58,7	11,50	2,70	41,5	58,5
Netherlands	1951-60	5,00	2,30	46,5	2,70	53,6	4,00	1,40	47,0	53,0
	1960-73	5,60	2,60	46,4	3,00	53,6	6,60	0,30	42,9	57,1
Norway	1953-65	5,40	2,88	53,3	2,52	46,7	5,10	0,80	40,0	60,0
	1949-59	3,40	2,50	73,5	0,90	26,5	2,00	0,50	30,0	70,0
United Kingdom	1949-59	2,50	1,20	48,0	1,30	52,0	3,10	0,60	30,0	70,0
	1960-73	3,80	2,10	55,3	1,70	44,7	4,60	0,00	38,7	61,3
United States	1947-60	3,70	1,40	37,5	2,30	62,9	4,00	1,40	39,3	60,7
	1960-73	4,30	1,30	30,2	3,00	69,8	4,00	2,20	41,4	58,6
Average		5,40	2,70	49,0	2,70	51,0	5,20	1,10	38,5	61,5
Developing										
Argentina	1950-60	3,30	1,05	31,8	2,25	68,2	2,65	1,10	-	-
	1960-74	4,10	0,70	17,1	3,30	82,9	3,80	2,20	-	-
Brazil	1950-60	6,80	3,65	53,7	3,15	46,3	3,10	2,80	-	-
	1960-74	7,30	1,60	21,9	5,70	78,1	7,50	3,30	-	-
Chile	1950-60	3,50	0,85	24,3	2,65	75,7	2,60	2,50	-	-
	1960-74	4,40	1,20	27,3	3,20	72,7	4,20	1,90	-	-
Columbia	1950-60	4,60	0,95	20,7	3,65	79,3	4,25	2,75	-	-
	1960-74	5,60	2,10	37,5	3,50	62,5	3,90	2,80	-	-
Equador	1950-62	4,75	2,18	46,2	2,54	53,8	2,82	3,41	38,0	62,0
Greece	1951-65	6,90	2,39	34,5	4,52	65,5	7,10	2,80	40,0	60,0
Honduras	1930-62	4,52	1,40	31,0	3,21	69,0	3,65	2,93	26,0	74,0
Hong Kong	1955-60	8,25	2,40	29,1	5,85	70,9	4,68	6,63	40,0	60,0
	1960-70	9,10	4,28	47,0	4,82	53,0	7,60	2,97	40,0	60,0
India	1959/60-1978/79	6,24	-0,18	-2,9	6,24	102,9	4,77	1,65	52,5	47,5
Ireland	1953-65	4,70	2,00	42,6	2,70	57,4	4,20	1,70	40,0	60,0
Israel	1952-58	9,80	3,90	39,8	5,90	60,2	11,80	3,20	30,0	70,0
	1960-65	11,00	3,40	30,9	7,60	69,1	13,10	5,00	30,0	70,0
Korea, Rep.	1955-60	4,22	2,00	47,4	2,22	52,6	2,18	2,25	40,0	60,0
	1960-73	9,70	4,10	42,3	5,50	57,7	6,60	5,00	36,7	63,3
Mexico	1950-60	5,65	1,60	28,3	4,05	71,7	5,20	2,65	-	-
	1960-74	5,60	2,10	37,5	3,50	62,5	3,90	2,80	-	-
Peru	1950-60	4,50	-0,70	-15,6	5,20	115,6	7,65	2,70	-	-

	1960-70	5,30	1,50	28,3	3,90	71,7	4,40	2,70	-	-
Philippines	1947-65	5,75	2,50	43,5	3,25	56,5	-	-	-	-
Singapore	1972-80	8,00	- 0,009	-0,1	8,01	100,1	9,48	5,52	61,1	38,9
Spain	1959-65	11,20	5,02	44,8	6,18	55,2	8,70	4,50	40,0	60,0
Taiwan	1955-60	5,24	3,12	59,5	2,12	40,5	2,68	1,75	40,0	60,0
Turkey	1963-75	6,40	2,223	34,8	4,17	65,2	6,28	1,02	55,0	45,0
Venezuela	1950-60	7,85	2,15	27,4	5,70	72,6	7,20	3,70	-	-
	1960-74	5,10	0,60	11,8	4,40	88,2	4,50	3,30	-	-
Average		6,30	2,00	31,0	4,30	69,0	5,50	3,30	45,30	54,7
Centrally planned										
Bulgaria	1953-65	12,50	3,30	26,4	9,20	73,6	11,60	7,60	40,0	60,0
Czechoslowakia	1953-65	7,00	2,74	39,1	4,26	60,9	6,60	2,70	40,0	60,0
Hungary	1953-65	6,50	1,78	27,4	4,72	72,6	7,30	3,00	40,0	60,0
Poland	1961-65	6,60	2,20	33,3	4,40	66,7	6,50	3,00	40,0	60,0
Romania	1953-65	11,10	5,32	47,9	5,73	52,1	8,30	4,10	40,0	60,0
U.S.S.R	1950-62	6,30	1,82	28,9	4,48	71,1	-	-	-	-
Yugoslavia	1953-63	11,80	4,78	40,5	7,02	59,5	7,50	6,70	40,0	60,0
Average		8,20	2,50	35,0	5,70	65,0	8,00	4,50	40,0	60,0

In dieser Tabelle werden die Ergebnisse unterschiedlicher Studien zusammengestellt. Auf deren einzelne Markierung und Nennung wird hier verzichtet.

Tabelle 131: Structure of Manufacturing Output According to Market Orientation. Pandey 2004: 33.
Erwähnt in Abschnitt 'F', 131.

Trade Classification Index	1980-81	1988-89	1996-97
Export promoting	19.5	3.1	24.8
Import competing	36.6	51.1	52.1
Export promoting, import competing	3.9	3.8	3.3
Non competing	40.1	41.9	19.8

Export promoting: Exports form more than 10 % of their output.
Import competing: Imports form more than 10 % of their output.
Non competing: The Rest.

Tabelle 132: Import penetration in the manufacturing industry. In: Pandey 2004: 39.
Erwähnt in Abschnitt 'F', 453, Abschnitt 'H', 814.

ASI code	Description			
ASI code	Description	1980-81 to 1988-89	1988-89 to 1996-97	1980-81 to 1996-97
20-21	Manufacture of food products	0.071	0.030	0.035
22	Manufacture of beverages, tobacco	0.000	0.017	0.003
23	Manufacture of cotton textiles	0.005	0.005	0.002
24	Manufacture of wool, silk and man made fibre textiles	0.048	0.024	0.027
25	Manufacture of jute and other vegetable fibre textiles	0.034	0.016	0.017
26	Manufacture of textiles products	0.008	0.020	0.097
27	Manufacture of wood and wood products, furnitures and fixtures	0.001	0.067	0.0033
28	Manufacture of paper etc.; printing etc.	0.083	0.092	0.096
29	Manufacture of leather etc.	0.001	0.017	0.028
30	Manufacture of basic chemicals, chemical products (except products of petroleum and oil)	0.045	0.149	0.166
31	Manufacture of rubber, plastic, petroleum and coal products	0.458	0.189	0.383
32	Manufacture of non-metallic mineral products	0.240	0.423	0.410
33	Manufacture of basic metal and alloy industries	0.125	0.122	0.135
34	Manufacture of metal products and parts	0.009	0.012	0.028
35-36	Manufacture of machinery and equipment	0.116	0.123	0.183
37	Manufacture of transport equipment	0.096	0.042	0.088
38	Other manufacturing industries	0.355	0.064	0.051
	All manufacturing	0.117	0.095	0.135

Tabelle 133: Growth in Output of Registered Manufacturing Sector.
In: Pandey 2004: 29.
Erwähnt in Abschnitt 'E', 387, Abschnitt 'F', 453.

ASI code	Description	Annual rates of growth		
		1980-81 to 1988-89	1988-89 to 1996-97	1980-81 to 1996-97
20-21	Manufacture of food products	10.62	7.52	12.26
22	Manufacture of beverages, tobacco	6.82	5.28	7.49
23	Manufacture of cotton textiles	2.50	5.66	4.64
24	Manufacture of wool, silk and man made fibre textiles	12.56	12.63	18.94
25	Manufacture of jute and other vegetable fibre textiles	-4.27	3.24	-1.07
26	Manufacture of textiles products	9.83	19.66	22.47
27	Manufacture of wood and wood products, furnitures and fixtures	5.33	-2.39	0.96
28	Manufacture of paper etc.; printing etc.	4.96	11.44	10.46
29	Manufacture of leather etc.	9.30	14.27	17.10
30	Manufacture of basic chemicals, chemical products (except products of petroleum and oil)	12.20	13.80	19.73
31	Manufacture of rubber, plastic, petroleum and coal products	11.17	12.30	17.23
32	Manufacture of non-metallic mineral products	15.63	7.22	15.94
33	Manufacture of basic metal and alloy industries	8.50	6.97	10.11
34	Manufacture of metal products and parts	5.89	8.20	8.98
35-36	Manufacture of machinery and equipment	9.41	10.06	13.52
37	Manufacture of transport equipment	12.12	19.06	24.83
38	Other manufacturing industries	46.86	11.78	51.40
	All manufacturing	9.69	10.46	14.13

Tabelle 134: Growth in Value Added of Registered Manufacturing Sector.
In: Pandey 2004: 31.
Erwähnt in Abschnitt 'E', 387, Abschnitt 'F', 453, 456.

ASI code	Description	Annual rates of growth 1980-81 to 1988-89	1988-89 to 1996-97	1980-81 to 1996-97
20-21	Manufacture of food products	17.24	8.96	19.28
22	Manufacture of beverages, tobacco	12.26	7.70	13.75
23	Manufacture of cotton textiles	-0.75	4.76	1.86
24	Manufacture of wool, silk and man made fibre textiles	11.34	12.74	17.56
25	Manufacture of jute and other vegetable fibre textiles	-5.02	1.31	-2.12
26	Manufacture of textiles products	19.32	25.90	42.63
27	Manufacture of wood and wood products, furnitures and fixtures	4.60	1.56	3.37
28	Manufacture of paper etc.; printing etc.	2.81	10.44	7.80
29	Manufacture of leather etc.	9.78	18.15	21.06
30	Manufacture of basic chemicals, chemical products (except products of petroleum and oil)	12.64	19.30	25.73
31	Manufacture of rubber, plastic, petroleum and coal products	24.38	18.40	39.32
32	Manufacture of non-metallic mineral products	14.81	7.10	15.16
33	Manufacture of basic metal and alloy industries	9.16	8.41	11.86
34	Manufacture of metal products and parts	6.98	7.35	9.22
35-36	Manufacture of machinery and equipment	8.78	8.45	11.59
37	Manufacture of transport equipment	7.86	20.35	20.51
38	Other manufacturing industries	44.19	8.45	41.25
	All manufacturing	9.85	12.17	15.80

Tabelle 135: Structure of Manufacturing Output.
In: Pandey 2004: 33.
Erwähnt in Abschnitt 'F', 453.

Classification	1980-81	1988-89	1996-97
Labor Intensive	20.3	17.8	17.4
Resource Intensive	33.8	34.2	29.1
Scale Intensive	33.1	35.4	41
Specialized Supplier Industries	12.8	12.7	12.5

Tabelle 136: Manufacturing industry import penetration ratios: imports/domestic demand, 1989-96 (%). In: Moreira/Correa 1998: 1863.
Erwähnt in Abschnitt 'F', 454.

Industries	1989	1991	1993	1995	1996
1. Industrial equipment and machinery, incl. parts	13,3	31,2	25,5	40,1	48,3
2. Electronic and communications equipment	11,6	27,3	24,0	35,5	41,0
3. Other vehicles (motorcycles, bicycles, etc.)	18,8	27,6	29,0	25,1	31,5
4. Chemical resins and fibers	6,3	12,1	14,2	26,8	30,4
5. Fertilizers	9,8	17,8	21,6	26,8	30,4
6. Chemicals and compounds	15,1	19,1	16,8	24,4	27,4
7. Motors and vehicle parts	6,0	17,1	14,7	20,3	23,6
8. Agricultural machinery and equipment incl. parts	1,7	13,3	7,1	15,0	22,1
9. Electric wires and cables	8,8	12,3	12,0	18,2	21,1
10. Natural fiber textile products	3,5	6,6	14,2	15,6	20,6
11. Rubber	4,8	6,5	7,8	20,0	20,1
12. Electric power equipment	8,2	15,6	13,8	15,8	19,9
13. Non-ferrous metals	8,0	11,4	14,6	20,5	18,8
14. Pharmaceuticals	6,9	11,5	8,5	11,2	14,0
15. TVs, radios and stereos	4,9	10,0	7,7	13,0	13,3
16. Glass products	4,0	7,6	6,8	14,7	12,8
17. Miscellaneous chemical products	5,7	4,8	8,3	13,3	12,5
18. Electric machinery and appliances	3,8	5,6	7,2	10,4	11,4
19. Synthetic fiber textile products	0,8	3,1	4,2	17,0	11,1
20. Petrochemicals	4,0	8,4	5,3	10,2	10,6
21. Automobiles, trucks and buses	0,0	1,9	4,8	14,3	10,2
22. Paper and paperboard products	1,4	4,5	3,7	8,4	9,6
23. Miscellaneous food products	3,0	4,1	3,4	8,5	8,8
24. Miscellaneous textile industries	1,0	2,7	2,4	6,9	8,2
25. Footwear	0,4	2,3	1,2	6,0	7,9
26. Plastics	0,5	1,8	2,3	6,3	7,3
27. Juices and seasonings	2,3	3,7	5,0	9,0	6,5
28. Timber	1,2	3,4	2,3	4,0	6,1
29. Other non-ferrous metals	1,8	3,0	2,5	4,6	6,0
30. Beverages	3,5	5,1	3,4	5,3	5,9
31. Dairy products	4,3	4,0	2,4	7,1	5,7
32. Miscellaneous metal products	1,5	3,8	3,3	4,4	5,4
33. Wood pulp	3,8	4,5	5,6	6,4	4,7
34. Toiletry	1,6	2,1	1,7	4,4	4,7
35. Steel products	1,9	2,8	3,2	4,7	4,3
36. Plastics sheets	0,2	0,9	0,7	6,3	4,1
37. Tobacco products	0,1	0,8	1,0	1,8	1,9
38. Cement	0,3	0,2	0,3	1,2	1,1
39. Concrete products	0,1	0,3	0,5	0,9	1,1
Manufacturing industry	4,8	8,6	8,8	14,6	15,5

Tabelle 137: Export intensity in the manufacturing industry. In: Pandey 2004: 39.
Erwähnt in Abschnitt 'F', 456.

ASI code	Description			
ASI code	Description	1980-81 to 1988-89	1988-89 to 1996-97	1980-81 to 1996-97
20-21	Manufacture of food products	0.129	0.071	0.113
22	Manufacture of beverages, tobacco	0.048	0.024	0.039
23	Manufacture of cotton textiles	0.045	0.013	0.162
24	Manufacture of wool, silk and man made fibre textiles	0.067	0.020	0.043
25	Manufacture of jute and other vegetable fibre textiles	0.146	0.074	0.069
26	Manufacture of textiles products	0.519	0.563	0.715
27	Manufacture of wood and wood products, furnitures and fixtures	0.004	0.073	0.031
28	Manufacture of paper etc.; printing etc.	0.006	0.006	0.017
29	Manufacture of leather etc.	0.159	0.381	0.371
30	Manufacture of basic chemicals, chemical products (except products of petroleum and oil)	0.028	0.057	0.104
31	Manufacture of rubber, plastic, petroleum and coal products	0.015	0.031	0.059
32	Manufacture of non-metallic mineral products	0.277	0.487	0.502
33	Manufacture of basic metal and alloy industries	0.003	0.017	0.064
34	Manufacture of metal products and parts	0.024	0.021	0.065
35-36	Manufacture of machinery and equipment	0.033	0.035	0.070
37	Manufacture of transport equipment	0.056	0.021	0.058
38	Other manufacturing industries	0.126	0.049	0.129
	All manufacturing	0.069	0.071	0.123

Tabelle 138: Comparative Costs of Factors (indexed as 100). Jha et al. 2004: 90.
Erwähnt in Abschnitt 'F', 457.

	India	China	Pakistan	Indonesia	Bangladesh	Sri Lanka
Raw material	100	87	99	100	102	101
Power	100	68	74	41	39	88
Dyes and Chemicals	100	85	101	102	106	112

Source: Gherzi Studie 2003.

Tabelle 139: Growth Rates before and after 1950 (Average Annual Rates of Growth). Aus Maddison (1970) In: Bruton 1998: 915.
Erwähnt in Abschnitt 'G', 466.

	GDP		Dollar Value of Exports	
	1913-50	1950-68	1913-37	1950-67
Argentine	3.0	3.0	1.6	.4
Brazil	4.6	5.3	.4	1.2
Ceylon	n.a.	3.6	2.1	.3
Chile	2.1	4.0	1.1	7.1
Columbia	3.7	4.6	4.1	1.5
Egypt	1.6	5.2	1.0	.6
Ghana	3.8	3.9	3.6	2.2
India	1.2	3.8	-.1	1.9
Malaya	4.3	4.1	4.2	.7
Mexico	2.6	6.2	1.6	4.7
Pakistan	1.2	4.1	-.1	1.2
Peru	3.2	5.4	3.2	8.6
Philippines	2.2	5.2	4.9	5.4
South Korea	n.a.	7.1	4.3	16.8
Taiwan	2.7	8.7	6.8	13.4
Thailand	n.a.	6.5	2.4	4.9
Turkey	n.a.	5.5	.7	4.1
Venezuela	n.a.	6.3	8.0	5.5

Tabelle 140: Wachstum des Bruttosozialprodukts in ausgewählten Entwicklungsländern in unterschiedlichen Zeitperioden, u.a. in denen, in denen eine Politik der Importsubstitution betrieben wurde. Daten aus Weltentwicklungsbericht 1979: 78-79, Weltentwicklungsbericht 1996.
Erwähnt in Abschnitt 'G', 466, 470, 561.

Country	1960-70	1970-76	1980-1985	1985-1994
Bangladesh	3,6	1,6	3,6	2,0
India	3,6	2,7	5,2	2,9
Pakistan	6,7	3,6	6,0	1,3
Tanzania	6,7	3,6	0,8	0,8
Indonesia	3,5	8,3	3,5	6,0
Kenya	7,1	4,8	3,1	0,0
Uganda	5,1	-0,1	4,9	2,3
Egypt	4,5	7,6	5,2	1,3
Nigeria	3,1	7,4	-3,4	1,2
Thailand	8,2	6,5	5,1	8,6
Bolivia	5,2	6,0	-4,5	1,7
Honduras	5,1	2,9	0,6	0,5
Philippines	5,1	2,9	-0,5	1,7
Columbia	5,1	6,5	1,9	2,4
Guatemala	5,6	5,9	-1,4	0,9
Ecuador	5,9	10,7	1,5	0,9
Paraguay	4,3	6,5	1,4	1,0
Korea Rep. of	8,5	10,3	7,9	7,8
Peru	5,4	5,7	-1,6	-2,0
Malaysia	6,5	7,8	5,5	5,6
Chile	4,2	-1,2	-1,1	6,5
China, P.R.	6,2	6,6	9,8	7,8
Taiwan	9,2	7,8		
Mexico	7,3	5,5	0,8	0,9
Brazil	8,0	10,6	1,3	-0,4
Argentina	4,2	3,2	-1,4	2,0
Yugoslavia	6,8	6,3	0,8	- (b)
Iran	11,3	8,9	-	-
Singapore	8,8	8,9	6,5	6,1
Spain	7,3	5,4	1,6	2,8
Portugal	6,3	5,2	0,9	4,0
Greece	6,9	5,2	1,0	1,3
Turkey	6,0	7,2	4,5	1,4
Israel	8,5	5,4	1,7	2,3

(b) Im Weltentwicklungsbericht 1996 nicht mehr aufgeführt, weil es nicht mehr als Staat besteht.

Tabelle 141: Brazil Main Manufacturing Export Branches 1961, 1973, 1978 (Value of Exports in US$ Millions 1980). In: Teitel/Thoumi 1986: 461.
Erwähnt in Abschnitt 'G', 467, 562, 564.

Industry (a)	1961 (b)	1973	1978
Cereals milling	48,4 (c)	2120,4	2369,3
Oils and fats	72,0 (d)	1076,4	1848,5
Automobiles	12,2	124,2	1034,0
Iron and Steel	,0	184,6	526,0
Cacao, chocolate etc.	148,3	104,6	460,1
Sugar refineries	156,5	996,8	453,8
Canned fruits and vegetables	14,3 (e)	124,3	441,6
Spinning, weaving, etc.	4,1	368,4	423,8
Shoes	0,5	153,5	340,5
Meat products	50,6 (f)	539,7	297,9
Oil refinery products	n.a.	117,9	290,8
Wood products	112,6 (g)	283,3	212,7
Radio, TV and communications equipment	0,2	95,6	208,0
Non-electrical machinery and equipment	3,1	68,9	188,7
Industrial machinery	3,8	48,0	181,7
Pulp and paper	0,3	67,7	167,5
Office machines	0,1	69,9	151,6
Chemical products n.e.c.	n.a.	68,8	142,9
Food products n.e.c.	n.a.	47,8	138,5
Shipbuilding	n.a.	5,9	135,7
Clothing	0,3	103,9	124,4
Basic chemical products	45,4 (h)	71,6	124,1
Leather	0,7	64,5	117,5
Electrical machinery	0,3	29,2	104,8
Total	673,7	7452,9	11700,0
Total manufactured exports	...	6953,9	10484,4
Share of total manufactured exports	...	0,93	0,90

(a) ISIC-Classification, numbers not reproduced here. (b) The 1961 data was not available according to ISIC; therefore, it is not strictly comparable with that for 1973 and 1978. (c) Soybeans, rice and corn products. (d) Castor oil and peanuts and peanut meal. (e) Oranges and orange juice. (f) Beef only. (g) Pinewood and wood products. (f) Inorganic chemical products; ethyl alcohol, menthol, tanning extracts, paints and kindred products; and essential oils.

Tabelle 142: Average Annual Rate of Export Growth, by Decades, 1950-1970, and Composition of Exports, 1970, Ten Countries. In: Krueger 1978: 19.
Erwähnt in Abschnitt 'G', 467, 553, 556.

Country	Average annual rate of growth of exports (dollar value)		Composition of Exports, 1970 (per cent of total dollar value)		
	1950-1960	1960-1970	Largest Export	Three largest Exports	Manufactured Exports
Brazil	-.5	8.0	34.2	47.5	11.2
Chile (a)	5.7	9.8	75.8	84.3	10.5
Columbia (b)	1.6	4.6	60.8	65.4	10.6
Egypt (c)	1.0	3.1	44.8	80.8	38.8
Ghana	4.4	-3.0	68.0	80.2	7.4
India (d)	1.5	4.2	12.4	27.0	14.7
Israel (e)	20.0	13.6	31.7	56.7	76.9
South Korea	1.7	41.7	21.3	40.5	83.6
Philippines (f)	5.4	6.6	23.5	61.4	17.3
Turkey	2.5	5.8	25.6	55.4	14.3

(a) Manufactured exports for Chile are for 1965, and the shares of largest and three largest are for 1969.
(b) For Colombia there are only two major exports; all others are treated as 'minor'. Manufactured export percentage was taken from Diaz-Alexandro, Table II-3.
(c) Egyptian data for 1968.
(d) Indian data in the first three columns are taken from Bhagwati/Srinivasan (1975), Table 9-1, and are for the year 1970/71.
(e) Israel's largest export is diamonds, which are imported, cut, and re-exported; they are of much less importance in terms of value added.
(f) The 'per cent' manufactured figure for the Philippines is 'minor exports' and includes all but the largest ten commodity exports given in Baldwin, Table 1-3.

Tabelle 143: Marktgröße in ausgewählten Entwicklungs- und Industrieländern. Bruttosozialprodukt und Pro-Kopf-Einkommen 1970, 1980, 1990. Aus: Für 1970 Weltentwicklungsbericht 1993: 294-295, Pro-Kopf-Einkommen aus World Tables 1990. Für 1980 Weltentwicklungsbericht 1982: 118-123. Für 1990 in $ 1990 Weltentwicklungsbericht 1992: 250, 254.
Erwähnt in Abschnitt 'G', 470.

Länder	1970		1980		1990	
	BSP Mrd. US$	Pro-Kopf US$	BSP Mrd. US$	Pro-Kopf US$	BSP Mrd. US$	Pro-Kopf US$
China	93	120	252	290	365	370
Indien	52	110	142	240	254	350
Mexiko	38	710	166	2090	238	2490
Brasilien	35	450	237	2050	414	2680
Argentinien	20	910	130	2390	93	2370
Nigeria	12	150	91	1010	34	290
Türkei	11	400	53	1470	96	1630
Indonesien	9	80	69	430	107	570
Korea	8	270	58	1520	236	5400
Thailand	7	210	33	670	80	1420
Kolumbien	7	349	29	1180	41	1260
Malaysia	4	390	23	1620	42	2320
Portugal	6	700	21	2370	57	4900
Spanien	37	-	198	5400	491	11020
Deutschland	184	-	819	13590	1488	22320
USA	1011	-	2587	11360	5392	21790

Kommentar: Teils sinkende BSP Werte wie für Nigeria oder Argentinien können durch die Berechnungsmethode der Weltbank erklärt werden, die auch Wechselkursveränderungen einbezieht, welche dann das Einkommensniveau beeinflussen. Hier geht es nur darum, ungefähre Anhaltspunkte zu gewinnen. Siehe z.B. die Erläuterung der Atlas-Berechnungsmethode in Weltentwicklungsbericht 1993: 360.

Tabelle 144: Sources of Growth for Sample Economies (percent). In Chenery et al. 1986: 158-159.
Erwähnt in Abschnitt 'G', 471, 525.

Economy and Sector	Growth rate	DD	EE	IS	IO	Total
Columbia (1953-70)						
Primary	4,5	12,7	9,1	0,5	0,1	22,4
Light Industry	6,8	15,3	1,5	1,5	3,0	21,3
Heavy Industry	11,1	9,0	0,8	4,5	1,7	16,0
Services	5,5	36,7	2,6	0,3	0,7	40,3
Total	5,9	73,7	14,0	6,8	5,5	100,0
Mexico (1950-75)						
Primary	4,8	12,8	0,7	-0,3	-0,5	12,7
Light Industry	6,0	17,7	0,4	0,5	0,7	19,3
Heavy Industry	10,8	16,7	1,8	2,9	1,3	22,7
Services	6,4	43,7	0,7	0,4	0,5	45,3
Total	6,5	90,9	3,6	3,5	2,0	100,0
Turkey (1953-73)						
Primary	2,5	14,9	1,2	0,2	-4,5	11,8
Light Industry	6,7	15,3	2,1	0,4	1,7	19,5
Heavy Industry	9,6	18,8	0,9	1,6	3,4	24,7
Services	6,7	38,3	2,8	0,2	2,7	44,0
Total	5,9	87,3	7,0	2,4	3,3	100,0
Yugoslavia (1962-72)						
Primary	2,6	10,1	3,9	-3,2	-4,6	6,2
Light Industry	11,0	17,7	6,2	-2,6	1,3	22,6
Heavy Industry	13,6	23,6	12,2	-6,1	4,4	34,1
Services	8,8	33,0	5,2	-1,3	0,2	37,1
Total	8,7	84,4	27,5	-13,2	1,3	100,0
Japan (1914-1935)						
Primary	1,9	7,6	2,8	-2,3	2,3	10,4
Light Industry	4,6	15,8	10,5	0,2	-0,4	26,1
Heavy Industry	8,1	15,2	4,4	1,9	-3,3	18,2
Services	4,2	35,2	9,0	-0,2	1,3	45,3
Total	4,1	73,8	26,7	-0,4	-0,1	100,0
Japan (1955-72)						
Primary	2,2	4,4	0,5	-1,5	-1,9	1,5
Light Industry	8,6	14,4	2,0	-0,7	1,1	16,8
Heavy Industry	18,0	30,9	8,4	-0,1	3,3	42,5
Services	11,4	35,7	3,0	-0,8	1,3	39,2
Total	11,5	85,4	13,9	-3,1	3,8	100,0
Korea (1955-73)						
Primary	5,7	12,0	3,0	-1,7	-2,5	10,8
Light Industry	13,6	19,7	15,1	0,0	-1,9	32,9
Heavy Industry	22,1	11,1	10,7	1,4	1,9	25,2
Services	10,3	25,6	6,2	0,2	-0,8	31,2
Total	11,2	68,4	35,0	-0,1	-3,3	100,0
Taiwan (1956-71)						
Primary	7,1	8,8	5,3	-0,2	-1,8	10,3
Light Industry	13,6	12,7	17,5	0,6	2,0	32,8
Heavy Industry	22,5	10,2	13,5	2,4	1,0	27,1
Services	9,7	23,6	7,1	0,1	-1,0	29,8
Total	12,0	55,3	43,4	1,1	0,2	100,0
Israel (1958-72)						
Primary	6,4	2,6	3,6	-0,3	-0,4	5,5
Light Industry	11,2	11,3	12,0	-0,2	1,2	22,5
Heavy Industry	14,3	18,7	6,3	-6,6	2,6	21,0
Services	8,9	39,3	13,9	-1,6	-0,6	51,0
Total	9,9	71,9	35,8	-10,5	2,8	100,0
Norway (1953-69)						
Primary	2,5	3,8	2,4	-1,7	0,3	4,8
Light Industry	3,7	14,0	6,2	-5,7	3,0	17,5
Heavy Industry	7,2	10,7	15,6	-2,2	2,2	26,3
Services	4,8	31,9	21,5	-2,7	0,7	51,4
Total	4,7	60,4	45,7	-12,3	6,2	100,0

DD – domestic demand; EE – export expansion; IS – import substitution; IO – input-output coefficients (that is, increasing use of intermediate produkts i.e. deepening of interindustry linkages

Tabelle 145: Sources of Growth in Manufacturing Output for Sample Economies. In: Chenery et al. 1986: 175.
Erwähnt in Abschnitt 'G', 471, 525.

Economy	Years (Episode)	Growth rate (a)	Source (b)			
			DD	EE	IS	IO
Columbia	1953-66 (1)	8,3	60,2	6,8	22,2	10,8
	1966-70 (2)	7,4	75,7	4,7	4,2	15,3
Mexico	1950-60 (1)	7,0	71,6	3,1	10,9	14,5
	1960-70 (2)	8,6	86,1	4,0	10,9	-0,9
	1970-75 (3)	7,2	81,4	7,9	2,4	8,3
Turkey	1953-63 (1)	6,4	80,9	2,4	9,1	7,6
	1963-68 (2)	9,9	75,1	4,5	10,5	9,9
	1968-73 (3)	9,6	76,2	10,4	-1,6	15,0
Yugoslavia	1962-66 (1)	16,6	73,7	24,8	-0,5	6,5
	1966-72 (2)	9,1	72,1	37,6	-22,1	12,4
Japan	1914-35 (1)	5,5	70,0	33,6	4,7	-8,9
	1955-60 (2)	12,6	76,2	11,9	-3,3	15,2
	1960-65 (3)	10,8	82,4	21,8	-0,4	-3,8
	1965-70 (4)	16,5	74,4	17,5	-1,5	9,6
Korea	1955-63 (1)	10,4	57,4	11,5	42,2	-11,2
	1963-70 (2)	18,9	70,0	30,2	-0,6	0,4
	1970-73 (3)	23,8	39,0	61,7	-2,6	1,9
Taiwan	1956-61 (1)	11,2	34,7	27,5	25,5	12,3
	1961-66 (2)	16,6	49,1	44,6	1,6	4,7
	1966-71 (3)	21,1	34,8	57,1	3,8	4,3
Israel	1958-65 (1)	13,6	57,0	26,5	11,7	4,8
	1965-72 (2)	11,3	75,8	50,0	-36,6	10,8
Norway	1953-61 (1)	5,0	65,1	36,5	-16,1	14,4
	1961-69 (2)	5,3	51,0	58,3	-19,4	10,0

(a) Average annual growth rates of total manufacturing output. (b) Expressed as percentages of change in total gross manufacturing output; add up to 100 percent. DD is domestic demand expansion, EE is export expansion, IS is import substitution, and IO is change in input-output coefficients.

Tabelle 146: Exportwachstum (f.o.b) in ausgewählten Ländern und Trends der nominalen und realen Wechselkurse. Exportwachstumsdaten aus: UNCTAD 1994: 14-21; UNCTAD 1996/1997: 14-21; sowie Trends der real effective exchange rate (REER) in Dean et al. 1994: 32, 56, 75, 85, 92-93; nominale Abwertung gegenüber Dollar siehe (a); sonst. Informationen siehe unten, Abwertung erfolgt gegenüber US$. Erwähnt in *Abschnitt 'G', 483, 510.*

Countries	Export 1980-1985	1985-1990	1990-1991	1991-1992	1992-1993	1993-1994	1994-1995	Nominal (a)/ sonst. Informationen
South Asia								
Bangladesh	4,6	11,9	1,0	24,2	8,3	17,1	19,2	-
- Trend	+	-	-	-	-	-	-	1991 Abwertung, d. progressive Abwertung 1992-1994; black market premium 45 %, 1990 165 % (c)
Sri Lanka	5,4	8,8	2,8	20,4	16,4	12,2	18,4	- 54 % (nominal, 1980-1993)
- Trend	+	--	+	+	+	-	-	ab 1984 Anpassungen, seit 1988 täglich; black market premium steigt 1990 (c)
India	2,4	15,7	-1,7	10,8	10,2	16,3	22,7	- 25 % (nominal, 1980-1993)
- Trend	/	--	--	--	--	-	-	1991 20 % Abwertung (c)
Pakistan	0,3	14,2	16,8	12,1	-8,6	10,1	8,5	-
- Trend	-	--	--	--	--	-	-	Seit Mitte 1980s managed float, Anpassungen; 1990 12,5 % Abwertung (c)
Africa								
Uganda	-8,7	6,7	-5,5	27,2	-9,9	136,9	8,7	-
- Trend	++	/	/	/	/	-	-	große Abwertung Mai 1987; black market premium davor 650 % (c)
Ghana	-16,1	7,0	12,0	-1,2	4,5	30,1	8,7	-
- Trend	++ d.	-	/	/	/	-	-	zwischen 1983-87: 7258 % nominale Abwertung; davor black market premium 1982 2000 % (d) 1995 Inflation 59,6 % wg. Geldmengen-ausweitung, Inflation sinkt, 1999 60 % Abwertung wirkt inflationär (i)
Zaire (f)	0,0	2,3	-17,1	-49,8	-10,8	13,9	4,5	-
- Trend	+ d. --	/	/	/	/	-	-	1984: 287 % nominale Abwertung; 1986 Inflation, Exportanreize fallen wieder, dann 1989 Hyperinflation bei politischer Krise (d)
Nigeria	-13,4	4,8	-10,3	-3,1	6,8	-5,5	13,5	-
- Trend	++	--	-	/	/	-	-	1987-88 338 % nominale Abwertung; davor black market premium 809 % (d)
Tanzania	-15,4	7,7	-17,5	21,6	-4,0	15,3	23,1	-
- Trend	++	--	/	/	/	-	-	1980-83 reale Wechselkurssteigerung um 74 %; black market premium 300 % (c); 1994 30 % Inflation, geringere reale Aufwertung, wieder nominelle Abwertung, Exporte brechen aber 1996 wieder ein (h)
Malawi	-1,6	8,4	-7,3	13,1	-18,7	1,6	24,6	-
- Trend	/	- d. +	+	-	-	-	-	1980/81 Krieg in Mozambique, BOP Krise d. Nahrungsmittelimporte für Flüchtlingen; 1984 Beginn von Abwertungen, 1988 15 % Abwertung, realer Wechselkurs steigt seit 1988, bis 1991 wieder auf 1984 Niveau (c)
South Africa	-7,6	7,2	-1,0	0,5	3,6	4,4	10,0	-
- Trend	/ d. -	+	/	/	+	-	-	Abwertungen seit 1983 (c)
Kenya	-4,5	-0,4	7,4	20,9	-0,2	20,4	16,4	

										Kommentar
- Trend	/	-	/							
Madagascar	-1,1	-5,3	-1,1	-12,0	-2,2	55,6			-9,4	15 % Sept., 14 % Dez. 1982; danach crawling peg (e); bis 1990 bis 93 deutliche Abwertungen; reale Löhne steigen 94 % zwischen 1994-98; Inflation sinkt aber von 45,6 % 93 auf 9 % 96; Exporte sinken nach 1996 wieder leicht ab (c)(i)
- Trend	/	-	-	+						1987-88 137 % nominale Abwertung, danach politische Krise, 1994 Stabilisierung, weitere Abwertung (d)
Latin America										
Argentina	-0,7	8,6	-1,6	3,6	4,5	19,4			33,9	
- Trend	-- d. +	-	+	+						3000 % Inflation 1989; 1000 % Abwertung 1990, seit 1992 peso statt austral, Überbewertung bleibt (c)
Brazil	5,1	7,6	0,7	13,2	7,8	12,9			6,8	
- Trend	-	+ (b)	--	-						1984-86 trotting peg Abwertung 1986: 226 % Inflation; 1990 2938 % Inflation, Reform 1990: black market premium über 100 % (c) trotzdem sinkender realer Wechselkurs weil die Preise trotz Inflation absinken (g)
Peru	-4,3	4,0	3,0	4,7	-0,6	29,6			22,4	
- Trend	+ d. -	+ d. ++	++	+						Abwertungen 1985, 1987, aber realer Wechselkurs steigt an; 1989 black market premium 185 % (c)
Venezuela	-6,6	6,3	-11,8	-14,7	5,7	9,6			14,7	
- Trend	+ d. -	-	/	+						Krise ab 1986: Inflation hoch von 11 % 1986 auf 84 % 1989; Verlust von Währungsreserven; 1989 Reformen: Abwertung; black market premium sinkt von 190 % 1988 auf 5 % 1990 (c)
Chile	-3,3	19,3	7,5	11,8	-7,8	26,1			39,1	- 96 % (nominal, 1980-1993)
- Trend	++ d. --	--	/	+						Abwertung seit 1985; 1988-1990 Kapitalzuflüsse, Aufwertungsdruck; realer Wechselkurs 1988-1990 halb so groß wie 1980 (c)
Colombia	0,0	11,0	6,9	-4,4	4,1	18,3			20,3	
- Trend	++ d. --	--	/	+						Abwertungen, realer Wechselkurs sinkt bis 1991 auf die Hälfte des 1984 erreichten Werts (c)
Costa Rica	-0,4	8,2	10,3	14,5	12,1	12,4			26,8	
- Trend	+ d.-d. +	--	-	/						seit 1980 crawling peg, Abwertung in kleinen Schritten, 1981 bis 85 steigt der reale Wechselkurs an, 1986 black market premium über 280 %, dies kehrt sich aber danach um (c)
Mexico	10,3	11,0	4,6	8,0	12,5	17,3			30,6	- 742 % (nom., 1980-1992, d. neue Währung)
- Trend	+ d.-d. +	- d. +	+	+						reale Abwertung zwischen 1986-87, danach Ansteig durch peg an Dollar, Inflation höher, Abwertung vis-a-vis Dollar nicht stark genug (c)
East Asia										
Korea	11,5	18,1	10,5	6,6	7,3	16,8			30,3	- 96 % (nominal, 1980-1993)
- Trend	+ d. -	- d. +	/	-						seit 1985 nominale und reale Abwertung des Won durch enge Bindung an Dollar; Kritik an unfaire Vorteile dadurch (c)
Malaysia	6,1	16,0	16,8	18,5	15,7	24,7			26,0	+ 10 % (nominal, 1980-1993)
- Trend	+	--	-	+						stabiler Wechselkurs in den achtziger Jahren (c)
Indonesia	-2,6	8,0	15,1	14,6	8,8	8,8			13,4	- 31 % (nominal, 1980-1993)
- Trend	+ d. -	--	/	-						seit 1978 managed float, 1986 31 % Abwertung, weitere Abwertungen gemäß

						Inflationsratendifferenzen mit wichtigen Handelpartnern (c)
Philippines	-3,7	13,7	8,7	11,2	13,7	20,0	31,6	- 36 % (nominal, 1980-1993)
- Trend	+ d.-d. +		--	/	+			1983 Inflation 56 %, Abwertung, realer Wechselkurs bleibt aber bestehen, ab 1986 fällt er, seit 1989 wieder steigende Inflation aber korrigierende nominale Abwertungen (c)
Thailand	1,5	28,0	23,2	14,2	13,3	22,7	25,1	+ 14 % (nominal, 1980-1993)
- Trend	+ d. -		-	/	-			1984 14 % Abwertung, eher graduelle nominale und reale Abwertung in der zweiten Hälfte der achtziger Jahre, aber sehr positive Bewertung d. Politik (s.o.) (c)
China	7,6	17,6	15,0	14,3	13,0	33,1	22,9	- 29 % (nominal, 1981-1993)
- Trend	--	-- d. +	-		-			1988, 1989 realer Anstieg, danach Abwertungsserie (c)

Es wird versucht die Wechselkurstrends (REER) von 1980 bis 1992 anzugeben, weil die absoluten Zahlen wenig aussagekräftig sind. Die Trends werden nach Intensität differenziert. Intensiv = doppelt Minus -- bzw. Plus ++, / bedeutet keine klare Tendenz, das Kürzel d. steht für dann, wenn zwei trennbare Tendenzen vorliegen, die etwa noch in die nächste Periode hineinwirken. + d.-d. + bedeutet erst Plus dann Minus dann Plus. Gemäß Theorie bedeutet Minus somit tendenziell, daß keine Gefahr besteht, daß sich der Wechselkurs gemäß heimischer inflationäre Vorgänge implizit aufwertet bzw. daß keine Gefahr besteht, daß sich die Anreize von handelbaren Güter wieder wegbewegen auf nicht-handelbare Güter. Abgelesen aus Dean et al. 1994: 32, 56, 75, 85, 92-93.

Folgende absolute Indexzahlen für reale Wechselkurse über den gesamten Zeitraum 1980 - 1992 (1980 =100) liegen weiterhin vor, Indexzahlen für 1992: In Südostasien: Indien 45; Pakistan 60; Bangladesh 83; Sri Lanka 93. Afrika: Uganda 25; Ghana 30; Nigeria 30; Malawi 90; Südafrika 80; Kenya 75; Madagascar 48; Tanzania 43; Zaire 43. Lateinamerika: Peru 290; Brasilien 80; Argentinien 80; Venezuela 50. Ostasien: Korea 92; Malaysia 78; Thailand 80; Philippinen 80; Indonesien 50; China 30. Dean et al. 1994: 32, 56, 75, 85, 92-93.

(a) nominale Auf oder Abwertung 1980-1993, gegenüber Dollar, der sich Ende der achtziger Jahren wieder auf einen 'normalen' Wert einpendelt. Zum Vergleich: Die Umtauschraten für DM sind 1980 1,82; 1993 1,66. Im Jahre 1985 mußte 2,94 DM für eine Dollar bezahlt werden. Daten aus: http://eh.net/hmit/exchangerates/exchange.
(b) + erst ab 1988.
(c) Dean et al. 1994: 19 (Bangladesh); 22-23 (Sri Lanka); 23 (India); 24-25 (Pakistan); 48-49 (Uganda); 47-48 (Tanzania); 44 (Malawi); 43 (Kenya); 62 (Argentinien); 63 (Brasilien); 64 (Chile); 67 (Peru); 65 (Kolumbien); 68 (Venezuela); 65-66 (Costa Rica); 66 (Mexico); 82 (Malaysia); 83 (Indonesien); 83 (Philippinen); 84 (Thailand); 85 (China).
(d) Sahn et al. 1997: 55-56, 59-60 (Ghana); 56, 68-69 (Zaire); 56, 67-68 (Tanzania); 56, 69-72 (Madagascar).
(e) Mosley et al. 1991: 275.
(f) Zaire heißt ab 1993 Demokratische Republik Kongo.
(g) Papageorgiou et al. 1991: 18-20; Edwards 1993a: 1369.
(h) Rankin et al. 2002: 5, Kanaan 2000: 31.
(i) Trade Policy Review Ghana 2001: 4-6.
(j) Trade Policy Review Kenya 2001: 3; Wagacha 2000: 12.

Tabelle 147: Brazil's legal tariff rate, 1966-77 (%).
In: Moreira 1995: 126, 198.
Erwähnt in Abschnitt 'G', 485, 556, 557, 558.

	1966	1967	1971	1975	1977	1980 (b)	1984 (b)	1989 (b)
Total Manufacturing	99	48	67 (a)	86,4 (b)	70,0	99,4	90,0	43,1
Capital goods for mnf.	49	36	43,2	41,0	60,6	62,9	83,3	69,4
Capital goods for agric.	32	25	44	38,7	41,3			
Interm. goods for mnf.	42	30,5	45,6	51,1	75,9	76,5	76,9	33
Intermed. goods for agric.	-	-	26,4	12,8	20,0			
Transport equipment	55	42	36,5	47,7	65,2	-	-	-
Consumer durables	80	64	100,7	115,2	140,2	n.a.	173,6	58,5
Consumer non-durables	73	54	102,7	10,5,7	154,4	n.a.	122,7	46,6

Note: Data for manufacturing is the sectoral average weighed by the 1970 output. For the rest of the data, simple averages. (a) 1973. (b) Ergänzt durch eine Tabelle, der einige Aufgliederungen fehlen, ebenfalls in Moreira 1995: 126.

Tabelle 148: Changes in legal tariff rates before and after tariff reform, 1967 (simple average rates). In: Frank et al. 1975: 60.
Erwähnt in Abschnitt 'G', 485, 528.

BTN Section	Old rate (percent)	New rate (percent)
1. Live animals and animal products	32.5	38.4
2. Vegetable products	38.5	36.8
3. Animal & vegetable fats and oils	39.6	42.3
4. Prepared foodstuffs, beverages, spirits, vinegar, and tobacco	84.3	95.1
5. Mineral products	15.9	25.2
6. Products of chemical and allied industries	27.6	29.7
7. Artificial resins and plastic materials	32.4	34.5
8. Raw hides and skins, leather, fur skins and articles thereof	55.2	58.1
9. Wood and articles of wood	40.1	44.2
10. Paper making material, paper and paperboard and articles thereof	43.0	54.2
11. Textiles and textile articles	59.0	71.0
12. Footwear, headgear, umbrellas, sunshades, whips, riding-crops	74.3	82.9
13. Articles of stone, plaster, cement, asbestos, mica etc.	48.9	53.8
14. Real pearls, precious stones and metals	43.7	36.1
15. Base metals and articles thereof	32.9	35.6
16. Machinery and mechanical appliances	27.4	30.6
17. Vehicles, aircraft, vessels, etc.	39.6	36.2
18. Optical, photographic, cinematographic, measuring, checking and precision instruments and apparatuses, etc.	44.4	40.4
19. Arms and ammunition	54.7	37.7
20. Miscellaneous manufactured articles	78.9	81.9
21. Works of art, collectors' pieces and antiques	0	0
Total number of items	(2,044)	(3,019)

Tabelle 149: Korea: Die Entwicklung der Importliberalisierung 1967 bis 1992.
In: Köllner 1992: 165.
Erwähnt in Abschnitt 'G', 485, 534, 535.

Jahr	Gesamtzahl der Importgüter	Automatisch genehmigte Importgüter	Beschränkte Importgüter	Verbotene Importgüter	Liberalisierungsquote (%)
1967	1.312	792	402	118	60,4
1868	1.312	756	479	71	57,6
1969	1.312	728	508	71	55,5
1970	1.312	712	526	73	54,3
1971	1.312	721	518	73	55,0
1972	1.312	668	571	73	50,9
1973	1.312	683	556	73	52,1
1974	1.312	665	574	73	50,7
1975	1.312	644	602	66	49,1
1976	1.312	669	579	64	51,0
1977	1.312	691	560	61	52,7
1978	1.097	712	385	0	64,9
1979	1.010	683	327	0	67,6
1980	7.465	5.183	2.282	0	69,4
1981	7.465	5.579	1.886	0	74,7
1982	7.560	5.791	1.769	0	76,6
1983	7.560	6.078	1.482	0	80,4
1984	7.915	6.712	1.203	0	84,8
1985	7.915	6.944	971	0	87,7
1986	7.915	7.252	663	0	91,6
1987	7.915	7.426	489	0	93,8
1988	7.915	7.553	362	0	95,4
1989	10.214	9.776	465	0	95,5
1990	10.274	9.898	376	0	96,3
1991	10.321	10.036	285	0	97,2
1992	10.321	10.079	242	0	97,7

Tabelle 150: Tariff rates and tariff revenues: Taiwan. In: Chen/Hou 1993: 340.
Erwähnt in Abschnitt 'G', 485, 548, 585.

Year	Nominal tariff rates (%) (a)	Average tariff burden (%) (b)	Tariff revenue as % of total tax revenue
1955	47,0	20,9	14,6
1961	38,8	12,8	17,3
1965	35,4	14,8	20,8
1971	39,1	11,3	19,3
1974	55,7	10,1	27,6
1975	52,7	11,4	23,8
1976	49,1	10,6	23,5
1977	46,2	10,8	23,3
1978	43,6	11,3	24,2
1979	39,1	10,6	23,6
1980	31,2	8,1	20,1
1981	31,2	7,5	17,6
1982	31,0	7,3	16,2
1983	31,0	7,7	17,4
1984	30,8	8,0	17,8
1985	26,2	7,7	16,0
1986	22,8	7,8	17,2
1987	19,4	7,0	15,2
1988	12,6	5,8	13,3
1989	9,7	7,0	13,2
1990	9,7	5,4	9,5

(a) The nominal tariff rate is the average rate of all tariff items in the tariff schedule. (b) The average tariff burden is the ratio of total tariff revenue to total value of merchandise imports before tariffs and hence does not take into account the effect of prohibitive tariff rates.

Tabelle 151: Trend movements of relative prices, nominal exchange rates, real effective exchange rate, and terms of trade for different regions (Cumulative percentage change). In: Aghevli/Montiel 1996: 622.
Erwähnt in Abschnitt 'G', 510.

		1978-81	1982-85	1986-89	1978-89
Industrial countries					
	Relative prices	-4.9	-7.1	-1.8	-13.7
	Nominal effective exchange rate	-5.9	-9.2	1.5	-13.6
	Real effective exchange rate	-1.1	-2.1	3.3	0.1
	Terms of trade	-0.7	2.3	9.8	5.1
Developing countries					
	Relative prices	-20.1	-30.9	-54.8	-105.8
	Nominal effective exchange rate	-15.6	-34.1	-74.7	-124.4
	Real effective exchange rate	4.5	-3.2	-19.9	-18.6
	Terms of trade	-12.4	2.1	-21.0	-31.4
Africa					
	Relative prices	-19.2	-21.8	-26.6	-67.6
	Nominal effective exchange rate	-8.3	-32.2	-56.4	-96.9
	Real effective exchange rate	10.8	-10.4	-29.8	-29.4
	Terms of trade	-22.4	9.1	-27.4	-41.0
Asia					
	Relative prices	-5.9	-8.2	-6.2	-20.2
	Nominal effective exchange rate	-12.8	-8.1	-27.4	-48.2
	Real effective exchange rate	-6.9	0.1	-21.2	-28.0
	Terms of trade	-7.0	8.4	-5.3	-3.9
Europe					
	Relative prices	-27.6	-30.1	-85.0	-142.8
	Nominal effective exchange rate	-27.9	-38.1	-90.1	-156.0
	Real effective exchange rate	-0.2	-8.0	-5.1	-13.3
	Terms of trade	-19.7	1.7	2.7	-15.2
Middle East					
	Relative prices	-16.8	-33.5	-49.1	-99.4
	Nominal effective exchange rate	-19.7	-19.2	-65.5	-104.4
	Real effective exchange rate	-3.0	14.3	-16.4	-5.1
	Terms of trade	20.7	-7.8	-58.9	-46.1
Western Hemisphere					
	Relative prices	-31.9	-58.9	-126.4	-217.2
	Nominal effective exchange rate	-22.8	-62.8	-136.6	-222.3
	Real effective exchange rate	9.0	-3.9	-10.3	-5.1
	Terms of trade	-18.8	-6.9	-7.1	-32.9

Tabelle 152: Economic Performance by Period. In: Rodrik 1999: 72-73.
Erwähnt in Abschnitt 'G', 524, 565.

	1960-73		1973-84		1984-94	
	GDP per worker	TFP	GDP per worker	TFP	GDP per worker	TFP
East Asia	4,2	1,3	4,0	0,5	4,4	1,6
Latin America	3,4	1,8	0,4	-1,1	0,1	-0,4
Middle East	4,7	2,3	0,5	-2,2	-1,1	-1,5
South Asia	1,8	0,1	2,5	1,2	2,7	1,5
Sub-Saharan Africa	1,9	0,3	-0,6	-2,0	-0,6	-0,4
East Asia						
China	2,2	1,4	4,3	2,2	8,0	4,6
Indonesia	2,5	1,1	4,3	0,5	3,7	0,9
South Korea	5,6	1,4	5,3	1,1	6,2	2,1
Malaysia	4,0	1,0	3,6	0,4	3,8	1,4
Philippines	2,5	0,7	1,2	-1,3	-0,3	-0,9
Singapore	5,9	0,9	4,3	1,0	6,0	3,1
Thailand	4,8	1,4	3,6	1,1	6,9	3,3
Taiwan	6,8	2,2	4,9	0,9	5,6	2,8
Latin America						
Argentina	2,6	0,2	0,4	-1,0	1,1	1,0
Bolivia	3,5	2,1	-0,6	-1,5	-0,1	0,8
Brazil	4,4	2,9	1,0	-0,8	0,5	-0,2
Chile	1,6	0,7	-0,6	-0,7	4,7	3,7
Colombia	2,9	1,9	1,2	0,0	1,8	1,0
Costa Rica	2,8	1,2	-0,5	-0,2	1,9	0,6
Dominican Rep.	4,6	2,5	0,8	-1,3	0,0	-1,0
Ecuador	4,4	3,3	1,7	-0,5	0,0	-0,1
Guatemala	3,2	1,9	0,5	-0,9	0,0	0,2
Guyana	0,4	0,2	-4,6	-4,3	-0,5	-0,3
Honduras	2,4	1,3	0,3	-1,1	-0,6	-1,2
Haiti	-0,2	-0,8	1,1	-1,5	-5,2	-5,2
Jamaica	3,3	1,5	-4,4	-4,0	0,6	0,8
Mexico	3,8	1,6	0,7	-0,8	-1,1	-1,8
Nicaragua	3,1	1,4	-3,2	-4,1	-5,7	-5,5
Panama	4,6	1,7	1,4	-0,2	-0,3	-0,6
Peru	2,6	1,4	-1,1	-2,2	-1,5	-1,3
Paraguay	2,0	0,8	3,1	0,0	0,6	-0,3
El Salvador	2,0	0,6	-2,4	-3,6	-0,2	-0,2
Trinidad and Tobago	3,3	2,0	3,9	1,2	-3,3	-2,8
Uruguay	0,4	0,1	0,5	-0,9	2,8	2,5
Venezuela	1,2	0,9	-3,1	-4,3	-0,6	-0,4
Middle East						
Cyprus	3,9	1,4	5,6	4,0	4,8	3,5
Algeria	2,3	1,6	2,4	-0,1	-3,3	-3,3
Egypt	3,0	1,8	6,2	2,3	0,0	-1,5
Iran	6,1	2,4	-2,9	-5,7	-2,2	-2,2
Israel	5,1	3,3	1,2	-0,1	2,7	1,9
Jordan	2,1	-0,9	6,7	2,3	-1,2	-2,9
Morocco	4,7	3,5	1,3	-0,5	0,9	0,3
Malta	3,7	1,9	6,6	4,9	3,9	2,0
Tunesia	4,1	2,3	2,2	0,2	0,7	0,1
South Asia						
Bangladesh	0,0	-0,6	2,5	1,8	1,1	0,7
India	1,8	0,1	2,4	1,0	3,1	1,6
Sri Lanka	2,1	1,0	3,2	0,7	2,7	1,0

Myanmar	0,5	0,1	3,5	1,9	-0,6	-1,6
Pakistan	3,9	0,2	2,8	2,0	2,7	1,5
Sub-Saharan Africa						
Côte d'Ivoire	5,9	3,3	0,5	-2,0	-2,4	-1,8
Cameroon	0,6	-0,8	6,7	3,4	-4,5	-5.7
Ethiopia	2,2	0,2	0,0	-0,9	-0,2	-1,6
Ghana	0,9	-1,0	-3,2	-3,2	1,8	1,1
Kenya	3,4	3,4	0,4	-0,1	0,1	0,4
Madagascar	0,3	-0,4	-2,0	-2,2	-0,9	-1,0
Mali	1,2	0,4	0,3	-0,2	0,9	0,4
Mozamique	0,3	-0,4	-2,0	-2,2	-0,9	-1,0
Mauritius	1,5	1,5	1,0	0,3	4,0	2,8
Malawi	3,3	0,2	1,5	0,0	-1,1	-0,8
Nigeria	1,2	0,9	-2,3	-4,6	1,3	2,0
Rwanda	-0,2	-0,8	1,7	-0,1	-3,6	-4,3
Sudan	-1,4	-3,7	2,1	0,2	-0,7	-0,7
Senegal	-0,5	-0,6	0,0	-0,2	0,2	-0,2
Sierra Leone	3,4	1,3	0,9	0,2	-0,3	-0,2
Uganda	0,7	-0,3	-2,9	-3,0	1,3	1,1
Tanzania	3,0	2,2	-1,1	-1,7	1,0	0,6
South Africa	2,3	0,9	1,0	-0,3	-2,0	-1,8
Zaire	2,4	2,2	-2,2	-3,4	-5,2	-5,9
Zambia	1,0	0,2	-2,3	-1,9	-2,5	-1,1
Zimbabwe	2,9	2,7	-0,8	-1,3	0,2	0,4

Tabelle 153: Trends in nominal effective exchange rates for exports and imports during the two periods 1964-1970 and 1977-1983 (won per dollar) Source: Bank of Korea. In: Kim 1991: 58.
Erwähnt in Abschnitt 'G', 530.

Date	1 Official rate	2 Net export subsidies (a)	3 Actual tariffs and equivalents (b)	4 Effective rates for Exports	5 Effective rates for Imports	6 Ratio of effective export rate to import rate (%)
Dec 1964	255.5	49.3	32.7	304.8	288.2	105.8
June 1965	271.1	9.9	27.7	281.0	298.8	94.0
Dec 1965	271.5	9.9	27.7	281.4	299.2	94.1
June 1966	270.9	12.5	25.1	283.4	296.0	95.7
Dec 1966	270.9	12.5	25.1	283.4	296.0	95.7
June 1967	269.2	20.0	25.5	289.2	294.7	98.1
Dec 1967	274.6	20.0	25.5	294.6	300.1	98.2
Dec 1968	281.5	18.2	25.9	299.7	307.4	97.5
Dec 1969	304.5	18.4	24.5	322.9	329.0	98.1
Dec 1970	316.7	20.8	25.7	337.5	324.4	98.6
Dec 1977	484.0	9.4	35.7	493.4	519.7	94.9
June 1978	484.0	11.0	42.9	495.0	526.9	93.9
Dec 1978	484.0	11.0	42.9	495.0	526.9	93.9
June 1979	484.0	11.0	36.0	495.0	520.0	95.2
Dec 1979	484.0	11.0	36.0	495.0	520.0	95.2
Dec 1980	659.9	20.6	34.4	680.5	694.3	98.0
Dec 1981	700.5	15.0	34.1	715.5	734.6	97.4
Dec 1982	748.8	3.0	41.8	751.8	790.6	95.1
Dec 1983	795.3	0.0	55.9	795.3	851.2	93.4

Column 4 is the sum of columns 1 and 2; column 5 is the sum of columns 1 and 3; column 6 is coumn 4 divided by column 5.

(a) The average value of net export subsidies per US dollar of exports for the respective years, not for the months indicated since such subsidies cannot be indicated by month.
(b) The average value of actual tariffs and tariff equivalents per US dollar of imports for the respective years, not the month indicated.

Tabelle 154: The Structure of Nominal and Effective Protection (%). In: Yoo 1993: 362-368. Erwähnt in Abschnitt 'G', 534, 535.

	1978			1982			1988	
	Tariffs	Actual Tariffs	Effective Protection	Tariffs	Actual Tariffs	Effective Protection	Tariffs	Actual Tariffs
Agriculture	25,8	20,6	64,6	18,7	14,8	82,7	23,1	14,4
Forestry	13,8	13,1	0,4	17,2	12,0	-0,1	15,3	10,9
Fishing	34,7	22,2	-0,5	29,7	28,4	-0,5	19,8	11,9
Mining	17,7	1,8	-1,5	4,2	3,2	-1,5	5,7	4,5
Manufacturing	40,8	25,1	24,4	31,9	21,2	31,5	18,3	12,4
Food	39,4	30,0	-28,8	21,4	19,0	-27,6	15,2	9,9
Beverage	125,0	18,1	4,8	126,7	24,1	-4,1	80,0	56,1
Tobacco	150,0	127,1	73,7	150,0	143,9	50,0	70,0	49,2
Textiles	49,2	29,8	5,5	40,3	29,3	5,3	19,0	11,7
Clothing	60,0	39,3	75,2	60,8	14,0	93,8	28,7	17,4
Footwear, leather	47,9	44,9	-6,1	51,4	38,8	-2,4	19,9	9,8
Wood	30,0	19,8	-9,3	25,8	22,3	6,5	17,1	13,7
Furniture	60,0	3,6	46,6	58,9	3,8	-2,1	19,5	9,2
Pulp, paper	36,4	26,3	36,2	37,8	22,9	22,9	18,2	14,4
Printing	8,1	3,5	-3,6	11,0	1,5	-11,7	3,1	4,2
Industrial chemicals	23,6	16,4	42,2	18,7	11,9	65,8	15,9	10,1
Other chemicals	35,9	34,6	45,4	31,9	30,7	35,9	19,4	14,6
Oil refining	20,4	7,4	26,1	6,2	4,0	681,9	9,8	8,5
Petrol., coal products	20,4	0,5	121,6	4,2	0,3	-0,2	0,7	0,8
Rubber products	50,0	27,3	-9,6	47,0	26,7	2,0	18,6	12,2
Plastic products	60,0	29,8	-3,9	60,0	33,2	-6,5	18,6	13,4
Pottery, china	60,0	20,8	23,1	60,0	20,1	15,4	25,5	18,9
Glass	45,5	32,4	15,4	42,4	32,6	8,8	19,3	12,2
Other nonmetal min. prod.	30,6	21,9	10,9	23,5	23,2	40,1	17,9	13,5
Iron & steel	20,8	13,6	24,7	14,7	10,5	31,5	11,6	7,0
Nonferrous metal	21,0	17,5	31,6	22,4	16,0	23,6	18,1	12,3
Fabricated metal	39,8	23,5	12,8	35,5	22,6	0	20,1	12,6
Nonelectrical mach.	23,6	13,3	44,2	18,1	9,6	22,0	18,5	10,1
Electrical mach.	36,5	27,3	105,4	38,6	22,5	44,8	19,9	20,4
Transport equip.	45,6	25,7	30,4	53,8	25,3	12,4	18,8	7,8
Prof. science equip.	34,5	28,1	102,6	29,5	21,6	42,8	21,0	10,7
Miscellaneous manuf.	63,2	25,9	5,9	58,5	30,2	-7,1	21,5	10,5
All industries	36,3	22,6	31,6	30,8	20,2	37,2	18,4	12,4
	(38,1)	(22,9)	(20,5)	(32,1)	(20,8)	(27,8)	(18,2)	(12,2)
Standard deviation	21,4	17,9	76,6	23,4	18,3	312,8	12,0	11,2
	(22,1)	(17,7)	(79,3)	(23,8)	(18,2)	323,6	(11,6)	(10,4)

Anmerkung: die nominalen durchschnittlichen Zölle sind womöglich gewichtet berechnet, korrigiert nach der Menge importierter Waren. Zumindest scheint dies für den Wert 'All industries' zu gelten, weil diesbezüglich darauf verwiesen wird, daß die Absenkung von 30,8 auf 18,4 durchschnittlichen Zolls im Jahre 1988 vom Autor darauf zurückgeführt wird, daß der Absenkung bezüglich des Maschinenbausektors ein asymmetrisch großes Gewicht zukommt, weil dieser Sektor viele Import aufweist. Yoo 1993: 366. Wäre dies so, müßten die Werte eigentlich noch zutreffender sein, als bei einer Berechnung der durchschnittlichen Werte, die durch die Anzahl jeder einzelnen Zollposition dividiert wird. Des Autors macht hierzu keine genauen Angaben. Weiterhin äußert sich Anne O. Krueger kritisch über einige Details dieses Artikels, unter anderem über den überhöht erscheinenden Wert von 681% Zollschutz für die Ölraffinerien im Jahre 1982, der ebenfalls nicht erklärt wird. Wie üblich sind die Zollhöhen, insbesondere die, die noch weitere Berechnungen erforderlich machen, eben die effektiven Protektionsraten, mit Vorsicht zu betrachten. Immerhin stellen die Werte Anhaltspunkte dar, die ein ungefähr richtiges Bild zu vermitteln scheinen.

Tabelle 155: Korea's effective protection rates (1) for the domestic market, 1968-82.
In: Moreira 1995: 58.
Erwähnt in Abschnitt 'G', 534.

Sector (ISIC)	1968	1978 (2)	1978 (3)	1982
Agriculture	19	57	77	74
Mining	4	-1.5	-26	-2
Processed foods	-18	-44	-29	-48
Beverages and tobacco	-19	33	28	15
Construction material	-11	12	-15	51
Interm. products I	-25	37	-38	62
Interm. products II	26	21	8	40
Consumer nondurables	-11	67	31.5	43
Consumer durables	64	243	131	52.5
Machinery	44	44	47	32
Transport equipment	163	327	135	124
Manufacturing	-1	32	5	28
All industries	11	39.7	30.6	n.a.

(1) Direkter Preisvergleich, Balassa Methode. (2) Geschätzt von Young, S. (1984). (3) Geschätzt von Nam (1981).

Tabelle 156: Coverage of Korea's contingent import control, 1981-1989. In number of items at the 8-digit level of CCCN. In: Moreira 1995: 187.
Erwähnt in Abschnitt 'G', 535.

Measure	1981	1982	1983	1984	1985	1986	1987	1989
Tariffs (a)								
(1) Emergency	300	12	104	23	7	2	7	n.a.
(2) Adjustment	-	-	-	14	7	5	-	-
(1)+(2) / total import items	4	0,2	1,3	0,5	0,2	0,1	0,1	n.a.
NTBs								
Import diversification (b)	205	209	174	168	160	162	n.a.	22
% total imp. items	20,3	20,7	17,2	16,6	15,8	15,0	n.a.	2,2
Surveillance (c)	193	201	161	125	118	106	57	25
% total import items	2,6	2,7	2,1	1,6	1,5	1,0	0,7	0,4 (e)
Special laws (d)	n.a.	1950	n.a.	n.a.	1875	n.a.	n.a.	n.a. (e)
% total import items	n.a.	26,1	n.a.	n.a.	23,6	26,0	n.a.	19,0 (e)

(a) 1981 – 1985 as of July 1of each year. 1986 – 87 as of December of each year. Emergency tariffs can be placed on any item. Adjustment tariffs are for newly liberalized items. (b) Aimed at reducing bilateral trade imbalances. At the 4-digit level of CCCN. (c) Liberalized items placed under government observation. Eliminated as of January 1. 1989. (d) Import restrictions on 'welfare' and national security grounds. (e) 1988.

Tabelle 157: Korea's merchandise imports by product group, 1980-1990 (US$ million and per cent). In: Trade Policy Review Korea 1990: 33.
Erwähnt in Abschnitt 'G', 535, 537.

	1980	1985	1990
Fuels	29.9	23.7	15.8
Other non-electric machinery	7.8	8.4	13.8
Office machinery and telecommunications	5.2	7.3	11.1
Chemicals	8.2	9.0	10.6
Raw materials	11.3	7.9	8.0
Other consumer goods	2.9	4.0	5.6
Food	9.8	5.8	5.6
Other semi-manufactures	3.1	4.0	5.0
Iron and steel	4.4	3.8	4.7
Ores and minerals	4.2	3.8	3.9
Other transport equipment	4.7	13.3	3.3
Electric machinery and apparatus	2.3	2.9	3.0
Textiles	1.8	2.1	2.8
Non-ferrous metals	1.6	1.5	2.7
Power generating machinery	1.4	1.5	1.7
Automotive products	1.0	0.8	1.3
Residual	0.2	0.3	0.8
Clothing	0.1	0.1	0.2
Total merchandise imports	100.0	100.0	100.0
Memorandum	Million dollars (c.i.f.)		
Total mercandise imports	22,243	31,136	69,844

Tabelle 158: Korea's and Brazil's export subsidies and export related imports as a percentage of manufactured exports (fob), 1969-85. In: Moreira 1995: 110.
Erwähnt in Abschnitt 'G', 536, 559, 560, 561.

Year	Korea (%)			Brazil (%)		
	Subsidies (1)		Imports (3) %	Subsidies (2)		Imports (3) %
	Net	Gross	of exp.	Net	Gross	of exp.
1969	6,4	27,8	10,8	10,8	42,7	2,34
1970	6,7	28,3	21,0	21,0	52,7	6,51
1971	6,6	29,6	22,3	22,3	53,1	8,05
1972	3,2	26,8	25,8	25,8	58,8	8,55
1973	2,2	23,7	24,1	24,1	58,3	11,69
1974	2,1	21,2	19,9	19,9	55,2	10,50
1975	2,7	16,7	25,3	25,3	56,0	16,28
1976	2,5	16,9	29,0	29,0	65,8	14,07
1977	1,9	19,2	33,5	33,5	72,5	9,37
1978	2,3	19,5	31,6	31,6	68,1	10,04
1979	2,3	20,2	30,3	30,3	67,5	n.a.
1980	3,3	21,3	7,4	7,4	45,1	n.a.
1981	2,2	n.a.	29,8	29,8	71,8	n.a.
1982	0,4	n.a.	34,6	34,6	76,7	n.a.
1983	0,0	n.a.	20,6	20,6	58,5	n.a.
1984	n.a.	n.a.	13,9	13,9	53,0	n.a.
1985	n.a.	n.a.	10,0	10,0	49,2	n.a.

(1) Korea data for total exports. Yet manufactured exports averaged 94 % during the period. Net subsidies include cash subsidies, export dollar premium, direct tax reduction and interest rate subsidy. Gross subsidies include net subsidy plus indirect tax exemption and tariff exemptions. (2) Net subsidies comprise direct tax reduction, tax credits and interest rate subsidy. Gross subsidies include net subsidies plus indirect tax and tariff exemptions. (3) Export-related imports consist of parts and raw material used in export production which were exempted from import and indirect taxes.

Tabelle 159: Ratio of imports to domestic production of final goods by sector for selected years (per cent). In: Kim 1991: 81.
Erwähnt in Abschnitt 'G', 536.

Sector	1966	1970	1975	1980
Agriculture, forestry and fishery	2.6	15.8	21.7	21.9
Mining	2.2	76.5	322.8	536.9
Processed food (including tobacco)	3.7	6.1	9.2	7.4
Textile products and apparel	3.5	7.6	5.4	4.0
Lumber and wood products	1.0	1.4	0.5	2.3
Pulp, paper, and allied products	6.3	19.5	19.2	16.9
Chemical and allied products	64.2	46.8	35.5	22.0
Petroleum and coal products	9.2	2.3	9.2	11.4
Nonmetallic mineral products	7.2	5.2	5.4	4.4
Iron and steel	34.7	48.5	32.9	18.6
Nonferrous metals	20.7	50.7	55.8	45.2
Metal products	49.9	55.3	14.4	12.0
General machinery	189.9	273.4	183.0	115.0
Electrical machinery	33.7	63.4	41.7	33.5
Transport equipment	71.9	58.3	63.7	47.6
Other manufacturing	2.2	4.0	8.8	8.6
All services	1.7	0.7	1.4	2.4
Total	7.3	12.5	17.6	16.1

Tabelle 160: Korea's export and import ratio by manufacturing sector, 1953-1983 (%). In: Moreira 1995: 169.
Erwähnt in Abschnitt 'G', 536, 560.

Import ratios (1)	1953	1960	1965	1972	1974	1980	1983
Total mnf.	10.2	12.1	10.2	15.3	24.1	16.8	17.6
HCI	26.0	33.3	23.6	33.0	39.0	23.8	23.8
Light	6.0	5.0	3.7	7.1	12.7	8.1	8.4
Exports (2)							
Total mnf.	1.1	0.8	5.3	17.9	26.5	17.5	21.1
HCI	1.0	0.6	3.5	14.0	22.3	19.0	22.0
Light	1.1	0.9	6.3	19.8	31.7	18.3	19.9

(1) Imports divided by the total domestic supply (2) Exports divided by total output.

Tabelle 161: Trends in nominal effective exchange rates for exports and imports during the two periods 1964-1970 and 1977-1983 (won per dollar) Source: Bank of Korea.
In: Kim 1991: 58.
Erwähnt in Abschnitt 'G', 536.

Date	1 Official rate	2 Net export subsidies (a)	3 Actual tariffs and equivalents (b)	4 Effective rates for Exports	5 Effective rates for Imports	6 Ratio of effective export rate to import rate (%)
Dec 1964	255.5	49.3	32.7	304.8	288.2	105.8
June 1965	271.1	9.9	27.7	281.0	298.8	94.0
Dec 1965	271.5	9.9	27.7	281.4	299.2	94.1
June 1966	270.9	12.5	25.1	283.4	296.0	95.7
Dec 1966	270.9	12.5	25.1	283.4	296.0	95.7
June 1967	269.2	20.0	25.5	289.2	294.7	98.1
Dec 1967	274.6	20.0	25.5	294.6	300.1	98.2
Dec 1968	281.5	18.2	25.9	299.7	307.4	97.5
Dec 1969	304.5	18.4	24.5	322.9	329.0	98.1
Dec 1970	316.7	20.8	25.7	337.5	324.4	98.6
Dec 1977	484.0	9.4	35.7	493.4	519.7	94.9
June 1978	484.0	11.0	42.9	495.0	526.9	93.9
Dec 1978	484.0	11.0	42.9	495.0	526.9	93.9
June 1979	484.0	11.0	36.0	495.0	520.0	95.2
Dec 1979	484.0	11.0	36.0	495.0	520.0	95.2
Dec 1980	659.9	20.6	34.4	680.5	694.3	98.0
Dec 1981	700.5	15.0	34.1	715.5	734.6	97.4
Dec 1982	748.8	3.0	41.8	751.8	790.6	95.1
Dec 1983	795.3	0.0	55.9	795.3	851.2	93.4

Column 4 is the sum of columns 1 and 2; column 5 is the sum of columns 1 and 3; column 6 is coumn 4 divided by column 5.

(a) The average value of net export subsidies per US dollar of exports for the respective years, not for the months indicated since such subsidies cannot be indicated by month.
(b) The average value of actual tariffs and tariff equivalents per US dollar of imports for the respective years, not the month indicated.

Tabelle 162: Die 10 bedeutendsten Exportwaren Südkoreas.
In: Seung 1996: 71.
Erwähnt in Abschnitt 'G', 537, 539.

1961		1970		1975	
1. Eisenerz	13,0	Textilien, Bekleidung	40,8	Textilien, Bekleidung	36,2
2. Wolfram	12,6	Sperrholz	11,0	Elektronische Produkte	8,9
3. Rohseide	6,7	Perücken	10,8	Stahlprodukte	4,6
4. Anthrazit	5,8	Eisenerz	5,9	Sperrholz	4,1
5. Tintenfisch	5,5	Elektronische Produkte	3,5	Schuhwerk	3,8
6. Sonst. lebende Fische	4,5	Süßwaren	2,3	Fische	2,7
7. Graphit	4,2	Schuhwerk	2,1	Schiffe	2,4
8. Sperrholz	3,3	Tabak und Tabakwaren	1,6	Metallprodukte	2,4
9. Getreide	3,3	Stahlprodukte	1,5	Petro-Produkte	1,9
10. Schweinehaare	3,0	Metallprodukte	1,5	Synthetische Harze	1,7
Zusammen	62,0		77,1		69,9
1980		1985		1992	
1. Textilien, Bekleidung	28,6	Textilien, Bekleidung	23,4	Elektronische Produkte	28,2
2. Elektronische Produkte	11,4	Schiffe	16,6	Textilien, Bekleidung	20,5
3. Stahlprodukte	10,6	Elektronische Produkte	14,1	Stahlprodukte	7,0
4. Schuhwerk	5,2	Stahlprodukte	8,1	Chemische Produkte	5,5
5. Schiffe	3,5	Schuhwerk	5,2	Schiffe	5,4
6. Synthetische Harze	3,3	Petro-Produkte	3,0	Schuhwerk	4,2
7. Metallprodukte	2,5	Synthetische Harze	2,4	Automobile	3,7
8. Sperrholz	2,0	Elektrische Produkte	2,0	Maschinen	3,2
9. Fische	2,0	Automobile	1,9	Petro-Produkte	2,2
10. Elektrische Produkte	1,9	Metallprodukte	1,7	Fischprodukte	2,0
Zusammen	71,0		78,5		81,8

Tabelle 163: Südkoreas Importabhängigkeitsgrad im Werkzeugmaschinenbereich 1960 bis 1995 (Einheit: %): In: Köllner 1998: 246.
Erwähnt in Abschnitt 'G', 538.

1960	1963	1966	1969	1970	1971	1972	1973	1975	1977	1979
34,7	60,2	66,3	69,9	68,3	88,0	91,6	86,7	88,8	74,9	75,5

1981	1983	1985	1987	1989	1990	1991	1992	1993	1994	1995
66,5	49,5	56,5	47,8	50,1	52,7	53,0	62,2	53,3	53,2	55,2

Tabelle 164: Brazil's effective purchase-power-parity exchange rates (1) 1954-1987 (1980 prices). In: Moreira 1995: 195.
Erwähnt in Abschnitt 'G', 558, 561.

Year	Exports (2)	Imports (3)	Official	Year	Exports (2)	Official
1954	23.9	53.7	m.r. (4)	1972	58.7	46.7
1955	29.3	63.8	m.r.	1973	57.8	46.6
1956	29.4	76.0	m.r.	1974	62.0	51.8
1957	31.3	97.3	m.r.	1975	61.0	48.9
1958	34.0	89.2	m.r.	1976	62.6	48.7
1959	41.7	104.3	m.r.	1977	64.5	48.5
1960	44.6	87.6	m.r.	1978	61.5	46.9
1961	49.5	117.9	m.r.	1979	64.1	49.7
1962	49.2	131.7	45.6	1980	56.5	52.7
1963	42.1	120.3	39.6	1981	67.4	52.8
1964	51.7	122.4	41.5	1982	74.3	56.2
1965	53.0	106.9	49.5	1983	83.8	70.4
1966	45.8	75.4	45.8	1984	77.8	68.4
1967	43.1	61.2	42.1	1985	79.0	72.3
1968	46.1	62.5	43.5	1986	n.a.	67.4
1969	53.4	70.8	48.2	1987	n.a.	62.9
1970	56.5	70.9	47.7	1988	n.a.	52.7
1971	58.2	n.a.	47.6	1989	n.a.	32.6

(1) Relevant exchange rate times the ratio of the average WPI of Brazil's major trade partners (EUA, UK, Germany, France, Italy, Netherlands) to Brazil's WPI. (2) Includes export bonuses and net subsidies. (3) Includes legal tariffs and surcharges. Not available for the post 1970 period. (4) Multiple rates.

Tabelle 165: Domestic market protection estimates for industry a 2 digit level, 1980-1981, and nominal export subsidy rates plus anti-export bias, 1981. Tyler 1985: 227, 234. Erwähnt in Abschnitt 'G', 558, 559, 560, 561, 562, 564.

Industry	Nominal legal tariff December 1980 (%)	Average implicit tariff (%)	Average implicit nominal protection (%)	Effective protection estimate (%)	Effective export promotion rate (%)	Anti-export bias (%)
Mining	27.0	-15.6	-3.6	-4.2	1.1	-5.4
Non-metallic minerals	107.5	-22.5	-17.7	-19.6	29.3	-48.9
Metallurgy	54.3	3.0	10.8	34.2	54.1	-20.0
Machinery	56.3	24.0	58.7	93.3	36.4	56.9
Electrical equipment	99.1	45.2	81.7	129.3	28.4	100.9
Transportation equipment	101.9	-16.7	-3.7	-6.5	39.1	-45.6
Lumber & wood	125.3	-8.9	-4.3	17.7	53.6	-35.9
Furniture	148.2	20.0	26.1	52.7	52.9	-0.3
Paper	120.3	-19.9	-16.1	-18.5	40.0	-58.4
Rubber	107.3	-23.3	-15.4	-21.4	28.5	-49.9
Leather	156.6	10.0	15.6	13.9	22.7	-8.8
Chemicals	50.3	40.7	55.1	86.4	15.5	70.9
Pharmaceutical products	27.9	79.0	97.4	116.3	22.5	93.8
Perfumery	160.5	28.5	35.1	91.6	57.0	34.5
Plastics	203.8	14.3	28.9	28.3	23.9	4.4
Textiles	167.3	20.6	25.2	36.7	36.7	0.0
Apparel	181.2	24.2	30.6	46.7	37.7	9.0
Food products	107.8	-21.3	-8.2	26.1	28.9	-2.8
Beverages	179.0	-9.9	-5.3	-1.1	29.6	-30.7
Tobacco	184.6	-3.6	1.3	5.7	16.0	-10.3
Printing&publishing	85.5	18.1	24.1	31.9	31.6	0.3
Miscellaneous	87.0	73.9	91.8	171.7	46.2	125.6
Averages						
Primary agriculture (a)	53.8	-22.2	-7.2	-8.2	-5.4	-4.8
Manufacturing	99.4	11.9	24.5	46.4	34.9	11.5
Capital goods	83.3	13.6	45.5	71.9	34.9	37.0
Intermediate products	76.5	5.6	25.2	42.0	34.7	7.2
Consumer goods	132.5	13.9	13.1	35.7	35.0	0.7

(a) Includes forestry and fishing, agriculture, and livestock and poultry.

Average implicit tariff: the proportional amount by which the domestic price exceeds the international price.
Average implicit nominal protection: implicit tariff plus domestic production subsidies, f.e. fiscal mechanisms or financial arrangements.
Effective protection estimate: nominal protection awarded to the final product plus input structure and the protection afforded to inputs
Effective export promotion rate: nominal export incentives, subsidies, taxes etc. plus other incentives or disincentives.
Anti-export bias: effective protection estimate minus effective export promotion rate. See Tyler 1985: 222-223.

Tabelle 166: Brazil's export and import ratios by manufacturing sector, 1949-1984 (%). In: Moreira 1995: 191.
Erwähnt in Abschnitt 'G', 560.

Import (1)	1949	1964	1967	1970	1974	1979	1984	1988	1990
Total mnf.	13.9	6.1	7.1	8.0 (8.8)	11.9 (12.2)	6.8 (7.4)	(5.1)	(4.4)	(5.7)
HCI	26.9	9.0	10.2	11.8	15.2	8.4	n.a.	n.a.	n.a.
Light	3.8	1.6	2.2	2.3	5.1	3.4	n.a	n.a	n.a
Export (2)									
Total mnf.	2.3	2.0	2.6	5.7 (4.5)	6.9 (6.4)	9.1 (8.0)	9.8 (16.0)	(9.8)	(9.3)
HCI	5.2	1.8	2.0	2.3	3.6	8.2	n.a.	n.a.	n.a.
Light	1.5	1.8	2.3	5.8	10.0	8.5	n.a	n.a	n.a

(1) Imports divided by the total domestic supply (2) Exports divided by total output.

Notes: (a) Heavy and chemical industry includes nonmetallic minerals, metallurgy, machinery, electrical and communications equipment, transport equipment, chemicals and pharmaceuticals. (b) Numbers in parantheses are from a recent BNDE study.

Tabelle 167: Classification of 41 developing countries by trade orientation 1973-85. Aus: Dodaro 1991: 1154-1157. (3) World Development Report 1978: 80-81. (4) Weltentwicklungsbericht 1982: 122-123, 126-127.
Erwähnt in Abschnitt 'G', 520, 561.

Orientation	Country	Nominal per capita GNP (1980) US Dollar	Price distortion index	(2)	Average real GDP growth rate (1971-81)	(2)	Average real merchandise exports growth rate (1970-81) (1)	(2)	Industry, percent of GDP (1960, 1976) (3)	GDP, Mio US $ (1980) (4)	Investment (1980) Mio. US $ (4)
Strongly outward oriented	Hong Kong	4,240	-		10,0	av. = 9,2	9,7 (10,3)	av. = 14,6	34, 34	20,230	**4,046**
	South Korea	1,520	1,57		9,0		22,0 (20,5)		19, 34	58,720	18,203
	Singapore	4,430	-		8,6		12,0 (11,9)		18, 35	10,480	4,506
Moderately outward oriented	Brazil	2,050	1,86	av. = 1,90	7,7	av. = 5,6	8,7 (7,3)	av. = 7,0	35, 39	237,930	**52,344**
	Chile	2,150	2,43		2,1		9,8 (11,6)		38, 39	28,080	5,054
	Israel	4,500	-		4,0		9,6 (8,4)		32, 43	15,340	3,375
	Malaysia	1,620	1,57		7,8		6,8 **(8,2)**		18, 30	23,600	**6,844**
	Thailand	670	1,43		7,2		11,8 **(9,4)**		19, 25	33,450	**9,031**
	Tunisia	1,310	1,57		7,4		4,0 (7,3)		18, 30	7,300	2,044
	Turkey	1,470	2,14		5,2		1,2 **(5,2)**		21, 28	53,820	**14,531**
	Uruguay	2,810	2,29		3,1		4,3 (9,2)		28, 32	8,430	1,517
Moderately inward oriented	Cameroon	670	1,57	av. = 1,87	6,3	av. = 5,1	4,9 (6,8)	av. = 3,6	10, 20	6,010	1,502
	Columbia	1,180	1,71		5,6		**1,6 (5,3)**		26, 30	29,570	**7,392**
	Costa Rica	1,730	-		5,2		4,0 (6,0)		19, 26	4,850	1,212
	Côte de' Ivoire	1,150	2,14		6,2		5,1 (5,0)		14, 20	7,030	1,968
	El Salvador	660	-		3,2		0,7 (3,7)		19, 21	3,390	406
	Guatemala	1,080	-		5,5		5,0 (5,4)			7,850	1,256
	Honduras	560	-		4,4		4,2 (4,4)		19, 28	2,230	624
	Indonesia	430	1,86		7,8		6,5 **(6,8)**		17, 34	69,800	**15,356**
	Kenya	420	1,71		6,2		-1,9 (0,7)		18, 23	5,990	1,317
	Mexico	2,090	1,86		6,5		15,3 (**8,2**)		29, 35	166,700	**46,676**

	Nicaragua	740	-	0,8	0,2 (-1,3)	21, 28	2,120	424
	Pakistan	300	2,29	5,0	3,0 (2,2)	16, 24	21,460	3,862
	Philippines	690	1,57	6,2	**7,7 (7,2)**	28, 34	35,490	**10,647**
	Senegal	450	2,29	2,0	-1,4 (2,9)	20, 24	2,650	397
	Sri Lanka	270	1,86	4,7	-1,5 (-1,7)	16, 21	3,760	1,353
	Yugoslavia	2,620	1,71	5,8	4,5 (4,0)	45, 43	62,150	21,752
Strongly inward oriented	Argentina	2,360	2,43	av. = 2,38 1,9	av. = 3,2 **9,4 (6,8)**	av. = -0,3 38, 41	130,920	**34,039**(5)
	Bangladesh	130	2,57	4,1	-0,7 (5,9)	8, 8	11,140	1,893
	Bolivia	570	2,29	4,4	-1,9 (1,9)	28, 32	6,100	793
	Burundi	200	-	3,5	n.a. (0,8)	...., 15	790	110
	Dominican Republic	1,160	-	6,3	3,8 (8,1)	23, 32	7,120	1,709
	Ethiopia	140	1,86	2,6	-0,8 (0,3)	12, 15	3,690	369
	Ghana	420	2,86	-0,3	-7,1 (-9,2)	19, 25	15,390	769
	India	240	1,86	3,6	**4,6 (8,4)**	20, 23	142,010	**29,822**
	Madagascar	350	-	0,3	-2,5 (-0,2)	10, 20	3,260	684
	Nigeria	1,010	2,71	4,5	0,5 (0,8)	11, 50	91,130	21,871
	Peru	930	2,29	3,1	4,6 (-0,3)	29, 31	19,240	3,078
	Sudan	410	-	6,2	-5,2 (-1,8)	15, 16	7,190	862
	Tanzania	280	2,57	4,2	-8,1 (-6,0)	11, 16	4,350	1,000
	Zambia	560	-	0,4	-0,2 (-0,9)	63, 41	3,240 (5)	680 (5)

(1) In parantheses export growth. (2) Simple average (5) für 1979, aus World Development Report 1981. Zum Vergleich: China 1980: GDP 252,230, Bruttoinlandsinvestitionen: 78,191 (Mill. US $).

Tabelle 168: Levels of Value Added per Hour Worked in Manufacturing Compared to the Total Economy (USA=100), 1950-1989.
Erwähnt in Abschnitt 'G', 565.

	1950		1973		1989	
	manufacturing	total economy	manufacturing	total economy	manufacturing	total economy
Brazil	20	17	40	25	27 (c)	25 (c)
India	4	4	5	4	6 (c)	4 (c)
Korea	5 (a)	10	11	15	18 (c)	21 (c)
France	32	36	62	63	76	85
Germany	39	28	76	60	79	77
Japan	18 (b)	12	57	38	80	52
Netherlands	40	42	80	71	85	84
United Kingdom	40	51	52	60	61	73
United States	100	100	100	100	100	100

(a) 1953; (b) 1955; (c) 1986. Aus: van Ark 1993: 109.

Tabelle 169: ICOP Estimates of Levels of Labor Productivity in Manufacturing, 1960-1998, USA = 100. Aus: Timmer/van Ark 2001.
Erwähnt Abschnitt 'G', 565.

	1960		1973		1987		1996	
	Value added per Person employed	Value added per hour	Value added per Person employed	Value added per hour	Value added per Person employed	Value added per hour	Value added per Person employed	Value added per hour
India -all firms -registered firms only (a)	2,1 6,7		2,6 (g) 7,0 (g)		2,2 8,4	 6,8	2,1 (i) 10,8 (i)	
China -all firms -large firms only					4,5 5,7	 4,9	6,4 (j)	
Indonesia -all firms -medium & large only	4,0 (e)		3,0 (h)		4,6 8,0	 6,3	5,0 (k) 11,2 (k)	
Hungary	17,6		16,7		20,1		25,2	
Poland	23,9		24,9		21,2		18,5	
East Germany	24,3		22,5		22,5	23,5	57,6	
Czechoslowakia	27,7		23,9		24,0	18,9		
Portugal	15,0		24,2		24,5		23,2	
USSR -all industry (d) -manufacturing only	27,2	27,3	25,5	26,8	26,1	27,7		
Mexico	36,8		35,3		25,5		25,4	
Korea	9,8 (f)	6,9 (f)	15,0	10,9	26,5	18,4	40,6	31,7
Taiwan	11,8 (f)	8,1 (f)	19,5	14,0	26,6	20,4	34,7	28,3
Brazil	41,8		46,3		32,7		21,9	
Spain	15,1		28,5		46,5		39,6	
Australia	40,7	39,6	43,1	43,8	48,4	49,9	45,5	47,3
United Kingdom	49,9	45,9	51,1	52,5	53,6	58,0	53,1	61.1
Finland	47,9	45,5	53,2	56,1	65,9	74,3	86,4	103,5
Sweden	53,6	55,3	73,0	88,3	68,4	87,4	83,1	99,4
West Germany	63,0	57,9	75,6	79,0	70,2	82,2	66,2	84,6
France	51,8	49,8	67,6	71,4	71,2	84,0	75,4	91,2
Japan	24,9	19,9	55,0	47,5	76,4	67,5	82,7	83,2
Canada	80,4	80,2	83,9	86,0	77,5	79,4	73,0	77,4
Belgium	42,1	42,2	57,6	67,0	78,5	99,8	80,7	104,0
Netherlands	54,4	50,2	79,3	87,0	83,3	105,4	82,8	108,9
United States	100,0	100,0	100,0	100,0	100,0	100,0	100,0	100,0

(a) establishments with 20 or more employees and establishments with between 10-20 employees using power; (b) enterprises above township level; (c) establishments with 20 or more employees except those in oil and gas refineries; (d) including mining and public utilities; (e) 1961; (f) 1963; (g) 1970; (h) 1971; (i) 1993; (j) 1994; (k) 1995.

Tabelle 170: Brazil's public sector share of gross capital formation, 1947-1987 (1). In: Moreira 1995: 193.
Erwähnt in Abschnitt 'G', 556.

	State firms (2)	Gov. budget	Public sector	Private sector	Total
1947-55	2.9	23.1	26.1	73.9	100
1956-64	9.3	23.8	33.1	66.9	100
1965-73	18.7	23.7	42.4	57.6	100
1974-79	22.1	14.7	36.9	63.1	100
1980-87	19.4	15.2	34.6	65.4	100

(1) Arithmetic average
(2) Over 1966-79, includes only the federal large state firms in steel, mining, petrochemicals, telecommunications, electricity and railroads.

Tabelle 171: Brazil and Korea R&D expenditures-to-sales ratios. In: Moreira 1995: 121.
Erwähnt in Abschnitt 'G', 568.

Sectors	Brazil (1982)	Korea (1983)
Metallurgy	0.2	0.4
Machinery	0.3	2.0
Electrical Equipment	0.4	3.0
Transport	0.4	1.5
Lumber	0.0	0.6
Rubber	0.0	1.0
Chemicals	0.0	0.5
Plastics	0.0	1.7
Textiles	0.0	0.7
Food	0.0	0.7
Manufacturing	0.1	0.8

Tabelle 172: The Scale of Production of Passenger Cars and Light Multiple-Usage Vehicles at the Firm and Model Level in Selected Countries, 1984. In: Fischer/Nunnenkamp et al. 1988: 77.
Erwähnt in Abschnitt 'G', 573.

	Total passenger car production	Mass produced cars (a)			Basic models per firm	Average volume of production per firm	Average volume of production per basic model
		firms	mass-produced basic models	volume of mass production			
	1000 units	number		1000 units	average number	1000 Units	
Brasil	679	4	21	676	5.3	169	32
Mexico	232	6	17	216	2.8	36	13
South Korea	159	2	4	156	2.0	78	39
India	86	4	4	85	1.0	21	21
Spain	1225	6	n.a.	1254	n.a.	209	n.a.
United States	7952	4	64	7742	16.0	1935	121
West Germany	3754	4	24	2819	6.0	705	117
Japan	7771	5	n.a.	7071	18.0	1414	134

(a) Hier werden nur die wichtigsten Hersteller in den jeweiligen Ländern einbezogen. Siehe für weitere Anmerkungen: Fischer/Nunnenkamp et al. 1988: 77.

Tabelle 173: The Automobile Industry in Developing Countries (1986). In: Rodrik 1988: 116.
Erwähnt in Abschnitt 'G', 573.

Country	Number of Firms	Number of Basic Models	Average Output per Model per Year
Argentina	4	6	20,357
Brazil	4	4	182,539
Chile	2	5	1,872
India	4	4	20,807
South Korea	3	3	70,494
Taiwan	6	6	19,783
Turkey	3	3	19,123
Venezuela	4	4	17,731

Source: Automobile International 1986.

Tabelle 174: Brazil: Exports 1990-1995 (FOB, im Millions of U.S. Dollars),
In: Bonelli 2000: 95.
Erwähnt in Abschnitt 'G', 576.

Categories	1990	1991	1992	1993	1994	1995
Agriculture	1,387	906	1,322	1,487	1,883	1,336
Extractive minerals	2,860	3,079	2,746	2,748	2,779	3,122
Nonmetallic minerals	241	258	321	431	438	481
Metallurgical products	5,389	6,053	6,253	6,350	6,535	7,197
Metal manufacturing	1,155	1,224	1,510	1,851	2,247	2.370
Electrical and communications equipment	1,444	1,534	1,727	1,917	1,934	2,141
Transport equipment	3,265	3,120	4,265	4,361	4,827	4,366
Wood products	426	443	554	833	1,044	1,082
Furniture	40	58	126	241	267	316
Pulp and paper	1,233	1,264	1,478	1,561	1,825	2,731
Rubber	284	337	443	505	550	578
Chemicals	2,591	2,350	2,594	2,900	3,237	3,363
Pharmaceuticals	69	90	99	105	123	157
Perfumes, soap, candles	37	49	73	118	120	134
Plastic products	37	45	90	116	120	110
Textiles	1,016	1,142	1,217	1,115	1,133	1,197
Clothing and foodwear	1,315	1,371	1,624	2,123	1,825	1,657
Hides and skins	301	319	408	421	481	593
Food products	6,732	6,158	6,861	7,406	9,734	10,821
Beverages	54	67	75	95	150	147
Tobacco products	594	799	960	880	1,010	1,145
Other	558	621	758	775	820	826
Scrap iron	5	15	3	6	21	7
Total	33,025	33,292	37,497	40,337	45,096	47,871

Tabelle 175: Brazil: Exports by principal commodity groups (In millions of U.S. dollars). IMF Country Report Brazil Selected Issues and Statistical Appendix January 2001: 240. *Erwähnt in Abschnitt 'G', 576.*

	1995	1996	1997	1998	1999
Total exports	46,506	47,747	52,994	51,140	48,011
Primary products	10,969	11,900	14,474	12,977	11,828
Soybeans and soybran	2,767	3,749	5,133	3,929	3,097
Iron ore	2,548	2,695	2,846	3,253	2,746
Coffee beans	1,970	1,719	2,745	2,332	2,230
Tobacco leaf	769	1,029	1,091	940	884
Raw sugar	408	0	0	0	0
Other	2,507	2,708	2,659	2,523	2,871
Industrial products	34,711	35,026	37,672	37,507	35,311
Semi-manufactures	9,146	8,613	8,478	8,120	7,982
Raw sugar (1)	1,042	1,191	1,045	1,096	1,162
Steel products	1,369	1,294	1,359	1,255	1,056
Paper paste	1,447	954	958	930	901
Iron products	838	871	876	888	730
Leather hides	566	678	739	657	595
Soybean oil	1,031	685	532	724	564
Cocoa products	92	115	108	131	90
Other	2,761	2,825	2,861	2,439	2,883
Manufactures	25,565	26,413	29,194	29,387	27,329
Transport equipment	3,211	3,721	5,620	8,203	7,119
Nonelectric machinery	3,904	4,180	4,531	4,339	3,970
Electric machinery	1,503	1,584	1,783	1,712	1,813
Airplanes	182	284	681	1,159	1,772
Footwear	1,499	1,650	1,594	1,387	1,342
Orange juice	1,132	1,453	1,058	1,262	1,235
Steel products (2)	1,809	1,723	1,397	1,465	1,204
Automobiles	1,040	1,247	2,488	1,619	1,138
Petroleum derivatives	839	949	988	865	1,118
Refined sugar	366	421	726	847	748
Processed beef	302	243	239	314	360
Soluble coffee	456	376	349	246	211
Cotton fabrics and yarn	299	278	246	224	197
Other textiles	1,142	1,014	1,021	889	813
Other	11,862	11,713	11,416	9,202	7,865
Other exports	826	821	848	656	872
Annual percentage change					
Total exports	6,8	2,7	11,0	-3,5	-6,1
Primary products	-0,8	8,5	21,6	-10,3	-8,9
Semi-manufactures	32,7	-5,8	-1,6	-4,2	-1,7
Manufactures	2,4	3,3	10,5	0,7	-7,0
Excluding automobiles and airplanes	4,0	2,2	4,6	2,2	-8,2
Total automobiles	-25,9	19,9	99,5	-34,9	-29,7

(1) Passenger and commercial vehicles. (2) Lamin. planos, tubos, barras e perfis de ferro/aco.

Tabelle 176: Production Costs of Boninas Laminada a Frio, Selected Countries, April 2001 (US$/dispatched tons). In: Ferraz et al. 2003: 27.
Erwähnt in Abschnitt 'G', 578.

	USA	Japan	Germany	UK	S. Korea	China	Brazil
Raw materials	115	106	109	105	112	118	103
Coal	27	27	26	24	28	28	37
Iron ore	55	56	62	58	59	75	40
Scrap / DRI	33	26	21	23	25	15	26
Other raw materials	172	150	148	153	134	152	135
Labour costs	154	142	136	113	62	26	57
Hourly wage	38	36	34	27,6	13	1,25	10,5
Total operational costs	441	398	392	371	308	297	295
Financial costs	39	60	40	46	42	50	67
Depreciation	29	40	30	26	30	30	32
Interest	10	20	10	20	12	10	35
Total cost	480	458	432	417	350	297	362

Tabelle 177: Characteristics of firms in the sample: nationality of ownership, level of exports and size. Modified: Ferraz et al. 1996: 149.
Erwähnt in Abschnitt 'G', 585.

	Intermediate goods	Durable Goods	Traditional goods	High technology goods	Average
	Aluminium Wood pulp Fertilizers Iron ore Vegetable oils Paper Petroleum Petrochemicals Iron and steel Fruit juices	Motor vehicles Motor vehicle parts Consumer electronics (a)	Slaughtering Leather footwear Diary products Wooden furniture Textiles (b) Wearing apparel	Automation Computers Telecommunication equipment Electrical power equipment Machine tools Agricultural machinery	
Nationality of ownership (No. of firms)	104	27	80	67	278
Brazilian	89.4	48.1	96.3	74.6	83.8
Foreign	10.6	51.9	3.8	25.4	16.2
Exports (No. of firms)	111	54	258	85	508
Percentage of sales:					
Under 5 %	**37.8**	**46.3**	**67.4**	**52.9**	56.3
5% - 20%	**20.7**	**31.5**	**13.2**	**29.4**	19.5
Over 20 %	41.5	22.2	19.3	17.7	24.2
Size (No. of firms)	111	54	258	85	508
Capital:					
Under US$ 10 million	10.8	24.1	57.0	51.8	42.5
US$10 million - US$100 million	36.9	50.0	34.9	37.6	37.4
Over US$ 100 million	52.3	25.9	8.1	10.6	20.1

(a) Television sets, radios and sound systems
(b) Cotton yarns and fabrics

Tabelle 178: Foreign firms (a) shares in exports of selected commodity groups (b) in Brazil, 1974-1985 (% of total exports of each group). In: Fritsch/Franco 1992: 212.
Erwähnt in Abschnitt 'G', 585.

	1974	1977	1980	1983	1984	1985
Basic products	11	14	16	15	15	15
Manufactures						
Equipment and instruments	67	64	62	62	67	63
Other	17	23	22	17	18	18
Total	17	22	25	22	23	23

(a) Foreign firms defined as those with over 25 % foreign control.
(b) Groups defined according to the Brazilian Commodity Nomenclature.

Tabelle 179: Export Shares (a) and the Structure of Exports (b) of Major Brazilian Automobile Companies, 1986.
Erwähnt in Abschnitt 'G', 586.

	Ford	General Motors	Fiat	VWB	MBB
Total exports (US$ million)	168,5	268,9	249,2	226,9	104,3
thereof (per cent)					
Vehicles	42	45	64	77	74
Parts	11	5	10	22	15
Components (c)	47	50	26	1	11
Export share (per cent)	14	21	32	13	12

(a) Share of exports in total sales (US$) in per cent. (b) Total exports US $ = 100). (c) Mainly engines.

Tabelle 180: Shares of developing countries in exports of manufacturers (percentages). Aus: Page 1994: 9.
Erwähnt in Abschnitt 'G', 587.

	1970	1975	1980	1985	1990
	Shares in total exports of manufacturers by developing countries				
Asia	52,4	62,8	71,8	71,2	82,7
Latin America	26,2	23,4	20,3	18,5	11.6
Africa	19,5	9,3	5,8	3,2	2,8
	Share in world exports of manufacturers				
LDCs (1)	7,0	7,4	10,0	13,3	17,1
Asia	3,7	4,7	7,2	9,5	14,1
Latin America	1,8	1,7	2,0	2,5	2,0
Africa	1,4	0,7	0,6	0,4	0,5

(1) Der damalige Sprachgebrauch nutzt LDCs als Abkürzung für less developed countries also weniger entwickelte Länder, bzw. Entwicklungsländer. Damit sind alle Entwicklungsländer gemeint. Heutzutage dient dieses Kürzel zur Abgrenzung der least-developed countries, also die Ländergruppe der am wenigsten entwickelten Ländern.

(Quelle: UN Monthly Bulletin of Statistics; UNCTAD: Handbook of International Trade and Development Statistics; IMF, International Financial Statistics)

Tabelle 181: Brazil: Exports and imports by principal commodity group, 1999 (In millions of U.S. dollars). IMF Country Report Brazil, January 2001 (Selected Issues and Statistical Appendix): 240.
Erwähnt in Abschnitt 'G', 587.

	1995	1996	1997	1998	1999
Total exports	46,506	47,747	52,994	51,140	48,011
Primary products	10,969	11,900	14,474	12,977	11,828
Soybeans and soybran	2,767	3,749	5,133	3,929	3,097
Iron ore	2,548	2,695	2,846	3,253	2,746
Coffee beans	1,970	1,719	2,745	2,332	2,230
Tobacco leaf	769	1,029	1,091	940	884
Raw sugar	408	0	0	0	0
Other	2,507	2,708	2,659	2,523	2,871
Industrial products	34,711	35,026	37,672	37,507	35,311
Semi-manufactures	9,146	8,613	8,478	8,120	7,982
Raw sugar (1)	1,042	1,191	1,045	1,096	1,162
Steel products	1,369	1,294	1,359	1,255	1,056
Paper paste	1,447	954	958	930	901
Iron products	838	871	876	888	730
Leather hides	566	678	739	657	595
Soybean oil	1,031	685	532	724	564
Cocoa products	92	115	108	131	90
Other	2,761	2,825	2,861	2,439	2,883
Manufactures	25,565	26,413	29,194	29,387	27,329
Transport equipment	3,211	3,721	5,620	8,203	7,119
Nonelectric machinery	3,904	4,180	4,531	4,339	3,970
Electric machinery	1,503	1,584	1,783	1,712	1,813
Airplanes	182	284	681	1,159	1,772
Footwear	1,499	1,650	1,594	1,387	1,342
Orange juice	1,132	1,453	1,058	1,262	1,235
Steel products (2)	1,809	1,723	1,397	1,465	1,204
Automobiles	1,040	1,247	2,488	1,619	1,138
Petroleum derivatives	839	949	988	865	1,118
Refined sugar	366	421	726	847	748
Processed beef	302	243	239	314	360
Soluble coffee	456	376	349	246	211
Cotton fabrics and yarn	299	278	246	224	197
Other textiles	1,142	1,014	1,021	889	813
Other	11,862	11,713	11,416	9,202	7,865
Other exports	826	821	848	656	872
Annual percentage change					
Total exports	6,8	2,7	11,0	-3,5	-6,1
Primary products	-0,8	8,5	21,6	-10,3	-8,9
Semi-manufactures	32,7	-5,8	-1,6	-4,2	-1,7
Manufactures	2,4	3,3	10,5	0,7	-7,0
Excluding automobiles and airplanes	4,0	2,2	4,6	2,2	-8,2
Total automobiles	-25,9	19,9	99,5	-34,9	-29,7

(1) Passenger and commercial vehicles. (2) Lamin. planos, tubos, barras e perfis de ferro/aco.

Tabelle 182: Manufacturing industry import penetration ratios: imports/domestic demand, 1989-96 (%). In: Moreira/Correa 1998: 1863.
Erwähnt in Abschnitt 'G', 587.

Industries	1989	1991	1993	1995	1996
1. Industrial equipment and machinery, incl. parts	13,3	31,2	25,5	40,1	48,3
2. Electronic and communications equipment	11,6	27,3	24,0	35,5	41,0
3. Other vehicles (motorcycles, bicycles, etc.)	18,8	27,6	29,0	25,1	31,5
4. Chemical resins and fibers	6,3	12,1	14,2	26,8	30,4
5. Fertilizers	9,8	17,8	21,6	26,8	30,4
6. Chemicals and compounds	15,1	19,1	16,8	24,4	27,4
7. Motors and vehicle parts	6,0	17,1	14,7	20,3	23,6
8. Agricultural machinery and equipment incl. parts	1,7	13,3	7,1	15,0	22,1
9. Electric wires and cables	8,8	12,3	12,0	18,2	21,1
10. Natural fiber textile products	3,5	6,6	14,2	15,6	20,6
11. Rubber	4,8	6,5	7,8	20,0	20,1
12. Electric power equipment	8,2	15,6	13,8	15,8	19,9
13. Non-ferrous metals	8,0	11,4	14,6	20,5	18,8
14. Pharmaceuticals	6,9	11,5	8,5	11,2	14,0
15. TVs, radios and stereos	4,9	10,0	7,7	13,0	13,3
16. Glass products	4,0	7,6	6,8	14,7	12,8
17. Miscellaneous chemical products	5,7	4,8	8,3	13,3	12,5
18. Electric machinery and appliances	3,8	5,6	7,2	10,4	11,4
19. Synthetic fiber textile products	0,8	3,1	4,2	17,0	11,1
20. Petrochemicals	4,0	8,4	5,3	10,2	10,6
21. Automobiles, trucks and buses	0,0	1,9	4,8	14,3	10,2
22. Paper and paperboard products	1,4	4,5	3,7	8,4	9,6
23. Miscellaneous food products	3,0	4,1	3,4	8,5	8,8
24. Miscellaneous textile industries	1,0	2,7	2,4	6,9	8,2
25. Footwear	0,4	2,3	1,2	6,0	7,9
26. Plastics	0,5	1,8	2,3	6,3	7,3
27. Juices and seasonings	2,3	3,7	5,0	9,0	6,5
28. Timber	1,2	3,4	2,3	4,0	6,1
29. Other non-ferrous metals	1,8	3,0	2,5	4,6	6,0
30. Beverages	3,5	5,1	3,4	5,3	5,9
31. Dairy products	4,3	4,0	2,4	7,1	5,7
32. Miscellaneous metal products	1,5	3,8	3,3	4,4	5,4
33. Wood pulp	3,8	4,5	5,6	6,4	4,7
34. Toiletry	1,6	2,1	1,7	4,4	4,7
35. Steel products	1,9	2,8	3,2	4,7	4,3
36. Plastics sheets	0,2	0,9	0,7	6,3	4,1
37. Tobacco products	0,1	0,8	1,0	1,8	1,9
38. Cement	0,3	0,2	0,3	1,2	1,1
39. Concrete products	0,1	0,3	0,5	0,9	1,1
Manufacturing industry	4,8	8,6	8,8	14,6	15,5

Tabelle 183: Brazil: Imports by End-Use. IMF Country Report Brazil Selected Issues and Statistical Appendix January 2001: 241.
Erwähnt in Abschnitt 'G', 587.

	1995	1996	1997	1998	1999
Total imports, f.o.b. (millions of US$)	49,972	53,346	59,745	57,734	49,224
Consumer goods	10,927	9,721	11,011	10,712	7,356
Foodstuffs	2,659	3,155	2,797	2,040	2,951
Apparel	804	862	979	681	424
Automobiles	3,040	1,562	2,641	2,677	1,214
Others	4,424	4,142	4,594	5,314	2,767
Raw materials	22,382	24,646	27,132	26,831	24,042
Grains	1,665	2,103	1,583	1,865	1,411
of which: Wheat	914	1,288	822	814	832
Fertilizers	661	860	1,021	954	864
Chemical products	6,287	7,150	8,111	8,357	8,223
Inorganic chemical products	638	562	553	543	504
Organic chemical products	2,987	3,185	3,488	3,446	3,267
Other chemical products	2,662	3,403	4,070	4,368	4,452
Cast iron and steel	699	793	1,254	1,375	871
Nonferrous metals	1,096	938	1,127	1,091	926
Coal	764	755	807	774	598
Others	11,210	12,047	13,229	12,397	11,149
Fuel and lubricants	5,217	6,228	5,597	4,107	4,257
Crude oil	2,587	3,459	3,220	1,965	2,169
Refined products	2,630	2,769	2,377	2,142	2,088
Capital goods	11,446	12,706	16,098	16,098	13,555
Transport equipment and components	5,940	4,510	6,456	6,793	4,651
Automotive vehicles, tractors etc.	5,567	3,979	5,409	5,666	3,440
Other	373	531	1,047	1,127	1,211
Machines and electric materials	5,729	6,876	8,505	7,758	7,443
Total imports (in per cent)	100,0	100,0	100,0	100,0	100,0
Consumer goods	21,9	17,6	17,2	20,1	8,9
Automobiles	6,1	2,9	4,4	4,6	2,5
Other	15,8	14,6	12,7	15,5	6,5
Raw materials	44,8	46,2	45,4	46,4	48,8
Fuels and lubricants	10,4	11,7	9,4	7,1	8,6
Capital goods	23,4	21,3	25,0	25,2	24,6
Transport equipment and components	11,9	8,5	10,8	11,8	9,4
Machines and electric materials	11,5	12,9	14,2	13,4	15,1
Total imports (Annual percentage change)	51,1	6,8	12,0	-3,4	-14,7
Consumer goods	97,2	-11,0	13,3	-2,7	-31,3
Automobiles	106,9	-48,6	69,1	1,4	-54,7
Other	93,7	-1,1	-2,4	17,5	-64,3
Raw materials	43,4	10,1	10,1	-1,2	-10,3
Fuels and lubricants	19,8	19,4	-10,1	-26,6	3,7
Capital goods	51,1	11,0	26,7	0,0	-15,8
Transport equipment and components	208,3	-24,1	43,1	5,2	-31,5
Machines and electrical materials	1,4	20,0	23,7	-8,8	-4,1

Tabelle 184: Brazil's composition of imports by end use (%), 1901-87.
In: Moreira 1995: 192.
Erwähnt in Abschnitt 'G', 587.

	1901-1907	1924-1929	1935-1939	1955	1964	1972	1974	1978	1982	1987
Food and beverages						7,3	7,1	8,7	8,3	7,4
Consumer goods	36,9	21,3	17,0	9,7	8,8	4,3	2,5	2,3	1,7	2,9
Durables	n.a.	n.a.	10,3	2,8	2,4	2,4	1,4	1,0	0,5	0,9
Non-durables (1)	n.a.	n.a.	6,7	6,9	6,4	1,9	1,2	1,3	1,1	2,0
Ind. supplies (2)	46,9	52,8	51,1	41,5	47,4	34,0	41,8	29,4	18,8	30,5
Fuel	8,2	11,1	12,2	21,5	20,4	12,6	22,8	32,5	53,4	32,3
Capital goods	7,1	14,8	26,3	27,3	23,4	37,7	22,9	24,2	15,6	22,6

(1) Includes food until 1964. (2) Includes raw material, intermediate goods minus fuel. Note: Percentages may not add to 100 % because of non specified goods. Definition of the categories among the sources are not strictly comparable.

Tabelle 185: Average annual growth rates of GDP, commodity production, exports and imports in constant prices (a). In: Gulhati et al. 1985: 10.
Erwähnt in Abschnitt 'G', 594.

Country	GDP (at market prices)		Commodity production (Agr. Min. Mfg.)		Exports (Goods and NFS)		Imports (Goods and NFS)	
	65/67-72/74	72/74-79/81	65/67-72/74	72/74-79/81	65/67-72/74	72/74-79/81	65/67-72/74	72/74-79/81
Kenya	8.6	4.8	7.2	4.1	4.3	0.3	5.1	-0.1
Tanzania	5.3	3.9	3.1	2.5	1.5	-11.0	5.7	-4.0
Uganda	3.4	-2.6	3.1	-3.1	-1.0	-9.3	-4.7	5.8
Malawi	5.9 (b)	5.3	4.6 (b)	4.2	5.7 (b)	7.1	6.8 (b)	2.4
Zambia	4.0 (c)	-0.8	3.3 (c)	-1.9	1.1 (c)	-2.2	-1.2 (c)	-8.6
Ethiopia	4.0	2.4	2.7	1.1	4.3	-0.8	0.5	5.9
Sudan	1.0	7.0	-0.9	4.8	0.9	-1.4	-5.6	8.4
Madagascar	-0.3	0.7	2.0 (c)	0.2	-1.9	0.5	-5.8 (c)	1.3
Somalia	2.3	5.2	-0.4	4.9 (d)	2.3	-8.7 (d)	3.9	5.1 (d)

(a) The base and terminal periods are three year averages to reduce the impact of erratic fluctuations on growth rates.
(b) 1967/69-1972/74 only
(c) 1970/72-1972/74 only
(d) 1972/74-1977/79 only

Tabelle 186: Vergleich ausgewählter afrikanischer Länder. Daten aus Weltentwicklungsbericht 1996: 222-251. Sowie Trade Policy Review, div. Ausgaben. Erwähnt in Abschnitt 'G', 595, 601, 605, 620, 628.

	Mauritius	Ghana	Kenya	Tanzania	Zambia
per capita GDP growth 1985-1994	5,8	1,4	0,0	0,8	-1,4
Population	1,1	16,6	26,0	28,8	9,2
GDP per capita 1994	3,150	239	580	945	753
GDP 1994	3,386	5,421	6,860	3,378	3,481
GDP 1980	1,132	4,445	7,265	5,702	3,884
growth of exports, 1980-1990	8,6	3,9	2,6	-1,8	-3,5
Exports 1994	1,347	1,431 (a)	1,609	519	993 (a)
Exports 1980	431	1,260	1,250	511	1,300
manufacturing share in GDP 1994	22	8	11	8	23
manufacturing share in GDP 1980	15	8	13	11	18
manufacturing share exports 1994	90	24	29 (c)	minimal (d)	9
manufacturing share exports 1980	27	1	12	14	6
Main export products (e)	agriculture 19 % (sugar 14 %); manufactures 80,8 % mostly textiles and clothing	gold (40,9 %), cocoa beans (26 %), other food (19,4 %), lumber (5,2 %), manufactures (decline from 1994 clothing 9,3 %, other 2,1 %, semi mnf 2,4 % to 1999: other 2,0 %, semi mnf 4,6 %)	tea (30 % 1998), coffee, pyrethrum, flowers, fruits, vegetables (agriculture 60 % of exports); soda ash, petroleum products, cement, clothing, leather products: manufacturing (share declines from 28 % 1993 to 23 % 1998)	cotton, now cashnew nuts, coffee, tea, tobacco, minerals (4,5 % 1998), manufactured products (6,2 % 1998)	copper, cobalt (2/3rd)

GDP- and exportdata in US$ Mio., the rest are percentages. Data from Weltentwicklungsbericht 1996: 222-251.

(a) Ghana for the year 1995 from Trade Policy Review Ghana 2001: 7.
(b) Zambia for the year 1996 from Trade Policy Review Zambia 2002: 5.
(c) A fall in exports of manufacturing products between 1993-1998 from 29 % to 25 % is reported in Trade Policy Review Kenya 2000: 8.
(d) Trade Policy Review Tanzania 2000: 7.
(e) Note the divergence concerning the numbers referring to manufactured export shares between WTO and World Bank data. Here: Trade Policy Reviews Mauritius 2001; Ghana 2001; Kenya 2000; Tanzania 2000; Zambia 2002.

Tabelle 187: Freight costs as a percentage of import value.
In UNIDO 2004: 84.
Erwähnt in Abschnitt 'G', 598.

Region	Freight costs (percent of import value)
World	6.11
Industrialized countries	5.12
Developing countries	8.70
North Africa	11.21
Indian Ocean countries	12.23
East Africa	12.35
Africa	12.65
Sub-Saharan Africa	13.84
West Africa	13.90
Southern Africa	16.42
Land-locked African countries	20.69

Tabelle 188: Other Determinants of Manufactured Exports for a Sample of Developing Countries (See notes for units of measure. Ratios are in percentages, as are the growth rates, which are annual averages for 1984-95). In: Elbadawi 2001: 20.
Erwähnt in Abschnitt 'G', 600.

	Ratio of gross domestic investment to GDP	Ratio of school enrolment to land per worker	Fax machines per 1000 people	Corruption	Paved roads
Burkina Faso					
1994/95 average	20.87	0.61	n.a.	4	17.35
Annual average growth	4.29	10.12	n.a.		-0.47
Cote d Ivoire					
1994/95 average	13.04	1.17	n.a.	2.79	9.50
Annual average growth	3.42	-0.04	n.a.		1.99
Kenya					
1994/95 average	20.55	2.71	0.14	2.81	13.70
Annual average growth	1.24	0.12	10.96		1.57
Mauritius					
1994/95 average	28.98	4.95	17.00	3.19	93.00
Annual average growth	2.00	3.46	177.08		n.a.
South Africa					
1994/95 average	17.95	1.13	2.11	5.64	41.50
Annual average growth	-1.99	3.70	24.44		n.a.
Tanzania					
1994/95 average	23.37	3.28	0.07	2.56	4.20
Annual average growth	3.14	-2.51	89.35		n.a.
Zimbabwe					
1994/95 average	23.66	1.97	0.35	2.94	51.45
Annual average growth	3.68	6.14	27.35		46.09
Tunisia					
1994/95 average	24.30	1.35	2.53	2.94	78.10
Annual average growth	-2.91	5.08	58.24		0.71
Chile					
1994/95 average	27.07	1.15	1.55		13.80
Annual average growth	6.90	-7.02	33.53		n.a.
Korea					
1994/95 average	36.55	11.37	8.67	2.38	76.90
Annual average growth	2.02	2.05	10.82		1.40
Malaysia					
1994/95 average	41.96	3.98	3.97	4.75	75.00
Annual average growth	2.92	-1.00	70.81		1.41
Thailand					
1994/95 average	40.94	1.77	1.48	3.19	96.05
Annual average growth	3.5	1.17	126.29		13.94
Indonesia					
1994/95 average	30.50	5.84	0.36	0.56	45.85
Annual average growth	2.02	3.96	55.49		-0.19

Source: World Bank data
Notes: n.a. not available

a) Gross domestic investment consists of outlays on additions to the fixed assets of the economy plus net changes in the level of inventories. Fixed assets cover land improvements (fences, ditches, drains etc.); plant, machinery, and equipment purchases; and the construction of roads, railways, and the like, including commercial and industrial buildings, offices, schools, hospitals, and private residence buildings.
b) Schooling to land per workier is given be the ratio of an index of primary school enrolments divided by the ratio of arable land per 100 workers.
b) The estimated number of facsimile machines connected to the public switched telephone network, per 1000 people. The growth rate for fax machines refers to 1990-95.
d) An index of corruption around the world published by Transparency International (high index means low corruption).
e) The percentage of paved roads that have been sealed with asphalt or similar road-building material. The growth rate for paved roads refers to 1990-95.

Tabelle 189: Number of commodities exported and indices of export commodity concentration in SSA adjusters: 1980 and 1990. In: Brownbridge/Harrigan 1996: 418. *Erwähnt in Abschnitt 'G', 602.*

Country	No. of commodities exported		Commodity concentr. index	
	1980	1990	1980	1990
Benin	30	29	0.415	0.482
Burkina Faso	43	23	0.476	0.481
Burundi	26	7	0.594	0.744
Cameroon	90	103	0.409	0.311
Central African Republic	15	25	0.415	0.588
Chad	15	17	0.794	0.688
Congo	29	34	0.890	0.797
Cote d'Ivoire	154	106	0.383	0.0345
Gabon	46	45	0.763	0.812
The Gambia	23	22	0.418	0.353
Ghana	55	54	0.729	0.450
Guinea	23	28	0.905	0.840
Guinea-Bisseau	22	n.a.	0.331	n.a.
Kenya	143	183	0.383	0.239
Madagascar	53	70	0.501	0.309
Malawi	47	35	0.409	0.656
Mali	40	41	0.477	0.565
Mauritania	24	20	0.661	0.621
Mozambique	n.a.		n.a.	
Niger	39	44	0.821	0.767
Nigeria	147	102	0.948	0.959
Rwanda	13	16	0.668	0.552
Senegal	113	106	0.271	0.251
Sierra Leone	39	16	0.444	0.458
Tanzania	83	66	0.286	0.250
Togo	51	47	0.468	0.468
Uganda	22	13	0.950	0.868
Zambia	49	33	0.717	0.931
Zimbabwe	87	170	0.257	0.245

Notes: n.a. not available. The number of commodities exported refers to products at the three digit SITC level, the value of which was greater than $ 50.0000 in 1980 or $ 100.000 in 1990 or was more than 0.3 % of the country's total exports. The export concentration index is a Hirschmann index which takes values between 0 and 1. Higher values of the index denote a greater commodity concentration of exports: i.e., a single commodity or a few commodities account for a larger proportion of total exports. Data Source: UNCTAD.

Tabelle 190: Developing country tariffs, 1985: regional averages and major importers. In: Page 1994. Aus: UNCTAD 1988.
Erwähnt in Abschnitt 'G', 466, 501, 603, Abschnitt 'H', 801, 812.

	Tariff rates	
Geographical region	Manufacturers	All sectors
Carribean	20	17
Central America	71	66
South America	55	51
Brazil	78,5	75,2
Argentina	41,2	38,6
Chile	19,7	20,2
Mexico	16,0	13,4
Venezuela	31,0	31,4
North Africa	45	39
Sub-Saharan Africa	37	36
Middle East	6	5
Other Asia	27	25
Hong Kong	3,7	2,5
Singapore	0,0	1,2
Malaysia	18,2	15,0
China	37,1	32,1
Thailand	41,2	36,9
South Korea	25,0	22,7
All regions	32	30

Tabelle 191: Adaptions under Liberalization (per cent of firms). Modified, percentage of firms not exporting added to table, numbers adding up to 100 per cent included, in order to show that a considerable part of the small enterprises remain passive. In: Parker et al. 1995: 57, 71.
Erwähnt in Abschnitt 'G', 619, 623.

	Ghana	Malawi	Mali	Senegal	Tanzania
Imported input use					
Increased	9	26	56	46	78
Fell	18	9	28	29	8
Changed product mix	38	50	20	56	24
Not changed product mix	62	50	80	64	76
Purchased new equipment	46	68	41	38	n.a.
No new equipment purchases	54	32	59	62	n.a.
Applied for a loan	47	50	27	47	57
Not applied for a loan	53	50	73	53	43
Percentage of firms not exporting	96	94	87	68	96

Tabelle 192: Efficiency and Firm Exporting.
In: Mengistae/Teal 1998: 34.
Erwähnt in Abschnitt 'G', 621.

Country	Exporting Firms	Non-Exporting Firms	All Firms
Cameroon	116	113	119
Cote d'Ivoire	261	197	238
Ghana	49	109	103
Kenya	152	132	140
Mauritius	na	na	394
Zambia	44	55	62
Zimbabwe	100	100	100

The numbers are index numbers of the level of firm efficiency in which Zimbabwe is taken as 100. Firm efficieny measures the extrent to which firms in other countries produce more, or less, output for given levels of inputs relative to Zimbabwe.

Tabelle 193: Countervailing Duty Cases. Number of countervailing duty cases, 1980-86.
In: Finger/Olechowski 1986: 157.
Erwähnt in Abschnitt 'H', 684, 763, 768.

	By	Against	
		Total	Excluding Chilean cases
I. Countries in which at least one countervailing duty case was initiated			
United States	281	11	1
Chile	140	0	0
Australia	20	2	2
Canada	11	11	11
European Community policies	7	11	6
Japan	1	2	1
Summary, Part I	460	28	21
As a percentage of all cases	100	6	7
II. Countries in which no CVD cases have been initiated			
Brazil	0	88	32
Spain	0	38	22
Argentina	0	32	6
Mexico	0	28	27
Peru	0	22	7
France	0	21	21
Korea	0	21	13
Other EEC member states	0	56	54
Other countries (40)	0		
Summary, Part II	0	432	299
As a percentage of all cases		94	93

Tabelle 194: Duration of Patents. GATT Document: Group on Negotiations on Goods. MTN.GNG/NG11/W/24/Rev.1, 15. September 1988: 58-60.
Erwähnungin Abschnitt 'H', 707; Abschnitt 'J', 1292.

Duration of Patents:

(a) Duration, counted from the filing date of the application:

(i) 20 years: Algeria; Belgium; Burundi; Chad; Denmark; Finland; France; Hungary; Israel; Italy (1); Monaco; Morocco; Netherlands; Nigeria; Norway; Rwanda; South Africa; Spain; Sudan; Sweden; Switzerland (2); United Kingdom; Zaire (except for medicine inventions for which the duration is 15 years from the filing of application); Zimbabwe; European Patent Convention;

(ii) 16 years: Bahamas; Jordan;

(iii) 15 years: Brazil; Barbados (3); Bulgaria; China; Czechoslovakia; Democratic People's Republic of Korea; Egypt (4); Iraq; Lebanon; Libya (5); Mongolia; Poland; Romania; Soviet Union; Syria; Thailand; Viet Nam;

(iv) 14 years: Malta (6); Mauritius (7);

(v) 10 years: OAPI (8); Cuba (9);

(vi) 5, 10, 15 years: Turkey (10)

(b) Duration, counted from the date following the filing date of the application:

(i) 20 years: Germany (Federal Republic of); Luxembourg;

(ii) 18 years: German Democratic Republic;

(iii) 15 years: Greece.

(c) Duration, counted from the publication date of the examined application (e.g., for opposition):

(i) 18 years: Austria, but not beyond 20 years from the filing date of the application;

(ii) 15 years: Japan, but not beyond 20 years from the filing date of the application;

(iii) 12 years: Republic of Korea, but not beyond 15 years from the filing of the application (10)

(d) Duration, counted from the publication date of the unexamined application:

(i) 7 years: Yugoslavia (publication occurs 18 month after the filing or priority date, unless the applicant requests an earlier publication, in which case, it would seem that duration is to be counted from such earlier publication date) (11).

(e) Duration, counted from the date the complete specification is lodged:

(i) 16 years: Australia (12), Ireland (13); Malawi (14); New Zealand (15), Zambia (16);

(ii) 14 years: India (except for process inventions for manufacturing food or medicine, for which the duration is five years from the date of sealing of the patent, or seven years from the date on which the complete specification was filed, whichever period is shorter)

(f) Duration, counted from the date of grant of the patent:

(i) 17 years: Canada; Philippines; United States of America (17);

(ii) 16 years: Bangladesh (18); Pakistan (19);

(iii) 15 years: Bolivia; Iceland; Malaysia; Portugal; Sri Lanka; Uruguay;

(iv) 14 years: Mexico; Trinidad and Tobago;

(v) 5, 10, or 20 years: Haiti (the law does not appear to indicated on what the actual duration depends);

(vi) 5, 10, or 15 years: Argentina, depending on the invention's merits and the whishes of the applicant (the decision is made by the National Directorate of Industrial Property); Dominican Republic;

(vii) 5 or 10 years: Venezuala, depending on the will of the applicant;

(viii) 5 years: Columbia (20); Ecuador (21); Peru (22).

(g) Duration, expiring on the same date as the corresponding patent in the United Kingdom: Cyprus; Ghana; Kenya; Uganda; United Republic of Tanzania.

Notes: (1) The Italian law also applies to the Holy See and San Marino
(2) The Swiss law also applies to Liechtenstein
(3) With the possibility of a five year extension. In Barbados, an extension is granted if the patent owner proves that the invention is being sufficiently used in the country at the date of the request or that there are circumstances that justify the failure to use the invention sufficiently in the country. In Egypt and Libya, an extension is granted if the invesion is of particular importance and if the patent holder proves that he has not secured an adequate return for his efforts and expense.
(4) With the possibility of an extension for a period apparantly not indicated in the law, on the grounds that the patent holder has not been adequately remunerated by the patent.
(5) With the possibility of up to a 14-year extension, on grounds apparently not indicated in the law.
(6) With the possibility of a five-year extension period for Benin, Burkina Faso, Cameroon, the Central African Republic, Congo, Cote d'Ivoire, Gabon, Mali, Mauritania, Niger, Senegal and Togo if the petitioner proves that the patented invention is being worked on the territory of one of the member states at the date of the request or that there are legitimate reasons for failing to work it. Chad is member of OAPI but is party to the Libreville Agreement which provides for a term of 20 years from filing without extension.
(7) With the possibility of a five-year extension, the law apparently not indicating the grounds therefor.
(8) Dpending on the applicant's request.
(9) The law does not appear to indicate on what the actual duration depends.
(10) In cases where the application is not published (e.g. secret patents), the duration is 12 years from the date of the grant of the patent.
(11) With the possibility of a seven-year extension if the patented invention is actually and seriously worked in the country.
(12) With the possibility of and extension, on grounds that the patent owner has been inadequately remunerated by the patent (in which case, the extension may be for a further five-year term, or, on exceptional cases, for 10 years) or on grounds of war loss (in which case, the extension is for such further term as the court thinks fit).
(13) With the possibility of a five-year or a 10-year extension. In Ireland, an extension is possible if the patent owner proves that he has not been sufficiently remunerated by the patent, and, in extending the term of the patent, due regard is taken of the merits of the invention. In New Zealand, an extension is possible if the patent owner proves that he has not been adequately remunerated by the patent or, if by reason of hostilities with any foreign State, he has suffered a loss or damage. In Zambia, an extension is possible if the patent owner proves that by reason of hostility with any foreign State he suffered loss and damage or he has not derived remuneration from the patent.
(14) With the possibility of an extension of five or 10 years or for the term of hostilities between Malawi and any foreign State if the patent owner has not obtained an adequate remuneration from the patent or if he has suffered a loss or damage because of the hostilities.
(15) With the possibility of an extension for certain patented inventions subjected to regulatory review before the commercial marketing or use, in which case the duration may be extended for a specific period of time (under normal circumstances, a time equal to the regulatory review which occurs after the patent is issued, provided that the period remaining in the term of the patent after the date of regulatory approval, when added to the regulatory review period, does not exceed 14 years). The possibility of such an extension usually applies to inventions related to a drug, food or cosmetics.
(16) With the possibility of a five-year or a 10 year extension if the patent owner proves that the patent has not been sufficiently remunarative.
(17) With the possibility of a five-year extension if the patent is adequately worked.

Tabelle 195: Recourse to Article XIX of the General Agreement on Tariffs and Trade, 1978-1987. Aus: IMF 1988: 137.
Erwähnt in Abschnitt 'H', 727, 728.

Country	Product	Measure	Year Introducted (Terminated)
Australia	Wool worsted yarns	Tariff Quota	1978
	Round blunt chainsaw files	Quantitative restriction	1978 (1978)
	Double-edged safety razor blades	Quantitative restriction	1978 (1982)
	Sheets and plates of iron and steel	Quantitative restriction	1978 (1980)
	Certain trucks and stackers	Quantitative restriction	1980 (1982)
	Files and rasps	Quantitative restriction	1976 (1978)
	Hoops and strips of iron and steel	Tariff Quota	1982 (1983)
	Certain filament lamps	Tariff Increase	1983
	Nonelectric domestic refrigerators	Tariff Increase	1983 (1985)
Austria	Broken rice	Quantitative restriction	1987
Canada	Footwear other than canvas and rubber	Quantitative restriction	1977 (1981)
	Nonleather footwear	Quantitative restriction	1981 (1)
	Leather footwear	Quantitative restriction	1982 (1)
	Yellow onions	Specific surtax	1982 (1983)
	Fresh, chilled, and frozen beef and veal	Quantitative restriction	1985 (1985)
Chile	Sugar	Tariff surcharge	1984
	Wheat	Tariff increase	1984
	Edible vegetable oils	Tariff increase	1985
European community	Preserved mushrooms	Quantitative restriction	1978 (1980)
	Yarn of synthetic fibers (UK only)	Quantitative restriction	1980 (1980)
	Cultivated mushrooms	Quantitative restriction	1980 (1984)
	Other cultivated mushrooms	Quantitative restriction	1980 (1980)
	Frozen cod fillets	Embargo	1981 (1981)
	Dried grapes	Compensatory tax	1982
	Certain tableware	Quantitative restriction	1983 (1983)
	Certain electronic quartz watches (France)	Quantitative restriction	1984
	Morello cherries	Tariff	1985
	Preserved raspberries	Tariff	1986
	Sweet potatoes	Quantitative restriction	1986
	Certain steel products	Quantitative restriction	1987
Finland	Porous fiberboard	Tariff surcharge	1986 (1986)
Iceland	Furniture, cupboards, and cabinets; window and doors	Import deposit	1979 (1980)
Norway	Various textile items	Quantitative restriction	1979 (1984)
Spain	Cheeses	Quantitative	1980 (1980)

		restriction	
South Africa	Certain footwear	Tariff increase	1984
	Malic acid	Tariff increase	1985
	Certain oil fatty acids, flasks, steel wire, plugs	Tariff increase	1986
Switzerland	Dessert grapes	Tariff increase	1982 (1982)
United States	CB Radio recievers	Tariff	1978 (1981)
	High-carbon forrochromium	Tariff	1978 (1982)
	Lag scews or bolts	Tariff	1979 (1982)
	Clothespins	Quantitative restriction	1979 (1984)
	Porcelain-on-steel cookware	Tariff	1980 (1984)
	Preserved mushrooms	Tariff	1980 (1983)
	Heavyweight motorcycles	Tariff increase	1983
	Certain speciality steels	Quantitative restriction	1983

Tabelle 196: Frequency of USDOC's Use of Observable Discretionary Practices, 1980-2000.
In: Blonigen 2003: 27.
Erwähnt in Abschnitt 'H', 740.

Year	Facts available	Adverse fact available	Constructed alue	Costs of roduction test	Third-country practices
1980	19.0	7.1	28.6	0.0	7.1
1981	8.1	0.0	29.7	10.8	5.4
1982	8.1	1.0	26.5	35.7	14.3
1983	4.8	1.9	41.7	49.5	11.7
1984	13.2	6.6	40.8	14.5	19.7
1985	21.9	7.3	37.5	41.7	8.3
1986	27.3	4.7	26.4	20.8	14.2
1987	35.1	13.5	16.2	35.1	2.7
1988	36.6	15.8	21.8	27.7	7.9
1989	41.7	16.7	20.8	18.8	20.8
1990	38.2	21.8	32.7	25.5	3.6
1991	25.4	20.3	20.3	20.3	15.3
1992	49.3	44.8	14.9	19.4	7.5
1993	49.6	34.3	32.3	39.4	4.0
1994	44.1	25.5	22.8	24.8	6.2
1995	29.7	27.0	35.1	27.0	0.0
1996	37.2	23.4	19.1	16.0	2.1
1997	35.9	35.9	59.0	59.0	10.3
1998	30.3	30.3	48.7	51.3	3.9
1999	45.1	45.1	15.4	20.9	0.0
2000	33.3	33.3	17.9	17.9	1.2

Notes: Author's calculations based on decision announcements by the USDOC in the Federal Register. Numbers are annual percent of cases employing the listed discretionary practice. Listed practices are not necessarily mutually exclusive as a case may employ more than one discretionary practice. Use of a practice for only part of a case (e.g., a subset of the investigated products) are included and treated identically to cases where the practice was fully used. 'Adverse Facts Available' numbers are a subset of 'Facts available' numbers.

Tabelle 197: Summary of Antidumping Investigations, 1995-1998.
In: Lindsey 1999: 8.
Erwähnt in Abschnitt 'H', 740, 741.

Calculation Methodology	Determinations (affirmative only in brackets)	Avg. Dumping Margins (affirmative only in brackets)
U.S. prices to home-market prices	4 (2)	4.00 % (7.36 %)
U.S. prices to third-country prices	1 (0)	0 % (0%)
U.S. prices to mixture of home-market prices, above-cost home-market prices and constructed value	31 (25)	14.59 % (17.95 %)
U.S. prices to mixture of third-country prices, above-cost third country prices and constructed value	2 (2)	7.94 % (7.94 %)
Constructed value	20 (14)	25.07 % (35.70 %)
Nonmarket economy	47 (28)	40.03 % (67.05 %)
'Facts available'	36 (36)	95.58 % (95.58 %)
Total	141 (107)	44.68 % (58.79 %)

Tabelle 198: Ranking of Countries by Numbers of Active Antidumping Measures. CBO AD Study 2001: 68.
Erwähnt in Abschnitt 'H', 753; Abschnitt 'J', 1080.

Country	Active measures on 12/31/99 (01/01/00)		Active measures on 12/31/94	
	Number	As percentage of world total	Number	As percentage of world total
United States	326 (267)	30.1 (26.1)	281	37.0
EC/U	148	13.7	138	18.1
South Africa	94	8.7	26 *	3.4
Canada	79	7.3	97	12.8
Mexico	71 (a)	6.6	49	6.5
India	60	5.5	5	0.7
Argentina	43	4.0	3	0.4
Brazil	39	3.6	20	2.6
Australia	38	3.5	75	9.9
Turkey	35	3.2	28	3.7
South Korea	26	2.4	7	0.9
New Zealand	21	1.9	21	2.8
Egypt	18 (b)	1.7	0 *	0
Colombia	14	1.3	5	0.7
Venezuela	14	1.3	2 *	0.3
Indonesia	14	1.3	0 *	0
Israel	9	0.8	0 *	0
Malaysia	9 (c)	0.8	0 *	0
Peru	8	0.7	0 *	0
Trinidad and Tobago	4	0.4	0	0
Thailand	4	0.4	1	0.1
Chile	2	0.2	1	0.1
Singapore	2	0.2	0	0
Japan	1	0.1	1	0.1
Guatemala	1	0.1	0 *	0
Nicaragua	1	0.1	0 *	0
Poland	1	0.1	0 *	0
All other reporting countries	0	0	0	0
Total, all countries	1,082 (1,023)	100.0	759	100.0

(a) One of the Mexican orders on 12/31/99 is against the EU as a whole.
(b) Three of the Egyptian orders on 12/31/99 are against the "EU other than France" as a whole.
(c) Two of the Malaysian orders on 12/31/99 are against the EU as a whole.
* Due to inadequate reporting the number could be somewhat higher than the number given here, but it is in most instances unlikely.

Tabelle 199: Antidumping and Antisubsidy Cases, 1980-92.
In: De Vault 1993: 741.
Erwähnt in Abschnitt 'H', 753.

Year initiated	Number of antidumping cases		Number of antisubsidy cases		Number of antidumping and antisubsidy cases	
	Total number	Number of steel cases	Total number	Number of steel cases	Total number	Number of steel cases
1980	37	9	79	0	116	9
1981	15	6	19	4	34	10
1982	65	49	144	117	209	166
1983	46	13	22	11	68	24
1984	74	49	51	21	125	70
1985	63	27	41	20	104	47
1986	71	3	29	5	100	8
1987	15	1	8	5	23	6
1988	42	4	13	4	55	8
1989	23	0	7	1	30	1
1990	43	7	8	3	51	10
1991	53	11	10	1	63	12
1992	99	65	44	40	143	105
Total	646	244	475	232	1,121	476

Tabelle 200: Target Industries of U.S. AD and CVD Investigations, 1980-1989.
In: Krishna 1997: 3.
Erwähnt in Abschnitt 'H', 753, 754.

Industry	AD	CVD
Chemicals	58	37
Food	16	45
Iron and steel	201	149
Leather	...	6
Machinery	8	6
Nonferrous metals	16	5
Oil country tubular goods	12	8
Textiles and apparel	15	6
Lumber	...	4
Other	125	34
All products	451	300

Tabelle 201: Countries that are the object of US antidumping and countervailing cases compared with the share they provide of US merchandizse imports (Antidumping and countervailing duty cases completed, 1980-1988). Finger/Murray 1990: 43.
Erwähnt in Abschnitt 'H', 754.

Country or group of countries	Total number of cases	Total cases against this country or group as a percentage of totals against all countries	Percentag of 1987 US merchandise imports that originate in this country or group	Percentages with restrictive outcomes (including voluntary export restraints)
All countries	774	100	100	70
Developed Countries	450	58	63	65
Developing Countries	286	37	36	75
Eastern European Countries	38	5	0.5	87
European Community	304	40	20	64
Brazil	56	7	2	79
South Africa	20	2.6	0.3	100
Korea	36	4.7	4.2	86
Mexico	35	4.5	4.9	91
Taiwan, China	29	3.7	6.1	62
Hong Kong	1	0.1	2.4	100
Singapore	6	0.8	1.5	67
Canada	35	5	18	54
Japan	49	6	21	69

Tabelle 202: Anti-dumping cases potentially involving monopolising behavior. In: OECD 1996g: 17.
Erwähnt in Abschnitt 'H', 755.

Country (period studied)	Total cases filed	Anti-dumping measures not imposed	Anti-dumping measures imposed	
			Total	Cases potentially involving monopolizing dumping
United States (1979-1989)	451	169	282	35 (d)
Canada (1980-1991)	155	63	92	0 (c)
Australia (1/9/88-31/12/91) (a)	40	20	20	5 (b)
European Union (1980-1989)	385	115	270	23 (e)
Total	1031	367	664	63

(a) The period studied is limited to September 1988 to end 1991, due to substantial change in the anti-dumping regime at the beginning of that period.

(b) The number of cases in which imports under simultaneous investigation originated from fewer than three countries and import penetration exceeded 15 per cent.

(c) The share of all imports of a particular product from a given challenged exporting country (as a percentage of domestic consumption) averaged across all products, was only 12.4 per cent. A multiplicity of international suppliers was found for most products subject to anti-dumping measures.

(d) The number of cases where imports under investigation originated from fewer than five countries, import penetration exceeded 20 per cent and the ratio of expenditure on long-lived machines and equipment (relative to total sales) was greater than th 4-digit SIC industry average of 0.25. (The latter is a measure of entry or exit barriers.) The number of cases would be 28 if a three-country screen rather a five-country screen had been applied.

(e) Cases in which (1) import penetration was projected to be greater than 40 per cent in the first year after the decision wether to take anti-dumping measures; and (2) involving three of fewer countries; and (3) seven or fewer firms involved in the anti-dumping proceeding; and either (4a) foreign firms had substantial (6.1 per cent or more) shares of the domestic market; or (4b) domestic concentration was high.

Tabelle 203: The Incidence of Preliminary and Final Duties per Sector and Country in 1990.
In: Schuhknecht 1990: 129.
Erwähnt in Abschnitt 'H', 759, Abschnitt 'I', 903.

Sector and products	Targets	Import value in million ECU, 1989
Consumer electronics (4 products):		1043
CD players	Japan, Korea	(320)
small colour TVs	Korea	(364)
cassettes	Japan, Korea, Hong Kong	(200) (a)
video cassettes	Korea, Hong Kong	(159) (a)
Computing machinery (1 product) DRAMS	Japan	300
Machinery (1 product) Ball bearings	Thailand	17
Chemicals (4 products)	CSFR, CIS, Indonesia, Thailand, Korea, Taiwan, China (2 x)	10
Steel (3 products)	Island, Norway, Sweden, Venezuela (2 x), Romania, Yugoslavia (2 x), Japan, Turkey	approx. 160 (b)
Other (7 products)	China (5 x), Japan (2 x), USA	271
Total: 20 products	17 countries	approx. 1800

(a) Import data from 1988.
(b) Excluding imports from Romania, import data for 1 product (pipes) from 1988. Source: Computed from EC's Official Journal and EUROSTAT, 6C, External Trade, 1988 and 1989.

Tabelle 204: Incidence of Less than Fair Value Cases on Imports of Manufactured Goods by Country Group (based on 1976 import figures). Aus: Finger 1981: 267.
Erwähnt in Abschnitt 'H', 762.

Country group	Imports covered by all cases as percent of total imports			Imports covered by affirmative cases as percent of total imports			Affirmative cases as percent all cases		
	Anti-dumping	Counter-vailing	Both	Anti-dumping	Counter-vailing	Both	Anti-dumping	Counter-vailing	Both
All countries									
All mfg. goods	16,4	7,1	23,5	0,5	1,4	1,8	2,7	19,7	7,9
excluding transport equipment	(4,9)	(8,9)	(13,8)	(0,6)	(1,8)	(2,3)	(11,5)	(19,8)	(16,8)
Developed countries									
All mfg. goods	23,0	8,5	31,50	0,6	1,1	1,7	2,6	12,3	5,2
excluding transport equipment	(7,5)	(12,0)	(19,4)	(0,8)	(1,5)	(2,3)	(11,5)	(12,3)	(11,9)
Developing countries (all manufactures)	0,4	3,6	4,0	0,1	2,3	2,4	21,0	63,6	59,7
Latin-American countries (all manufactures)	0,1	0,8	0,8	0,0	0,4	0,4	0,0	46,2	42,8

Tabelle 205: Country Incidence of Antidumping and Countervailing Duty Cases Combined (January 1975-December 1979).
Erwähnt in Abschnitt 'H', 762.

Country	Total imports (millions)	Imports under less than fair value cases					
		All cases (LFV imports)			Affirmative cases		
		Value (millions)	Percent of total imports	Value (millions)	Percent of total imports	Percent of all LFV imports
Belgium-Luxembourg	1,131.1	795.6	70.3	13.6	1.2	1.7
Pakistan	70.0	44.0	62.8	0.0	0.0	0.0
Germany (FR)	5,700.1	3,508.8	61.6	66.5	1.2	1.9
France	2,540.6	1,123.3	44.2	21.8	0.9	1.9
Japan	15,683.1	6,176.8	39.4	422.0	2.7	6.8
Netherlands	1,094.3	420.6	38.4	75.4	6.9	17.9
Sweden	925.6	291.9	31.5	3.1	0.3	1.1
Uruguay	62.4	19.6	31.5	19.6	31.5	100.0
Italy	2,543.7	621.9	24.4	30.9	1.2	5.0
Austria	241.8	54.5	22.6	15.2	6.3	27.9
India	710.2	121.9	17.2	0.0	0.0	0.0
Canada	26,826.8	4,217.2	15.7	196.7	0.7	4.7
Finland	190.1	28.2	14.8	26.2	13.8	92.9
China (Formosa)	2,999.3	437.6	14.6	372.1	12.4	85.0
United Kingdom	4,228.9	601.0	14.0	44.3	1.0	7.4
Denmark	564.6	77.5	13.7	77.1	13.6	99.4
Spain	928.2	113.4	12.2	72.7	7.8	64.1
South Korea	2,440.0	211.4	8.7	131.6	5.4	62.3
Argentina	309.9	22.2	7.2	3.3	1.1	14.8
Mexico	3,606.3	202.3	5.6	1.3	0.0	0.6
South Africa	995.6	34.4	3.5	0.0	0.0	0.0
Hungary	49.0	1.1	2.3	0.0	0.0	0.0
Norway	646.8	14.3	2.2	14.3	2.2	100.0
Romania	198.7	3.8	1.9	0.0	0.0	0.0
Switzerland	1,041.4	16.5	1.6	15.2	1.5	92.3
Brazil	1,739.9	26.4	1.5	8.0	0.5	30.2
Ireland	206.4	2.1	1.0	2.1	1.0	100.0
Poland	318.8	2.4	0.8	2.4	0.8	100.0
Colombia	657.4	3.7	0.6	3.7	0.6	100.0
Israel	424.2	2.3	0.5	0.0	0.0	0.0
Philippines	887.6	3.2	0.4	0.0	0.0	0.0
Yugoslavia	387.2	0.8	0.2	0.8	0.2	100.0
Australia	1,214.0	0.7	0.1	0.0	0.0	0.0

Tabelle 206: Anteil des Staates an der Finanzierung der Forschung im Unternehmenssektor (vH). In: Bletschacher/Klodt 1992: 64.
Erwähnt in Abschnitt 'H', 772.

	1980	1990
Vereinigte Staaten	31,5	33,0
Japan	1,9	1,5 (a)
Bundesrepublik Deutschland	17,6	10,8
Frankreich	24,0	20,8 (a)
Vereinigtes Königreich	29,2 (b)	16,5 (a)
Italien	9,3	16,6
Niederlande	5,8	13,2 (a)

(a) 1988. (b) 1978.

Tabelle 207: Commercial Jet Aircraft: Relative Market Shares, 1974-86 (In percent and in number ordered). Aus: IMF 1988: 168.
Erwähnt in Abschnitt 'H', 774.

	1974	1975	1976	1977	1978	1979	1980	1981	1982	1983	1984	1985	1986
All aircraft													
Airbus	1	4	5	5	14	15	6	29	13	-	22	9	25
Boing	70	69	72	67	68	68	81	57	62	56	50	61	47
Lockheed	5	6	4	1	4	3	5	4	-	-	2	-	-
McDonnel Douglas	24	21	19	27	14	14	8	10	25	44	26	30	28
	100	100	100	100	100	100	100	1000	100	100	100	100	100
Total number ordered	237	212	197	336	623	754	465	315	87	339	297	315	724
Wide-bodied aircraft													
A 300, A 310	1	19	23	19	28	37	19	53	30	0	29	33	11
747	38	50	29	38	27	25	38	15	47	68	29	45	61
767	-	-	-	-	26	14	26	9	6	29	4	7	12
L-1011	19	29	19	5	8	8	16	9	-	-	8	-	-
DC-10	42	2	29	38	11	16	1	14	17	3	30	15	16
	100	100	100	100	100	100	100	100	100	100	100	100	100
Total number ordered	67	42	42	91	303	307	137	127	36	34	70	73	152

Tabelle 208: Subsidies to the steel industry in the European Community, Mio. DM
Erwähnt in Abschnitt 'H', 775, 778, 779, Abschnitt 'I', 864.

Country	1975-1979	1980-1985	Total
Belgium	2,725	10,017	12,742
Denmark	115	191	306
France	2,060	21,515	23,575
Fr Germany	922	6,320	7,242
Ireland	76	621	697
Italy	4,327	28,317	32,644
Luxembourg	33	1,485	1,518
Netherlands	33	1,073	1,095
United Kingdom	13,852	13,275	27,127
Total	24,132	82,814	106,946

Aus: Wirtschaftsvereinigung Eisen- und Stahlindustrie, Flankenschutz durch die Politik bleibt unverzichtbar, Düsseldorf, 1987, Anhang Tabelle 5. In: Oberender/Rüter 1993: 78. Detaillierter, mit Angabe der Unternehmen, aber gleichen Zahlen: Rosenstock 1995: 202.

Tabelle 209: Crude steel production of public companies in % of total crude national steel production in the European Communiy, 1988.
Erwähnt in Abschnitt 'H', 777, 780, 793.

Country	Share of total production	Most important public companies
Belgium	40,2 %	Cockerill-Sambre
	31,3 %	Arbed Sidmar (1)
Denmark	100,0 %	Det Danske-Stlevalsevaerk
France	92,1 % (2)	Usinor-Sacilor
Ireland	100,0 %	Irish Steel
Italy	49,8 %	ILVA
Luxembourg	100,0 %	Arbed
Netherlands	96,4 %	Hoogovens
Spain	28,0 %	Ensidesa

(1) The main shareholders of Sidmar are Arbed (Luxembourg), ILVA (Italy) and the Flemisch regional government.
(2) This figure represents the status of 1988.

Aus: International Iron and Steel Industry, World Steel in Figures 1990, Brussels. Aus: Oberender/Rüter 1993: 74.

Tabelle 210: Staatliche Hilfen für den Neubau von Schiffen in den EG-Ländern 1974-1986 (vH der Baupreise). In: Soltwedel et al. 1988: 166.
Erwähnt in Abschnitt 'H', 781.

	Belgien		Bundes-republik		Dänemark		Frankreich	
	Schiffe für inländ-ische Reeder	exportierte Schiffe	Schiffe für inländ-ische Reeder	exportierte Schiffe	Schiffe für inländ-ische Reeder	exportierte Schiffe	Schiffe für inländ-ische Reeder	exportierte Schiffe
1974	.	6 (a)	10	4	.	13	.	.
1975	.	6 (a)	10 (a)	4 (a)	.	9	.	.
1976	15	4 (a)	10 (a)	4 (a)	.	4	6-19 (a)	4 (a)
1977	15	4 (a)	19 (a)	4 (a)	.	4 (a)	.	.
1978	15	4 (a)	20 (a)	4 (a)	.	4 (a)	.	.
1979	19	4 (a)	26 (a)	14 (a)	15	6	28-48 (a)	14-34
1980	42	5	27 (a)	15 (a)	60	32	34-48 (a)	23-37
1981	47	5	25	13	61	33	44-57	42
1982	36	5	22 (a)	7 (a)	59	38	41-54	39
1983	24	7	18 (a)	7 (a)	29	19	47	35
1984	27	10	23 (a)	12 (a)	29	18	39-52	37
1985	19-24	7	22 (a)	10 (a)	16	10	20-45	20-30
1986	18-23	7	18 (a)	7 (a)	30-31	7	15-40 (a)	15-40 (a)

	Irland		Italien		Nieder-lande		GB	
	Schiffe für inländ-ische Reeder	exportierte Schiffe	Schiffe für inländ-ische Reeder	exportierte Schiffe	Schiffe für inländ-ische Reeder	exportierte Schiffe	Schiffe für inländ-ische Reeder	exportierte Schiffe
1974	.	.	.	14	.	4 (a)	17	17
1975	.	.	.	14	.	4 (a)	14	14
1976	.	.	.	14	.	.	10	10
1977	.	.	.	.	.	.	.	.
1978	.	.	.	19-28	15-36 (a)	10-31 (a)	14-32 (a)	14-32 (a)
1979	.	.	.	19-28	8-11	.	.	.
1980	.	.	.	38-45	38-45	.	.	.
1981	.	.	56	56	32	22	39	39
1982	.	.	52	52	28	18	31	31
1983	27	25	52	52	24 (a)	14 (a)	22	23
1984	.	.	39	39	25 (a)	15 (a)	19	20
1985	.	.	.	.	.	.	.	.
1986	.	.	31-53	21-40	30-35 (a)	12-17 (a)	26 (b)	27 (b)

(a) Fördersatz, der möglich wäre, wenn die Zinsverbilligung im Rahmen von Finanzierungsbeihilfen 2 Prozentpunkte (ab 1982: 2,5 Prozentpunkte für exportierte Schiffe im Fall Belgiens, der Bundesrepublik, Frankreichs, der Niederlande und des Vereinigten Königreichs) betrüge; da in den betreffenden Jahren die Kapitalmarktzinsen um weniger als 2 Prozentsätze über dem OECD-Limit (8 vH) lagen, ist nicht ausgeschlossen, daß der tatsächliche Fördersatz geringfügig niedriger war. – (b) Höchstsatz, tatsächlicher Satz vermutlich niedriger.

Tabelle 211: Entwicklung des EG-Haushalts nach Obergruppen 1971-1992 (Mill. ECU).
In: Klodt/Stehn 1992: 53.
Erwähnt in Abschnitt 'H', 782, 783, 785.

	1971	1980	1984	1988	1992
EAGFL, Abteilung Garantie	1756,0	11485,5	18333,0	27500,0	35093,0
Agrarstrukturen		460,0	810,1	1201,6	
Regionalpolitik	118,0 (a)	1484,7	2267,4	4006,3	17585,3 (a)
Sozialpolitik		972,7	2059,9	3119,4	
Forschung, Energie	64,0	443,4	1018,3	1360,4	2834,3
Anderes	269,0	2645,6	4785,8	8156,5	10605,3
Insgesamt	2207,0	17491,9	29264,5	45344,2	66117,9

EAGFL = Europäischer Ausrichtungs- und Garantiefonds für die Landwirtschaft
(a) Agrarstrukturen, Regionalpolitik und Sozialpolitik zusammengefaßt.

Tabelle 212: The scale and redistributive effects of the Structural Fund transfers in the European Community in 1992.
Aus: Costello 1993: 276.
Erwähnt in Abschnitt 'H', 782.

	B	DK	D	GR	E	F	IRL	I	L	NL	P	UK	EUR12
Income differential per capita (%)	5,05	8,91	12,31	-47,79	-19,54	9,13	-30,99	4,05	35,18	3,26	-42,92	1,35	
Gross transfers (MioECU)	218	97	1898	1840	3529	1655	1013	2745	17	202	1918	1608	16740
Net transfers (MioECU)	-338	-262	-2427	1647	2166	-2207	891	-26	-23	-699	1750	-473	0
as % of GDP	-0,20	-0,23	-0,18	2,81	0,46	-0,22	2,38	-0,00	-0,28	-0,29	2,72	-0,05	0,31
Redistributive effect	4,11	2,87	1,65	3,06	1,89	2,57	5,29	0,07	1,09	9,21	3,62	3,97	

Nicht die gesamte Tabelle ist reproduziert

Tabelle 213: Indikatoren zu den FuE-Aktivitäten in Industrieländern 1980 und 1986. Aus: Klodt et al. 1988: 6. Erwähnt in Abschnitt 'H', 785, 791.

		Bundesrepublik	Frankreich	Vereinigtes Königreich	Italien	Belgien	Niederlande	Vereinigte Staaten	Japan
FuE-Ausgaben insgesamt (Mill US $)	1980	11897 (a)	8586	11490 (b)	3342	985 (a)	2332	64189	20294
	1986	19774 (c)	15500	14359 (c)	8149	1494 (d)	3446 (c)	117100	41784
Anteil der FuE Ausgaben am BIP (vH)	1980	2,5	1,8	2,4 (b)	0,7	1,4 (a)	1,9 (a)	2,4	2,2
	1986	2,7	2,3	2,3 (c)	1,3	1,5 (d)	2,1 (c)	2,8	2,8
Durchführung von FuE darunter : (vH)									
Unternehmen	1980	69,3 (b)	60,4	61,8 (b)	59,0	69,6 (a)	51,6	69,3	59,9
	1986	72,2 (c)	58,7 (c)	63,1 (c)	58,1	.	56,2 (c)	71,4	66,6
Hochschulen	1980	16,5 (b)	16,2	13,3 (b)	16,1	20,6 (a)	24,3	14,6	25,5
	1986	14,9 (c)	15,0 (c)	13,6 (c)	17,7	.	23,3 (c)	13,7	19,9
Finanzierung von FuE darunter (vH)									
Unternehmen	1980	58,0 (b)	40,9 (b)	41,4 (b)	51,1 (b)	65,8 (a)	45,2	48,2	60,9
	1986	60,9 (c)	41,2	46,1 (c)	41,0	.	50,2 (c)	47,4	68,9 (c)
Staat	1980	40,3 (b)	53,4 (b)	49,0	47,2 (b)	31,0	47,8	49,3	26,9
	1986	37,6 (c)	52,8	43,4 (c)	55,3	.	45,0 (c)	50,3	21,0
Staatliche FuE-Förderung der Unternehmen insgesamt (Mill. US $)	1985	2223	2035	2105	675	60	132	20215	434
darunter: (vH)									
Landwirtschaft, Bergbau		7,0 (d)	1,6	.	0,3	1,2	.	0,2	
Verarbeitende Industrie insgesamt		78,1 (d)	95,6	96,6	93,0	85,4	.	94,8 (d)	83,4
Elektronische Ausrüstungen und Komponenten		31,1 (d,e)	32,4	37,2	17,5	20,5	.	25,4 (d)	9,7
Chemische Industrie		6,6 (d)	4,3	0,7	8,2	26,0	.	.	7,8
Luft- und Raumfahrzeugbau		20,1 (d)	49,0	43,2	28,4	1,5	.	51,0 (d)	0,1
Maschinenbau		9,1 (d)	6,0	11,1	15,4	6,6	.	8,8 (d)	5,6
Dienstleistungen		9,4 (d)	2,8	2,7	6,7	13,6	.	5,2 (d)	14,3
Anteil staatlicher FuE-Ausgaben für	1980	12,2	37,2	54,2	2,7	0,3	3,1	47,0	2,3
Verteidigung an allen staatlichen FuE-Ausgaben	1986	17,0 (h)	36,8 (h)	54,3	15,4 (h)	0,2 (h)	5,8 (h)	74,9	2,8

Tabelle 214: Direct and indirect R&D support to manufacturing industry. Reported expenditure in billion US$. In current US$, average of daily rates. In: OECD 1998a: 196.
Erwähnt in Abschnitt 'H', 786.

	1989	1990	1991	1992	1993	Total 1989-1993
Direct R&D supports (282 progammes) (NCG)	6.4	7.4	8.7	9.2	8.3	40.0
R&D contracts to manufacturing industry	19.3	17.8	17.5	16.7	17.2	88.5
Space agencies: contracts awarded by/procurement of	4.9	5.9	5.6	6.5	6.4	29.3
Public support to intermediary R&D institutions	0.8	0.9	0.9	1	1	4.6
R&D defense procurement expenditure	28.9	30	28.4	29	29.5	145.8

Tabelle 215: Budget authority for R&D by function and character of work: Anticipated levels for FY 1998. Aus: http://www.nsf.gov/sbe/srs/.
Erwähnt in Abschnitt 'H', 790.

Budge Function	Basic research	Applied research	Development	R&D total
	Millions of dollar			
Total	15,710	15,570	42,359	73,639
National Defense	1,099	4,308	34,463	39,871
Nondefense (total)	14,611	11,261	7,895	33,768
Health	7,361	4,618	1,578	13,557
Space research and technology	1,658	1,591	5,015	8,265
Energy	257	370	516	1,143
General science	3,944	266	0	4,210
National resources and environment	156	1,667	191	2,015
Transportation	459	1,258	203	1,920
Agriculture	560	589	94	1,243
All other	216	902	297	1,415

Tabelle 216: Preliminary federal obligation for research and development and for R&D plant, by agency, category, and performer: FY 2000. Aus: http://www.nsf.gov/sbe/srs/.
Erwähnt in Abschnitt 'H', 790.

Agency and category	Performer							
	Total performers	Federal intramural	Industrial firms	Universities and colleges	Federal extramural			
					All FFRDCs	Other nonprofits	State and local governments	Foreign
	(In millions of current dollars)							
Agency								
Total	77,186	18,118	32,157	15,339	7,407	3,483	422	260
DoD	34,475	7,906	24,254	1,383	670	134	4	123
HHS	16,361	3,406	885	9,208	256	2,386	172	49
NASA	9,695	2,356	4,735	787	1,389	370	13	47
DOE	7,458	667	1,226	648	4,868	46	3	1
NSF	2,890	23	158	2,329	189	175	4	11
USDA	1,709	1,211	11	475	0	7	1	4
All other	4,597	2,549	888	509	36	366	224	25
Category								
Development	77,186	18,118	32,157	15,339	7,407	3,483	422	260
Total research	40,425	8,866	26,930	1,769	1,935	711	75	138
Basic research	34,680	8,776	4,710	13,422	4,543	2,762	346	122
Applied research	18,209	3,336	1,440	9,227	2,437	1,624	88	58
R&D plant	16,470	5,440	3,270	4,195	2,106	1,138	258	64
	2,081	477	517	147	929	10	1	0

FFRDCs: Federally Funded Reseach and Development Centers; DoD: Department of Defense; HHS: U.S. Department of Health and Human Services; NASA: National Aeronautics and Space Agency; DOE: Department of the Environment; NSF: National Science Foundation; USDA: United States Department of Agriculture.

Tabelle 217: Government finance of capital formation as a percentage of total gross capital formation. Aus: Hufbauer/Erb 1984: 3.
Erwähnt in Abschnitt 'H', 791.

Country	1964	1968	1972	1976	1979
Japan	13,9	11,7	15,4	16,2	19,3
Italy	n.a.	n.a.	14,0	14,5	14,5
GB	20,9	25,4	23,8	22,2	14,1
Germany	17,0	15,0	14,8	15,5	14,1
France	15,6	17,4	14,3	13,5	12,9
Canada	16,7	18,3	16,9	13,7	12,2
USA	15,6	14,9	11,9	11,2	8,6

Tabelle 218: Subsidies as shown in national account statistics as percentage of GDP
Erwähnt in Abschnitt 'H', 791.

Country	1952	1956	1960	1964	1968	1972	1976	1980	1984	1988	1992	1994	1997
Italy	0,89	1,30	1,51	1,23	1,67	2,29	2,60	3,01	3,49	2,89	2,34	2,41	1,90
France	1,71	2,71	1,62	2,03	2,62	1,99	2,68	2,51	3,00	2,51	2,20	2,33	2,72
Canada	0,41	0,39	0,81	0,85	0,87	0,83	1,73	2,34	2,80	1,76	1,79	1,25	0,95
GB	2,68	1,76	1,93	1,56	2,06	1,82	2,78	2,32	2,44	1,32	1,15	1,12	1,03
Germany	0,65	0,20	0,79	0,99	1,44	1,48	1,49	1,59	2,07	2,27	1,94	2,07	1,84
Japan	0,79	0,26	0,34	0,65	1,11	1,12	1,32	1,32	1,28	0.91	0,70	0,72	0,70
USA	0,11	0,20	0,25	0,44	0,50	0,59	0,34	0,43	0,61	0,65	0,53	0,50	0,42

Aus: OECD 1999. Berechnungen des Verfassers. Germany bis 1988 als BRD. Siehe zu den Zahlen bis 1980, die ebenso auf OECD National Account Statistics beruhen. Hufbauer/Erb 1984: 3.

Tabelle 219: OECD-Total. Main aggregates based on exchange rates. Billions of US dollars. Aus: OECD 1999: 18-19.
Erwähnt in Abschnitt 'H', 791.

	1960	1969	1970	1975	1980	1985	1990	1995	1997
Subventionen	8,49	31,34	33,28	73,68	134,92	206,34	252,52	317,02	485,86
GDP	1125,32	2447,91	2701,16	4678,78	7981,86	11820,96	16941,12	24214,13	34614,45
Subventionen/GDP	0,7	1,2	1,2	1,5	1,6	1,7	1,4	1,3	1,4

Tabelle 220: Sektorale, regionale und allgemeine Subventionen in Deutschland 1993. Aus: Krieger-Boden/Lammers 1993: 15. Erwähnt in Abschnitt 'H', 792.

	Subventionen								Anteile		
	insgesamt	sektorale	regionale	allgemeine					sektorale Subventionen	regionale Subventionen	allgemeine Subventionen
				insgesamt	beschäftigungs-politisch	darunter:					
						Investitions-förderung	FuE-Förderung	Mittelstands-förderung		vH	
Subventionen insgesamt	215985	162987	23404	29794	6310	12314	4920	1656	75,5	10,8	13,8
Finanzhilfe	168474	133677	7959	27038	6310	11129	4915	656	79,3	4,7	16,0
darunter:											
Bund (a)	41501	34770	-	6732	677	864	4587	308	83,8	-	16,2
Länder (a)	50203	39908	6559	3737	1654	365	327	349	79,5	13,1	7,4
Gemeinden	9416	9416	-	-	-	-	-	-	100,0	-	-
EU	13463	13463	-	-	-	-	-	-	100,0	-	-
Treuhandanstalt	29580	29580	-	-	-	-	-	-	100,0	-	-
Bundesanstalt f. Arbeit	4520	740	-	3780	3780	-	-	-	16,4	-	83,6
Kohlepfennig	5800	5800	-	-	-	-	-	-	100,0	-	-
ERP	13991	-	1400	12591	-	9900	1	-c	-	10,0	90,0
Steuervergünstigungen	47511	29310	15445	2756	-	1185	5	1000	61,7	32,5	5,8

(a) Die Finanzhilfen werden der Gebietskörperschaft zugeordnet, von der sie ausgezahlt werden, (b) geschätzt, (c) Die ERP Darlehen dienen überwiegend der Mittelstandsförderung, sie werden hier unter dem zusätzlich verfolgen Zielen subsumiert.

Tabelle 221: Sektorspezifische Subventionen nach ausgewählten Wirtschaftsbereichen 1981, 1986 und 1993.
Aus Krieger-Boden/Lammers 1993: 16.
Erwähnt in Abschnitt 'H', 792.

	Subventionen			Anteile		
	1981	1986	1993	1981	1986	1993
			Mill. DM			vH
Land- und Forstwirtschaft, Fischerei	15142	23151	31606	16,1	20,0	20,6
Energie- und Wasserversorgung	2197	2860	945	2,3	2,5	0,6
Bergbau	5896	7038	11792	6,3	6,1	7,7
Schiffbau	855	475	700	0,9	0,4	0,4
Luft- und Raumfahrzeugbau	703	569	386	0,7	0,5	0,3
Verkehr	17145	19132	27645	18,2	16,5	18,0
Wohnungsvermietung	20696	22112	31554	22,0	19,1	20,5
Dienstleistungen für den privaten Haushalt	9075	11233	12458	9,6	9,7	8,1
Sonstige Dienstleistungen	6011	6972	1360	6,4	6,0	0,9
Sonstige sektoral verfaßte Subventionen	16542	22066	5546	17,5	19,1	3,6
Unternehmen der Treuhandanstalt	-	-	29580	-	-	19,3
Insgesamt	94262	115608	153571	100.0	100.0	100.0
Nachrichtlich:				.	.	.
Branchenübergreifende Subventionen	1699	2322	62414	.	.	.
Alle Subventionen	95961	117930	215985	.	.	.

(a) Ohne Nachrichtenübermittlung, (b) Ohne Wohnungsvermietung, (c) Einschließlich einiger sonstiger sektoraler Subventionen, die keiner einzelnen Branche zugeordnet werden können.

Tabelle 222: Subventionen in Deutschland nach unterschiedlichen Kategorien und Erfassungskonzepten (Mrd. DM). Aus: DIW-Subventionsabbau 1999.
Erwähnt in Abschnitt 'H', 792.

	1980	1990 (a)	1993	1994	1995	1996	1997	1997 in vH des BIP
Steuervergünstigungen für Unternehmen								
nach DIW	28,8	35,9	47,9	49,0	50,7	53,7	.	1,52 (c)
nach IfW	35,1	44,9	45,2	44,7	47,9	48,6	45,5	1,25
Steuervergünstigungen in erweiterter Abgrenzung nach IfW	.	57,9	57,8	61,7	62,7	62,6	60,1	1,65
Finanzhilfen des Bundes an Unternehmen (b)								
nach DIW	33,5	46,9	94,7	107,4	93,6	99,1	.	2,80 (c)
nach IfW	.	.	95,4	99,6	73,8	71,7	75,0	2,06
Finanzhilfen des Bundes (b), der Länder und Gemeinden an Unternehmen nach IfW	62,5	82,8	153,0	157,7	131,0	139,0	141,7	3,89
Finanzhilfen insgesamt in erweiterter Abgrenzen nach IfW	.	.	249,1	250,9	222,7	230,1	230,9	6,34

(a) Früheres Bundesgebiet, (b) Einschließlich der Finanzhilfen der EU, des ERP-Sondervermögens, der Bundesanstalt für Arbeit, der Treuhandanstalt sowie des Ausgleichsfonds zur Sicherung des Steinkohleeinsatzes; IfW-Zahlen ab 1993 ohne ERP-Sondervermögen, (c) 1996.

Tabelle 223: Numbers employed, value added and gross fixed capital formation (CFCF) in European public enterprises, 1991. In: Parker 1998: 11.
Erwähnt in Abschnitt 'H', 796.

	Share of non-agricultural employment (%)	Value added as a % of total manufacturing and service industy (a current prices)	Share in non-agricultural CFCF (%)
Belgium	9,8	7,5	8,4
Denmark	8,2	8,7	17,6
France	13,4	15,1	24,2 (a)
Greece	14,7	17	30
Ireland	8,7	11,5	16,9
Italy	13,5	20	23,5
Luxembourg	3,0	5,2 (b)	4,6
Netherlands	5,1	8,0	9,2
Portugal	10,6	21,5	30,0
Spain	6,0	7,5 to 8,5	12,5 to 13
UK	4,6	4,0	5,0

a Total CFCF
b Percentage share in non-agricultural turnover

Tabelle 224: Output and investment shares of public enterprises. In: Chang/Singh 1994: 73-76. Aus Short 1984.
Erwähnt in Abschnitt 'E', 419, Abschnitt 'H', 796.

Country	Years	Percentage share in GDP at factor cost	Percentage share in gross fixed capital formation	Overall surplus/deficit (h)
World (*)		9,4	13,4	-0,2
Industrialized Countries (*)		9,6	11,1	1,7
Australia	1974-77	9,2	18,7	-3,5
Austria (a)	1976-77	14,5	19,2	-
Belgium	1974-77	-	12,6	-0,9
Canada (b)	1974-77	-	14,7	-2,8
Denmark	1974	6,3	8,3	-
Finland (b)	1974-75	-	13,6	-2,6
France	1974	11,9	14,0	-1,8
Germany (a)	1976-77	10,3	12,3	-
Ireland	1974-77	-	13,1	-
Italy (a)	1974-77	7,7	17,2	-3,5
Japan (b)	1974-77	-	11,6	-3,4
Luxembourg	1974	-	9,2	-
Netherlands (b)	1971-73	3,6	13,8	-0,5
Norway	1974-77	-	17,7	-2,7 (i)
Spain (a)	1979	4,1	16,6	-3,1
Sweden (a)	1978-80	6,0	15,3	-
United Kingdom	1974-77	11,3	18,6	-1,9
United States of America (b)	1974-77	-	4,9	-0,7
Developing Countries (*)		8,6	27,0	
Oil exporting countries				
Algeria	1974-77	-	70,2	-
Venezuela	1974-77	15,0	22,3	-5,2
Middle East				
Egypt	1976-79	-	47,8	-
Africa (*)		17,5	32,4	-
Benin (a, d)	1976	7,6	-	-
Botswana (a)	1974-77	7,7	16,5	-4,7
Ethiopia	1976-77	-	17,6	-
Gambia	1978-80	-	36,5	-4,9 (1979)
Guinea (a)	1979	25,0	-	-8,0 (1976-77)
Cote d' Ivoire (a)	1974-77	-	28,8	-3,5
Kenya	1974-77	-	18,1	-
Liberia	1974-1976	-	14,1	-
Malawi	1974-77	-	28,1	-2,5
Mali (d)	1974-77	-	31,1	-5,9 (1975-77)
Mauritius	1977-79	-	14,4	-
Senegal (a)	1974	19,9	17,9	2,2
Sierra Leone	1979	7,6	19,6	-
Tanzania, United Rep. of	1974-77	12,3	30,3	-2,8 (1974-75) (j)
Togo	1980	11,8	-	-
Tunisia	1978-79	25,4	44,6	-
Zambia	1972	37,8	49,7	-3.4
Asia (*)		8,0	27,7	-5,6
Bangladesh	1974	5,7	31,0	-
India	1974-77	9,8	33,8	-6,3

Korea, Rep. of (b)	1974-77	6,4	33,8	-5,4
Myanmar	1974-77	-	39,6	-1,2
Nepal	1974-75	1,3	-	-2,1
Pakistan	1974-75	6,0	33,3	-
Papua New Guinea	1977	-	18,8	-
Philippines (b)	1974-77	1,7	9,5	-
Sri Lanka	1974	9,9	15,7	-
Taiwan, Province of China	1974-77	13,6	35,0	-7,3
Thailand	1970-73	3,6	8,5	-1,1
Europe (*)		6,6	23,4	
Greece (b)	1975	5,8	10,8	-1,6
Malta (e)	1974-77	3,8	11,6	-
Portugal (b)	1976	14,3	31,0	-8,1
Turkey (a, f)	1974-77	5,8	23,5	-7,0
Western Hemisphere (*)		6,6	22,5	-2,5
Argentine (d)	1976-77	4,8	20,7	-3,1
Bahamas	1975-77	-	20,4	-1,9
Bolivia (a)	1974-77	12,1	40,9	-4,4
Brazil	1980	-	22,8	-1,7
Chile (d)	1974-77	15,2	20,0	-0,2
Columbia	1974-77	1,9 (c)	10,3	-0,9
Costa Rica	1977-79	-	19,6	-4,4
Dominica	1975-77	-	25,5	-4,4
Dominican Republic (d)	1974-77	-	11,1	-0,2
Guatemala	1978-80	1,1	13,3	-1,8 (1975-77)
Guyana	1974-77	22,8	38,3	-6,6
Haiti (b, d)	1976-77	-	16,3	-2,0
Honduras	1978-79	-	14,6	-2,3
Jamaica (b, d)	1976-77	-	40,1	-4,3
Mexico	1975-77	6,1 (g)	27,0	-3,9 (d)
Panama (b)	1974-77	-	32,7	-7,1
Paraguay (a)	1974-77	2,7	10,4	-1,6
Peru	1974-77	-	22,1	-4,8
St. Lucia	1975-77	-	12,3	-4,6
Uruguay	1974-77	-	16,6	-0,8

(*) Weighted average for 1974-77 or closest available period using GDP at market prices and Gross Fixed Capital Formation (CFCF) expressed in US dollars for 1974-77 for weights.

a Share in GDP at market prices
b Share in Gross Domestic Capital Formation (rather than CFCF).
c Excludes public enterprises at the regional or local level
d Major enterprises only
e Excludes industrial enterprises
f Figures relate to State economic enterprises
g Twenty-two major enterprises only
h Excluding government capital transfers
i Central government enterprises only
j Figures include parastatal enterprises only; exludes former East African Community enterprises

Tabelle 225: Major-signatory contracts awarded under the Code on Government Procurement, 1983 (in millions of SDR). Aus: Grieco 1990: 147.
Erwähnt in Abschnitt 'H', 797.

Value of contracts awarded by code covered entities	EC	USA	Japan	Canada	The Nordics	Switzerland	Austria
(A) Above 150.000 SDR Threshold	3,409.3	16,663.6	1,223.0	358.4	364.4	114.5	36.6
(B) Below 150.000 SDR Threshold	6,100.6	6,160.8	1,945.0	449.9	1,072.4	141.7	130.2
Total value of contracts by code covered entities	9,509.9	22,824.4	3,168.0	808.3	1,436.8	256.2	166.8
Above threshold contracts/total (A as percent of C)	35.9	73.0	38.6	44.3	25.4	44.7	21.9

Der damalige Wechselkurs lautet $ 1.126 = SDR 1. Grieco 1990: 165.

Tabelle 226: Average Tariff Levels in Selected Countries (in percent). In: Irwin 1994: 31.
Erwähnt in Abschnitt 'H', 797, 807.

	1913	1925	1927	1931	1952
Belgium	6	7	11	17	n.a.
France	14	9	23	38	19
Germany	12	15	24	40	16
Italy	17	16	27	48	24
Netherlands	2	4	n.a.	n.a.	n.a.
United Kingdom	n.a.	4	n.a.	17	17
United States	32	26	n.a.	n.a.	16

Note: Not all years are comparable. Calculations for 1913 and 1925 are from the League of Nations as reported in GATT (1953, p. 62), also the source for the 1952 GATT calculation. For 1927 and 1931 tariff data, see Leipmann (1938), p. 415, and Kitson and Solomou (1990), pp. 65-66, for the United Kingdom in 1932.

Tabelle 227: Überblick über die GATT-Verhandlungsrunden und ihre wichtigsten Charakteristika.
Erwähnt in Abschnitt 'H', 798, 799, 806, 807.

Verhandlungsrunde/ Zeitraum	durchschnittliches Zollsenkungen, in Prozent	EWG bzw. EG: gewogene Durchschnitts- zollsätze, in Prozent (a)	Wert des von den Zollsenkungen erfaßten Handels in Mrd. US-Dollar (b)	Regulierungsinhalt
1. Genf 1947	19-20		10,0	Ausschließlich: Zollsenkungen
2. Annecy 1949	2		-	
3. Torquay 1950/51	3		-	
4. Genf 1955/56	2-3		2,5	
5. 'Dillon' 1961/62	7	12	4,9	
6. Kennedy 1964/67 (Umsetzung bis 1972)	35	9	40,0	Einbeziehung der nichttarifären Handelshemnisse, Verhandlungen auf multilateraler Basis
7. Tokio 1973/79 (Umsetzung bis 1987)	34	6	148,0	
8. Uruguay 1986/94	40 (auf niedrigem Niveau)			'new issues': Agrarhandel, Dienstleistungen, geistiges Eigentum, Investitionen

Modifiziert: basierend auf Kareseit 1998: 55-70, Hauser/Schanz 1995: 42. (a) Aus: Werner/Willms 1984: 1. (b) Aus: Müller 1983. 57

Tabelle 228: Penetration rates. Proportion of domestic demand accounted for by imports (as percentages). Total Industry. Buigues/Goybet 1985: 230.
Erwähnt in Abschnitt 'H', 799.

	1973	1979	1980	1981	1982	1983	1984	1985	Difference 1979-73	Difference 1985-79
EUR7	8.7	10.4	11.1	11.3	11.4	11.9	13.1	13.1	+ 1.7	+ 2.7
USA	6.3	8.7	9.3	9.5	9.6	10.0	11.7	12.3	+ 2.4	+3.6
Japan	4.9	5.1	5.2	4.9	5.2	4.9	5.1	4.8	+ 0.2	- 0.3

Tabelle 229: Nominal and effective rates of protection in the United States, by commodity group, 1964 and 1972 (a). In: Baldwin 1970: 165.
Erwähnt in Abschnitt 'H', 800.

Commodity group (b)	Nominal rate, tariffs only (c)		Effective Rate (d)			
			Tariff and nontariff measures		Nontariff measures only	
	1964 (1)	1972 (2)	1964 (3)	1972 (4)	1964 (5)	1972 (6)
Primary products	.08 (.014)	.07 (.14)	.18	.17	.08	.08
Intermediate and consumer groups	.10 (.13)	.07 (.11)	.22	.18	.04	.07
Capital goods	.11	.06	.15	.07	-0.1	-0.1
Average	.10	.06 (.10)	.20	.15	0.3	0.5

(a) Rates for 1972 include the effects of reductions agreed to in the Kennedy Round of GATT negotiations.
(b) Primary products include industries 1-10 (exept 4) from the 1958 input-output table; intermediate and consumer products govver industries 13-42; and capital goods cover industries 43-64. See Baldwin 1970: 163-164.
(c) Figures in parantheses are nominal rates based on both tariff and non-tariff measures; they are given only for groups that include industries where the effects ot nontariff measures were estimated.
(d) Nontrade inputs are treated like trade inputs and excluded from value added, as suggested by Balassa, 'Tariff Protection in Industrial Countries,' and Basevi, 'United States Tariff Structure'.

Tabelle 230: Kennedy round tariff reductions on imports from less developed countries in important commodity groups (1964 imports into US, EEC, UK, Japan, Sweden, Switzerland). Aus: Evans 1971: 251.
Erwähnt in Abschnitt 'H', 800.

Group	Kennedy round action				
	No reduction	Reduced less than half	Reduced by half	Reduced more than half	Eliminated
	(percent of imports in group)				
Tropical products	50,5	34,5	4,0	4,5	6,0
Processed foods	43,5	13,0	33,5	1,0	9,0
Nonferrous metals and products	37,5	27,0	33,5	0,0	2,0
Cotton yarn and fabrics	22,5	73,5	4,0	0,0	0,0
Clothing (a)	19,0	71,5	7,0	0,0	0,0
Other Textiles	12,5	29,0	7,0	0,0	51,5
Leather and manufactures	23,0	22,0	53,0	1,0	1,0

(a) Information unavailable for 2,5 % of imports of this group.

Tabelle 231: Ausfuhr der Entwicklungsländer in Industrieländer von 1955 – 1980 (in Mrd. US$). In: Werner/Willms 1984. 1955 und 1963 einschließlich Ölländer bzw. OPEC, danach ohne diese Länder.
Erwähnt in Abschnitt 'H', 800.

Warengruppen	1955	1963	1970	1973	1976	1980
Primärgüter						
-mit Öl, ohne Ernährung	4,51	4,52	5,25	8,14	10,70	18,00
-ohne Öl, mit Ernährung	11,24	12,48	14,87	24,03	33,70	52,50
-mit Öl, mit Ernährung	14,6	19,0	16,85	28,35	48,00	89,50
-Mineralöl	3,36	6,52	1,98	4,32	14,30	37,00
-Ernährung	6,73	7,96	9,62	15,89	23,00	34,50
-Holz	0,33	0,49	0,73	1,73	1,40	-
-Fasern	1,59	1,49	1,25	1,88	1,63	-
-Erze, Mineralien	1,04	1,41	2,50	3,19	5,00	8,00
-sonstige Rohstoffe	1,55	1,13	0,77	1,34	2,67	10,00
Verarbeitete Güter	1,91	3,08	9,11	18,89	30,75	63,45
Halbwaren	1,69	2,43	5,61	9,43	12,15	23,95
Kunststoffe und andere chemische Halbwaren	0,11	0,13	0,27	0,58	1,30	4,00
Holzwaren incl. Papier	0,03	0,08	0,31	0,79	0,75	-
Textilien	0,21	0,53	0,82	2,10	2,75	4,70
Eisen und Stahl	0,03	0,07	0,27	0,49	0,80	2,00
Nicht-Eisenmetalle	1,16	1,28	3,22	3,77	4,10	7,00
Andere Halbwaren	0,15	0,34	0,72	1,70	2,45	6,25
Fertigwaren	0,22	0,65	3,50	9,46	18,6	29,50
a) *Konsumgüter*	0,19	0,57	2,85	7,15	14,2	26,80
-Kunststoffwaren	0,02	0,07	0,13	0,23	0,30	-
-Bekleidung	0,04	0,21	1,13	3,23	6,80	12,00
-Haushaltsgeräte	-	0,03	0,26	1,30	2,60	5,30
-sonstige Konsumgüter	0,13	0,26	1,33	2,39	4,50	9,50
b) *Investitionsgüter*	0,03	0,08	0,65	2,31	4,40	12,70
-Spezialmaschinen	0,01	-	0,07	0,24	0,30	0,90
-Büro- und Kommunikationsgeräte	-	-	0,19	0,97	1,85	5,70
-Straßenfahrzeuge	-	-	0,03	0,11	0,20	0,60
-sonstige Transportausrüstung	-	-	0,07	0,16	0,35	-
-Maschinen	0,02	0,08	0,29	0,83	1,70	5,50
Gesamtexporte, ohne Öl, ohne Ernährung	6,52	7,60	14,36	27,03	41,45	81,45
ohne Öl, mit Ernährung	13,25	15,56	23,98	42,92	64,45	115,95
Gesamtexporte (mit Öl, mit Ernährung)	16,51	22,08	25,96	47,24	78,75	152,95

Tabelle 232: Unweighted average tariffs by country and sector: per cent. (In parantheses, average total import charges). Data for 1989. Modified, average import charges not reproduced, not all countries reproduced: In: Erzan et al. 1989: 49.
Erwähnt in Abschnitt 'H', 801, 812.

Country	Food	Agric. raw materials	Mineral fuels	Ores and metals Total	Iron, Steel, NFM	Manufacturing Total	Chemical products	Other manuf.	Mach. & Equip.	Others	All sectors
Argentina	21	25	25	28	29	28	21	33	25	22	27
Bangladesh	64	66	36	42	50	101	55	140	65	29	86
Bolivia	20	20	20	20	20	20	20	20	20	20	20
Brazil	52	43	19	30	36	62	41	77	51	69	55
Chile	35	35	35	35	35	34	35	34	34	31	35
Columbia	32	24	15	25	30	43	27	55	34	49	38
Egypt	30	15	6	12	14	46	15	73	22	19	38
Ghana	29	30	30	30	30	30	30	30	31	29	30
Malaysia	10	7	7	7	8	16	10	21	11	11	14
Mexico	32	14	8	12	14	35	19	49	22	38	30
Nigeria	42	29	23	29	30	38	26	48	28	34	37
Pakistan	81	48	38	57	68	84	56	112	52	57	77
Philippines	35	23	17	16	17	29	18	38	23	39	28
Korea	28	14	10	15	18	24	20	27	21	5	23
Singapore	0	0	2	0	0	0	0	1	0	0	0
Thailand	40	24	7	13	17	33	26	41	23	18	31
Tanzania	40	37	41	20	20	32	19	37	33	4	32
Venezuela	39	34	21	17	19	30	24	44	18	17	30
Zaire	37	12	6	15	15	35	11	49	28	32	31
Zimbabwe	9	1	2	2	3	10	2	17	6	12	9

Tabelle 233: Importance of the GSP for the Developing Countries in 1980. Some indicators with reference to the imports of OECD preference-giving countries (a) (percentages): In: OECD1983a: 95.
Erwähnt in Abschnitt 'H', 802.

	Average annual import growth 1976 - 1980		Ratio of GSP to total imports
	Total	under GSP (b)	1980
All beneficiaries	20.2	26.7	8.3
Ten largest beneficiares (1980 list)	22.2 (c)	25.6 (c)	18.9
South Korea	17.5	25.3	30.1
Taiwan	24.8	29.5	31.2
Hong Kong	20.6	26.2	20.5
Brazil	18.2	27.8	13.8
India	11.5	25.0	25.3
Singapore	29.2	25.6	16.7
China	(c)	(c)	13.4
Yugoslavia	15.6	11.4	27.6
Mexico	35.9	22.8	6.1
Philippines	23.8	36.1	18.3
Next ten beneficiaries (1980 list)	24.2	28.1 (d)	8.6
Malaysia	26.0	13.3	9.7
Romania	18.7	16.4	24.6
Venezuela	22.8	33.8	6.1
Thailand	22.6	31.4 (d)	15.0
Argentina	15.3	27.6	14.1
Israel	21.4	29.9	32.5
Indonesia	32.9	28.3 (d)	1.8
Pakistan	22.6	22.3	33.5
Colombia	25.1	58.1	9.5
Chile	25.2	44.8	7.9
The least developed countries (1980 list)	9.3	44.3 (d)	15.1

(a) Including in each case only those preference-giving countries for which the developing country concerned is a GSP beneficiary. (b) The contribution of New Zealand to these rates is an estimate. (c) Growth rates for imports from China have not been included as China was not a beneficiary of any GSP scheme until the end of 1978. (d) For 1977-1980.

Tabelle 234: Durchschnittliche Zollsätze; Zollsenkungsraten (%) für alle Länder nach den Zollsenkungen der Tokiorunde für Waren unterschiedlichen Verarbeitungsgrades, gewichtet (g) und ungewichtet (u). Gekürzt: Werner/Willms 1984: 9.
Erwähnt in Abschnitt 'H', 807.

	Alle Waren		Rohstoffe		Halbwaren		Fertigwaren	
	Senkungsrate	Zollsatz	Senkungsrate	Zollsatz	Senkungsrate	Zollsatz	Senkungsrate	Zollsatz
g	34	4,7	64	0,3	30	4,0	34	6,5
u	39	6,4	37	1,6	36	6,2	40	7,1

Tabelle 235: Nominelle Zollsätze der EG vor und nach den Zollsatzsenkungen im Rahmen der Tokio-Runde nach Industriebereichen und nach Verarbeitungsstufen. Modifiziert, u.a. gekürzte Tabelle von: Werner/Willms 1984: 19-20.
Erwähnt in Abschnitt 'H', 807.

SITC Erwähnt in Abschnitt	Produktionsbereich, Gütergruppe	Info: EG-Importe aus Entwicklungsländern in Mrd. US$ (1978)	Nominalzollsätze in v.H. vor den Zollsatzsenkungen (1979)	Nominalzollsätze in v.H. nach den Zollsatzsenkungen (1987)
in: 26; 65; 84	**Textilien, Bekleidung**			
26 ohne 266 f.	- Naturfasern (Wolle, Baumwolle, Flachs u.a.)	1,2	0	0
266 f., 651-657	- Synth.-Fasern, Garne, Stoffe	2	1,5-24 (a) (10-18)	1,4-17 (a) (5-13)
84	-Bekleidung a. Hüte, Schals, Handschuhe, Strümpfe b. sonstige Bekleidung, ohne Schuhe, Sportschuhe	3	5-10,5 16-20	0-10 (4,9-6) 4,9-20
	Metalle, Maschinen, Transportausrüstung			
28	- Erze, Schrott	2	0	0
67	- ver- und bearbeitete unedle Metalle	2,5	1,5-12 (6-10)	1,4-10 (3-7)
694 ff., 72-77	- Werkzeug, Maschinen	1,7	2,5-14 (4-8)	2,2-12 (3-6)
78-79, 697; 71	- Transportausrüstung, Haushaltswaren	1,7	3-22 Durchschnitt 8,4	2,5-20 Durchschnitt 6,2
	Chemie	0,7		
in: 27 f.: Abschn. 3	- mineral. Grundstoffe		fast alle 0	
51 f.	- Elemente, Zusammensetzungen (b)		0-18,4 Durchschnitt 10,7	0-17,5 Durchschnitt 7
58	- Kunststoffe (c)		10-18,4 Durchschnitt 13,5	6,3-12,5 Durchschnitt 8,6
54 f.	- Med. und pharmaz. Produkte, Parfümeriewaren, Farben		4,5-23,8 Durchschnitt 10,7	3,5-10 Durchschnitt 6,5
	Holz, Möbel, vorwiegend aus Holz			
in: 63	- Holz, unbearbeitet		fast alle 0	

in: 63	- Bretter, Furniere usw.		3-12 Durchschnitt 6,6	0-10 Durchschnitt 3,7
82	- Möbel, Möbelteile		8,5	5,6
	weitere Fertigwaren, ohne Differenzierung nach Bearbeitungsgrad			
716,; 77	-Elektroartikel		4-20 (5,5-10,5)	3,2-8,9 (4,4-6,3)
76	- Radio, Telegraphentechnik, -kommunikation		5,5-14 (6,5-10)	4,1-14 (4,6-7)
77	- Elektroindustrie/-technik		5,5-15 Durchschnitt 9,5	4,1-10 Durchschnitt 6,4
88	- Optische, feinmechanische Kontroll- und wiss. Instrumente		viele 7-9	viele 4,9-6,5
885	- Uhren		5,5-10,5 viele 10 Durchschnitt 9	4,1-6,3 viele 6,2 Durchschnitt 5,8
898	- Musikinstrumente, Geräte		3,5-10,5 (7-10,5)	2,9-7 (4,9-6,3)
894	- Spielzeug, Sportgeräte		5-19 (8,5-16) Durchschnitt 11,1	3,8-8,7 (5-8) Durchschnitt 6,3
75	- Büroartikel		2-13 viele 7-8,5 Durchschnitt 7	1,8-7,2 viele 4,5-5,6 Durchschnitt 4,9

Zum Verständnis: Die erstgenannten Zollsätze außerhalb der Klammern geben den niedrigsten und höchsten Zollsatz an. Die Zollsätze in Klammern geben den Bereich an, indem sich fast alle Zollsätze bewegen. Wenn die Zollsätze stark streuen, wird der durchschnittliche Zollsatz als ungewichtetes arithmetisches Mittel angegeben.

(a) Zum Teil Zollaussetzungen für den Veredelungsverkehr.
(b) Extreme Unterschiede: Der Zollsatz für Bromide soll von 18,4 auf 8,6 % sinken, der von Phenobarbital von 17,6 auf 17,5 %. Es überwiegen die Fälle starker Senkungen (etwa um 50 %) bei überdurchschnittlich hohen Zollsätzen (über 11 %), sodaß nach den Zollaussetzungen der weitaus größte Teil dieser Zollsätze nur noch zwischen 4 und 8 % schwanken soll (vorher zwischen 6 und 16 %).
(c) Waren aus Kunststoffen werden in der Regel mit einem niedrigeren Zollsatz verzollt als ihr Input 'Kunststoff'. Die Durchschnittszollsätze gelten für 'Kunststoffe und Waren daraus'. Alle Positionen der Tarifnummer 39.02 C, die die meisten Kunststoffe umfaßt, sollen nach der Zollsatzsenkung mit 12,5 % verzollt werden.

Tabelle 236: Post-Tokyo Round, applied, and GSP tariffs in selected industrial countries (percentages). In Page 1994: 13.
Erwähnt in Abschnitt 'H', 807.

Product group	MFN tariffs				Average applied				GSP tariffs			
	EC	Japan	US	All developed	EC	Japan	US	All developed	EC	Japan	US	All developed
All food items	3,7	9,7	4,1	6,4	4,4	9,4	3,5	5,3	5,0	11,1	3,6	5,5
Food and live animals	3,2	10,0	3,8	6,5	4,8	9,7	3,2	5,3	5,1	11,7	3,4	5,6
Oilseeds and nuts	10,3	5,6	1,4	5,3	4,9	4,8	1,0	4,0	6,2	5,0	0,3	4,5
Animal and vegetable oils	0,1	0,3	0,9	0,1	0,0	0,3	1,0	0,2	0,0	1,2	0,1	0,4
Agriculture raw materials	3,4	0,7	0,3	0,8	0,4	0,3	0,3	0,5	0,5	0,5	0,1	0,5
Ores and metals	2,8	2,5	1,9	2,3	0,7	1,8	2,2	1,5	0,5	1,3	1,1	0,9
Iron and steel	5,5	5,0	4,3	5,1	2,3	2,9	5,0	3,4	3,3	2,0	3,5	3,0
Nonferrous metals	3,2	5,5	0,7	2,3	0,5	4,3	0,7	1,3	0,5	3,1	0.3	1,1
Fuels	0,1	1,5	0,4	1,1	0,3	1,2	0,4	0,6	0,2	1,3	0,3	0,6
Chemicals	8,4	5,5	3,7	5,8	3,4	4,8	3,9	3,1	4,1	5,1	1,0	3,7
Manufactures excl. chemicals	8,1	5,7	5,6	7,0	4,6	4,6	4,9	4,7	6,4	4,2	6,6	6,7
Leather	10,2	11,9	4,2	5,1	2,1	10,7	2,7	3,1	2,8	8,4	1,4	3,2
Textile yarn and fabrics	17,3	8,6	10,6	11,7	5,3	7,1	12,1	7,9	7,6	6,1	9,0	8,4
Clothing	19,9	15,0	20,3	17,5	7,3	10,0	18,1	11,9	9,3	8,6	17,8	14,6
Footwear	22,5	14,2	11,7	13,4	6,5	12,5	9,5	9,0	9,1	7,9	9,4	10,1
Other items	4,8	2,3	n.a.	n.a.	0,1	0,7	3,6	3,3	0,1	1,0	0,4	3,8
All products	4,2	3,5	3,9	4,7	2,5	3,1	3,8	3,0	2,1	2,3	3,6	2,7
Developing country weights	3,2	3,0	4,9	n.a.	2,1	2,4	4,5	n.a.	2,1	2,3	3,6	2,7

Auch in: Finger/Olechechowski 1987.

Tabelle 237: Distribution of 'high tariff' and other imports in EC, Japan and US, from world and developing countries, 1984. Aus: Page 1994: 14.
Erwähnt in Abschnitt 'H', 807.

Post-Tokyo MFN tariff rates	Percentage of all tariff lines (a)	Percentage of total imports from world (a)	Percentage of total imports from developing countries (a)	Percentage share of developing countries in total imports
EC				
'high tariff' items (above 10 %)	21.5	9.3	10.7	45.9
lower tariff items (10 % or less)	66.9	88.3	86.9	39.4
All (b)	100.0	100.0	100.0	40.0
Japan				
'high tariff' items (above 10 %)	17.1	6.6	5.0	44.4
lower tariff items (10 % or less)	82.8	92.7	94.4	59.4
All	100.0	100.0	100.0	58.3
US				
'high tariff' items (above 10 %)	16.0	7.9	11.4	53.5
lower tariff items (10% or less)	83.1	89.7	87.0	35.8
All (b)	100.0	100.0	100.0	36.9

(a) Owing to tariff-lines with no post-Tokyo MFN rates available the shares do not add to 100%
(b) All items include also those tariff-lines for which no post-Tokyo MFN rates were available
In: Page (1994) aus UNCTAD, 1988. Protectionism and Structural Adjustment, Statistical and Information Index, TD/B/1160/Add.1, UNCTAD, Geneva.

Tabelle 238: Southern import penetration ratios (%). In: Wood 1994: 97.
Erwähnt in Abschnitt 'H', 810.

	1959-69	1969-70	1980-81	1984-85	1988-89
Primary products (UNCTAD)	11.6	12.9	26.5	20.5	16.7
Manufactures (including processed primary products)					
UNCTAD estimates	1.2	1.4	2.0	2.9	3.3
OECD estimates		1.7	3.2	3.7	
Hughes and Waelbroeck estimates		1.7	3.4		

Notes: The Southern import penetration ratio is calculated as the share of imports from developing countries in total developed-country apparent consumption of the goods concerned. Apparent consumption is output plus imports minus exports.

Tabelle 239: Bindings before and after the Uruguay Round. All merchandise trade.
In: Finger et al. 1996: 24-25.
Erwähnt in Abschnitt 'H', 812.

	Percentage of imports GATT bound				
	Total pre - UR	Total post - UR	Above applied rates	At applied rates	Below applied rates
Argentina	17.1	100.0	99.8	0.2	0.0
Australia	33.3	97.2	30.9	22.9	43.3
Austria	91.1	100.0	52.9	25.7	12.0
Brazil	16.0	100.0	71.8	5.8	0.6
Canada	96.4	96.8	42.7	31.8	21.4
Chile	100.0	100.0	99.7	0.3	0.0
Colombia	4.4	100.0	97.6	1.9	0.5
Czech Slovak CU	96.2	100.0	0.8	33.1	66.2
El Salvador	97.8	97.8	96.8	0.5	0.5
European Union	98.2	100.0	15.8	42.9	38.6
Finland	97.4	100.0	40.4	46.5	12.5
Hong Kong	0.8	27.9	0.0	27.9	0.0
Hungary	87.1	94.4	4.9	39.6	49.9
Iceland	79.9	86.9	49.8	36.2	0.9
India	11.6	58.5	16.5	8.8	29.1
Indonesia	29.7	93.4	88.5	2.4	2.5
Jamaica	0.0	100.0	100.0	0	0
Japan	72.7	83.4	1.9	42.3	38.1
Korea, Republic of	21.3	83.2	5.7	13.2	64.2
Macau	0.0	20.8	0.0	20.8	0.0
Malaysia	1.6	77.4	30.6	17.0	26.1
Mexico	100.0	100.0	97.5	2.4	0.1
New Zealand	61.1	100.0	42.3	45.8	10.1
Norway	96.9	100.0	34.4	53.3	11.7
Peru	17.1	100.0	98.3	0.8	0.2
Philippines	9.7	60.6	16.6	27.4	16.5
Poland	0.0	91.3	46.1	16.9	28.3
Romania	9.8	100.0	87.5	11.6	1.0
Senegal	39.1	58.3	25.4	32.9	0.0
Singapore	0.4	66.0	43.9	15.5	5.6
Sri Lanka	9.9	26.7	9.3	12.5	0.1
Sweden	96.0	99.5	47.1	34.4	15.6
Switzerland	94.2	96.5	61.7	18.2	12.1
Thailand	7.5	64.3	8.3	12.2	40.1
Tunisia	0.0	67.9	46.0	21.5	0.4
Turkey	35.6	45.1	3.2	5.7	36.1
United States	91.5	92.5	13.6	41.4	37.4
Uruguay	13.3	100.0	84.9	15.1	0.1
Venezuela	100.0	100.0	89.9	3.1	6.3
Zimbabwe	9.8	14.7	5.9	6.7	2.0

Tabelle 240: Bound tariffs on industrial products. Simple averages by country and MFN category (percentage). WTO 2001a: 11. Erwähnt in Abschnitt 'H', 813.

Import markets	1 Wood pulp, paper and furniture	2 Textiles and clothing	3 Leather, rubber, footwear and footwear and travel goods	4 Metals	5 Chemicals and photographic supplies	6 Transport equipment	7 Non-electric machinery	8 Electric machinery	9 Mineral products and precious stones and precious metals	10 Manufactured articles not elsewhere specified	11 Fish and fish product
North America											
Canada	1.3	12.4	7.6	2.8	4.5	6.8	3.6	5.2	3.1	4.2	1.8
United States	0.6	8.9	8.4	1.8	3.7	2.7	1.2	2.1	3.3	3.0	2.2
Latin America											
Argentina	29.4	35.0	35.0	34.4	23.5	34.6	34.9	34.7	32.8	33.7	34.5
Brazil	27.7	34.9	34.7	33.4	22.7	33.6	32.6	31.9	33.5	33.5	33.4
Chile	25.0	25.0	25.0	25.0	25.0	24.9	25.0	25.0	24.9	25.0	25.0
Colombia	35.0	36.8	35.2	35.0	35.0	35.8	35.0	35.0	35.1	35.0	47.7
Costa Rica	44.2	45.1	45.9	44.5	43.5	49.6	44.2	43.3	44.6	44.7	46.3
El Salvador	35.3	38.6	40.8	35.0	37.7	35.8	32.6	34.6	37.7	38.2	45.0
Jamaica	50.0	50.0	50.0	50.0	50.0	50.0	50.0	50.0	50.0	50.0	50.6
Mexico	34.0	35.0	34.8	34.7	35.2	35.8	35.0	34.1	34.4	34.6	35.0
Peru	30.0	30.0	30.0	30.0	30.0	30.0	30.0	30.0	30.0	30.0	30.0
Venezuela	33.7	34.9	34.5	33.6	34.1	33.6	33.2	33.9	34.1	33.4	33.8
Western Europe											
European Union	0.7	7.9	4.8	1.6	4.8	4.7	1.8	3.3	2.4	2.7	11.8
Iceland	11.9	9.7	13.8	6.8	2.8	17.1	7.0	19.4	11.5	21.9	3.6
Norway	0.4	8.5	2.2	1.1	3.0	3.3	2.7	2.7	0.7	2.2	7.3
Switzerland	2.1	4.6	2.0	1.1	1.5	2.2	0.6	0.7	1.5	1.3	0.5
Turkey	40.5	80.3	79.9	30.4	29.0	25.8	23.7	26.6	39.4	43.3	26.2
Eastern Europe											
Czech Republic	5.5	6.2	3.8	3.8	4.0	6.2	3.8	4.2	3.4	3.6	0.2
Hungary	5.4	8.1	6.7	4.9	5.5	15.9	8.4	9.5	5.0	7.8	17.1

Poland	8.0	13.1	11.9	9.9	8.7	16.1	8.9	9.7	6.9	11.6	16.3
Romania	31.4	32.9	30.7	31.7	30.6	32.1	29.5	27.3	32.2	29.3	28.1
Slovak Republic	5.5	6.2	3.8	3.8	4.0	6.2	3.8	4.2	3.4	3.6	0.2
Asia											
Australia	7.0	28.8	17.5	4.5	9.2	15.1	9.1	13.3	7.0	7.0	0.8
Hong Kong, China	0.0	0.0	0.0	0.0	0.0	0.0	0.0	0.0	0.0	0.0	0.0
India	56.4	87.8	67.8	58.3	44.1	53.9	36.2	44.8	47.2	72.4	68.6
Indonesia	39.6	39.9	39.6	36.4	37.4	58.5	36.6	38.7	39.2	36.9	40.0
Japan	1.2	6.8	15.7	0.9	2.4	0.0	0.0	0.2	1.0	1.1	6.2
Korea, Republic of	4.8	18.2	16.7	7.7	6.7	24.6	11.1	16.1	10.4	11.4	19.1
Macau, China	0.0	0.0	0.0	0.0	0.0	0.0	0.0	0.0	0.0	0.0	0.0
Malaysia	19.8	20.7	19.1	14.2	15.4	29.8	10.9	14.1	14.7	12.6	14.5
New Zealand	4.5	21.9	19.1	11.2	6.1	17.0	15.1	16.1	7.6	11.7	2.8
Philippines	31.8	27.7	32.7	22.9	22.6	26.1	22.0	26.2	28.5	29.5	29.4
Singapore	3.1	7.8	3.4	3.2	5.0	4.4	4.3	4.9	1.2	1.2	9.8
Sri Lanka	32.6	45.0	43.0	16.6	15.8	18.3	12.8	20.4	26.2	27.1	49.2
Thailand	21.3	29.2	34.1	25.6	29.3	38.5	23.4	30.5	25.9	29.5	12.5
Africa											
Cameroon	21.8	22.8	21.2	15.9	11.6	14.9	12.2	16.8	18.5	22.9	23.8
Chad	21.8	22.7	21.2	15.9	11.6	20.2	12.2	16.8	18.5	22.9	23.8
Gabon	15.5	15.1	15.0	15.2	15.2	15.0	15.2	15.0	16.1	18.5	15.0
Senegal	17.6	16.1	16.3	15.1	15.2	14.1	6.7	7.2	15.1	15.0	12.9
South Africa	9.2	27.7	23.1	14.1	13.9	23.3	12.0	17.4	11.5	14.8	22.5
Tunisia	34.2	56.3	36.1	25.6	26.5	25.5	25.2	29.1	28.9	32.5	41.2
Zimbabwe	12.6	21.4	13.1	9.1	5.5	10.1	6.3	12.3	7.6	15.5	3.1

Tabelle 241: Applied tariffs on industrial products (a). Simple averages by country and MTN category. Bacchetta/Bora 2003: 20. Erwähnt in Abschnitt 'H', 813.

Import markets	1 Wood pulp, paper and furniture	2 Textiles and clothing	3 Leather, rubber, footwear and footwear and travel goods	4 Metals	5 Chemicals and photographic supplies	6 Transport equipment	7 Non-electric machinery	8 Electric machinery	9 Mineral products and precious stones and precious metals	10 Manufactured articles not elsewhere specified	11 Fish and fish product
North America											
Canada (2002)	2.1	10.6	6.6	2.6	3.4	5.3	1.8	2.4	2.1	2.9	1.5
United States	1.1	9.4	6.4	2.3	4.0	2.7	1.3	2.0	3.4	2.3	2.2
Latin America											
Brazil	13.1	19.8	15.8	14.1	10.0	18.6	13.5	15.3	9.9	16.3	12.3
Mexico (2000)	15.4	24.0	20.7	15.6	11.5	17.3	13.2	16.1	15.2	17.9	27.1
Europe											
European Union	2.3	8.6	4.9	2.4	4.6	4.7	1.7	2.8	2.4	2.5	12.2
Poland (2002)	8.5	14.0	12.7	11.0	8.5	19.4	7.9	8.3	7.9	10.5	18.3
Turkey (1999)	3.1	15.3	8.0	5.6	4.8	5.7	1.8	2.8	2.5	2.4	49.8
Asia											
Australia	3.5	12.3	6.8	3.5	1.9	5.5	3.4	3.4	1.9	1.6	0.1
China (1997)	13.9	27.0	17.3	9.9	11.2	28.8	14.3	15.6	12.2	17.7	21.2
India (1997)	29.6	43.6	36.7	32.2	34.4	37.2	27.1	34.8	36.7	37.0	19.9
Japan (2000)	1.9	8.5	11.6	1.6	2.5	0.0	0.0	0.2	1.0	1.2	5.9
Korea, Republic of	5.6	9.8	8.8	6.2	7.3	5.9	6.3	5.7	6.0	6.7	16.9
Malaysia (2000)	2.4	15.3	12.8	10.7	5.8	50.7	6.3	10.9	11.6	7.3	4.2
Chinese Taipei	4.8	10.1	6.2	6.0	3.9	14.1	4.9	5.6	4.5	4.7	27.1
Thailand (1999)	32.1	69.2	58.1	23.2	32.1	54.3	32.8	41.2	28.8	41.2	59.0

(a) For the year 2001 except where otherwise indicated in parenthesis. Source: WTO Integrated Database.

Tabelle 242: Sub-Saharan tariff averages, applied ad valorem tariff rates. ILEAP 2004: 73. *Erwähnt in Abschnitt 'H', 813.*

Country	Agriculture	Industrial
	Percent	
WTO Members (applied ad valorem tariff rates)		
Benin	14.91	11.51
Botswana	10.61	7.66
Burkina Faso	14.91	11.51
Cameroon	23.46	17.17
Central African Republic	23.46	17.17
Chad	23.46	17.17
Congo	23.46	17.17
Cote d'Ivoire	14.91	11.51
Djibouti	22.07	32.00
Gabon	23.46	17.17
Ghana	19.64	13.89
Guinea	6.62	6.44
Guinea-Bissau	14.91	11.51
Kenya	23.23	18.46
Lesotho	10.61	7.66
Madagascar	5.71	4.44
Malawi	15.28	12.75
Mali	14.91	11.51
Mauritania	14.36	10.30
Mauritius	20.84	18.70
Mozambique	21.91	12.50
Namibia	10.61	7.66
Niger	14.61	11.51
Nigeria	32.71	25.01
Rwanda	13.14	9.35
Senegal	14.91	11.51
South Africa	10.61	7.66
Swaziland	10.61	7.66
Tanzania	21.60	15.49
Togo	14.91	11.51
Uganda	12.90	8.42
Zambia	19.61	13.18
Zimbabwe	25.80	18.60
Average	17.12	13.21
WTO members (bound ad valorem tariff cielings)		
Angola	13.33	80.00
Burundi	100.00	100.00
Congo, Dem. Rep.	55.00	100.00
Gambia	110.00	-
Sierra Leone	40.00	50.00
Average	63.67	82.50

Tabelle 243: Applied tariffs on selected product groups, simple averages by importer, 2003.
In: Mayer 2004: 6.
Erwähnt in Abschnitt 'H', 813.

	Manufactures		Textiles		Clothing	
	Simple averages	Share of tariff lines above 15%	Simple averages	Share of tariff lines above 15 %	Simple average	Share of tariff lines above 5%
Developed countries						
Australia (2004)	5.6	6.7	10.1	4.0	19.7	68.0
Canada	4.2	7.8	8.5	7.9	14.3	65.4
European Union (2002)	1.3	0.6	2.8	0.0	3.8	0.0
Japan	3.2	10.1	5.6	3.9	12.1	37.6
United States (2004)	3.3	4.2	6.9	4.4	10.3	20.6
Developing countries						
Brazil	14.71	45.0	17.1	86.7	20.0	100.0
China (2004)	9.7	15.1	11.4	11.4	17.0	89.7
India (2001)	30.8	93.5	29.3	98.3	34.0	95.9
Malaysia (2002)	8.0	30.3	14.3	57.0	14.6	53.1
Mexico	18.5	51.3	21.5	87.4	34.3	98.2
Republic of Korea	7.8	0.4	9.5	0.0	12.5	0.0
Taiwan Province of China	5.7	3.4	8.8	3.4	11.9	14.3
Thailand (2001)	14.6	51.6	17.0	70.1	35.3	84.4
Tunisia	24.5	65.8	31.3	83.7	41.3	96.0
Turkey	1.7	0.6	2.9	0.0	5.4	0.0
Countries in Central and Eastern Europe						
Czech Republic	5.0	1.4	6.5	2.9	8.4	1.6
Poland	2.4	3.5	2.4	3.7	8.2	46.7
Romania (2001)	10.7	22.1	14.9	41.6	21.9	63.6

Tabelle 244: Applied tariffs on industrial products (a). Tariff peaks (Share of tariff lines above 15 % by country and MTN category) (percentage) Bacchetta/Bora 2003: 21.
Erwähnt in Abschnitt 'H', 813.

	1	2	3	4	5	6	7	8	9	10	11
Import markets	Wood pulp, paper and furniture	Textiles and clothing	Leather, rubber, footwear and travel goods	Metals	Chemicals and photographic supplies	Transport equipment	Non-electric machinery	Electric machinery	Mineral products and precious stones and precious metals	Manufactured articles not elsewhere specified	Fish and fish product
North America											
Canada (2002)	0.6	41.9	18.8	0.0	0.0	6.3	0.0	0.0	0.8	1.6	0.0
United States	0.0	16.8	9.1	0.0	0.0	5.7	0.0	0.0	2.9	0.4	1.1
Latin America											
Brazil	36.2	92.8	60.0	48.1	26.6	54.2	23.3	60.1	21.0	65.8	16.3
Mexico (2000)	40.5	87.7	62.5	45.0	23.5	60.4	40.3	56.8	45.4	58.6	93.5
Europe											
European Union	0.0	0.0	10.4	0.0	0.0	6.2	0.0	0.0	0.0	0.0	23.4
Poland (2002)	0.4	44.6	33.9	0.2	1.5	28.0	0.1	10.6	7.3	13.7	35.7
Turkey (1999)	0.2	10.9	30.5	8.6	0.0	13.2	0.0	0.0	1.2	0.2	96.4
Asia											
Australia	0.0	24.2	2.4	0.0	0.1	0.0	0.0	0.0	0.0	0.0	0.0
China (1997)	36.1	87.4	50.0	12.8	18.0	53.1	33.7	34.5	28.3	52.5	71.6
India (1997)	83.9	99.9	82.9	91.3	96.2	84.4	98.3	96.5	88.4	99.1	16.8
Japan (2000)	0.0	2.2	30.8	0.0	0.0	0.0	0.0	0.0	0.0	0.0	0.0
Korea, Republic of	0.0	0.0	5.8	0.0	0.0	0.0	0.0	0.0	0.0	0.0	68.6
Malaysia (2000)	8.9	44.2	42.1	35.2	19.4	64.8	20.9	32.3	32.5	20.1	12.8
Chinese Taipei	2.2	11.3	1.1	0.0	0.2	37.3	2.3	1.2	0.6	1.5	60.7
Thailand (1999)	40.1	62.6	64.2	60.6	79.6	76.7	99.9	91.8	54.8	85.4	85.1

(a) For the year 2001 except where otherwise indicated in parenthesis. Source: WTO Integrated Database.

Tabelle 245: Federal Republic of Germany: Nominal and Effective Protection in Industry (in percent).
Erwähnt in Abschnitt 'I', 824.

	Nominal Protection		Effective Protection		
	Tariffs	Tariffs and NTBs	Tariffs and NTBS	Subsidies	Total effective protection
Industry average	7,9	11,2	22,4	9,2	31,6
Standard deviation	(2,9)	(10,8)	(39,8)	(27,0)	(62,9)
Coefficient of variation	(0,4)	(1,0)	(1,8)	(2,9)	(2,0)
Of which:					
Coal	...	44,2	189,2	147,6	336,8
Iron and steel	6,4	20,0	43,1	14,9	58,0
Automobiles	10,3	10,3	9,9	1,0	10,9
Shipbuilding	2,7	2,7	-6,5	1,0	19,5
Aircraft	7,2	7,2	15,8	26,0	45.4
Electronics	7,0	7,0	6,0	29,6	9,6
Textiles	13,0	34,4	71,2	2,1	73,3
Clothing	15,3	44,7	120,0	2,9	122,9

Aus: IMF 1988: 125.

Tabelle 246: EU State aid and other instruments of protection, by industry. In: Messerlin 1999: 181. Erwähnt in Abschnitt "I", 824, 825, 856.

ISCIC Code	Sectors	Case load	Forms of aid (4)					Avg number of forms	Tariffs		Antidumping cases			VERs
									Base rate	Bound rate	No of cases	DUM (2)	ADM (2)	(3)
No		No	I	II	III	IV	All							
(1)														
1000	Agriculture	2		1	1		2	1,0	11,60	9,78				Yes
311	Food Products (1)	1		1	1		2	2,0	-	-	4	25,4	-	
3113	Fruits and Vegetables	1		2			2	2,0	-	-				Yes
3114	Fish industries	2		1		1	2	1,0	14,28	13,30				Yes
3118	Sugar industry	1	1	1			2	2,0	-	-				Yes
3133	Beer	1			2		2	2,0	-	-				?
320	Textiles and apparel (1)	4		1	5	3	9	2,3	10,46	8,11				Yes
3210	Textiles	4	3	1	2	2	8	2,0	10,08	7,62	13	32,7	26,3	Yes
3220	Apparel	2	1		1		2	1,0	12,28	10,48				Yes
3240	Footwear	1	2				2	2,0	10,83	9,44	2	6,1	6,7	?
3311	Sawmills	2		2	2		4	2,0	5,27	2,26	19	31,1	-	?
3411	Pulp and paper	4	3	1	2		6	1,5	6,50	3,09	3	7,7	-	?
351	Basic chemicals (1)	1	1		1		2	2,0	7,19	4,87				
3511	Industrial chemicals	1			1		1	1,0	7,12	4,84	105	41,3	20,2	
3512	Fertilizers	1			1		1	1,0	4,88	4,32	19	43,3	22,3	
3513	Synthetic products	9	1	7	3	1	12	1,3	8,28	5,23	31	26,6	11,6	
3520	Other chemicals	1			1		1	1,0	6,39	3,40	6	83,6	-	
3522	Drugs and medicines	2	1	1		1	3	1,5	6,21	0,38	4	93,8	-	Yes
3530	Petroleum refineries	1		1			1	1,0	4,62	2,92				
3540	Petroleum and coal	3		2		1	3	1,0	2,14	1,27				
3610	Pottery and china	3	2			3	5	1,7	8,42	5,90	2	26,5	26,5	
3620	Glass industry	7	1	3	5	1	10	1,4	6,94	4,51	13	42,5	17,5	
3692	Cement, lime and plaster	1	1	1			2	2,0	2,74	1,42	5	37,7	-	
3710	Iron and steel	5	2	1	3	3	9	1,8	4,87	0,24	43	30,2	26,2	Yes
3720	Non-ferrous metals	4	1	2	1	1	5	1,3	4,61	3,03	14	16,2	-	
3812	Metal furniture	1		1			1	1,0	5,61	2,25				
3813	Structural metal products	1			1		1	1,0	4,66	2,17				
3822	Agricultural machinery	3	1	1	4	1	7	2,3	3,67	0,40				
3824	Industrial machinery	2	3		1	1	5	2,5	3,99	1,38	4	19,1	21,2	Yes

3832	Radio and TV	1		1	1		1,0	6,73	4,32	20	27,2	22,7	Yes
3841	Shipbuilding	4		4	4		1,0	2,88	1,75				Yes
3843	Motor vehicles	8	4	2	6	1	13	1,6	9,08	6,58				Yes
3853	Watches and clocks	1				1	1	1,0	5,45	3,49	1	19,5	-	-
	Maritime Services	3		2	3	1	6	2,0	-	-	2	-	-	Yes
	Airlines	1	2			1	3	3,0	-	-	0	-	-	Yes
	Others Services	2		1	1		2	1,0	-	-	0	-	-	Yes
	Horizontal Cases	12	4	6	9		19	1,6	-	-	0	-	-	
	Total	193	3	4	5	2	161	1,6			310			20
			4	7	6	4								

(1) ISIC-4-digit (ISIC-3-digit correspond to cases involving a wide range of products).
(2) DUM: dumping margin; ADM: ad valorem equivalent of known anti-dumping measures.
(3) Yes: VERs have been observed
(4) The four forms of state aid: I: Asset re-evaluation, capital grant, capital injection, debt conversion; II: Direct subsidy, foregone recovery, subsidy to input; III: Interest subsidy, preferential loan, low interest operation, parafiscal charge, tax concession, preferential tariff; IV: State guarantee, state participation, other forms.
(5) Sabena case
(6) French horse betting (PMU) and Greek films
(7) Regional aid (5 cases), labor (2), taxation (1), natural disaster (1), global schemes (3).

Tabelle 247: Produktion japanischer Unternehmen im Vereinigten Königreich (in Stück). Daten aus: Auto International in Zahlen, div. Jahrgänge.
Erwähnt in Abschnitt 'I', 842.

Jahr	Toyota	Honda	Rover Group -of which Honda	Nissan	Insgesamt
1988	-	-	-	56.542	56.542
1989	-	-	-	77.282	77.282
1990	-	-	26.454	76.190	102.644
1991	-	-	35.952	124.666	160.618
1992	-	1.001	32.444	179.009	212.454
1993	37.314	32.139	18.406	246.281	334.140
1994	85.467	42.805	8.726	204.944	341.942
1995	88.440	91.084	2.199	215.346	397.069
1996	116.973	105.801	-	231.627	454.401
1997	104.615	108.097	-	271.666	484.378
1998	172.342	112.089	-	288.818	573.249
1999	178.660	114.479	-	271.157	564.296

Tabelle 248: Sample of Instances of EC Surveillance. Modifiziert durch weitere Informationen, die aus dem Artikel entnommen sind, aus Winters 1994: 220-222, 226.
Erwähnt in Abschnitt 'I', 851, 895, 898, 900, 902.

Product	Initial Regulation	Cited Exporters	Period	Type of Measure
Slide Fasteners	P: 646/75	All	1975-79	
Phosphate Fertilizers	P: 440/77	All	1977-83	
Titanium		All	1987	
Footwear	P: 716/78 (5/78-10/78) R: 78/560 (after 10/78)	DCs	1978-87	
Certain Machine Tools	R: 536/81 R: 653/83	Japan	1981-87 (1981-82, 1986-87) 1983-87 (1986-87)	continuation of moderation
Color TVs	R: 537/81 P: 1245/87 (after 3/87)	Japan	1981-87 (1981-82, 1986-87)	moderation set for two years 1984; renewable for third year
Cathode Ray Tubes for Color TV		Japan	1983, 1984, 1985	specific level of moderation
Quartz Watches	R: 653/83	Japan	1983-87	VERs
Hi-fi Equipment	R. 653/83	Japan	1983-87 (1986-87)	VERs
Light Commercial Vehicles (Vans)	R: 3544/82	Japan	1983-87 (1986-87)	generel export moderation
Motorcycles	R: 3543/82	Japan	1983-87 (1986-87)	VERs
Videocassette Recorders	R: 235/86	Korea Japan	1986-87 1983	1987 Antidumping Investigations ad hoc price and quantity assurance

Tabelle 249: United States – Apparent Supply of Steel Mill Products. 1977-86 (in thousand of tons). Aus: IMF 1988: 160.
Erwähnt in Abschnitt 'I', 854, 855, 859.

	Net shipments	Exports	Imports	Apparent Supply	Import share
1986	70.263	929	20.692	90.026	23.0
1985	73.043	932	24.256	96.367	25.2
1984	73.0739	980	26.163	98.922	26.4
1983	67.583	1.119	17.070	83.454	20.5
1982	61.567	1.842	16.663	76.388	21.8
1980	83.853	4.101	15.495	95.247	16.3
1977	91.147	2.003	19.307	108.451	17.8

Tabelle 250: Major EC imports of steel products. 1000 Tonnes. World: % of EC apparent consumption.
In: Messerlin 1999: 186.
Erwähnt in *Abschnitt "I", 855, 857*.

Year	EC apparent consumption	EC imports from:									
		World (1)	World (2)	Western Europe non-EEA	Central Europe	Former Soviet Union	Africa	Japan	Asia less Japan	USA	American continent less USA
1975	74962	6145 (8,2)	3385 (4,5)	26	1207	42	118	1548	104	45	76
1979	92401	9416 (10,2)	4629 (5,0)	350	2581	163	298	601	77	140	290
1980	85986	8992 (10,5)	4766 (5,5)	153	2080	269	275	562	343	359	563
1981	81689	6566 (8,0)	2681 (3,3)	45	1925	106	89	164	15	125	186
1982	77637	8736 (11,3)	4246 (5,5)	102	2130	128	369	237	120	96	978
1983	75465	8491 (11,3)	3693 (4,9)	345	1815	282	284	255	84	71	456
1984	80050	8087 (10,1)	3164 (4,0)	194	1880	74	243	212	7	89	461
1985	79151	8616 (10,9)	3404 (4,3)	201	1779	120	323	287	46	64	554
1986	89219	9281 (10,4)	5065 (5,7)	458	2000	243	482	393	180	116	1166
1987	90257	8833 (9,8)	4638 (5,1)	655	1923	330	476	210	189	93	757
1988	103737	9695 (9,3)	5497 (5,3)	939	2090	442	393	152	193	116	1165
1989	110444	10734 (9,7)	6381 (5,8)	890	2110	538	434	165	192	393	1641
1990	108573	11625 (10,7)	7011 (6,5)	1351	2427	691	361	127	280	174	1558
1991	109603	10709 (9,8)	5630 (5,1)	525	2208	1129	277	114	148	209	923
1992	109217	12502 (11,4)	7258 (6,6)	468	-	-	613	113	318	117	1069

(1) At current EC borders. (2) At constant borders of the EEA.

Tabelle 251: Steel: World Exports, Imports, and Trade Balance. 1980-88 (In million of ingot tons equivalent). Aus: IMF 1988: 159.
Erwähnt in Abschnitt 'I', 855, 859.

	1980	1982	1983	1984	1985	1986	1987	1988 (1)
Exports								
OECD	103.0	96.7	101.2	111.7	115.4	100.4	98.1	...
United States	4.8	2.3	1.5	1.1	1.1	1.2	1.4	1.5
European Community (10)	36.6	33.9	34.5	40.1	...	...	...	...
European Community (12)	...	...	...	...	50.0	39.7	39.9	40.0
Japan	38.6	37.2	40.1	41.2	41.0	37.3	32.8	31.8
Canada	...	4.6	3.5	4.0	4.1	4.5	5.2	...
Australia. New Zealand	...	1.8	1.7	1.3	2.0	2.0	2.1	...
Other OECD	23.0	16.9	19.9	24.0	17.2	15.7	16.7	...
Developing countries	36.9	19.4	23.2	23.3	25.3	24.3	26.2	...
Others (2)	...	23.2	27.4	28.3	33.1	35.8	34.2	...
World	139.9	139.3	151.8	163.3	173.8	160.4	158.5	...
Imports								
OECD	52.4	52.6	53.7	68.0	63.7	61.1	65.2	...
United States	17.9	19.3	19.7	30.3	28.1	23.9	23.5	24.0
European Community (10)	13.5	13.0	13.0	12.5	...	...	...	...
European Community (12)	...	...	...	...	12.1	14.2	13.7	14.2
Japan	1.5	2.6	3.6	5.2	3.8	4.3	6.5	7.5
Canada	...	1.4	1.6	2.5	3.1	2.8	3.9	...
Australia. New Zealand	...	1.7	1.4	1.8	1.7	1.6	1.8	...
Other OECD	19.5	14.5	14.4	15.7	14.9	14.3	15.8	...
Developing countries	84.9	57.2	54.6	51.4	52.6	45.6	46.7	...
Others (2)	...	30.0	39.4	41.3	56.6	52.7	44.7	...
World	137.3	139.8	147.7	160.7	172.8	159.4	156.6	...
Net exports								
OECD	50.6	44.1	47.5	43.7	51.7	39.3	32.9	31.5
United States	-13.1	-17.0	-18.2	-29.2	-0.27	-22.1	-22.1	-22.5
European Community (10)	23.1	20.9	21.5	27.6	-	-	....	-
European Community (12)	...	...	...	...	38.0	25.5	26.2	25.8
Japan	37.1	34.6	36.5	36.0	37.2	33.0	26.3	24.3
Canada	-	3.2	1.9	1.5	1.0	1.7	1.3	1.3
Australia. New Zealand	-	0.1	0.3	-0.5	0.3	0.4	0.3	0.4
Other OECD	3.5	2.4	5.5	8.3	2.3	1.4	0.9	2.2
Developing countries	-40.6	-37.8	-31.4	-28.1	-27.3	-21.3	-20.5	-18.4
Others (2) (3)	-10.0	-6.3	-12.0	-13.0	-23.5	-17.0	-10.5	-11.1

(1) OECD Projections
(2) Includes South Africa. U.S.S.R. other East European Countries. China. and the Democratic Peoples's Republic of Korea (North Korea).
(3) Includes small amounts from unspecified sources for 1980 and 1982.

Tabelle 252: Import Quotas Provided in Bilateral Agreements with the European Community 1979 and 1982 (1000tons).
Erwähnt in Abschnitt 'I', 856.

Country	Import Quotas for constant quota	countries
	1979	1982
Total of which:	5110	7913
Hungary	264	371
Czechosovakia	612	637
Romania	324	394
Bulgaria	492	252
Poland	456	420
Austria	312	1017
Finland	312	389
Norway	192	568
Sweden	588	879
Spain	744	780
Japan	492	1220
South Korea	72	225
Australia	132	407
Brazil	-	253

Aus: Fischer/Nunnenkamp et al. 1988: 256.

Tabelle 253: The 1984 Steel Pact Agreement of the United States compared wirth Market Shares of Respective Countries (per cent of US annual consumption). Aus: Fischer/Nunnenkamp et al. 1988: 254.
Erwähnt in Abschnitt 'I', 853, 865.

Country	Market shares				Pact agreement
	1982	1983	1984 (a)		
Total of which:	21,8	20,5	26,1		17-20
Japan	6,3	5,1	6,7		5,8
South Korea	1,4	2,1	2,4		1,9
Brazil	0,8	1,5	1,4		0,8
Spain	0,7	0,7	1,6		0,67
South Africa	0,7	0,7	0,7		0,42
Mexico	0,1	0,8	0,9		0,36
Australia	0,2	0,2	0,3		0,18
Argentina	0,2	0,3	0,3		n.a.
Finland	0,2	0,2	0,4		n.a.
Canada	2,4	2,9	3,2		n.a.
EC (b)	7,3	4,9	5,9		5,9

(a) 1984 values include only first nine month. (b) EC values are subject to the 1982 US-EC arrangement.

Tabelle 254: Anteile am Inlandsverbrauch in der Gruppe der nordatlantischen Industrieländer (NAIL) (in %) Aus: Weltentwicklungsbericht 1987: 168.
Erwähnt in Abschnitt 'I', 866, 876.

Warenart und Herkunft	Anteile am Inlandsverbrauch		
	1975	1983	Veränderung 1975-1983
Textilien			
Inland	83,9	80,6	-3,3
NAIL	14,8	16,0	1,2
übrige Länder	1,3	3,4	2,1
Bekleidung			
Inland	78,6	69,3	-9,3
NAIL	12,0	13,0	1,0
übrige Länder	9,4	17,7	8,3
Schuhwerk			
Inland	73,1	56,1	-17,0
NAIL	18,5	23,9	5,4
übrige Länder	8,4	20,0	11,6
Stahl			
Inland	85,0	84,5	-0,5
NAIL	13,8	14,4	0,6
übrige Länder	1,2	1,1	-0,1

Anmerkung: Zu den nordatlantischen Industrienländern (NAIL) gehören die europäischen OECD-Mitgliedsländer, Kanada und die Vereingten Staaten.

Tabelle 255: Agrarzölle nach der Umsetzung der Reduktionsverpflichtungen im Jahr 2000, in Prozent (nach Tangermann 1995: 38)
Erwähnt in Abschnitt 'I', 868.

Produkt	EU	Japan	USA
Weizen (common wheat)	56,5	259,3	1,8
Gerste	90,0	151,7	0,6
Mais (nicht zur Aussaat)	86,1	3,4	2,0
Reis (nicht zur Aussaat)	13,0	k.A.	8,3
Sojabohnen	0,0	0,0	0,0
Kaffee (nicht geröstet)	0,0	0,0	0,0
Kaffee (geröstet)	7,5	12,0	0,0
Tee	0,0	17,0	6,4
Kakaobohnen	0,0	0,0	0,0
Bananen, grün	145,6	27,5	0,0
Rohrzucker (nicht raffiniert)	41,0	115,4	58,5
Tabak	18,4	17,8	7,9
Rindfleisch (Rümpfe)	87,8	50,0	26,4
Schweinefleisch (Rümpfe)	28,6	136,3	0,0
Hühnerfleisch (nicht gestückelt)	16,1	11,9	5,2
Butter	66,5	307,2	46,6
Magermilchpulver	119,5	337,0	74,1
Ungewichteter Durchschnitt aller Agrarprodukte	17,7	40,2	7,9

Tabelle 256: Spitzenzölle auf Agrarprodukte in der EU nach Produkten, zum Vergleich Summe der Spitzenzölle Japans und der USA (nach UNCTAD 1999a: 14)
Erwähnt in Abschnitt 'I', 868.

Produktgruppe	Anzahl der Tarife						Anzahl Spitzen	Anteil an allen Spitzen
	Gesamt	12-19%	20-29%	30-99%	100-299%	>= 300%		
Fleisch, Lebendvieh etc.	351	52	68	79	13	1	213	16,2
Fisch und Krustentiere	373	96	45				141	10,7
Milchprodukte	197	14	21	77	9		121	9,2
Obst und Gemüse	407	116	10	5	1		132	10
Getreide, Mehl etc.	174	21	29	75			125	9,5
Pflanzl. Öle, Fette, Ölsaaten	211	14		8	1	1	24	1,8
Verarb. Fleisch, Fisch etc.	105	33	17	8			58	4,4
Zucker, Kakao und Verarb.	75	10	34	6			50	3,8
Verarb. Obst, Gemüse	310	140	70	39	1		250	19
Andere Nahrungsindustrieprod.	90	16	27	8			51	3,9
Getränke und Tabak	202	48	9	15	2		74	5,6
Andere Agrarprodukte	231	12	4	14	4		34	2,6
Gesamt: Agrar-/Fischprodukte	2726	572	334	334	31	2	1273	96,8
Japan: Agrar-/Fischprodukte	1897	204	299	111	81	65	760	85,1
USA: Agrar-/Fischprodukte	1779	138	70	99	15	11	333	36,6

Tabelle 257: Nettoexportmengen (X-M) in 1000 t und Selbstversorgungsgrad (SV) in % bei ausgewählten Agrarprodukten, Bundesrepublik und EG, 1958/59 bis 1988/89. In: Henrichsmeyer/Witzke 1991: 175.
Erwähnt in Abschnitt 'I', 868.

		Getreide X-M SV	Zucker X-M SV	Pfl. Öle X-M SV	Fleisch X-M SV	Butter X-M SV
EG-6	58/59-62/63	-10594	27	-1876	-518	15
		0,84	1,02	0,44	0,95	1,02
	67/68-70/71	-7762	296	-924	-615	115
		0,91	1,03	0,74	0,93	1,10
	76/77-79/80	-2568	2512	-502	-296	272
		0,97	1,41	0,87	0,98	1,27
	85/86-88/89	12417	1675	10	468	292
		1,14	1,35	1,04	1,03	1,11
EG-9	76/77-79/80	-7981	1255	-998	-188	159
		0,93	1,16	0,80	0,99	1,13
EG-12	85/86-88/89	14743	920	-194	872	408
		1,10	1,09	1,00	1,03	1,13

Tabelle 258: Struktur der Weltexporte, 1970, 1980, 1986. Industrieländer: Nordamerika, Europa, UdSSR, Australien, Neuseeland, Japan, Israel, Südafrika. In: Henrichsmeyer/Witzke 1991: 169.
Erwähnt in Abschnitt 'I', 869.

Importeure		Industrieländer		Entwicklungsländer		Welt	
Exporteure		Mrd. US$	Anteil (%)	Mrd. US$	Anteil (%)	Mrd. US$	Anteil (%)
Industrie-länder	1970	205	66	48	16	253	82
	1980	1076	54	337	17	1413	71
	1986	1310	62	337	16	1647	78
Entwicklungs-länder	1970	45	14	13	4	57	18
	1980	420	21	151	8	571	29
	1986	307	15	145	7	452	22
Welt	1970	249	80	61	20	310	100
	1980	1496	75	488	25	1984	100
	1986	1617	77	481	23	2099	100

Tabelle 259: Imports from major LDC debtors to th OCED subject to access barriers, 1982 ($US billion and percentages). Aus: OECD 1985: 181.
Erwähnt in Abschnitt 'I', 870.

	Brazil	Mexico	Argentina	Chile	Korea	Indonesia	Philipines	Yugoslavia	All
Manufactured imports affected by non-tariff barriers (1) ($US billion)	1.8	0.4	0.2	0.01	6.8	0.2	0.6	0.8	10.8
--As % of total OECD manufactured imports from that country	42.9	8.2	22.2	14.3	58.1	40.0	30.0	34.8	40.6
Agricultural imports (2) affected by non-tariff barriers ($US billion)	3.2	1.4	2.0	0.6	0.9	0.6	1.4	0.3	10.4
--As % of total OECD agricultural imports from that country	51.6	73.7	100.0	95.0	98.0	54.5	93.3	68.2	74.8
Manufactured and agricultural imports affected by non-tariff barriers (1) (2) as % of total OECD imports from that country	35.7	8.0	55.0	21.0	58.3	4.3	41.7	31.4	25.3

1. Textiles, clothing, iron and steel, footwear, consumer electronics.
2. Meat, cereals, sugar, fish, vegetables and fruit, animal feeds, tobacco, vegetable oils.

Tabelle 260: Nominal tariff rates (a) on textiles and apparel.
In: Cline 1987: 163.
Erwähnt in Abschnitt 'I', 871, 877.

	Textiles			
	Thread and yarn	Fabrics	Apparel	All manufactures
United States				
1962	11,5	24,0	22,0	11,5
1973 (b)	14,5	19,0	27,0	11,5
1987 (c)	9,0	11,5	22,5	6,5
European Communities				
1962	3,0	17,5	18,5	18,5
1973 (b)	8,0	14,5	16,5	9,5
1987 (c)	7,0	10,5	13,5	6,5
Japan				
1962	2,5	19,5	25,0	16,0
1973 (b)	9,0	12,0	18,0	11,0
1987 (c)	7,0	9,5	14,0	6,5

Source: GATT: Textiles and Clothing, pp. 67-69.

(a) The greater of simple and weighted averages.
(b) Pre-Tokyo Round.
(c) Post-Tokyo Round.

Tabelle 261: Average Landed Prices in the European Community for 'Sensitive' Categories of Clothing, 1980 (European units of account). Aus: Wolf et al. 1984: 95.
Erwähnt in Abschnitt 'I', 871.

	T-Shirts etc. (a)	Jerseys (a)	Trousers (a)	Blouses (a)	Shirts (a)
European Community					
Belgium-Luxembourg	4,3	7,0	8,4	6,5	6,2
Denmark	3,3	6,7	8,1	6,1	3,4
France	5,1	9,0	9,5	10,1	7,7
Germany	4,7	8,6	10,5	9,4	5,2
Ireland	2,2	6,5	6,9	7,0	7,2
Italy	2,8	5,1	9,0	6,8	7,2
Netherlands	1,8	5,4	8,6	<u>3,9</u>	4,6
United Kingdom	3,7	10,1	9,6	6,2	7,0
Other European Countries					
Austria	5,5	12,0	10,4	11,3	4,0
Greece	1,4	3,5	7,5	4,4	<u>2,5</u>
Portugal	1,5	3,5	7,0	4,4	4,6
United States (b)	<u>1,2</u>	<u>3,0</u>	<u>5,7</u>	4,2	3,0
Restricted Developing Countries (bc)					
Hong Kong (bc)	2,6	4,8	4,5	4,1	3,5
India (bc)	1,1	2,7	3,7	3,0	2,8
South Korea (bc)	2,1	3,1	4,3	2,3	2,7
Taiwan (bd)	2,1	3,5	3,7	2,5	2,5

Note: The figures are average landed prices, before VAT and duty. The figures for members of the European Union are for their exports to one another. The cheapest unresticted supplier is underlined.

(a) These are categories 4 to 8 (inclusive) of the European Community's classification of MFA products.
(b) Exports from these countries pay duty of 17 per cent, except for jerseys (for which duty is 10,5 or 18 per cent).
(c) These countries face MFA or similar restrictions.
(d) Taiwanese products pay 21 per cent duty (20 per cent on shirts).

Tabelle 262: Einfuhr in vH des Inlandsverbrauchs für ausgewählte Industriezweige. Vom Verfasser berechnet ist der Anteil der Entwicklungsländer am Inlandsverbrauch. Daten aus Dicke et al. 1976: 165, 178, 184-187.
Erwähnt in Abschnitt 'I', 875.

	1965	1972
BRD Einfuhr aus Entwicklungsländern (in DM)		
Textil	615.368.000	1.360.621.000
Bekleidung	165.101.000	1.096.987.000
Schuhe	13.291.000	179.058.000
Anteil der Entwicklungsländer an den Einfuhren in diesen Bereichen		
Textil	12,5 %	15,4 %
Bekleidung	14,5 %	27,5 %
Schuhe	3,1 %	4,7 %
Einfuhr als Anteil des Inlandsverbrauchs alle Länder für BRD		
Textil	18,2 %	30,6 %
Bekleidung	5,7 %	20,7 %
Schuhe	7,5 %	27,6 %
Einfuhr durch Entwicklungsländer als Anteil des Inlandverbrauchs der BRD		
Textil	2,2 %	4,7 %
Bekleidung	0,8 %	5,7 %
Schuhe	2,3 %	11,4 %

Tabelle 263: Imports of apparel from non-OECD sources as percentage of US apparent consumption. (a). In Cline 1987: 64.
Erwähnt in Abschnitt 'I', 875, 877, 881, 882.

Year	Actual	Three-moving average	Predicted (b)	Percentage change, predicted
1971	3,7	3,6	3,6	23,2
1972	4,4	4,4	4,4	22,1
1973	5,0	5,0	5,3	20,8
1974	5,8	5,8	6,3	19,3
1975	6,7	7,0	7,4	17,6
1976	8,6	7,9	8,6	15,8
1977	8,3	9,0	9,8	13,9
1978	10,3	9,8	10,9	11,9
1979	10,9	10,9	12,0	10,0
1980	11,5	11,6	13,0	8,2
1981	12,5	12,2	13,9	6,6
1982	12,5	12,9	14,6	5,2
1983	13,7	14,3	15,3	4,0
1984	16,7	n.a.	15,6	3,0

(a) Imports on customs value basis, exluding insurance, freight, duties.
(b) Based on regression estimate of logistics curve. See appendix A.

Tabelle 264: Adjusted import penetration ratios, value basis (percentage) (a). Aus: Cline 1987: 49.
Erwähnt in Abschnitt 'I', 876.

Period	Textiles	Apparel	Textiles and Apparel
1961-65 (b)	6,0	3,7	4,9
1966-70 (b)	5,7	6,0	5,9
1971-75 (b)	5,8	10,7	8,2
1976-79 (b)	5,2	16,3	10,8
1980	5,6	18,4	12,1
1981	6,3	19,5	13,2
1982	5,9	19,9	13,7
1983	6,0	21,6	14,4
1984	7,9	27,3	18,6
1985	8,5	29,6	20,5
1986	9,5	31,1	22,0

Tabelle 265: Annual growth rates of real US imports of textiles and apparel (percentage) (a). Cline 1987: 170.
Erwähnt in Abschnitt 'I', 876, 878, 882.

	SYE (b)	Textile-apparel deflator	Wholesale price deflator
Textiles			
1961-72	16,1 (c)	5,9	4,2
1972-77	-9,1	-4,9	-9,3
1977-81	-2,1	4,3	0,4
1981-86	21,9	12,7	12,6
Apparel			
1961-72	18,3 (c)	13,8	14,8
1972-77	2,9	11,1	6,7
1977-81	4,7	6,8	1,9
1981-86	12,9	16,4	17,4

(a) Calculated form log-linear regressions for each period.
(b) Square yard equivalents
(c) 1964-72.

Tabelle 266: Importe, Komsumption und Marktanteile.
In: Hufbauer et al. 1986: 117-153.
Erwähnt in Abschnitt 'I', 876, 877.

Year	Imports from all sources		Imports affected (a)	Apparent consumption		Market share	
	Volume (mill. pounds)	Value (bill. dollars)	Volume (mill. pounds)	Volume (mill. pounds)	Value (b) (billion dollars)	Imports/ apparent consumption, percentage (volume)	Imports/ apparent csumption, percentage (value) (c)
VERs							
1960	416	0,873	252	6,563	28,5	6,3	3,0
During LTA							
1972	1,187	3,2	950	12,335	56,5	9,6	5,6
During MFA I							
1974	948	3,7	758	11,240	62,5	8,4	5,9
1975	979	3,7	776	10,826	62,1	9,0	5,9
1976	1,287	4,9	1,034	12,095	71,1	10,6	6,8
1977	1,317	5,4	1,005	12,734	86,8	10,3	6,2
During MFA II							
1978	1,617	7,1	1,268	13,197	93,0	12,3	7,6
1979	1,381	7,2	1,128	13,064	94,7	10,6	7,6
1980	1,455	8,2	1,190	12,026	98,3	12,1	8,3
1981	1,715	9,5	1,458	12,246	107,4	14,0	8,8
Begin of MFA IV							
1984	1,992	16,5	2,225	14,636	131,6	20,4	12,5

(a) Leider liegen keine Zahlen zu den Werten der von den Beschränkungen erfaßten Importen vor. Somit kann hier nur ein Eindruck von Größenordnungen vermittelt werden.
(b) These figures are derived from the value of imports and domestic output, with an adjustment for exports.
(c) Wohlgemerkt, leider nur Zahlen in bezug auf die gesamten Importe und nicht nur in bezug auf die von Beschränkungen erfaßten Importe.

Tabelle 267: Output, Beschäftigung, Löhne, Profite, Kapazitätsauslastung. Aus: Hufbauer et al. 1986: 132-134. Erwähnt in Abschnitt "I", 876, 878.

Year	Output of domestic industry Volume (mill. pounds) (a)	Value (bill. dollars) Textiles	Value (bill. dollars) Apparel	Employment in domestic industry (thousand production workers) Textiles	Employment in domestic industry (thousand production workers) Apparel	Wages (dollars pro hour) Textiles	Wages (dollars pro hour) Apparel	Industry profits (million dollars) (b) Textiles	Industry profits (million dollars) (b) Apparel	Industry capacity utilization (textiles only, average in December) Percentage
VER										
1960	6,477	13,8	13,8	924,0	1098,0	1,61	1,59	659	320	93
During LTA										
1972	11,649	28,0	27,8	985,7	1208,0	2,75	2,53	1024	1077	91
During MFA I										
1974	11,102	32,8	30,6	965,0	1174,9	3,20	2,97	995	915	69
1975	10,553	31,1	31,4	867,9	1066,0	3,42	3,17	720	1244	85
1976	11,617	36,4	34,8	918,8	1134,3	3,69	3,40	1440	1422	84
1977	12,167	40,6	40,2	910,2	1316,3	4,07	3,56	1924	1818	87
During MFA II										
1978	12,391	42,3	42,7	899,1	1332,3	4,41	3,80	1918	1634	85
1979	12,773	45,1	43,0	885,1	1304,3	4,75	3,97	1998	1617	82
1980	11,890	47,2	45,8	847,7	1263,5	5,28	4,25	1408	1825	80
1981	11,548	50,1	49,8	823,0	1244,4	5,58	4,53	1300	2020	75
Begin of MFA III										
1983 (c)	12,000	57,8	57,3	726,0	1215,0	6,18	5,48	2697	-	86

(a) These figures reflect mill consumption of cotton, wool, and man-made fibres.
(b) Net profits before taxes.
(c) Teils Zahlen für 1984.

Tabelle 268: Trade and domestic consumption: textiles (million dollars). Nominal prices.
Gekürzt, aus: Cline 1987: 35.
Erwähnt in Abschnitt 'I', 877.

Year	Imports	Exports	Apparent Consumption (a)	Imports/Consumption (percentage)
1961	590	320	13,151	4,5
1965	858	391	17,547	4,9
1970	1,058	461	21,706	4,9
1975	1,107	1,157	29,158	3,8
1980	2,034	2,488	44,320	4,6
1983	2,557	1,560	51,482	5,0
1986	4,322	1,751	54,488	7,9

(a) Equals production plus imports minus exports.

Tabelle 269: Trade and domestic consumption: apparel (million dollars). Gekürzt, aus Cline 1987: 40.
Erwähnt in Abschnitt 'I', 877.

Year	Imports	Exports	Apparent Consumption (a)	Imports/Consumption (percentage)
1961	283	159	13,212	2,1
1965	568	177	16,817	3,4
1970	1,286	250	21,430	6,0
1975	2,775	603	29,270	9,5
1980	6,543	1,604	45,232	14,5
1983	10,018	1,049	58,392	17,2
1986	17,744	1,102	69,965	25,4

(a) Equals production plus imports minus exports.

Tabelle 270: Production, investment and employment: textiles and apparel, 1960-86.
Gekürzt, aus Cline 1987: 27.
Erwähnt in Abschnitt 'I', 878.

Year	Textiles				Apparel			
	Production	Production at constant 1982 prices	Investment (mill. $)	Employment (thousand workers)	Production	Production at constant 1982 prices	Investment (mill. $)	Employment (thousand workers)
1960	12,629	21,103	417	874,6	12,999	30,867	86	1,234
1965	17,080	33,634	618	893,2	16,426	36,271	168	1,335
1970	21,112	38,110	811	924,5	20,394	34,765	299	1,341
1975	29,208	41,832	997	835,1	27,098	40,270	381	1,214
1980	44,774	49,423	1,487	817,5	40,293	45,742	608	1,307
1983	50,147	48,498	n.a.	670,2	50,784	48,551	n.a.	1,142
1986	51,917	49,210	n.a.	668,9	53,323	49,548	n.a.	1,133

Tabelle 271: Beschäftigungsniveaus und Arbeitsplatzverluste in der Schuh-, Textil- und Bekleidungsindustrie. Aus: OECD Industrial Structure, div. Jg. In Tausend.
Erwähnt in Abschnitt 'I', 878, 892.

	1970	1980	1985	1990 (a)	1997 (a)
Deutschland -Beschäftigung	1236,5 (g)	637,0	485,9	423,4	245,4
Exporte (Mrd. DM)		18,3	24,1	35,7	
- Textil		12,1	15,5	23,0	-
- Bekleidung		4,6	6,0	9,3	
Importe		33,5	35,0	59,8	
- Textil		17,3	18,3	28,2	-
- Bekleidung		10,5	11,0	21,8	
Italien		579,0	493,0	(c) 520,0	(d) 495,5
Frankreich		667,9	514,5	411,2	280,2
Belgien		(b) 120,2	112,2	(f) 101,0	-
UK		727,9	572,0		387,0
Japan		1290,0	1242,0	-	809,8
Kanada		214,4	197,0	-	145,0
United States		2362,0	1870,0	1751,0	(e) 1650,0

(a) Neue Industrieklassenabgrenzung. ISIC Rev. 3, (b) Zahl aus dem Jahr 1981.. (c) Zahl aus dem Jahr 1988. (d) Zahl aus dem Jahr 1994. (e) Zahl aus dem Jahr 1995. (f) Letzte verfügbare Zahl für Belgien für 1989. (g) Zahl aus Dicke et al. 1976: 217.

Tabelle 272: European Community: Voluntary Export Restraint Arrangements, September 1987. Aus: IMF 1988: 92 (Quelle dort GATT. Review of Developments in the Trading System, Geneva 1987).
Erwähnt in Abschnitt 'I', 895, 900.

Major known VERs (excluding the MFA)	World-wide	EC-total	EC-wide	National	Restrained Exporters
Total	135	69	49	20	Industrial countries (32); developing countries (25); Easter European countries (12)
Steel	38	12	12	-	Industrial countries (4); developing countries (3); Eastern european countries (5)
Agriculture and food products	20	19	19	-	Industrial countries (8); developing countries (5); Eastern european countries (6)
Automobiles and transport equipment	14	11	2	9 (France, Italy, GB, Spain, Portugal)	Industrial countries (11)
Textiles and clothing	28	7	7	-	Developing countries (7)
Electronic products	11	8	5	3 (France, Italy, GB)	Industrial countries (5); developing countries (3)
Footwear	8	5	1(1)	4 (France, GB)	Developing countries (5)
Machine tools	7	3	2	1 (GB)	Industrial countries (3)
Other	9	4	1	3 (Benelux, Denmark, GB)	Industrial countries (1); developing countries (2); Eastern european countries (1)

(1) Industry-to-Industry arrangement

Tabelle 273: Voluntary Export Restraints and Similar Restraint Arrangements in the EC, as of Mid-1990. Aus: Schuknecht 1992: 116-117.
Erwähnt in Abschnitt 'I', 895, 900, 902, 908.

Targets	Initiator	Products	Type
Agriculture:			
All suppliers (a)	EC	sheep/goats	VER (b)
Argentina, Australia, Chile, New Zealand,	EC	dessert apples	IRA (c)
South Africa, Korea	EC	frozen squid	IRA
Footwear:			
Korea, Taiwan	EC	footwear, no slippers	VER
China	France	slippers, sandales	IRA
Korea	Ireland	footwear	IRA
CSFR, Romania	UK	footwear	IRA
Textiles outside MFA:			
Bulgaria	EC	MFA textiles/clothing	VER
Soviet Union	EC	MFA textiles/clothing	VER
Japan	EC	textiles/clothing	IRA (d)
Cyprus	EC	textiles/clothing	IRA
Egypt	EC	textiles/clothing	IRA
Malta	EC	textiles/clothing	IRA
Morocco	EC	textiles/clothing	IRA
Tunisia	EC	textiles/clothing	IRA
Turkey	EC	textiles/clothing	IRA
Yugoslavia	EC	textiles/clothing	VER
Steel/Steel product:			
Austria	EC	steel	IRA
Brazil	EC	pig iron – steel	VER
Bulgaria	EC	steel	VER
CSFR	EC	steel	VER
Finland	EC	steel	IRA
Hungary	EC	steel	VER
Japan	EC	steel	IRA
Poland	EC	steel	VER
Romania	EC	steel	VER
Sweden	EC	steel	IRA
USA	EC	steel/steel products	VER
Machinery:			
Japan	EC	machine tools	VER
Japan	EC	machining centres	VER
Japan	EC	NC lathes	VER
Japan	EC	forklift trucks	VER
Japan	EC	ball bearings	IRA (d)
Japan	France	NC lathes, machining centres	VER
Electrical and electronic household equipment:	EC	color TV sets	VER
Japan	EC	color TV tubes	VER
Japan	EC	video tape recorders	VER
Japan	EC	mircowave ovens	IRA (d)
Korea	EC	video tape recorders	VER
Korea	Germany	color TV sets	IRA
Japan	France	TV tubes	IRA
Japan	EC	video tape recorders	IRA
Japan			
Vehicles:			
Japan	EC	passenger cars	VER
Japan	EC	commercial vehicles	VER
Japan	EC	motorcycles	Ver

Japan	UK	passenger cars, commercial, four-wheel drive vehicles automobiles	IRA
Japan	Belgium		IRA
Other products:			
Japan	EC	metal flatware	IRA
Korea	Benelux	metal flatware	IRA
Singapore, Taiwan Thailand	France	umbrellas	IRA
Japan	UK	pottery	IRA

(a) Argentina, Australia, Austria, Bulgaria, CSFR, Hungary, Iceland, New Zealand, Poland, Romania, Yugoslavia.
(b) VER = all formal restraint arrangements, i.e. VERs, Orderly Marketing Agreements, Community Export Monitoring, and Formal Restraint Agreements.
(c) IRA = all informal restraint arrangements, i.e. export forecasts, export ceilings, informal restraint arrangements, industry to industry arrangements, autolimitations, reference prices or price fixings, export cartels, export moderation.
(d) The EC Commisssion or national government is not aware of these restraints.

Tabelle 274: Importanteile bedeutender Schuhexporteure auf wichtigen Absatzmärkten des deutschen Schuhgewerbes (1). Aus: Neckermann/Wessels 1988: 151.
Erwähnt in Abschnitt 'I', 897.

Exporteur	Jahr	Importeur Niederlande	Österreich	Schweiz	Belgien/ Luxem.	Frankreich	USA	Großbritannien	EG (2)	OECD
Italien	1971	36,8	37,9	39,5	36,3	61,7	38,0	26,4	52,7	39,8
	1985	36,2	54,0	48,1	46,3	60,5	15,2	40,9	45,0	28,5
Taiwan	1971	1,6	0,4	0,3	0,6	1,8	8,7	2,0	1,2	5,1
	1985	5,7	3,5	5,4	3,2	2,4	30,9	7,3	5,4	18,9
Südkorea	1971	0,0	0,0	0,1	0,0	0,1	3,5	0,1	0,1	1,8
	1985	2,8	2,0	1,9	1,0	4,4	19,2	4,2	3,5	12,5
Brasilien	1971	0,0	0,0	0,0	0,0	0,0	3,1	0,2	0,0	1,4
	1985	0,3	0,0	0,1	0,0	1,0	15,3	4,3	1,1	8,1
Spanien	1971	3,9	2,9	1,1	1,2	4,1	16,7	5,6	3,4	9,1
	1985	5,9	1,5	1,8	2,6	6,2	7,3	9,4	6,9	6,4
Frankreich	1971	15,3	4,9	11,7	31,1	-	2,2	8,1	15,0	7,7
	1985	7,1	3,6	9,3	17,5	-	2,1	6,4	6,2	4,0
BRD	1971	24,1	13,5	13,6	11,3	11,0	2,2	1,1	6,5	4,3
	1985	17,6	25,3	16,8	6,5	2,8	0,4	2,4	3,9	2,8
Portugal	1971	0,0	1,0	0,2	0,0	0,0	0,1	2,0	0,0	0,5
	1985	5,2	2,1	1,3	3,3	6,4	0,4	4,8	4,6	2,4
Österreich	1971	0,7	-	17,6	0,1	0,3	0,6	4,7	1,1	2,6
	1985	0,9	-	8,2	0,4	0,9	0,1	2,2	3,1	1,7
Ürige Länder	1971	17,6	39,4	15,9	19,4	21,0	24,9	49,8	20,0	27,9
	1985	16,4	8,1	7,1	17,1	15,3	9,2	18,1	20,2	14,7
Importolumen in Mill. US$	1971	80	23	67	85	83	758	132	590	1819
	1985	422	219	320	370	878	6104	865	4644	12719

(1) Anteile in vH berechnet auf US-Dollar Basis (c.i.f.) Exporteure in der Reihenfolge ihrer Bedeutung für den gesamten OECD Import von Schuhen im Jahr 1985. (2) Ohne Portugal und Spanien.

Tabelle 275: Industrialized countries' import tariffs and domestic excise taxes on selected tropical products (mid-1980s). In: Valdes/Zietz 1995: 921.
Erwähnt in Abschnitt 'D', 169, Abschnitt 'H', 808.

	EC		Australia	Canada	Japan		U.S.
Commodity	Tariff (%)	Tax (%)	Tariff (%)	Tariff (%)	Tariff (%)	Tax (%)	Tariff (%)
Coffee							
Green	5.0	15.0	2.0	0.5	20.0	5.0	
Roasted	15.0	0.2	2.0			5.0	
Cocoa							
Beans	2.9		2.0				
Butter	12.0	0.2			2.5		
Powder	16.0	2.6		10.0	21.5	5.0	3.0
Tea	0.2	15.5			20.7		
Cotton					0.4		
Groundnuts			10.0				14.0
Groundnut oil	10.0		10.0	7.5	6.6		5.1
Palm oil	6.0		2.0	10.0	7.0		2.7
Tobacco leaves	23.0		12.8	7.7			11.5

Tabelle 276: Pervasiveness of different types of NTBs in OECD countries: the "Quad". In: OECD 1996a: 46. Erwähnt in Abschnitt "I", 911, 919.

NTB categories	USA				EU				Japan				Kanada			
	F		IC		F		IC		F		IC		F		IC	
	1989	1993	1989	1993	1989	1993	1989	1993	1989	1993	1989	1993	1989	1993	1989	1993
All NTBs	25,5	22,9	16,7	17,0	26,6	23,7	13,2	11,1	13,1	12,2	8,6	8,1	11,1	11,0	5,7	4,5
-- Core NTBs	25,5	22,9	16,6	17,0	25,2	21,8	10,9	9,0	12,5	11,3	7,4	3,8	8,9	8,2	4,1	2,5
Quantitative restrictions (QRs)	20,4	18,1	13,7	10,2	19,5	17,2	7,8	7,1	11,7	10,5	6,6	3,0	6,6	6,8	3,0	1,7
-- Export restraints	29,5	13,1	12,9	10,1	15,5	13,9	6,2	5,6	0,3	0,1	0,2	0,0	4,8	5,8	1,2	1,4
-- Non-automatic licensing	0,0	0,0	0,0	0,0	4,4	3,5	2,2	1,7	8,9	8,9	1,3	1,3	2,6	0,2	0,7	0,0
-- Other QRs	6,6	5,6	1,1	0,2	0,2	0,2	0,1	0,0	2,8	1,6	5,4	1,7	0,8	0,8	1,1	0,3
Price control measures (PCMs)	17,8	10,8	3,6	7,3	12,4	8,4	6,0	3,5	0,8	0,9	0,7	0,8	2,4	1,4	1,1	0,8
-- Variable Charge	0,1	0,0	0,1	0,0	6,3	5,4	1,8	1,5	0,8	0,9	0,7	0,8	0,0	0,0	0,0	0,0
-- AD/CVs and VEPRs	17,8	10,8	3,4	7,3	2,6	1,9	2,2	1,3	0,0	0,0	0,0	0,0	2,4	1,4	1,1	0,8
-- Other PCMs	0,0	0,0	0,0	0,0	4,3	1,1	2,1	0,6	0,0	0,0	0,0	0,0	0,0	0,0	0,0	0,0

(1) F = Frequency Ratio, (2) IC = Import coverage ratio

Tabelle 277: Share of Imports of Industrial Countries Subject to Non-Barriers, 1983 (per cent) (a). Aus: Donges 1986: 7.
Erwähnt in Abschnitt 'I', 912.

Importer	Exporter (b)	Fuels	Agricultural products	Manufactures Total	Textiles	All goods Total	Textiles
Sixteen major industrial country markets (c)	DCs	59,5	40,5	14,5	23,3	21,0	17,1
	LDCs	51,9	31,2	21,3	57,2	34,3	22,5
	World	43,0	36,1	16,1	44,8	27,1	18,6
of which:							
France	DCs	78,2	53,3	25,0	21,9	31,3	27,4
	LDCs	78,1	28,1	33,0	64,6	50,1	28,6
	World	91,0	37,8	27,4	48,4	57,1	28,1
GB	DCs	0	44,5	13,2	26,0	15,4	17,0
	LDCs	0	24,4	30,4	78,6	23,3	27,4
	World	0	34,9	14,8	59,6	14,3	17,5
BRD	DCs	0	28,5	13,3	8,8	13,7	14,5
	LDCs	0	16,6	30,2	71,9	18,1	23,9
	World	0	22,3	18,5	57,0	12,4	18,3
EC-9	DCs	14,7	47,7	15,2	15,6	18,6	18,9
	LDCs	22,3	26,9	29,9	68,0	25,4	26,9
	World	24,4	36,4	18,7	52,0	22,3	21,1
Japan	DCs	52,8	36,8	9,7	11,0	21,4	16,9
	LDCs	6,7	53,3	4,4	13,0	12,1	17,5
	World	7,0	42,9	7,7	11,8	11,9	16,9
USA	DCs	99,8	23,5	16,5	31,1	26,0	16,6
	LDCs	99,9	25,1	18,6	64,0	54,0	18,9
	World	100,0	24,2	17,1	57,0	43,0	17,3

Tabelle 278: Nutzung von NTBs seitens der Industrieländer, Prozent des Importwerts.
Aus: Finger/Olechowski 1987: 46.
Erwähnt in Abschnitt 'I', 912.

Product category	Percent of value of imports from					
	All countries		Industrial countries		Developing countries	
	1981	1984	1981	1984	1981	1984
All products	17	18	17	17	18	19
Agricultural products	39	38	47	44	31	33
Fuels and ores	15	13	20	18	9	10
Industrial goods	15	16	12	14	22	21
-Textiles	48	50	23	25	62	62
-Iron and Steel	23	4	44	2	47	4
-Footwear	46	4	44	2	47	4
-Electrical machines	7	9	8	10	6	7
-Vehicles	31	29	32	30	6	3

Tabelle 279: Korean Exports under NTBs by Major Trading Partners.
In: Nam 1993: 197.
Erwähnt in Abschnitt 'I', 912.

	1976	1981	1985	1987	1989
Exports to the U.S.: Total exports (million U.S. dollars)	2,493	5,661	10,754	18,311	20,639
Exports under NTBs (million U.S. dollar)	935	2,412	4,656	4,855	4,072
Share (=B/A) (%)	37,5	42,6	43,3	26,5	19,7
Share (%) of exports under NTBs to other industrial countries					
Canada	39,3	45,6	31,1	42,9	23,9
EC	31,6	39,3	29,5	41,0	22,3
Japan	14,5	48,5	32,0	19,4	23,7
19 industrial countries (a)	27,8	45,8	36,6	31,0	22,3 (b)

(a) The nineteen industrial countries are the United States, Canada, Japan, Australia, New Zealand, Germany, the United Kingdom, France, the Netherlands, Belgium, Luxembourg, Denmark, Italy, Greece, Ireland, Finland, Norway, Sweden, Austria. (b) Of the nineteen counries, New Zealand is omitted.

Note: NTBs here include VERs, Ads, CVDs, safeguard actions, and other import restriction under administrative or unfair trade regulations in force or under investigation.

Tabelle 280: Anteile der Importe der Industrieländer, der nichttarifären Handelshemmnissen unterliegt, 1983.
Erwähnt in Abschnitt 'I', 919.

Importmarkt	Prozent der Importe aus:		
	Industrieländer	allen Entwicklungsländer	Hauptschuldnerländer
EG	10,2	21,8	24,9
Japan	9,3	10,5	9,6
Vereinigte Staaten	7,7	12,9	14,5
Industrieländer insgesamt	10,5	19,8	21,9

Aus: Weltentwicklungsbericht 1985: 46.

Tabelle 281: Schutzklauselnutzung 1995-2005: Quelle: various Reports of the WTO Committee on Safeguards.
Erwähnt in Abschnitt 'J', 945, 970, 973, 975.

Time frame for report/Reporting member	Definitive safeguard measure (including recommendations of imposition, provisional measure excluded)	Expired or terminated measures (only those notified in writing)
2005 G/L/761 26 October 2004 - 3 November 2005		
Chile	Wheat flour; 04/03/2005 (G/SG/N/10/CHL/6+Suppl.1&2)	
European Communities	Salmon; 06/02/2005 (G/SG/N/10/EEC/3 +Suppl.1-3)	Salmon terminated: 27/04/2005 G/SG/N/10/EEC/3/Suppl.3
Indonesia	Ceramic tableware; 10/05/2005 (G/SG/N/10/IDN/1)	
Jordan	Insecticides; 16/10/2005 (G/SG/N/10/JOR/5 +Suppl.1)	
Morocco	Ceramic tiles; 01/09/2005 (G/SG/N/10/MAR/2)	The measure is not imposed as of 3 November 2005
Turkey	Actice earth and clay; 08/07/2005 (G/SG/N/10/TUR/1+Corr.1)	
Turkey	Certain voltmeters and ammeters; 12/08/2005 (G/SG/N/10/TUR/2)	
2004 G/L/703 21 October 2003 – 25 October 2004		
Brazil	Toys; 19 December 2003; G/SG/N/10/BRA/2/Suppl.2	
Ecuador	Smooth ceramics; 25 Februar 2004; G/SG/N/10/ECU/3	
European Communities	Mandarins; 16 March 2004; G/SG/N/10/EEC/2 + Suppl. 1	
Hungary	White sugar; 28 November 2003; G/SG/N/10/HUN/3	Terminated April 2004
Jamaica	Cement; 23 April 2004; G/SG/N/10/JAM/1 + Corr. 1	Cement terminated: 15 September 2004; G/SG/N/9/JAM/1
Philippines	Grey Portland cement; 18 March, 2004; G/SG/N/10/PHL/2/Suppl. 1	
Philippines	Float glass; 26 May 2004; G/SG/N/10/PHL/3 + Corr. 1	
Philippines	Figured glass; 26 May 2004; G/SG/N/10/PHL/4	
Philippines	Glass mirrors; 26 May 2004; G/SG/N/10/PHL/5	
Poland	Matches; 9 December 2003; G/SG/N/10/POL/4	Terminated April 2004
2003 G/L/651 29 October 2002 – 20 October 2003		
Bulgaria	Crown corks; 14 January 2003; G/SG/N/10/BGR/1	
Bulgaria	Ammonium nitrate; 3 February 2003; G/SG/N/10/BGR/2	
Chile	Fructose; 27 February 2003; G/SG/N/10/CHL/5/Suppl. 2	
Czech Republic	Sugar; 25 February 2003; G/SG/N/10/CZE/4	
Czech Republic	Tubes and pipes; 28 February 2003;	

	G/SG/N/10/CZE/5	
Czech Republic	Ammonium nitrate; 4 September 2003; G/SG/N/10/CZE/6	
Ecuador	Fibreboard; 8 October 2003; G/SG/N/10/ECU/2/Suppl.1	
Hungary	Steel; 7 April 2003; G/SG/N/10/HUN/1	
Hungary	Ammonium nitrate; 20 June 2003; G/SG/N/10/HUN/2	
India	Epichlorohydrin; 18 December 2002; G/SG/N/10/IND/8	
Jordan	Sanitary Ware Products; 21 February 2003; G/SG/N/10/JOR/4	
Jordan	Pasta; 24 February 2003; G/SG/N/10/JOR/3	
Latvia	Live pig and pork; 23 June 2003; G/SG/N/10/LVA/3	
Moldova	Sugar; 30 September 2003; G/SG/N/10/MDA/1	
People's Republic of China	Steel; 5 November 2002; G/SG/N/10/CHN/1	Steel terminated; 4 February, 2004; G/SG/N/10/CHN/1/Suppl. 1
Philippines	Cement; 10 July 2003; G/SG/N/10/PHL/2	
Poland	Steel; 27 March 2003; G/SG/N/10/POL/1	
Poland	Calcium carbide; 28 August 2003; G/SG/N/10/POL/3	
Poland	Water heaters; 14 August 2003; G/SG/N/10/POL/2	
Slovak Republic	Ammonium nitrate; 14 April 2003; G/SG/N/10/SVK/2	
2002 G/L/583 30 October 2001–28 October 2002		
Brazil	Coconuts; 01/09/2002; G/SG/N/10/BRA/3	
Chile	Steel; 07/2002; G/SG/N/10/CHL/4	
Chile	Fructose; 30/08/2002; G/SG/N/10/CHL/5	
Czech Republic	Cocoa Powder; 14/06/2002; G/SG/N/10/CZE/3	
Ecuador	Matches; 24/10/2002; G/SG/N/10/ECU/1	
European Communities	Steel; 29/09/2002; G/SG/N/10/EEC/1/Suppl.1	Certain steel products terminated; 19 December, 2004 G/SG/N/10/EEC/1/Suppl.2
India	Gamma Ferric Oxide (GFO)/Magnetic Iron Oxide (MIO) ; 24 January 2001; G/SG/N/10/IND/7	
Jordan	Magnetic tapes; 01/05/2002; G/SG/N/10/JOR/2	
Lithuania	Pastry yeast; 01/03/2002; G/SG/N/10/LTU/1	
Philippines	Ceramic floor and wall tiles; 11/04/2002; G/SG/N/10/PHL/1	
USA	Certain steel products; 20 March 2002 G/SG/N/10/USA/6	Certain steel products terminated; 12 December 2004 G/SG/N/10/USA/6/Suppl.8
2001 G/L/494 10 November 2000 – 29 October 2001		
Argentina	Peaches; 08/08/2001; G/SG/N/10/ARG/3	
Argentina	Motorcycles; 22/06/2001; G/SG/N/10/ARG/2	
Chile	Liquid/powdered milk; 10/01/2001; G/SG/N/10/CHL/3	
Czech Republic	Isoglucose; 26/07/200; G/SG/N/10/CZE/2	
Egypt	Powdered milk; 12/04/2001; G/SG/N/10/EGY/4	

Jordan	Biscuits; 01/09/2001; G/SG/N/10/JOR/1	
Morocco	Bananas; 04/200; G/SG/N/10/MAR/1	
Slovak Republic	Sugar; 01/05/2001; G/SG/N/10/SVK/1	
2000 G/L/409 26 October 1999 - 9 November 2000		
Chile	Wheat, wheat flour, cane beet/sugar, edible vegetable oils Affirmative(G/SG/N/10/CHL/1 & Suppl.1) 22.01.2000 Tariff increase	
Egypt	Common fluorescent lamps; (G/SG/N/10/EGY/2 & Suppl.1) 27.02.2000 Tariff increase	
India	Carbon Black; (G/SG/N/10/IND/2) 28.02.99 Tariff increase	
India	Acetone; (G/SG/N/10/IND/6) 27.01.2000Tariff increase	
Korea	Garlic; (G/SG/N/10/KOR/2 + Suppl.1) 01.06.2000 Tariff increase	
Latvia	Swine meat; (G/SG/N/10/LVA/1 & Suppl.1) 18.12.99 Variable customs duty	Swine meat terminated 01.06.2000 (G/SG/N/10/LVA/2)
USA	Line pipe; (G/SG/N/10/USA/5) 01.03.2000 Tariff increase	
USA	Steel wire rod; (G/SG/N/10/USA/4) 01.03.2000 Tariff quota	
1999 G/L/338 6 November 1998- 22 October 1999		
Czech Republic	Cane beet, sugar; (G/SG/N/10/CZE/1), tariff rate quota	
India	Acetylene Black; (G/SG/10/IND/1 & Suppl.1) 10.12.98 Tariff increase	
India	Slabstock polyol; (G/SG/N/10/IND/3 & Suppl.1) 24.12.98 Tariff increase	
India	Propylene glycol (G/SG/N/10/IND/4 & Suppl.1) 24.12.98 Tariff increase	
India	Phenol; (G/SG/N/10/IND/5) 30.06.99Tariff increase	
USA	Lamb meat; (G/SG/N10/USA/3 & Suppl.1) 22.07.99 Tariff quota	
Egypt	Safety matches; (G/SG/N/10/EGY/1), 19.02.1999 tariff increase	
1998 G/L/272 23 October 1997-5 November 1998		
Argentina	footwear; (G/SG/N/10/ARG/1 & Corr.1 & Suppl.1 + Suppl.2)	
Brazil	toys; (G/SG/N/10/BRA/1)	
USA	Wheat gluten; (G/SG/N/10/USA/2 & Suppl.1 + Corr. 1), 01.06.98, 3 yr. + 1 day QR	
1997 G/L/200 November 1996 - October 1997		
Brazil	Toys; (G/SG/N/10/BRA/1), tariff increase	
Korea	Diary products; (G/SG/N/10/KOR/1 + Corr.1 + Suppl.1 + Suppl.1/Corr.1) 01.03.97 Import quota	Measure terminated 20.05.2000
Argentina	Footwear; (G/SG/N/10/ARG/1 + Corr.1 + Suppl.1 + Suppl.2), tariff increase, converted	

	into tariff rate quote 1998	
1996 G/L/129 November 1995- October 1996		
USA	Brooms; (G/SG/N/10/USA/1), 28.11.96 tariff increase	Measure terminated 03.12.98 (G/SG/N/10/USA/1/Suppl.1)
G/L/32 (1995) January 1995- November 1995		
European Community	notified pre-existing safeguard measures (G/SG/N/2 and addenda)	
Korea	notified pre-existing safeguard measures (G/SG/N/2 and addenda)	

1996 klammert Brasilien Entwicklungsländer von seiner Schutzklausel für Spielzeug aus, die USA in bezug auf Weizeneiweiß. G/L/272, S. 3, Para. 20,

1997 klammert die USA Three of these notifications, from Brazil on toys (G/SG/N/11/BRA/1), from Korea on dairy products (G/SG/N/11/KOR/1), and from the United States on broom corn brooms (G/SG/N/11/USA/1) were reviewed at the Committee's 5 May 1997 regular meeting (G/SG/M/9). The fourth, from Argentina on footwear (G/SG/N/11/ARG/1 + Corr.1 + Suppl.1 + Suppl.2) was reviewed at the Committee's 22 October 1997 regular meeting (G/SG/M/10). siehe 17.

1998: Two notifications concerning non-application of a safeguard measure to developing country Members were received and reviewed during the period. These were from Brazil on toys (G/SG/N/11/BRA/1/Suppl.1), and from the United States on wheat gluten (G/SG/N/11/USA/2).

1999: Six notifications concerning the non-application of a safeguard measure to developing country Members were received during the period. These were from Argentina on footwear, from the Czech Republic on cane/beet sugar, and from the United States on lamb meat and wheat gluten. The above notifications from Argentina and the United States were reviewed by the Committee during the period.

2000: 18. ine notifications concerning the non-application of a safeguard measure to developing country Members were received during the period. These were from Argentina on footwear, from the Czech Republic on sugar, from Korea on garlic, and from the United States on line pipe and wheat gluten.

2001: During the period under review, the Committee received 13 notifications concerning the non-application of a safeguard measure to developing country Members. These were from Argentina on motorcycles and peaches, Chile on liquid / powdered milk, synthetic socks, wheat, wheat flour, sugar and edible vegetable oils, the Czech Republic on isoglucose, Japan on tatami-omote, welsh onions and shiitake mushrooms, the Slovak Republic on sugar, and the United States on wheat gluten.

2002: During the period under review, the Committee received 21 notifications concerning the non-application of a safeguard measure to developing country Members. These were from Brazil on coconuts; from Chile on certain steel products; from the Czech Republic on cocoa powder; from the European Communities on certain steel products; from Hungary on certain steel products; from India on acetone; from the People's Republic of China on certain steel products; from the Philippines on ceramic floor tiles; from Poland on certain steel products; and from the United States on certain steel products, lamb meat, and line pipe.

Tabelle 282: International Use of Antidumping and the Global Antidumping Database. Modified, rank added. In: Bown 1996: 7.
Erwähnt in Abschnitt 'J', 1001, 1109.

Rank	Country	Number of Antidumping Investigations, 1995-2004	Number of Antidumping Measures Imposed, 1995-2004
1	India	400	302
2	United States	354	219
3	European Union	303	193
4	Argentina	192	139
5	South Africa	173	113
6	Australia	172	54
7	Canada	133	80
8	Brazil	116	62
9	China (since 2001)	99	52
10	Turkey	89	77
11	Mexico	79	69
12	South Korea	77	43
13	Indonesia	60	23
14	Peru	55	34
15	New Zealand	47	14
16	Egypt	38	30
17	Venezuela	34	25
18	Thailand	34	23
19	Malaysia	31	18
20	Israel	27	15
21	Colombia	23	11
22	Taiwan (since 2000)	8	2
23	Japan	3	3
	Other WTO Members	102	55
Total		2646	1656

Tabelle 283: Targeted: Imposing vs. targeted countries by level of development. Partially reproduced. In: Zanardi 2005: 29.
Erwähnt in Abschnitt 'J', 1002.

1988-1994				
Imposing/Targeted	Developed countries	Developing countries	Countries in transition	Total
Developed countries	219 (39%)	217 (38%)	128 (23%)	564 (100 %)
Developing countries	54 (43%)	35 (28%)	36 (29%)	125 (100 %)
Countries in transition	0	0	0	0
Total	273 (40%)	252 (37%)	164 (24%)	689 (100 %)
1995-2001				
Imposing/Targeted	Developed countries	Developing countries	Countries in transition	Total
Developed countries	168 (28%)	232 (39%)	195 (33%)	595 (100 %)
Developing countries	173 (32%)	184 (34%)	187 (34%)	544 (100 %)
Countries in transition	7 (39%)	5 (28%)	6 (33%)	18 (100 %)
Total	348 (30%)	421 (36%)	388 (34%)	1157 (100 %)

Tabelle 284: Intensities (per value of exports) for countries affected by AD investigations. In: Zanardi 2005: 33.
Erwähnt in Abschnitt 'J', 1002.

Rank	Country	1995-2001 Per value of exports	Ranking in initiations
1	Serbia/Montenegro	2685	52
2	Latvia	2302	38
3	Moldova	2270	61
4	Macedonia	2007	49
5	Ukraine	1454	12
6	Kazakhstan	1011	28
7	Lithuania	863	43
8	Romania	863	25
9	Belarus	821	35
10	India	788	8
11	Egypt	752	42
12	Bulgaria	648	40
13	Indonesia	540	7
14	China	529	1
15	Brazil	505	11
16	Uzbekistan	475	64
17	Spain	470	14
18	South Africa	465	17
19	Thailand	446	10
20	Chile	435	27
21	Turkey	408	20
22	South Korea	405	2
23	Croatia	359	53
24	Portugal	348	55
25	Poland	345	22
26	Slovak Rep.	339	41
27	Russia	334	6
28	Pakistan	325	44
29	Greece	312	54
30	Trinidad Tobago	290	71
31	Taiwan	283	5
32	Czech Rep.	236	29
33	Argentina	221	30
34	Netherlands	217	21
35	Hungary	211	36
36	Venezuela	187	37
37	Austria	183	34
38	Malaysia	167	16
39	EEC total	151	
40	New Zealand	150	51
41	Denmark	138	46
42	Belgium Luxembourg	132	32/67
43	Italy	131	15
44	United Kingdom	126	13
45	Iran	118	48
46	Finland	118	47
47	Germany	115	9
48	Colombia	109	57
49	France	108	18
50	Mexico	97	19
51	Slovenia	95	70
52	Australia	90	31
53	Israel	87	50

54	Sweden	87	39
55	Japan	79	4
56	Ireland	62	60
57	USA	61	3
58	Saudi Arabia	51	45
59	Singapore	44	33
60	Hong Kong	42	23
62	Canada	31	26
62	Philippines	30	69
63	Switzerland	21	56
64	Norway	17	68

Tabelle 285: Intensities of initiations (per value of imports) of AD investigations. In: Zanardi 2005: 32.
Erwähnt in Abschnitt 'J', 1003.

	1988-1994			1995-2001	
Country	Per value of imports	Ranking in initiations	Country	Per value of imports	Ranking in initiations
Poland (a)	4106	12	South Africa	1345	4
Argentina (a)	2009	9	Argentina	1309	5
South Africa (a)	1710	8	Lithuania (a)	1267	24
Australia	1436	2	India	964	3
Peru (a)	1141	15	Trinidad Tobago	698	25
Turkey (a)	953	6	New Zealand	606	11
New Zealand	864	10	Peru	597	16
Colombia (a)	591	14	Nicaragua (a)	566	30
Brazil	549	7	Egypt (a)	510	14
Mexico	540	5	Australia	419	6
Venezuela (a)	230	20	Venezuela	402	17
Canada	229	4	Brazil	331	8
EEC	146	3	Costa Rica (a)	277	26
Chile (a)	129	23	Colombia	260	22
USA	122	1	Paraguay (a)	231	35
Taiwan	122	11	Indonesia	204	12
Thailand (a)	94	22	Chile	203	21
India	86	16	Uruguay	191	32
Finland	73	19	Israel	176	15
South Korea	48	13	Ukraine (a)	172	31
Sweden	38	17	Panama (a)	160	34
Austria	36	18	Philippines	128	20
Japan	5	21	Canada	111	7
			Turkey	102	19
			Mexico	102	9
			South Korea	76	10
			Jamaica	73	40
			Taiwan	72	13
			Guatemala (a)	62	39
			Ecuador (a)	59	38
			USA	53	2
			China (a)	50	18
			Malaysia	45	23
			EEC	44	1
			Russia (a)	32	36
			Czech Rep. (a)	29	29
			Poland (a)	27	27
			Slovenia	23	41
			Thailand	14	28
			Singapore	4	37
			Japan	1	33

(a) The value has not been calculated on the whole period because of missing data or because the country did not haave an AD during the full sample.

Tabelle 286: Definitive Anti-Dumping Measures in Force, including Under-Takings (As of 31 December 1999). In: UNCTAD 2000: 26.
Erwähnt in Abschnitt 'J', 1080.

Measures maintained by parties			Affected parties		
	Number of measures	Percentage of total		Number of measures	Percentage of total
United States (a)	315	29.2	China	198	18.3
EU	189	17.5	EU (b)	167	15.4
South Africa	86	8	Japan	82	7.6
Mexico	80	7.4	Taiwan	59	5.5
Canada	79	7.3	United States	56	5.2
India	64	6	Rep. of Korea	52	5
Argentina	45	4	Brazil	43	4
Australia	44	4	India	33	3.1
Brazil	38	3.5	Russian Fed.	33	3.1
Turkey	36	3.3	Thailand	29	2.7
Rep. of Korea	26	2.4	Romania	20	2
Other	78	7.4	Other	308	28
Total	1080	100	Total	1080	100

(a) Measures in force as of 30 June 1999.
(b) Including measures affecting its individual members states.

Tabelle 287: Long-term development of subsidy levels in developed countries, 1950-2004 (Percentages, subsidies as ratio of GDP). In: WTO 2006: 113.
Erwähnt in Abschnitt 'J', 1197.

	1950-60	1960-69	1970-79	1980-89	1990-99	2000-04
Austria		2.0	2.3	2.9	2.9	3.1
Belgium		2.0	3.3	3.5	2.1	1.5
France			2.2	2.8	1.8	1.3
Germany	0.5	1.4	2.2	2.2	2.0	1.5
Italy			2.5	3.4	1.9	1.1
Spain			1.2	2.3	1.9	1.1
Sweden			2.8	4.6	3.9	1.5
United Kingdom	1.8	1.9	2.4	1.9	0.8	0.6
EU 12			2.2	2.8	2.0	1.4
EU 15			2.3	2.8	1.9	1.2
Norway	4.5	3.9	5.2	4.5	3.7	2.2
Switzerland					4.1	4.0
Australia			1.1	1.6	1.3	1.3
Japan	0.4	0.8	1.3	1.2	0.8	0.8
Canada	0.4		1.6	2.4	1.3	1.2
United States	0.1	0.4	0.4	0.5	0.5	0.4

Tabelle 288: Subsidy expenditure according to different sources, 1998-2002 (Period averages, billion dollars). WTO 2006: 115.
Erwähnt in Abschnitt 'J', 1197.

	National Accounts Data (NACC)	National/supra national review	WTO notifications
Developed countries			
Australia	4.7	2.3 (a)	0.3
Canada	7.7		0.9
EU (15) total	109.0		96.3
EU (15) community level			82.4
EU (15) member level		80.3 (b)	13.9
Germany	33.7	56.9 (c)	3.1
Japan	34.3		4.2
Norway	4.1		2.9
Switzerland	10.8		0.7
United States (all)	43.5		16.3
United States (federal)	41.5		16.2
Developing economies			
Brazil	2.0		1.7
China	13.5 (d)		
India	12.2		
Korea, Republic of	1.0		1.3
South Africa	0.9		

(a) Mainly federal level, not all sectors. (b) Including partly estimated railway subsidies. (c) All government levels (incl. EU) and all sectors. (d) State level, referring to 2000-2002.

Tabelle 289: Percentage of Notifications by Stated Objective in 2004. In: G/TBT/15, 4 March 2005: 4.
Erwähnt in Abschnitt 'J', 1230.

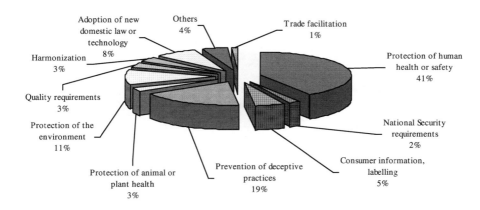

Quelle: WTO.

Tabelle 290: Patente, 1992. In: OECD 1994a.
Erwähnt in Abschnitt 'J', 1288.

Country	National Patent Applications	Resident Patent Applications	Autosufficiency ratio (resident/national patent applications)
Australia	28307	7897	0,28
Austria	43359	2147	0,05
Belgium	44854	788	0,02
Canada	43729	2873	0,07
Denmark	39311	1222	0,03
Finland	14781	2067	0,14
France	78753	12693	0,16
Germany	98940	34587	0,35
Greece	35943	366	0,01
Iceland	149	28	0,19
Ireland	14647	754	0,05
Italy	63261	7750	0,12
Japan	383926	337577	0,88
Luxembourg	35526	4	0,00
Mexico	7695	565	0,07
Netherlands	49376	1859	0,04
New Zealand	4545	1031	0,23
Norway	13979	954	0,07
Portugal	13290	72	0,01
Spain	48900	2101	0,04
Sweden	46969	3371	0,07
Switzerland	46666	3306	0,07
Turkey	1252	189	0,15
United Kingdom	89748	18961	0,21
United States	185957	92683	0,50
Total OECD	1433857	535845	0,37
North America	207799	96121	0,46
EC	405809	81157	0,20
Nordic countries	108884	7642	0,07

Tabelle 291: Filings by Technical Field. In: WIPO 2005: 5.
Erwähnt in Abschnitt 'J', 1288, 1335.

Filings by Technical Field		2001	2002	2003	2004	2005	2005 (Percent)
A61K	Preparations for Medical, Dental, or Toilet Purposes	5,284	6,082	7,071	6,768	6,449	5.1
G06F	Electric Digital Data Processing	8,018	7,993	6,951	6,428	5,784	4.6
H04L	Transmission of Digital Information e.g. Telecommunications	2,646	3,078	2,958	3,088	3,425	2.7
C07D	Heterocyclic Compounds	2,479	2,563	2,612	3,110	3,173	2.5
H01L	Semiconductor Devices; Electric Solid State Devices not Otherwise Provided for	2,129	2,651	2,921	3,092	3,097	2.5
G01N	Investigating or Analysing Materials by Determining their Chemical or Physical Properties	2,359	2,746	2,922	2,857	2,848	2.3
A61B	Diagnosis; Surgery; Identification	1,960	2,089	2,391	2,561	2,633	2.1
H04N	Pictorial communication, e.g. Television	1,771	1,783	2,030	1,871	1,915	1.5
C12N	Micro-Organisms or Enzymes; Compositions thereof	3,963	3,494	2,547	2,197	1,905	1.5
A61F	Filters Implantable into Blood Vessels; Prostheses; Devices Providing Patency to, or Preventing Collapsing of Tubular Structures of the Body	1,326	1,263	1,511	1,520	1,566	1.2
C07C	Acyclic or Carbocyclic Compounds	1,508	1,412	1,501	1,476	1,476	1.2
H04Q	Selecting	1,479	1,447	1,406	1,396	1,444	1.2
G02B	Optical Elements, Systems, or Apparatus	1,170	1,606	1,583	1,453	1,437	1.1
H04B	Transmission	1,457	1,516	1,545	1,505	1,434	1.1
C12Q	Measuring or Testing Processes Involving Enzymes or Micro-Organisms	1,295	1,502	1,615	1,137	1,464	0.9
Others		60,753	62,941	68,416	71,740	85,569	68.3
Total		99,597	104,166	109,980	112,526	125,292	

Tabelle 292: Summarized Results of Concordance for EPO Patents 1998-1999. Johnson 2002: 30-33. IOM: Industry of Manufacture; SOU Sector of Use.
Erwähnt in Abschnitt 'J', 1288, 1335.

Sector		Total by IOM		Total of SOU	
1	A - Agriculture, hunting and forestry	10	0.04	338	1.36
2	01 - Agriculture, hunting and related	10	0.04	309	1.24
3	011 - Growing of crops; market gardening	1	0.00	162	0.65
4	0111 - Growing of cereals and other crops	0	0.00	137	0.55
5	0112 - Growing of vegetables, horticultural	1	0.00	23	0.009
6	0113 - Growing of fruit, nuts, beverage	0	0.00	2	0.01
7	02 - Forestry, logging and related service	0	0.0	-	29
8	B - Fishing	0	0.00	29	0.12
9	05 - Fishing, operation of fish hatcheries	0	0.00	29	0.12
10	C - Mining and quarrying	6	0.02	254	1.02
11	10 - Mining of coal and lignite	3	0.01	6	0.02
12	11 - Extraction of crude petroleum, nat gas	2	0.01	194	0.78
13	12 - Mining of uranium and thorium ores	0	0.00	2	0.01
14	13 - Mining of metal ores	1	0.00	31	0.12
15	14 - Other mining and quarrying	0	0.00	9	0.04
16	D - Manufacturing	24915	99.94	17092	68.56
17	15 - Manufacture of food products	133	0.53	469	1.88
18	16 - Manufacture of tobacco products	8	0.03	34	0.13
19	17 - Manufacture of textiles	158	0.63	223	0.89
20	18 - Manufacture of wearing apparel	29	0.12	66	0.26
21	19 - Tanning and dressing of leather	42	0.17	59	0.24
22	20 - Manufacture of wood products	53	0.21	89	0.36
23	21 - Manufacture of paper products	187	0.75	304	1.22
24	22 - Publishing, printing and reproduction	89	0.36	439	1.76
25	23 - Manufacture of coke, refined petroleum	56	0.22	157	0.63
26	**24 - Manufacture of chemical products**	**4929**	**19.77**	**2851**	**11.43**
27	241 - Manufacture of basic chemicals	2 103	8.44	887	3.56
28	242 - Manufacture of other chemical	2 825	11.33	1880	7.54
29	2421 - Manufacture of pesticides	89	0.36	142	0.57
30	2422 - Manufacture of paints	248	1.00	153	0.61
31	2423 - Manufacture of pharmaceuticals	1 498	6.01	1 104	4.43
32	2424 - Manufacture of soap and	199	0.80	175	0.70
33	2429 - Manufacture of other chemical	791	3.17	307	1.23
34	243 - Manufacture of man-made fibres	0	0.00	83	0.33
35	25 - Manufacture of rubber and plastics	714	2.86	747	3.00
36	26 - Manufacture of other non-metallic	271	1.09	247	0.99
37	**27 - Manufacture of basic metals**	**146**	**0.59**	**257**	**1.03**
38	271 - Manufacture of basic iron and steel	94	0.38	137	0.55
39	272 - Manufacture of basic precious metals	41	0.16	74	0.30
40	273 - Casting of metals	11	0.05	46	0.19
41	2731 - Casting of iron and steel	11	0.05	46	0.19
42	2732 - Casting of non-ferrous metals	0	0.00	0	0.00
43	28 - Manufacture of fabricated metal	837	3.36	466	1.87
44	29 - Manufacture of machinery	6 472	25.96	3 697	14.83
45	30 - Manufacture of office machinery	1 305	5.24	1 449	5.81
46	**31 - Manufacture of electrical machinery**	**90**	**0.36**	**76**	**0.30**
47	3130 - Manufacture of insulated wire, cable	90	0.36	76	0.30
48	**32 - Manufacture of radio, television**	**2 049**	**8.22**	**1 665**	**6.68**
49	321 - Manufacture of electronic valves	1 279	5.13	553	2.22

50	322 - Manufacture of television, radio lines	409	1.64	530	2.13
51	323 - Manufacture of television, radio recvr	361	1.45	582	2.33
52	33 - Manufacture of medical instruments	2 173	8.72	723	2.90
53	331 - Manufacture of medical	2 075	8.32	666	2.67
54	3311 - Manufacture of medical and surgical	0	0.00	0	0.00
55	3312 - Manufacture of instruments	2 075	8.32	666	2.67
56	3313 - Manufacture of industrial process	0	0.00	0	0.00
57	332 - Manufacture of optical instruments	75	0.30	39	0.16
58	333 - Manufacture of watches and clocks	24	0.10	18	0.07
59	**34 - Manufacture of motor vehicles**	**1 144**	**4.59**	**1 596**	**6.40**
60	35 - Manufacture of other transport equip	186	0.75	288	1.16
61	351 - Building and repairing of ships	32	0.13	48	0.19
62	352 - Manufacture of railway	82	0.33	106	0.43
63	353 - Manufacture of aircraft	72	0.29	133	0.53
64	359 - Manufacture of transport equipment	0	0.00	0	0.00
65	36 - Manufacture of furniture; man. n.e.c.	2 483	9.96	447	1.79
66	37 - Recycling	0	0.00	1	0.00
67	E - Electricity, gas and water supply			499	2.00
68	40 - Electricity, gas, steam, hot water			0	0.00
69	41 - Collection, purification of water			0	0.00
70	F - Construction			1 129	4.53
71	45 - Construction			1 129	4.53
72	G - Wholesale and retail trade			361	1.45
73	50 - Sale, maintenance and repair of			50	0.20
74	51 - Wholesale trade			61	0.25
75	515 - Wholesale of machinery			61	0.25
76	52 - Retail trade			180	0.72
77	H - Hotels and restaurants			96	0.38
78	55 - Hotels and restaurants			96	0.38
79	I - Transport, storage and communications			532	2.13
80	60 - Land transport; transport via pipelines			145	0.58
81	61 - Water transport			14	0.06
82	62 - Air transport			26	0.11
83	63 - Supporting and auxiliary transport			52	0.21
84	64 - Post and telecommunications			288	1.16
85	641 - Post and courier activities			15	0.06
86	642 - Telecommunications			274	1.10
87	J - Financial intermediation			38	0.15
88	65 - Financial intermediation			37	0.15
89	66 - Insurance and pension funding			0	0.00
90	67 - Activities auxiliary to financial			0	0.00
91	K - Real estate renting and business activ			545	2.18
92	70 - Real estate activities			7	0.03
93	71 - Renting of machinery and equipment			0	0.00
94	7123 - Renting of office machinery			0	0.00
95	72 - Computer and related activities			0	0.00
96	721 - Hardware consultancy			0	0.00
97	722 - Software consultancy and supply			0	0.00
98	723 - Data processing			0	0.00
99	724 - Data base activities			0	0.00
100	725 - Maintenance of office machinery			0	0.00
101	729 - Other computer related activities			0	0.00
102	73 - Research and development			230	0.92
103	74 - Other business activities			283	1.14
104	741 - Legal, accounting, consultancy			2	0.01
105	742 - Architectural, engineering			50	0.20
106	743 - Advertising			20	0.08
107	749 - Business activities n.e.c.			211	0.85

108	L - Public administration and defense			163	0.65
109	75 - Public administration and defense			163	0.65
110	M - Education			13	0.05
111	80 - Education			6	0.03
112	801 - Primary education			0	0.00
113	802 - Secondary education			0	0.00
114	803 - Higher education			5	0.02
115	809 - Adult and other education			1	0.01
116	N - Health and social work			2 322	9.32
117	85 - Health and social work			2 322	9.32
118	O - Other community activities			1 506	6.04
119	90 - Sewage and refuse disposal			17	0.07
120	91 - Activities of membership orgs			1	0.00
121	92 - Recreational, cultural and sporting			104	0.42
122	93 - Other service activities			1 384	5.55
123	P - Private households			14	0.05
124	95 - Private households			14	0.05
125	Q - Extra-territorial organizations			0	0.00
126	99 - Extra-territorial organizations			0	0.00
Totals		24 931	100.00	24 931	100.00

Tabelle 293: PCT International Application Top 15 Countries. In: WIPO 2005: 3; (a) aus: WIPO 2006: 37-38.
Erwähnt in Abschnitt 'J', 1288.

	2001	2002	2003	2004	2005	Resident applications 2004 (a)
European Patent Office Member States	40,633	42,447	43,205	44,010	47,239	32,178
United States of America	43,055	41,294	41,026	43,342	46,019	189,536
Japan	11,904	14,063	17,414	20,263	24,815	368,416
Germany	14,031	14,326	14,662	15,213	15,995	44,448
France	4,707	5,089	5,171	5,184	5,737	14,230
United Kingdom	5,482	5,376	5,206	5,028	5,114	19,178
Republic of Korea	2,324	2,520	2,949	3,556	4,685	105,250
Netherlands	3,410	3,977	4,479	4,283	4,516	2,187
Switzerland	2,349	2,755	2,861	2,899	3,259	1,600
Sweden	3,421	2,990	2,612	2,849	2,855	2,768
China	1,731	1,018	1,295	1,705	2,500	65,786
Italy	1,623	1,982	2,163	2,192	2,354	6,300
Canada	2,114	2,260	2,270	2,104	2,321	3,900
Australia	1,664	1,759	1,680	1,837	1,984	9,640
Finland	1,696	1,762	1,557	1,672	1,888	2,011
All others	3,720	3,573	3,833	5,096	6,208	-
Total	108,231	110,391	115,202	122,640	135,602	-

Tabelle 294: Key Indicators on World GDP, Population and GERD (a), 2002. In: UNESCO 2005: 4. Erwähnt in Abschnitt 'J', 1288.

	GDP (in billions)	% world GDP	Population (in millions)	% world population	GERD (in billions)	% world GERD	%GERD/ GDP	GERD per inhabitant
World	47599.4	100.0	6176.2	100.0	829.9	100.0	1.7	134.4
Developed countries	28256.5	59.4	1195.1	19.3	645.8	77.8	2.3	540.4
Developing countries	18606.5	39.1	4294.2	69.5	183.6	22.1	1.0	42.8
Less-Developed countries	736.4	1.5	686.9	11.1	0.5	0.1	0.1	0.7
Americas	14949.2	31.4	849.7	13.8	328.8	39.6	2.2	387.0
North America	11321.6	23.8	319.8	5.2	307.2	37.0	2.7	960.5
Latin America and the Caribbean	3627.5	7.6	530.0	8.6	21.7	2.6	0.6	40.9
Europe	13285.8	27.9	795.0	12.9	226.2	27.3	1.7	284.6
European Union	10706.4	22.5	453.7	7.3	195.9	23.6	1.8	431.8
Comm. of Ind. States in Europe	1460.0	3.1	207.0	3.4	17.9	2.2	1.2	86.6
Central, Eastern and Other Europe	1119.4	2.4	134.4	2.2	12.4	1.5	1.1	92.6
Africa	1760.0	3.7	832.2	13.4	4.6	0.6	0.3	5.6
Sub-Saharan countries	1096.9	2.3	644.0	10.4	3.5	0.4	0.3	5.5
Arab States Africa	663.1	1.4	188.2	3.0	1.2	0.1	0.2	6.5
Asia	16964.9	35.6	3667.5	59.4	261.5	31.5	1.5	71.3
Comm. of Ind. States in Asia	207.9	0.4	72.6	1.2	0.7	0.1	0.4	10.3
Newly Indust. Asia	2305.5	4.8	374.6	6.1	53.5	6.4	2.3	142.8
Arab States Asia	556.0	1.2	103.9	1.7	0.6	0.1	0.1	6.2
Other Asia	1720.0	3.6	653.7	10.6	1.4	0.2	0.1	2.1
Oceania	639.5	1.3	31.8	0.5	8.7	1.1	1.4	274.2
Other groupings								
Arab States All	1219.1	2.6	292.0	4.7	1.9	0.2	0.2	6.4
Comm. of Ind. States all	1667.9	3.5	279.6	4.5	18.7	2.2	1.1	66.8
OECD	28540.0	60.0	1144.1	18.5	655.1	78.9	2.3	572.6
Selected countries								
Argentina	386.6	0.8	36.5	0.6	1.6	0.2	0.4	44.0
Brazil (b)	1300.3	2.7	174.5	2.8	13.1	1.6	1.0	75.0
China	5791.7	12.2	1280.4	20.7	72.0	8.7	1.2	56.2
Egypt (b)	252.9	0.5	66.4	1.1	0.4	0.1	0.2	6.6
France	1608.8	3.4	59.5	1.0	35.2	4.2	2.2	591.5
Germany	2226.1	4.7	82.5	1.3	56.0	6.7	2.5	678.3
India (b)	2777.8	5.8	1048.6	17.0	20.8	2.5	0.7	19.8

Israel	124.8	0.3	6.6	0.1	6.1	0.7	4.9	922.4
Japan	3481.3	7.3	127.2	2.1	106.4	12.8	3.1	836.6
Mexico	887.1	1.9	100.8	1.6	3.5	0.4	0.4	34.7
Russian Federation	1164.7	2.4	144.1	2.3	14.7	1.8	1.3	102.3
South Africa	444.8	0.9	45.3	0.7	3.1	0.4	0.7	68.7
United Kingdom	1574.5	3.3	59.2	1.0	29.0	3.5	1.8	490.4
United States of America	10414.3	21.9	288.4	4.7	290.1	35.0	2.8	1005.9

(a) Gross domestic expenditure on R&D (GERD) is total intramural expenditure on R&D performed on the national territory during a given period, it includes business, government and university funds.
(b) GERD figures for Brazil, India and Egypt are all for 2000.
Note: For Asia, the sub-regional totals do not include China, India or Japan in any of the tables in the present chapter.

Tabelle 295: Estimated static rent transfer from TRIPS-induced strengthening of 1988 patent laws. Maskus 2002: 184.
Erwähnt in Abschnitt 'J', 1331.

Country	Outward transfer	Inward transfer	Net transfer
USA	92	5,852	5,760
Germany	599	1,827	1,228
France	0	831	831
Italy	0	277	277
Sweden	13	230	217
Switzerland	474	510	36
Panama	0	0.3	0.3
Australia	177	154	-23
Ireland	71	12	-59
New Zealand	79	8	-71
Israel	125	32	-93
Colombia	132	2	-130
Portugal	138	0	-138
Netherlands	453	314	-139
South Africa	183	15	-168
Greece	197	2	-195
Finland	281	47	-234
Norway	277	25	-252
Denmark	330	77	-253
Austria	358	83	-275
Belgium	470	111	-359
India	430	0	-430
South Korea	457	3	-454
Spain	512	31	-481
Mexico	527	1	-526
Japan	1,202	613	-589
UK	1,221	588	-633
Canada	1,225	85	-1,040
Brazil	1,714	7	-1,707

Tabelle 296: Technology license payments abroad by income level and region, 1985 and 1998. UNIDO Industrial Development Report, 2002/2003: 158.
Erwähnt in Abschnitt 'J', 1332.

Country group, income level or region	1985 (a)				1998 (a)				Growth rate (percent)
	Value (billions of dollars)	World shares (percent)	Developing economies shares (percent)	Per capita value (dollars)	Value (billions of dollars)	World shares (percent)	Developing economies' shares (percent)	Per capita value (dollars)	
World	11,091.8	100	na	2.6	70,471.0	100	na	14.2	16.7
Industrialized economies	9,286.9	83.7	na	12	54,825.4	77.8	na	66.2	15.9
Transition economies					583.8	0.8	na	2.5	19.3
Developing economies	1,804.9	16.3	100	0.6	15,061.8	21.4	100	3.9	18.7
High- and upper middle income	1,230.1	11.1	68.2	3.2	11,409.7	16.2	75.8	23.6	13.9
Lower middle income	539.9	4.9	29.9	1.0	2,937.8	4.2	19.5	4.3	26.1
Low income	34.9	0.3	1.9	-	714.3	1.0	4.7	0.2	19.0
Low income (without China and India)	9.7	0.1	0.5	-	93.5	0.1	0.6	0.1	42.3
Least developed countries (b)	0.2	-	-	-	21.8	-	0.1	0.1	42.39
East Asia					11,568.3	16.4	76.8	7.1	
East Asia (without China)	942.3	8.5	52.2	2.7	11,248.3	15.8	74.0	26.6	22.9
South Asia	25.1	0.2	1.4	0	225,6	0.3	1.5	0.2	20.1
Latin America and the Carribean	696.9	6.3	38.6	1.9	2,348.8	3.3	15.6	5.3	10.7
Latin America and the Carribean (without Mexico)	554.9	5.0	30.7	1.9	1,847.8	2.6	12.3	5.2	10.5
Sub-Saharan Africa	127.8	1.2	7.1	0.4	229.0	0.3	1.5	0.6	5.0
Sub-Sahara Africa (without South Africa	7.5	0.1	0.4	-	63.6	0.1	0.4	0.2	19.5
Middle East and North Africa and Turkey	12.8	0.1	0.7	0.1	690.1	1.0	4.6	3.0	39.4

(a) When data for 1985 and 1998 were not available, data for the closest period were used.
(b) Includes only 12 of 49 least developed countries.

Tabelle 297: Complaining Parties in WTO disputes. Leitner/Lester 2006: 221.
Erwähnt in Abschnitt 'J', 931.

	1995	1996	1997	1998	1999	2000	2001	2002	2003	2004	2005	Total
Brazil	1	0	4	1	0	7	4	5	0	0	0	22
Canada	5	3	1	4	2	1	3	4	1	2	0	26
Chile	1	0	1	0	0	1	3	2	1	0	1	10
European Communites	2	7	16	16	6	8	1	4	3	5	2	70
India	1	4	0	3	1	2	2	2	0	1	0	16
Japan	1	3	1	1	2	1	0	2	0	1	0	12
Korea	0	0	2	0	1	3	0	1	3	2	0	12
Mexico	2	3	0	0	3	1	1	0	3	0	2	15
United States	6	17	17	10	10	8	1	4	3	4	1	81
Other - Developed	0	2	5	2	3	1	0	4	1	0	1	19
Other - Developing	9	12	3	4	6	9	9	9	11	3	4	79
Other - Least	0	0	0	0	0	0	0	0	0	1	0	1
Total	28	51	50	41	34	42	24	37	26	19	11	363

Tabelle 298: Abbau der innergemeinschaftlichen Zölle In: Smeets 1996: 63.
Erwähnt in Abschnitt 'H', 799.

Datum	vertraglich vorgesehene Liberalisierung (in %)	tatsächliche Liberalisierung (in %)	
		Industrieprodukte	Agrarprodukte
1.1.1959	10	10	10
1.7.1960	20	20	20
1.1.1961	20	30	25
1.1.1962	30	40	35
1.7.1962	30	50	35
1.7.1963	40	60	45
1.1.1965	50	70	55
1.1.1966	60	80	65
1.7.1967	1)	85	75
1.7.1968	1)	100	100
1.1.1970	100		

1) Auf Vorschlag der Kommission festzusetzen

Tabelle 299: Korea: Nominal Protection, Effective Protection, and Effective Subsidy Rates, by Industry Group, 1968. In: Westphal/Kim in Balassa et al. 1981: 230.
Erwähnt in Abschnitt 'G', 530.

Industry group	Nominal protection				Effective protection				Effective subsidy			
	Legal tariff		Nominal		Balassa			Corden	Balassa			Corden
	D	A	D	A	E	D	A	A	E	D	A	A
Agriculture, forestry, fishing (I)	37	36	17	17	-16	19	18	17	-10	23	22	21
Mining & Energy (IV)	12	10	9	7	-1	4	3	3	3	5	5	4
Primary activities (I+IV)	35	34	17	16	-8	18	17	16	-3	22	21	20
Processed foods (II)	61	57	3	3	-3	-18	-17	-13	2	-25	-23	-18
Beverages & tobacco (III)	141	135	2	2	-2	-19	-19	-15	15	-26	-24	-19
Construction materials (V)	32	31	4	4	-5	-11	-11	-9	6	-17	-16	-12
Intermediate products I (VIA)	37	31	3	2	31	-25	-19	-14	43	-30	-22	-16
Intermediate products II (VIB)	59	53	21	19	0	26	24	16	17	20	19	13
Nondurable consumer goods (V)	92	68	12	9	-2	-11	-9	-7	5	-21	-15	-11
Consumer durables (VIII)	98	78	39	31	-5	64	51	32	2	38	31	19
Machinery (IX)	53	49	30	28	-13	44	43	28	5	31	31	20
Transport equipment (X)	62	62	55	54	-53 (a)	163	164	83	-23 (a)	159	159	80
Manufacturing (II,III, V-X)	68	59	12	11	3	-1	-1	-1	12	-9	-7	-5
Primary production plus processed foods (I, II, IV)	41	39	14	13	-6	14	13	12	-1	17	16	15
Manufacturing, less beverages and tobacco (II, V-X)	61	52	13	11	3	1	1	1	12	-7	-5	-3
All industries, less beverages and tobacco (I, II, IV-X)	50	45	15	13	0	12	11	9	8	11	11	10
Manufacturing, less beverages and tobacco and processed foods (V-X)	60	51	16	13	4	6	6	4	14	-2	0	0
All industries (I-X)	54	49	14	13	0	11	10	8	9	10	10	9

Note: The initials used in the column headings are D for domestic sales, E for export sales, and A for all sales. Because of rounding, zero denotes any value greater than or equal to -0.5 and less than 0.5.

(a) Estimated value added in exports at exporters' producer prices and at world prices are both negative; as is explained in the text, the algebraic sign of the effective incentive rate has thus been reversed from that given by the conventional formula.

Tabelle 300: Manufactures and Semimanufactures of Export Interest to Developing Countries: Competitiveness and Nontariff Barriers (1968). Aus: Walter 1971: 204. Erwähnt in Abschnitt 'I', 911.

SITC No.	Product Desciption	Competitive Position	NTB Factor	SITC No.	Product Description	Competitive Position	NTB Factor
841	Clothing	19,0	71,1	013	Preserved meats	5,2	78,0
657	Carpets	18,0	25,0	012	Dried and salted meats	5,2	97,5
243	Shaped Wood	16,3	15,0	724	Telecom apparatus	4,9	42,0
899	Other products	16,0	8,3	599	Other chemicals	4,7	10,5
831	Travel goods	13,9	0,0	431	Oils, fats and waxes	4,7	7,1
653	Woven noncotton fabrics	13,2	60,3	696	Cutlery	4,5	2,1
032	Preserved fish	12,8	37,5	665	Glassware	4,1	1,7
897	Jewelery	12,5	25,0	551	Essential oils	4,0	5,0
632	Wood products	12,5	2,7	821	Furniture	3,5	0,0
651	Yarn and thread	12,4	19,4	521	Tar, etc. from coal	3,4	6,7
656	Bags, sacks, linens	12,2	24,3	072.3	Cocoa butter	3,2	15,0
053	Preserved fruit	12,2	47,5	073	Chocolate	3,2	34,7
055	Preserved vegetables	12,2	46,3	071.3	Coffee extracts	3,0	44,6
894	Toys and sporting goods	11,8	6,7	661	Lime, cement, etc.	2,8	0,0
532	Tanning and dying extracts	11,5	2,5	541	Medicinal products	2,8	55,5
655	Special textile fabrics	10,0	15,6	861	Scientific instruments	2,7	4,8
663	Mineral manucturers nes	9,3	0,1	641	Paper and paperboard	2,3	4,7
851	Footwear	9,2	17,5	513	Inorganic chemicals, oxides	2,3	10,8
652	Woven cotton	7,8	117,1	514	Other inorganic chemicals	2,3	10,5
099	Other food products	7,6	21,3	629	Rubber products	2,2	10,2
052	Dried fruit	7,5	23,5	251	Pulp and waste paper	2,0	0,0
892	Printed Matter	7,5	5,0	266	Synthetic fibers	2,0	4,3
893	Plastic products	7,5	5,0	678	Iron, steel tubes and pipes	1,7	23,0
631	Veneers and plywood	6,6	0,8	512	Organic chemicals	1,6	18,2
611	Leather	6,6	3,3	671	Pig iron	1,4	0,0
697	Household metal products	6,5	1,9	673	Iron and steel bars	0,1	30,0
698	Other metal products	6,4	1,5	674	Iron and steel plates, sheets	0,1	30,0
561	Manufactures fertilizers	5,9	23,0	533	Pigments, paints, varnishes	<0,1	4,3
812	Light and sanitary fittings	5,7	8,8	642	Art. of paper, pulp, paperboard	<0,1	0,0
661	Clay products	5,7	4,4	712	Agric. machinery, implements	<0,1	0,7

Für weitere 63 Kategorien wurden keine komparativen Vorteile gemessen. In bezug darauf sind 15 Kategorien NTBs ausgesetzt und die restlichen 48 nicht. Für weitere Kommentare siehe den Artikel.

Tabelle 301: Illustrative Matrix of Technological Capabilities.
In: Lall 1990: 21; Lall 1992: 167.
Erwähnt in Abschnitt 'F', 430.

			Functional					
			Investment		Production			
			Preinvestment	Project Execution	Process Engineering	Product Engineering	Industrial Engineering	Linkages with Economy
Degree of complexity	Basic	Simple routine (routine based)	Prefeasibility and feasibility studies, site selection, scheduling of investment	Civil contruction, ancilliary services, equipment erection, commissioning	Debugging, balancing, quality control, preventive maintenance, assimilation of process technology	Assimilation of product design, minor adaption to market needs	Work flow, scheduling, time-motion studies, inventory control	Local procurement of goods and services, infor-mation exchange with suppliers
	Intermed	Adaptive duplicative (Search based)	Search for technology source, negotiation of contract, bargaining suitable terms, information systems	Equipment procurement, detailed engineering, training and recruitment of skilled personnel	Equipment stretching, process adaption and cost saving, licensing new technology	Product quality improvement, licensing and assimilating new imported product technology	Monitoring productivity, improved coordination	Technology transfer of local suppliers, coordinated design, S&T links
	Advanced	Innovative risky (Research based)		Basic process design, equipment design and supply	In-house process innovation, basic research	In-house product innovation, basic research		Turnkey capability, cooperative R&D, licensing own technology to others

Tabelle 302: Tabelle Zölle nach Produktgruppen in den Vereinigten Staaten, Japan und der EG (vH). Bletschacher/Klodt 1992: 68.
Erwähnt in Abschnitt 'G', 466, Abschnitt 'I', 845.

	Vereinigte Staaten	Japan	EG
	1988	1989	1985
Industriewaren insgesamt	6,6	5,3	6,3
Elektronische Halbleiter	0,0	0,0 (a)	14,0
Luft- und Raumfahrzeuge	2,8	2,1	6,5
Straßenfahrzeuge	2,5	0,6	10,0
Textilien	9,9	9,0	9.7
Bekleidung	13,9	13,1	12,5

(a) Allgemeiner Zoll von 15 vH bis auf weiteres ausgesetzt.

Im Halbleiter und Automobilbereich kommen signifikante nichttariffäre Handelshemmnisse dazu. In: Bletschacher/Klodt 1992: 68.

Tabelle 303: Brazil's imports and export structure by main categories, 1946 - 1996 (US$ Million and % of total exports). Modifiziert, aus: Moreira 1995: 190.
Erwähnt in Abschnitt 'G', 564.

Categories	1946	1950	1955	1964	1974	1980	1987	1992	1996
Total imports (f)	674,0	1085,0	1305,8	1263,4	14162,7	24948,8	16577,8	23115,3	56947,0
Total exports	985,3	1355,5	1423,0	1429,8	7950,0	20132,0	26228,6	36186,8	47762,0
Primary and semi-manufactures (a)	912,6 (92,6)	1339,5 (98,8)	1407,8 (98,9)	1353,5 (94,7)	6030,3 (75,8)	12541,9 (62,3)	13223,1 (50,4)	-	-
Coffee	(35,3)	(63,9)	(58,9)	(53,1)	(12,3)	(13,7)	(8,3)	-	-
Manufactured products (b)	72,7 (7,4)	16,0 (1,2)	15,2 (1,1)	76,3 (5,3)	1920,6 (24,1)	7590,1 (37,7)	13005,5 (49,6)	-	-
Motor Vehicles -Pass. Vehicles (c) -Parts	-	-	2 (d)	9,46 (e)	152,0 188,9	1039,9 431,3	324,7 610,3	761,4 1953,8	619,2 3124,6

(a) SITC divisions 0,1,2,3,4,9,68 (b) SITC divisions 5 to 8 minus 68. (c) SITC division 732 bzw. 781 for motor vehicles, divisions 7328, 73289 bzw. 784, 7841, 7842, 7849 for parts. Eigene Hinzufügung unter Rückgriff auf dieselbe Quelle wie im Original, ohne Trucks, Busse etc., nämlich UN International Trade Statistics Yearbook, div. Ausgaben. (d) keine Aufgliederung, 1956. (e) keine Aufgliederung in Teile. (f) Eigene Ergänzung, s.o.

Tabelle 304: War damage and reconstruction. Crafts/Toniolo 1996: 4.
Erwähnt in Abschnitt 'H', 799.

	Pre-war year when GDP was the same as 1945 (1)	Year when GDP recovered the highest prewar level (2)	Annual rate of GDP growth during 'reconstruction' (1945 to year in col. (2)) (3)
Austria	1886	1951	15.2
Belgium (a)	1924	1948	6.0
Denmark	1936	1946	13.5
Finland	1938	1945	
France	1891	1949	19.0
Germany	1908 (b)	1951	13.5
Italy	1909	1950	11.2
Netherlands	1912	1947	39.8
Norway	1937	1946	9.7
Sweden	never		
Switzerland	never		
United Kingdom	never		

(a) Interpolations
(b) Relative to 1946.

Tabelle 305: Die effektive Gesamtprotektion der Industriezweige der Bundesrepublik Deutschland 1958, 1964, 1970. In: Hiemenz/von Rabenau 1973: 204-205.
Erwähnt in Abschnitt 'H', 799.

Industriezweig	Effektive	Gesamtprotektion	gegenüber Einfuhren	aus
	1958	1964		1970
	Drittländern	Drittländern	EWG-Ländern	Drittländern
Bergbauliche Erzeugnisse	0,8 (b)	52,2 (b)	3,6 (b)	102,1 (b)
Steinkohlebergbau, Kokerei	0,5	65,6	4,1	128,3
Braun- und Pechkohlenbergbau	-2,2	-3,4	-0,2	-2,9
Erdöl, Erdgas u. bituminöse Gesteine	-	-	-	-
Sonstiger Bergbau	5,4	3,1	2,9	2,5
Grundstoff- und Produktionsgüterindustrien	23,5	30,2	5,3	19,4
Steine und Erden	1,6	12,0	0,4	4,4
Eisen- und Stahlerzeugung	33,3	39,4	5,9	23,8
Eisen-, Stahl- u. Tempergießereien	13,4	23,4	5,9	23,8
Ziehereien und Kaltwalzwerke	5,6	8,5	3,9	7,3
NE-Metallerzeugung	31,4	68,2	22,8	30,3
NE-Metallgießerei	35,6	73,7	14,8	39,4
Mineralölverarbeitung	-	60,5	0,8	168,4
Chemie und Kohlewertstoffe	18,0	24,6	5,1	16,0
Säge und Holzbearbeitungswerke	15,9	19,0	3,6	13,1
Zellstoff-, Papier-, Pappeerzeugung	51,3	53,5	5,6	42,1
Gummi- und Asbestverarbeitung	27,8	29,2	5,1	15,7
Investitionsgüterindustrien	5,5	9,3	1,0	7,4
Stahl- und Leichtmetallbau	0,6	5,8	0,2	3,0
Stahlverformung	16,6	21,0	3,9	12,3
Maschinenbau	0,8	4,0	0,4	3,7
Straßenfahrzeugbau	11,0	14,5	2,3	9,4
Schiffbau	(-14,9)	(-14,6)	(-2,9)	(-10,9)
Luftfahrzeugbau	(24,0)	(1,8)	(3,4)	(73,2)
Elektrotechnik	5,1	9,2	-0,4	8,1
Feinmechanik, Optik	3,4	7,9	1,2	4,5
Uhren	2,7	5,8	1,2	4,5
EBM-Waren	8,4	15,3	2,5	11,0
Verbrauchsgüterindustrien	20,4	24,4	3,6	20,6
Feinkeramische Erzeugnisse	9,5	18,3	1,7	18,7
Glas und Glaswaren	16,7	22,8	3,0	15,1
Holzverarbeitung	23,1	24,3	2,1	17,5
Musikinstrumente, Sport, Spielwaren	6,3	13,8	2,8	10,6
Papier- und Pappeverarbeitung	29,7	29,2	5,9	27,4
Druckerei, Vervielfältigung	4,3	9,6	1,3	8,3
Kunststoffverarbeitung	8,8	13,0	1,6	9,5
Leder (Herstellung, Veredelung)	11,6	13,0	3,1	11,2
Lederverarbeitung	21,0	26,3	3,8	19,1
Schuhe	26,2	30,6	4,4	15,1
Textilien	24,9	29,3	5,2	25,6
Bekleidung	20,9	26,0	3,2	25,1
Industrie insgesamt	14,9 (b,c)	22,1 (b,c)	3,4 (b,c)	19,3 (b,c)

(a) Unter Zugrundelegung der Input/Output-Matrix des Ifo-Instituts für die Jahre 1961-1964
(b) Ohne Erdöl, Erdgas und bit. Gestein. (c) Ohne Mineralölverarbeitung
Für den Schiffbau und den Luftfahrzeugbau bestehen substantielle Subventionen, über die jedoch keine systematischen Informationen vorlagen.

Tabelle 306: Reciprocal tariff concessions recieved and given at the Uruguay Round. In: Finger et al. 1999: 22.
Erwähnt in Abschnitt 'H', 813.

	Percent tariff reduction (a)			Mercantilist balance, in percentage point dollars (b)		
	Recieved	Given	Recieved minus Given	Concessions Given	Concessions Given	Recieved minus Given, as percent of Recieved
Australia	0.76	3.35	-2.59	21032	88162	-319
Austria	2.64	3.74	-1.11	74602	108820	-46
Canada	0.22	0.89	-0.67	5291	26205	-395
European Union	1.94	2.19	-0.26	578816	627939	-8
Finland	3.47	2.52	0.95	63924	44021	31
Hong Kong	2.36	0.00	2.36	60258	0	100
Iceland	1.59	0.20	1.39	2151	299	86
Japan	2.06	1.06	1.00	481006	143142	70
New Zealand	0.84	0.83	0.01	5126	4155	19
Norway	1.15	2.17	-1.03	24250	44263	-83
Singapore	1.96	0.85	1.11	50294	32741	35
Switzerland	2.15	0.89	1.25	100659	46829	53
United States	1.21	1.07	0.14	214791	283580	-32
Czech&Slovak CU	2.06	1.05	1.01	9773	7312	25
Hungary	1.82	1.69	0.13	7755	13727	77
Poland	1.36	1.26	0.09	8609	7112	17
Argentina (c)	0.98	0.00	0.98	6331	0	100
Brazil	1.37	0.00	1.36	38037	98	100
Chile (c)	0.50	0.00	0.50	3291	0	100
Colombia	1.25	0.02	1.23	6323	81	99
India	1.22	6.16	-4.94	14380	67172	-367
Indonesia	0.87	0.25	0.63	16222	3355	79
Korea Rep.	1.87	5.99	-4.12	100809	262918	-161
Malaysia	1.46	1.97	-0.51	36108	28966	20
Mexico	0.16	0.00	0.16	960	3	100
Peru	0.57	0.03	0.54	1586	58	96
Philippines	2.43	1.29	1.14	19748	12847	35
Sri Lanka	1.36	0.01	1.35	1595	33	98
Thailand	1.33	5.93	-4.60	20564	95953	-367
Tunisia	1.42	0.02	1.40	2506	72	97
Turkey	1.72	3.00	-1.27	12557	32661	-160
Uruguay	0.52	0.00	0.51	772	6	99
Venezuela	0.21	0.13	0.08	2051	806	61
	Sum abs diff/Sum of rec'vd, as % = 137			Sum abs diff/Sum of rec'vd, as % = 58		
	Overlap index - 42			Overlap index - 29		

(a) Weighted average of change measured as dT/(1+T avg)*100, where T avg is the average of the before and after change rates, calculated across all tariff lines, including those on which there was not reduction.
(b) Tariff cut measured in the first or second column multiplied by the value (in millions of dollars) of the imports or exports to which the importing country applies mfn tariff rates.

Tabelle 307: Shares of Intra-Industry Trade in Total Trade for Consumer Goods, Semi-Fabricated Goods and Investment Goods in 1980. In: Culem/Lundberg 1986: 118. *Erwähnt in Abschnitt 'D', 220.*

Country	All goods	Consumer goods (C)	Semi-fabricated goods (S)	Investment goods (I)	LDC	DC
Australia	35.8	18.6	53.9	32.8	I	S
Belgium	79.7	84.5	76.4	77.0	S	C
Canada	58.5	72.3	43.9	59.0	S	C
France	80.4	70.9	86.2	85.8	S	S
Germany	65.4	62.0	71.4	60.3	S	S
Italy	65.4	51.7	75.5	70.2	S	I
Japan	28.8	18.4	38.0	31.5	S	I
Netherlands	74.2	69.0	74.7	85.8	S	I
Sweden	66.5	67.3	59.2	79.7	S	I
U.K.	79.1	78.6	78.8	80.0	I	I
USA	60.7	63.1	63.4	54.0	C	S
Number of products	81	36	28	17		

Tabelle 308: U.S. Economy, products sold i.e. value of Shipments, 1997 and 2002. ($ 1000)
(a) Census of Manufacturing.
Erwähnt in Abschnitt 'D', 246.

NAICS Code	Industrie	1997	2002
31-33	Manufacturing	3 834 700 920	3 916 136 712
311	Food mfg	421 737 017	458 786 540
312	Beverages & tobacco mfg.	96 971 368	105 714 263
313	Textile mills	58 707 401	45 652 142
314	Textile product mills	31 051 835	32 273 047
315	Apparel mfg	68 018 116	44 521 126
316	Leather & allied products (incl. footwear) mfg	10 876 510	5 254 100
321	Wood product mfg	88 470 180	89 085 026
322	Paper mfg	150 295 890	153 766 022
323	Printing & related support acticities	97 485 138	95 726 203
324	Petroleum & coal products mfg	177 393 098	215 312 899
325	Chemical mfg	415 616 508	460 424 786
- 3254	- Pharmaceutical & medicine	92 932 786	140 557 276
326	Plastics & rubber products mfg	159 161 346	174 369 289
327	Nonmetallic mineral product mfg	86 464 708	95 261 480
331	Primary metal mfg	168 117 728	139 343 112
- 3311	- Iron & Steel mills & ferroalloy mfg	58 383 159	47 040 728
- 3313	- Alumina & aluminium production and processing	32 550 279	28 262 020
- 3314	- Nonferrous metal (except aluminium) production & processing	29 616 370	22 252 493
332	Fabricated metal product mfg	242 813 453	247 059 502
333	Machinery	270 687 165	252 476 407
- 3336	- Engine, turbine & power transmission	30 508 866	38 463 675
334	Computer & electronic product mfg	439 381 300	358 414 047
- 3341	- Computer & peripheral equipment manufacturing	110 054 987	73 667 620
- 3342	- Communications apparatus (incl. telephone, radio, TV) mfg	82 852 421	64 987 314
- 3343	- Audio & video equip. mfg	8 226 685	8 879 264
- 3344	Semiconductors & other electronic component mfg	139 083 873	110 476 817
335	Electrical equipment, appliance (u.a. houshold) & component mfg	112 116 267	102 879 191
336	Transportation equipment	575 306 996	636 758 285
- 3364	Aerospace product and parts manufacturing	120 438 212	124 402 031
337	Furniture & related product mfg	64 299 098	75 964 713
339	Miscellaneous mfg	99 729 798	126 094 532
- 3391	Medical equipment and supplies manufacturing	44 893 840	61 928 760

(a) Value of shipments: This item covers the received or receivable net selling values, f.o.b. plant (exclusive of freight and taxes), of all products shipped, both primary and secondary. Kurz: Shipped bedeutet nicht exportiert, sondern verkauft.

Tabelle 309: Pro-Kopf-Ausgaben für Regionalförderung in ausgewählten EG-Mitgliedsstaaten 1981, 1983, 1987 und 1988. Nettozuschußäquivalent in englischen Pfund (Preise von 1988). Aus: Klodt/Stehn 1992: 74.
Erwähnt in Abschnitt 'H', 783.

	1981	1983	1987	1988
Belgien	15	10	8	17
BRD	7	7	8	10
Dänemark	2	1	2	1
Frankreich	3	3	1	2
Irland	73	30	38	30
Italien	49	54	44	53
Luxemburg	16	14	61	79
Niederlande	8	6	4	8
Vereinigtes Königreich	20	15	11	11